SEVENTY-SECOND ANNUAL ISSUE

THE MINISTERS MANUAL

1997 EDITION

Edited by

JAMES W. COX

JAMES W. COX, a leading authority on preaching and one of the most influential teachers in the field of homiletics, is a senior professor at Southern Baptist Theological Seminary in Louisville, Kentucky. He is the author of *Surprised by God: A Guide to Biblical Preaching, Learning to Speak Effectively, Preaching: A Comprehensive Approach to the Design and Delivery of Sermons,* and *Handbook of Themes for Preaching.*

HarperSanFrancisco
An Imprint of HarperCollins*Publishers*

Editors of THE MINISTERS MANUAL

G. B. F. Hallock, D.D., 1926–1958
M. K. W. Heicher, Ph.D., 1943–1968
Charles L. Wallis, M.A., M.Div., 1969–1983
James W. Cox, M.Div., Ph.D.

Translations of the Bible referred to and quoted from in this book may
be indicated by their standard abbreviations, such as NRSV (New
Revised Standard Version) and NIV (New International Version). In
addition, some contributors have made their own translations and
others have used a mixed text.

Other acknowledgments begin on page 327.

THE MINISTERS MANUAL FOR 1997. Copyright © 1996 by James W.
Cox. All rights reserved. Printed in the United States of America. No
part of this book may be used or reproduced in any manner whatsoever
without written permission except in the case of brief quotations embodied in critical articles and reviews. For information address Harper-
Collins Publishers, 10 East 53rd Street, New York, NY 10022.

HarperCollins Web Site: http://www.harpercollins.com
HarperCollins®, ® ®, and HarperSanFrancisco™ are trademarks of
HarperCollins Publishers Inc.

FIRST EDITION

Library of Congress Cataloging Card Number
25-21658
ISSN 0738-5323
ISBN 0–06–061623–7 (cloth)

96 97 98 99 00 HAD 10 9 8 7 6 5 4 3 2 1

CONTENTS

PREFACE

It has been gratifying to hear from pastors, teachers, musicians, and others, in many parts of the world, that *The Ministers Manual* has been a valuable resource in their service to the Church. However, this volume as rendered could not have been produced without the contributions of scores of individuals whose work has enriched its pages. To them the readers and the editor are deeply indebted.

From the very beginning of this editorial work, I have been encouraged and assisted by my wife, Patricia, and our lawyer son Kenneth. Dr. Lee McGlone and Clara McCartt have, for many years, contributed significantly. The Southern Baptist Theological Seminary, where I have taught since 1959, has provided valuable secretarial assistance in producing the manuscript. The present volume was word-processed by Elizabeth Beauchamp, Nancy Callicott, and Bev Tillman. To all of these people and the authors and publishers whose works have been quoted and highlighted in the several volumes, I am deeply grateful. And I wish to thank the fine folk at HarperSanFrancisco for giving me the opportunity to compile and publish *The Ministers Manual* and for their patient cooperation in bringing each issue to completion.

The next annual issues of *The Ministers Manual* are scheduled for publication by Jossey-Bass Inc., Publishers of San Francisco, and I anticipate a pleasant and productive relationship with them, such as I have enjoyed with the people at HarperSanFrancisco.

James W. Cox
The Southern Baptist Theological Seminary
2825 Lexington Road
Louisville, Kentucky 40280

SECTION I.
General Aids and Resources
Civil Year Calendars

1997

JANUARY
S M T W T F S
1 2 3 4
5 6 7 8 9 10 11
12 13 14 15 16 17 18
19 20 21 22 23 24 25
26 27 28 29 30 31

FEBRUARY
S M T W T F S
1
2 3 4 5 6 7 8
9 10 11 12 13 14 15
16 17 18 19 20 21 22
23 24 25 26 27 28

MARCH
S M T W T F S
1
2 3 4 5 6 7 8
9 10 11 12 13 14 15
16 17 18 19 20 21 22
23 24 25 26 27 28 29
30 31

APRIL
S M T W T F S
1 2 3 4 5
6 7 8 9 10 11 12
13 14 15 16 17 18 19
20 21 22 23 24 25 26
27 28 29 30

MAY
S M T W T F S
1 2 3
4 5 6 7 8 9 10
11 12 13 14 15 16 17
18 19 20 21 22 23 24
25 26 27 28 29 30 31

JUNE
S M T W T F S
1 2 3 4 5 6 7
8 9 10 11 12 13 14
15 16 17 18 19 20 21
22 23 24 25 26 27 28
29 30

JULY
S M T W T F S
1 2 3 4 5
6 7 8 9 10 11 12
13 14 15 16 17 18 19
20 21 22 23 24 25 26
27 28 29 30 31

AUGUST
S M T W T F S
1 2
3 4 5 6 7 8 9
10 11 12 13 14 15 16
17 18 19 20 21 22 23
24 25 26 27 28 29 30
31

SEPTEMBER
S M T W T F S
1 2 3 4 5 6
7 8 9 10 11 12 13
14 15 16 17 18 19 20
21 22 23 24 25 26 27
28 29 30

OCTOBER
S M T W T F S
1 2 3 4
5 6 7 8 9 10 11
12 13 14 15 16 17 18
19 20 21 22 23 24 25
26 27 28 29 30 31

NOVEMBER
S M T W T F S
1
2 3 4 5 6 7 8
9 10 11 12 13 14 15
16 17 18 19 20 21 22
23 24 25 26 27 28 29
30

DECEMBER
S M T W T F S
1 2 3 4 5 6
7 8 9 10 11 12 13
14 15 16 17 18 19 20
21 22 23 24 25 26 27
28 29 30 31

1998

JANUARY
S M T W T F S
1 2 3
4 5 6 7 8 9 10
11 12 13 14 15 16 17
18 19 20 21 22 23 24
25 26 27 28 29 30 31

FEBRUARY
S M T W T F S
1 2 3 4 5 6 7
8 9 10 11 12 13 14
15 16 17 18 19 20 21
22 23 24 25 26 27 28

MARCH
S M T W T F S
1 2 3 4 5 6 7
8 9 10 11 12 13 14
15 16 17 18 19 20 21
22 23 24 25 26 27 28
29 30 31

APRIL
S M T W T F S
1 2 3 4
5 6 7 8 9 10 11
12 13 14 15 16 17 18
19 20 21 22 23 24 25
26 27 28 29 30

MAY
S M T W T F S
1 2
3 4 5 6 7 8 9
10 11 12 13 14 15 16
17 18 19 20 21 22 23
24 25 26 27 28 29 30
31

JUNE
S M T W T F S
1 2 3 4 5 6
7 8 9 10 11 12 13
14 15 16 17 18 19 20
21 22 23 24 25 26 27
28 29 30

JULY
S M T W T F S
1 2 3 4
5 6 7 8 9 10 11
12 13 14 15 16 17 18
19 20 21 22 23 24 25
26 27 28 29 30 31

AUGUST
S M T W T F S
1
2 3 4 5 6 7 8
9 10 11 12 13 14 15
16 17 18 19 20 21 22
23 24 25 26 27 28 29
30 31

SEPTEMBER
S M T W T F S
1 2 3 4 5
6 7 8 9 10 11 12
13 14 15 16 17 18 19
20 21 22 23 24 25 26
27 28 29 30

OCTOBER
S M T W T F S
1 2 3
4 5 6 7 8 9 10
11 12 13 14 15 16 17
18 19 20 21 22 23 24
25 26 27 28 29 30 31

NOVEMBER
S M T W T F S
1 2 3 4 5 6 7
8 9 10 11 12 13 14
15 16 17 18 19 20 21
22 23 24 25 26 27 28
29 30

DECEMBER
S M T W T F S
1 2 3 4 5
6 7 8 9 10 11 12
13 14 15 16 17 18 19
20 21 22 23 24 25 26
27 28 29 30 31

Church and Civic Calendar for 1997

JANUARY

1	New Year's Day
	The Name of Jesus
5	Twelfth Night
6	Epiphany
7	Eastern Orthodox
	Christmas
18	Confession of St. Peter
20	Martin Luther King Jr. Day
25	Conversion of St. Paul

FEBRUARY

1	National Freedom Day
2	Presentation of Jesus in the Temple
	Groundhog Day
3	Four Chaplains Memorial Day
12	Ash Wednesday
	Lincoln's Birthday
14	St. Valentine's Day
16	First Sunday in Lent
17	Presidents Day
22	Washington's Birthday
23	Second Sunday in Lent

MARCH

2	Third Sunday in Lent
9	Fourth Sunday in Lent
16	Fifth Sunday in Lent
17	St. Patrick's Day
19	Joseph, Husband of Mary
23	Palm/Passion Sunday
23–29	Holy Week
	Purim
27	Maundy Thursday
28	Good Friday
30	Easter

APRIL

6	Daylight Saving Time Begins
14	Pan-American Day
22	Passover
25	St. Mark, Evangelist
27	Orthodox Easter

MAY

1	Law Day
	Loyalty Day
	May Day
	St. Philip and St. James, Apostles
1–5	Cinco de Mayo Celebration
8	Ascension Day
11	Mother's Day
	Festival of the Christian Home
18	Pentecost
25	Trinity Sunday
26	Memorial Day

JUNE

8	Children's Sunday
11	First Day of Shavuot
15	Father's Day
29	St. Peter and St. Paul, Apostles

JULY

1	Canada Day
4	Independence Day
22	St. Mary Magdalene
25	St. James the Elder

AUGUST

4	Civic Holiday (Canada)
6	The Transfiguration
14	Atlantic Charter Day
15	Mary, the Mother of Jesus
24	St. Bartholomew, Apostle
26	Women Equality Day
31	Labor Sunday

SEPTEMBER

1	Labor Day
7	Grandparents' Day
	Rally Day
8	Birth of Virgin Mary
17	Citizenship Day
21	St. Matthew, Apostle and
	Evangelist
	Christian Education Sunday
	Gold Star Mother's Day
29	St. Michael and All Angels

OCTOBER

2–3	Rosh Hashanah

5 World Communion Sunday
11 Yom Kippur
12 Laity Sunday
13 Columbus Day (observed)
   Thanksgiving Day (Canada)
16 Sukkoth
   World Food Day
18 St. Luke, Evangelist
24 United Nations Day
26 Daylight Saving Time Ends
28 St. Simon and St. Jude, Apostles
31 National UNICEF Day
   Reformation Day
   Halloween

NOVEMBER

1 All Saints' Day
2 All Souls' Day
4 Election Day
9 Stewardship Sunday
11 Armistice Day
   Veterans Day

Remembrance Day (Canada)
21 Presentation of the Virgin Mary
   in the Temple
23 Thanksgiving Sunday
   Bible Sunday
27 Thanksgiving Day
30 First Sunday of Advent
   St. Andrew, Apostle

DECEMBER

7 Second Sunday of Advent
14 Third Sunday of Advent
15 Bill of Rights Day
21 Fourth Sunday of Advent
   Forefathers' Day
24 Christmas Eve
25 Christmas
26 Boxing Day (Canada)
   St. Stephen, Deacon and Martyr
27 St. John, Apostle and Evangelist
28 The Holy Innocents, Martyrs
31 New Year's Eve Watch Night

The Revised Common Lectionary for 1997

The following Scripture lessons are commended for use in public worship by various Protestant churches and the Roman Catholic church and include first, second, Gospel readings, and Psalms, according to Cycle B from January 6 to November 29 and according to Cycle C from November 30 to December 31. (Copyright 1992 Consultation on Common Texts.)

EPIPHANY SEASON

Jan. 5: Jer. 31:7–14; Ps. 147:12–20; Eph. 1:3–14; John 1: (1–9) 10–18.
Jan. 12 (Epiphany): Isa. 60:1–6; Ps. 72:1–7, 10–14; Eph. 3:1–12; Matt. 2:1–12.
Jan. 19: 1 Sam. 3:1–10; Ps. 138:1–6, 13–18; 1 Cor. 6:12–20; John 1:43–51.
Jan. 26: Jonah 3:1–5, 10; Ps. 62:5–12; 1 Cor. 7:29–31; Mark 1:14–20.
Feb. 2: Deut. 18:15–20; Ps. 111; 1 Cor. 8:1–13; Mark 1:21–28.
Feb. 9: Isa. 40:21–31; Ps. 147:1–11, 20c; 1 Cor. 9:16–23; Mark 1:29–39.

LENT

Feb. 12 (Ash Wednesday): Joel 2:1–2, 12–17; Ps. 51:1–17; 2 Cor. 5:20b–6:10; Matt. 6:1–6, 16–21.
Feb. 16: Gen. 9:8–17; Ps. 25:1–10; 1 Pet. 3:18–22; Mark 1:9–15.
Feb. 23: Gen. 17:1–7, 15–16; Ps. 22:23–31; Rom. 4:13–25; Mark 8:31–38.
Mar. 2: Exod. 20:1–17; Ps. 18; 1 Cor. 1:18–25; John 2:13–22.
Mar. 9: Num. 21:4–9; Ps. 107:1–3, 17–22; Eph. 2:1–10; John 3:14–21.
Mar. 16: Jer. 31:31–34; Ps. 51:1–12; Heb. 5:5–10; John 12:20–33.

HOLY WEEK

Mar. 23 (Palm/Passion Sunday): Mark 11:1–11; Ps. 118:1–2, 19–29; (Passion) Isa. 50:4–9a; Ps. 31:9–16.
Mar. 24 (Monday): Isa. 42:1–9; Ps. 36:5–11; Heb. 9:11–15; John 12:1–11.
Mar. 25 (Tuesday): Isa. 49:1–7; Ps. 71:1–14; 1 Cor. 1:18–31; John 12:20–36.

Mar. 26 (Wednesday): Isa. 50:4–9a; Ps. 70; Heb. 12:1–3; John 13:21–32.

Mar. 27 (Thursday): Exod. 12:1–4 (5–10), 11–14; Ps. 116:1–2, 12–19; 1 Cor. 11:23–26; John 13:1–17, 31b–35.

Mar. 28 (Good Friday): Isa. 52:13–53:12; Ps. 22; Heb. 10:16–25 (alt.); Heb. 14–16; 5:7–9 (alt.); John 18:1–19:42.

Mar. 29 (Holy Saturday): Job 14:1–14 (alt.); Lam. 3:1–9, 19–24; Ps. 31:1–4, 15–16; 1 Peter 4:1–8; Matt. 27:57–66 (alt.); John 19:38–42 (alt.).

SEASON OF EASTER

Mar. 29–30 (Easter Vigil): Gen. 1:1–2, 4a; Ps. 136:1–9, 23–26; Gen. 7:1–5, 11–18; 8:6–18; 9:8–13; Ps. 46; Gen. 22:1–18; Ps. 16; Exod. 14:10–31; 15:20–21; Exod. 15:1b–13, 17–18 (resp.); Isa. 55:1–11; Isa. 12:2–6 (resp.); Bar. 3:9–15, 32–4:4 (alt.); Prov. 8:1–8, 19–21; 9:4–6 (alt.); Ps. 19; Ezek. 36:24–28; Pss. 42–43; Ezek. 37:1–14; Ps. 143; Zeph. 3:14–20; Ps. 98; Rom. 6:3–11; Ps. 114; Luke 24:1–12.

Mar. 30 (Easter Sunday): Acts 10:34–43 (alt.); Isa. 65:17–25 (alt.); Ps. 118:1–2, 14–24; 1 Cor. 15:19–26 (alt.); Acts 10:34–43 (alt.); John 20:1–18 (alt.); Luke 24:1–12 (alt.).

Mar. 30 (Easter Evening): Isa. 25:6–9; Ps. 114; 1 Cor. 5:6b–8; Luke 24:13–49.

Apr. 6: Acts 4:32–35; Ps. 133; 1 John 1:1–2:2; John 20:19–31.

Apr. 13: Acts 3:12–14; Ps. 4; 1 John 3:1–7; Luke 24:36b–48.

Apr. 20: Acts 4:5–12; Ps. 23; 1 John 3:16–24; John 10:11–18.

Apr. 27: Acts 8:26–40; Ps. 22:25–31; 1 John 4:7–21; John 15:1–8.

May 4: Acts 10:44–48; Ps. 98; 1 John 5:1–6; John 15:9–17.

May 11: Acts 1:15–17, 21–26; Ps. 1; 1 John 5:9–13; John 17:6–19.

SEASON OF PENTECOST

May 18: Ezek. 37:1–14 or Acts 2:1–2; Ps. 104:24–34, 35b; Rom. 8:22–27; John 15:26–27; 16:4b–15.

May 25: Isa. 6:1–8; Ps. 29; Rom. 8:12–17; John 3:1–17.

June 1: 1 Sam. 3:1–10 (11–20); Ps. 139:1–6, 13–18; 2 Cor. 4:5–12; Mark 2:23–3:6.

June 8: 1 Sam. 8:4–11 (12–15); 16–20 (11:14–15); Ps. 138; 2 Cor. 4:13–5:1; Mark 3:20–35.

June 15: 1 Sam. 15:34–16:13; Ps. 20; 2 Cor. 5:6–10 (11–13), 14–17; Mark 4:26–34.

June 22: 1 Sam. 17 (1a, 4–11, 19–23) 32–49; Ps. 9:9–20; 2 Cor. 6:1–13; Mark 4:35–41.

June 29: 2 Sam. 1:1, 17–27; Ps. 130; 2 Cor. 8:7–15; Mark 5:21–43.

July 6: 2 Sam. 5:1–5, 9–10; Ps. 48; 2 Cor. 12:2–10; Mark 6:1–13.

July 13: 2 Sam. 6:1–5, 12b–19; Ps. 24; Eph. 1:3–14; Mark 6:14–29.

July 20: 2 Sam. 7:1–14a; Ps. 89:20–37; Eph. 2:11–22; Mark 6:30–34, 53–56.

July 27: 2 Sam. 11:1–15; Ps. 14; Eph. 3:14–21; John 6:1–21.

Aug. 3: 2 Sam. 11:26–12:13a; Ps. 51:1–12; Eph. 4:1–16; John 6:24–35.

Aug. 10: 2 Sam. 18:5–9, 15, 31–33; Ps. 130; Eph. 4:25–5:2; John 6:35; 41–51.

Aug. 17: 1 Kings 2:10–12; 3:3–14; Ps. 111; Eph. 5:15–20; John 6:51–58.

Aug. 24: 1 Kings 8: (1, 6, 10–11) 22–30, 41–43; Ps. 84; Eph. 6:10–20; John 6:56–69.

Aug. 31: Song of Songs 2:8–13; Ps. 45:1–2, 6–9; James 1:17–27; Mark 7:1–8, 14–15, 21–23.

Sept. 7: Prov. 22:1–2, 8–9, 22–23; Ps. 125; James 2:1–10 (11–13), 14–17; Mark 7:24–37.

Sept. 14: Prov. 1:20–33; Ps. 19; James 3:1–12; Mark 8:27–38.

Sept. 21: Prov. 31:10–31; Ps. 1; James 3:13–4:13, 7–8a; Mark 9:30–37.

Sept. 28: Esther 7:1–6, 9–10; 9:20–22; Ps. 124; James 5:13–20; Mark 9:38–50.

Oct. 5: Job 1:1; 2:1–10; Ps. 26; Heb. 1:1–4; 2:5–12; Mark 10:2–16.

Oct. 12: Job 23:1–9, 16–17; Ps. 22:1–15; Heb. 4:12–16; Mark 10:17–31.

Oct. 19: Job 38:1–7 (34–41); Ps. 104:1–9, 24, 35c; Heb. 5:1–10; Mark 10:35–45.

Oct. 26: Job 42:1–6, 10–17; Ps. 34:1–8 (19–22); Heb. 7:23–28; Mark 10:46–52.

Nov. 2: Ruth 1:1–18; Ps. 146; Heb. 9:11–14; Mark 12:28–34.

Nov. 9: Ruth 3:1–5; 4:13–17; Ps. 127; Heb. 9:24–28; Mark 12:38–44.

Nov. 16: 1 Sam. 1:4–20; Ps. 16; Heb. 10:11–14 (15–18), 19–25; Mark 13:1–8.

Nov. 23 (Christ the King): 2 Sam. 23:1–7;
Ps. 132:1–12 (13–18); Rev. 1:4b–8; John
18:33–37.
Nov. 27 (Thanksgiving): Joel 2:21–27; Ps.
126; 1 Tim. 2:1–7; Matt. 6:25–33.

ADVENT AND CHRISTMAS SEASON

Nov. 30: Jer. 33:14–16; Ps. 25:1–10; 1
Thess. 3:9–13; Luke 21:25–36.
Dec. 7: Mal. 3:1–4; Luke 1:68–79; Phil.
1:3–11; Luke 3:1–6.

Dec. 14: Zeph. 3:14–20; Isa. 12:2–6; Phil.
1:3–11; Luke 3:1–6.
Dec. 21: Mic. 5:2–5a; Luke 1:47–55; Heb.
10:5–10; Luke 1:39–45 (46–55).
Dec. 25 (Christmas Day): Isa. 9:2–7; Ps. 96;
Titus 2:11–14; Luke 2:1–14 (15–20) or
Isa. 62:6–12; Ps. 97; Titus 3:4–7; Luke
2:(1–7) 8–20 or Isa. 52:7–10; Ps. 98;
Heb. 1:1–4 (5–12); John 1:1–14.
Dec. 28: 1 Sam. 2:18–20, 26; Ps. 148; Col.
3:12–17; Luke 2:41–52.

Four-Year Church Calendar

	1997	1998	1999	2000
Ash Wednesday	February 12	February 25	February 17	March 8
Palm Sunday	March 23	April 5	March 28	April 16
Good Friday	March 28	April 10	April 2	April 21
Easter	March 30	April 12	April 4	April 23
Ascension Day	May 8	May 21	May 13	June 1
Pentecost	May 18	May 31	May 23	June 11
Trinity Sunday	May 25	June 7	May 30	June 18
Thanksgiving	November 27	November 26	November 25	November 23
Advent Sunday	November 30	November 29	November 28	December 3

Forty-Year Easter Calendar

1997 March 30	2007 April 8	2017 April 16	2027 March 28
1998 April 12	2008 March 23	2018 April 1	2028 April 16
1999 April 4	2009 April 12	2019 April 21	2029 April 1
2000 April 23	2010 April 4	2020 April 12	2030 April 21
2001 April 18	2011 April 24	2021 April 4	2031 April 13
2002 March 31	2012 April 8	2022 April 17	2032 March 28
2003 April 20	2013 March 31	2023 April 9	2033 April 17
2004 April 11	2014 April 20	2024 March 31	2034 April 9
2005 March 27	2015 April 5	2025 April 20	2035 March 25
2006 April 16	2016 March 27	2026 April 5	2036 April 13

Traditional Wedding Anniversary Identifications

1 Paper	7 Wool	13 Lace	35 Coral
2 Cotton	8 Bronze	14 Ivory	40 Ruby
3 Leather	9 Pottery	15 Crystal	45 Sapphire
4 Linen	10 Tin	20 China	50 Gold
5 Wood	11 Steel	25 Silver	55 Emerald
6 Iron	12 Silk	30 Pearl	60 Diamond

Colors Appropriate for Days and Seasons

White.   Symbolizes purity, perfection, and joy and identifies festivals marking events, except Good Friday, in the life of Jesus: Christmas, Epiphany, Easter, Eastertide, Ascension Day; also Trinity Sunday, All Saints' Day, weddings, funerals. Gold may also be used.

Red.   Symbolizes the Holy Spirit, martyrdom, and the love of God: Good Friday, Pentecost, and Sundays following.

Violet.   Symbolizes penitence: Advent, Lent.

Green.   Symbolizes mission to the world, hope, regeneration, nurture, and growth: Epiphany season, Kingdomtide, Rural Life Sunday, Labor Sunday, Thanksgiving Sunday.

Blue.   Advent, in some churches.

Flowers in Season Appropriate for Church Use

January. Carnation or snowdrop.
February. Violet or primrose.
March. Jonquil or daffodil.
April. Lily, sweet pea, or daisy.
May. Lily of the valley or hawthorn.
June. Rose or honeysuckle.

July. Larkspur or water lily.
August. Gladiolus poppy.
September. Aster or morning glory.
October. Calendula or cosmos.
November. Chrysanthemum.
December. Narcissus, holly, or poinsettia.

Historical, Cultural, and Religious Anniversaries in 1997

Compiled by Kenneth M. Cox

10 Years (1987). *March 10:* The Vatican issues document regarding procreation, condemning "test-tube" fertilization and artificial insemination and advocating laws prohibiting surrogate motherhood. *March 19:* Evangelist Jim Bakker resigns his PTL ministry amid brewing scandal. *October 19:* U.S. stock market crashes, as the Dow Jones Industrial Average falls nearly 23 percent.

25 Years (1972). *February 20:* President Nixon arrives in Peking, meets with Chairman Mao Tse-tung and Premier Chou Enlai, ending U.S. hostility toward People's Republic of China. *May 15:* Alabama Governor George Wallace, campaigning for Democratic presidential nomination, is shot by Arthur Bremer in Laurel, Maryland. *May 22:* President Nixon arrives in Moscow, confers with Communist Party Secretary Leonid Brezhnev, becoming first U.S. President to visit the Soviet Union. *June 17:* Arrests of five men inside Democratic Party national headquarters in Watergate apartment complex mark beginning of Watergate affair. *September 5:* PLO terrorists murder eleven Israeli athletes at summer Olympic Games in Munich. *October 5:* Congregationalists and English Presbyterians join as United Reformed Church in England and Wales. Debut: *Ms.* magazine.

50 Years (1947). *March 12:* President Truman, in speech to Congress, outlines "Truman Doctrine," to provide aid to Greece and Turkey to help prevent Communist infiltration. *June 23:* Taft-Hartley Act passes over President Truman's veto, increasing restrictions on organized labor. Bedouin boy discovers Dead Sea Scrolls of parchment written in first century B.C. by Jews of Essene sect, containing nearly all of Old Testament book of Isaiah. Jackie Robinson joins Brooklyn Dodgers, becoming first black baseball player in major leagues. Debut: Everglades National Park.

75 Years (1922). *February 1:* Washington Conference among Britain, France, Italy, Japan, and U.S. restricts submarine warfare and use of poison gas. *March:* Irish Republican Army, militant arm of Sinn Fein political party, is formally constituted "to safeguard the honor and independence of the Irish Republic." *March 15:* Kingdom of Egypt proclaimed, after Britain terminates protectorate. *November:* King Tutankha-

men's tomb discovered at Luxor. Debuts: British Broadcasting Corporation; *Reader's Digest.*

100 Years (1897). *June 2:* Mark Twain cables *The New York Times* from London: "The report of my death was an exaggeration." *June 16:* Treaty annexes Hawaiian Islands to U.S. Zionism formally established at International Jewish Congress in Basel. Debuts: Boston Marathon; cathode-ray tube; "The Katzenjammer Kids" cartoon; Waldorf-Astoria Hotel.

125 Years (1872). *June:* Jesse James gang robs its first U.S. passenger train. *June 25:* Jesuits expelled from Germany under imperial law as part of new Kulturkampf. Pittsburgh evangelist Charles Taze Russell's

"The Object and Manner of Our Lord's Return" announces second coming of Christ in fall of 1874 without mankind's awareness. Debuts: Vanderbilt University; Yellowstone National Park.

150 Years (1847). *November:* Donner Party trapped by deep snow in Sierra Nevada; about half survive, some by eating flesh of those who died. Fifteen thousand Mormons arrive on shores of Great Salt Lake in Mexican territory soon to be ceded to U.S., and Brigham Young establishes himself as president of independent nation. English novelist publishes *Wuthering Heights.* United Presbyterian Church is formed. Debuts: American Medical Association; nitroglycerine; ring doughnuts.

Anniversaries of Hymn Writers and Hymn-Tune Composers in 1997

Compiled by Hugh T. McElrath

25 Years (1972) *Death* of Jack D. Scholfield (b. 1882), author-composer "Saved, Saved"–RAPTURE

50 Years (1947) *Birth* of Barry Braman, composer PORTALS ("Creator of the Universe"); Ruth Duck, author of "Arise, your light is come," "To God compose a song of joy," "Lead on, O cloud of presence," "As grain on scattered hillsides," and others; David L. Edwards, author-composer "You have called me"–KAY'S SONG, "Fill the world with love"–COMPASSION, "Some there are that by their living"–GREENCASTLE, and others; James Gestmenian, author-composer "God of Abraham and Sarah"–CONSTANTINE, author "The weaver's shuttle softly flies"; Daniel L. Schutte, author-composer "Here I am, Lord"–HERE I AM, LORD; Russell E. Sonafrank II, author "Bless God, O my God."

Death of Percy C. Buck (b. 1871), composer GONFALON ROYAL ("The royal banners forward go"); Will H. Houghton (b. 1887), composer LEAD ME ("Lead me to some soul today"); Timothy Tingfang Lew (b. 1891), author original "The Bread of life, for all men broken"); Sydney H. Nicholson (b. 1875), composer BOW BRICKHILL ("We sing the praise of Him who died"), CHISTLEHURST ("Hail the day that sees Him rise"), CRUCIFER ("Lift high the

cross"), FENITON ("Christ upon the mountain peak"), and others.

75 Years (1922) *Birth* of Doris Akers, author-composer "Sweet, sweet spirit"–MANNA; Colbert S. Cartwright, author "Be in our midst, O Christ"; Edith Sinclair Downing, author "When, like the woman at the well," "God, who summons through all ages"; Robert E. Kreutz, composer FINEST WHEAT ("You satisfy the hungry heart"); Keith Landis, author-composer "Make a joyful noise"–JOYFUL NOISE, "Christ, the world's true light is waking"–RAFFERTY, "Behold the face of God"–CHARLOTTE, "God so loved the world," "Yesterday, Today, Forever"–RANDLES, and others.

Death of Myles Birket Foster (b. 1851), composer CRUCIS MILITES ("Soldiers of the cross, arise!"), CRUCIS VICTORIA ("Lift up your headsm ye gates of brass"), SALVATOR ("When the Lord of love was here"); William Herbert Jude (b. 1851), composer GALILEE ("Jesus calls us o'er the tumult"). Johnson Oatman, Jr. (b. 1856), author "Count your blessings," "He included me," "Higher ground," "No, not one," and others; Denis Wortman (b. 1835), author "God of the prophets, bless the prophet's sons."

100 Years (1897) *Birth* of Purd E. Deitz (d. 1987), author "We would be building"; Ellis Govan, author "I will not be afraid."

Death of Frederick C. Atkinson (b. 1841), composer MORECAMBE ("Spirit of God, descend upon my heart"); Jane L. Borthwick (b. 1813), translator "Be still, my soul," "Jesus, still lead on," "My Jesus, as Thou wilt," and others; Frances E. Cox (b. 1812), translator "Jesus lives!" "Now rest beneath night's shadows," "Sing praise to God who reigns above," and others; Emily Elizabeth Steele Elliott (b. 1836), author "Thou didst leave Thy throne and Thy kingly crown"; William Walsham How (b. 1823), author "For all the saints," "O Jesus, Thou art standing," "O Word of God incarnate," "We give Thee but Thine own," and others; Jean Ingelow (b. 1820), author "And didst Thou love the race that loved not Thee?"; Francis T. Palgrave (b. 1824), author "Christ in Clara H. Scott (b. 1841), author-composer "Open my eyes, that I may see" SCOTT; Lawrence Tuttiett (b. 1825), author "Father, let me dedicate," and others.

125 Years (1872) *Birth* of Cyril A. Alington (d. 1955), author "Good Christian men, rejoice and sing"; John S. Arkwright (d. 1954), author "O valiant hearts, who to your glory came"; John M. C. Crum (d. 1958), author "Now the green blade riseth"; Hugh T. Kerr (d. 1950), author "God our life, through all the circling years"; William C. Piggott (d. 1943), author "For those we love within the vail"; H. Wheeler Robinson (d. 1945), author "O Thou whose love has brought us here"; Edward Shillito (d. 1948), author "Away with gloom, away with doubt"; Edward Shillito (d. 1948), composer DOWN AMPNEY ("Come down, O love divine"), KING'S WESTON ("At the name of Jesus, every knee shall bow" and others), THE CALL ("Come, my way, my truth, my life"); adapter and harmonizer FOREST GREEN ("O little town of Bethlehem" and others), KINGSFOLD ("O sing a song of Bethlehem") and others, KING'S LYNN ("God God of earth and altar"), and others, LASST UNS ERFREUEN ("All creatures of our God and king" and others), MIT FREUDEN ZART ("Sing praise to God who reigns above" and others), MONK'S GATE ("He who would valiant be" and others), THIS ENDRIS NYGHT ("I come, the great Redeemer cries").

Death of John Bowring (b. 1792), author "God is love, His mercy brightens," "In the cross of Christ I glory," "Watchman, tell us of the night," and others; Henry F. Chorley (b. 1808), author "God the omnipotent! King who ordainest"; Nicolai F. S. Gruntvig (b. 1783), author original of "Built on the rock"; Thomas Hastings (b. 1784), composer ORTONVILLE ("Majestic sweetness sits enthroned"), and others, RETREAT ("From every stormy wind that blows"), and others, TOPLADY ("Rock of Ages"); Charles Jeffries (b. 1896), author "Speak forth your word, O Father"; Conrad Kocker (b. 1786), composer DIX ("For the beauty of the earth," "As with gladness men of old"; Mary Macdonald (b. 1789), author "Child in the manger"; Norman McLeof (b. 1812), author "Courage, brother, do not stumble."

150 Years (1847) *Birth* of Henry Scott Holland (d. 1918), author "Judge eternal, throned in splendor"; William Boyd (d. 1928), composer PENTECOST ("Let there be light, O God of hosts"), and others; Alfred Scott-Gatty (d. 1918), composer WELWYN ("Observer man, fold to thy heart thy brother," "Lord of true light, we gratefully adore Thee"); Will L. Thompson (d. 1909), author-composer "Jesus is all the world to me"—ELIZABETH, "Softly and tenderly Jesus is calling" —THOMPSON and others; Samuel A. Ward (d. 1903), composer, MATERNA ("O beautiful for spacious skies"); Winfield S. Weeden (d. 1908), composer SURRENDER ("I surrender all"); SUNLIGHT IN MY SOUL ("I wandered in the shades of night").

Death of William Crotch (b. 1775), composer SIDON ("Lord, it belongs not to my care"), OLD 134th (ST. MICHAEL) ("Stand up and bless the Lord"), and others; Franz Michael Franzen (b. 1772), author original of "Prepare the way, O Zion"; Henry Francis Lyte (b. 1793), author "Abide with me," "God of mercy, God of grace," "Jesus, I my cross have taken," "Praise, my soul, the King of heaven," and others; Felix Mendelssohn (b. 1809), composer MENDELSSOHN ("Hark! the herald angels sing", ALMIGHTY FATHER ("Almighty Father, hear our prayer"); Dorothy A. Thrupp (b. 1779), author "Saviour, like a shepherd, lead us."

175 Years (1822) *Birth* of John E. Gould (d. 1875), composer PILOT (Jesus Saviour,

pilot me"); Thomas Hughes (d. 1896), author "O God of truth, whose living word"; William Dunn Longstaff (d. 1896), author "Take time to be holy"; George Hunt Smyttan (d. 1870), author "Forty days and forty nights."

200 Years (1797) *Birth* of William Bullock (d. 1874), author "We love the place, O Lord"; Edward Mote (d. 1874), author "My hope is built"; Death of Meyer Leoni (b. 1751), transcriber of LEONE ("The God of Abraham praise").

225 Years (1772) *Birth* of William Walford (d. 1850), author "Sweet hour of prayer."

250 Years (1747) *Birth* of Joseph Bromehead (d. 1826), author "Jerusalem, my happy home"; Johann A. P. Schultz (d. 1800), author-composer "Oh, come, little children"–SCHULTZ.

275 Years (1722) *Birth* of Peter Williams (d. 1796), translator "Guide me, O Thou great Jehovah"; Christopher Smart (d. 1771), author "Awake, arise, lift up your voice," "Hearken to the anthem glorious," "Where is this stupendous stranger?" "We sing of God, the mighty source of all things."

300 Years (1697) *Birth* of Katharina von Schlegel (d. unknown), author original of "Be still, my soul"; Gerjard Tersteegen (d. 1769), author original of "God himself is with us," and others. *Death* of Jean Baptiste de Santeuil (b. 1630), author original of "Captains of the saintly band."

325 Years (1672) *Birth* of Joseph Addison (d. 1719), author "The spacious firmament on high," "When all Thy mercies, O my God," and others; Benjamin Schmolk (d. 1737), author original of "My Jesus, as Thou wilt"; Johann Christoph Schwedler (d. 1730), author original of "Ask ye what great thing I know." *Death* of Heinrich Schutz (b. 1585), composer PSALM 84 ("How lovely is your dwelling"), and other psalm tunes.

350 Years (1647) *Death* of John Milton, Sr. (b. 1563), harmonizer YORK ("The Lord will come and not be slow"), and others; Johann Heerman (b. 1585), author original of "Ah, holy Jesus, how hast Thou offended."

375 Years (1622) *Birth* of Henry Vaughan (d. 1695), author "Lord, when Thou didst Thyself undress" and "My soul, there is a country."

425 Years (1572) *Death* of Claude Goudimel (b. 1514), harmonizer GENEVA 42 and other Genevan metrical psalm tunes.

1600 Years (397) *Death* of Ambrose, Bishop of Milan (b. 340), author of original "O splendor of God's glory bright," "O Trinity of blessed light," and others.

Quotable Quotations

1. That which we really know about God is not what we have been clever enough to find out, but what the Divine Charity has secretly revealed.–Evelyn Underhill

2. Vice knows she's ugly, so puts on her Mask.–Benjamin Franklin

3. No man can think clearly when his fists are clenched.–George Jean Nathan.

4. There is no man suddenly either excellently good or extremely evil.–Sir Philip Sidney

5. According to Gandhi, the seven sins are wealth without works, pleasure without conscience, knowledge without character, commerce without morality, science without humanity, worship without sacrifice, and politics without principle.–Jimmy Carter

6. The best sin of the pious man is to become the proud man.–Dorothy L. Sayers

7. A Church is faithful not by refusing to change but by being willing to grow.–Eugene C. Kennedy

8. When an evil act has been committed, the person who blames himself for that act (that is, hates his action *and* himself) will focus on his own worthlessness rather than on how to correct the act in the future.–Paul A. Hauck

9. Man is the only animal that blushes or needs to.–Mark Twain

10. The best cure for worry, depression, melancholy, brooding, is to go deliberately forth and try to lift with one's sympathy the gloom of somebody else.–Arnold Bennett

11. A child miseducated is a child lost.–John F. Kennedy

12. Tempt not a desperate man.–William Shakespeare

13. Whatever a man sows, that shall he

reap. The law of Karma is inexorable and impossible of evasion. There is hardly any need for God to interfere. He laid down the rules and, as it were, retired.–Mohandas K. Gandhi

14. The intellectual emancipation of women may actually be the crucial step in ushering in one of the noblest chapters in the history of the Christian faith.–D. Elton Trueblood

15. Flattery is all right–if you don't inhale.–Adlai Stevenson

16. Without the work of God's Spirit in opening our hearts, we cannot really understand the Bible.–Emil Brunner

17. When peace has been broken anywhere, the peace of all countries everywhere is in danger.–Franklin D. Roosevelt

18. In science we have been reading only the notes to a poem; in Christianity we find the poem itself.–C. S. Lewis

19. Judge a man by his questions rather than by his answers.–Voltaire

20. Few things are harder to put up with than a good example.–Mark Twain

21. I don't know the answers, but I know the Answerer. It's not what you know but who you know that counts.–Peter Kreeft

22. Alone we can do so little; together we can do so much.–Helen Keller

23. If we want a love that will protect the soul from wounds, we must love something other than God.–Simone Weil

24. Although God is good, this does not mean that he is goody-good or that all he does is pleasant and agreeable to human tastes.–Victor White

25. Nothing is worse than active ignorance.–Goethe

26. The heart has its reasons which reason knows nothing of.–Blaise Pascal

27. It is worse than useless for Christians to talk about the importance of Christian morality unless they are prepared to take their stand upon the fundamentals of Christian theology.–Dorothy L. Sayers

28. The value of marriage is not that adults produce children but that children produce adults.–Peter de Vries

29. The desire for truth is the desire for God.–John Macquarrie

30. As scarce as truth is, the supply has always been in excess of the demand.–Josh Billings

31. The only way to have a friend is to be one.–Ralph Waldo Emerson

32. In prayer we shift the center of living from self-consciousness to self-surrender.–Abraham J. Heschel

33. We have just enough religion to make us hate, but not enough to love one another.–Jonathan Swift

34. Wherever I have studied adults, I have found impressions left on them from their early childhood and lasting forever.–Alfred Adler

35. Wisdom don't consist in knowing more that is new, but in knowing less that is false.–Josh Billings

36. The Kingdom of God actually exists wherever living faith and living love grows out of communion with God.–Emil Brunner

37. No one has mastered the art of living who has not mastered the art of dying.–Peter Kreeft

38. Seize upon truth, wherever it is found, amongst your friends, amongst your foes, on Christian or on heathen ground; the flower's divine where'er it grows.–Isaac Watts

39. There are no hopeless situations. There are only men and women who have grown hopeless about them.–Anonymous

40. Every calamity is a spur and valuable hint.–Ralph Waldo Emerson

41. A man may go to Heaven with half the pains which it costs him to purchase Hell.–Henry Fielding

42. Sex prejudice is so ingrained in our society that many who practice it are simply unaware that they are hurting women. *It is the last socially acceptable prejudice.*–Bernice Sandler

43. For our race the Kingdom of God can only come by the Cross, by crisis, by a breach with the natural life, though not a disruption of it. It is this new relation to a Holy Creator and His eternity that gives the final value to life's chief assets and its best dreams.–P. T. Forsyth

44. Happy the Man, and happy he alone
He who can call today his own;
He who, secure within, can say,

Tomorrow do thy worst, for I have liv'd today.
                                    –Horace

45. The faith that makes men whole makes room for questions and for the blessing of endless discovery and surprise.– Eugene C. Kennedy

46. Only prayer can wear away our native resistance to God.–Ian Shevill

47. A spoonful of honey will catch more flies than a gallon of vinegar.–Benjamin Franklin

48. Do not fight doubts with reasons or with arguments; but fight them with deeds. –Jacques Benigne Bossuet

49. To pray is to expose oneself to the promptings of God; and, by the same token, to become less suggestible to the low persuasions of the world.–George A. Buttrick

50. Is it progress if a cannibal uses a fork?–Stanislaw J. Lec

51. There is no more fertile source of disruption in marriage today than this inability to distinguish between the reality of love and the feeling of love. Christian marriage is founded not primarily on a feeling or an emotion, but on a relation, a convenantal bond in which two people have committed themselves to each other before God to hold to each other through all the changing weather of their human feeling.–James E. Smart

52. Every difficulty slurred over will be a ghost to disturb your repose later on.– Chopin

53. Very few of us would be Christians today if there had not been missionaries yesterday.–Roy L. Smith

54. Prayer is a space in which to become truly human.–David Jenkins

55. A Christian man is the most free lord of all, and subject to none; a Christian man is the most dutiful servant of all, and subject to everyone.–Martin Luther

56. We never love our neighbor so truly, as when our love for him is prompted by the love of God.–Francois Fenelon

57. The moral sense, or conscience, is as much a part of man as his leg or arm.– Thomas Jefferson

58. Change is certain. Progress is not.– E. H. Carr

59. Creation is simply an act of divine love and cannot be accounted for on any other supposition than that of immense and eternal love.–F. W. Faber

60. Gossip is when you hear something you like about someone you don't.–Earl Wilson

61. That which seems the height of absurdity in one generation often becomes the height of wisdom in the next.–Attributed to John Stuart Mill

62. Usually a person with an unswerving belief in a God of justice and goodness is one who was blessed with a loving and incorruptible parent.–Karl Menninger

63. A spiritual person feels himself to be "more at home" in the universe than unspiritual persons do. He has a certain serenity and inward peace which others cannot help envying and even admiring.–H. H. Price

64. To some people, roses have thorns. To others, thorns have roses.–Peter Kreeft

65. The louder he talked of his honor, the faster we counted our spoons.–Ralph Waldo Emerson

66. Education is a loan to be repaid with gift of self.–Lady Bird Johnson

67. Between a man and his wife nothing ought to rule but love.–William Penn

68. If you think education is expensive– try ignorance.–Derek Bok

69. To achieve great things we must live as though we were never going to die.– Marquis de Vauvenargues

70. God does not guarantee to any of us freedom from sickness or death. . . . Sickness is no more a sign of deficiency in faith or piety than health is proof of faith and piety.–Frank Stagg

71. Wherever there is uncertainty, hope springs eternal. The irreligious individual no less than the religious plans for a happy landing.–Gordon W. Allport

72. Prayer, as petition and intercession, helps to make the human reality, and not only that part of it actively engaged in prayer.–John Macquarrie

73. Happiness is good health and a bad memory.–Ingrid Bergman

74. The church with no great anguish on

its heart has no great music on its lips.–Karl Barth

75. Don't be humble; you're not that great.–Golda Meir

76. God does not die on the day when we cease to believe in a personal deity, but we die on the day when our lives cease to be illumined by the steady radiance, renewed daily, of a wonder, the source of which is beyond all reason.–Dag Hammarskjold

77. Content makes poor men rich; Discontent makes rich men poor.–Benjamin Franklin

78. God is the creator of laughter that is good.–Philo

79. In order to be happy oneself it is necessary to make at least one other person happy.–Theodore Reik

80. The greatest happiness you can have is knowing that you do not necessarily require happiness.–William Saroyan

81. Give me a firm place to stand, and I will move the earth.–Archimedes

82. I believe the life of the Spirit is something we break into as we break out of ourselves through trying to love more deeply and truly.–Eugene C. Kennedy

83. The trouble with most of us is that we would rather be ruined by praise than saved by criticism.–Norman Vincent Peale

84. Where love is, there is God also.–Leo Tolstoy

85. In all ranks of life the human heart yearns for the beautiful; and the beautiful things that God makes are his gift to all alike.–Harriet Beecher Stowe

86. I have never smoked in my life and look forward to a time when the world will look back in amazement and disgust to a practice so unnatural and offensive.–George Bernard Shaw

87. I am as certain as that I live that nothing is so near to me as God.–Meister Eckhart

88. The universe is like a safe to which there is a combination, but the combination is locked up in the safe.–Peter de Vries

89. This time, like all times, is a very good one, if we but know what to do with it.–Ralph Waldo Emerson

90. Time heals what reason cannot.–Seneca

91. Consecration is handing God a blank sheet to fill in with your name signed at the bottom.–M. H. Miller

92. Guilt is the gift that keeps on giving.–Erma Bombeck

93. Sin is not hurtful because it is forbidden but it is forbidden because it's hurtful.–Benjamin Franklin

94. When a needy person stands at your door God himself stands at his side.–Hebrew proverb

95. He was a bold man that first ate an oyster.–Jonathan Swift

96. At fifty, everyone has the face he deserves.–George Orwell

97. If it be *things* that slay you, what matter whether things you have, or things you have not?–George Macdonald

98. Love is what you've been through with somebody.–James Thurber

99. Thou hast given so much to me. . . . Give one thing more–a grateful heart.–George Herbert

100. Labor to keep alive in your breast that little spark of celestial fire called conscience.–George Washington

Questions of Life and Religion

These questions may be useful to prime homiletic pumps, as discussion starters, or for study and youth groups.

1. Why do people of every culture pray?

2. What was the purpose of Jesus' miracles?

3. Are dramatic signs needed to bring us to faith?

4. What are the false trails to avoid in the "pursuit of happiness"?

5. Is fear a necessary part of life?

6. How can we deal with confusion and indecision?

7. Are there special indications of God's "call" to special Christian service?

8. How may God be involved in whatever work we do?

9. Is there a way to get beyond our self-centeredness?

10. Can we really accept ourselves?

11. How can we build up a treasury of good memories?

12. Does humor contribute to a sense of wholeness in life?

13. How can we best prepare for old age?

14. What can our children teach us?

15. What does it mean to worship God?

16. Who are and who are not God's people?

17. Are there other helpful images of God in addition to "Father"?

18. What are some special gifts of God to people for God's service?

19. How can we know that we are forgiven?

20. In what ways were the temptations of Jesus like our own temptations?

21. Is the evil thought as bad as the evil deed?

22. What is the right way for a Christian to handle a personal enemy?

23. Why is the institution of marriage to be held in high honor?

24. What do we mean when we say that God was enfleshed or incarnate in Jesus of Nazareth?

25. In what ways is the Church unavoidably related to the world?

26. What can we do to get God to approve of us and grant us salvation?

27. What kind of rewards can we expect in heaven?

28. How can we prepare ourselves to receive Holy Communion most fittingly?

29. Why is "the blood of Christ" emphasized in Scripture and song?

30. Is it true and helpful to think of Jesus as a Friend and Presence?

31. What are some practical things we can do to minister to people who have lost a loved one in death?

32. Should we expect forgiveness to be easy?

33. What should be our attitude if our best efforts for our Lord seem to fail?

34. What is the Church?

35. Is thanksgiving a neglected element of our personal prayers?

36. How can we make right decisions in a complex society?

37. Are we in some ways practitioners of idolatry today?

38. In ethical dilemmas, when, if ever, does the end justify the means?

39. What is the simplest irreducible minimum of Christian belief?

40. How should we calculate our Christian financial stewardship?

41. What is our missionary obligation as Christians to people of other religious faiths?

42. Are self-esteem and humility in conflict?

43. How can we maintain a good conscience?

44. Is there such a thing as "sick religion"?

45. What are the evidences of a true conversion?

46. Are there legitimate and creative uses of anger?

47. What can we say about the near-death experiences of people who come back to report on the afterlife?

48. How does humor help in daily life?

49. Is depression a matter of religious concern?

50. How is God's providence manifested?

51. What can permanently break the cycle of addiction?

52. In what ways is Jesus' style of dealing with people desirable for our own behavior?

53. What will heaven be like?

54. How are we to understand the Final Judgment?

55. Is the pastor supposed to be also a prophet?

56. How can church members prepare themselves to hear sermons?

57. What does prayer change?

58. How can I determine if the Holy Spirit is leading me?

59. Are we ever truly free?

60. Is being "born again" for *all* Christians?

61. How desirable is "tough love" in the home?

62. How much do we really need to know about God?

63. What can our troubles teach us?

64. How can one reach one's greatest potential as a human being?

65. What are the essentials of a happy marriage?

66. Is eternal life a present possession?

67. How can we overcome our fears?

68. Is our physical health a matter of religious concern?

69. How does God protect us?

70. What should we do when everything seems to go wrong?

71. Why do people suffer?

72. Is God personal?

73. Is it possible to live one day at a time?

74. How do God's deliverances arrive?

75. How valuable is the individual?

76. Can we resolve the struggle between the new and the old?

77. What are some basic guidelines for understanding the Bible?

78. What was involved in the writing of the Scriptures?

79. How far can we go with the crowd?

80. What are the differences between belief and faith?

81. Is Christian hope wishful thinking?

82. How does Christian love, as Paul saw it, differ from other expressions of love?

83. Does criticism have a healthful role in the church?

84. What are our obligations as religious people to the government?

85. Do the order and beauty of God's creation contribute to our religious experience?

86. Why does God sometimes seem silent?

87. Is the Christian way the only way?

88. What is sanctification?

89. Do we find God or does God find us?

90. What are the sources of a pastor's authority?

91. Are the people of all nations and races kin?

92. How can we overcome temptation?

93. Does the church still need reformation?

94. What message does Jesus' resurrection send to all our human needs?

95. What should we do when we have sinned?

96. Do religious faith and practice enlarge or narrow life?

97. What does every Christian marriage need?

98. Why does the Cross of Christ have a lasting appeal?

99. Is joy a continuing possibility for the believer?

100. How can we overcome divisions in the household of faith?

Biblical Benedictions and Blessings

The Lord watch between me and thee, when we are absent from one another.– Gen. 31:49

The Lord bless thee, and keep thee; the Lord make his face to shine upon thee, and be gracious unto thee; the Lord lift up his countenance upon thee, and give thee peace.–Num. 6:24–26

The Lord our God be with us, as he was with our fathers; let him not leave us, nor forsake us; that he may incline our hearts unto him, to walk in all his ways, and to keep his commandments, and his statutes, and his judgments, which he commanded our fathers.–1 Kings 8:57–58

Let the words of my mouth, and the meditation of my heart, be acceptable in thy sight, O Lord, my strength, and my redeemer.–Ps. 19:14

Now the God of patience and consolation grant you to be likeminded one toward another according to Christ Jesus; that ye may with one mind and one mouth glorify God, even the Father of our Lord Jesus Christ. Now the God of hope fill you with all joy and peace in believing, that ye may abound in hope, through the power of the Holy Ghost. Now the God of peace be with you.–Rom. 15:5–6, 13, 33

Now to him that is of power to establish you according to my gospel and the teaching of Jesus Christ, according to the revelation of the mystery, which was kept secret since the world began, but now is manifest, and by the scriptures of the prophets, according to the commandment of the everlasting God, made known to all nations for the obedience of faith: To God only wise, be glory through Jesus Christ for ever.– Rom. 16:25–27

Grace be unto you, and peace, from God our Father, and from the Lord Jesus Christ.–1 Cor. 1:3

The grace of the Lord Jesus Christ and the love of God, and the communion of the Holy Ghost, be with you all.–2 Cor. 13:14

Peace be to the brethren, and love with faith, from God the Father and the Lord Jesus Christ. Grace be with all them that love our Lord Jesus Christ in sincerity.– Eph. 6:23–24

And the peace of God, which passeth all understanding, shall keep your hearts and minds through Christ Jesus. Finally, brethren, whatsoever things are true, whatsoever things are honest, whatsoever things are just; whatsoever things are pure, whatsoever things are lovely, whatsoever things are of good report; if there be any virtue, and if there be any praise, think on these things. Those things, which ye have both learned and received, and heard, and seen in me, do; and the God of peace shall be with you.–Phil. 4:7–9

Wherefore also we pray always for you, that our God would count you worthy of this calling, and fulfill all the good pleasure of this goodness, and the work of faith with power; that the name of our Lord Jesus Christ may be glorified in you, and ye in him, according to the grace of our God and the Lord Jesus Christ.–2 Thess. 1:11–12

Now the Lord of peace himself give you peace always by all means. The Lord be with you all. The grace of our Lord Jesus Christ be with you all.–2 Thess. 3:16–18

Grace, mercy, and peace, from God our Father and Jesus Christ our Lord.–1 Tim. 1:2

Now the God of peace, that brought again from the dead our Lord Jesus, that great shepherd of the sheep, through the blood of the everlasting covenant, make you perfect in every good work to do his will, working in you that which is well-pleasing in his sight, through Jesus Christ, to whom be glory for ever and ever.–Heb. 13:20–21

The God of all grace, who hath called us unto his eternal glory by Christ Jesus, after that ye have suffered a while, make you perfect, establish, strengthen, settle you. To him be glory and dominion for ever and ever. Greet ye one another with a kiss of charity. Peace be with you all that are in Christ Jesus.–1 Pet. 5:10–11, 14

Grace be with you, mercy, and peace, from God the Father, and from the Lord Jesus Christ, the Son of the Father, in truth and love.–2 John 3

Now unto him that is able to keep you from falling, and to present you faultless before the presence of his glory with exceeding joy, to the only wise God our Savior, be glory and majesty, dominion and power, both now and ever.—Jude 24–25

Grace be unto you, and peace, from him which was, and which is to come; and from the seven Spirits which are before his throne; and from Jesus Christ, who is the faithful witness, and the first begotten of the dead, and the prince of the kings of the earth. Unto him that loved us, and washed us from our sins in his own blood, and hath made us kings and priests unto God and his Father; to him be glory and dominion for ever and ever.—Rev. 1:4–6

SECTION II.

Sermons and Homiletic and Worship Aids for Fifty-two Sundays

SUNDAY: JANUARY FIFTH

SERVICE OF WORSHIP

Sermon: Depending on God
TEXT: Ps. 91

One of the things that religious people talk a lot about is dependence upon God. We sing hymns about it; we imply it in our prayers; we preach sermons about it constantly. But isn't it possible to be too dependent upon God?

Americans in an adult congregation like this, if they spoke what was really on their minds, might be a little suspicious of the psalmist who wrote in the Ninety-first Psalm, "I will say of the Lord, He is my refuge and my fortress: my God; in Him will I trust." They might say it, or read it in concert as part of the service but make the mental reservation to themselves that the psalmist might have done better if he had trusted less in God and done something about it himself. So this question, Isn't it possible to be too dependent upon God? is one that deserves serious consideration.

I. The answer, of course, is yes *and* no. If you depend on God, for instance, to get you through an examination (if you happen to be a student) the following day and have not opened any of the books through the preceding year that have to do with the subject in hand, you are depending upon God altogether too much. Or if you depend on God to save a man who has been struck down by a truck and is bleeding to death and do nothing whatsoever to stop the bleeding, you are depending on Him far too much.

But if *after* and *while* you do everything you can in a situation you depend on God, you cannot depend upon Him too much, because everything you are and everything you have or can ever hope to be come ultimately from God. From Him your life, your thoughts, your imagination are derived, and upon His energies you are completely and utterly dependent.

II. This raises another question. Where does this whole idea of depending upon God come from?

a. When you stop to think about it and look into your selves and into what you know about life, you realize at once that it comes right out of our human situation, just as spontaneously as the grass comes out of the earth. No one thought it up; it came up all by itself as soon as human beings had the wits to take it in.

We are born completely helpless; I think no one would question that. A baby can do nothing for itself; it is dependent entirely upon its parents or upon some older person to take care of its needs. As we grow up we learn in a marvelous way, and very quickly, to do a great many things for ourselves. After about fifteen or sixteen years, when we can do so much to help ourselves, we are sometimes misled into believing that we are not dependent upon anything, that we can do everything that is required under any emergency and do not need to acknowledge any dependence upon anyone or anything outside ourselves. We then, of course, have to learn all over again that

17

while we can help ourselves in many of the daily tasks of life, we never become completely independent, and the older we grow, I think, the more we realize how dependent we really are.

The people who have made the most of life are the people, aren't they, who have made the most graceful submission to the larger forces that mysteriously press upon them from all sides and that they never completely understand—at least, they never presume to understand them—but with which they make some satisfactory, secret terms.

b. You find this, this dependence upon God, this sense of depending upon the larger forces outside oneself, not only in pious people. Think of all the creative artists that you have ever known or heard about or read about and the evidence they have left of the process by which they work. You would agree that there is one thing that they have in common, one thing that they all agree to, and that is that they are in the very nature of their lives agents of communication. They are not imitators of anything; they are channels through which something greater is communicated to the world, and therefore, they are constantly aware of the fact that they are dependent upon this source outside themselves.

c. And another thing we might notice about it is that you don't grow out of this sense of dependence upon God, you grow up into it; and the older you get, the more you are aware of it.

One of the most interesting people, in American history, we have ever produced is Benjamin Franklin. His friends all thought of him as a freethinker; he belonged to no church and subscribed to no creed, and as far as they knew did not practice any of the ordinary religious techniques of life. When the Convention was meeting to draw up the Constitution of the United States, they were amazed when he stood up in the Convention and made a resolution that each one of its sessions begin with prayer, after which he said, "The longer I live, the more convincing proofs I see of this truth; that God governs in the affairs of men."

The longer you live, the more convincing proofs become that there are forces outside yourself that in the long run govern the world.

III. There is still one other question that I should like to raise, and that is, What sort of help can we expect from God?

a. The man who wrote the Ninety-first Psalm, if you remember the psalm, had a very definite expectation. He expected immunity against all disaster. He even goes so far as to say, "There shall no evil happen unto him, neither shall any plague come nigh his dwelling."

I don't know how you feel when you read that, but I have always wondered about it. I used to think that this was all the result of the author's imagination and an exaggerated statement brought about by his enthusiasm, but, again, as I grow older, I think there is something in it, and it is this: It is true, isn't it, that people who lose themselves in something great and significant have a greater power of resistance than other people. At least, doesn't it seem that way from your observations? I wonder whether there isn't something to be said for the fact that the more you submerge yourself in some great interest the greater your resistance is to the things that are likely to strike you down. The more you trust in God, the more you stave off the inroads of disaster.

b. The reason for it, I suppose, is that it eliminates fear. A person who really trusts in God is not a fearful person, and fear is something like a lightning rod, it draws disaster to itself; but, unlike a lightning rod, it does not drain the disaster off into the harmless soil of the earth but concentrates it and magnifies it at the place where it can do the most damage.

c. There is another kind of help we need even more, and this we can speak of with greater assurance. It is not so much immunity against disaster—which I think we cannot guarantee people, rather I cannot honestly do it—but rather the enlargement of our power to meet the demands of life when they come. That, I can speak of with absolute confidence. Depending on my own efforts, nothing happens; depending on God, anything may happen.

I know that there are people here in this congregation who could say the same thing about themselves. Placed in other situations in life where they were facing circumstances for which they had not at all adequate resources, they realized that by themselves alone they could not do it, and yet when they recognized that fact and acknowledged that they depended ultimately upon a God who could help them, somehow, from somewhere, through them came the energies that they themselves could not have dreamed possible.

d. The psalm, interestingly and, I think, encouragingly to us, ends on that note, and I end on that note. It begins with a man speaking to God in all confidence, "In God is my hope and my strength, my refuge, my fortress, in Him will I trust and He will deliver me from all the disasters of life." It is not always the will of God to get us *out* of trouble; there are times when it is His will to see us *through* trouble.—Theodore Parker Ferris

Illustrations

HOW TO "DEPEND." It is as if a man were sailing a boat. If he depended upon the wind to such an extent that he didn't do one thing to raise a sail, you would say that he was depending upon the wind too much. But if, after and while he is raising his sail and adjusting it to the wind, he depends on the wind in the sense that he knows he is dependent on it and that, therefore, to the degree to which he understands the ways of the wind and cooperates with its ways will he sail forward, then he cannot depend on the wind too much.— Theodore Parker Ferris

TRUST. A mystical Dominican monk, Meister Eckhart by name, gives this as his testament of faith, "Trust and perfect love is demonstrated when a man has great hope and confidence in God. There is nothing to test the perfection of love better than trust. Wholehearted love for another person carries confidence with it. Whatever one dares to trust God for, he really finds in God and a thousand times more."—Harold A. Bosley

SERMON SUGGESTIONS

Topic: A Threefold Prayer
TEXT: Num. 6:22–27
(1) Security—that God will "keep" us in all circumstances. (2) Grace—that God will favor us despite our unworthiness. (3) Peace —that God will enable us to enjoy the fullness of his blessing (cf. John 14:27).

Topic: Patience
TEXT: Gal. 5:22
(1) Patience with self. (2) Patience with others. (3) Patience with God.—Dan Baumann

Worship Aids

CALL TO WORSHIP. "The Lord is in his holy temple: let all the earth keep silence before him" (Hab. 2:20).

INVOCATION. O Lord of the past and the future, we are grateful for this time of worship, for the memories it evokes, the opportunities it presents, the insights it brings, the challenges it engenders, the Savior it glorifies.—E. Lee Phillips

OFFERTORY SENTENCE. "They voluntarily gave according to their means, and even beyond their means, begging us earnestly for the privilege of sharing in this ministry to the saints" (2 Cor. 8:3–4 NRSV).

OFFERTORY PRAYER. Lord, let our offering ring with gratitude for the past, dedication to the possibilities of the present, and hope for the potentials of the future through our blessed Savior, the same yesterday, today, and forever.—E. Lee Phillips

PRAYER. Today, Father, give us a vision greater than we have possessed, that we may see clearly what you want to accomplish through each of us and all of us as a church. Grant us the faith to realize that with you anything is possible. Open our eyes to the scope of your love for all people in every circumstance and culture that we may not be afraid to reach out to them, in the name of the lord, and share his love in positive, redeeming ways. Extend our hands in giving, that the work to which you have called us and the challenges we have already accepted may be brought to fulfillment even as new ones are undertaken. Bless us as we listen for word from you and make the commitments that will bring significance to all the coming days.–Henry Fields

LECTIONARY MESSAGE

Topic: Becoming Children of God
TEXT: John 1:(1–9)10–18
Other Readings: Jer. 31:7–14; Ps. 147:12–20; Eph. 1:3–14
The first chapter of John does for the New Testament what the first chapter of Genesis does for the Old Testament–begin at the very beginning of the Universe. But John goes even further back than Genesis. He begins *before* the beginning, with the formation of the very concept of creation in the thought of God and his active, personalized participation in all of existence.
I. The creating Word was from the beginning with God, and was God.
a. Not concerned with Earth, Sun, Moon, Air, Light, Water, Animals, and Man as physical realities, John describes the fulfillment of God's spiritual necessity, the true Light of Man, not perceived as a physical phenomenon but as the glowing inner spirit capable of God's fellowship.
b. We should know John the Baptist rather as John the Witness. His true purpose was to spread knowledge of the true Light so that all persons might believe in the Light that lights every person coming into the world.
c. John had to bear his witness because, although the Light came into the world and unto his own people, the world, and even his own people, did not know or receive him.
II. The crucial realization must be that the Word, Creator, Life, and Light became one of us, a man, so that–*if* we receive him–we can and do become spiritually alive for eternity.
a. Becoming the children of God is not something persons can do for themselves.

Although we know of the act of God, in the greatest event ever to occur in this world, in becoming man and visiting the earth, we cannot merely by our desires reverse the process and become members of God's family, like him.
b. We must recognize God's reason for sending his Son. Our motives in seeking to become children of God may impel us to mighty and self-sacrificing acts, but they affect only our lives among other humans. We must become hungry for more than God's constant expression of the Word of love, through creation, provision, prophet, and law, which have been evidence of his presence with us always, and let him tell us of his eternally unique love shown in coming as a man.
c. We cannot know the mind of God. Although we can know the wondrous marvel contained in Christ's becoming man as far as men and the earth are concerned, we cannot imagine how it seemed to God. We must accept that he came to claim "his own." We are all "his own," because the Jews among whom he was born are truly representative of all mankind.
III. Our great need makes us truly his, as Peter declared (6:68), "Lord, to whom shall we go? Thou hast the words of eternal life."
a. We are his forever, as forever we need his forgiving salvation, his insight, his wisdom. So he comes to us, his own.
b. The words of verse 12 bear an awesome burden of realization for us–"As many as received him . . ." We and all people can have power over God–we can refuse to receive him. Such is the power of the free will that God has given to each of us that we can frustrate his eternal plan, his incarnation, his great love and sacrifice, merely by saying no to him. "As many as received him . . ." he endlessly blessed by the unique gift, given in the only way known to human or divine intelligence that we can accept, to become children of God. We must receive him in order to possess his life.
c. Hundreds and thousands followed Jesus to have illness cured, to have limbs healed, to have life restored, and he fulfilled their needs. He comes to us all–he has found us where we are. Can we receive it all with one word? We must only say, "Yes."–John R. Rodman

SUNDAY: JANUARY TWELFTH

SERVICE OF WORSHIP

Sermon: The Validity of a Vision
TEXT: Matt. 3:16–17 NEB

In the New Testament being saved is a process; a Christian is not to be defined as a person who has had one supreme moment of decision that labels him or her as among the saved, but one who is on what the Bible calls the "way of salvation."

I want to talk today about the validity of what I'm calling a "vision": the abrupt, unexpected awareness of the unseen world, the invasion of our souls by the Spirit of God, or the sudden encounter with a living Christ.

Some years ago the validity of this kind of experience was ruled out in the name of rationalism and the scientific approach. Today it is dawning on more and more thinking people that the most real world of all is not only that which is disclosed to us by the marvelous discoveries of science, but the dimension of goodness, truth, and beauty that breaks through to us in the vision of God.

I don't know if you have ever given much attention to the story of Jesus' baptism in the River Jordan, although all Gospel writers record that it was the first event of his public ministry. You may never have heard a sermon on the subject. There's enough in this story to keep a preacher going for twenty years, let alone twenty minutes, but I have only one main theme today—the baptism of Jesus as a vision of God.

I. Some may be shocked at the idea that Jesus could ever have one of these visionary experiences I have been talking about. But that is to deny the incarnation. He "was made flesh and dwelt among us." We are told, "As Jesus grew up he advanced in wisdom and in favor with God and man." You can't "advance in wisdom" if you were never ignorant, which disposes of the notion that Jesus, as Son of God, must have known Einstein's theory of relativity in his cradle.

a. What brought him out that day from Nazareth to join the crowds that swarmed around John on the banks of the Jordan River? I believe it was his growing conviction that, whatever God had in store for him, he was going to give himself totally, in life and death, for other people. That, he said, was what God required of him, and so it could be said that at this moment of his baptism in water he was being ordained to that sacrificial ministry that would end with his baptism in his own blood "shed for us."

b. Jesus emerged from the waters of the Jordan with the shining eyes of one who has seen God, and the burning conviction of one who has heard him speak. From now on he broke with family life he had known in Nazareth and went out in total trust to preach and to heal and announce the gospel of God's reconciling love. In his vision, we read, "heaven opened, and he saw the Spirit of God descending like a dove to alight upon him." The next time he returned to his old synagogue in Nazareth he preached from this text: "The Spirit of God is upon me because he has anointed me; he has sent me to announce good tidings to the poor, to proclaim release for the prisoners, and recovery of sight for the blind; to let the broken victims go free."

II. How do you find language to express a vision like this? Surely only by symbols and poetic imagery. Does anyone imagine that we decide upon the validity of such a vision by subjecting the description to the kind of analysis we give to a legal document? Do we seek to determine its truth by asking questions like, Was there really a dove to be seen that day and how long did he walk around with it nestling on his head?

a. More and more people are now realizing how we have been brainwashed by the dogma that only those things that can be seen and measured, analyzed by our instruments and verified by our logic, are real and true.

"The heavens opened; he saw the Spirit of God descending on him like a dove . . ." That's the only way to describe the kind of experience that moves us to our depths and changes the course of our lives.

b. I doubt if there is anyone here who has never known the moment of vision or heard the voice that comes with it. Can you not think now of some moment when for you "the heavens opened"? It might have been unexpectedly in a service of worship. It might have been a chance remark, a scribble on a wall, the sight of a newborn baby, or the lifeless body of a father or mother. The vision strikes most often in ordinary time, I think, rather than at Christmas or Easter. Always with the vision comes the call–to realize afresh who we really are and what we are to do with our lives.

III. Didn't this happen to the young Jesus of Nazareth, when the vision came as he emerged from the waters of Jordan? It is not presumptuous to say that he knew then who he was–"This is my Son, my beloved, on whom my favor rests." And he knew what he had to do. At whatever the cost might be, he was to seek and save those who were lost.

His was a unique relationship with God, and his was a unique calling as Savior of the world. But every moment that may be given to us when the heavens open and the Spirit comes near is a reassurance that we too are truly sons and daughters of God, and we too are being dedicated to the service of his Kingdom. Whether such moments are rare or fairly frequent is not of our choosing. As Hamlet said, "The readiness is all." That's why we're here.–David H. C. Read

Illustrations

HOW THE CALL CAME.   Ida Scudder said when she was a young girl beginning college there were two things she would never do: be a doctor and go back to India where her parents lived. However, one day she received word that her mother was gravely ill, and she had to go back to India to care for her precious relative. Ida's father was a doctor. He was called out to care for a patient one night, and Ida was left alone. A Hindu man whose wife was having a baby knocked at the door. The Hindu law forbade a man's looking at another man's wife –so he needed Ida! Regretfully Ida had to tell the concerned husband that she could not go, because she was not a doctor. The same situation repeated itself twice more that night as frantic men came seeking help for their wives. The next morning Ida's father found out that both mother and child had died in each case. Those three knocks at the door called Ida Scudder into medical missions where she continued the famous

Scudder tradition in India.–*Adult Life and Work Lesson Annual* (1992–93)

SCIENCE AND RELIGION.   Science and religion need each other today for the kind of understanding that can save our world. It was Albert Einstein who said. "Religion without science is lame, but science without religion is blind."–David H. C. Read

SERMON SUGGESTIONS

Topic: Doing God's Will
  TEXT: Deut. 30:9–20
  (1) Requires a deliberate turning, verse 10. (2) Is clear and simple enough for the doing, verses 11–14. (3) Has obvious consequences, verse 16.

Topic: Two Hills
  TEXT: Matt. 5:1–2, 43–44; Luke 23:34
  (1) Where Jesus taught love and forgiveness. (2) Where Jesus practiced love and forgiveness.–Chester E. Swor

Worship Aids

CALL TO WORSHIP.   "They that sow in tears shall reap in joy" (Ps. 126:5).

INVOCATION.   Move deeply in our souls, O Lord. Seal in us the truth of Scripture that through this hour of worship we might seek thy will and find it through him who found us all in the cross.–E. Lee Phillips

OFFERTORY SENTENCE.   "Happy are all who fear the Lord, who conform to his ways. You will enjoy the fruit of your labours, you will be happy and prosperous" (Ps. 128:1–2 REB).

OFFERTORY PRAYER.   In the first glimmers of this new year, we are grateful, Father, that we have the opportunity to bring our tithes and offerings before you. Keep us faithful in our giving throughout the months ahead. Inspire us to meet the needs of our decisions as we serve you in the world, and bless those who benefit from our gifts given in Christ's name.—Henry Fields

PRAYER. Dear Father, hold us within your providential hand; guide us when perplexed; free us from all fatal ills of the heart in this world and the next; and through the power of your Holy Spirit, provide your strength to help us overcome our greatest fears, and keep us close to Christ and his courage, in whose name we pray, saying, Our Father . . . —Albert J. D. Walsh

LECTIONARY MESSAGE

Topic: After His Birth, They Sought Him
TEXT: Matt. 2:1–12
Other Readings: Isa. 60:1–6; Ps. 72:1–7, 10–14; Eph. 3:1–12

The birth of Jesus Christ did not occur in an arena of peace but in an era of desperate, nearly universal, suffering. Feelings of such desperation are difficult to recapture once the terror has past. Some "night dream" pain remains for the immediate survivors, but much of the horror dies with the events. New generations escape most of the miseries of the past, but some are later tortured by the bent and warped lives of the survivors, for generations. Almost no evil seems ever to be lost. Its residual influence remains. So grows mankind's accumulated and ongoing inhumanity to one another.

In our affluent Western culture, the terrors of oppression are mostly distant, easily forgotten images viewed mostly from the nearly silent television set. But there really was a time when all of life was uncomfortable, miserable, and terror-filled for ordinary citizens. When Jesus Christ was born, the only protection from the evils perpetrated by legitimated authorities was to be found in a person's hope. The people could only wait for God.

First-century Hebrews had known oppression for generations, but they had some slender hope. Their great prophet Isaiah had said, "The light will come." Just as in creation, the blackness of chaos was to be shattered again by the brilliant, creative light of the word of God. A messiah would come in the future to create a kingdom of light, of righteousness, and of peace.

The child was born, and they called his name, Jesus.

But that's an old story now. Christmas came to our Western world this year with all the monotony an overfamiliar story can muster, leaving us with a predictable old story's low expectations (cf. Fred Craddock). Nevertheless, here and there, some still seek spiritual nurture in Jesus Christ in the ongoing story that began at the manger in Bethlehem of Judah in the days of Herod the king.

I. *Seekers of worship.* Some sought him in order to worship him. (a) The villagers and shepherds from the surrounding hills sought him out and worshiped him. Even in that obscure village of Judah at a time of oppression and massive poverty among the common people, he was welcomed with awe and wonder. (b) No seeker was to be excluded. The prayerful cries of the ordinary citizens had been made unceasingly to the God of Abraham, Isaac, and Jacob. The names of the great prophets of old were invoked. Isaiah had predicted that all nations would recognize the birth of the child King. It was the sign of God's promise of a new order of peace for all (Isa. 9:6–12; 60:3). O how they longed for the fulfillment of that prophecy! (c) Foreign seekers were also welcomed. This child king was not to be exclusively for the Hebrews but for people of every nation on earth. Representatives from distant lands came. The star had been ignored by Israel's own scholars. The magi, astronomers from the Eastern world, came bearing gifts; these gentiles from afar participated with joy at the coming of the light of God.

Who alive in Bethlehem of Judea during those days could know of the vast civilization to grow based on the teachings of this child? Who could predict even the wonders of the next four decades, or that this child was to conquer death? Who could have imagined the profound movements launched in future time in the name of this, Jesus.

II. *Seekers of destruction.* Some sought him under pretense of worship. In every generation there are those who have built their power bases and sustain their personal security by acts of tyranny. This is especially true when peacemaking, law-abiding citizens accumulate the fruits of uninterrupted labor only to have them ruthlessly seized by aggressive thieves. (a) Tyrants sought to destroy him. Herod sought Jesus in response to his anger, jealousy, and fear. And he lied to enlist foreign strangers in his deadly plans. (b) Herod sent his destroyers after Jesus' birth. Their assignment was to murder him. They thought nothing of destroying helpless infants. They were butchers in a search for targets upon whom to vent their accumulated internal rage; how could sane men participate in such ghastly deeds? (c) The high priests and scribes of the Jewish faith must have had some stake in seeking him, if only to demonstrate the truth or falsehood of their prophetic traditions, to maintain creditability with their countrymen, to assist Herod in order to maintain their places of privilege, to calm their fears related to loss of power. (d) Anyone sensing the power of Jesus would gravitate to him, if for nothing else to draw off his power for their own ends; from every generation they come.

III. *Just plain seekers.* (a) Some nominal Christians still seek the Christ of Bethlehem to renew and deepen faith and commitment to God. Occasionally, something stirs some Christians, calling them from "couch-potato worship and service." They are reminded that Christianity is not a spectator sport, called to seek Jesus again, challenged to reevaluate the gifts in their hands useful for the work of Christ. (b) Frequently some who have never considered becoming Christians are moved to faith at the anniversary season of the birth of Jesus. They respond in the hope of salvation, of peace, of the promise of justice. They celebrate newfound awareness that spirituality is the center of all of

life. When they do trust Jesus Christ for salvation, in him they find what all of us seek: a loving, forgiving, existence-changing savior whose life and teaching are the soul of this and all future life.

One day I watched the Philadelphia Eagles football team summer training camp in action. As I watched, Bill Slazak, my high school assistant football coach, joined me. The linemen were working out close to the fence. I remarked how strong, competitive, and energetic they were, and that they must be "the greatest." Bill said, "No, Walter, they are men still 'trying out' for the team." The real team was out on the field, in light gym suits, running mock plays to the cadence call of their coaches. For more than an hour, they ran up and down, looking for all the world as if they were doing the same thing over and over again.

Bill told me they were perfecting a series of plays. At each signal, every player had a specific assignment, ever so slightly different than the one before. They looked like men just doing wind sprints, but they were professionals perfecting their nearly flawless craft. They critically analyzed even their best performances and practiced to make them better.

You, too, are seekers of Christ, seeking him through Christ-like living and service every day. You use only the gifts God has given you. But no matter how often you perform, or how lovingly Jesus' message of "well done" is spoken in your hearts, critical analysis is indicated and improved performance tomorrow.

We who have made professions of faith in Jesus are all professional Christians, called to lay our gifts daily before Jesus' manger or cross. May God give you strength for your service to mankind in Jesus' name, today and every day to come.–Walter C. Jackson

SUNDAY: JANUARY NINETEENTH

SERVICE OF WORSHIP

Sermon: On Human Worth

TEXT: Heb. 2:6

This message has one major purpose. It is designed to convince you that God loves you and that you are of infinite worth to him. It may be one of the most important messages you will ever hear. It can change your life if you can believe it and receive it.

Low self-esteem has a devastating effect on a person. Many people go through life with a defeatist attitude because of it. They don't try to do or become anything worthwhile, because they believe that they will fail. They give up before they start. These same people can accept anything negative directed toward them but nothing positive. They are receptive to criticism but not to compliments, to hate but not to love. They are like vacuum cleaners that suck up only the negative.

I. The World Speaks of Little Worth

a. There are many negative voices in our world that have brainwashed millions of people into believing that they have little or no worth. The voice of the world is like a newspaper—we will think only negative.

Negative voices are not confined solely to the world. Some forms of religion seem to emphasize the negative qualities of human beings while totally ignoring the good in them. Humanity is often referred to as a sinner, a worm, a dirty little anarchist in whom no good can be found. But this is only half the truth. The same human being who is a sinner, a worm, a dirty little anarchist, has the potential of being a child of the King, a joyful creature, and a coworker with God.

Great sorrow come from humanity's negative image. The Bible says, "Love your neighbor as yourself" (Matt. 19:19). If you do not have a healthy love for yourself, you cannot love your neighbor. In other words, if you don't feel good about yourself, it is highly unlikely that you will feel good about anyone else.

b. The greatest tragedy of overemphasizing the negative aspects of humanity is that, in some cases, it can cause people to be in-capable of feeling God's love. Most religious people who emphasize the negative aspects of human beings do so in order to lead a person to accept Christ and experience the love and forgiveness of God. However, this can be self-defeating. It can lead people to feel so ashamed, so guilty, and so low that they can never mentally accept the fact that God has forgiven them or that God loves them. This is tragic.

II. The Bible Speaks of Great Worth

a. You are of great worth to God. God loves you dearly. When I say "you," I mean you personally. This message is not for others; it is for you. In keeping with the basic teachings of the Bible, I am saying to you that God loves you dearly and that you are of great worth to him.

b. Your great worth to God can clearly be seen in the Scriptures. In Matt. 12:12, Jesus stated that you are worth far more than animals. In Mark 8:36, Jesus asked, "And how does a man benefit if he gains the whole world and loses his soul in the process? For is anything worth more than his soul?" In the book of Mark, Jesus taught that you are worth more than religious institutions. "The Sabbath was made to benefit man, and not man to benefit the Sabbath" (2:27).

III. God Has Acted to Enhance Worth

a. Human worth can be seen in creation. The Bible teaches us that human beings are noble creatures. Mankind alone on the face of the earth has the intelligence to differentiate between right and wrong. Of all God's creatures, mankind alone has freedom. We have the freedom to make choices that will determine our fate for all eternity. In addition to intelligence and freedom, a human being has a spiritual nature.

b. God's estimate of human worth can be seen in incarnation. God loved mankind so much that he left the comfort and glory of heaven to come into our world. Christ had two purposes in coming. Both are related to people. He came to serve . . . and to save. If people were not of infinite value to God, then Jesus would not have come.

c. God's estimate of human worth can be seen in the crucifixion. Nowhere is God's love for mankind more clear than at Calvary. God loved us so much that he gave his Son Jesus for our sins.

IV. Even today you should know that you are worth much to God. He has left his church in the world for your salvation and growth. God calls, leads, and encourages you to follow him. If God did not feel that you were of great worth, he would not work so hard to bring you to salvation. Although you may doubt many things, don't doubt these two facts: God loves you, and you are of infinite worth to him.—Robert G. Wilkerson

Illustrations

TURNING TO GOD.   F. B. Speakman said, "Someone has imagined God first fashioning man, and one of the host of heaven, watching, exclaiming in alarm, but you are giving this creature freedom! He will never be wise enough or strong enough to handle it. He will think himself a God. He will boast in his own self-sufficiency. How can you gamble that he will ever return to you?" And God replies, "I have left him unfinished within. I have left him with deep needs that only I can satisfy, that out of his desire and homesickness of soul, he will turn to me."—Robert G. Wilkerson

"IN CHRIST," ACCORDING TO PAUL. He knows nothing of a mysticism that stops short of faith's final goal. Behind every expression of his intense intimacy with Jesus stands the great ultimate fact of God Himself. Indeed, as we have already seen, the nature that can impart itself to believing souls in the way in which, by the plain testimony of experience, Christ's nature can and does impart itself proves itself *ipso facto* to be divine. Hence the more any man comes to be "in Christ," the more is he "in God." There are not two experiences, but one.—James S. Stewart

SERMON SUGGESTIONS

Topic: Prescription for Success
TEXT: Josh. 1:9
(1) Stop, look, and listen for God's guidance, verse 9a. (2) Take yourself in hand and be decisive and bold, verse 9b. (3) Count on the unfailing presence of God in all—even the worst circumstances, verse 9c.

Topic: Bought with a Price
TEXT: 1 Cor. 6:19–20
Paul was dealing with the sins of the flesh, manifested in selfish individualism. (1) "Ye are not your own." (2) "For ye are bought with a price." (3) "Therefore glorify God."—D. M. Baillie

Worship Aids

CALL TO WORSHIP.   "Seek the Lord, and his strength: seek his face evermore" (Ps. 105:4).

INVOCATION.   We come now to this place of worship, Father, yearning to be met by your love and grace as your spirit abides with us. We bring all that we are and all that we do, that in this sacred place we may be blessed and encouraged. Our lives are in need of direction. Our hopes await some measure of fulfillment. Our very souls long for assurance and an anchor amid the chances and changes of life. Let us here be met with life-changing power and certainty, as we lift our hearts and voices in praise and prayer.—Henry Fields

OFFERTORY SENTENCE.   "But my God shall supply all your needs according to his riches in glory by Christ Jesus" (Phil. 4:19).

OFFERTORY PRAYER.   Do mighty good with our offering, O Lord. Bind up the wounds of the afflicted, challenge unchecked evil, spread the gospel of Jesus Christ, change doubters into believers and

believers into saints, for thy name's sake.–
E. Lee Phillips

PRAYER. Eternal Father, the wonder of
whose being became real for us in the face
of Jesus Christ, we bless you for the visitation among us of your providence in him
and the companionship of his spirit with us
as we walk the common road of life. With
him ahead of us, ever steadfast and with his
eyes set toward the Jerusalem of our times,
we neither shrink back nor are we afraid, for
no one who has chosen his example has
ever felt let down. We thank you that, in this
age of doubt and uncertainty when our spiritual visions are very few or clouded, there
rises before us the strong Son of God who is
and remains the hero and healer of our
race. Help us to live like him among all the
pressures and complexities of our careers
and even the ever so many errands of the
daily round. Let us under the lure and spell
of his great example accept our part in the
high calling of simply doing good. May we
match with his our human strength to climb
the path of duty, to spend and to be spent in
our useful actions for the care and cure of
all, and with words and works of kindness to
touch and uplift the hearts of friend and foe
alike. Give us, like Jesus, to have meek and
lowly hearts, to befriend the friendless, and
by our union with you, our Father, to become anchors of stability amid the ceaseless
chaos of these days. Send forth your love to
us in abundant measure and in the name of
your Son, our Lord, may we be always
in your service glad and free.–Donald
Macleod

LECTIONARY MESSAGE

Topic: Being Found, and Finding
TEXT: John 1:43–51
Other Readings: 1 Sam. 3:1–10 (11–20); Ps.
139:1–6, 13–18; 1 Cor. 6:12–20

First being found, and then finding themselves, were the experiences of both Philip
and Nathanael.

I. God has always found those for whom
he had plans and work to be done.

a. God knew where to find Adam and
Eve in the Garden of Eden, and he knew of
their fear of being found after their disobedience. He had to ask them "searching"
questions in order to get them to confront
themselves in his presence.

b. God knows where you are, he has
found you out, and he knows what fears you
may have of facing him. He provided a
cover for Adam and Eve, and he punished
their tempter. He had plans for them, and
he has plans for you. He will provide for
your life and service just as he did for them.

c. Jesus knew Philip was to be his follower and helper, he knew where to find
him, and he deliberately went to Galilee, to
Bethsaida, just above the northwest edge of
the sea, and found Philip.

II. Philip in turn, being found, found another.

a. Nathanael, however, was prejudiced
because of Jesus' hometown. He asked,
"Can there any good thing come out of
Nazareth?" There are so many causes of
prejudice, which is the forming of opinions
without specific knowledge. We, like
Nathanael, may be prejudiced at least tenta-
tively on the basis of someone's origin or
residence. Other influences may be occupation, education or its lack, relatives, appearance or clothing, race, religion, or gender.

b. Like Nathanael, we may come close to
missing out on our own most valuable discovery because of our unfounded prejudices.

III. The best test of truth is personal discovery.

a. There are many sources of knowledge.
For most of the facts we know, our sources
must be the words of others, simply because
they concern things of which we could have
no personal knowledge. Consider the history of our country and of the world. Consider all the sciences and mathematics.
Knowing family members or even the time
and place of one's own birth depends on
hearsay, or what others have told us.

b. Although fear may cause one to hide
or conceal, drive one to seek truth by stren-
uous searching, or lead one to achieve
greatly through education and hard work, it
cannot cause faith or lead to belief. Nothing
can do that as well as personal experience.

One may cite an old adage, "The burned child respects the fire."

c. Perhaps the only way to come to belief and faith is through personal experience. How fortunate we are to follow a Lord of whom we, like Philip, are not afraid to say, "Come and see." We have an open and inviting faith. Jesus sought people in order to change their lives and their eternities, but no matter what others tell us about who he is or what he does, we truly believe only when we try him. Jesus is his own best evidence and proof. We need not fear disappointing friends or loved ones when we say, "Come and see." Numerous times we hear the openness of our faith: "Prove all things . . ." (1 Thess. 5:21); "Prove me now herewith, saith the Lord of hosts" (Mal. 3:10); "Beloved, . . . try the spirits . . ." (1 John 4:1); "Go . . . and tell . . . what things ye have seen and heard . . ." (Luke 7:22). We need now, having been found by Jesus ourselves, to go and find others to receive his gifts and do his service.—John R. Rodman

SUNDAY: JANUARY TWENTY-SIXTH

SERVICE OF WORSHIP

Sermon: From Innocent Service to Committed Obedience

TEXT: 1 Sam. 3:1–10

Samuel, of whom is said the same thing that Luke says about Jesus, that he "grew on, and was in favor both with the Lord, and also with men" (2:26), had been promised by his parents to serve in the Lord's house; but he had much yet to learn about service.

I. The "Precious" Word of the Lord

a. There have been other times like that: the Middle Ages; the fourteenth and fifteenth centuries, the days of Wycliffe and Huss; and pioneer days in the New World. But *now* is a time of danger for the word of the Lord, when governmental "separation of church and state" enforcement forbids use and teaching just where and when it is needed most. Children are ridiculed for Bible use in schools. Now, when more translations and versions are available in more attractive and readable formats than ever before, use of the Bible for instruction in what it teaches is under a cloud of restriction. As described in Ps. 74:9, 10, "We see not our signs: no more is there a prophet. . . . O God, how long shall the adversary reproach? Shall the enemy blaspheme thy name for ever?"

b. Interest in God's word today is derogated because of the influence of secular society and philosophy. The influential voice of today is anti-Biblical because of the idea abroad that there is no absolute standard of truth and morality. A large majority of today's adults have grown up in a self-serving time, when anything people did that felt good to them was not only permissible but necessary, even if harmful to others. Permissiveness in child rearing has taught that there is no need of a word to live by except that of self-satisfaction. Courts have come to recognize any personal condition, even self-induced intoxication or even a deprived or abused childhood, as justifying the most heinous crimes against others. Today, God's word is "precious" because there is no open "vision" of our society's desperate need. History seems to be changing: the nation that was founded on God's Word is now rejecting it as a basis for laws and commerce.

II. The Call of the Lord

a. The call of God came early in the morning, while the previous evening's lamp was still burning near the Ark. The Lord made it personal. Samuel was innocent and eager but so far knew only ordinary service to an earthly, fading master. He went naturally to him.

b. The scripture says Samuel did not yet know the Lord and had not received the revelation of his word. We need to inquire earnestly how many there are among us, teaching in church schools and weekday schools, preparing and serving meals in church "fellowship" halls, beautifully laundering sacerdotal linens for services of the Lord's Supper, arranging carefully selected flowers on chancel stands, and repairing or maintaining church buildings and equipment–devoted servants of all their friends in the church–who have not yet received a personal calling from God.

III. Hearing and Answering

a. An experienced guide came to Samuel's aid. All those who hear God's personal call to service benefit if they have one or more of those who recognize the Lord's voice from personal experience nearby to give direction. But God is still able to awaken spiritual consciousness in lonely, isolated, or even incarcerated men and women by the power of his Spirit and Word.

b. Samuel personally responded to God's call. He was one who had no reservation. He responded and saw God standing by him. He had an individual relationship with the Lord of the universe! He had indeed a new life. Everything changes when one hears and answers God's call–all the elements of life take on different values, as they are seen to add to or detract from the value of one's fulfillment of God's requests. The call is answered by commitment, the total reorientation of principles of using energy and time. Continued preparation and personal sacrifice become the order of each day, and events are judged in the light of eternity above the here and now. "Speak, Lord, for *thy servant* heareth."–John R. Rodman

Illustrations

LIVING OUT OUR COVENANT. If, therefore, the next few weeks, the next year, the next few years, or even the rest of our lives (as was the case for Moses) seem to be like a wilderness, as we chart a new life, begin a new way, search for new truth, live out a new covenant, we can remember that it is quite all right to be in the wilderness. Some pretty good people have been there before us and are still there with us, folk like Moses, Abraham, Jesus.

It's okay to be in the wilderness, for even there are the certainty and the reality of God's presence for the journey. On their pilgrimage the children of Israel had the symbols of manna, and the pillar of cloud by day, and the pillar of fire by night. We, too, have symbols or signs on our pilgrimage. We have a rainbow that comes in the storm. We still have bread, wine, a towel, and a basin. We have, most of all, a cross.–Robert T. Young

END AND MEANS. Eternally speaking, there is only one means and there is only one end: the means and the end are one and the same thing. There is only one end: the genuine Good; and only one means: this, to be willing to use those means which genuinely are good–but the genuine Good is precisely the end. In time and on earth one distinguishes between the two and considers that the end is more important than the means. One thinks that the end is the main thing and demands of one who is striving that he reach the end. He need not be so particular about the means. Yet this is not so, and to gain an end in this fashion is an unholy act of impatience. In the judgment of eternity the relation between the end and the means is rather the reverse of this.– Soren Kierkegaard

SERMON SUGGESTIONS

Topic: Freedom That Knows No Bounds
TEXT: Judges 21:25
(1) It may seem to hold great promise. (2) It has painful consequences: social chaos; personal internal conflict. (3) It can, after suffering, come to terms with truth: by law, by human leadership; by recognition of the Lord's sovereignty.

Topic: Why Life Is Worth Living
TEXT: Matt. 27:19–26
(1) We don't have to deny our guilt. (2) We don't have to remove our guilt by ourselves. (3) We don't have to be overcome with fear. (4) We don't have to live for ourselves.–Gerhard Aho

Worship Aids

CALL TO WORSHIP. "O I will sing unto the Lord as long as I live: I will sing praise to my God while I have my being. My meditation of him shall be sweet: I will be glad in the Lord" (Ps. 104:33–34).

INVOCATION. Because you have revealed yourself in Jesus Christ, we can praise you freely and lovingly, O God. All that the people of old believed and hoped about you, however dimly perceived, was confirmed in your Son in a fullness that challenges our highest thoughts and our deepest devotion. So let the story unfold for us in ever-new chapters, and we will continually praise you.

OFFERTORY SENTENCE. "Thanks be to God for his indescribable gift" (2 Cor. 9:15 NIV).

OFFERTORY PRAYER. Blessed Lord, though some give meagerly, others generously, and a few sacrificially, take all we bring and all the reason for our gifts and build a mighty kingdom against which the gates of hell cannot prevail!–E. Lee Phillips

PRAYER. We thank thee, O God, for the people with open minds, who have been willing to listen, and see, and take risks. In our own time there are so many questions that we cannot answer, so many moves that we hardly know which one to make. Give us the open-mindedness, the willingness to listen; and then, if it be thy will, give us the courage and the grace to make the plunge. Amen.–Theodore Parker Ferris

LECTIONARY MESSAGE

Topic: Jesus Came Preaching
TEXT: Mark 1:14–20
Other Readings: Jonah 3:1–5, 10; Ps. 62:5–12; 1 Cor. 7:29–31
The setting of our message is somewhere near Capernaum and Bethsaida, a fishing village near the former. After the arrest of John the Baptist by Herod Philip, Jesus had departed from Judea and turned northward into Galilee, where he had spent most of his first thirty years.

In this striking and very important Gospel of Mark, the writer of which we believe to be John Mark, we find some very interesting and striking elements. It is the first Gospel and is the briefest. It forms the framework for the Gospels of Matthew and Luke, but it spends far more time in relating the miracles of Jesus than it does on the narrative carried by the other two synoptists. He does not say anything about the birth and early childhood of Jesus. He uses the present tense and the historical present in relating much of what took place, and we find a sense of movement and of challenge in reading it.

We glean two main thoughts from our text: the first is the message of the Master; the other is to the messengers he called to assist him.

I. First, We Take a Peek at the Message He Proclaimed

Mark, according to many New Testament scholars, was giving his readers the bare bones of Christ's ministry and message for the Christians at home. He wastes no time on background or lengthy descriptions and moves directly into what he wishes to say. Observe the words: "After John had been arrested, Jesus came in to Galilee proclaiming the gospel (good news) of God, and saying, 'The time is fulfilled, and the kingdom of God is at hand.'"

Mark gives reasons for John the Baptist's arrest but merely notes it and moves with the story of Jesus into Galilee with the straightforward manner of his work and message.

It is about the preaching of Jesus on the theme of God's kingdom. Now his kingdom, as we will learn later, was not of political or material matters but of spiritual and eternal matters of the soul and of persons' living now in the way God wants them to live. It is the rule of God in one's life, which is within oneself when one permits Christ to indwell one's life. It is for the present; it is a continuing concept, and it is to be consummated in the future.

II. Second Is a Word to the Messengers
Jesus knew that he would not remain on earth and that he must have his followers to

assist in the task. So he called his first four messengers: Peter and Andrew, and James and John, sons of Zebedee. Although they had met Jesus and had become his followers after Jesus' baptism by John the Baptist, they had not been called to a life of service and ministry of healing and preaching until this time.

Jesus said to the two fisherman who had been casting their nets into the lake, "Follow me, and I will make you to become fishers of men." To this they responded, and Mark says, "And they immediately left their nets and followed him." A little later he spotted James and John mending their nets, and he called them. Again listen to Mark: "And they left their father Zebedee in the boat with the hired servants, and followed him."

Evidently there was no hesitation, no arguing the matter with one another or with family members. It seemed that they were ready to go and went.

We often wonder how Jesus came to call the various men to serve among the twelve. Why, for instance, did he not call some of the religious leaders in Jerusalem or in Ca-pernaum or elsewhere? Why fishermen? Why a tax collector? Why a zealot? Even, why Judas Iscariot?

We will never know in this world, but we accept his judgment and knowledge of those he called. He called those who would, according to tradition, give their lives for him and his kingdom, men who would write such books as Matthew, John, and Peter. Each of them would make a particular contribution to our Lord's kingdom.

III. Conclusion

Thus, we find the message of our Lord as being the Kingdom of God and the way one may enter: through repentance toward sin and faith in Jesus Christ as Savior and Lord.

So came the messengers, at that time only the four; but soon others would be added to the list, and then still others, and from the tiny beginning, the followers and messengers have multiplied into the millions, scattered over all the world. But there is room for more, and always the invitation continues from our Lord: "Follow me, and I will make you to become fishers of men."– G. Allen West, Jr.

SUNDAY: FEBRUARY SECOND

SERVICE OF WORSHIP

Sermon: Make Love Your Aim

TEXT: 1 Cor. 12:31b–14:1a

There is nothing like a good church fight, and that congregation in Corinth fought with the best. Paul writes to ameliorate the crisis. He insists that just as our bodies possess many parts, each vital to functioning of the whole body, so no one dare exclude anyone's spiritual gifts and witness from what he calls the body of Christ: the church.

Following this brilliant image of a body, Paul says, but if you really want to discern who is doing the will of God and following the way of Christ, if you really want to bring unity through your diversity, let me show you, truly, the highest way.

I. "If I speak with the tongues of mortals and of angels, but have not love, I am a noisy gong or clanging cymbal." Paul tells us that a community claiming Christian discipleship is a community itself living the re-creative and redemptive power of the resurrected Christ in a fallen world. By faith he affirms that the self-centeredness, the warped vision, the egoistic claims operating from within our hearts–casting shadows over our best intentions and frequently over our most treasured relationships–are themselves conquered by the power of God alive and at work among us through the Spirit of Christ.

a. And therefore, and speaking of himself, pointing to the loveless risks of his own vocation, Paul says, essentially, "I may possess surpassing eloquence: I may be gifted with brilliant turns of phrase and luminous metaphors: I may bring people to their feet with thunderous rhetoric and dazzling allusions–but, if I provide nothing assuring you of the love God has for each of you and for this congregation enabling you to love one another and to serve the world, then, the radiant purpose of my discourse ignored, I am nothing more than a harsh and blaring cacophony, a dissonant, meaningless clamor."

b. And Paul continues, "If I can interpret the scriptures lucidly and with erudition; if I share with you the intricacies of arcane theology; if I exhibit faith trusting enough to change and ennoble the worst of circumstances—I may demonstrate a lustrous intellect and transcendent religious commitment. But if I bring you no confidence of the saving love of God embracing every life here, seeking to bind you into a joyful and mutually supportive body loving one another through miscommunication, budget crunches, personal oversights, and human stupidity, then I offer nothing but a long line of zeroes."

c. And, "If I, for a great cause, give away all I have, if I risk my own death for the sake of others, I may make a difference in a terrible situation, but if my action plays to some pride-filled heroism, some world-defined martyrdom, and is neither born of love nor creates the opportunity for justice or reconciliation, then although the publicity may be intense, the event inspiring, my gain in reputation great, my gain before God is empty, void, nil."

II. Now, after rooting matters of Christian witness in a creative, love-forged community, Paul continues by describing the kind of behavior the love of Christ enables us to exercise among ourselves and with one another. He believes by the grace and power of Jesus Christ we in the Christian community are liberated to love one another.

a. "Jesus Christ is patient and kind; Jesus Christ is not jealous or boastful, Jesus Christ is not arrogant or rude. Jesus Christ does not insist on his own way, in not irritable or resentful, does not rejoice in the wrong but rejoices in the right, Jesus Christ bears all things, believes all things, hopes all things, endures all things." That is Paul affirming the sovereignty of Christ's love over the things within us raising the barriers separating us from one another.

b. "Love is patient—long suffering." If by Christ's spirit we are freed up from our-

selves for the service and love of our neighbor, then the only ones before us are God and our neighbor, and we live for the other patiently.

c. We continue. He names those things in our viscera wrestling for control and frequently winning in our encounter with others.

Jealousy, envy: the resentment of other's gifts, successes, luck; a dissatisfaction with our place and invidious pursuit for greater recognition, honor, privilege.

Love is not arrogant, not pretentious. Love suffers fools gladly.

Love does not insist on its own way. Love is not irritable. Love does not rejoice at wrong, but rejoices in the right.

And Paul affirms: "Love bears all things, believes all things, hopes all things, endures all things." This he says in the face of all the failures, the dangers, the impatiences, the sin seeking to divide and shatter us all of the time, confessing in faith the victory and triumph of the love of Christ finally and ultimately over our self-oriented, self-generated, divisive and fragmenting furies.

III. And finally, wrapping it all up: "Love never ends." As for our most popular readings of the human condition, profound as they may be, they are limited and ultimately inadequate. As for our most exquisite spiritual and aesthetic expressions, many of them beautiful beyond words, in light of eternity they too drift in the shadows. As for our knowledge, it cannot fathom what is truly worth knowing; it is woefully partial and veiled until we fully enter the loving and creative community God has in store for us. This side of heaven, spiritually speaking, we are like children, perceiving and speaking as children; when God's loving dominion grasps us all, it will be as if we have finally matured. What we understand now of God's love for us is as if we were staring into a cracked mirror, distorted, backwards, obscured, but then coherent, unblemished, intimate, as if face-to-face. Now we know only of the Divine person and future in part; then we will grasp God's fullness, just as God knows us now to our very depths. So faith, hope, love, these three abide . . . but the greatest of these, the ground beneath and the impulse behind all else, is love. Make love your aim!–James W. Crawford

Illustrations

LOVE LASTS.   During my college years a graduation speaker told of an immensely rewarding experience. A lady in the church of which he was minister baked a chocolate cake and brought it to the church office, saying that she wanted him and his family to have it. He expressed his appreciation and then, because it was midmorning and not yet time to go home for lunch, set the cake on a table beside a window that opened on a vacant lot where neighborhood children often played. During the morning he happened to notice that several boys from the not-too-well-to-do neighborhood had stopped their game and were looking longingly at the cake. On an impulse, the minister invited the boys in and shared the cake with them. It was soon gone, but the wonderful memories of a happy group of neighborhood children never left him; he told our graduating class months later that he was still enjoying the cake. A generation later, I am still enjoying the cake that they never saw or tasted. How different the destiny of this cake if the preacher had kept it for himself and his family.–Batsell Barrett Baxter

TO LOVE IS TO RISK.   In the measure that you are really alive, you are risking, for you take all sorts of chances without knowing how they will come out. To marry is to risk: you surrender your private self to a community of selves, risk your individual life in the hope of finding it more fully with another; and today the odds are only 50–50. To love is to risk: you open yourself to all the burden that being loved lays on you, and uncounted men and women crumble under it. To be a top-flight doctor or lawyer, to be in politics or business, is a risk: you may end up terribly narrow and one-sided, closed to everything save a spastic colon or a court case, public applause or private enterprise. To be a priest is to risk: too many of us are crotchety, peevish, self-centered bachelors incapable of loving or being

loved. Simply to be free is to risk: you can say no to God, betray your dearest friend with a kiss. In a word, to live humanly is to launch out into a large unknown.–Walter J. Burghardt, S.J.

SERMON SUGGESTIONS

Topic: Holy—But Stained!
TEXT: Exod. 28:38
The religion of the Hebrews provided not only for forgiveness for the plain wickedness of the people when they were penitent, but forgiveness also for the stains that sometimes disfigured holy things. Are we guilty of iniquity in holy things? (1) In our penitence. (2) In our worship. (3) In our prayers. (4) In our service. (5) In our giving.–W. E. Sangster

Topic: Wanted Today: A Revival Like Pentecost
TEXT: Acts 2:1
(1) It began with united prayer. (2) It calls for fervent preaching. (3) It comes through personal work. (4) It leads to widespread repentance.–Andrew W. Blackwood

Worship Aids

CALL TO WORSHIP.   "I will praise thee, O Lord, with my whole heart; I will show forth all thy marvelous works" (Ps. 9:1).

INVOCATION.   Our Lord and our God, let your love that we have known in Jesus Christ so fill us with praise that there will be no end of it when we leave this holy place. Help us to translate what we believe and feel and sing about into deeds of love and mercy.

OFFERTORY SENTENCE.   "Every one of us shall give account of himself to God" (Rom. 14:12).

OFFERTORY PRAYER.   Almighty God, use our gifts this day to say what we cannot say, to go where we cannot go, to do what we cannot do, because the power of the gospel is unlimited, the Holy Spirit unbound, and the word of the Lord abides forever.–E. Lee Phillips

PRAYER. O God, when we move through the valley of suffering, sorrow and disappointment, help us to be quiet, to trust in the goodness of thy being and love; to wait upon thee; to do nothing quickly, rashly; and then to go forward, believing that all things will work together for good to those who love thee and try to do thy will. We ask this in the name of him who when things did not go well for him, thought about it, asked that the cup be taken from him, and then said, thy will, not mine, be done.–Theodore Parker Ferris

LECTIONARY MESSAGE

Topic: Making Room in the Heart of God
TEXT: Mark 1:21–28
Other Readings: Deut. 18:15–20; Ps. 111; 1 Cor. 8:1–13
I. The Right Place to Be
a. The synagogue of Jews, like the church of Christians, consists in physical assembly (as the Greek name denotes, it is a "leading together," just as the Church–*ekklesia*–is a "calling out") and in the persons of those assembled, as well as in the religious worship those persons engage in. As the building becomes associated with the gathering together and with the spiritual worship, it becomes known by the name. The Church assembles at the church for church.
b. The synagogue in the time of Jesus was a place for the publishing of the Law and Prophets and for the worship of God. As such, the Spirit of God ought to prevail purely in it within the spirits of the worshipers. So, at Capernaum, it was perfectly fitting that Jesus, at the invitation of the ruler of the synagogue, should teach and apply God's truth to human lives. And he did so with an authority confirming the presence of his Father.
c. The Spirit of God is in the place be-

cause he lives in the hearts and minds of those who have pure hearts and are ready to meet God. Even one who is ignorant of God, one who is conscious of impure aspects of his life or knows of his moral and ethical offenses, may be suitably present in the place of worship to receive instruction and to find spiritual power to correct his life.
II. The Wrong Condition
a. Jesus was interrupted in his teaching by an unclean spirit. This spirit even called out to Jesus to leave him alone, saying he had nothing to do with Jesus, recognizing in him the holiness of God himself. The spirit was in a man who was in the right place in the wrong condition. His condition was "out of place," not only in the presence of Jesus, but also in the place of God's worshiping congregation.
b. The Jews had always had strict provisions regarding cleanness and uncleanness, since the very beginning when Cain's offering was not acceptable in God's service because of what was in his heart. The result of uncleanness was exclusion from the fellowship and worship of the sanctuary. It could be caused in the ceremonial sense by association with blood, death, or certain animals. It could be purified by ceremonial acts of washing and sacrifice.
c. This man's defiant spirit was intolerable in the worship, just as Jesus was intolerable to him. He forces us to recognize that defiant spirits may be present even in holy places among holy spirits today. His question, "What have we to do with thee?" was indicative of the essence of rebellion against God that is part of many natures. But Jesus has something to do with him.
III. Jesus and the Way to Holiness
a. The man's uncleanness was actually sin, being defiance and opposition to the Spirit of God. But God has always provided a way to become purified, physically and ceremonially. He eternally fulfilled the promise of sacrifices by giving his Son to do what mere offerings could not–heal our tremendous guilt of sin, cast out uncleanness, and enter in with cleansing grace and power.
b. We all are involved in the type of un-

cleanness that cannot be cured by soap and water. In the power of Christ, which is ours by the prayer of request, his spirit will cast out our unwilling, defiant, rebellious spirits and make us want what is the fruit of his spirit—love, joy, peace, longsuffering, gentleness, goodness, and faith (Gal. 5:22). As the unclean spirit "tore" the man and cried out, anyone may feel pain and trouble in changing. But the result is a good life and glory to God.—John R. Rodman

SUNDAY: FEBRUARY NINTH

SERVICE OF WORSHIP

Sermon: The Life of Prayer and the World of Action

TEXT: Isa. 60:1-3

There have always been critics of religion who feared that people of prayer permit prayer to become a substitute for real action in the world around them. We have to admit that the possibility exists.

I. The biblical view of prayer is that it leads directly to action. It may be communion of "the alone with the Alone," but it does not remain alone for very long. The idea that praying is for escapists, for people who want to avoid contact with the hard, cruel facts of life, is simply mistaken.

a. Consider Jesus, for instance. He began his ministry by going into the wilderness to pray. But he ended his ministry by entering the turbulent city to face the evil men who were corrupting the simple faith of the people.

Again and again, the Master confirmed a singular rhythm in his life-style; from his hours of aloneness, when he worshiped the Father and sought the Father's will in his life, he returned invariably to a hectic ministry among the sick, the degenerate, and the victimized inhabitants of what was still, despite our romanticized view of it, a dark and barbaric land.

b. It was to be the same for his disciples, once they were put in charge. They were all at prayer, the book of Acts tell us, when the Holy Spirit broke over them like a tidal wave of fire, baptizing them with courage and the urgency of bearing witness to all they had seen and heard during those extraordinary years with Jesus. Later, Peter was at prayer when he had a remarkable vision confirming God's acceptance of the Gentiles; Paul was similarly at his prayers when he felt compelled to go to Rome, even as a prisoner, in order to share his experience of the gospel with those in the imperial city.

c. Prayer, for these early giants of the faith, was not merely a means of personal integration, of self-understanding and consolation, as it is often viewed today; it was an embarking of the self upon dangerous voyages over uncharted seas and through dark, primeval woods, untracked by any previous traveler except the Savior himself, who, they always felt, had gone ahead of them and waited for them there, encouraging them when obstacles were most severe. Prayer was no retreat from the world of action. If anything it plunged them into the very heart of that world. Instead of shielding them from trouble, it invited trouble, it courted trouble, it guaranteed trouble.

II. Prayer and action belong together, you see. Each serves the other. Prayer without action misses the point of prayer and never arrives at its fullness, the surrender of the self to God as an act of love. Action without prayer, on the other hand, is always imprudent, unimaginative, and lacking in the power of the Holy Spirit, so that it becomes lost in a welter of confusion and misdirection. Prayer leads us into creative action in behalf of the needy world around us.

a. Think of the enormous needs today. There is the need for food. Millions of people in the world go to bed at night with hunger pangs. They eat grass and stones and chips of wood to give their intestines something with which to keep busy. We forget the need for food in the world. We may complain about the rise in energy prices, but we have the energy. We forget the people who don't. There is the need for love. Our world is teeming with people who feel cut off, alone, rootless in an alien society.

b. What is the answer to all of these tremendous needs? We know God's answer:

Arise, shine; for your light has come,
and the glory of the Lord has risen
upon you.
For behold, darkness shall cover the earth,
and thick darkness the peoples;
but the Lord will arise upon you.
And nations shall come to your light,
and kings to the brightness of your rising.

(Isaiah 60:1–3)

The early Christians, who were people of prayer and devotion, heard this word and responded. Their lives were transformed by it. They rose above the greedy, dark culture of their time to become guiding lights of morality, courage, and unselfishness. And now it is ours to do something.

c. The thing about prayer is that it is the way we can turn the unlimited resources of God into saving the world around us. When we truly pray, when we open ourselves to God without reservation, it is like turning a valve in the largest dam in the world, so that the tremendous power embraced behind the dam is suddenly released through the aperture the valve was controlling and goes shooting forth with incredible energy into the valley below. We are not the power. We do not have to be powerful in ourselves. All we have to do is be an opening, and let God do the rest.

III. Do you see? It is what we must do for the world. Hundreds of us, thousands of us, must become openings for God. We must perforate the barrier between his resources and our world's needs so that he is able to pour through into our world with all his healing power.

In the end, it all has to do with love: God's love for the world. Our love for the world. Our opening ourselves to God, so that his love can reach the world through us. This is what it means to become Christians,

for it is what Christ did. By praying constantly, he became the perfect opening. God came into the world through him. We call that the Good News. But it is only part of the Good News. The other part is, God comes into the world through us too!–John Killinger

Illustrations

PRAYER AND REALITY.   It is a mere caricature of prayer to regard it as emergency signals that we send out to God in difficult situations. Prayer is a fundamental style of thinking, passionate and compassionate, responsible and thankful, that is deeply rooted in our humanity and that manifests itself not only among believers but also among serious-minded people who do not profess any religious faith. Yet it seems to me that if we follow out the instinct to pray that is in all of us, it will finally bring us to faith in God. Michael Novak remarks, "It is in prayer that one comes to know God best." And he goes on to ask the very significant question whether people do not pray because they do not believe in God, or whether they do not believe in God because they have given up (or never learned) prayer. To pray is to think in such a way that we dwell with reality, and faith's name for reality is God.–John Macquarrie

LOVE AND REALITY.   Jesus does not demand that men love their brethren because from a transcendent perspective all men are equal, but because the God of the historic and cosmic process is one who avenges all lovelessness, all lack of forgiveness because selfishness, self-assertion lead to destruction. The laws of God are not the laws of moral perfection, but the laws of reality. The Sermon on the Mount does not tell men what to do in order that they may live up to the moral ideal, but what to do in a world where hatred as well as murder, lasciviousness as well as adultery have terrible destructive consequences. The morality of the Sermon on the Mount does not stand on its own bottom, it stands upon the foundations of reality.–H. Richard Niebuhr

SERMON SUGGESTIONS

Topic: Expanding Horizons
TEXT: Ps. 31:8
(1) The roominess of the life of faith. (2) The illimitable realm of prayer. (3) The unexplored area of Christian fellowship. (4) The untrammeled plateaus of immortal hope.—Edgar De Witt Jones

Topic: Jesus and the Reality of Suffering
TEXT: 2 Cor. 4:1–6
(1) The open face of Jesus Christ (John 1:14b). (2) The set face of Jesus Christ (Luke 9:51 and Heb. 12:2). (3) The silent face of Jesus Christ (Matt. 17:12–14). (4) The suffering face of Jesus Christ (John 11:35 and many others). (5) The transforming face of Jesus Christ (2 Cor. 3:12–13, 16, 18; 1 John 3:1–3).—Wayne E. Oates

Worship Aids

CALL TO WORSHIP. "Blessed are they that do his commandments, that they may have right to the tree of life, and may enter in through the gates into the city" (Rev. 22:14).

INVOCATION. O God, how can we worship you unless you put your praise into our hearts? How can we obey you unless the love of Christ constrains us? We confess our coldness of heart and ask you to "kindle a flame of sacred love" within us, so that we may glorify your name.

OFFERTORY SENTENCE. "And he said to them all, If any man will come after me, let him deny himself, and take up his cross daily, and follow me" (Luke 9:23).

OFFERTORY PRAYER. Ever-living and ever-giving God, you have made us a part of what you are doing in the world and have given meaning to our life here on earth. May the offerings that we bring, extensions of our strength and labors, enter into your purpose and bring blessing wherever they are used.

PRAYER. Our heavenly Father, we praise you for your infinite wisdom, while we stand in awe of the mystery of your ways. Again and again in the history of the world and in our personal and private stories you have proven that your way is best. Still, we often reluctantly conclude and confess that you have been at work in all things to accomplish your good and gracious purpose.

We thank you for the wisdom of the cross by which you have purchased our salvation and in which you freely give us all things. We thank you for the wisdom of our own cross, which we often fail to understand and even rebel against. Yet grant to us the grace not to crucify Christ afresh to ourselves by any reckless thought of your power to overrule our sins. And grant to us the grace not to add to the burden of the crosses that others must bear in their brave and costly discipleship.—James W. Cox

LECTIONARY MESSAGE

Topic: On with the Task
TEXT: Mark 1:29–39
Other Readings: Isa. 40:21–31; Ps. 147:1–11, 20c; 1 Cor. 9:16–23

Some people may think that because of the times in which Jesus lived everything moved slowly and not much could be accomplished in a day like ours. But that idea is soon put to rest when we look at the extremely busy day when John Mark presents Jesus opening his Galilean ministry.

Following his schedule of preaching and the calling of his first four disciples, Jesus went to Capernaum and to the synagogue, where he taught as one having authority. In the midst of his message, a man with an evil spirit interrupted the meeting, and Jesus said, "Be silent." Then he cast out the demon and healed the man. All in the building were astonished at his teaching with such authority and showing his power over a demon-possessed man. "And his fame spread everywhere."

From there our text picks up, and we are told that Jesus went with Simon and Andrew along with James and John.

I. The Busy Day Continues

First, someone told him that Peter's mother-in-law was ill and in bed with a fever. Jesus went to her, took her by the hand, and helped her to her feet, and "the fever left her and she waited upon [served] the people." Again we see the writing ability of Mark in presenting that story all in the space of two short verses (1:30–31).

Second, Mark moves on to the evening when people were bringing their sick, infirm, and demon-possessed to Simon's house for Jesus to heal them. "And he would not permit the demons to speak, because they knew him." One can imagine the physical and emotional drain placed upon Jesus during that hard day of speaking, teaching, healing. Then finally came a time of rest.

II. Early the Next Morning He Went to Be Alone and Pray

It was evidently before dawn when he left the house and sought a place where he could be alone and commune with his Father. Sometime later Simon found him and wondered why he was out so early, telling him that many people had already gathered at the house to be healed.

This should be a lesson to all of God's children: Jesus, the Son of God, felt the necessity to be alone with his Father; in a time when he was very busy, he still sought and found rest for a while. How much more should we feel that necessity of being alone with our Father in heaven to share our heartaches, our joys, and our needs with him, and to listen for his word to us!

But the Master was thinking of another day and of others who needed him. Listen to him: "Let us go on to the next towns, that I may preach there also; for that is why I came out" (RSV). There it is again for us to ponder. His mission was to proclaim the Good News of hope, and peace, and salvation. Mark adds, "And he went throughout all Galilee, preaching in their synagogues and casting out demons."

III. Conclusion

One can understand the weariness of Jesus after such a day, and it will be that way for almost three and a half years. He had to keep moving, but in the meantime the hostility of some of the religious leaders would rise and make his task even more difficult. How are we doing today? Have we, too, become weary in well-doing and stand in need of the refreshing encouragement of the Father? Then let us move closer to him in prayer and listen for his voice to speak to us. —G. Allen West, Jr.

SUNDAY: FEBRUARY SIXTEENTH

SERVICE OF WORSHIP

Sermon: The Great Requirement

TEXT: Deut. 18:15–20

I. God's Promise and Requirement

The words of that Prophet here promised are to be the touchstones of all human life. Because of the terror inspired in his people by the fire, God had promised not to speak to them again as on Sinai. Moses here repeats the promise God made there, that he would raise up a Prophet who would speak all the truth necessary for his people: "He shall speak unto them all that I shall command him." Then, these very serious words

were spoken: "Whosoever will not hearken unto my words which he shall speak in my name, *I will require it of him.*" Other words of judgment had promised excommunication, exile, or death for those who did not obey the words God's messenger delivered in his name, as for those who were not afflicted in their souls on the Day of Atonement, promising that any such one "shall be cut off from among his people" (Lev. 23:29).

II. The Source of Rightness

a. Confusion about the means of godly forgiveness, righteousness, and salvation is found in the secular world of competing philosophies and ethical systems. Sadder yet, uncertainty is often seen among those of Christian family inheritance, where right behavior is often instilled or commanded apart from or independent of its only true source. In other words, obedience to a set of rules is required of those who have no strength or even incentive adequate for compliance.

b. Laws and rules are essential for any social or community existence. When God gave rules for his people's lives, he gave words of explanation and reason. He attached to them promises of reward and also, inevitably, punishment, so that those who obeyed were accepted and blessed by him, while those who ignored the instruction were penalized or punished. Obviously one source of acceptance has always been obedient compliance.

c. The function of this Prophet was to deliver God's word. The duty of the hearer was to accept and obey that word. Failure resulted in judgment. The great "requirement" promised is what awaits wholesale humanity, for "all have sinned and come short of the glory of God" (Rom. 3:23), and "all we like sheep have gone astray; we have turned every one to his own way" (Isa. 53:6). Our obedience has never been more than partial, and our failures have blighted our world with horrible social ailments.

III. Our Living Hope

a. Those under the judgment of God, those of whom God requires and exacts strict obedience, have another source of righteousness and forgiveness. It is always, and still is, God's pleasure to redeem and accept one who hears his word. All scripture reveals that what God wants is the spirit of man, the believing and willing response of the heart, and that God himself provides what he requires. The Word written on tables of the heart is the source of righteousness. Let him who suffers from his own or another's sinfulness turn to the spirit of God's word and adopt that spirit as his own.

b. The utmost obedience is satisfied by a human heart's being conformed to God's word. It is the working of that word to set a wayward wayfarer on the path that leads to blessing and honor. The reformed life is made possible by the transformation of a person's standard of choice from his own desires or those he sees others expressing to a new standard of the word of God. His decisions are tested by whether or not God would be pleased, and his actions thereafter in kind from those of the unbelievers. But now we know that in the birth of God's Son, we have the Living Word, the savior who gave his life in fulfillment of all the Father required. We can now enter into that transformation by confessing our need and believing in him. We thank God for his redeeming Word, delivering us from the great requirement.–John Rodman

Illustrations

A PLACE TO STAND.   New strength came into my ministry both public and private when I saw that either I had to reject Christ and the admiring talk, or accept Him on His own terms. As though illumined by a great light, I saw that He did not ask for admiration; He asked for commitment! To the perplexed, the confused, the distraught, He said and still says, "Come to me." In all the relativities of this world there is, if Christ is right, one solid place. He offers "rest," not in the sense of passivity, but in that of a place to stand, a center of trustworthiness in the midst of the world's confusion.–Elton Trueblood

HAVING AND BEING.   The man who buys is to be as though he does not own. For the man who owns is the one who claims to be a master before God. He confuses what he is with what he has. He thus links his own destiny to what he has. This is the problem of "where your treasure is, there will your heart be also." To have a sense of ownership is to be a dispossession of the self. This is a radical judgment on the total enterprise of modern civilization, which is totally oriented to achieving possession of the world. The more man does this, the more alienated he is. The experience of a century and a half strictly confirms the proclamation of the gospel in this regard.

Once again, God does not tell us this in order to prevent us from enjoying things. He does so in order that man may simply be. Now as those who are freed by Christ we can be only as those who do not possess. –Jacques Ellul

SERMON SUGGESTIONS

Topic: Remember Your Mountains
TEXT: Ps. 36:6

A mountain is a constant quantity, and so is God's justice. (1) There is Mount Sinai, where the Ten Commandments were given. They were termini of thought, moral conclusions due to the upsurge of God's spirit in the soul. (2) The supreme mountain to remember is Calvary, where God did full justice to the pitiful human situation. It is the height of the Divine love which is God's justice grasping with ungrudging sacrifice those who are going under, in order to give them a masterly standing which will share in the Divine nature.–Arthur A. Cowan

Topic: Faith and Doubt
TEXT: Mark 9:24

(1) Everybody doubts. (2) Everybody believes. (3) The faith and the doubt come to a crux in Jesus Christ. The doubt is honestly admitted; the faith is courageously held. (4) Can the tension be resolved? Not fully in this life but yet with great measure of certitude. What we need is a strategy rather than a proof, a strategy and a certain valor of the spirit. (5) The man confessed his doubts and faced them: "Help my unbelief!" Augustine spoke a final word: A man doubts, therefore God is.–George A. Buttrick

Worship Aids

CALL TO WORSHIP.   "'I have set before you life and death, blessing and cursing,' saith the Lord, 'therefore choose life'" (Deut. 30:19b).

INVOCATION.   O God of peace, quiet the conflicts warring within our hearts, as both the flesh and the spirit struggle for ascendancy. Give us grace through this experience of worship to the end that we can follow after the spirit and so reject the demands of the flesh.

OFFERTORY SENTENCE.   "Every one of us shall give account of himself to God" (Rom. 14:12).

OFFERTORY PRAYER.   Our Father, help us to realize that every day in our lives is a judgment day, that we are making decisions for which we are accountable to you. Give us the reverence and the wisdom to make every decision in the awareness of your saving presence.

PRAYER.   Almighty God, Lord of the universe, God of our salvation, we praise you for your mighty power, your steadfast love, and your redemptive presence among us. We lift out voices to you in song; we lift our hands to you in prayer; we bring our gifts to you in offering. We acknowledge that you are our creator; you are our redeemer; you have brought us through many trials; you have given us good things of this world to enjoy. We belong to you. Yet we confess that we have often failed to hearken to your voice. Sometimes we have been preoccupied with business, conflicts in our home, or trouble with a neighbor or business associate. Some of us may even have let our hearts gradually harden against you through accumulations of bitterness and envy. Forgive us, put us on right paths again, and restore to us the joy of your salvation.–James W. Cox

LECTIONARY MESSAGE

Topic: The Baptism of Jesus and What Follows
TEXT: Mark 1:9–13
Other Readings: Gen. 9:8–17; Ps. 25:1–10; 1 Pet. 3:18–22

The message will focus on two major events that took place immediately before the Master began his Galilean ministry: they were his baptism at the hands of John the Baptist and the temptations he endured from Satan. What do the two have in common? If we keep reading, we may find some important ties.

First, then, the baptism of Jesus.

Mark is now considered the first of the Gospels, and it is the shortest, the most succinct, the most action-laden of the four. The words catch our attention as we read, "immediately," "straightway," "forthwith." We note the use of the present tense and Mark's use of the historical present. His Gospel outline or presentation is used both by Matthew and Luke for the general framework of their Gospels.

Our text reads, "At that time Jesus came from Nazareth and was baptized by John in the Jordan. As Jesus was coming up out of the water, he saw heaven torn open and the Spirit descend on him like a dove. And a voice from heaven, 'You are my Son, whom I love; with you I am well pleased.'"

I. *First, consider the one doing the baptizing:* it was John the Baptist, the one who was kin to Jesus through their mothers. John was one promised, a prophet to prepare the way of Christ's coming. He was the Elijah promised in Malachi. As a prophet he came unusually dressed, with beard and long hair. He was one of whom Jesus said, "Among those born of women there has not risen anyone greater that John the Baptist; yet he who is least in the kingdom of heaven is greater that he." Mark further reports that he was without fear in his dynamic preaching against the sins of the religious leaders and even of the puppet ruler, King Herod Philip. And he baptized those who came at his preaching asking forgiveness, a baptism of repentance it was called.

Jesus came to him for baptism. John naturally demurred, for he felt that Jesus should be baptizing him. But Jesus said, "Let it be so now; it is proper for us to do this to fulfill all righteousness." Why did Jesus come to John to be baptized? Did he have sins that should be repented of and for which to ask forgiveness? No! Did he come to serve as an example to us of baptism? Maybe so. Is the answer found in his words to John? Why had Jesus come to earth as the Incarnate Son of God? Was it not to seek and to save people from their sins? Was it not to bring them into a right relationship with God the Father? What, then, did he need to do in order to bring that about? He tells us in other places that he must suffer and be

killed and rise again on the third day. Therein was the heart of the gospel, his atonement for mankind. Hence, he was saying to John, we must do this, for it is the dedication of myself to the Father and to my life's purpose, my mission. And John baptized Him!

II. *What followed that wonderful moment?* the dove that came down upon him, the symbol of peace and of the Holy Spirit. Even though the Holy Spirit had conceived in his mother, Mary, and had been with him throughout his life, yet here was a visible symbol of the Presence. But there was more —a voice from heaven giving approval, affirmation: "This is my Son, whom I love; with him I am well pleased."

Jesus had come at the beginning of his ministry to dedicate himself to a mission that would require his all, his very life. And the Father and the Spirit are present to affirm him in that task and purpose. What a high and holy moment!

Who have come on after him to follow as his disciples? What has that baptism meant to us? It is an act of obedience to his command to follow him and be his servants. It is to mark out the fact that in his death, burial, and resurrection, we have followed him symbolically in the baptismal act. It has introduced us into the fellowship of God's family, the Church, and it has marked us publicly from that moment on as belonging to him, if indeed our faith is real and truly in him.

And what does that baptism mean to you? Can you look back to whatever time or whatever moment you may have found Christ as Savior and Lord of your life and say, "Thank you, Lord, for that holy and meaningful hour"?

But something else took place following the baptism. It was his being led into the wilderness area not far from the place where he was baptized. There he spent forty days and nights with God the Father. But another was present—Satan, the deceiver, the tempter, the evil one. That enemy of God and of humanity did his best to get Jesus to compromise himself as to his relationship to the Father God and to his life's purpose. He quoted, rather, misquoted, Scripture to get

Jesus to succumb to his wiles. But Jesus came out of it a winner. Even so, Luke says that he lifted Jesus for a season.

And the significance of that event for us? Satan never gives up in trying to get to us. Often, when we've had some joy-filled and glorious experience with God, we are walking on air and think we stand tall, only to be next facing some powerful temptation from Satan. So it was with our Lord. And so it is with all of us.

Let us pray that when that time may come, God will give us the strength to withstand Satan's attack and give us the victory. —G. Allen West, Jr.

SUNDAY: FEBRUARY TWENTY-THIRD

SERVICE OF WORSHIP

Sermon: Home Again for the Heart
TEXT: Jer. 31:1–14

The words of our text, while appearing in the words of a great and well-known Hebrew prophet, directed explicitly to a captive Hebrew populace, constitute a promise and a prophecy to God's people of every time, every place, and every condition. We as Christian believers may apply them and their loving graciousness to ourselves and our conditions and hopes.

I. God's love is shown in the words of this prophecy, an early announcement of the grace of Christ's gospel; they are the words of the one who made all things and of Christ, without whom "nothing was made that was made," together with the Spirit, guaranteeing to every one who hears him the love that draws us to him.

a. God never gives up on his own. "I have loved thee; I have drawn thee" are his words to all who hear, all who accept by faith his care for them. Nothing in the world can compare to being loved with the love of God. Such love can wipe away a lifetime of degraded and despicable activities when one answers his call.

b. God brings his loved ones to a time of restoration. He promises once again the joy of living, even to the enjoyment of the ordinary affairs of life. Cast adrift in a roaring torrent, fallen into a bottomless crevice of ice and snow, alone on a battlefield overrun by the enemy—in any of the extremities of life, we cry aloud for restoration, for rescue; at all cost of future self-determination, we offer everything we hope to have for one more chance at life. That is what God offers and promises to his people, whatever their situation, because of his "everlasting" love—love that had no beginning, takes no time off, and has no ending. He frees his own from the "hands stronger than" they.

II. God's provision is more than restoration—it is complete newness of life.

a. He saves all who say, "Arise, let us go to Zion to the Lord our God." They feel the captivity, the homesickness of the "north country," far from home; they shall come. They are in other lands, continents, and islands; they shall come. They are blind; they shall come. They are lame; they shall come. Woman are pregnant and giving birth; they shall come.

b. What they come to is what we all long for. The physical provisions God makes for us are metaphors for our souls' welfare.

1. A straight way by the rivers of water is the provision for those who have been crowded into corners, have taken dark byways, have struggled with unknown paths in strange places. The rivers of water are life-giving refreshment.

2. Ways without stumbling give hope to all who have fallen over hidden obstacles, stepped into ditches, or fallen into traps lying hidden from the innocent and unwary. God's ways are ways of protected trust and restored innocence.

3. God will seek out every last one, "as a shepherd his flock." Those who are dangerously lost can especially appreciate, like a bleating sheep, the anxiety of heart, hoping to be found. It is as though having been lost or exiled is the only way we can truly appreciate, like bleating sheep, the anxiety of

heart, hoping to be found. It is as though having been lost or exiled is the only way we can truly appreciate a home place for our souls. None can claim to have clung faithfully and unerringly to the way of pure faithfulness, the way of God. We all know what being lost means.

4. The good life will be restored like a garden that is watered. All shall enjoy the fruits of labor—the wheat, wine, and oil, the flocks and herds. Everyone who answers God's call to return to the Lord who gave him life will know the safety and security of salvation. Life's greatest enemy is the sin that is always "stronger than we," and God's rescue from that is a return to the heart's true home.

5. "My people shall be satisfied with my goodness, saith the Lord." How many parents would give their own lives to be able to guide their children safely "through the perils of childhood and the temptations of youth," to keep them from being hurt or lost! Their only hope is to lead them surely to the Lord who alone satisfies and eternally loves them. God would never say, "I don't love you anymore," without adding, "I couldn't love you more than I already love you."—John R. Rodman

Illustrations

THE FINALITY OF CHRIST. To claim finality for Jesus Christ is not to assert either that the majority of men will someday be Christians, or to assert that all others will be damned. It is to claim that commitment to him is the way in which men can become truly aligned to the ultimate end for which all things were made. The church which believes this will not be afraid to address confidently to every generation and every people the call which it has received from him: Follow me.—Lesslie Newbegin

GLEANING FOR GOD. We slander people when we say they do not want the Christ. It is nonsense, it is not true. I will not hear them libeled. They do want God, they do want the Bible, they are not hostile to Jesus Christ, but they do hate the poor caricature they see of him in the lives of so

many of us who profess to follow him; they hate that, but they do not hate Jesus; they respond to Jesus, and they know Jesus when they see him. And I have lived to learn that there are far more people who will come and sit in your pew if you ask them than you dream of.—Gipsy Smith

SERMON SUGGESTIONS

Topic: Wit's End Corner
TEXT: Exod. 14:1–14
(1) It is the place to which God sometimes leads us, verses 1–4a. (2) It is the place where God tests us (vv. 4b–9). (3) It is the place where we sometimes fail the Lord (vv. 10–12). (4) It is the place where God undertakes for us (vv. 13–14).—James Braga

Topic: The Christian Secret of Radiance
TEXT: Luke 24:13–35
(1) Being with the Living Christ. (2) Understanding the Scripture. (3) Engaging in Christian service. (4) Living in Christian hope.—Andrew W. Blackwood

Worship Aids

CALL TO WORSHIP. "Whatsoever ye do in word or deed, do all in the name of the Lord Jesus, giving thanks to God and the Father by him" (Col. 3:17).

INVOCATION. O God, open our hearts to thee, that we may be led by thy Spirit to render to thee true worship. Receive, we pray, the words from our voices, the gifts from our hands, and the service from our daily living.

OFFERTORY SENTENCE. "Where your treasure is, there will your heart be also" (Matt. 6:21).

OFFERTORY PRAYER. Lord, we have professed to have surrendered our all to you. Help us to know if it is really true or if there are still miles to travel in our stewardship, and then strengthen our true desires to make what we are and what we have available for your service.

PRAYER. Long have we heard that Jesus is the way, the truth, and the life, Father. Grant us the grace that enables us to follow him, to learn from him, and to live in him as we venture into the days before us.

Give us the vision to walk in his ways. Open our minds to truth, that we may not fall into falsehood. Fill our hearts with love, that we may overcome hate and its attendant ravages and that in him we may live lives of righteousness, peace, and love.

Help us, Father, to translate Christ's spirit into deeds of compassion and service. May we never be merely hearers of his word and not doers of it also. Generate in us a compassion for the needs of our fellow pilgrims which will go forth to care for their need. Give us a concern for the burdened which will strengthen us to help them carry their heavy loads. Give us a caring for the lonely which will populate their loneliness with friendly presence. Give us a heart for the lost which will go out into all climates to gently lead them into the fold of your grace and forgiveness.

Father, in a world which is a mixture of good and evil, light and darkness, pray keep our faith and hopes burning bright, that we may be light bearers in the darkness and the bringer of good news, with all its promise and hope, to people everywhere.–Henry Fields

LECTIONARY MESSAGE

Topic: The Heart of the Gospel
TEXT: Mark 8: 31–38
Other Readings: Gen. 17:1–7, 15–16; Ps. 22:23–31; Rom. 4:13–25

The words in these eight verses of our Scripture passage are marked with spiritual dynamite. Jesus and his disciples were in the region of Caesarea-Philippi in northern Galilee. He had just asked them what men were saying as to who he was and then what they, the disciples, said he was. Peter responded strongly, "You are the Messiah." Matthews adds other details, but Mark gives the essence.

"He then began to teach them that the Son of Man must suffer many things and be rejected by the elders, chief priests and teachers of the law, and that he must be killed and after three days rise again" (Mark 8:31 NIV). That was the message–and what a message. The remaining verses of the text are addressed to the messengers, the disciples, and to all of us who follow in their train.

I. The Message Here Is the Heart of the Gospel
Jesus uses the title he most frequently used of himself, "Son of Man." As such, he was representative Man, fully man, perfect man. "For the Son of Man must suffer many things"–suffer the humiliation of coming from heaven's glory to earth's sinful state in becoming a man; suffer the insults, shame, and humiliating treatment from religious leaders of Israel, and later from the people; suffer the shameful treatment and epithets thrown at him.

And then, being rejected by elders, the chief priests, and the scribes was heartbreaking. We are reminded of what the author, John, wrote in his prologue: "He was in the world, and the world was made by him, yet the world knew him not. He came to his own home, and his own people received him not." It was so with the rich young ruler and with the greedy rich farmer. And it is still so today, for there are millions who still have not received him.

The next words, "and be killed," tell the story of what he had to do in order to secure the freedom of God's people from sin, death, and the grave. He paid the price with his life for our lives. On the cross, atonement was made for the sins of the whole world, for your sins and mine.

The final words in the message are these: "and rise on the third day." There is the hope. There is where he would say just before his death on the cross, "It is finished." The work of redemption was over, for the Son of Man had given his all that the world might have salvation, life eternal! And it all sprang from the love and heart of God. That is the message in a nutshell, the good news of the gospel.

It was so vital that Jesus repeated essentially the same words a second and a third time in Mark and in parallel passages of Matthew and Luke. And the apostle Paul picks up on those words regarding the gospel in First Corinthians 15:1–4. And his disciples still found it difficult to accept his words; they didn't want to hear them, for they didn't know that he *had* to die if humanity's sins were taken away, and that he must rise from the grave, victorious over death and over human and Satanic power.

II. Jesus Speaks on Discipleship

He laid down the cost-conditions of discipleship in clear-cut, simple, but demanding terms.

a. *The first is self-denial.* In recent years, we've heard very little of denying ourselves for anything, and certainly not for Christian service. From the servant role, we've gone to the chairman-of-the-board style of leadership for pastors and other types of leadership in our denomination. We hear little of being caring, loving, warmhearted pastors. We have moved from the prophetic role of preaching, the expositor role in Bible truths, to the television-actor-style communicator. But we hear little of self-denial. This same change has also been seen in physicians and in those in various other professional roles. Where do we find any longer the people coming because of self-denial?

b. *The second is cross-bearing.* We've denigrated the meaning of the cross. Now it is more or less a token relationship, something nice to have and look at or wear, but very little concern is given to what it meant to our Master and to many of his disciples then and since.

The cross meant death of the cruelest and most painful placed upon human beings. But it meant death. Here for Christ's followers today, it still means death to the world's way, death to Satan's ways, death to the former way of life; and it may mean physical death to the disciple. So it was with Bonhoeffer and a host of others who gave their lives for Jesus our Lord. The question here: Are we willing to give our lives for him?

c. *Follow me.* There are the last words in this series of three conditions laid down by our Lord. Follow him to the hard places, to the troubled areas of the world, to the small churches in the area. And what word is there for laypersons? What and where do we see any word to them of sacrifices to be made for our Lord? Have we watered down the message so much that there is no challenge in it for anyone?

There are other instructions from our Master in this brief passage:

The life-death principle: "For whoever would save his life will lose it; and whoever loses it for my sake and the gospel's will find it."

The profit-loss principle: "For what does it profit a man, to gain the whole world and forfeit his life?"

The sheer value of a human life: "For what can a man give in exchange for his life?"

Finally, the matter of shame: "For whoever is ashamed of me and of my words in this adulterous and sinful generation, of him will the Son of Man be ashamed when he comes in the glory of the Father with the holy angels."

III. Conclusion

The message found here is the heart of the Gospel. The words to the disciples concerning their ministry and discipleship demand uncompromising love for our Lord, a turning to him with singleness of heart and purpose, and the willingness to give ourselves to him as completely as possible.—G. Allen West

SUNDAY: MARCH SECOND

SERVICE OF WORSHIP

Sermon: Four Ways to Be a More Caring Person

TEXT: Selections from Philippians

This morning I want to think with you about how to be a more caring person. I recognize that some of you are already caring persons. Others of us could be far more caring. Some of us are almost totally unaware of the feelings and pain of the other people around us. The purpose of the message this morning is to help us grow in some neglected area of our lives. There are four ways to be a more caring person.

I. Cultivate and Communicate Awareness

Step number one is to cultivate and communicate awareness. Cultivate an awareness, a sensitivity to the people around you. What are their joys and sorrows? Put yourself in someone's place and try to see how that feels.

a. Behind Paul's letter to the Philippians, there is a beautiful story of awareness. When the little congregation at Philippi heard that Paul was being kept under guard in Rome, they decided to do something to help him. They sent one of their young members to care for Paul. They sent a number of gifts with Epaphroditus, but most of all they sent a person. While he was in Rome, Epaphroditus became very ill. He nearly died. Paul prayed for him and he got better, but he was never the same.

b. Paul was a sensitive and caring person. He was aware that this young man had to return to Philippi to really recover. Out of this sensitive awareness, Paul did a beautiful thing. It was something that maintained the young man's dignity and confirmed his integrity. Paul wrote the Philippians a letter to rebuild one broken life, to comfort one hurting person. Notice that Paul made it clear that it was his decision, not Epaphroditus's, for Epaphroditus to return home. Notice too the words of positive affirmation, "my brother and fellow worker and fellow soldier, and your messenger." Paul was saying by implication, "Don't treat him with contempt. Give

him a hero's welcome." Listen to the concluding verses of the chapter, "So receive him in the Lord with all joy; and honor such men, for he nearly died for the work of Christ, risking his life to complete your service to me" (Phil. 2:30).

c. Isn't that beautiful? It comforts me to know that Paul was aware of some sickly, drooping, discouraged, despondent young man. It comforts me to know that Jesus was aware of a poor woman who had been sick for so long. It comforts me to know that he was aware of a tax collector name Zacchaeus. It comforts me to know that Jesus was aware of little children, of blind beggers, of lepers, and of a thief on a cross.

There is someone in your circle of friends who needs your awareness. The first way to become a caring person is to cultivate and then communicate awareness.

II. Express Positive Expectations

The second step is to express positive expectations. I am reading from verse 19, "I hope in the Lord Jesus to send Timothy to you soon, so that I may be cheered by news of you." Paul wanted to communicate this caring to the little congregation.

a. Notice the positive expectation that surrounds Timothy's visit, "that I may be cheered by news of you" (Phil. 2:19). Paul expected good news, not a word of disaster. He didn't say, "I am sending Timothy to you to check up on things because I know everything is falling apart and that the church is probably in a terrible mess." Expectations are tremendously important for positive or negative results!

b. Remember how Paul began his letter with a positive statement, "I thank my God in all my remembrance of you, . . . thankful for your partnership in the gospel from the first day until now. And I am sure that he who began a good work in you will bring it to completion at the day of Jesus Christ" (Phil 1:3–6). Paul communicated positive expectations.

III. Affirm Strengths

The third step in becoming a more caring person is to look for, find, and confirm strengths in the other person. Most people already know their faults. It is not your mission to correct every person you meet.

a. Paul moves, in his letter to the Philippians, from the statement of positive expectations to strength affirmation. Notice verse 20. "I have no one like him [Timothy], who will be genuinely anxious for your welfare" (Phil. 2:20). What a beautiful introduction! Paul doesn't introduce Timothy as a brilliant organizer, as a skilled negotiator, as a brilliant preacher, as a great scholar, as a famous teacher. Paul affirms Timothy's greatest strength: He was an authentically caring person. He was "anxious for your welfare." There are so many people who desperately need to meet someone who will genuinely care about them.

b. Become a more caring person! This is a great pull of the New Testament, the magnetism of Jesus. It is certainly part of what it means to have the mind of Christ. Look for, find, and affirm strengths in other people.

IV. The fourth way to become a more caring person is to appreciate yourself. Paul had positive self-esteem without being neurotically self-centered. It takes a certain courage to say, as Paul says in chapter 3, verse 17, "Brethren, join in imitating me, and mark those who so lives as you have an example in us."

a. When Paul was attacked by the Corinthians, they really worked him over. They accused him of being funny-looking, of being dishonest, of being deceptive, and of being of no account as a preacher. Paul refuses to slink away with his head tucked down between his shoulders. He stands tall. He faces his critics. This is what he says, "I think that I am not in the least inferior to these superlative apostles" (2 Cor. 11:5).

b. Don't let your life be intimidated by the world's negative. In the name of Jesus, in the power of his Spirit, affirm yourself! Paul goes on to say that self-worth doesn't depend upon the accomplishments of the flesh. In chapter 3 he tells us that he puts no confidence in the flesh, "Though I myself have reason for confidence in the flesh, also. If any other man thinks he has reason for confidence in the flesh, I have more: circumcised on the eighth day, of the People of Israel, of the tribe of Benjamin, a Hebrew

born of Hebrews; as to the law a Pharisee, as to zeal a persecutor of the church, as to righteousness under the law blameless. But whatever gain I had, I counted as loss for the sake of Christ. Indeed I count everything as loss because of the surpassing worth of knowing Christ Jesus my Lord" (Phil. 3:4–11).

c. Appreciate who you are in Jesus Christ! Understand that your worth is not measured by the standards of the world. You are somebody because of the love of God. Appreciate yourself! Do you really believe that Jesus Christ died for you? Do you really know that the Holy Spirit lives within you? Do you know that you are a creation of God? Do you know that it is all right to feel good about yourself?—Joe A. Harding

Illustrations

LIFE TOUCHING LIFE. No one is equipped to help others unless something of this inward power that was in Jesus is in him also. For it is only life that can touch life. There is no force in things to raise the sunken spirit, no balm in Gilead to cure the wounded will. Flame must be kindled by flame. It is the touch of man that heals. Psychologists and psychiatrists are agreed that we must get a new hope and sense of power into the lives of people if they are to get well and strong. They are also agreed that this new and quickened hope can be given only through the impact upon the life needing it by the life of one who possesses it.—Raymond Calkins

REDEMPTIVE AFFIRMATION. A number of years ago two young men with a long history of crime and delinquency robbed the YMCA on the Lower East Side of New York City. On the way out, they saw a man at a telephone switchboard. They were frightened and concluded that he must be calling the police. They grabbed him and beat him savagely with brass knuckles and a blackjack. Thinking him to be dead, they stuffed him behind a radiator near the swimming pool and left.

Later that evening Gertrude Ederle, the famous channel swimmer, was walking by the pool; she stepped in some blood, slipped, screamed, and then found Donald Tippet's body. He was rushed to the hospital, where for days he lingered between life and death. Eventually he lived, but one eye had been so badly damaged that it could not be saved. Meanwhile the two young men were caught and brought to trial. Their past record assured that they would get a long sentence. Donald Tippet did an amazing thing. He asked that the two young men be paroled to him. He believed in them, believed that they would change; and he gave them his confidence.

One boy refused to change and soon was caught for another crime. The other boy was receptive to trust and confidence. He went to college. Eventually he went to medical school and became a surgeon–an eye surgeon.

The late Bishop Everett Palmer wrote of this surgeon, "I wonder if he ever performs one of those delicate operations without stopping to think of that night in the YMCA and of a young man, who later became Bishop Donald Tippet of the San Francisco area, whose confidence changed his life.– Joe A. Harding

SERMON SUGGESTIONS

Topic: How God Takes Care of You
TEXT: Ps. 91

(1) By giving you an unending supply of courage–plain, everyday courage. (2) By giving us the ability to adjust to our frustrations and then gradually devise ways by which to outwit them. (3) By persistently trying to lead other people to do for us what we must have done but cannot do for ourselves.–James Gordon Gilkey

Topic: One Thing I Do
TEXT: Phil. 3:13–14

(1) Paul is describing what we would call his "identity crisis." This involved an act of will based upon faith. (2) Paul describes his inner discovery that such a choice means rejection of past goals. (3) Such a decision for

Paul, and for anyone, means taking the risk of making a personal commitment in faith to what one has come to know to be the source and center of one's life.–Ganse Little

Worship Aids

CALL TO WORSHIP.   "The Lord is my light and my salvation; whom shall I fear? the Lord is the strength of my life; of whom shall I be afraid?" (Ps. 27:1).

INVOCATION.   O Lord, we would sing of your mercies; we would make known your faithfulness. Tune our hearts and open our lips, so that the world may hear the joyful sound.

OFFERTORY SENTENCE.   "God is able to make all grace abound toward you; that ye, always having all sufficiency in all things, may abound to every good work" (2 Cor. 9:8).

OFFERTORY PRAYER.   God grant that we may never be speechless when we can say a good word for the Lord Jesus Christ, or without means when we are called upon to meet some need. As we receive, so let us give.

PRAYER.   O Lord, our God, we confess to thee all our evil; all our unworthiness; all that is weak in us from infirmity; all our trangressions, even the most heinous. We desire to hide none of these from thine eyes, nor from our own. We would look upon the face of our sins, and acknowledge them, and turn away from them, and be cured of every desire that leads us to them. Grant that we may every day, more than for silver or for gold, more than for food or for raiment, crave those dispositions which shall make us worthy to be called the sons of God. May we count nothing so precious to be as that which makes us better. May we look upon life as but for this end. In all our gettings, may we get understanding. Whatever we lose, so that we retain thy favor, may we consider ourselves rich; and whatever we gain, if by it we fail of thy favor, may we consider ourselves poor. Grant that we may see from day to day thy work growing in more tenderness of conscience, in more gentleness of disposition, in more fruitfulness of a true beneficence. May we more and more know the sacred word of life, not for ourselves, but for others. May we follow thee, if need be, through sorrow. May we not be afraid of the cross of Christ. May we desire to bear it. May we desire to take reproach for his sake. May we become like him in rebuking all evil; in seeking to heal it; in being witnesses against it.

Grant thy blessing to rest upon every one in thy presence. Give wisdom to the conscience that is burdened. Give light to all that are darkened. Give to every one that needs confirmation the word of faith. Disclose thyself to those that look for thee and cannot find thee. Grant that those who are seeking the right way may be lead by the very hand of God, and find the way of wisdom. May those that are tempted be able to resist temptation. May those that are fallen not be destroyed. May they be lifted up by the mercy of God, and turn to better ways.–
Henry Ward Beecher

LECTIONARY MESSAGE

Topic: What Sign Can You Give Us?
TEXT: John 2:13–22
Other Readings: Exod. 20:1–17; Ps. 19; 1 Cor. 1:18–25

The Gospel of John, often called The Fourth Gospel, is at once seemingly the most simple and yet most profound of the Gospels. It is the only one that specifically gives the purpose in writing (see 20:30–31). He discusses many of the miracles as "signs," as well may be the case in the passage used here.

Our message is built around the "cleaning of the Temple" by Jesus. He had gone there at the time of the Passover and found a marketplace of sellers, animals, and birds.

I. The Temple Scene and Reaction of Our Lord

The time was Passover, or the spring season, which brought to Jerusalem thousands of pilgrims to make their sacrifices and to take part in the celebration of one of two great religious festivals of the Jewish people.

One would expect a deeply religious atmosphere surrounding the temple area, but it was a mass of animals, oxen, sheep, and pigeons. The pilgrims would have had no way to bring their animals or birds for the sacrifice, and so they would wait until they arrived to buy them from the sellers. And the sellers had moved from the countryside into the city and then into the temple area itself, but not into the Temple. There they made their sales to the people. Some sources have said that they were charging outrageous prices to the pilgrims, but as today when the Kentucky Derby is run or major events take place in other cities, the prices for hotel rooms and certain items are raised because it is the time to make money. Then there were the money-changers. The Jewish religious leaders had declared that no coins from other countries could be given as a temple offering. Thus the money was changed into the Jewish coins, and the rate of exchange was high.

Not only did Jesus not like to see the animals and birds and money-changers there, but their ethical practices were a far cry from what they should have been. Another matter was that such practices discouraged the pilgrims from worship.

Jesus therefore took a rope and drove out the animals, overturned the money-changers' tables, and ordered the sellers and others to clear out! The synoptics place their story of the cleansing of the Temple immediately following the royal entry of Jesus into the city and just a week before his crucifixion and resurrection. Some say that there was only one such cleansing. But it is difficult to explain only one.

II. The Religious Leaders Demand an Answer for Jesus' Action

They came to him and asked point-blank, "Where did you get the authority for your action; give us a sign of it?" His disciples recalled a prophecy in the Old Testament: "Zeal for your house will consume me."

Jesus answered his critics: "Destroy this house and I will raise it again."

The religious said, "It has taken forty-six years to build this temple. Are you going to raise it again in three days?"

Then the writer, John, interprets: "But the temple He was speaking of was his own body. After his resurrection his disciples recalled what he had said, and they believed the Scripture and the words that Jesus had spoken."

Throughout the Gospel of John we find this style of writing. The presentation of the event, the reaction of the people to the event, and the response of Jesus to them, with an interpretation given from time to time by the writer.

III. Conclusion

The Temple had been cleansed. The action of Jesus was courageous and bold and drew the fire of the Establishment. They challenged his authority. And he came back to talk about the temple of the body, his own, and after death, his resurrection. They asked for a sign, and he gave them the greatest sign of all, his being raised from the grave, victor over death, Satan, the grave. And it is he and he alone who can bring victory for those who trust in him for Life everlasting.—G. Allen West, Jr.

SUNDAY: MARCH NINTH

SERVICE OF WORSHIP

Sermon: What Are Your Plans?
TEXT: Luke 12:16–21
Said Isaac Watts:

There are a number of us creep
Into this world, to eat and sleep
And know no reason why we're born,
But only to consume the corn,
Devour the cattle, fowl, and fish,
And leave behind an empty dish.

. . . .

Then if their tombstone, when they die,
Be n't taught to flatter and to lie,
There's nothing better will be said
Than that "they've eat up all their bread,
Drunk up their drink, and gone to bed."

Earthbound people are shortsighted people. They believe only in what they can see, love only what they can use, and worship only what they have accumulated. Earthbound people, life is more than what you see, more than what you can use, and more than what you have.

Life is more than verbs. Think about nouns. Verbs express action. But nouns are the subjects of sentences, and they put verbs like *see, use,* and *have* to work. Don't be a prisoner of verbs like earthbound people of the past and present.

In our text, Jesus painted the picture of a successful earthbound person. He was a master of economics. He knew how to multiply dollars. In an inflationary world, he took no losses, for his dollars multiplied geometrically.

This earthbound man stimulated the economy. The construction industry loved him. He was always building bigger and better barns. The carpenters' union thought well of him. He was fighting unemployment by giving unemployed carpenters a job.

He was an efficiency expert, a successful planner and organizer, and a genius in management techniques. He was industrious, always providing the best for his family. The best food, the best clothes, the best medical and dental care, the best schools, and the best vacations were theirs.

This earthbound man was too busy to worship God once or twice a year with his nominally churchgoing family. In fact, he was a practical man, who told his family to be careful of cults and Christians. "Regular church attendance is a dangerous thing. Drink shallow draughts from the gospel stream, or don't drink at all," was his advice to his family.

This earthbound man was too busy for the Lion's, the Rotary, or the Kiwanis clubs. Now and then he would contribute liquor and money to the campaign of a conservative political candidate who promised to preserve the economic status quo.

Good Mr. Earthbound enjoyed excellent health, but he didn't know who gave him that health. He was smiled upon by nature.

The sun sent enough heat rays not to burn up his crops. The wind held back destructive tornadoes from his farm. The rain refused to drown his crops. The stock market was kind to his investments.

With all of this going for him, Mr. Earthbound said, "I'm doing better than those poor church folk who pray all the time and borrow money from me." Poor Mr. Earthbound didn't know that God told mercy to smile on him so he would have time to repent of his sins and be saved.

What sins did he commit? Yes, he was a sinner, although he was morally upright. He was a sinner even though he did not cheat but earned his wealth by the sweat of his brow. He was a sinner, even though he was no hypocrite who felt repentance on Sunday for what he did on Saturday and would do again on Monday.

He was a sinner, even though he was rich in his intellectual orientation, rich in his economic relationships, and rich in his social and cultural relationships.

He was not rich toward God, who is the Giver of the opportunity for success. God is the Giver of talent. Every good and perfect gift comes from God.

Mr. Earthbound was so nearsighted that his whole orientation was thing-centered rather than God-centered. His focus was on barns, fruits, goods, possessions, and external happiness. His externally based happiness was related to his internal self-centeredness. His sin was also the sin of self-centeredness. "My barns, my ease, my drink, my making merry, my earthbound, my heavenly retirement, my power to give myself a future that I think I can control, including any variables that you church people call God . . ."

But, without warning and without an opportunity for him to hire a lawyer to negotiate a contract for an extension of his life on earth, God spoke to him: "Thou fool, this night thy soul shall be required of thee: then whose . . ." When God called him a fool, he was startled. He thought God was calling the wrong man. The last time anyone had called him a fool was when he was a child. But God said, "Thou fool." The Chamber of Commerce called him successful. But God said, "Thou fool."

His young protégés in business called him wise; his children called him Daddy; his wife called him My Darling, but God said, "Thou fool, . . . I am changing your plans. I am altering your agenda. I have already advised death to knock on your door. Medicine can't save you. Human know-how can't redeem you. The preacher can eulogize you at your funeral, and the choir can sing for you, but their prayers can't save you! Thou fool, . . . tonight I am calling you into courts on nonexistence."

Conclusion: What are your plans? Have you made the right plans? Who is your travel agent? Do you have a confirmed reservation? Is your ticket paid for? –J. Alfred Smith, Sr.

Illustrations

A DAY FOR CREATIVE DETACHMENT. Like the beginning of creation, the Lord's Day is the first day. It is the day on which God would accomplish new things among people. In this sense, Calvin, for instance, understood the Lord's Day as a day of rest, for in it people are to surrender their confidence in their own achievements, thereby opening themselves to the workings of God. We cease our labors, he says, and are gathered together, that God may work in us. What mattered to Calvin was not a Sabbath rest, or a vacation from responsibilities, but an occasion for gatherings genuinely open to God's grace. Hence, for Calvin, the day is truly the Lord's Day, to be spent with the Lord's people; and it is to be free from self-preoccupations, whether of labor or of leisure. This day, given as it is, provides opportunity for people to recognize God's works among them.–John E. Burkhart

OPPORTUNITY. You must have heard the story of the eager young man who visited the aged James Russell Lowell at the turn of the century. Thrilled again at his stories of the struggle against slavery, the young man exclaimed, "How I wish I could have stood at your side then!" The aged warrior for righteousness stepped to the window, pulled aside the curtain to reveal the smoking stacks of a great industrial plant with wretched hovels housing its workers, and he asked, "What more do you want?"—Harold A. Bosley

SERMON SUGGESTIONS

Topic: A Good Old Age

TEXT: Gen. 25:8; Philem. 9

(1) The prime creative force of good old age is faith. (2) A good old age is thus an old age which, by the influence of great ideas, has attached the gains of experiences each to the other, so that at last they have made life a unit. (4) A good old age is an old age with the memory of a well-spent life behind it. (5) A good old age is an old age conscious of its special privileges and duties—the everlasting time, which we call years; a height for discovery of truth, and for large visions of God. (6) A good old age means a Christian old age, by the masterful working of God in the mind and heart.—Frank W. Gunsaulus

Topic: The Dynamic of Prayer

TEXT: Matt. 21:22

(1) Jesus promises that prayer gives us *the ability to do.* (2) Prayer is *the ability to accept,* and in accepting, *to transform.* (3) Prayer brings *the ability to bear.*—William Barclay

Worship Aids

CALL TO WORSHIP.   "Let us draw near with a true heart in full assurance of faith, having our hearts sprinkled from an evil conscience, and our bodies washed with pure water. Let us hold fast the profession of our faith without wavering (for he is faithful that promised); and let us consider one another to provoke unto love and to good works" (Heb. 10:22–24).

INVOCATION.   Lord, thou hast withheld nothing we need and given us more than we could ever deserve; therefore, we do not withhold our great praise of thee and we sing of thy salvation. Great thou art and

greatly to be praised, O Lord of hosts.—E. Lee Phillips.

OFFERTORY SENTENCE.   "May God, the giver of hope, fill you with all joy and peace because you trust in Him—so that you may be overflowing with hope through the power of the Holy Spirit" (Rom. 15:13 Weymouth).

OFFERTORY PRAYER.   Lord, let our gifts express our beliefs that in Christ is life, joyous and eternal, in the Bible is truth for now and always, through the Holy Spirit is guidance and undergirding that cannot fail; and let us give accordingly.—E. Lee Phillips

PRAYER.   Here we are, Father, coming to you with all of life's package. Some bring needs to be met. Others bring joys to share. Others come singing songs of thanksgiving for blessings received. Still others enter softly with deep hurts to be healed. There are those who linger beside graves of sorrow, wounded to the core, and who cannot as yet make the journey back into the full fellowship of faith. The young come with their dreams. The midlifers come with their realities. The older faithful come with their memories and expectations of a yet closer walk with you.

Here this morning is the casual believer who haunts the periphery of the faith and cannot as yet commit fully to Christ's lordship and faithful fellowship with your people. Seekers are among us, wanting clear answers to murky issues, assurance for their questing souls, and sometimes demanding packaged faith according to their dictates. Guilty hearts are here, folks who have willfully and inadvertently broken your heart and the hearts of others by their actions and words, needing the healing balm of forgiveness and restitution. Young and tender hearts are here today, ready for that sacred moment when the call of commitment to Christ meets the readiness to answer and rise up to follow him through life. The lonely are here, hoping against hope that some friendship will eradicate the loneliness.

We are all here, Father, coming from every walk of life, every area of need, every place of hope and longing. Here in your blessed presence we wait, believing in faith that you will speak softly and kindly to our yearning hearts and souls, meeting us as we are and leading us to where you would have us be by the power and spirit of Jesus.— Henry Fields

LECTIONARY MESSAGE

Topic: The Only Son of God
TEXT: John 3:14–21
Other Readings: Num. 21:4–9; Ps. 107:1–3, 17–22; Eph. 2:1–10

The blurred spiritualities that characterize our age need to confront the clarity of the gospel. The cross of Christ offers a dying world the opportunity for eternal life. The gospel calls persons living in the shadows to walk in the light of God's love.

John's proclamation of Jesus as "the only Son of God" (v. 18, cf. v. 16) challenges both the culture-bound piety of Christians and the pluralistic vagueness of contemporary culture. The Son of Man who was lifted up is the Son of God who reveals love and light.

I. Lifted Up (vv. 14–15)

The biblical story of Moses raising up a bronze serpent on a pole in the desert (Num. 21:4–9) foreshadows God's redemption through Christ. Through Moses' action God brings healing to Israelites bitten by poisonous snakes. Moses "lifting up" the serpent is a type of Jesus (veiled as "the Son of Man") being "lifted up" on the cross. The correspondence between these two biblical events reminds us of God's continuing saving purpose across the Scriptures.

As Israelites bitten by the serpents are to "look at the serpent of bronze and live" (Num. 21:9), so we who hear these words are urged to look at Jesus lifted up on the cross and receive eternal life. The cross of Jesus is God's remedy for the "poisonous bite" of sin.

The lifting up of the Son of Man has two dimensions. Jesus was (1) lifted up to die on the cross and (2) lifted up from death in the resurrection. The raising up of Jesus to suf-

fering and death is thus fused with his exaltation to glory. Christ's crucifixion and resurrection together form the one saving event through which believers may have eternal life in him.

II. Love (v. 16)

This famous one-verse summary of the gospel declares that God's love for a lost world is the starting point for understanding and believing in Jesus. Both the life and death of Jesus originate in God's great love for the world. God's love is not just an abstract attribute of God's divine being; it is expressed in action in human history. The incarnation and crucifixion of Jesus unite in revealing the cost of God's love. This divine love for a disobedient world forms "the background of the canvas on which the rest of the Gospel is painted" (George Beasley-Murray, *John*, p. 51).

God offers unconditional love in the gift of the Son. God's love is directed to all the world. The gospel is not just for a few select persons, although many will not accept the gift offered in Christ. Love by nature carries the possibility of rejection.

Those who believe in Christ will find eternal life as they accept God's gift. Eternal life is not just a future promise of God to be received at the end of the age. Rather, eternal life is a present reality that we can receive now. Both God's saving work in Christ and our human response of faith are part of the process of salvation. God's gift must be accepted by faith in Christ if we are to experience eternal life.

III. Light (vv. 17–21)

The mission of God's only Son is to bring light into darkness (cf. John 1:5). The sending of the Son expresses God's positive purpose of salvation (v. 17). God's goal is not condemnation but salvation.

As the light shines, people either move toward the light or away from it. The consequences are absolute—light or darkness, living eternally or perishing under condemnation. So although God sends the Son for salvation (v. 17), Christ's coming is also the occasion for judgment (v. 19). This dark side of God's revelation in Christ is the inevitable outcome of turning away from the light. To reject Christ is to reject God's offer of forgiveness.

Fearing exposure of their evil deeds (v. 20), people hate the light and are tragically separated from it. It is not that God seeks to condemn them, for God freely offers them the gift of life. Unbelievers are "condemned already" (v. 18) in the darkness of their unbelief.

In contrast, believers "who do what is true"—who live their lives according to the truth—"come to the light" (v. 21). They have nothing to fear from the light and habitually seek to do what the truth demands. Their deeds have been accomplished in God through Christ and so will be revealed in the light.

Believing the gospel and living the Christian life are directly connected. No separation is allowed between theology and ethics, between Christian doctrine and Christian practice. Right believing (orthodoxy) and right living (orthopraxy) belong together.

Into our world full of vagueness and shadows, the gospel light shines with striking clarity. The only Son of God, who was lifted up on the cross, calls us to receive God's love and live in the light.—Charles J. Scalise

SUNDAY: MARCH SIXTEENTH

SERVICE OF WORSHIP

Sermon: To Be Content
TEXT: Phil. 4:1–7

In the middle of the fourth chapter of Philippians, we read an amazing statement. This is verse 11: "Not that I complain of want; for I have learned, in whatever state I am, *to be content*." I want to think with you about this great theme, "To Be Content."

I must tell you in all honesty that I am really listening beside you in this congregation this morning. I am not preaching down to you. I am listening beside you, because I need in my own life what I hear this text saying to us. In fact, I am really excited about sharing with you this good news. There are three beautiful gifts that are offered to us in these opening verses of chapter 4.

I. First, there is the gift of affirmation. I hear God speaking an affirming, uplifting, inspiring word. "Therefore, my brethren, whom I love and long for, my joy and crown, stand firm thus in the Lord, my beloved" (Phil. 4:1).

a. Focus with me, for a moment, upon a very brief but important scene from the ministry of Jesus. Jesus had been teaching the multitudes and was surrounded by people. His mother and brothers had come from Nazareth to take him home, because he seemed to be beside himself. A man brought a message that said, "Your mother and brothers are outside asking to speak to you." Jesus replied to the man who brought the message, "Who is my mother, and who are my brothers?" Now listen to Matt. 12:49–50, "*And stretching out his hand* toward his disciples, he said, 'Here are my mother and my brothers! For whoever does the will of my Father in heaven is my brother, and sister, and mother.'"

b. Notice very carefully the outstretched hand of Jesus. See this very clearly in your imagination. The hand of the Pharisee was clenched in anger. The hand of the scribe was pointed in accusation. The hand of the sinner was twisted in anxiety and guilt. The hand of Jesus was stretched out toward people. Think of the times that Jesus stretched out his hands. There was a poor leper crying by the side of the road, "Lord, if you will, you can make me clean." He stretched out his hand and touched blind Bartimaeus, and he received his sight! Then he touched the ears of a deaf man and the bent back of a woman who had been twisted for eighteen years. He reached out and touched the children and blessed them. He stretched out his hands on the cross. Then he stretched out his hand to Thomas and said, "Put your finger here, and see my hands; . . . do not be faithless, but believing" (John 20:27). He is here today touching people.

c. He is here this morning, stretching out his hand, saying, "my sister—my brother!" Perhaps you think of him in great theological categories as Prophet, as Priest, as King, as Savior, as Lord. That is wonderful! But do not miss his words. Stretching out his hand, He says to you, "You are my sister—you are my brother."

Affirmation is powerful. It is healing. It is beautiful. It is God's gift to you today. "My beloved whom I love and long for, and my joy and crown . . . my beloved . . . my true yoke-fellow . . . turn today—at this moment—and receive your gift of grace, your affirmation, form the Lord of all creation."

II. Next is the gift of decisiveness: "Stand firm . . . stand firm thus in the Lord." The pressure is great. If you stand for something, you will not fall for anything.

a. The place where we need to stand firm is the place where we are getting the pressure. Where is the world pushing or shoving in your life? Have you ever noticed that evil is terribly pushy? Sin is always shoving on us. The gambling interests are pushing and shoving. Immorality keeps pushing. Racial prejudice and discrimination is always shoving at us.

b. Paul gives this tremendous reminder that we don't have to give way to pressure or to surrender our conviction of our faith. "To stand firm thus in the Lord" means to have the certainty that we don't have to be pushed around any longer. You remember the word of Jesus, "Let your yes be yes and your no be no." He didn't say, "Let your yes be yes and your no be maybe!" You will never be contented with yourself as long as you are compromising and falling below the standards that you know to be in your best interest and in the best interest of others. The gift of decisiveness—of standing firm in a age of pressure to take the line of least resistance—is God's gift. Receive this beautiful gift.

III. The third gift is the gift of reconciliation, forgiveness, harmony, and agreement. It is the gift of getting along with those who differ from us. Let me read verse 2 of chapter 4. "I entreat Eudoia and I entreat Syntyche to agree in the Lord."

a. Now we don't know much about Eudoia and Syntyche. They appear in this brief reference in the New Testament, and then they drop out of sight. Paul says they labored side by side with him together with Clement. He said their names were in the Book of Life. They had a problem. They had some sort of misunderstanding or disagreement or confusion, and they got mad at each other. They refused to forgive. Bitter words were spoken. People took sides. The church was divided. Paul was so concerned about this matter that he mentioned it in his letter. I was wondering what it would have been like to be seated in the congregation and to have been Eudodia and Syntyche when that letter was read. That would clearly have gotten your attention! What would happen if the pastor one day said, "I entreat Bill and I entreat Mary to agree in the Lord. There has been enough of this argument! Get it together! Well, I am not going to do that, but at least there is some apostolic precedent.

b. The bond of bitterness can be broken. Maybe that is exactly what God wants to give to you today. Maybe he wants you to understand the situation in a totally new light. I do know that he has three beautiful gifts. When we receive them, we begin to experience a new depth of inner joy and peace, which is exactly what is meant by the words "to be content." The gift of reconciliation, the gift of decisiveness, and the gift of affirmation are God's great gifts. Right now there is one who reaches out his hand toward you and speaks very quietly some very powerful words, "You are my sister—you are my brother." Perhaps, like the old violin, you have been battered and torn. Perhaps you too need the touch of the Master's hand! He is here today—reaching out *to you!*—Joe A. Harding

Illustrations

THE BASIS OF CONTENTMENT.   Let us think hard while we think, and as honestly as we can, but when we have come to the limit of our power and our thought can go no further, let us stop thinking and yield ourselves up to the joy of God's presence. Let us work hard while we work, and as effectively as we can, but when we have come to the end of our strength and can do no more, let us stop working and watch God at work. Let us cast all our care on him who careth for us, confident that in his good time he will give us light and peace.

In the last analysis it comes to this: either there is a God or there is not; either we are alone in the universe, facing its unsolved mysteries and its appalling tragedies with only the help that comes from other mortals as ignorant and as helpless as we, or there is Some One who hears when we speak and can answer when we call.

In prayer we put this supreme issue to the test. Prayer introduces us to the Great Companion who meets our human need with his divine response. The man who has learned to pray is no longer alone in the universe. He is living in his Father's house.—William Adams Brown

ACCEPTANCE.   A little Mexican boy was badly burned—so badly burned that his face was totally disfigured. His family, parents, brothers, and sisters were all killed in the terrible fire. He alone was left. He had no home. He was a beggar, living like a frightened animal, rejected by one person after another. One day he heard sounds of laughter and children playing. He looked over a wall to see happy children in an orphanage. They had a home. That was what he wanted above everything else. The doors were locked, and he didn't know how to get in. He saw the priest, the father, walking alone in the fields. You will remember the moment that the camera catches little Alfredo—the scene is shown in slow motion —as he ran and fell at the feet of the priest. The father wants to receive this boy into the orphanage. The scars are so terrible. He wonders if the other boys will accept him. A rejection experience would be even more devastating. The father gathers the children together and explains to them the story of Alfredo. "Oh yes, we will accept him. We will be glad to receive him." "But," says the father, "you have never seen anyone so badly burned as this boy. I will leave it to you to decide." Alfredo was brought in. The children looked with horror at the scars, at the terrible ugliness. Alfredo stood there with his head bowed in the agony of that moment. Finally, after what seemed like an eternity of silence, one little boy moved. He came forward. He simply took Alfredo by the hand and said, "You are my brother." Then the film moves very quickly to a joyous conclusion with a fiesta—the joy, the singing, the dancing, and the fireworks—and you see in the closing scene a smiling Alfredo by the side of his newfound friend. The narrator says, "And Alfredo was received into the family."—Joe A. Harding

SERMON SUGGESTIONS

Topic: The Offering of Isaac
TEXT: Gen. 22:1–19

(1) For Abraham, all God's promise were riding on Isaac. (2) But God spoke and said, "Kill him off!" (3) Then, of all things, Abraham moves to obey God! (4) But God provides a substitute lamb to sacrifice. (5) God set Abraham free from blind obedience to faith. (6) We are free to trust God, too.—David Buttrick, as summarized by Donald L. Hamilton

Topic: The Basis of Certainty
TEXT: 1 John 3:14; 2 Tim. 1:12; 1 John 3:24; John 17:3; Phil. 3:8

(1) The character of God himself. (2) The covenant of God, especially his covenant as revealed in the Sacrament of Baptism. (3) The conviction of the Spirit about Christ.— Bryan Green

Worship Aids

CALL TO WORSHIP.   "Because he hath set his love upon me, therefore will I deliver him: I will set him on high, because he hath known my name" (Ps. 91:14).

INVOCATION.   Lord of life, mercifully bring us to repentance, quietly stir us to resolve, mightily challenge us, redemptively fill us, powerfully use us, for in your will is our peace.—E. Lee Phillips

OFFERTORY SENTENCE.   "Be ye steadfast, unmovable, always abounding in the work of the Lord, forasmuch as ye know that your labor is not vain in the Lord" (1 Cor. 15:58).

OFFERTORY PRAYER. Lord, let what we believe and what we pray merge to make the difference in what we give for Jesus' sake.–E. Lee Phillips

PRAYER. O Savior of the world, in whom we find love to live and faith to die, we have your word that if you would be lifted up from the earth, you would draw all of us to yourself. Unveil for us afresh the "wondrous Cross on which the young Prince of glory died" so we shall see and feel how love was given to the loveless and in dying, desolate and forsaken, you yielded your soul to God. Help us in our time to die more and more to self and to live daily unto righteousness. Give us to trust more earnestly in your work of grace and through it, as in ages past, may all loyal hearts be heirs of your fullness and once and for all set free. Keep us and possess us as your own forever, and may we live to the end in the solemn thought that they who die believing die safely through your love.–Donald Macleod

LECTIONARY MESSAGE

Topic: The Glorified Son of Man
TEXT: John 12:20–33

Other Readings: Jer. 31:31–34; Ps. 51:1–12; Heb. 5:5–10

We customarily say "the hour has come" when referring to the arrival of an event of some seriousness and importance. It may be a joyous event–like a wedding. It may be a sad event–like saying good-bye. For Jesus, the request of some Greeks at a festival elicits the phrase. At the Passover Jesus solemnly declares "the hour has come" (v. 23) for the event of his death on the cross.

I. Greeks (vv. 20–22)

The coming of the Greeks to Jesus provides concrete evidence of the truth of the Pharisees' exasperated observation, "Look, the world has gone after him!" (v. 19). In the Gospel of John the Greeks represent the coming of the gentile nations to Christ. Because Jesus is the Savior of the world, ultimately all people will owe their allegiance to him.

In the midst of this high Jewish festival, these Greek worshipers wonder, "Will Jesus accept Gentiles like us?" The safe thing to do is first make a polite request of one of Jesus' disciples. So they ask Philip (who has a Greek name) to introduce them and arrange for them to see Jesus. After consultation, Philip and Andrew (a second disciple with a Greek name) cooperate like a team in presenting the Greeks' request to Jesus.

II. Grain (vv. 23–26)

The text does not record whether Jesus actually met with the Greeks. Rather, the occasion of their coming provided Jesus with an opportunity to declare how the Greeks–and the gentile world as a whole–will be able to see him. "The hour has come for the Son of Man to be glorified" (v. 23). It is only as the glorified Son of Man that Jesus can bring redemption to the peoples of the earth.

The hour of the Son of Man's glorification is the hour of Jesus' death. The glory of Jesus is shown in his death on the cross, not just in his resurrection and ascension. As a grain of wheat must be buried and die in order to produce a harvest, so Jesus must die and be buried in order to bear the fruit of salvation (cf. 1 Cor. 15:35–37).

Jesus' identification of himself with a grain of wheat contrasts dramatically with his role in the famous parable of the sower. As Matthew 13:37 interprets that parable, "The one who *sows* the good seed is the Son of Man." In our text, Jesus is not the sower of much seed but is instead a single kernel of seed that must die to produce much fruit.

The example of the grain of wheat reminds us that God gives life through death. Hidden within the graphic death of Jesus lies the miracle of resurrection. So the law of nature mirrors the operation of God's grace.

Christ's disciples are called to renounce their involvement in "their life in this world" (v. 25) and follow Jesus in a life of servanthood (v. 26). We are to follow the way of the cross. This way of self-sacrifice is not only a command but also a promise. For if we follow Christ, we will receive the blessing of his presence and the honor of the Father (v. 26). Self-denying service of Christ leads us through the path of suffering to the glory of God.

III. Glory (vv. 27–33)

Jesus' prayer (vv. 27–28a) gives us a glimpse into the agony of his soul as he faces the approaching reality of his suffering and death. Despite all the inner turmoil, Jesus reaffirms his mission and expresses his complete obedience to God's will.

In praying, "Father, glorify your name" (v. 28), Jesus confirms his commitment to undergo the trials and ultimately the death that lies ahead. The Father's glory will be revealed in the death and resurrection of the Son.

Glorifying God's name is not only the foundation of Jesus' mission but lies at the heart of the life and service of those who follow Christ. Jesus here models for us how to live in the presence of God when we confront the stressful days of life and the reality of death. Sharing Christ's glory also entails sharing the sufferings that an ungodly world inflicts upon those who follow the way of the cross.

The heavenly response to Jesus' prayer, though not comprehended by the crowd (v. 29), nevertheless comes for their sake (v. 30; cf. 11:42). The voice (v. 28) affirms God the Father's continuing embrace of Jesus' ministry, both in the past ("I have glorified it") and in the future ("I will glorify it again").

The death and resurrection of Jesus constitute the turning point of history. The lifting up of the Son of Man is "the judgment of this world" (v. 31). The "ruler of this world" (Satan) is cast out and the Son of Man exalted. The bad news of this judgment is the exposure of sin and its deserved punishment. The good news is that at the cross God gives the Son who bears the judgment for us.

The glorified Son of Man "will draw all people" to himself (v. 32). All of the ways in which we learn to trust Christ and serve him are included in this drawing power of the cross. Those who believe in Christ will no longer "walk in the darkness of sin" (v. 35, cf. v. 46) but will "become children of light" (v. 36).

The cruel lifting up of Jesus on the cross has become God's exaltation of the Messiah before all the nations. God's victory may seem slow in coming, but it has already been won by the glorified Son of Man.—Charles J. Scalise

SUNDAY: MARCH TWENTY-THIRD

SERVICE OF WORSHIP

Sermon: Ride on . . . to Live!
TEXT: John 12:12–19

On this very day Jesus Christ has been coming to us again. On this Palm Sunday, we anticipate Good Friday and its cross. So it is easy for us to have a mental picture of Jesus coming to us in his humility. We can visualize him with his face turned steadfastly toward Jerusalem and his crucifixion. But his coming to us is much more than this. It is more than a vividly imagined event, more than a warm sentiment that dissolves us into ecstasy. His presence is real. He comes to us with the same work to be done, with the same life to live, and with the same death to die. But that is not all. Today he confronts again in us the same attitudes as those held by his friends and his enemies in the days of his flesh.

And now we look at Palm Sunday through the eyes of the writer of the Fourth Gospel.

During the closing days of his earthly ministry Jesus' raising of Lazarus caused great excitement among many people. Some were overjoyed. Mary and Martha, the sisters of Lazarus, could not find enough words and time to thank Jesus for what he had done for them. And there were others who went into Jerusalem and spread abroad the story of the most wonderful event they had ever witnessed. But not all were happy. John tells us that Jesus' enemies determined to kill him when he raised Lazarus from the dead. Besides that, these men planned to put Lazarus to death also.

With events shaping up for a showdown, Jesus entered Jerusalem, riding an ass's colt, and the crowds went wild. The fickle majority, a convinced minority, the twelve disciples, and the Pharisees constituted the groups involved with Jesus on Palm Sunday. Two thousand years ago, you and I would easily have been in one group or another. Today we are in such groups as Jesus Christ passes through our midst again.

I. Are you in the group that opposes Christ? I hope not, and you probably are not. But we cannot rule out the possibility that even if we imagine that we would never "hurt a hair of him," we might oppose him.

When Jesus was here in the flesh, opposition to him was direct. "Now the chief priests and the Pharisees had been given orders that if anyone knew where he was, he should let then know, so that they night arrest him (John 11:57 RSV). After Palm Sunday, with all its tumult and shouting, some of the Pharisees despaired of doing anything with Jesus. They said to one another, "You see that you can do nothing; look, the world has gone after him: (John 12:19 RSV). Yet, the enemies of Jesus did not give up: "So the band of soldiers and their captain and the officers of the Jews seized Jesus and bound him" (John 18:12 RSV).

Opposition to Jesus Christ today is more subtle and sophisticated. He is not here among us physically, so we cannot crucify him again. But why did anyone oppose him in the first place? Were the reasons then any different essentially from the reasons that explain our stance toward many of the issues of our own day? Was not Jesus opposed because he threatened existing structures? Were not his opponents principally those who had considerable vested interests in these structures? Did they not fear that the revolutionary changes Jesus seemed to favor would precipitate conflict? The opposition to Jesus was easy to explain, and credible! Jesus' opponents said, "What are we to do? For this man performs many signs. If we let him go in thus, every one will believe in him, and the Romans will come and destroy both our holy place and our nation" (John 11:48 RSV).

Now, honestly, we are no different, are we? For centuries some Christians tried to blame the Jewish people for the crucifixion of Jesus, calling the Jews "Christ killers." But what did this age-old slander accomplish? It only served to blind generations of church people to the fact that they too, Gentiles or whatnot, were capable of crucifying Jesus Christ.

How do we oppose Jesus Christ today? We may prefer a Christianity that is tamed and domesticated by political traditions, by denominational biases, by racial prejudices, by social stratifications, and by personal ambitions. We may not want anyone to take religion outside the walls of the church building. So, when the judging and redeeming message of Jesus Christ begins to make itself felt where custom and habit are deeply entrenched, we may find ourselves opposing him. But it is far more likely that our opposition to him will be a simple, uncomplicated refusal to do what the lordship of Christ and Christian love require in concrete instances. We will reject a clear command, or we will decide a matter by looking the other way.

Religion is no guarantee that one will not line up against Christ. The Pharisees were good men, praying men, men scrupulous in their financial stewardship. Yet they were opposed to Jesus. They rejected in public and private ways that judging and saving presence, and so have his opponents of whatever century.

II. You and I may not oppose Jesus Christ, but are we in the group that praises him superficially? Certain people were excited by the news that Jesus was coming to grips with some of the vital issues of life. He had fed the hungry thousands. He had healed the sick. He had even raised the dead. The raising of Lazarus caused no end of talk about Jesus in Jerusalem. His name was on the lips of young and old alike. You can imagine one of them saying, "This is what we have been working for and waiting for all our lives–freedom from hunger and sickness and the fear of death. Jesus can answer all our human problems. Perhaps the Messiah has come." Back and forth like a shuttlecock flew the rumors, and each time they caught another person in the warp and woof of popular enthusiasm.

Could it be that some of the problems the churches face today stem from the superficial attractiveness of church membership, to which some persons have yielded with no real concern for the deeper meaning of it?

Christ was the answer to many of the superficial questions we were asking, but too many of us never got around to asking the basic questions of our existence.

The biggest job facing the church today is not that of converting the world, but that of converting us who are already in the church.

III. Now you and I may belong neither to a group that opposes Jesus Christ nor to a group that is enchanted with him for a while, only to fall aside soon or late. Are we among those who take him seriously?

Those who witnessed Jesus' raising of Lazarus took Jesus seriously. What they saw and heard and felt, they could never forget. It was a part of their fund of experience. Moth and rust could not corrupt it, and the thief of time could not take it away. Every thought about God and about life would, from that time forward, have to be with reference to what Jesus did at Bethany. Those witnesses were the persons who spread the report in Jerusalem of what Jesus had done. But all of this did not mean that the witnesses were necessarily converted by what they had seen, heard, and felt.

We too may be profoundly impressed with the evidence for the Christian faith. We have accepted a certain set of facts and subscribed to a certain set of doctrines. We know the Bible well and can argue glibly about it. We may even be theological students or theological professors. (And I do not have to tell you, there are definite advantages to having a sound religious upbringing!) But is there nothing more to faith than knowing a great number of important facts and assenting to a system of beautiful beliefs?

Do you take Jesus Christ seriously? Can you read and discuss the Bible intelligently? Does your ethical life correspond to your beliefs? If so, then you may not be far from the kingdom of God. You may be in it. There are many such people in the kingdom of God. To them, the Christian faith is a reasonable way of believing. To them. the Christian life is a responsible way of living. They accept the faith and live the life. It is as simple as that. On the other hand, there are those who are ever learning, as the apostle Paul put it, ever learning but never able

to come to knowledge of the truth. They would agree with almost anything reasonable that you might say about Christian faith and perhaps insist that they would not want to live in a community or a country that did not have such faith. But for them the Christian faith remains a matter for discussion and a question yet to be settled.

IV. So, we may oppose Jesus; we may lightly praise him; or we may be everlastingly haunted by his reality but never quite committed to him. On the other hand, could we be among those who are truly his friends, truly sharing his cross?

The disciples of Jesus, excepting Judas Iscariot, were willing to go with him to the death. It is strange, is it not, that no matter how many wandering stars blazed and flickered and disappeared about Jesus, those disciples kept their courses around him, like planets around a central sun, in spite of cloud and storm and darkness? But should it be strange and incredible?

The Christian faith is certainly not something to be opposed. And just as surely, it is not something merely to rave about with hollow praise or with which to play intellectual games. The Christian faith is to be lived and died for. We sing in our Palm Sunday hymn, "Ride on to die!" Where did this idea come from, if not from Jesus himself? He said, "Truly, truly, I say to you, unless a grain of wheat falls into the earth and dies, it remains alone; but if it dies, it bears much fruit" (John 12:24 RSV). In the Synoptic Gospels, Jesus says in one form or other, "Take up your cross and follow me"–and a cross means death!

Now if Christian discipleship meant death and nothing more, it would be a form of suicide and totally reprehensible. And unfortunately that is all that some persons see in it: the death of happiness, the death of friendship, the death of human striving, the death of freedom. But Jesus referred to his crucifixion as his glorification. To die with Jesus really means to give up self. This may not be required all at once. It seldom is. We may have to die daily, giving a bit of self here, a bit there, until it all adds up to what can only be called "taking up his cross" or offering ourself as "a living sacrifice."

You and I can take our stand this side of the resurrection of our Lord and see that the call to death is actually a summons to life. Crucifixion is actually glorification. Our meager self-denials and sufferings are gaining for us a richness of life out of all proportion to what we give up. So the words of the hymn, "Ride on to die!" really mean, "Ride on to live!" for the cross of humiliation has opened the door to the triumph of the resurrection. And to those of us who walk with him, he says, "Because I live, you will live also" (John 14:19 RSV)–James W. Cox

Illustrations

THE "CALL." One day in the last century a lad sat in the gallery of the British House of Commons and listened to the majestic eloquence of John Bright. He went back home with the resolve in his heart that he was going to be a lawyer. The day before he was to sign the articles in a law office, he was walking through his native city when he came face-to-face with his Sunday school teacher. He said, "I am signing the articles in a law office tomorrow." The Sunday school teacher said, "That is a great profession," and then his face clouded and he continued, "but Henry, I have always hoped that you would be a minister of Christ." In deep thought, the youth went to his home, and there in solitude he heard the call of the Eternal ringing in the chambers of his soul "as clearly as the morning bell rings in the valleys of Switzerland," and John Henry Jowett entered the Christian ministry. In Great Britain, and in America, he exercised a ministry second to none in the twentieth century.–John Sutherland Bonnell

CONVICTIONS. There's a story told of Heinrich Heine. The German-Jewish poet was standing with a friend before the great cathedral of Amiens. When the friend asked, "Why can't people build piles like this anymore?" Heine replied, "My dear friend, in those days people had convictions. We moderns have opinions, and it takes more than opinions to build a Gothic cathedral."–William Sloane Coffin

SERMON SUGGESTIONS

Topic: The Godly Life
TEXT: Dan. 9:15b

The godly life is always marked by the genuine confession of sin. (1) It could not be godly without getting rid of sin. (2) It could not get rid of sin without confession. (3) It could not confess without dropping all self-righteousness. (4) It could not drop all self-righteousness without casting itself on God's mercy.–Donald L. Hamilton

Topic: The Crucial Question
TEXT: Matt. 27:22

(1) There is the answer of rejection. (2) There is the answer of neutrality. (3) There is the answer of commitment.–John N. Gladstone

Worship Aids

CALL TO WORSHIP. "Blessed be the King that cometh in the name of the Lord; peace in heaven, and glory in the highest" (Luke 19:28).

INVOCATION. Lord of life, with hosannas we praise and magnify your name this day. Allow our rejoicing to mingle with confession and our praise with dedication to the honor and glory of our savior, Christ Jesus.–E. Lee Phillips

OFFERTORY SENTENCE. "He that taketh not his cross, and followeth after me, is not worthy of me" (Matt. 10:38).

OFFERTORY PRAYER. Lord, let us not be tempted to give less and expect more, to withdraw where we should extend, rather let us be found giving beyond our limits that we may receive beyond our dreams through the Savior, who gave his life a ransom for many.–E. Lee Phillips

PRAYER. Eternal God, in whose will is our peace and who is worthy of a greater love than we can either give or understand, we bring you thankful hearts in this hour of worship and present them as our morning sacrifice. We bless you for the fruits of faith and for the timely consciousness that we owe to them the unsearchable riches of Christ. We praise you for what he has revealed to us of your love and for the clear vision of ourselves which his pure and noble life has brought. We remember in our deepest thoughts in this season of the year the terrible cost to him of our redemption: the agony in the garden . . . the desertion of his friends . . . the mockery . . . the scourge . . . the crown of thorns . . . the brutal cross . . . the cruel nails . . . the thirst . . . the pain . . . the death—all for us. In humility and with a sense of shame, we acknowledge your unspeakable gift.

In sober gratitude we name in our hearts all the spiritual benefits that have come to us through his incarnate life: the news and high regard for the preciousness of every person; all just laws and humane institutions for the relief and benefit of our people; spiritual fellowship received from you and which we ourselves are led to give and share for the healing and strengthening of the poor in heart and dispossessed of life's necessities; and that uncommon example of a sinless brother laying down his life for his guilty friends.

Dear Lord, whose name we bear, we pray you to take us by the hand in this holy season of the year and lead us imaginatively to the hill of Calvary. Help us to see in the Cross—as we can nowhere else—what sin and hate can do. May his pain open our cold and selfish hearts; may the stark realism of it all destroy our casual indifference and give us new sympathy for the hopeless faces turning to us today in their desperation.—Donald Macleod

LECTIONARY MESSAGE

Topic: The Crucified King of Israel
TEXT: Mark 14:1–15:47 (Focal: Mark 15:16–39)
Other Readings: Mark 11:1–11; Ps. 118:1–2, 19–29; Isa. 50:4–9a; Ps. 31:9–16; Phil. 2:5–11

Mark's direct, vivid Gospel brings Jesus, the crucified King of Israel, before our eyes. Crucifixion was such a shameful and feared form of death that Roman citizens were exempt from this form of execution. Such a humiliating death should not be the fate of kings.

Because Jesus is the true king of Israel, Mark emphasizes the great irony in Jesus' crucifixion as "the King of the Jews" (vv. 18, 26). The irony leads us to see the truth about Jesus. What his enemies say and do in scorn points us to the true king, who gives his life for others. The Son of God is mocked, executed, taunted, and abandoned.

I. Mocked (vv. 16–20)
Mark focuses upon the humiliating ridicule—the mental and emotional abuse—Jesus endures, rather than the physical agonies of his crucifixion. The soldiers mock the idea of Jesus as king. In contrast to the mockery in Jesus' trial before the high priest (14:65), the political rather than the prophetic aspects of Jesus' identity as Messiah are attacked.

The soldiers make Jesus appear to be a clown who is pretending to be a king. The twisted crown of thorns (v. 17) dramatically and painfully satirizes crowns with radiating points, which were used to portray a monarch's royal glory. Contemptuously saluting him as "king of the Jews" (v. 18), the soldiers make false sign of obeisance (v. 19). They strike him with a reed (mock scepter—Matt. 27:29) and punctuate their ridicule with spit.

Jesus' silent enduring of all these cruel insults highlights his nobility in contrast with his accusers (cf. Isa. 50:6). Christ's patient suffering draws our hearts toward him.

II. Executed (vv. 21–26)
The cruel Roman humiliation of Jesus has rendered him so physically helpless that the soldiers force Simon of Cyrene, a passerby, to carry the beam of Jesus' cross. Despite his physical weakness, Jesus refuses the offer of drugged wine, which would reduce his awareness of pain and suffering.

The simplest possible terms—"And they crucified him" (v. 24)—describe the terrible act of his execution. The completeness of Jesus' public humiliation is portrayed by accounts of the soldiers gambling for his clothes at the scene of the cross.

The official charge against Jesus—"The King of the Jews" (v. 26)—not only announces his execution as a Jewish political subversive, but reveals his true identity as the messianic king of Israel. One brief phrase both specifies the crime and reveals the truth. The sign above the Crucified King's head calls us to be his subjects.

III. Taunted (vv. 27–32)

The merciless taunting of Jesus not only originates from the soldiers and religious authorities, but even from people passing by (v. 29), and the two bandits crucified with him (v. 32) participate in the heartless ridicule.

The sarcastic address to Jesus, "You who would destroy this temple and build it in three days" (v. 29), not only recalls Jesus' trial before the Jewish leaders (14:57–59), but foreshadows his death and resurrection and their consequences. The traditional restrictions upon worship of God in the Temple will pass away, symbolized by the tearing in two of the temple curtain (v. 38). Jesus' resurrection offers a new way to approach God—through the new "temple" of his glorified body (cf. 14:58 and John 2:19–21).

With great irony the redemptive nature of the cross is unconsciously articulated by those who taunt Jesus: "He saved others; he cannot save himself" (v. 31). The mockers view their challenge to Jesus as perfectly logical. In their view, his fate in being crucified plainly reveals that Jesus has been deceiving himself with messianic claims. His crucifixion proves he is a helpless impostor. The taunters, however, do not understand that it is precisely the work of the Messiah "to give his life a ransom for many" (10:45). If Jesus had saved himself from death, he would not have saved us.

IV. Abandoned (vv. 33–39)

The only words of Jesus on the cross that Mark records are those of his cry of desolation in verse 34. Hanging on the cross in agony through the three long hours of darkness, Jesus, the Son of God, sees himself forsaken by God. It is as if the light of God has been temporarily withdrawn. As Vincent Taylor comments, "The least inadequate interpretations are those which find . . . a sense of desolation in which Jesus felt the horror of sin so deeply that for a time the closeness of His communion with the Father was obscured" (*The Gospel According to St. Mark*, p. 594).

Jesus' words, however, are not simply a shout of despair. They are also a quotation of Scripture. In the midst of his intense suffering, Jesus loudly exclaims the first verse of Psalm 22, a prayer that expresses the suffering of a righteous person attacked by enemies.

Yet even this direct use of Scripture is misunderstood by those standing by, who think Jesus is appealing to Elijah to come and save him (vv. 35–36). An anonymous bystander (perhaps a soldier) offers Jesus sour wine and a final taunt about Elijah's taking Jesus down from the cross.

Thus, mocked by his executioners and taunted by his enemies, the true King of Israel dies, abandoned by his people and apparently even by God. His violent death comes with sudden intensity.

A centurion—one of the gentile soldiers who executed Jesus—ironically declares the true identity of Jesus (v. 39). A Roman centurion is the only human character in Mark's Gospel to use the title "Son of God" to describe Jesus (cf. 1:1). As we stand at the foot of the cross two thousand years later and behold again the crucified King of Israel, who do we confess him to be?—Charles J. Scalise

SUNDAY: MARCH THIRTIETH

Sermon: Take a Stranger to Lunch

TEXT: Luke 24:13–34; also 1 Cor. 15: 19–26

Two people walking down the Road to Emmaus—that's the scene that is set for us in the Gospel lesson for this morning. We don't know who they were, except that they were followers of Jesus; not among the twelve disciples but among the group called the followers, those who followed him all the way from Galilee through all the towns, all the way to Jerusalem. We do know that one of them was named Cleopas. The text tells us that.

They had been knocked down by an express train, then dragged by a freight train, the gaiety pressed out of them. There was nothing left for them in Jerusalem, nothing worth staying there for. It was over for them. It was finished. So they were heading home. That is their situation.

Everything they had placed their hopes on was gone now. Just wiped out in one sudden, ruthless blow. There is nothing you can do about those things. You know that. They just happen. They come from nowhere. One day everything looks so hopeful, our Lord entering the city triumphantly. The next day, it is all gone. That is the way it was for them.

There are some stories in the Bible that are not going to happen to you. They are simply there for the record. There are others that are there because they do happen to you. You just need to have your eyes opened.

I. From the very beginning, the Church saw the Emmaus Road story as a model of Holy Communion. Jesus joins us as the Host in the sacrament. He takes the bread, he blesses it, he breaks it, and he hands it to them. That is what he did at Emmaus. That is the description in the story. There isn't a Christian in the world who doesn't know what comes next. He said, "This is my body broken for you."

a. Luke says that if you want to know where to find the resurrected Christ in this world, get yourself to Holy Communion. You will meet him there in the breaking of bread.

b. That is not the only place that it happens. People have experienced the real presence of Christ almost anywhere, which is what he promised. "I will not leave you desolate. I will come to you." It means that not only is the Supper at Emmaus a model of Holy Communion, but Holy Communion is a model of all human experience. If we can experience him in the sacrament of the Lord's Supper, we can experience him in the common meals we eat with one another.

II. He comes to us not only as we kneel at the alter. I have known people who had the experience of his coming to them as they stood at the kitchen sink.

a. It can happen when we least expect it. There is a sign in this story. It is a wonderful symbol. It is unmistakable. You can call it "the presence of the stranger."

That was the rule, you know, among those people in the ancient world, in the Middle East. It is still the rule in the Middle East. It is called hospitality. You always offer it. "Will you eat with us." You sense, when you read that, that they are almost saying "I hope he says no." But you are supposed to ask. So, "Will you eat with us?"

b. The presence of the stranger: it is an unmistakable sign. It takes us back to the Book of Genesis and the story of Abraham and Sarah. They too, had a great promise. They were supposed to have a child, an heir. Now it looked as though it wouldn't happen.

Three strangers appear. Abraham practices hospitality. "Will you eat with us?" Sarah fixes a meal. It was while they were eating the meal that the strangers renewed the promise. "God has not forgotten you." At last it is going to happen. They are going to have a child. The strangers are messengers from God. We call them angels. They are bearers of hope to these people.

We don't know when it will happen, under what circumstances it will happen, or what form it will take when it happens. So be ready for a stranger.

III. There is one more way of looking at this story. We can approach it from another angle. If Jesus works through the stranger, then maybe Jesus will work through you.

a. It was promised, you know. "I will not leave you desolate. I will come to you." Not only will Christ come to us through the stranger, Christ calls us to be the stranger to somebody else. Christ wants to use you as a means of touching someone else.

b. It can happen, you know. The resurrected Christ can use you. It can happen anywhere, at any time. Take a person to lunch. Write a note to somebody. You know who it is you ought to write to. Write the note. Or, sit by a stranger on a plane and ask, "How have you been?" You could experience the power of the universe working through you.—Mark Trotter

Illustrations

DOUBTS AND QUESTIONS. I was asked to confer with a young mother who had been admitted to one of our hospitals for psychiatric care. In addition to her medical problems, she was confused and doubted her faith in God. She had many questions about which she wished to talk with a minister. Her physician asked me to confer with her. When I encouraged her to express her questionings and doubts concerning God, she became quite fearful. She said, "In my home, religion was always a matter my father settled for us, and there was no questioning allowed. We would never have dared to express our doubts to our father." I pointed out to her that this was one of the main differences between God and her father. God could stand being questioned and her father could not. It is an act of real faith to bring one's doubts to God in face-to-face prayer. Likewise, she could never become a person in her own right before God as long as her father did all her thinking for her.—Wayne E. Oates

BELIEVE IT OR NOT. The person can be defined as a believing phenomenon, as one who must believe in order to live at all. Believing is as fundamental as loving in the human situation, but few songs and little poetry are written about it. Believing, in fact, seems to be the subject rather of exhortation than celebration. You are free to love, but you must believe. Man has experienced such an imperative about belief that he has only slowly come to inspect it as his means of tapping into and freely symbolizing his identity and the meaning of his universe.—Eugene C. Kennedy

SERMON SUGGESTIONS

Topic: No Better Time
TEXT: Eccl. 3:1–11
(1) The perils of postponement. (2) The benefits of the favorable moment.

Topic: The Resurrection of Christ
TEXT: Matt. 28:1–15
(1) It completed his work of atonement and stamped it with divine approval (Rom. 4:24f., 8:44; 2 Cor. 5:15). (2) It is the ground and pledge of his people's resurrection. (a) Of their spiritual resurrection, to walk in newness of life (Rom. 6:4; Col. 2:12f., 3:1–4). (b) Of the resurrection of the body (1 Cor. 15:20; 1 Thess. 4:14; Phil. 3:10f.). (3) It is represented in baptism (Rom. and Col. as above). (4) It is celebrated on the Lord's Day.—John A. Broadus

Worship Aids

CALL TO WORSHIP. "The kingdom of the world has become the kingdom of our Lord and of his Christ, and he will reign for ever and ever" (Rev. 11:15).

INVOCATION. Lord, as thou didst raise thy son Jesus victorious over sin and death, raise in us all that is holy and righteous, that transcending the travails of this world, we might live victorious and triumphant lives through Christ our Lord.—E. Lee Phillips

OFFERTORY SENTENCE. "Thou art worthy, O Lord, to receive glory and honor and power: for thou hast created all things, and for thy pleasure they are and were created" (Rev. 4:11).

OFFERTORY PRAYER. To thee, creator God, heavenly Father, we bring in worship and dedication a portion of the things that thou hast created and put in our care. Bless them that they may continue to fulfill thy purpose.

PRAYER.   Almighty God, the true light of life, whose power no earthly force can challenge and whose reign over and among us no alien god can shake, we bless you for the saving work of your Son whom heaven has enthroned as King of kings and Lord of lords. We sing the praise of him who died but is now alive forevermore. We rejoice in his living presence which we feel in church, in groups at prayer, and in our solitary vigil when we retreat and are alone with him. We are stirred over what a friend we have found in Jesus and how through his Easter triumph our work, our worship, and our living of these days are sanctified and blessed abundantly. Glad are our hearts today as we lift our songs to heaven, and before all who will see and hear we leap with joy and declare our God is alive!—Donald Macleod

LECTIONARY MESSAGE

Topic: The Risen Rabbi

TEXT: John 20:1–18

Other Readings: Acts 10:34–43; Ps. 118:1–2, 14–24; 1 Cor. 15:1–11

We are so familiar with the Easter stories that we have difficulty perceiving the complete surprise—the utter astonishment—of the early disciples at the resurrection of Jesus. Unlike us, they did not know the end of the story. They did not expect Jesus to be raised from the dead. An empty tomb led them to suspect a missing corpse, not a resurrected body. This Easter we are especially focusing on Mary Magdalene's story of the Risen Rabbi.

I. Discovering the Empty Tomb (vv. 1–10)

In the predawn darkness Mary discovers that the tomb has been opened. The stone door has been removed. (The Greek perfect participle in v. 1 pictures the stone "lifted up," as if it were taken out of a groove.)

Mary immediately runs to tell Simon Peter and the Beloved Disciple ("the other disciple") the news of the empty tomb.

Mary's use of "we" in her message in verse 2 implies that she was not alone at the tomb (cf. Matt. 28:1; Mark 16:1–2; Luke 24:1–3).

Mary, Peter, and the Beloved Disciple were afraid that Jesus' body had been taken by grave robbers or enemies. It seemed the most reasonable explanation for the empty tomb. When first Peter and then the Beloved Disciple enter the tomb, however, it does not look like a grave robbery. The costly linen wrappings of the body are lying together in one location, while the cloth that covered Jesus' head ("the napkin") is "rolled up" in a separate place (vv. 5–7). As the great preacher of the ancient church, John Chrysostom observed, "If anyone had removed the body, he would not have stripped it first, nor would he have taken the trouble to remove and roll up the napkin and put it in a place by itself" (*Sermons on John,* 85:4, as quoted in George Beasley-Murray, *John,* p. 372).

The resurrected Jesus has cast off his grave clothes, in dramatic contrast to Lazarus, who emerged from the tomb with "his hands and feet bound with strips of cloth, and his face wrapped in a cloth" (11:44). Jesus' bodily resurrection is not merely a physical resuscitation.

Peter sees the evidence in the empty tomb but does not seem to grasp the miracle of the resurrection (cf. Luke 24:12). The Beloved Disciple, however, sees and immediately believes (v. 8). When persons earnestly seeking Christ today examine the evidence of the empty tomb at second hand, some remain uncomprehending, while others receive the gift of faith.

Verse 9 reminds us of the role of Scripture —at this early date, the books of the Old Testament—in confirming faith (cf. Luke 24:47). Even the Beloved Disciple still has much to learn from Scripture to strengthen and support his faith. Seeking to understand God's purpose in Christ challenges all Christians to know the Scriptures more deeply.

The two disciples head for their homes (v. 10), but Mary—still stricken with grief—remains.

II. Looking for the Missing Body (vv. 11–15)

Mary's grieving has found a new concern. She is not simply weeping because Jesus is dead but because even his body has vanished. When Mary looks in the tomb (vv. 11–12), she does not see only grave clothes, but angels! God has been the agent here, not grave robbers. Yet Mary still keeps looking for the missing body. Her response to the angels' question (v. 13) reveals that the possibility of resurrection has not occurred to her. Like Mary, we must overcome our obsession with the missing body in order to recognize the risen Lord.

Mary is so preoccupied with her own conception of what has happened to Jesus that she does not recognize him (v. 14). Even when Jesus stands before her and speaks, she assumes he is the gardener (v. 15). Because the tomb is in a garden (19–41), Mary thinks this stranger might have carried the body of Jesus away and knows where she might find it. Faith in the risen Lord cannot be compelled by miraculous appearance; it is a gift from God.

III. Encountering the Risen Lord (vv. 16–17a)

Only when Jesus calls Mary's name does she recognize him. As John 10:3 describes, the shepherd "calls his own sheep by name." So, Jesus calls each of us by name to be his disciples. Jesus takes the initiative to seek a personal relationship with us. The question is whether we will "know his voice" and "follow him" (10:4).

Mary enthusiastically responds to Jesus as her "Rabbi." (*Rabbouni* is an elaborated form, which literally means "my Teacher.") This glad exclamation—"Teacher!"—points to Mary's unexpectedly renewed and deepened relationship with Jesus. The pain of her grieving has become joy (cf. 16:20).

After recognizing Jesus (probably with some form of touching) Mary wants to grasp hold of him and never let him go. Now that Jesus is alive, Mary does not want to lose him again. She wants to cling tightly to him. Jesus, however, instructs her to let him go, as he is in the process of ascending to the Father.

Jesus is departing to God. The time for remaining with Jesus has not yet arrived. The relationship between the Lord and his disciples will move away from physical contact toward real spiritual presence.

IV. Announcing the Good News (vv. 17b–18)

Mary is to go and tell the disciples about Christ's resurrection and ascension. When all we desire to do is hold onto Jesus for ourselves, he gently commands us to share the good news with others.

The words she brings from Jesus include the first time the Fourth Gospel explicitly calls God the "Father" of *believers* ("my Father and your Father"). The intimate relationship between the Father and the Son is being extended to include Christ's followers. Our place as God's adopted sons and daughters is based upon the risen Christ's interaction with the Father.

Mary is immediately obedient to Jesus' command. Her testimony to the resurrection is based upon her personal experience. "I have seen the Lord" provides the foundation for Mary's announcing the good news of Easter.

The resurrection surprised the earliest disciples. Does it amaze us today that Jesus chose to announce the good news through the witness of a woman who testified to her experience with the Risen Rabbi?—Charles J. Scalise

SUNDAY: APRIL SIXTH

SERVICE OF WORSHIP

Sermon: Times of Refreshing

TEXT: Acts 3:12–19

Our bad choices have tarnished, stunted, and endangered our lives. The Jews to whom Peter addressed his criticism, following the amazing healing of a lame beggar at the temple gate, could not yet see the creative power of Christ. Their eyes were blinded by their bad decision to have a murderer released to them and having Christ crucified. Decisions we have made have left us in times of languor and suffering.

I. Lives Can Be Healed by Jesus Christ

a. Peter had nothing to give the lame man except his own tremendous faith. He told the Jews, "His name through faith in his name has made this man strong," referring to the name of the creator and king of life, Jesus Christ. The faith was that of Peter and John. If the lame man had known faith, he would have been walking already.

b. Whereas the lame man was suffering through no known fault of his own, perhaps through an accident or a congenital illness, we have brought suffering on ourselves. Nevertheless, our suffering and blight can be healed by the Prince of Life, just as his could be, by faith.

c. The healing of one person draws a crowd. Of course, this was a well-known person, seen daily by all who came to the Temple, and the change in him was bound to be noticed and marveled at. Many who know us and see us daily would wonder to see us walking by faith.

II. Good Acts Still Mystify People Who Do Not Know the Source

a. Many of us, in our families, in our community and church agencies, have so habitually, so assiduously, and so creatively done good things for those in need of help that the rest of us may lose sight of the great power of goodness responsible for their lives.

b. It is necessary for all of us to give credit where due, not to accept accolades as our personal honors but to acknowledge the force of daily faith in Christ for urging, guiding, and sustaining whatever good we do.

III. Repentance Is the Secret of Times of Refreshing

a. We cannot continue to glorify God if we continue to languish in tarnished lives. We must heed Peter's call (v. 19) to "repent and be converted" so that our bad decisions and their results, even if chosen in ignorance (a lame excuse), as Peter says the Jews had done, "may be blotted out."

b. Some travelers who were enjoying good fellowship over their lunches so much that they brought reflected joy to a lone nearby diner were much surprised when they stopped to pay their bill to find that the lone diner, out of joy caught from them, had paid it for them. Most of us have obligations for all we have benefited from in life; yet it is hard to realize that for the debt we owe for sin, another one has already paid our bill.

c. When an honest worker has made an expensive error, one that costs his employer more than he could repay, he can expect at best to be fired. But if the employer sees repentance and honest sorrow, he can be sure of gratitude and enduring loyalty if he simply says, "I forgive you—I know you didn't mean to harm me—continue your duties as before."

We must prepare ourselves for the "times of refreshing" coming from the presence of the Lord by honest repentance, acknowledging the power that can heal and renew our lives.—John R. Rodman

Illustrations

HOW WE RELATE TO GOD.   Man's relationship to God is not established by a code of law, without his being personally involved. He must submit himself, not simply to the law, but to God: to accept, that is, what God demands of him in a wholly personal way.

That is why Jesus does not attempt to talk learnedly of God, to proclaim universal, all-embracing moral principles, to present man with a new system. He does not give directives for all spheres of life. Jesus is not a legislator and does not want to be one. He neither binds people again to the old legal system nor issues a new law embracing all spheres of life. He does not compose either a moral theology or a code of conduct. He issues neither moral nor ritual instructions as to how people are to pray, fast, observe sacred times and respect sacred places. Even the "Our Father," not recorded at all by the earliest evangelist, is not reproduced as a single, binding form of words but in different versions in Luke (probably original) and Matthew. Jesus is not concerned about repeating a prayer in the same words. And the commandment of love particularly is not to become a new law.—Hans Küng

LIVING EXPERIENCE.   If I want to sell you on Oysters Rockefeller or Veal Piccata, I don't hand you a recipe; I let you smell it, taste it, savor it. If you are to grasp the horrors of the Holocaust, it's not enough to read "six million were exterminated"; you must see the gas ovens, the mountains of human bones. To appreciate Handel's *Messiah*, the score is not enough; you have to drink it in with your ears. Naked knowledge is not unimportant, but it's only a beginning. You know best when you are one with what you know: with the things of God, with the people of God, with God Himself. You know best when you love.—Walter J. Burghardt, S.J.

SERMON SUGGESTIONS

Topic: The Best Kind of Happiness
TEXT: Ps. 1
(1) The gradual steps downward in sin implied, verse 1. (2) The gradual steps upward in righteousness specified: (a) opening one's heart to the will of God as revealed in Scripture, verse 2; (b) nurturing the good thing that has begun to grow, verse 3a; (c) enjoying the right kind of success, verse 3b. (3) The great difference to be expected in contrasts: the futility of a godless life; the immeasurable richness of a life that God has been invited to share, verses 4–6.

Topic: The Great Difference
TEXT: 2 Cor. 5:17; Col. 3:1
(1) We want God, but often on our own terms. (2) A genuine encounter with God in

Jesus Christ makes everything different: a new style of life; proceeding from a transformed character; issuing in self-denying creative love.

Worship Aids

CALL TO WORSHIP.   "Then said Jesus to them again. Peace be unto you; as my Father hath sent me, even so send I you. And when he said this, he breathed on them, and saith unto them, Receive ye the Holy Ghost" (John 20:21–22).

INVOCATION.   Holy God, who alone knowest what this hour of worship might begin, what hearts lift, what hopes engender, what visions bring; make us open and available and honest before the leading of the Holy Spirit.—E. Lee Phillips

OFFERTORY SENTENCE.   "If a brother or sister be naked, and destitute of daily food, and one of you say unto them, Depart in peace, be ye warmed and filled; notwithstanding ye give them not those things which are needful to the body; what doth it profit? Even so faith, if it hath not works, is dead, being alone" (James 2:15–17).

OFFERTORY PRAYER.   We learned from you to give, Father, but we have not yet learned to give completely as you gave when Christ came to live and walk among us and show us what true giving is all about. This morning let us come a little closer to what you desire as we give generously and in love for his sake as well as our own.—Henry Fields

PRAYER.   Almighty God, make the nearness of the living Christ to become more real so that our coldness may be overtaken by warmth, our stumbling corrected by our being lifted up, and our tears and sorrow wiped away through hope. May we become humble in his presence, and through our surrender to his call may we rise to share in the victory of his will in every decision and crisis of life. Change our lives so that we ourselves may become life changers who bear others' burdens, offer a cup of water to a thirsty one, and nourish always a vision of the larger good. Help us so to work, and pray, and serve until we shall all come "in the unity of faith unto the measure of the stature of the fullness of Christ." Lord, we believe; bear with us through our unbelief. O Risen Savior, lead us to believe in you that we may own your life.—Donald Macleod

LECTIONARY MESSAGE

Topic: On Seeing and Believing
TEXT: John 20:19–31
Other Readings: Acts 4:32–35; Ps. 133; 1 John 1:1–2:2

Our pragmatic, materialistic world proclaims that "seeing is believing." People seek physical evidence to prove or disprove faith. The story of Thomas coming to believe in the risen Lord shows us that the relationships between faith and sight are not so simple. The message is directed especially to those readers of John's Gospel who —like all of us—were *not* present for Jesus' Easter evening appearance.

I. Seeing and Believing (vv. 19–23)

Meeting in fear behind locked doors, the disciples are in desperate need of an empowering faith. The risen Lord appears, not in some distant vision, but coming and standing among them (v. 19). Jesus' miraculous presence in their midst surpasses his previous capacity to be with his disciples.

Jesus comes seeking to renew a personal relationship with his followers. He brings them both a greeting and a sense of God's peace. When we are afraid, the presence of the risen Lord can come among us with the gift of God's peace. As George Beasley-Murray observes, "'shalom!' . . . is supremely the Easter greeting" (*John,* p. 379).

Jesus shows the disciples "his hands and his side" (v. 20). When they see the identifying marks of his crucifixion, the disciples immediately rejoice. Their seeing has led to believing!

The wounds of the crucifixion in the glorified body of the resurrected Jesus assure Christ's followers that the crucified Son of Man and the risen Lord of glory are one. Jesus is really alive. The disciples are not merely seeing an apparition. (Further confirmation is offered by Jesus' breathing on the disciples in v. 22.) When we see that the same Jesus who died for us has been raised, we should respond with rejoicing (v. 20).

As soon as the disciples have recognized the Lord, Christ commissions them to continue his mission in the world (v. 21). "As the Father has sent me, so I send you" is the Fourth Gospel's parallel to Matthew's Great Commission (Matt. 28:19–20). The Father's sending of the Son authorizes Jesus' sending his followers on mission. Seeing and believing result in action.

The disciples will be empowered for this mission by receiving the gift of the Holy Spirit (v. 22). Just as God in creation breathed the breath of life into Adam (Gen. 2:7), so Jesus in the new creation breathes the Spirit on his disciples. The Spirit will assist the disciples in witnessing to their faith in a world that has been hostile to Christ and his message. Through the presence of the Spirit, Christ's disciples will proclaim both the gospel message of forgiveness of sins to those who receive Christ's word and God's judgment to those who reject it (v. 23). Seeing and believing are expressed in empowered witness.

II. Seeing Is Believing (vv. 24–25)

Thomas was present for the seeing and believing experience of the other disciples with the risen Lord. All of their testimony put together ("We have seen the Lord"–v. 25; cf. Mary in v. 18) could not convince Thomas. He had predicted disaster when Jesus returned to Judea (11:16), and his fears had proven true when Jesus was crucified in Jerusalem.

So Thomas demands positive proof of Jesus' resurrection. No contemporary skeptic could be more direct or pointed in his or her remarks. For Thomas, seeing is believing!

Jesus spoke negatively of such an attitude in John 4:48, when he declared to the royal official, "Unless you see signs and wonders you will not believe." Doubtful skepticism can easily become hardened into continual unbelief.

III. Believing Because of Seeing (vv. 26–28)

Jesus accepts Thomas's challenge, appearing the next Sunday evening to Thomas and the other disciples. Thomas is at the crossroads between faith and unbelief. Jesus offers Thomas the tangible proof he demands with words that both encourage Thomas to have faith and reprove him for his doubt. Jesus' exhortation, "Do not doubt but believe" (v. 27), although specifically addressed to Thomas, applies to all of Christ's followers who are struggling with doubt regarding the resurrection (cf. Matt. 28:17). The resurrected Lord calls us to move away from our doubts and toward a life of faith.

The text has no indication that Thomas actually touched Jesus' wounds. Thomas turns out not to be as persistent a doubter as he originally seemed. Apparently, seeing the wounds on the body of the risen Lord was enough. Thomas believes because of seeing!

Thomas's response to Jesus is a soul-wrenching confession of faith (v. 28). Thomas is not merely admitting the fact of Jesus' resurrection. Thomas is personally committing himself in faith to this risen Jesus whom he has now personally seen. Jesus has become *"My* Lord and *my* God" to Thomas (cf. Ps. 35:23). The personal pronouns reveal the transformation that has occurred. The skeptical doubter is now a passionate believer.

Thomas's confession of faith was heard by early Christians as standing against the claims of Roman emperors (like Domitian) to be "our Lord and God." Our Christian faith must be strengthened against the divine pretenses of political leaders. Christ, not Caesar, is Lord.

IV. Believing Beyond Seeing (vv. 29–31)

What is the situation of those, like us, who do not have the opportunity of believing because we have seen the risen Lord? Unlike Thomas, we do not believe because of seeing. Unlike the disciples, we are not privileged with a seeing that leads to believing. Perhaps our experience of faith is closest to the Easter morning experience of the Beloved Disciple at the empty tomb (v. 8), where he saw only empty grave wrappings but believed the promise of Jesus (cf. 14:28–29). In any case, we are blessed by Jesus for believing on the word of the gospel. Our believing is beyond seeing!

Instead of blessing Thomas for his confession of faith, Jesus reserves the blessing—his final beatitude—for us. "Blessed are those who have not seen and yet have come to believe" (v. 29). We can share in the faith of Thomas and the disciples without duplicating their experience.

The stories of Jesus recorded in the Fourth Gospel are not just records of events witnessed by the disciples. Rather, they are selected "signs" (v. 30) pointing to faith in Jesus. The Gospel of John has itself been written so that readers may come to share this faith of the disciples that Jesus is "the Christ, the Son of God" (v. 31). As those whose believing is beyond seeing, we are invited to receive the gift of "life in his name." —Charles J. Scalise

SUNDAY: APRIL THIRTEENTH

SERVICE OF WORSHIP

Sermon: The Freedom from Want

Text: Ps. 23; also Eph. 5:8–14

This opening line of a very familiar psalm catches again our attention and our imagination: "The Lord is my shepherd; I shall not want." But as soon as we say it or read it, there is something that says to us, "Can that really be true?" Because we live in a time when our wants seem to multiply, not diminish. From cradle to grave our wants are always before us.

I. What does it mean to say that God is my shepherd? The Israelite was a nomad. For him God was like a shepherd who took care of the sheep. The sheep were not "anxious" about tomorrow because they sensed that the shepherd would take care of them.

a. Who is the good shepherd? According to the Old and New Testaments, the shepherd God is the One who feeds us and nourishes us. The word *ruach,* which is the Old Testament word for shepherd, means "one who feeds, one who teaches, one who nourishes." The shepherd is the One who gives us the bread that will not pass away. Do you remember that sign of the cross on the bread? It is a living reminder that we hunger not just for bread alone but for every word that proceeds out of the mouth of God. When we begin to skimp on that kind of food, we are asking for trouble, for soul trouble. When we think that we can get by with an hour of feeding a week, we begin to be malnourished. We need to feed on the word of God.

b. Sometimes I ask people in a counseling situation, "What nourishes you?" That's really important to me because we center just on problems. The problems are going to come and go. There'll be new problems next week. The question is, What nourishes you and feeds you so that you may overcome the problem? He's the bread of life. He is the One who feeds us so that we can meet the problems each day. Jesus Christ was the good shepherd. He was the one who has compassion upon the multitude. In one passage it says that because he had compassion, "He fed them," and in another place it says, "He taught them." *Ruach,* the good shepherd—He is the one who can feed us so that we will not be in want.

II. The second thing that we know about the shepherd is this: He is the guide. He is the one who leads us.

a. The God whom we know in Jesus Christ is the One who leads us in the big things and the small. Do you remember Saul of Tarsus and his conversion experience? There were two questions that Saul asked: Who are you? and What should I do? God is more than willing to lead us and to answer the question, What should I do? but it begins with the question, Who are you? The more we discover that we are not our own god, we are not our own shepherd, we are not our own savior, we are able to know that He will lead in the next step of the way.

b. Sheep, I am told, can only see ten or fifteen feet ahead. I think they can see farther ahead than I can, because I always want to know what will happen two steps down the road. Yet my experience is that

God gives enough light for the next step, and when I take it the miracle is that there is just enough light for the step after that. We are the sheep of His hand, the people of His pasture, and we are those who are guided each step of the way.

III. The last great significance of the shepherd image is that He is not only the one who feeds us and guides us but He is the One who guards us. He guards us from the very things that can destroy. But we're not exactly the same as sheep, and we can make conscious decisions to take up the enemies of our souls and the noxious weeds and to feed on them. We can nurse resentment so it chokes and kills the life of the spirit. So the Lord can't be our shepherd if we don't allow Him to be. He will not take care of the noxious weeds of jealousy and resentment and bitterness unless we turn them over. But when we do, we know that He guards us from falling.

The Lord is my shepherd. Have we gotten too sophisticated for that message? Have we grown too much spiritually to be brought back again to the basics that only in trusting Him will I receive the freedom from want that is His and His alone to give? May that be His gift to each one of us this day.—Gary D. Stratman

Illustrations

THE VITAL IMAGE.　　My youngest son and I were in a museum. We had a day to look at some of the sights of a city, and he picked out, as his first choice, a museum. He said it sounded really good because "it's a museum of antiques." Well it turned out to be a museum of antiquities, but to a child there may not be much difference. There we saw a stone that came from the early centuries of Christianity, and on that stone was carved a cross. Before bread was baked for a journey, the dough was pressed upon that stone, causing the sign of the cross to appear on the bread. Those who were on a journey could then be reminded that it was the good shepherd, even Jesus Christ, who gave Himself for us that would meet not only their physical but their spiritual needs. "The Lord is my shepherd; I shall not want." What we often do is start with the second phrase, "I shall not want," and we forget that it is the Lord's being our shepherd that causes us not to want. Remember this: As much as the Lord is our shepherd, then in that same amount will we not want. As much as we allow the Lord to be our shepherd, in that same measure we will not want. We can't have one without the other. The Lord is my shepherd.—Gary D. Stratman

UNTIL HE FINDS IT.   We didn't have a hundred sheep. But we did have three children, and the youngest was lost.

Having dropped our five-year-old son at the YMCA for a weekly activity class, I went back later to pick him up. But this time he wasn't out front where he usually waited with the rest of the kids. I hurried through the building, but he was nowhere to be found. My throat tightened with anxiety as I scoured the neighborhood between the Y and our apartment, three miles away. We called the police, then telephoned the homes of all his friends. No one had seen him. Our apprehension mounted by the minute.

Even today, after twenty-seven years, I remember the overwhelming sense of relief that washed over me when, in the gathering dust, I caught sight of that familiar little figure trudging along the railroad tracks toward home. In that moment, I think I understood just how intensely the Good Shepherd longs for the return of His wayward sheep.—Lucien E. Coleman, Jr.

SERMON SUGGESTIONS

Topic: Listening—A Spiritual Discipline
TEXT: Ps. 66:16–19; Rom. 10:14–17
(1) An avenue to knowing oneself. (2) A means of ministering to others. (3) A way of witnessing about the gospel. (4) The method for interpreting the Bible. (5) The starting point for obeying God.—C. Welton Gaddy

Topic: The Essential Elements in a Vital Christian Experience
TEXT: Acts 19:21
(1) A great need. (2) A great salvation. (3) A great gratitude. (4) A great compulsion.—Harry Emerson Fosdick

Worship Aids

CALL TO WORSHIP.   "Let the people praise thee, O God; let all people praise thee" (Ps. 67:5).

INVOCATION.   Almighty God, heavenly Father, open our hearts to what you have done for us, what you are doing even now, and what you promise to us for the future—then we can only praise your name. Let this service of worship remind us of your goodness and so call forth our praise.

OFFERTORY SENTENCE.   "Let the people praise thee, O God; let all the people praise thee. Then shall all the earth yield her increase; and God, even our own God, shall bless us" (Ps. 67:5–6).

OFFERTORY PRAYER.   We acknowledge, O Lord, the link between faith and blessing. Because of you, when we are weak we become strong; when we are poor the kingdom of God belongs to us. Grant that our increase also may become a blessing to us as we invest it in the life and work of your kingdom.

PRAYER.   Lead us, we pray, into the most holy of places this morning, Father. Let the consciousness of your presence fill our minds so that everything which is flippant and frivolous may be banished from our souls. Deliver us from carelessly approaching such holy times. Redeem us from our irreverent habits. Break up the bondage of any custom which has become our foe. May we never be imprisoned by the letter of the law, but rather be set free to be all possible in your name by the grace of Christ. Quicken our memories this morning to recall the many times you have intervened with us and for us. Remind us of the boundless presence of your strength and comfort when we face the disasters of life. Let the warmth of divine solace scatter sorrow's shadows where those shadows exist this morning. Let the glory of forgiveness be experienced as we lay our sinful burdens at the cross this sacred day. Encircle us with the wonder of your love that we may indeed learn to love as Christ loved.–Henry Fields

LECTIONARY MESSAGE

Topic: Your Personal Commission
TEXT: Luke 24:36b–48
Other Readings: Acts 3:12–14; Ps. 4; 1 John 3:1–7

A commissioning ceremony is an exciting event in a military service. It is a one-time occurrence in the life of any officer. Although promotions may follow and rank may bring increases in authority and responsibility, the commissioning is a landmark event.

I. Qualifications

a. Conviction that what you are doing is important is a necessary attribute of an officer in any endeavor. The most challenging task of instructors is the motivation if their students, because the students can do more than they think possible if they are dedicated and convinced that learning the subject is important or essential to them. Any teachers worthy of their job constantly illustrate and emphasize the value of their subject to the students, beginning with their success in the course and in the completion of a grade or a degree, and also in their personal, family, employment, career, and public life. The first qualification, if not the only one, for commissioning by Jesus is experiential conviction of the blessing of one's own salvation.

b. Confirmation of one's own ability to serve is a great help. The disciples who recognized Jesus in their meal together first responded by going to Jerusalem to give witness, realizing that they had possession of earth-shaking, life-making knowledge that everyone should have. They knew he was alive, and they had energy to go and tell about him.

c. Personal dedication leads to the assumption of the duties involved in the office. The official vows in the oath of office are necessarily a personal promise to perform, without which one could not be trusted with responsible leadership. Occa-

sionally the regret is uttered that Jesus had only human beings to do his work in the world, frail as we all are. And yet no great world cause, no job worth doing, can be done without human agents who take to heart the importance of their own efforts in its accomplishment.

II. Preparation

a. Personal proof of the presence of Jesus cemented these disciples' faith in the knowledge of the Scriptures. To see him as he "opened their understanding, that they might understand the scriptures" that he had just reviewed with them was to be fully prepared for the task.

b. They had known the Scriptures all their lives, but his course of instruction, beginning in the law of Moses and going to the prophets and the psalms, about what concerned him touched fire to the dry wood they had known. Their refresher course under the Master Teacher brought all their knowledge and experience into fresh focus.

c. As one is trained in fundamentals and given specific task experience and practice, one is made ready for the recognition of a commission.

III. Appointment

a. Every commission in an American federal service is an official appointment by the highest governing officials, and their signatures testify that they "repose trust and confidence" in the appointee. And the confidence expressed is in the fitness of the appointee to function in a specific capacity, to do a certain job and do it well.

b. Every commission involves not only performance but also leadership. Every talent, skill, ability, and bit of knowledge is directed toward accomplishment and toward inspiring others who follow to accomplish in their turn the same necessary work.

c. Jesus told these disciples that it behooved him to suffer and to rise from death on the third day and that repentance and remission of sins should be preached in his name among all nations, beginning at Jerusalem. And then he gave to them the Great Commission, as he gives it to you all who believe: *"Ye are witnesses of these things."*
–John R. Rodman

SUNDAY: APRIL TWENTIETH

SERVICE OF WORSHIP

Sermon: Who We Really Are

TEXT: Luke 6:39–49 NRSV; Job 8:11–15 KJV

Hypocrisy is one of those subjects that makes anyone shudder who isn't a hypocrite! Certainly, to be charged with being a hypocrite is one of the most damning accusations that can be hurled at people who claim to try and be who God would have them to be.

I. A lot of people on the periphery of the Church and those who are flat out no longer involved love to harp on the theme of hypocrisy among the church members.

a. In fact, I do believe the single most used excuse for not participating in the life of a church by those who once participated to some extent somewhere is the hypocrisy thing.

b. "I don't go to church anymore because of the hypocrites there; it's as simple as that," they say. And what I say, in response, is, "You know, I've known very few hypocrites in any of the churches in which I've been involved. Now, I'm imperfect, and so are many of the people with whom I've served; in fact, *all* the Christians I've ever known have been imperfect. Only a handful have ever claimed otherwise, and—my goodness—were they ever tough on the rest of us poor sinners. We may have a few of the holier-than-thou types in the Church, but we surely do need plenty of sinners around to keep them in the minority!"

II. A hypocrite is not someone who is imperfect and owns it. A hypocrite is someone who is imperfect and who pretends to be above this human condition and above those who admit who and what they are.

a. The Greek word *hypokritēs,* from which we get our English word *hypocrite* meant "actor." In and of itself, an actor is not a bad thing, of course; and the word, originally, was not pejorative in any way. But, in time, the word *could* be used with a negative connotation, in the sense that "the stage is a sham and the actor a deceiver."

No one who is, in any sense, in tune with the will of God wants to be a hypocrite, can even stand the tension of pretense. The matter is worse than simply carrying out the phoniness itself. Jesus said that one day the jig will be up, and not only will hypocrites be known for who they really are, but also—and this is the worst—the lies upon which they have built their lives will prove to be no foundation at all; everything will come apart. They'll be in for utter destruction.

III. Now, what all of this points to is the fact that we have to know and own *who we really are.* We must discover our true selves, and we must not claim more for ourselves than is justifiable. In part, to help alleviate the need some may feel to take up the facade of hypocrisy, the Church should help us in our quest.

a. Under the worst of circumstances, however, the Church has not done so well at this. The Church has not always made us comfortable with our seeking for self-understanding or with the results of the search. Some churches are only comfortable with certain kinds of sins; other sins, they won't tolerate—unless they're being committed by some people, other than the paid ministers, who are important to the life of the congregation.

b. Under the best of circumstances, the Church is a community of love and acceptance wherein we are nurtured into the discovery of *who we really are* and blessed when we own what we find–warts and all. The Church won't let us forget that we never are and never have been perfect persons; the best we will ever be are sinners who have worth because God loves us and because God's grace gives us life.

IV. Hear Jesus' word for us today. As long as we are trying our best to hear and do what he tells us to do, we are happily received as his disciples. When we fail to live up to our calling–and from time to time we will fail–as long as we own our shortcomings and try to correct them, we are not excluded from the family of faith. One more thing: whatever our spiritual and moral achievements may be, we never use them to try to pretend that we are perfect or that we are, in any sense, better or more deserving of God's love than anyone else; that is a foundation for living that will cave in one of these days, and then everyone will know that we have based our lives on hypocrisy and not on our best efforts to live according to what Jesus has taught.

May that not be true for any of us, and if there is any danger of that, let today be the day we make things right with our Lord and our sisters and brothers in his community.– David Albert Farmer

Illustrations

HYPOCRITES. A church in New Orleans used to run an ad in the Saturday newspaper's religion section. The ad read, "Come, join the other hypocrites at First Church." Under the pastor's name, it said, "Chief hypocrite."–David Albert Farmer

THE INNOVATOR. The peril of the Church in every age is being intolerable of the innovator. When Peter had a vision from heaven bidding him broaden out and receive a new group into the Church, he replied: "Not so, Lord, for I have never." His tradition and habit were to limit God's activity. A Christian Church, with room in it for Jesus of Nazareth, must safeguard the liberty of the unsettling critic. He may seem, and sometimes he is, a fool; but even when tactless and unwise, he may be a messenger of God. Our Father employs odd agents. See that we make the Church open-minded. –Henry Sloane Coffin

SERMON SUGGESTIONS

Topic: Expanding Horizons
TEXT: Ps. 31:8

(1) The roominess of the life of faith. (2) The illimitable realm of prayer. (3) The unexplored area of Christian fellowship. (4) The untrammeled plateaus of immortal hope.–Edgar De Witt Jones

Topic: The Christian Secret of Radiance
TEXT: Luke 24:13–35

(1) Being with the Living Christ. (2) Understanding the Scriptures. (3) Engaging in Christian service. (4) Living in Christian hope.–Andrew W. Blackwood

Worship Aids

CALL TO WORSHIP. "He was in the world, and the world was made through him, yet the world knew him not. He came to his own home, and his own people received him not. But to all who received him, who believed in his name, he gave power to become children of God" (John 1:10–12 RSV).

INVOCATION. O God, we call to you out of the turmoil of our world. Great forces of evil and great forces of good compete in our personal lives and in the life of the larger world. Help us to find the key to victory in the midst of it all as we look to you.

OFFERTORY SENTENCE. "You shall receive power when the Holy Spirit has come upon you; and you shall be my witnesses in Jerusalem and in all Judea and Samaria and to the end of the earth" (Acts 1:8 RSV).

OFFERTORY PRAYER. Our Father, let these offerings go forth into all the world with your blessing, so that your witnesses may speak the saving truth that affirms all the good and challenges all the evil. We thank you for giving us this partnership with you in what you are doing on this earth.

PRAYER. May our souls find a resting place, Father, not in creeds and designed statements of faith, but in you and you alone.

Some come here today worn and weary with the burdens of life. There is no seeking to turn aside from the common struggles of life. We do not seek rest from mental and manual toil. The rest we long for is deeper than struggle and toil. It is a longing for satisfying rest that settles our souls, an inner rest which is the reward of those who bring their desires into harmony with your purpose and commit themselves to doing your will. Let that inner peace and rest come as we wait together in your presence today.

Some come here restless because they have wandered far from you. Deceived by the glamour of cheap joys, many have tried to satisfy themselves with the husks of life, but there is still the deeper hunger for the very bread which you alone can give. Ashamed and homesick, they feel a longing for your presence too deep to be uttered. Give folks courage to arise and go to the father and say, "Make me content to abide within the shelter and love of your grace and to live within the limits of your law."

Give your blessings to the church, we pray. As it seeks to bring restless people back to their moorings, from which they have drifted, give it guidance, compassion, forgiveness, and love to accomplish the purpose. Create through the church a fellowship that cannot be broken, a longing that will never give up on anyone and a winsome love that will exemplify Christ.

Whether our pathways through the coming week lead us into green pastures and beside still water or through dark valleys and mountainous disappointments and difficulties, give us the ability to keep our hearts and minds set on you.—Henry Fields

LECTIONARY MESSAGE

Topic: Increasing the Value of Jesus
  TEXT: John 10:11–18
  Other Readings: Acts 4:5–12; Ps. 23; 1 John 3:16–24
  Suppose you're scheduled for heart surgery tomorrow. Today it came to your attention that the surgeon scheduled to perform the operation had lost every patient in doing this procedure. A dozen questions would arise in your mind. When it comes to our physical care, we want someone who is approved, knowledgeable, skillful, and caring.

Jesus taught his followers that the well-being of our souls is even more important than the welfare of our bodies. It bothered Jesus that so many were willing to turn over the care of their souls to uncaring and destructive leaders. They were like sheep being handled by shabby shepherds. Jesus tagged some shepherds as unfit and vicious, verses 2 and 10a. Other shepherds were interested only in the paycheck and not the safety of the sheep, verse 12. After all, they didn't own the sheep; they were just tenant shepherds. Philip Keller writes about those kinds of hired hands in his book *A Shepherd Looks at Psalm 23* (pp. 28–29).

Jesus saw the human family as being mismanaged by unauthorized and uncaring soul-carers. His heart was moved with compassion. So he came to be the "True Shepherd," verse 2. In contrast with the deceitful entrance of the false shepherds, Jesus came the right way, verse 2. The prophets had predicted the way the shepherd would come to the sheep. They had foretold where he would be born, whom he would be born to, and the unusual character of his birth. He was also ushered in by the one sent to identify him, John the Baptist. John opened the door; he cried, "Prepare the way of the Lord."

Then Jesus claimed to be "Good Shepherd," verse 11. This goodness was evidenced by his personal relationship with each of the sheep, verse 3. He knew his sheep by name. He knew the nature and needs of each sheep. He's good because he willingly placed himself in jeopardy for the sheep. But if we are to show the proper commitment to Jesus, words like *true* and *good* might be too tame. We need to elevate him in our life to be more than just the "right one," as compared with Buddha or Muhammad. We must speak of Jesus as more than good as we would speak of one who is kind. One of those who heard Jesus first speak these words later wrote about the shepherding role of Jesus. He chose not to use the words *true* or *good* shepherd but elevated Christ's role to "chief" shepherd (1 Pet. 5:4).

Then there's the book called Hebrews, designed to show the superiority of Jesus. In its closing benediction, the writer calls Jesus "the great shepherd of the sheep" (Heb. 13:20).

Why did they not use the words *true* or *good?* What made them elevate Jesus to be the chief and the great? I believe that their growing understanding of this very conversation with Jesus was responsible. At the first hearing, the radical aspects of the message did not sink in, verse 6. But as they came to grips with his words, they elevated Jesus from the *true one* and the *good one* to the *great one* and the *chief one*.

There are three seeds in this passage that if planted in the soil of the mind will grow into a bouquet of praise to the Lord Jesus Christ and increase his worth as the Shepherd of the soul.

I. Jesus Will Increase When You Accept the Mystery of His Will

The death of Jesus Christ can be approached in many ways. He was nailed to the cross because of the envious religious leaders. He was killed because of the weak-kneed politicians such as Herod and Pilate. He was the object of Satan's cruel scheme to destroy the seed of Eve. Jesus was the offering of a Holy God for the punishment of broken law. All of these, and no doubt others, could be supported by the Bible as reasons for Calvary. But Jesus wanted his followers to know that he gave myself voluntarily. He could have resisted, he could have been rescued, he could have said no, but his love for you and me took him to the cross. Five times in this passage Jesus spoke of the voluntary aspect of his death (10:11, 15, 17–18). The New Testament writers were quick to point this out: "He loved me and gave himself for me" (see Gal. 2:20; Rom. 5:8). Beyond the substitutionary giving of himself, there is the age-long and worldwide activity of Jesus.

II. Jesus Will Increase When You Appreciate the Magnitude of His Work (v. 16)

The KJV gave two different words in verse 16 one meaning. They translated both words "flock." The first word should be "fold," or "pen," while the second is "flock." Jesus was predicting that there would be many folds, pens, within the one flock. The diversity within the church of God bothers some. They see it as confusing and divisive, but Jesus saw the folds as different pens within one flock shepherded by himself. He realized that believers would find certain truths to be more important than others. He was aware that strong personalities would emerge and gather folds of like-minded people. There is a saying, "If you have one believer you have a Christian, if you have two believers you have a church, and if you have three believers you have two churches." The unity Jesus prayed for was not for every believer to be in one fold, but for every believer to recognize the One Flock over which he was the One Shepherd (John 17:20–21).

III. Jesus Will Increase When You Announce the Measure of His Worth (vv. 19–21)

Jesus is great because he is the dividing line among the peoples of the earth. It is said that he lived a long time ago, that his views are ancient, and that faith in him does not square with the twentieth-century culture. Yet it can't be denied that his claims are still being accepted. People are still claiming that their lives are being changed. "A demon cannot open the eyes of a blind man, can he?" Truly he was, as the religious leaders of his day claimed, a maniac, or he was in truth all he claimed to be, the Good, True Shepherd who gave his life for the sheep.–James Lemuel Higgs

SUNDAY: APRIL TWENTY-SEVENTH

SERVICE OF WORSHIP

Sermon: Living on the Watch

TEXT: Eph. 5:15–20; 6:18–20

I. As Christians, we cannot afford to ignore the strong biblical affirmation of the world in creation, "God saw everything that he had made, and indeed, it was very good," and in redemption, "For God so loved the world that he gave his only Son." At the same time, as Christians, we cannot afford to ignore the strong biblical warnings about the darkness of evil that permeates the atmosphere in which we live. It appears that Paul leans toward the dark side in his view of the world. The Christian goes into the world as a soldier goes into battle. We are advised to "Put on the whole armor of God . . . to stand against the wiles of the devil." The armor is for defense against the "spiritual forces of evil in the heavenly places." Perhaps David Koresh had a more literal interpretation of the "whole armor of God" than I do. Shortly before the holocaust in Waco, *Time* ran a brief cover story, "In the Name of God: what happens when believers embrace the dark side of faith." The article linked the bombing of the World

Trade Center in New York, ethnic cleansing in Bosnia, and the Branch Davidian disaster in a world of volatile emotions and religious extremism: "If you scratch any aggressive tribalism, or nationalism, you usually find beneath its surface a religious core, some older binding energy of belief or superstition, previous to civic consciousness, previous almost to thought. Here is the paradox of God-love as a life-force, the deepest well of compassion, that is capable of transforming itself into a death-force, with the peculiar annihilating energies of belief." Simultaneously the world is becoming more secular and more religious, and the result is a world more polarized. Religious extremists are declaring war on the world and/or anyone who gets in their way. The motor that drives militant Christian sects is a distortion of the biblical warnings about the world. The whole armor of God does not include a paranoid view of the world. How does one justify killing in the name of God? Two ideas stand in the background. God is a warrior intent on the absolute destruction of his enemies. The world, at least the world of people and ideas different from ours, is the enemy of God, a place of darkness.

In spite of the military image in Ephesians, not one ounce of violence is implied or allowed for the Christian soldier. Because our struggle is not against blood and flesh but against principalities and powers, our struggle can never degenerate into physical warfare or into hatred of the world. Ephesians follows the pattern of Pauline epistles in moving from faith to ethics. The armor of God is a rhetorical device to sum up Christian behavior. Because of the connection between the conclusion and the body of the Epistle, we have drawn interpretation of the armor of God out of the well of earlier statements in Ephesians. Taken as a whole, Ephesians champions the cause of peace. We are commissioned to save the world, not to destroy it. We are called to live on the watch, to keep alert, to be careful how we live. In typical Pauline parlance, we are to be in the world but not of the world.

II. a. We live in tension with the world. We cannot live at war with the world. There is a difference. On hearing that Margaret Fuller had finally accepted the universe, Thomas Carlyle was said to have ex-claimed, "Egad, she'd better!" This is the only world we have. Acceptance is something of a necessity. All of us live here. If we choose to reject the world, we have two choices—destruction of the world or of ourselves. Jim Jones and David Koresh chose both. Demagogues have exploited the fears and prejudices of people through the ages. The most effective have made their case out of the apocalyptic literature of the Bible. If the future of this world is terminal, the hope is in another world. We cannot understand Daniel and Revelation apart from the crisis historical events that produced them.

To look beyond political leaders and world governments for the hope is always valid. To rest our hope in neither the United States nor the United Nations acknowledges that salvation comes from a higher source than any human institution. To take steps toward war with the world denies the world-saving mission of Christ. Rejection of the world must eventually mean rejection of life itself. If we judge the world by human behavior, we can easily make the Branch Davidian case. The babies who died in Waco as well as the babies who died in Union, South Carolina, are enough to cause anyone to pause before giving a stamp of approval to life on this planet. Although it is the only place, the world is a threatening place to live. Bad things happen to good people, and good people—at least religious people—do bad things. The irony of demonizing the world is that religion comes to create the very evil that it describes. The worst evil and the worst cynicism grows out of the behavior of religious people in the name of God.

b. We must learn to live on the watch. I learned a lot of military-style language playing high school football. When we were running sprints, the coach would yell with great urgency, "Move out." If a ball was punted or thrown toward a group that was occupied with another game or drill, the call was, "Heads up!" or "Headache!" The sense of emergency was important to avoid the immediate threat of catching a football in the head. The warnings on the field were quite different from the typical parental caution before taking the family car on a date. The word that I eventually adopted as the expected parental advice was, "Be careful."

What is the difference? One is an alert to an imminent threat, while the other is a general word of caution about possible hazards. Some overprotective parents would prefer to be the eyes, ears, and minds of their children, to always be present to yell the appropriate warning when danger threatens. Eventually all of us have to trust our young adults to be alert to the risks of life and to take the appropriate measures when temptations and challenges arise. Decisions are made in the spirit of the values that have been learned and modeled. I am not sure which we trust the least, the world and its threat or our values and their strength to stand. The Christian world mission calls us out of our seclusion to live in the world. We should not underestimate the power to change the world in the Christian witness to authentic values.

To take the whole armor of God finally comes down to being careful how to live. The language of Ephesians is "to watch" and to "be alert." I cannot think of any counsel more relevant to the time in which we live than to call us away from our intoxication into soberness. The Spirit of God does not scramble our heads and cast our gaze on the world of our dreams. To be filled with the Spirit of God or to pray in the Spirit is to live a sober life with a sharp mind and a determined commitment to the calling of God in Christ.—Larry Dipboye

Illustrations

CREATIVE THOUGHT.   True faith can grow and mature only if it includes the elements of paradox and creative doubt. Hence the insistence of orthodoxy that God cannot be known by the mind, but is known in the obscurity of faith, in the way of ignorance, in the darkness. Such doubt is not the enemy of faith but an essential element within it. For faith in God does not bring the false peace of answered questions and resolved paradoxes. Rather, it can be seen as a process of "unceasing interrogation." Alan Ecclestone has expressed its character well. The spirit enters into our lives and puts disturbing questions. Without such creative doubt, religion becomes hard and cruel, degenerating into the spurious security that breeds intolerance and persecution. Without doubt, there is a loss of inner reality and of inspirational power to religious language. The whole of spiritual life must suffer from, and be seriously harmed by, the repression of doubt.—Kenneth Leech

THE STRONGER GOD.   I remember the friend of mine who returned from a visit to the Soviet Union in the 1970s (on a trip sponsored by the National Council of Churches) announcing to us that the church was mostly "irrelevant because the only people there are little old ladies." Looking back now at the collapse of communism, the embarrassment of those seminary professors who advocated this god as the savior of Latin America, the difficulties of rebuilding the Soviet Union after a long period of spiritual bankruptcy, I hope my friend would now say, "Thank God for the little old ladies." They bet on the stronger of two gods and won. Their existence provided a continuing, visible, political rebuke to the Soviets.—William H. Williamson

SERMON SUGGESTIONS

Topic: A Vision of the Almighty
    TEXT: Isa. 6:1
    (1) What the prophet saw of God. (2) What the prophet saw of himself. (3) What the prophet saw of a needy world.

Topic: A Creative Fellowship
    TEXT: Various
    (1) The fellowship of faith (Gal. 3:28). (2) The fellowship of prayer (Acts 1:14). (3) The fellowship of worship (Matt. 18:20; Heb. 10:25). (4) The fellowship of service (2 Cor. 8:3–4).

Worship Aids

CALL TO WORSHIP.   "In the shadow of thy wings will I make my refuge" (Ps. 57:1).

INVOCATION.   Meet us in a special way this morning, Father, as we gather to wait, watch, and worship in your presence. There are times when it seems that your face is hidden from us, and we know that such happens because of our sins. In the blindness of our hearts we forget your mercy and forgiveness. This morning we ask that you cleanse us from our offenses, deliver us from our selfish thoughts, remove us from our base, destructive desires, and inspire us to draw near to you in all humbleness and meekness. We long to come near to your presence that we may confess our sins and faults and experience the wonder of your forgiving grace.—Henry Fields

OFFERTORY SENTENCE. "They shall appear before the Lord empty-handed; every man shall give as he is able, according to the blessing of the Lord your God which he has given you" (Deut. 16:16b–17 RSV).

OFFERTORY PRAYER. O Lord, you have blessed us in ways that we cannot number or describe. Now bless us again as we bring to you these tithes and offerings, and bless all of those whose lives are touched and changed by our gifts.

PRAYER. Look upon us, O God, with understanding and patience as we try to find our way through the frightening tangle of international affairs. Clarify our vision of the truth; help us to see in Jesus him in whom violence found no place; and as we follow him, step by step, imperfectly though faithfully, may we gradually rule it out of our lives.—Theodore Parker Ferris

LECTIONARY MESSAGE

Topic: My Father, The Gardener

TEXT: John 15:1–8

Other Readings: Acts 2:26–40; Ps. 22:25–31; 1 John 4:7–21

I was only a boy of ten when my father pastored a church in the small sawmill town of Dierks, Arkansas. It seemed as if each family had a cow, a few pigs, and a garden. I still remember helping my dad dig up the potatoes and onions. One day our work was interrupted when he said, "Let's go to the post office." I remember the teasing he took from the men as they pointed to his blue bibbed overalls. "Is that any way for a preacher to dress?" He was a gardener on that day.

Jesus used that image when he taught his twelve followers that the heavenly Father wanted them to be productive. "My Father is the Gardener . . . and you are his chosen garden."

Our fathers do have a profound effect on us. If they are good gardeners of lives, they will help their children to be productive people. If they fail to garden well, they can hinder their children in many areas of their lives.

But Jesus has brought us all good news. He introduced us to a perfect Father. He wants us to pray, "Our Father in heaven." All of us, whether we had a good father or not, need to focus first on the Heavenly Father. Instead of focusing on the earthly fathers and projecting our impressions of them upon the Heavenly Father, let's begin with him. Let's be fair and be glad that there's a Perfect Father and that he wants to be the Gardener of our lives.

John 15 shows us how the Father, the Gardener, grows us into productive people.

I. He Graciously Attached Us to the True Vine

"I am the true vine" is contrasted with the vines that served as symbols or foreshadowings. God had given the nation Israel the opportunity to point to the coming vine. Isaiah sang about it in Isaiah 5. The vine was the emblem on the coins of the Maccabees. One of the glories of the Temple in Jerusalem was the great golden vine relief that was upon the front wall of the worship center. Jesus was saying that all of this pointed to him, the True Vine, the one through whom the life of God flowed. His Father, the Gardener, in pure grace, took lifeless branches and united them to the vine (Rom. 6:5). That is union; and the branch is to stay close to the vine, which is communion. The word *remain, abide,* or *live in* is repeated eleven times in chapter 15.

II. His Father the Gardener Wisely Tends the Branches

Some branches are lifted up (v. 2). The word *airo* has four basic meanings: (1) to lift up or pick up; (2) to lift up figuratively, as in lifting one's eyes or voice; (3) to lift up with the idea of carrying away; or (4) to remove. Most of the translations have chosen the fourth usage, but I think the primary use of the word deserves consideration here. The gardener picks up the drooping branch, the branch dragging on the ground, so that it can get air and sun and come to fruitage. Here in California we are accustomed to seeing the vines grown vertically, but in Palestine I've seen vineyards growing horizontally. The vineyardman must go and lift the branches touching the ground and prop them up with forked sticks. The Father does that to the discouraged disciple or the drooping follower.

At times he comes with a knife, cutting off some of the live stems because he wants to strengthen the branch. A skilled pruner makes the difference between a poor crop and a good crop. They are trained for two or three years to know *what, where,* and *how* to make the cut. The hand of our Father, the Gardener, cuts away the unproductive, the superfluous, and the sapping parts of our lives. He removes the sucker sprouts that draw off the vital strength of the branch. He severs the debilitating relationships, the burdensome things, the meaningless pursuits. This surgery can leave us confused, even angry and hurt. But it is done with divine wisdom and love. This process is explained carefully in Hebrews 12:4b–11.

III. He Also Proudly Rejoices over the Branches

Not only does the Father plant the branches and tend to the branches, but he is happy for the fruit. What is that fruit? I have sometimes thought it meant other souls that were brought to Jesus. I heard when I was younger, "Apple trees reproduce apple trees

and orange trees reproduce orange trees. So believers produce believers." And I'm sure that this happens, but I've come to believe that the fruit the Father is looking for is the reproduction of his Son in us (Rom. 8:29 and 2 Cor. 3:18). In Jesus the fullness of the Spirit dwelled. In Galatians the ninefold fruits of the Spirit are mentioned (5:22). It follows that the Gardener wants us to have the fruit of the Holy Spirit, which is the manifestation of the life of Jesus in us. Even in this Upper Room discourse in John's Gospel, the first three of the fruits of the spirit are identified: his peace (14:27), his love (15:9), and his joy (15:11). As the Father was supremely glorified in the obedience of Jesus (13:31f.; 17:1, 4), so he is glorified in lives that reproduce the obedient life of Jesus (8:31). How the people of this hungry and hurting world need to see the beauty of Jesus lived out in front of them! Although, looking at this teaching from an individual standpoint, I think it was addressed to the church, God's vineyard. Churches are planted and pruned, and hardships are to bring them to increased commitment to the Vine, the Lord Jesus. Each must allow the Gardener to shape his branches that more and better fruit might come forth.

There is no real future for the branch outside of Jesus. There may have been colorful days, leaves, dwelling in the empty vines of this world, but eternal fruit comes only in knowing "My Father–The Gardener."–James Lemuel Higgs

SUNDAY: MAY FOURTH

SERVICE OF WORSHIP

Sermon: Happy Though Married
TEXT: 1 Cor. 13

There may not be a single marriage so perfect that it cannot stand improvement. Marriage is not to be endured; it is to be enjoyed. Furthermore, one can ask, is it not as much a minister's responsibility to help a couple stay happily married as it is to marry them in the first place?

I. To be happy though married requires time working at your marriage. Great mar-

riages don't just happen! Just as it takes time to trim the lamp of friendship, so it takes time to nurture and bring to flower this deepest of life's relationships.

a. If the flame of love begins to flicker in a marriage, it may be because the husband or the wife (or both) takes the other for granted. That love may be a glowing flame, there are few things more important than spending some moments together each day.

Unless a husband and wife deliberately decide and plan to have some time together, the chances are that they will not. It may be a few moments over a cup of coffee. It may be ten o'clock each night after the children are in bed. It may be the lingering minutes spent over a meal in a restaurant. It may be a walk hand-in-hand after supper while watching the glory of the setting sun. Whatever the occasion, it needs to be more than a casual contact; it ought to be an intimate sharing—a genuine communion of person with person. In marriage, a couple either grows together or grows apart.

b. If you are not at home with your mate, if you do not feel free to relax in his or her presence, it may that you do not spend enough time together to get to know each other properly. To be happy in marriage requires more than the sharing of superficialities; it demands nothing short of genuine communion. Such communion takes time. In this connection, we need to realize, too, that marriage cannot be preserved against the future but has to be won fresh each day.

II. To be happy through married, one needs to see marriage as the greatest of life's relationships rather than as a job. Marriage is much more than the sum total of many separate responsibilities and obligations. It is a growing, developing, reciprocal relationship.

a. Marriage is not something that man has invented; it is what God has intended from the very beginning. Only when God made woman, who was of the same nature (the meaning of taking a rib from Adam to make Eve), could there be the kind of partnership and communion that God intended for the highest and noblest of His creatures. Do you have this perspective on marriage? Unless you do, you are cheating yourselves!

b. It is of help, also, to note that in the Bible the relationship between a man and a woman in marriage is the continuous analogy of the deepest relationship in life—the relationship between God and man. In the Old Testament, one should recall that God was partner to a marriage in which Israel was the bride. In the New Testament, the analogy is used to illustrate Christ's relationship to the Church.

c. The God-ordained nature of this relationship is further explained by Christ. He speaks of how God made them from the beginning male and female; and, "for this reason a man shall leave his father and mother,

and be joined to his wife; and, the two shall become one." The apostle Paul confesses that this is a deep mystery, and so it is. In the very nature of our creation, we are made for each other, not only physically, but in our entire person; we complement each other.

Marriage is not just a physical union, although this is important and good. No, marriage is a new community of mind, body, spirit, and feeling; if it is not, then it is not a Christian marriage. This new community that comes into existence is the family.

III. To be happy though married, one needs to bring those personal resources that make possible the fulfillment of this highest of life's relationships.

a. The greatest resource that anyone can bring to the marriage relationship is not a new house, a good job, economic security, or a beautiful face, an attractive figure, or an expensive wardrobe; it is an authentic self. If you are not a real person, anything else you contribute will never make up this deficiency. Until you have a self to give, you are not really capable of this relationship. Until you have gotten yourself off your hands, you do not have a self that you are free to give.

b. When Jesus said, "Forget yourself and follow me," He was not just talking about discipleship; He was seeking to free the "you" that you might give yourself to all of life's relationships. There is nothing wrong with marriage; in fact, it is capable of bringing the greatest happiness, satisfaction, and fulfillment known. Where there is marital disappointment, difficulty, and frustration, it is usually because one partner (or both) has not become free to give his or her self to the other.

c. The wedding liturgy reminds us of the resources that are needed to fulfill the marriage vows. It speaks of the "resourcefulness of Christian love."

Of course, this is the love of God. It is a completely unselfish, mature love; it is the expression of one who has discovered the freedom to be. To be open to God in such a way that we can mediate His love to each other in the marriage relationship is surely the very nature of our calling as husband and wife.

Without this resource—without the continuous experience of God's perennial love, the possibility of two different persons' coming together to find fulfillment in the intimacy of marriage is but a frustration. Marriage is the celebration of His love and grace in the greatest intimacies of which a man and a woman are capable. "This is of the Lord's doing; and, it is marvelous in our eyes!"–John Thompson

Illustrations

LAUGHTER. Laughter is hope's last weapon. Crowded on all sides with idiocy and ugliness, pushed to concede that the final apocalypse seems to be upon us, we seem nonetheless to nourish laughter as our only remaining defense. In the presence of disaster and death, we laugh instead of crossing ourselves. Or perhaps better stated, our laughter is our way of crossing ourselves. It shows that despite the disappearance of any empirical basis for hope, we have not stopped hoping.–Harvey Cox

PRAISING PEOPLE. "Praise," says George Meredith, "is our fructifying sun." It is–in every sphere of life. Nothing nerves for heroic struggle like praise. Parents know the kindling effect of praise upon their children. A good name given makes men seek to be worthy of a yet better name. Perhaps we may have chilled aspiration and curbed enthusiasm for holiness in some life by refusing to utter the well-deserved, "I praise you."–Dinsdale T. Young

SERMON SUGGESTIONS

Topic: Why Dr. Eliphaz's Patient Grew Worse Instead of Better
TEXT: Job 14:1–5
(1) He diagnosed the case wrongly. (2) He applied the wrong medicine. (3) He only distressed the patient the more. (4) It was God who cured him in the end.–R.C.H. Lenski

Topic: This Is Your Day of Victory
TEXT: Luke 22:24–34
(1) Christ knows our limitations (Matt. 26:34). (2) Christ shows us the way of victory (Matt. 26:44). (3) Christ restores us when we fail (John 21:15–17).

Worship Aids

CALL TO WORSHIP. "Show me thy ways, O Lord; teach me thy paths" (Ps. 25:4).

INVOCATION. O thou who hast cried out in the wilderness of this world and arrested the vagrant thoughts and affections of those who were far from thee and hast made the desert like the garden of the Lord when people have obeyed thee, grant us in these confusing days ears to hear thy voice, hearts to obey thy will, and tongues to repeat after thee thy truth.

OFFERTORY SENTENCE. "'Why spend money on what does not satisfy? Why spend your wages and still be hungry? Listen to me,' says the Lord, 'and do what I say, and you will enjoy the best food of all'" (Isa. 55:2 TEV).

OFFERTORY PRAYER. We confess, O Lord, that it is difficult to understand that our faithful stewardship of time, talents, money, and influence brings greater rewards than our grasping selfishness. Enlighten us and deepen our devotion to you, so that we may find the truly abundant life.

PRAYER. Every day, O Lord, your hand of grace is upon us. We receive blessing upon blessing from you. Not a moment goes by that is not touched by your providence. We are the beneficiaries of your mercies throughout the ages. Yet we must confess that we sometimes walk about in your wonderful world as if you were not real or did not care. We let the anxieties and responsibilities of life dull our sensitivity to you. Forgive us our sin, for we *have* sinned; and open our eyes and our hearts to you once more. Give us another opportunity to walk with you, assured of your presence; to talk with you, assured that you hear us; to work with you, assured that what we do counts.

LECTIONARY MESSAGE

Topic: The Branches and the Branches

TEXT: John 15:9–17

Other Readings: Acts 10:44–48; Ps. 48; 1 John 5:1–6

The first eight verses of this chapter explain the close connection that the believer enjoys with Christ. That union is so integral that Paul likens it to the intimacy that a husband and wife experience (Eph. 5:31–32). In the second section, beginning with verse 9, Jesus turns from the connection of the vine and the branches to the relationship of the branches and the branches. The fruit expected by the heavenly farmer is a growing likeness to the Son of God, as suggested in John 17:11, "My life is on display in them" (*The Message,* by Eugene Peterson). See also Romans 8:29 and 2 Corinthians 3:18. That image will be evidenced by an obedient spirit. Such obedience will focus on the new commandment given by Jesus in the words "Love one another. As I have loved you, so you must love one another" (John 13:34). This is reiterated when he says, "My command is this: Love each other as I have loved you" (v. 12). The imperatives remove the optional and occasional actions. They call for a lifestyle of love.

This obedience is a joyful privilege and not a painful duty, as seen in verse 11, and is motivated by a deep friendship that the believer has with the Savior. Bring up a memory of a very close friend, and remember how you analyzed the desires of your friend so that you might delight that one with a gift. To love our fellow believers brings special delight to our friend Jesus. John Wesley described his conversion as the time when he exchanged the faith of a servant for the faith of a son.

It is hard for us to associate love or friendship with a command because we are programmed by much of the media to identify love with our feelings. But the love for the branches is a commitment to be for one another. It doesn't so much call us to like one another, but to work for one another's wellbeing. Some branches are more difficult to love than others. Perhaps the branches are a bit twisted, ungovernable, or immature. This may demand the phrase that is often heard today: "tough love." One sermon title that fits this is "Everyone Has Someone." The sermon asserted that each of us has someone in our lives who is very hard to love. With this in mind, the love Jesus expects may require pain. Perhaps we need that lesson early in our Christian life. It happened that way for one candidate for baptism. As he was preparing to receive the ritual, the administrant gave him words of encouragement and challenge. Then the bishop prepared to administer baptism. In order to free his hands, he stuck his staff into the ground. He didn't realize that he had accidentally stuck his staff right through the foot of the baptismal candidate. The man grimaced in pain but did not say a word. Afterward the bishop saw what he had done and was very sorry. The remorseful bishop asked the man, "Why in heaven's name didn't you say something?" The candidate responded, "Well, I thought it was just part of the ritual."

An insightful book, *Father Make Us One,* by Floyde McClung, says that the unity of the church that the Bible calls for is "doing love." Love is an activity and at times may be like work. There are several keys in 1 Corinthians 13 that open doors of love toward others. One mentioned is to always believe the best in someone. It requires that we give the branch another chance. Our constant love prayer calls for the Lord to renew our trust relationship with our fellow believers. Though there will be quiet debate among the hearers whether the expectation of the Head of the church is impossible, they are to be reminded that the resources for loving the difficult are available from the indwelling Holy Spirit (Rom. 5:4).

Christians often try to manufacture love by legislative methods, in which all are asked to conform to the same wording, dressing, speaking, or thinking. Others seem to remove all the boundaries because they believe love and convictions are inimical. But the church is called upon to love revealed truth and to speak the truth tenderly and respectfully. The unity expected is not uniformity but an understanding of our common life in Jesus Christ. The strongest motivation for me to love difficult people is the fact that Jesus loved me, a loveless one (Rom. 5:8).

The branches have to forgive one another. Being willing to forgive may be the biggest factor in "doing love." Corrie Ten Boom went throughout Europe after World War II preaching forgiveness. After one message, she saw a former cruel Nazi officer coming toward her. As he drew near to affirm her message on forgiveness, extending his hand, she remembered the cruel treatment directed by this man toward her sister Betsy. She admitted it took a long time for her to be able to reach out her hand to shake his.

Yes, Jesus has called us to a radical love.

The church is to be unique. Our love cannot be based only on emotions or offered on the basis of "because you have treated me so kindly," or "if you will do this," but rather "in spite" of our differences. "I love you" (see Luke 8:32).–James Lemuel Higgs

SUNDAY: MAY ELEVENTH

SERVICE OF WORSHIP

Sermon: The Cradle of Civilization

TEXT: Gen. 21:9–21

I. William Ross Wallace coined the nineteenth-century proverb, "The hand that rocks the cradle is the hand that rules the world," attributing both power and responsibility to mothers that they do not always possess. There is a subtle rejection here. It is the myth of maternal control, which has often been the occasion of condemning witches, setting the blame for human failure, and attributing the power behind ambition to the hand that rocks the cradle. I have no doubt that the basic building block of civilization is the family, but there is a larger context. Family is more than a mother, and family is often the victim of conditions and children under influences beyond parental control. Both civilization and uncivilization are cradles in the community in which lives are shaped. Our children are affected by community values, attitudes, and expectations.

We should not be surprised when the violence of the world visits the children. The shooting death of an eleven-year-old boy in Chicago seems far removed from where we live. He was the product of poverty, the ghetto jungle, a mother with a crack habit, and the violent gang that executed him. At the time of his murder, he was a fugitive wanted for murder. The violent world of the big-city street visits the suburbs and pours daily from the entertainment center in your family room. Guns and violence have never been as available to children or more of a threat than they are today. Our world drifts toward genocide.

II. The story was not the front page of yesterday's newspaper but in the biblical message of the founding of Israel. With good cause, we are normally occupied with the miraculous parenthood of Abraham and Sarah and the destiny of Isaac. Normally, I would address the preferred situation of Mother's Day, thinking that you would more likely find your family mirrored in Sarah than in Hagar, but there are more mothers like Hagar than Sarah in our world. Ignorance and neglect of Hagar and Ishmael sounds a prophetic note in the events of world history and stands in radical contrast with the response of God to one who is named Ishmael, "God hears." Abraham, "father of the nations," is the peacemaker who sent the sons of his concubines away from Isaac with gifts. Although Ishmael later joined Isaac in the burial of Abraham, the son of Hagar, traditionally the father of the Arabic nations, was always less than a son, left to grow up with the limited resources of an outcast mother. Perhaps the hostility today of Arabic nations toward the West is suggestive of the rejection of Ishmael. Does our text reveal a root cause of a contemporary world problem that we continue to ignore? I would not suggest that we should or could go back in history to undo the wrongs of our forebears. A greater cause is before us. Hagar and Ishmael continue to be driven into the desert. The fact the desert is now a city or a suburb does not matter. The Mother's Day call to love our mothers is appropriate. Can you hear the

Word of God calling us to love someone else's mother and some other mother's child? We are called to care about the rejected children of the concubines of our world.

a. *The perfect family is myth.* Waldo Beach traces the gradual evolution of the American family of six or more to the present ideal of two parents, a son and a daughter. The perfect family is modeled on the billboard, an exact fit for a compact car off for a picnic. Now for the truth! There are far more Hagars and Ishmaels than Sarahs and Isaacs in the world, and I dare suggest that much of the time you find more in common with the imperfect family. The myth of the perfect family may be more a burden than a boost. To be sure, the best way to be family is with one whole mother, one whole father, a reasonable number of children, and adequate resources to care for everyone. Even with all of the right pieces in place, ideal families are not always ideal. Successful parents are sometimes guilty of sacrificing their children on the altar of their own accomplishments. Drugs, violence, promiscuity, and AIDS visit ideal families. The move to quarantine children from the world by rejecting public education and retreating behind walls of social, economic, and religious segregation may cause more harm than good. Realities do not go away by denial. The child's game "hide-and-seek" carries over into life. That which is hidden is often sought and usually found.

Hagar and Ishmael had an ideal family by the standards of time until the hostility of Sarah caused them to be driven away. The subtle suggestion that only Isaac counts often justifies our entrenched rejection of Hagar's plight. The deprived existence of this single mother cannot be waved off as her own fault. An alarming number of women and children are the victims of cruel persons and circumstances over which they have no control. The single parent can no longer be ignored as the exception to our definition of family. What makes a family ideal? By the numbers, more children are growing up in a single-parent environment. If Abraham had been a more responsible father, we might have a different international situation today. Instead of concentrating attention on protecting Isaac from Ishmael, maybe we ought to help Ishmael.

b. *The troubled family needs help.* The raging issue deciding national policy is a question of personal responsibility. No one should be excused for behavior that victimizes others. To concentrate on punishing the criminal ignores at least half of the truth. Abraham must own a share of the responsibility for the struggle of Hagar and Ishmael. I hear that poverty should not cause people to be mean. I agree. Look again. Does poverty create a community of meanness? Yes! We are responsible. Children of America are nurtured in poverty. Who cares?

Bastard is indeed an obscenity. Spoken in derogation of children even in the Old Testament, the word is an indictment more of the one who uses it than of the one accused. Isaac and Ishmael are two children, a child of privilege and a child of rejection, but God has created one world that they must share. Marian Wright-Edelman, president of The Children's Defense Fund, sounds an alarm for America: 100,000 children are homeless, child poverty reached a thirty-year high in 1994, 9.4 million children were without health insurance in 1993, every fourteen minutes a child dies, every sixty-four seconds a baby is born to a teenage mother, and every thirteen hours a child is murdered and every ninety-eight seconds a child is killed by gunfire. Who cares? The moment Isaac was born, Ishmael was stigmatized with illegitimacy. In the obsession with the miracle of Isaac's birth, we must not forget the miraculous preservation of Ishmael. I suspect that in the eyes of God children are always worth saving. "God hears" Ishmael in the wilderness even if Abraham and Sarah can close their ears, and God hears the cries of thousands of Ishmaels who are ignored by the rest of us. Sometimes God provides a well, sometimes a Christian with a cup of cold water.—Larry Dipboye

Illustrations

WHAT IS LOVE? What some call love is only a projection of their own ego into other persons; their enjoyment is not the *Thou* of the other person, but their own Egos in the Thou. They marry not to love but to be loved; they are in love not with a person but with a nerve-ending. That is why as soon as the other person ceases to give them pleasure, they leave that person and marry again and again. Carnal experience is replaceable, but not persons. If it were a person that is loved, the person would *always* be loved, because persons are unique. No one can replace your mother! No one can replace God!

BUILDING IS DIFFICULT. We learned in our infancy a lesson that we should not have forgotten in our maturity: it is far, far easier to knock something down that to build it up. As infants, we came equipped with the convulsive movement of hand and foot that easily topples a pile of blocks. But we early found it a quite different matter to take up one block after another and build a pyramid. We had to learn how to do that! In similar fashion, we are good at saying what we do not believe, but we stumble and stutter over what we do believe. Yet we shall not find our way out of the confusion in which we live until we are able to do just that.—Harold A. Bosley

SERMON SUGGESTIONS

Topic: Songs in the Night
TEXT: Job 35:10

(1) God is the author of songs in the night. (a) God is the subject of the songs. (b) God is the one who inspires these songs. (2) We sing about three things: the yesterday that is over; the night itself; or the morrow that is to come. (3) These are the excellencies of these songs: (a) They are hearty. (b) They show that we have real faith in God. (c) They prove that we have true courage. (4) When we sing in the night, (a) it will cheer ourselves; (b) it will delight God; (c) it will cheer our companion; and (d) it is one of the best arguments for our religion.—Charles Haddon Spurgeon

Topic: The Light of Faith
TEXT: Heb. 11:1

(1) Faith challenged by life's many problems. (2) Faith encouraged by loving parents and trustworthy friends. (3) Faith defined by God's revelation in Jesus Christ. (4) Faith experienced in daring commitment to Jesus Christ, who (a) makes us confident and expectant, and who (b) pours his love into our hearts and actions.

Worship Aids

CALL TO WORSHIP. "Thy laws are a wondrous mystery—my soul obeys them—the interpretation of thy words enlightens and instructs the open-minded; and I am open, eager, panting for thy commands" (Ps. 119:129–131, Moffatt).

INVOCATION. Almighty God, we adore thee, we praise thee, we worship thee, we honor thee. Thou givest strength to the faith and hope to the weary. Thou art more than we can comprehend, yet so real that we could never deny thee. We honor thee with our worship and our praise.—E. Lee Phillips

OFFERTORY SENTENCE. "Take ye from among you an offering unto the Lord: whosoever is of a willing heart, let him bring it" (Exod. 35:5).

OFFERTORY PRAYER. Lord, you have been gracious to us. You have given to us out of your riches. Now we return to you for your use a portion of what we have received. As you have willingly blessed us, may we in this way joyously bless your holy name.

PRAYER. Eternal God, Who hast revealed Thyself to the ever-changing lives of men in a Word that stands fast forever, speak now to our hearts as we wait upon Thee. Remind us of all Thy mercies, which have shone forth Thy love in the past, and in that love make us, on the holy ground of each present day, steadfast and very sure. Keep us, we pray Thee, from thinking too poorly of ourselves whom Thou dost honor with Thy care and tenderness. Fit us for the full stature that is ours, whatever be our lot, by cleansing us from all sin. Hold steadily before our eyes that pure will of Thine for us until we learn to choose it above all wealth and the esteem of men. Make our timorous faith more sure, and our high if bewildered loyalties firm. Hearten us by Thine own undiscouraged presence here in the place whereon we stand: and in Thy word, by which the heavens and the earth are held in store, bring us to find joy for our sorrow, strength for our weaknesses, and hope again for all the hopes we have lost; through Jesus Christ, our Lord and Saviour.–Paul Scherer

LECTIONARY MESSAGE

Topic: The Prayer Requests of Jesus
TEXT: John 17:6–19
Other Readings: Acts 1:15–17, 21–26; Psalm 1; 1 John 5:19–13

"Our Father in Heaven" introduces what is commonly called "The Lord's Prayer"; it was given as a pattern for prayers. According to Luke 6:9, the prayer in John 17 is truly the personal prayer of Jesus. In it he reveals the deepest desires and concerns of his heart. It is not unlike a pastoral prayer, since it was prayed aloud so that his little flock could hear. They would always remember how he consecrated himself in preparation for Calvary. It was a prayer offered between heaven and earth, for the Savior's mind was already contemplating his return to the Father: "I am coming to you now" (v. 13).

The value of prayer may be pointed out by asking, Why did Jesus pray? He was divine. John claimed throughout his Gospel that Jesus was the "I Am" (the Light, the Water of Life, the Way, the Truth, the true Bread from heaven, the Door, the Shepherd, etc.). It would be assumed that no one so great need pray. The life of Jesus indicates that prayer was essential for him. Then how much more do we the weaker need to pray. *Communication* and *intimacy* are hot words today. When two people are in a trust relationship they communicate their deepest feelings. They share their inmost thoughts. No one enjoyed the closeness with God more than Jesus. That closeness naturally erupted into conversation.

A second reason Jesus prayed was to show his gratitude to the Father for the favors granted to him. While the words *thanks, grateful,* or *appreciation* are not in the text, variations of the word *give* are many. Jesus wanted to acknowledge that all he had came from the generous heart of his father (vv. 2, 6, 7, and 8).

Have you ever asked, "What do you give the person who has everything?" What could the Father give to his Son, the heir of all things? Jesus was delighted that the Father had given him people. He was also thankful that he had been granted the power to change people's lives. He was empowered to bring people into tune with their Creator (vv. 2 and 6). This brought immense joy to Jesus. The gladness of the heart of Jesus was that eleven men understood (16:29–30 and 17:8). That these few caught on would seem meager to some, but to Jesus it was a miracle of revelation.

The communicator recognizes that the first part of the prayer is for Jesus himself and the last part is for us who have come to faith through the witness of the apostles. In the middle section, verses 6–19, we find Jesus asking the Father for help. He foresees the disciples' walking a "tight-rope." They are "in the world" (v. 14). Jesus knew that this was a precarious role for them. Society at enmity with the Father's plan would deny them, discourage them, and destroy them. Last year my wife and I visited a foreign country. It is perceived as a nation that is a friend of the United States. They certainly welcome the financial assistance and trade agreements with the United States. One afternoon I was standing on the corner of a busy street. I was wearing my San Francisco Giants ball cap. As I stood there relaxing, a carful of students drove by, and they shouted, "Get out of our country, go back to your home!" It wasn't that they knew me. It wasn't that I had ever done anything against them. But I represented a country that they resented. Jesus knew that his apostles would be persecuted for representing his right to rule in the hearts of people.

It is significant that Jesus did not pray for the world (v. 9) but for his agents in the world (v. 18). The eleven were his good news messengers to a bad news society. They were to be the Daniels of their day, that is, a foreigner bringing the light of the One God to a darkened land. The passion of Jesus was based on the protective care he had given the apostles the past three years. They were not aware of how he had fended off evil assaults. They had been like chicks gathered under his strong wing (v. 12). But his departure would remove the visible shield, and he interceded for the Father to protect them.

Not only did he pray for their protection, but for their sanctification (v. 17). Sometimes the word *sanctified* is presented in such a way that it scares the listeners. The hearers think that a religious fumigation will be required. They feel that all evil must be washed away. The basic idea to *sanctify* is to be set apart for a special task and to be by the word of God. Paul rated the reading, studying, and obedience to the word as the best way to be fully committed and equipped (2 Tim. 3:16). The companion lectionary text in Psalm 1 outlines this same thought; that is, the one who meditates and keeps the law of God will be fruitful and favored.

Notice that Jesus prays with faith. He recognizes that his eleven will succeed (v. 20). They will be kept, and they will be productive. He had already prayed that these unschooled followers would become the best thing ever to happen to the world.

It is always helpful to us to know that Jesus prays for us. This prayer is an example of the intercession that Jesus makes for his people. He prayed that we would be protected, committed, and productive (Hebrews 7:25), "because he always lives to intercede for them."–James Lemuel Higgs

SUNDAY: MAY EIGHTEENTH

SERVICE OF WORSHIP

Sermon: Exit Here

TEXT: John 14:1–4, 15–27

The message of John 14 has found a classic application in the Christian funeral: "Do not let your hearts be troubled"–words of hope in the face of despair, a message of strength to people who have been run over by death and life. When we are thrust suddenly into the maze of grief, we search desperately for a way out. We seek help from professionals in counseling, who bring to our ignorance insight into human behavior and provide a mirror of self-understanding. We ask Job's question with a new urgency: "If a man dies, shall he live again?" We search desperately for maps through the jungle with specific directions on where to turn, how to act, and what to do. We naturally seek out others who have walked our path or who are fellow pilgrims in the journey of grief. We reach for palliative treatment. Some medicine is not designed to heal. Sometimes we hear the word of comfort from Jesus as just another soothing balm for our fragmented spirits.

On Pentecost we are here to declare that the gospel is more than an anesthetic for pain. The Spirit of God promised by the Christ is the presence of God for our loneliness, hope for our despair, peace for our distress, integrity for our fragmented souls, and the unity of the body of Christ for scattered individuals in the church.

I. *Easter is fulfilled at Pentecost.* Fred Craddock proclaimed, "Easter is completed at Pentecost. Without Pentecost, Easter means the departure of Christ, leaving behind the confused and uncertain disciples who can do no better than return to fishing." John alone reports the message of preparation for Jesus' departure that culminates in the cross and resurrection of Christ. At least three generations separate Easter from the writing of the Gospel of John. Paralysis had closed in on some Christians. The hope for an immediate return of Christ was fading. Christians were still trapped in a maze of grief, searching desperately for the door leading out and on with life. The Church was coming to realize that the resurrection of Christ was not a return to life as it had once been. Easter did not undo the cross. Christians needed to hear a new word of encouragement from Christ to get on with life, to keep on toward the Kingdom that Christ proclaimed.

Mark's Gospel takes us closer to the historical reality of the man Jesus than John. Mark paints, in simple, clear strokes, a portrait of Jesus in the flesh. The Jesus we meet in John is a transcendent, heavenly Christ. We are more likely to see visions than to smell campfires, but John is a bridge to our time and need. We live closer to Pentecost than to Easter. The watershed is portrayed in Acts as the disciples gathered with a backward gaze, "Is this the time when you will restore the kingdom to Israel?" Jesus turns the vision forward to Pentecost. The word is onward—to Jerusalem, Judea, Samaria, and to the ends of the earth.

II. *Life goes on.* The classical application of Christ's words of comfort to our experience of loss is valid. The eternal hope of Christians does not erase the fact of separation. With the death of Jesus, like the death of your friend or beloved, everything changes. We can never go back to life as it was and recover days of being together like those we once knew and accepted as normal. Separation in death was a hard reality even for disciples of the risen Christ. In grief we often long for contact with our departed companions. The need of communion exploited by spiritualists and entrepreneurs was answered in Christian history by the doctrine of the communion of the saints. Even if we could call up the spirits of the dead, would this be enough? The resurrection appearances of Jesus were brief and scattered, limited to a few days after his death. A false hope developed that the return of Christ was imminent, that the way out was in, that the way forward was backward. The return of Christ was often misconstrued as the return of the good old days of yore. John's Gospel came late enough to offer a corrective for Christians of the first century and for people like us who continue to stand gazing into space waiting for the calendar to reverse.

The resurrection of Christ is without question the central event of the New Testament, but the gospel does not stop on Easter morning. Neither should we. To believe in eternal life through the God who raised up Christ is the basis of the Christian hope, but it is not enough. Like the Christians of the first century, we want an immediate fulfillment of the ultimate hope. We need to hear the command of Christ to go on and the promise of the Spirit to lead us. I began to defy the rules of safety and gravity as a teenager, leaping over as many steps as possible in ascending or descending any stair-

case. Seven-inch steps were too slow and tedious for my impatience to get to the landing. They get more reasonable every day. The kingdom comes by careful steps taken at the right time and level. Neither early nor later Christians can skip to the top. The living Christ who was known in the breaking of bread and perceived in the gathering of disciples continues to abide with his church in the Spirit.

III. *Christ abides in the Spirit.* The agony of slavery in America was more than the physical abuse of hard labor and the dehumanizing experience of becoming property. A song from the heart of slavery expresses the sense of abandonment that Christ addressed, "Sometimes I feel like a motherless child a long way from home." Christ detected the disciples' fear as he promised, "I will not leave you orphaned." The eternal Spirit of God abides with us. This is not a new idea, certainly not a different God. The Spirit of God was not created, invented, or discovered after Easter. Jesus charged Nicodemus to be born of the Spirit and advised the Samaritan woman, "God is spirit." The Spirit of God descended, affirming Jesus at his baptism. In the beginning, the Spirit of God was the dynamic presence of God brooding over the waters of chaos creating light and life, and God who is spirit breathed (spirited) life into the man. The same God who was present with us in Jesus continues to be present among us. The same God who breathed life into your beloved, who was the source of daily wisdom and strength, who was the bond of unity between you, continues to be your source of strength to continue with life.

The word of Christ for the epoch of separation and the maze of grief is, "Exit here!" You can wander endlessly in the wilderness, longing for life to return to the way it was, or you can follow Christ on the way out of the darkness. The truth is, nothing remains constant in life, but God abides. The alpha and omega, the beginning and end, is our constant in the chaos of change. The promise of Christ to all who wander through the corridors of grief is that the Spirit of God is with you forever: "You know him, because he abides with you, and he will be in you."—Larry Dipboye

Illustrations

WHAT IS GOD LIKE? Jesus is the final and supreme revelation of God, because Jesus Christ is God is human flesh. "He that hath seen the Father." When you read the four Gospels and watch Jesus Christ in his life on earth, you are seeing a revelation of what God is like. He takes up a little child in His arms. He stops to listen to the needs of a beggar. He heals the sick. He forgives the sinful. He attends a wedding feast. He goes to a house where death has come and brings comfort. This is God: helping people like us to carry the burdens of life.—Warren W. Wiersbe

CONFLICT AND WORRY. When Paul was confronted with an ugly situation of hostility and divisions in First Church Corinth, he could have responded in a variety of ways. He could have told the Corinthians, "Obey your leaders. Do what they tell you to do and stop all this bickering." Or he could have said, "People like you are a disgrace to the church and ought to burn in hell because of your pettiness."

Instead, Paul decided to pick up on the images of baptism as grafting onto a body, in the same way that a tree may be grafted in order to produce better fruit. He says, "For just as the body is one and has many members, and all the members of the body, though many, are one body, so it is with Christ. For by one Spirit we were all baptized into one body—Jews or Greeks, slaves or free—and all were made to drink of one Spirit" (1 Cor. 12:12–13).—William H. Willimon

SERMON SUGGESTIONS

Topic: Zion's Joy and God's
Text: Zeph. 3:14, 17
(1) God's joy over Zion. (2) Zion's joy in God.—Alexander Maclaren

Topic: With Christ as Head of the Church
Text: Col. 1:18
The church will (1) Have his spirit; (2) Seek to know his will; (3) Obey him; (4) Coordinate its actions; (5) Express itself in individual as well as corporate devotion.

Worship Aids

CALL TO WORSHIP. "The Lord is my strength and my shield; my heart trusted in him, and I am helped; therefore my heart greatly rejoiceth; and with my song will I praise him" (Ps. 28:7).

INVOCATION. How can we enter into your presence, Father? We are so small and you are so great. We are such sinners and you are sinless perfection. We are so limited and you are infinite. Our knowledge is so little and yours is eternal. Yet we come because we have need to link our lives with everlasting greatness, discover limitless power, and experience undying love. Meet us in this sacred place today. Stir our hearts with the presence of your holy spirit. Whisper the wonder of forgiveness to us anew. Call the unsaved with words of power and grace, and prepare us to be deliverers of your truth to those in our homes, in our schools, in our work, in our community, and to the uttermost parts of the world. Set our hearts afire with the desire to tell the wonders of Christ.—Henry Fields

OFFERTORY SENTENCE. "Set your affection on things above, not on things on the earth" (Col. 3:2).

OFFERTORY PRAYER. Because we love you, O Lord, we now bring to you these offerings. May our love for you never wane.

PRAYER. Father, as on that first Pentecost you made possible the coming together of all believers as one body, working together to accomplish the purposes of the church, so bring us together in these days. Give us the desire and courage to unite behind the decisions of the church that through what we do we may glorify your name and prepare the way for future generations to know, serve, and praise you. Now we ask that you refresh our faith, renew our vision, rekindle our courage, and as we are blessed by your spirit, lead us to build your church.—Henry Fields

LECTIONARY MESSAGE

Topic: (Pentecost): The Power Source of the Church

TEXT: John 15:26–16:16

Other Readings: Ezek. 37:1–14 or Acts 2:1–21; Ps. 104:24–34, 35b; Rom. 8:22–27.

"What will happen to the Billy Graham Association when Dr. Graham dies?" He is known around the world. His personal magnitude and his spiritual depth have created a following that few personalities have enjoyed. Who could possibly duplicate that leadership?

On a greater scale Jesus faced this problem as his death and return to heaven drew near. He tried to discuss this matter with his twelve followers, but they were preoccupied with their own welfare. "What's going to happen to us?" (John 16:5–6).

Like a dying mother with small children trying to prepare them for her death, Jesus tenderly showed his followers what would happen to them after he returned to heaven. Jesus wanted them to know that their anxiety about the future was unwarranted. His departure was for their good (16:7a). It would benefit them, him, and us. They were to face extreme persecution (16:1–3). He wanted them to be aware that it would not be easy. He didn't want them to be surprised. The book of Acts certified this prediction. Like small children they were unaware of the evil directed toward them during those past three years. Jesus had shielded them. He had stood between them and evil (16:4). But now they needed to know that they would be looked upon as foreigners (15:9). Their opponents would not need a reason to hate them. But they would be assigned a defender (14:16–18). The Holy Spirit would be their strengthener, a heavenly legal assistant. The Holy Spirit would also give them the emotional courage and the divine arguments to withstand the opposition.

Then Jesus showed them that his departure would be good for Him. He would rejoin the Father and have the glory he had enjoyed before he came to earth (John 17:5). He would undertake the role of praying for His followers (1 John 2:1).

Another major desire of Jesus was to reach the people of the world with the message of his death, his resurrection, and his return. He planned to do this through his witnesses (Acts 1:8). It was through the lives of the apostles that the Spirit would challenge the ideas of an unbelieving world (16:8). The Holy Spirit would serve in this capacity as a prosecuting attorney through his followers. The areas of accusation would be their viewpoint of sin (16:9). The sin under consideration is the worst sin, the unforgivable sin, that is, unbelief in Jesus, God's offering for sin (John 3:18–21). Then there was the issue of righteousness (v. 10). It is not unrighteousness that the Spirit uncovers, but righteousness: first, to show that a righteousness accepted by a Holy God is available, and then to show that it is only available in him who has gone to the Father (see Phil. 3:9). The remaining indictment is judgment. This charge of the Holy Spirit discredits the idea that a loving God will not hold people accountable. Jesus said that the ruler of evil has been judged (v. 11 and 12:31). Upon the return of Jesus, the Devil will receive the final sentence.

The coming of the Holy Spirit enabled the apostles to carry out their commission to be witnesses of all the things they had seen and heard of Jesus. But today on Pentecost Sunday we need to know that we are greatly benefited. The exodus of Jesus was for our good (16:12–15). When you hold a Bible in your hand, you have one of the benefits of the Savior's departure. The article *the* in verse 13 does not appear in the NIV, but the RSV realized its value, "He will guide you into all the truth." I suggest that "the truth" means the whole body of New Testament revelation. In John 14:26 Jesus promised that the Holy Spirit would "remind you everything I have said to you." In addition he would reveal the things to come.

When the Holy Spirit came fully upon the apostles, they were empowered as convinced witnesses, and they powerfully confronted the world of unbelievers. They had phenomenal results. Acts 2:37 shows the incredible conviction that fell on the audience at Pentecost. The hearers cried out, "Brothers, what shall we do?" The Spirit became the prosecuting attorney, exposing, refuting, and convincing. The world may think that it is judging Christians, but it is the Christians who are passing judgment on the world as they witness to Jesus. The purpose is to bring salvation, not condemnation. The Holy Spirit is still wanting to indwell individuals who want to glorify God. When a person believes in Jesus as his or her One and Only Savior, that person has been the object of the convicting and converting power of the Holy Spirit. Then the Spirit wants to use that person's testimony and the Word of God to bring others to saving faith.

In 1989 the well-known California historian Kevin Starr brought an address to our church on our 140th anniversary. As he reviewed the beginnings of our church and traced its ups and downs, he concluded with words I shall never forget. He asked, "Do you know why the First Baptist Church of San Francisco is still here?" He then proceeded to answer his own question, "It isn't because of its buildings, its beautiful stained glass windows, its famous organ, its choir, or its preachers. There is only one reason: It's because of the Holy Spirit.–James Lemuel Higgs

SUNDAY: MAY TWENTY-FIFTH

SERVICE OF WORSHIP

Sermon: Counting God
TEXT: Rom. 8:1–11

At the ripe age of twenty-two, my first experience as a pastor was in a farming community a few miles from Dallas. When I arrived on the scene, Ewell was a deacon and teacher of the men's Bible class. After a tragic accident in a propane truck that took the life of his brother, Ewell adjusted his commitments in life and became a strong leader in our little church. He was a skilled carpenter. As we worked together on several projects around the church on Saturdays, our work chatter often revolved around faith issues. I still hold Ewell and his theology in the highest esteem. One day he told about his ordination service. The church had a visiting evangelist, a real fireball preacher who had stomped everyone's toes right up to their eyeballs. The last service of the revival was to be Ewell's ordination. Ewell gave his testimony and allowed that he wasn't educated and didn't know that Bible very well, but he loved the Lord and would do his best to be a good deacon. The evangelist then cross-examined the candidate before the congregation. His first question (or command) was, "Explain the Trinity!" Ewell replied that he didn't know that he could. He had never understood the Trinity, and if he did, he wasn't sure he could explain it. This humble response

evoked an angry lecture and rejection of the ordination. He called for the church to call the service to a halt. The church (all two families) decided that they had had enough. They proceeded with the ordination and sent the visiting preacher off to his mission of steam-cleaning the world. The pastor later reassured Ewell that the Trinity exceeded the mental grasp of most seminary professors and that he could be a Christian and a deacon without mastering this difficult theological question.

I. *Is the Trinity riddle or reality?* Is this the test of one's theological agility or a measure of one's ability to believe the incomprehensible? In 1963, Bishop John A. T. Robinson suggested the abandonment of much of our traditional language about God. He even suggested that we drop the word *God* until we have purged it of all misguided traditions. Bishop James Pike followed with the judgment that the Holy Trinity is an old bottle that is eventually going to burst and for which we should have no regrets. One searches in vain for the word *trinity* in the Bible, even in the New Testament passages that refer to the Three–Father, Son, and Spirit. Obviously the Old Testament contains no reference to the Three. The plurality of God at creation, "Let us make humankind in our image, according to our likeness," is just grammar, with no enumeration of deities, and certainly not a reflection of the Trinity. Historians generally agree that the Trinity did not become orthodox doctrine until the Council of Nicaea, A.D. 325. An exposition of the academic analysis of the creeds revolving around two Greek words might prove to be medically inadvisable on a hot summer day.

Maybe that is our problem. Although the Trinity is not a simple fact or an obvious biblical doctrine, it is not a ridiculous puzzle or a practical joke passed down from earlier Christian generations. Figures, word pictures, and mental images are necessary tools in the attempt to proclaim that God we cannot see, hear, or hold. The very instant we attempt to speak of Almighty God we are in over our heads. We might do well to adopt the humility of Augustine: "We do not speak to exhaust the mystery; we speak to keep from being silent." We can mentally reduce God to our level of comprehension, or we can recognize that true worship always reaches beyond our grasp. The focus of worship is always beyond what and who we are.

II. *We begin with mystery.* I have a confession. I have found myself forced to speak of the Trinity in my pastor's class with our children. It is with children that I most often find confusion with church language and the need to explain it. The Three—Father, Son, and Holy Spirit—are familiar to any child who has grown in the church, and sometimes we are guilty of dismissing children with a sweep of the hand as if God were obvious or perfectly understood by everyone else. Our children deserve adult companions in the struggle to know God. We may not come with simple explanations, and we should not substitute stork stories. To confess our limits is not only honest but helpful in accepting our difference from God.

The Trinity is about God's saving work. Paul draws from the deep well of Christian experience. God is not a thing to be managed or defined. We cannot describe God the way we describe a Tinkertoy or even a sunset. God is person, but not one of the boys. To simply describe the eternal God in human terms would be a major understatement. The Trinity emerges with a thousand years of experience. To begin at the beginning, God is Creator (Father) of all that is, the God of creation. The Jews probably knew God as Savior in the Exodus before they could imagine the enormous propor-

tions of creation. The Gospels declare that Jesus was a man sent by God to reveal the Father. We celebrate his coming in Advent and Christmas. He was Immanuel, "God with us." The clearest picture of God in all of human history is in the person of Christ. In Jesus we meet the mind of God. Jesus declared, "I and my Father are one." The God of Creation, who sent Jesus into our human world, is not only God over us. God is present and active in his world and abides with us in the Spirit: "If the Spirit of him who raised Jesus from the dead dwells in you, he who raised Christ from the dead will give life to your mortals' bodies also through his Spirit that dwells in you."

III. *God is known in community.* The Old Testament emerged in a polytheistic culture. The generic word for god *(Elohim)* is plural and could refer either to the God or the gods. For most of the Old Testament, multiple gods are not denied, but the exclusive worship of "Jahweh," God of the Jews, was the divine command. Isaiah could ridicule the process of manufacturing gods in a pagan world with the clear understanding that God has made us. Confession of the mystery of God is the beginning of wisdom. Leslie Weatherhead could even write about "the Christian agnostic" in humility about the nature of God. He commented on living near the sea and the mystery of the ocean. A beaker of water would reveal the chemical content, "But what can a beaker of saltwater tell me about what goes on the vast, silent depths of the ocean?" (p. 38).

Only as the New Testament unfolds with the focus of God in Christ and God present in the Spirit does the question of Trinity confront us. In our struggle with the mathematics of deity, we miss God altogether. Don't bother to count God. We do not discover, create, or otherwise invent God. God comes to us. The Bible describes a God who wants to be known, who reveals himself in our history, in our experience. Walter Brueggemann observed in Genesis that the human part of creation is in the image of God only in the plural of humankind. Only in relation with others does one express the creative grace of love. Because we do not live in a vacuum of isolation, we know God in the community of faith where God's love is.—Larry Dipboye

Illustrations

THE BETTER NEWS OF THE TRINITY. It is good news to learn that God is One. But as you see, there is still better news in the message that the One God is Father, Son, and Holy Spirit, when you really understand it. Of course to say merely "three in one and one in three"–that in itself means nothing. But when it comes at the end of the story, it tells you everything. It tells you of what God is, in His eternal and infinite love; and of what God does still today, dwelling with us as truly as He dwelt among men nineteen centuries ago, and the same forevermore. So to those who know the story, the doctrine of the Trinity sums up the whole gospel. And the Church never tires of singing in gratitude, "Glory be to the Father, and to the Son, and to the Holy Ghost: as it was in the beginning, is now, and ever shall be, world without end."–D. M. Baillie

MYSTERY AND FAITH. It is truth, rather than explanations of truths, by which we are saved. The bee does not analyze the flower, it extracts the sweetness. So do you. You do not say, "I will not touch a fragment of my dinner till I understand its chemical components"; you would, under such conditions, be liable to a prolonged and irritating fast. You are sustained by the food you do not comprehend. It may be even so with the religion of Christ. I know little of flowers botanically; their germs and their species often puzzle me, but I understand them sympathetically. So approach the Christian faith; though much of mystery be associated with it, bless its beauty, and revel in its fragrance. Accept great, reposeful truths, and be content to wait for full explanations. In religion "What?" is more important than "How?"–Dinsdale T. Young

SERMON SUGGESTIONS

Topic: Once Upon a Time in Damascus and Samaria

TEXT: 2 Kings 5:1–19

(1) There was a mighty general, who was stricken with leprosy. (2) There was a little Jewish maid, who knew her religion. (3) There was a foolish Israelite king, who forgot his God. (4) There was a wise prophet, who voiced the Word of God. (5) There were sensible heathen servants, who helped their foolish master. (6) There was that mighty general again, who now believed and confessed the true God.–R. C. H. Lenski

Topic: They Gird the Earth with Valor

TEXT: Matt. 28:16–20

The baptized have upon them the name of the triune God. (1) They proclaim a message of good news. (2) They fulfill a mission of universal scope. (3) They obey a mandate without alternative. (4) They receive a promise that makes the challenge both "doable" and rewarding.

Worship Aids

CALL TO WORSHIP. "While I live will I praise the Lord: I will sing praises unto my God while I have any being" (Ps. 146:2).

INVOCATION. Lord, we know in quietness and confidence is our strength, in prayer and praise is our refreshment, in singing and giving is our joy. Lead this service to be all it can be through the Spirit and the Son.–E. Lee Phillips

OFFERTORY SENTENCE. "It is required in stewards, that a man be found faithful" (1 Cor. 4:2).

OFFERTORY PRAYER. Lord, watch over what we bring, us who bring it, and those who receive it, that God might be glorified and the cross of Christ uplifted.–E. Lee Phillips

PRAYER. O Lord, our God, Creator of heaven and earth, through whom we enjoy the privileges of humanity and the joys of salvation, all praise and glory to your being: regnant in holiness, clothed in mystery, wrapped in light ineffable and love untainted.

Forgive us for being so caught up in the pull of our times that we are more affixed to things than principles and the superficial than the profound. Pardon us that the allure of false gods is not unknown to us, that often we are so divided in our priorities that what matters most often receives our least attention. The poor and disfranchised, the grief-stricken and depressed, the spiritually empty and sincerely deceived are all about us, and we have done so little.

Call us back from our wandering by that Light emanating from Calvary, which dispels every darkness, enabling the weak and enabling the faithful through the power of the Holy Spirit.

We are thankful this day for loved ones in our past who shaped and cared for us, who saw to it that we found our way to God and knew the rudiments of righteous living.

Teach us to pray, that the effectual fervent prayers of righteous persons may avail much. Teach us to share, so that the best we know may enrich a new generation that will need all the wisdom they can get. Teach us to love until all littleness of spirit is changed into practical deeds of peace and justice and reconciliation. Commune with us when we beseech you and seek you and desire to be with you, to learn your precepts, obey your counsel, and rest in your peace.

And come to us when we are not thinking of you and have failed to ask you in and gone our own way, that the chastisements of your love, and the directives of your Word, and the undauntable tug of your compassion may bring us around.—E. Lee Phillips

LECTIONARY MESSAGE

Topic: The Mystery of Grace

TEXT: John 3:1–17

Other Readings: Isa. 6:1–8; Ps. 29; Rom. 8:12–17

Our purpose here is to sketch an overview that will serve to "prime the pump" as you prepare to preach from this intriguing question-and-answer period that Jesus hosted from one Nicodemus, "a ruler of the Jews." This Fourth Gospel is interpreted by many present-day Bible scholars as "a book of the Church." There is no doubt that John's record bears the imprint of how the early church saw Jesus of Nazareth. This incident is found only in John's Gospel.

Nicodemus's queries were not mere rhetorical questions but the crying out of the soul for life—for the something more that people were discovering in the young rabbi

—"The people heard him gladly for he spoke as one having authority." The authority of the Law was paling in the presence of the strange God of grace that the young Nazarene was proclaiming and demonstrating—not only to Jews but wherever there was need that caught his attention.

For many the Gospel reaches its climax in verses 16 and 17. All that has come before is a prologue, and all that follows is but commentary on this great theme: "God so loved the world that he gave his only Son . . ." As so decisively enunciated in these verses, God's love is of such a nature, so great, that he wills life not death for all who believe in his Son. Not for the world's condemnation, but for its life, salvation, God gives to the uttermost.

In verse 2 it is noted that Nicodemus was a nocturnal visitor. Perhaps more has been made of this fact than the reporting warrants. However, it should be noted that in 19:39, where Nicodemus reappears as one concerned for the proper burial of Jesus, he *is* identified as "who first came to Jesus by night." The assumption through the ages of his nocturnal inquiry is that Nicodemus feared the ridicule of his compatriots, or perhaps, even more serious, his position of leadership among them.

For the writer of the Fourth Gospel, "night" may symbolize the darkness of the intelligentsia, especially their literalism. Such possibility of interpretation is in keeping with John's portrayal of the Messiah's appearance as "light shining in darkness." Nicodemus is very much "in the dark" when it comes to comprehending the true nature of Jesus' mission.

There is no indication that Nicodemus was other than an earnest inquirer, deliberate and honest in his questioning, and not one seeking to subvert the young teacher's ministry, as some Pharisees were prone to do. He was not argumentative, but conscientiously seeking the wisdom of the young rabbi as to the meaning of it all.

It is interesting that Nicodemus's encounter is without locale, but at its conclusion Jesus and his disciples are reported as going "into the land of Judea" (v. 22).

In this encounter do we not learn that the light by which some see, blinds others who are not ready to receive—to stretch the imagination—to grasp the radical dimension of Jesus' teaching? These blind are so often among the learned. And Nicodemus, in one way or another, represents the intelligentsia—those who are not willing to enter the Kingdom themselves and are a stumbling block to those who want to.

The metaphorical interpretation seems so in keeping with the nature of John's writing—more mythical than literal, more philosophical than historical, universal rather than Jewish. In Nicodemus's reluctance—slowness of heart, dull-mindedness—are we not confronted with our own infidelity?

This story has haunted the Church for nearly twenty centuries, and *we* still don't know what to make of it as we seek to fathom its depths and scale the heights of its profundity. Its obscurity, perhaps, speaks of the mystery of the grace by which God saves us. Until we realize that grace is not a riddle to be solved but a gift to be received, we, too, live in the darkness that Nicodemus confesses, "How *can* these things be?"—John Thompson

SUNDAY: JUNE FIRST

SERVICE OF WORSHIP

Sermon: The Cross As a Crown

TEXT: John 12:20–36

The cross is the central symbol of Christianity. It is a startling symbol when one realizes that the cross was an ugly and tortuous means of execution. The Romans chose this method and used it as their way to punish criminals, runaway slaves, and rebels. Jesus met his death in this cruel manner, his crucifixion becoming even more horrible in the eyes of Jewish people because of an ancient teaching found in the law of Moses. That teaching said, "Anyone hung on a tree is under God's curse."

The Roman practice of crucifixion that Jesus endured began with scourging, or flogging with a whip. The condemned person then was forced to carry his own cross to the place of execution, usually outside the city but in a conspicuous place set apart for that purpose. Before being nailed to the cross, the condemned was offered a medicated cup of vinegar as a kind of anesthetic to ease the subsequent pain. Ordinarily, to hasten death, Roman soldiers would break the legs of those hanging on the crosses. Jesus was spared that indignity because death came quickly for him. His side was pierced by a soldier's spear, however, in proof of his death. A flow of blood and water from that wound suggests that Jesus literally died of a broken heart—a ruptured heart. By any measure or description, dying on a cross was a gruesome and awful thing. Yet that cross has become the central symbol of Christianity.

It was not always so. Jesus' disciples and the growing company of early Christians felt revulsion when considering this device. They would not be found wearing crosses as pendants or placing them in their centers of worship. The apostle Paul, it is true, developed some positive interpretations of the cross, speaking of its power as well as of its challenge to a skeptical world. But the New Testament also speaks of the shame of the cross, a shame Jesus endured for the sake of others.

I. What Kind of Symbol?

It remained for nearly three hundred years to pass before the cross came into use as the chief emblem of Christianity. The Emperor Constantine caused it to happen. According to tradition, on the eve of a crucial battle Constantine saw a flaming cross in the heavens bearing a Latin inscription that said, *In hoc signo vinces.* Those words mean, "By this sign thou shalt conquer." The tradition goes on to say that the very next night Jesus himself appeared in a vision. He ordered Constantine to take for his standard the sign of the cross. The emperor, only recently converted to Christianity, at once ordered a new standard to be crafted and carried by the Roman legions. This Labarum, as it was called, remained the sign or emblem of the Roman army until the downfall of the Western Empire in 476 A.D. The Labarum was made like a banner bearing an embroidered monogram of the first two Greek letters of the title Christos. Those letters, the chi and the rho, when superimposed one over the other, give the appearance of a cross. From that usage as a military insignia, other usages followed. The cross in various designs came to symbolize Christianity, and that still is common practice, to this day.

Constantine did Christianity no favor, however, in elevating the cross as a sign of conquest. What originally was an evidence of surrender and sacrifice suddenly was turned into one of triumphalist religion. "By this sign conquer," shouted the emperor to his troops. And for all the later centuries, people and nations have trumpeted the same. The Crusades of the Middle Ages sought to purge Europe of non-Christian religions and to do so by battle if necessary. Nineteenth-century imperialism carried forward some of the same sentiment, conquering in the name of Christ. The cross, sadly, has been used to bludgeon non-Christians. It happens in our own time when the so-called religious Right seeks to impose its particular agenda upon all of us as the law of the land. As I say, Constantine did Christianity no favor when he envisioned the cross as a symbol of conquering might.

Surrender and sacrifice are the true meanings of the cross; that is what Jesus represented as he hung there. Surrender was real as Jesus relinquished his own desires, his own will, for what he believed was the will of God. At the time of his arrest in the Garden of Gethsemane Jesus struggled with the impulse for self-preservation versus his calling from God to demonstrate saving, redeeming love by offering up his life. Agitated and in deep distress, Jesus prayed that the ordeal of suffering he knew was awaiting him might pass. "Father," he prayed, "for you all things are possible; remove this cup from me; yet not what I want, but what you want." That prayer was repeated, leading at last to Jesus' acceptance of the worst that his enemies could inflict. From Gethsemane to Calvary—from the garden of prayer to the hill of crucifixion—Jesus' experience of surrender proved real.

Sacrifice, the other meaning of the cross, was explained by Jesus to his followers at an earlier time when he said, "No one has greater love than this, to lay down one's life for one's friends." Jesus indicated that he voluntarily would die, as evidence of love and as proof of God's desire to draw all people to himself and a testimony to the need and power of forgiveness for humanity's sins. The apostle Paul reflected on Jesus' sacrifice by saying, "While we were still weak, at the right time, Christ died for the ungodly, indeed, rarely will anyone die for a righteous person—though perhaps for a good person someone might actually dare to die. But God proves his love for us in that while we were still sinners Christ died for us." Paul affirmed that this action made reconciliation possible, reconciliation between human beings and God. It was as if Jesus from the cross connected earth and heaven, taking the hands of his human friends and placing them in the hands of God. He sacrificed himself for this blessed union.

II. A Glorious Fulfillment

In contemporary terms, the cross still means surrender and sacrifice. It decidedly does not mean conquest, although, yes, there is victory associated with it. The cross led to the glory of Resurrection, a crown of glory—for Jesus and for all creation. That became a victory, in the sense of fulfillment. God fulfilled his intended purpose through Jesus' death and resurrection. But those steps of surrender and sacrifice lay behind that fulfillment. When understood in this way, the cross as the central symbol of Christianity becomes extremely significant for us today.

We are able to say and sing with John Bowring, "In the cross of Christ I glory . . ." Or we resonate with the words of another hymn: "Upon that cross of Jesus,/Mine eyes at times can see/The very dying form of One/Who suffered there for me;/And from my stricken heart with tears/Two wonders I confess:/The wonders of redeeming love/And my unworthiness."

These affirmations become the part of personal faith; accordingly, the cross takes its preeminent place in our spiritual lives. We may decide to wear it, to wear the cross as a visible reminder. It becomes a reminder that we are to bear its meanings in everyday affairs. For us, the cross calls us first to surrender, to surrender our own agenda, our own ambitions, our own will to the will of God. Then it calls us to sacrifice, to offer personal sacrifices of love and service in behalf of others. "Who gives all," wrote the poet, "and gives with spirit willing. . . . Shall find in sacrifice supreme delight." Contemplation of the cross leads to that glad result; sacrifices of our love and service become, for us, crowns of glory. The cross anticipates a crown as we strive to bear its meanings of surrender and sacrifice in daily life.

With the writer George MacLeod, we can say in conclusion that "the cross needs to be raised again at the center of the market place as well as on the steeple of the church." This spokesman continues by saying, "Christ was not crucified in a cathedral between two candles but on a cross between two thieves; on the town garbage heap; at a crossroads so cosmopolitan that they had to write his title in Hebrew and in Latin and in Greek . . . at the kind of place where cynics talk smut, and thieves curse, and soldiers gamble. . . . That is where he died. And that is what he died about." It was a violent, wrenching death. But it heralded a radiance, a peace, a joy that through all time and eternity abide.

The cross remains central to your Christian experience, and mine.—John H. Townsend

Illustrations

ARE PREACHERS COWARDS? As a young preacher I thought that there weren't more prophets in pulpits because preachers were cowards. The way I figured it, preachers were afraid to speak out for fear that they would lose their jobs. Later, I came to see that this was not so. What keeps preachers from speaking the truth, the reason we often take the safe way out and make it all sound sweeter and easier than it is on Sunday morning, is that we have come to love these people we serve. It is tough to say unpleasant things to people we have grown to love.

So congregations must be warned against the homiletical tendency to divorce Sunday morning from Monday morning, our terrible need to tie it all up with a neat bow and make it all appear easier, less challenging, less demanding, less open-ended than the gospel really is.—William H. Willimon

INFLUENCE.   Genuine goodness is often contagious. We recall that scene in *Tom Brown's School Days*. There had come to Rugby a small boy whose name was Arthur. He was a slender little chap, who would not make much of a showing on the football field. He went around the first day very much overawed by the other boys. It was a new experience for him, because he had been delicately reared. But when he was ready for bed, he dropped down upon his knees and said his prayers, as he had been taught to do. Instead of jeers of laughter, or shoes thrown at him, as he had feared, there came a hush over the whole room. There was a feeling of respect for the young chap who had the moral courage to be true to his own sense of right. And before the week was gone, all but three or four of the entire group were doing the same thing, as they had wanted to do all along. They too knelt before their Maker, to thank him for the blessing they had received during the day, and to ask for strength to run straight the next day.—Charles R. Brown

SERMON SUGGESTIONS

Topic: Fresh Every Morning
    TEXT: Exod. 16:19–20

(1) People seek protection against the future. (2) Physical security does not settle the main problem. (3) The important things cannot be gathered in advance. (4) God provides for us daily.—Gerald Kennedy

Topic: Right or Wrong
    TEXT: 1 Thess. 5:21–22. In trying to tell right from wrong, (1) We have to begin with God. (2) Then we can apply some simple tests: (a) What does conscience say? (b) What does the Bible say? (c) What do mature, clear-thinking Christians say? (d) What

will be the consequences to others, to one-self, to the purpose of God as we know it?

Worship Aids

CALL TO WORSHIP.   "From the rising of the sun unto the going down on the same the Lord's name is to be praised" (Ps. 113:3).

INVOCATION.   Holy, holy, holy, Lord God of Hosts. Speak to us here in this place filled with bright memories, holy commit-ments, and deep resolves, now as we pray and wait.–E. Lee Phillips

OFFERTORY SENTENCE.   "The Lord is good to all; and his tender mercies are over all his works" (Ps. 145:9).

OFFERTORY PRAYER.   Father, receive and bless the offerings of our prayers, our praise, our obedience, and our material sub-stance. You have made all of them possible. Magnify them now and in the good works of tomorrow, to the end that your name may be glorified throughout the world.

PRAYER.   O God, who gives life to the world; who breathed your spirit into man and woman, created them in your own image, and made them living souls: we thank you for the life you give, for the signs of life all around us. Were it not for you, O God, there would be no life in the plant world or the animal world. Because you continue to serve as the great life source, we enjoy fruits and vegetables, milk and cheese, eggs and ice cream, and all the good things we often take for granted.

We thank you for the life you give us. Help us to use that life, O God, in a way that is pleasing to you. Enable us to discover the gifts and talents you have placed within us; direct us in putting those gifts to work in the work of the church and for the good of the community.

We pray for those persons whose lives are not what they should be. We intercede for those whose bodies are plagued with illness

or incurable disease. We pray for those who have lost hope. And we pray for those per-sons–both women and children–who are victims of domestic violence, those persons who fear constant threats, injury, abuse, or perhaps desertion from those of their own household. Where there is pain, sadness, anger, and confusion, bring your healing, O God. May your goodness and mercy follow each of these all the days of their lives.– Randy Hammer

LECTIONARY MESSAGE

Topic: The Greater Issues
    TEXT: Mark 2:23–3:6
    Other Readings: 1 Sam. 3:1–10 (11–20); Ps. 139:1–6, 13–18; 2 Cor. 4:5–12
    The Gospel lesson includes two incidents in which Jesus and his followers are accused of violating the Sabbath. The first is a dese-cration by the disciples; the second is by the Master–healing on the Sabbath. They vio-late the Sabbath, for both actions are con-sidered "work" according to ceremonial law. Actually, these incidents conclude a compilation of a series of conflicts between Jesus and the religious leaders of the day.
    Mark 2:23–28 is the account of the disci-ples plucking grain on the Sabbath. As is true of the other incidents compiled in this conflict section, the locale or time is not noted.
    There is no objection to the disciples tak-ing the grain along the way and husking it by rubbing it between their hands and eat-ing. Actually, such is permitted, as noted in Deut. 23:25, and is quite characteristic of the humanitarian legislation found in this book.
    The controversy is provoked by the tim-ing; it was work and thus violated the fourth commandment. Two other actions of the dis-ciples aroused the ire of the scribes and Pharisees: their failure to fast and their eat-ing with unwashed hands. In all three of these instances, Jesus defended his followers.
    Evidently the disciples as a whole were members of the "people of the land," who did not adhere strictly to the ceremonial law.
    Although the incident is not dated, the fact that the grain was ripe indicates that it was about the time of the Passover. These

data are helpful in determining the chronology of the life of Jesus. This episode probably took place about a year before his final days in Jerusalem.

As recorded in verse 24, the Pharisees are eager to make a public example of these Sabbath-violators and discredit their leader.

In verses 25 and 26 Jesus defends the action of his followers by reference to no less than King David, who, when fleeing from Saul, took holy bread, "the bread of the Presence," eating it himself and sharing it with his bodyguard. According to the law, only priests were permitted to partake of this holy bread.

The reference here to the priest as "Abiathar" is incorrect and is probably a textual corruption. Matthew and Luke closely follow Mark's wording of this incident, but neither has the name of the priest. As read in 1 Sam. 21:1–7, the priest was Ahimelech.

It is more than interesting that Jesus raises no protest to say that the action of his followers was not work. He granted that they had violated the Sabbath, but under certain circumstances such violations were justifiable, per the example of David. The rabbinic teaching on this matter, with which Jesus was no doubt familiar, justified the suspension of the Torah when life was endangered—"the laws were given that men might live by them and not die by them." Although Jesus' view was in line with contemporary rabbinic teaching that ritual laws were subject to human needs, he went much further in application—in fact, so far as to give a new and independent teaching.

As recorded in verse 28, Jesus uses this incident as the backdrop for enunciating a universal principle—the Sabbath is made for man and not man for the Sabbath. The only justification for laws and institutions is that they serve human needs.

The phrase "son of man" in verse 28 presents some difficulty in interpretation, but Bible scholars seem to agree that this is a mistranslation of the Arabic idiom that meant simply "man." The meaning then is not that Jesus claimed a personal authority over the Sabbath but "that man is lord even over the Sabbath."

The chapter division here is not helpful, for the incident of Jesus' healing on the Sabbath is the fifth and the last of the conflict episodes in this series. As true of the previous incidents, the matter of time and place are not mentioned, so this healing is related to the preceding stories only in subject.

Healing was legally treated as work and was therefore prohibited on the Sabbath. There were several occasions when Jesus thus violated the Sabbath; Luke records two others—Luke 13:10f. and 14:1f.

We may well ask a question: What was the purpose of the Pharisees at this juncture in the ministry of the young Nazarene—to destroy him or merely ridicule him before the populace? According to the older law, a violator of the Sabbath was subject to the death penalty (see Exod. 31:14 and 35:2). If this was the intent of the accusers, they were foiled, for the authorities did nothing. And it was not for violating the Sabbath that Jesus was finally arrested and tried. Their purpose was more likely to prove Jesus a false prophet and deceiver of the people by pointing to his deliberate disregard for the Torah.

In the text, the discussion as to whether the act should be done precedes the cure, but in two instances of healing on the Sabbath in Luke's Gospel, the disputation follows, which seems more natural. But literal accuracy is beside the point.

In the defense of his act Jesus does not argue as to whether healing is "work" but accepts the protest of the Pharisees as legitimate in keeping the current ceremonial law. But he uses the occasion to raise a much greater issue: Is it right or wrong to do good on the Sabbath?

Verse 6 is the conclusion not only to this incident but to the whole series of conflict narratives in 2:1–3:6.

That opposition to Jesus and his ministry is snowballing is noted in that strange bedfellows are beginning to forget their differences and collaborate for his demise.—John Thompson

SUNDAY: JUNE EIGHTH

SERVICE OF WORSHIP

Sermon: Going Both Miles of the Christian Life

TEXT: Matt. 5:38–48 RSV

Nestled in a memorable list of pungent commands by Jesus is this one small sentence, which has stirred the imagination and imitation of untold human beings across the centuries: "If any one forces you to go one mile, go with him two miles" (v. 41). Many people have been so struck by what Jesus said that they have felt this concept uniquely sums up the Christian way of life. I invite you to take a hard look with me at this verse and at our religious mileage charts. I find that my chart has a habit of becoming distorted.

I. The First Mile of Obligation

a. For one thing, I find I must be careful to walk the first mile in the Christian life before I attempt to walk the second. That may sound strange, but how tempting it can be to leapfrog the first mile of obligation to get to the second mile of opportunity. How attractive it can be to get to the extraordinary before we've been faithful in the ordinary.

Why would a person be tempted to bypass the first mile? Frankly, you can get tired on it. It can seem tedious. Seldom are people applauded for walking that mile of obligation. But wouldn't the church move closer to God's purpose if we Christians deferred the idealism of the second mile until we pursued the hard realities of the first mile? Consider that proposition in relation to ordinary areas of life.

b. For instance, in the home, our responsibility as parents and children is not something extraordinary. Nothing is quite as hollow as the family member who accuses other family members of ingratitude. This may be the parent who says, "Just look how much we sacrifice for you!" The obvious retort is, What are parents for? Our children did not ask to be born. We brought them into the world. We have basic obligations to them.

Likewise, the child is truly impoverished who whines, "Just look how much my friends have that I don't get!" Commitment to the welfare of your family is a first mile of the Christian life.

Consider the first mile in another area: simple integrity in daily work. An office manager complained that a Christian employee spent too much time during business hours telephoning and writing letters about church matters. Being a bit of a cynic, the manager said, "You Christians might be more honest if you were less religious and gave a fair day's work for a fair day's pay."

There's no doubt that Jesus called us to the second mile, but not before we have walked the first mile. Check up on yourself. Is it tempting to leapfrog the mile of obligation to get to the mile of opportunity?

II. The Second Mile of Opportunity

a. But there's a second possible pitfall in responding to Jesus' challenge. It is to assume that we ourselves can accomplish the second mile he talked about. It is enjoyable to go further and to do more for people–if they respond positively. It can be greatly rewarding to do acts of kindness–for people who appreciate them. We all like that kind of affirmation.

But look with me at the context of our Scripture. Jesus was not showing appreciated acts of unusual kindness. He said, "Do not resist one who is evil. But if any one strikes you on the right cheek, turn to him the other also; and if any one would sue you and take your coat, let him have your cloak as well. . . . But I say unto you" (Matt. 5: 39–44).

b. So, Jesus was not showing appreciated acts of unusual kindness. He was showing a Christian person facing people who don't like him, who don't appreciate what he does, and who, when he does them good, may go off and laugh at him. I have yet to find a person who by himself can keep up that kind of Christian response for very long. It's understandable to go the second mile when it's appreciated, but not when it's humiliating.

In this sermon, Jesus is proclaiming the absolute demand of God on our lives. He is talking to us who have a high opinion of our own ability to live an extraordinary moral life. He is saying that we can be unrealistically optimistic about our ability to travel the second mile.

III. The Will to Surrender

a. Long-distance runners talk about catching a second wind. After running awhile their legs get heavy; their breathing becomes labored; and they slow down. But suddenly, they gain access to new strength. Their legs are no longer weary; they breathe more easily; and they pick up speed. They have caught their second wind!

The demand of God is that Christians travel two miles. The reality of human nature is that we ourselves cannot accomplish this. But the gift of God is that a spiritual second wind is available in every Christian.

b. The demand of God is that Christians travel two miles. The reality is that the Christian can do this only through the gift and power of the Spirit of God.

I challenge you to ensure that the deep covenant you have made with God in Christ finds growing expression in both miles of the Christian life. You are called to walk the first mile of obligation before you walk the second mile of opportunity. You are called to go the second mile not only when it's appreciated but when it's humiliating. The appropriate response to the two miles demanded of every Christian lies not in struggle but in surrender—your continuing surrender to the second Wind that is in you. In the will to surrender, we can find strength to live.—J. Altus Newell

Illustrations

GLAD?—MAYBE!   I have always been puzzled by that word in the New Testament which tells us that claim needs to be revised in the light of the Gospel records themselves. It would be far truer to fact if it could be enlarged to read, "The common people heard him gladly until they understood what he meant; then, like the rich young ruler, they went away sorrowing, for all of them were involved in many things they did not want to give up in order to follow him, or to enter the kingdom, or to possess eternal life.—Harold A. Bosley

THE IMPORTANT FIRST MILE.   Some time ago I was asked to speak for a church's spring revival. Just as I opened my eyes after the benediction in the first service, a man of tremendous size was barreling down on me. I sent up a holy telegram, "Lord, help him to be able to stop in time!" He pulled up two inches from my face, pinned me to the platform, and begin telling me about his plans for the revival. He had organized a prayer meeting for 5:00 A.M. every morning of the week. He had me scheduled for all the civic clubs, the high school, and the PTA. Fortunately, the pastor finally managed a rescue and later related some things about this member. He will organize an all-night prayer meeting on a moment's notice. He will travel many miles to attend services in other towns. He will go to South America on layman's crusades. He will lead any special cause. But he cannot be counted on for regular participation in his church. He does not attend Sunday school except on unusual occasions. He does not support the church financially except when there is a special project. This charming fellow is an expert at traveling the second mile. Somehow he has forgotten to walk the first mile.— J. Altus Newell

SERMON SUGGESTIONS

Topic: Facing the Red Sea

TEXT: Exod. 14

(1) The people said, "Go back." (2) Moses said, "Stand still." (3) God said, "Go forward."—W. E. Sangster

Topic: What Do You Think of Yourself?

TEXT: Rom. 12:3 Phillips

(1) We can have exaggerated ideas of our importance. (2) God can give us a true view of what we mean to him and to others.

Worship Aids

CALL TO WORSHIP.   "Rejoice, inasmuch as ye are partakers of Christ's sufferings; that, when his glory shall be revealed, ye may be glad also with exceeding joy" (1 Pet. 4:13).

INVOCATION.   Great God our heavenly Father, as we steal away from the din of the world, do thou fill our souls with the bliss of heaven, that in praise and prayer we might go forth in the earth renewed to proclaim the grace of undying love.—E. Lee Phillips

OFFERTORY SENTENCE.   "If he will obey my voice indeed, and keep my covenant, then ye shall be a peculiar treasure unto me above all people: for all the earth is mine: and ye shall be unto me a kingdom of priests, and an holy nation" (Exod. 19:5–6a).

OFFERTORY PRAYER.   Help us as individuals and as a congregation, O Lord, to see what is in our power to be and to do for thee. Let our obedient stewardship prepare us for the good and gracious service thou hast for us.

PRAYER.   Teach us, Lord,
          to serve you as you deserve,
          to give and not to count the
            cost,
          to fight and not heed the
            wounds,
          to toil and not to seek for rest,
          to labour and not to seek for
            any reward
          save that of knowing that we
            do your will.
                —Saint Ignatius Loyola
                    (1491–1556)

LECTIONARY MESSAGE

Options: Facing Troubles at Home
TEXT: Mark 3:20–35

Dealing with troubles at home is not something that is a modern phenomenon. The Bible reveals that homes have been places where conflict is met, managed or mismanaged. The books of Kings and Chronicles reveal that home life among the mighty was no bed of roses. Intrigue and rejection fill the pages of the accounts of the mightiest of Israel. Usually trouble in the home spilled over into the public sector and brought havoc to the nation. Such is still the case. Our age faces the trauma of breakdown in public life, which is frightening beyond imagination. Yet, if we can believe the experts on violence, much of the public havoc can be traced to the conflict and trouble which arise in the home.

It is interesting that even the home of the Lord Jesus did not escape its share of trouble and conflict. Both Mark and Luke tell us of the rejection that He received from those among whom He had grown up, the people of His hometown. That would be bad enough, but he also had to face the rejection of His family as well as that of the religious leaders.

I. Note the family rejection (vv. 21, 31–32). One can only wonder what thoughts were racing through their minds as they heard of the return of Mary's boy to His home turf. Looking at His life from a purely human standpoint, it would seem that He was wasting it with rootless wanderings and itinerant preachings. Indeed, they likely felt that He had joined some cult dominated by evil powers that gained recognition by doing magic tricks with no God-accepted basis. After all, He had been caught straightening out crooked limbs, making blind folks see, and healing devastating diseases. Nothing like that was done by the orthodox religious leaders who were revered and trusted. That was the work of those who were looked upon as the ones walking in the shadows of evil's darkness.

Then there was the fact that He had walked away from the family business, just left it behind to wander around the countryside doing all sorts of strange things. Had he stayed at home He could have had a steady income, community acceptance, and security for the future. His leaving and subsequent activities had brought embarrassment to His family and caused those who knew Him well to think that He had entered the land of the demented.

Not only that, but He had taken up with a rough crowd—fishermen, tax collectors, revolutionaries, and who knew what else the ones He called His closest friends actually did. They simply were not the most acceptable companions for people raised in a "better environment." Thus, the family voted to go and rescue Jesus from Himself.

Misunderstandings of what we are about in life create conflicts in the home. Choose a vocation different from that expected by family and community or make some choice that does not fit into the social structure of home, and conflict results.

II. Then, note the rejection of the religious leaders (v. 22). Frankly, Jesus must have frightened them down to the tassels on the hems of their robes. He was a definite threat to their way of life and especially their teachings. Not only did He challenge what they were proclaiming as eternal truth, He gave some powerful substitutes in place of their declaration. Through Jesus, fresh breezes were blowing across the hot, barren desert of religious truth and practice. Traditionalists knew that He had to be stopped, or they were finished. Thus they came to tiny Nazareth all the way from Jerusalem, following and observing and listening to Him. Likely there were some religious leaders present that day in Nazareth who knew Jesus well.

Why, they had taught Him in synagogue school. They had watched Him develop into a deeply religious young man who revered the great teachings and traditions of the faith. But now they joined the voices of other teachers, saying that He performed His mighty works by the power of the prince of devils.

Attributing evil purposes to good deeds and intentions is still a way in which some folks seek to eliminate those with whom they disagree. Fame and success that come from following nontraditional pathways seem to always bring the ire of the orthodox down upon the one who threatens them.

III. Now hear Jesus' response (vv. 34–35). While He loved His hometown, His family and friends, He knew that a higher calling of God demanded a new understanding of who family and friends really were. He knew that everlasting family ties come, not necessarily from the family into which we are born, but from those who do the will of God, who constantly seek to know, do, and understand God's truth. Such folks indeed constitute a family where conflicts are ably resolved and where acceptance is offered without demeaning restrictions. Truly, whoever does the will of the Father becomes not only Jesus' brother and sister and mother but that of every follower of His as well.—Henry Fields

SUNDAY: JUNE FIFTEENTH

SERVICE OF WORSHIP

Sermon: Our Father—The *Real* One
    TEXT: Matt. 6:9

Our Father. It is impossible, if one reads the Gospels carefully, to imagine prayer apart from the Fatherhood of God. Jesus' entire practice of prayer was rooted in a sense of intimacy with God as his heavenly Father.

I. This becomes even more interesting when we realize how Jesus felt about earthly father-son relationships.

a. "What man of you," he said, "if his son asks him for bread, will give him a stone? Or if he asks for a fish, will give him a serpent? If you then, who are evil, know how to give good gifts to your children, how much more will your Father who is in heaven give good things to those who ask him!" (Matt. 7:9–11) You . . . *who are evil.* Imagine that! We hope that Jesus meant that earthly fathers are enmeshed in a world that is often evil and ungodly. Earthly fathers, he seems to have been saying, are severely limited by their nature or environment.

b. Now add to this another saying. Jesus was discoursing about the scribes and Pharisees, who love earthly authority. "You are not to be called rabbi," he said to his disciples, "for you have one teacher, and you are all brethren" (Matt. 23:8). That is, they were advised not to seek titles for themselves but to be content to dwell together as brothers or equals. Then this: "And call no man your father on earth, for you have one Father, who is in heaven" (Matt. 23:9).

c. Did Jesus attempt systematically to alienate his followers from their earthly fathers? What was he hoping to do?

The answer lies in the Hebrew concept of the father. The father was the dominant figure in his child's life and the one through whom "the blessing" passed to the child. The father's blessing was considered very important. Of course it was primarily a psychological matter, a state of mind; but who would gainsay the importance of a state of mind, or its role in determining a son's destiny?

Maybe you haven't considered it, but the idea of the father's blessing still has a lot of significance today.

d. But Jesus knew the state of the world, the way things are. He knew that human fathers are unreliable, at best, and that even if they do give their blessings these are not always enough.

II. Not even the blessing of a good earthly father is enough.

a. Jesus understood this, and that is why he counseled his followers, "Call no man your father on earth." He wasn't against fathers. He merely knew their inadequacy. He knew that no earthly father can love enough and give enough to suffice for all our needs, at every moment of our lives. Only the heavenly Father is equal to this.

For Jesus to call our God our heavenly Father was to make the most audacious theological statement that could ever be made. Think about it—the God who created the world and cast the nebulae in space, the God who heard the prayers of the first man and woman on earth and who seeds the intricacies of the future, the God whose majesty is seen from the highest mountain and inhabits the jeweled depths of the darkest ocean, the God who led the Hebrews out of captivity in Egypt and spoke when Jesus was baptized to say, "This is my beloved Son, listen to him"—*our Father.*

b. If it doesn't make shivers run up and down your spine, then you have not properly understood. To think that the God of all this depth and power and resourcefulness should be our Father, the One with whom we are privileged to live in an attitude of intimacy and relationship, is enough to stagger our minds, to make them recoil from sheer insufficiency. *Our Father:* it is confession, praise, triumph, unbelievable fortune, overwhelming good news! Who could ever have hoped or dreamed that the God of the universe, the God of *all* universe, should be *our Father?!*

c. What a difference it makes in the life of prayer! Not believe in prayer? Why, when one realizes he is our Father, one can do nothing else but pray. Not have time to pray? Why, when we have discovered our true relationship to him, we shall want to pray all the time. Not know how to pray? Why, no one has trouble talking or listening to a real Father. When we are able to say *Our Father* and know it and mean it in all sincerity, prayer becomes to us the most natural activity in all the world—far more natural than most of the things we do in the run of a day. Then we would rather pray than eat or sleep or watch TV, for prayer is our line of connection to the heavenly Father.

III. The real test of his *Our Father* thinking came, of course, on the Cross. If he was ever going to decide he was wrong about the Father's care and presence, it was there. No crueler instrument of death ever existed. Talk about a deterrent to crime—the Romans often lined whole roadways with such crosses to remind the populace that resistance and insurrection would be met with pitiless torture. As Jesus saw such death looming before him, he went into the Garden of Gethsemane to pray. Saint Luke says it was his custom. Only this time he prostrated himself and cried out, "O Father, if it be thy will, let this cup pass from me."

a. *O Father.* The heavenly father. The real Father, One who cared for him beyond any earthly father. The One in whose power he had lived, to whom he had prayed for years. The One who had altered the very course of history, and could alter it now, if he would.

But he didn't. The soldiers came. There was a farce of a trial. The crowd was whipped into a frenzy, crying, "Crucify him! Crucify him!" And, reality of realities, Jesus found himself stripped and laid on a cross, staring dizzily into the cirrus clouds floating overhead as men drove spikes of pure pain into his hands and feet. Where was his Father then? If he was ever going to renounce this Father as a figment of his youthful imagination, as a pious concoction of his religious mind, it was now, as his body was raised on the gallows and his whole life clambered down to the vanishing point.

b. But Jesus didn't, did he? "Father," he prayed, "forgive them, for they know not what they do" (Luke 23:34). And then, as he died, "Father, into thy hands I commend my spirit" (Luke 23:46).

A Father to be trusted in death as much as in life.

A Father beyond all fathers, a Father who would not die, a Father who would always be there, forever and ever, world without end.

Our Father.

The world begins when we can truly say it.—John Killinger

Illustrations

WHAT EASTER MADE CLEAR.   All this, which the disciples most assuredly experienced, but which, because their eyes were strangely "holden," they had not yet taken in, suddenly dawned upon them in the light of Easter. The whole life of the wandering Savior, who had gone through the land healing, helping, forgiving, and bestowing new beginnings, suddenly became transparent to them. It was as if hitherto they had seen the colored windows in the sanctuary of this unique life only from the outside. The panes were dark and the language of the pictures was obscure. But when these people were transported to the interior of this mystery on Easter morning, the pictures sprang into life and took on sight and speech. That which had seemed gray to them before, the mute, empty meaninglessness of which had plunged them into the panic of Golgotha and caused them to doubt everything, now became for them an eloquent and compelling sign. Suddenly they realized they had not really known him at all. True, their hearts had burned within them, and they dimly felt that they were walking in the shadow of a mighty figure; but not till now did they discover who it was that walked with them there. Afterward the light came into his enigmatic words and acts and the heavens opened above the one they thought was only one of themselves, even though the greatest among men—now he turned out to be the "totally Other," who came from the eternity of the Father and shared for a little while their life on earth.—Helmut Thielicke

LOVE UNEXPRESSED.   A women I knew in Paris, France, had left home at an early age because she did not feel that her father loved her. In her thirties, she suffered from acute depression and malaise. She traveled back to the States, had a tearful reunion with her father, and came back much elated at his assurance that he had always loved her, though he had difficulty expressing his emotions. "Still," she said, "I will never be the woman I might have been if I had only grown up with this assurance. I am already marked for life."—John Killinger

SERMON SUGGESTIONS

Topic: God for Us Forever
    TEXT: Ps. 139:5
    (1) Behind: All my yesterdays are covered. He saves me from my soiled past. (2) Before: All my tomorrows are anticipated. He is undertaking for my future. (3) Just here: In this very present he lays his hand upon me.—W. E. Sangster

Topic: The Good Shepherd
    TEXT: John 10:11, 14
    (1) Saves his sheep (v. 9). (2) Knows his sheep (vv. 3 and 14). (3) Leads his sheep (vv. 3b–4). (4) Keeps his sheep (vv. 27–30). (5) Lays down his life for his sheep (v. 11).

Worship Aids

CALL TO WORSHIP.   "How precious is thy steadfast love, O God! The children of men take refuge in the shadow of thy wings" (Ps. 36:7).

INVOCATION.   In this place, O Lord, we find security in you. Our lives are hid with Christ in you. Yet our secret lives burst out everywhere in obedience and service if they are truly yours. Deepen our lives with you, so that they may be as shining lights and glorify your name.

OFFERTORY SENTENCE.   "There are varieties of working, but it is the same God who inspires them all in every one" (1 Cor. 12:6 RSV).

OFFERTORY PRAYER.   Help us, Father, to declare your faithfulness by our own faithfulness in our giving, whether our gifts are great or small may they be used for your glory as they are blessed by you for the on-going of your kingdom among people of the world.–Henry Fields

PRAYER.   Dear Lord, and Father of mankind, forgive our foolish ways. . . . How foolish our ways when life is frenetic and we are so frantic that we are all but beside ourselves. How foolish our ways when those nearest and dearest to us come knocking at the door of our life only to find nobody home. How foolish our ways when we neglect those relationships where there is meaning and life. How foolish to gain the world and lose the self–the greatest gift we will ever know.

O Father, we have come here to find our self. It is so easy to get lost in the labyrinth of the things that entice us. Here we have been confronted with our deepest need–"Be still and know that I am God."

Drop thy still dews of quietness
Till all our strivings cease;
Take from our souls the strain and stress,
And let our ordered lives confess
The beauty of thy peace.
                    –John G. Whittier, 1807–1892

The beauty of your peace is life ordered after your love–we are no longer orphans but your children. Once we were no people, but now we are Your people; once we had not received mercy, but now we have received mercy that we may declare the wonderful deeds of him who called us out of darkness into Your marvelous light. How different our beginnings, how varied the roads we have traveled, but what joy to share the household of faith in this time and place.

We praise you for all of those who have been loving in leading us to the family of faith–parents, teachers, pastors, counselors, friends. May we be as faithful to *our* responsibility and opportunity.

On this day with a special thank you to fathers, may we be reminded that you have ordained the family for the welfare and happiness of humankind–that through the family your fatherly intention toward all your children is revealed. Whatever our responsibility or opportunity in the home, make us strong to do your will–to love with the love that believes all, that hopes all, that endures all, that perseveres through all estrangements.–John Thompson

LECTIONARY MESSAGE

Topic: How the Kingdom Grows
TEXT: Mark 4:26–34

Most Christian traditions emphasize the responsibility of the individual to be busy about the business of building the kingdom of God. In some instances, this emphasis has become a mandate that is the only focal point of the group. We all have been victims of those who feel that their sole responsibility is to inaugurate and build the kingdom of God in this generation. Their zeal is to be admired, but their reason and method most times leave negative attitudes about the true nature of the kingdom. Think for a moment about this parable of Jesus, which gives us a vivid picture of how the kingdom grows.

I. Kingdom growth is a cooperative effort. Drawing from the field of agriculture, Jesus leads his followers to understand that the kingdom grows through our cooperation with God and his provisions. The farmer casts his seeds upon the earth, goes about his other pursuits, and leaves the rest to the care of the creator. He knows that the rains will fall, the sun will shine, and the seeds buried in the earth will sprout and grow. The farmer does not make any of that happen. He does not have the power to do so. He simply brings the seeds to the field, plants them, and trusts God to do all else in the growth department.

That, said Jesus, is how the kingdom grows. We are called upon to cooperate in that we plant the seed. We tell the good news. In God's time it brings forth fruit in the kingdom.

One lesson we all need to learn is that we do not own the kingdom. We cannot generate or create the kingdom. It is not ours; it is God's. He has invited us to be a part of his kingdom. He has asked that we assist in planting the seed that his kingdom might grow throughout the world. But the kingdom is his and his alone. We are simply those who plant the seed. It is God who gives the increase.

We must also learn that while God brings the growth, we have a responsibility to be diligent in our care of the kingdom. Every farmer knows that it is only as he plows the field and tends the growing crop, keeping the weeds and briars out, that the tender plants will have a chance to mature. Such care of God's kingdom is a part of the cooperation needed for his kingdom to come among us and grow. Once the seeds are planted and sprout, God still depends on his people to manage his kingdom.

II. Kingdom growth begins very small. In a parable of the mustard seed (vv. 30–32), Jesus lets us know that the smallest effort can produce a large result. The mustard seed is so small that when held in your hand it can hardly be seen. Yet when it is full-grown, it provides nesting places for the birds.

We have all heard others say that they cannot do much in the church. The reasons given range from lack of talent to fear of talking to people. It may be factual that someone cannot do much. Yet Christ is saying in this parable that the very smallest talent, the very smallest effort can produce something of infinite worth in the kingdom of God.

Who knows what some small gesture of friendship, some momentary word of encouragement, some kind deed hastily done, or some small act of bravery has done to bring growth to another? Who knows how many people have been brought to faith in Christ because of some tiny seed that took root in the heart of another and a life was turned Godward, a soul born into the kingdom. Nothing that we do in God's name and Spirit is too small to be used in his kingdom. Who of us can measure what growth it will produce?

III. All can be part of helping the kingdom to grow. From the least to the greatest, we can all make a conscious effort every day to do what we can to enhance the kingdom of God on earth. We cannot create it, but we can labor in it. We cannot make the kingdom grow, but we can plant the seeds, trusting God to give the increase.

Silently, imperceptibly the kingdom grows. Even the smallest seed planted in hope, entrusted to God's power and nurtured by his grace, coupled with our effort, will produce growth beyond imagination. Growth cannot be forced, but it will come if we join God in the cooperative effort of enhancing the kingdom.—Henry Fields

SUNDAY: JUNE TWENTY-SECOND

SERVICE OF WORSHIP

Sermon: Rock-Bottom Pricing
  TEXT: Matt. 7:24–27
Jesus knew the nature of some of the Galileans who would hastily build on the sandy embankments of dry streams in the rainless months of summer. By midwinter's rain, their foundations would erode, and their houses would collapse into a pile of rocky ruin.

Yet Jesus was not cautioning His hearers about failed construction codes, or merely accusing stupid builders of their foolishness, or warning us about the weather's treachery and vacillation. His bottom line had a cost affixed to it. "Listen to Me," He seemed to say, "Wise up. You get what you pay for. Build on solid rock."

I. Yet we continue to ignore our Lord's advice!

a. Everywhere we turn, whether it is society as a whole or specific institution within it, we are ignoring the need for rock-hard foundations. As society becomes more accepting of life-styles that fail to meet the standards of Scripture, every home and even the Church are in danger of building the future upon unsteady sand. When it comes to the Church, it is not a matter of democratic niceties but an issue about foundations. It's not a justice issue or one that depends on the latest polls. Jesus warns us about the "foolish man who built his house on sand. The rain fell, and the floods came, and the winds blew and beat against that house, and it fell—and great was its fall," He said. Instead of sandy sentiment, Jesus insists we build on sturdier stuff—the rock foundation of Scripture, the bedrock of the Bible.

b. If we avoid the solid rock of the Bible to build our future on the shifting sands of social sentimentality alone or the political correctness that is currently popular, we can expect Jesus' prophecy to be fulfilled—again! It's God's Word up against the latest public mood swing—and what will you settle for?

We build on sand every time we neglect providing children with substantive foundations in God's Word through Sunday School, Day School, and Vacation Bible School. We build our own adult lives on sand when we personally ignore Bible study and prayer, worship and the sacraments. We build flimsy homes when we insist morality is unimportant and concern about ethics is unnecessary, when we fail to support the Church with generosity, as well as our missions abroad and our ministries to the homeless and others. We have become so enamored of the bottom line that we've forgotten the cost to be paid if we exchange rock-bottom pricing for unstable sand. Isn't that what's happening to our public institutions of human services, to worthwhile welfare and health programs and our agencies for the aging? Instead of keeping sound foundations, we're moving over to the precarious site on unstable ground.

II. Friend, the basis of the gospel is love. It is love that instructs us to stick with solid foundations instead of flimsy ones. It's love that makes us willing to stick with moral values as well as solid scriptural interpretation. We are to love God and do so by loving others.

a. We are not to turn that love into hate and thereby brutalize and isolate those who think differently than we do. Love gives us no right to belittle others or treat them shamefully. But loving them as God's creations does not mean we are to build our own lives on what may appear to be less than solid foundations. We are to love and minister to gays and lesbians as Jesus would have us. We are to love and care for materialists and drug addicts, criminals and sectarians—without trading our solid foundations in God's Word for theirs built on sand.

b. Our love, founded on God's love and the love Christ shared in His death and resurrection, is meant to weather the blustery winds and terrifying rains and instant floods that attempt to dislodge us from biblical soundness. Hold on! There are storms abrewing!

III. But if there are floods that destroy, there is one that builds up. If there is rain that kills, there is water that gives life.

a. It is in the Sacrament of Baptism that we experience Christ taming the tempest all over again to enable us to sail smoothly through life's storms to eternity. It is in this gracious gift that we are rinsed clean of sin's stain, and the seed of faith is watered so that it may grow and produce fruit. It is this water of Baptism that solidifies into the rock-bottom price of salvation, for in it is the costly price of Christ's sacrifice. In it is the abundance of His love. In this gift we find waterproofing for future storms by being watered down by the Spirit through this sacred second birth. Here is water upon which to walk as Jesus did upon the sea—and to walk all the way into eternity. Here is liquid upon which to set sail as Noah did in sailing the ark—and bringing his passengers to safe landing.

b. Friends, check your foundation! If you're not built on the rock, watch out! You're bound to collapse. But if you structure your life and hopes on this Word that is the gospel, you will find you are able to weather every storm that assails you. There is no greater consideration for parents to make than the foundation upon which they and their children are building their family home.

Jesus put it this way, "Everyone then who hears these words of Mine and acts on them will be like a wise man who built his house on rock." That's the rock-bottom price for salvation. It's the bedrock that weathers the tumult.—Richard Andersen

Illustrations

THE SERMON AND THE PREACHER. Matthew relates the sermon inseparable to the Preacher, and relates ethics inseparable to christology. To be sure, there is no explicit christology in the Sermon on the Mount. The subject matter of the sermon is not the person of Christ but the kind of life Christ's disciples are called to live. But the demands of the sermon are incomprehensible apart from the implicit christology found there (see 5:1–12, 17–20, 21–48; 7:21–27). One cannot avoid christology and appeal only to the teaching or great principle of Jesus, for these are inseparable from the claims of his person. But for Matthew the converse is also true: "Correct" christological understanding can never be a substitute for the kind of ethical living to which Jesus calls his disciples. Christology and ethics, like christology and discipleship, are inseparable for Matthew.—*The New Interpreter's Bible*

THE HOPE OF THE WORLD.   Recall what George Bernard Shaw said. You do not go to George Bernard Shaw for sentimental opinions. "I am ready to admit," he wrote, "that after contemplating the world and human nature for nearly sixty years, I see no way out of the world's misery but the way which would have been found by Christ's will if he had undertaken the work of a modern practical statesman." "Though we crucified Christ on a stick, he somehow managed to get hold of the right end of it, and . . . if we were better men we might try his plan."—Harry Emerson Fosdick

SERMON SUGGESTIONS

Topic: How to Begin with God
TEXT: Isa. 40:25–31
(1) Humbly. (2) Confidently. (3) Decisively.

Topic: Costly Devotion
TEXT: John 12:1–8
(1) *Jesus and his friends.* (a) Martha served—did the practical thing. (b) Mary anointed him—did the unexpected. (2) *Significance of Mary's deed.* (a) She loved Jesus for what he did for her and her family—raised Lazarus; glorified God. (c) She anticipated his suffering and death—gradual dawning. (3) *How to honor Christ today—doing "the unexpected."* (a) By nobility. (b) By generous self-denial. (c) By radiant testimony.

Worship Aids

CALL TO WORSHIP.   "The Lord hath done great things for us; whereof we are glad" (Ps. 126:3).

INVOCATION.   Father, we are thankful for this world in which we live, for its beauty, its vastness, its supportive wealth, and its many challenges. As we view all the demands of life on this earth, we are made aware of our littleness. Yet, through Christ we know the greatness of your life which gives worth and meaning to our small lives. This morning as we worship may we find sufficient faith to see you more clearly, sufficient confidence to know that we can worship you only, strong enough love to serve you always and enough wisdom to acknowledge you as lord in all of our life situations.—Henry Fields

OFFERTORY SENTENCE.   "He raises the poor from the dust; he lifts the needy from their misery and makes them companions of princes" (Ps. 113:7–8a TEV).

OFFERTORY PRAYER.   God of grace, take what we give and what we wish we could give, our gifts and our hopes, and merge them to make of ourselves and this church an oblation of praise to Christ our King.—E. Lee Phillips

PRAYER.   O Christ, thou hast bidden us pray for the coming of thy Father's kingdom, in which his righteous will shall be done on earth. We have treasured thy words, but we have forgotten their meaning, and thy great hope has grown dim in thy Church. We bless thee for the inspired souls of all ages who saw afar the shining city of God, and by faith left the profit of the present to follow their vision. We rejoice that today the hope of these lonely hearts is becoming the clear faith of millions. Help us, O Lord, in the courage of faith to seize what has now come so near, that the glad day of

God may dawn at last. As we have mastered Nature that we might gain wealth, help us now to master the social relations of mankind that we may gain justice and a world of brothers. For what shall it profit our nation if it gain numbers and riches, and lose the sense of the living God and the joy of human brotherhood?

Make us determined to live by truth not by lies, to found our common life on the eternal foundations of righteousness and love, and no longer to prop the tottering house of wrong by legalized cruelty and force. Help us to make the welfare of all the supreme law of our land, that so our commonwealth may be built strong and secure on the love of all its citizens. Cast down the thone of Mammon, who ever grinds the life of men, and set up thy throne, O Christ, for thou didst die that men might live. Show thy erring children at last the way from the City of Destruction to the City of Love, and fulfill the longings of the prophets of humanity. Our Master, once more we make thy faith our prayer: "Thy kingdom come! Thy will be done on earth!"—Walter Rauschenbusch

LECTIONARY MESSAGE

Topic: Crossing the Sea
  Text: Mark 4:35-41
  Other Readings: 1 Sam. 17:1a, 4-11, 19-23, 32-49; Ps. 9:4-20; 2 Cor. 6:1-13

There is mystery and wonder about the Lord stilling the storm that so suddenly swept across the Sea of Galilee. Traditionally, as we read verses 35-41 in the fourth chapter of Mark's Gospel, we center our thoughts and interpretations on that momentous miracle. Yet there is much more food for thought to be found in these words.

I. In these words we see something of the vision of the Lord. Consider "Let us go across to the other side" (4:35). There was a restlessness in the heart of Jesus. Throughout the story of his life he is always moving on to another place, another challenge, another need. For him, the horizon did not end where he was at the moment. He was not satisfied to settle down and concentrate on only a select few. He knew that his purpose was to tell the truth of God to every

soul, and to do that he must ever be going on to the next place, the next challenge.

The words "let us go" must never be ignored by the Lord's church but must ever be a warning. It is easy to become established, to get involved in a settled ministry, to stagnate in a maze of routines and forget the horizons to which we have been called. We followers of the Lord must always be ready to cross over to new challenges, new places, and new possibilities so that his kingdom may become a reality everywhere.

II. Again, we see the security of Jesus. He had no fear of leaving the accepting crowd gathered around him. He knew that there were other crowds to meet, other places to proclaim God's truth. Unlike us, he did not need the crowd to feed his ego or give him a sense of worth. To him, they were as sheep without a shepherd, and it was his responsibility to tend the sheep wherever they were found. So he courageously left the acceptance of one crowd to face whatever might lie over the horizon or on the other side of the sea. From him we need to learn that the packed house is not our security; rather our security lies in forgetting the praise of the crowd and following wherever the shadow of the cross falls, even when it is away from the teeming, demanding crowds.

III. Then, in these words, we see the inevitability of the rising storm. It is not uncommon for the placid Sea of Galilee to be suddenly churned into a frenzy of whitecaps and swamping waves. The surrounding hills and mountains act as a funnel to channel the winds across the lake, making it a treacherous body of water. Anytime a boat sets out across those waters, there is danger of its being caught in a storm of devastating proportions.

Is that not also the case when we venture after Christ across the sea of life? Inevitably there will come storms that sweep upon us when we least expect them. The gospel truth always runs counter to much that is accepted practice by the world. To proclaim it, live it, and seek to effect its powerful change in any situation will ultimately provide the stuff of which storms are made. Those who declare the truth of Christ will, like Paul and his companions, be accused of turning the world upside down. Such always raises storm winds. When the storms begin to rage, we, like the disciples of this account, cry out in our fear and distress, "Do you not care that we perish?" For we cannot manage the storms alone. In the midst of them we often feel like a small leaf being buffeted in every direction without hope of survival.

IV. When such is the case, however, we, like those fearful sailors on that storm-tossed sea, have with us the presence of one who can manage the most powerful storms we may encounter. Over and over he has spoken to the storms that arise and brought calm. Sometimes his "Peace, bestill" is spoken directly to our fearful souls, so that we may be able to handle the circumstances creating the storm; other times those words are spoken to forces beyond us so that the way may be prepared for the storm to pass. No matter where the winds of adversity arise or how strong they blow, if we have him with us in the boat, we can know the peace that passes understanding and the hope that will not fade. Do you not hear him asking anew, "Why are you afraid? Do you have no faith?" He who calls us to new horizons, who is secure in God's power and who yet speaks calming words to deadly storms is with us. Therefore, we need not be afraid.—Henry Fields

SUNDAY: JUNE TWENTY-NINTH

SERVICE OF WORSHIP

Sermon: We Are Heirs

TEXT: Gal. 3:23–4:7

I. We come together not as creditors but as debtors. The ledger is out of balance. We carry far more liabilities than assets. Our inheritance is a reminder of debt. We are not in any sense of the word "self-made." Remembering those who have died that others may live is a worthy ritual in gratitude. We are reminded that freedom comes at a great price. We are indebted to numerous others for the place and the liberty that we enjoy, and we are reminded of a treasure that must be claimed and preserved by every generation. The power to remember distinguishes humanity from other forms of life on the planet, and the significance of history separates biblical religion from other forms of worship. The Jews stood apart because they had learned to remember. Unlike the gods of their neighbors, Jahweh was known through events in history. Statements of Jewish faith were seldom philosophical. Revelation was anecdotal. The power and love of God were illustrated by remembered experience of the Jewish family. Stories about people, heroes and villains, and the patterns of divine purpose that unfolded in the life of the family-nation were vehicles to carry the Word of God. God was evident in the collective experience of Israel.

Of course, real history is not always sweetness and light. The down side of tradition was a religion sometimes tainted by national bigotry. Honesty required a record of personal failure along with the national heritage of divine guidance. As often as the Jews were called to gratitude for their fathers, they were warned about the failures of previous generations. The call to remember noted the persons and behaviors to avoid as well as the models for faithfulness to covenant. We too could stand to learn from the mistakes of biblical history. Any nation should hesitate before leaping to claim exclusive divine rights or "Christian" identity. The danger of holding history in reverence is that one begins not only to worship at the altars of tradition but to presume upon the future. Gratitude gives way to arrogance. We begin to live out of past accomplishments rather than present commitments. Paul's calling as apostle to the Gentiles required a reassessment of his own inheritance. For Galatian Gentiles treated as second-class Christians by the Jewish faction, Paul found a new connection to the legacy of promise that had been the exclusive claim of his own people: "As many of you as were baptized into Christ have clothed yourself with Christ." No human distinctions count for anything—national identity, social status, gender. "All of you are one in Christ Jesus."

II. a. We are in debt to our ancestors. Heritage extends the meaning of life beyond the boundaries of birth and death. Like trees, people grow from roots. Not a one of us is here by personal effort or initiative. We are the offspring of our biological and spiritual forebears. Thus, Paul refused to discount the importance of the foundation that was laid by the children of Abraham or to burn the bridge between Christ and the Jews when addressing the late entrance of Gentiles into the Jewish heritage. We are derived from others. A significant part of personal identity is in biological and spiritual ancestors who lived and died long before we were born. That is why we develop an interest in history and genealogy as we turn toward the senior years of life. History does not serve those who prefer remembering to doing. History serves those who are willing to learn from the past before deciding the future. Just as we do not create ourselves from nothing, we do not live out our existence from zero. Fortunately, every generation can benefit from the past. We can share in the experience of the larger family. The wheel does not have to be reinvented by each person or by each generation. The Covenant with Abraham was big enough to bless all of the nations of every generation implied in his name. On the other hand, Abraham was just a man. We do not have to repeat the Patriarch's blunders and failures.

After describing the great heroes of faith who have laid the foundations on which we build, the Hebrew Christians were reminded that they are surrounded by a cloud of witnesses, suggesting we are enveloped by history and watched by our forebears in faith. Nationality, biology, and social identity count for nothing. The key is spiritual identity. Appearance is nil. We reflect the image of our spiritual forebears in our commitments and actions. A few years ago Virginia Baptists retrieved from Baptist history a form of communication called a "memorial" which was addressed to Southern Baptists in general, the Executive Committee in particular. A memorial was an anchor in time, an appeal to the memory of Baptist identity in history. The name *Baptist* does not matter if we have thrown away the substance of our faith, especially our commitment to religious liberty. The children of God live in the image of their Father.

b. We are in debt to the children we are sending into tomorrow. We have received more than land, privilege, and freedom from our ancestors. We have inherited a responsibility for the future. We are the ancestors to whom future generations will look for clues to faith and promise, thus, we are reminded that every gift carries a responsibility. While we are blessed beyond measure, we are also burdened beyond comprehension. As heirs of promise, we are laying the foundations on which our children will build tomorrow. I came up behind a rather impressive motor home at a stop light. Because of my personal interest in RVs, I was admiring the style and size when my eye fell on the bumper sticker: "We are spending our children's inheritance." My first mental response was, "Good for you." As I grow closer to the age of my traveling mentors, I am growing more concerned about what we are leaving future generations. The national debt, a bankrupt Social Security system, and depleted Medicare programs are far from the basic issue. We owe our children an inheritance that money cannot buy. The issue is not dollars; it is values. With the phenomenal shift of population in the nation and in our church toward senior citizens, we cannot afford to draw an artificial line that says, "I am no longer responsible." The most productive years of our Christian lives can be our retirement years when we have more time to invest in our children.

c. We are in debt to the God of creation. Ultimately, we are the children of God. We are prevented from worshiping the idols of our ancestors at the altars of history and from the fear of failure by an eternal vision of the God who transcends all generations. Ultimately our identity reaches far beyond Abraham and his heritage. We are the children of God. Only as Paul could think higher than national heritage could he find fellowship with gentile believers. A sense of the eternal raises our vision to include all of creation in the promise of God. The genealogical quest is fun and informative, but it serves to distinguish and separate from the rest of humanity. Only as we know ourselves as the children of God do we find redemptive love big enough to include the whole family of faith.–Larry Dipboye

Illustrations

HOW TO BE RICH.   When Jesus said to the rich young man, "Go and sell all that thou hast and give to the poor," he had simply found a man who did not know how to be rich. There was nothing to do with that man but to send him back to the preparatory school of poverty. To make that special treatment of a single man the universal rule of human life would be to shut up one of the great higher schools of human character in sheer despair. Sometimes perhaps a rich man feels that if he could get rid of his money he could be a strong and unselfish man. It is the old delusion. The sinner in the tropics thinks he could be a saint at the North Pole. It is only that he knows how the sun burns, but has never felt how the frost freezes. There is a special strength and a particular unselfishness that the rich man's wealth makes possible for him. It is his duty to seek after them, and never rest till he has found them; not to make himself poor, but to know how to be rich is the problem of his life.–Phillips Brooks

MY BROTHER'S BROTHER.   Dr. Charles Reynolds Brown, the brilliant and beloved former dean of Yale Divinity School, once answered this question, "Am I my brother's keeper?" with an emphatic, "No." Then he added, "I must be my brother's brother." Back of his answer was, I presume, his recognition that there are certain dangers involved in assuming responsibility for another's welfare.

One danger is that of annoying interference with the other person's freedom and activity. One day I rode in a railroad coach with a mother and her four children. They were a noisy crew, and the mother was about the noisiest of the lot. She was incessantly calling out, "Stop that. . . . Take your hand off that. . . ." In the whole trip of over a hundred miles, I did not observe those children do one thing in which the mother joined encouragingly. Her attitude was like that of another nagging mother, whose little

son had gotten out of her sight. She called to the lad's older sister and said, "Mary, go see what Johnny is doing and tell him to quit." Such a parental attitude stultifies the character of both parent and child.–Ralph W. Sockman

SERMON SUGGESTIONS

Topic: The Missionary Call of the Old Testament
TEXT: Jonah 1:1, 2, 3; 3:1, 2
(1) God's universal love. (2) All people are capable of receiving God's love and responding to it. (3) Jonah's heedlessness arose from unwillingness, but ours springs from indifference.–J. D. Jones

Topic: The Lord God Omnipotent Reigneth
TEXT: Rev. 19:6
Three tremendous consequences: (1) The liberation of life–release from petty worries; release from the fears of life; release from self-contempt. (2) The doom of sin. (3) The comfort of sorrow.–James S. Stewart

Worship Aids

CALL TO WORSHIP.   "Show me thy ways, O Lord, teach me thy paths. Lead me in thy truth, and teach me: for thou art the God of my salvation; on thee do I wait all the day" (Ps. 25:4–5).

INVOCATION.   Grant us this hour of confession and praise, O Lord, not as we deserve, but as with humble and obedient hearts, we desire, through our obedient and living Savior.–E. Lee Phillips

OFFERTORY SENTENCE.   "Greater love hath no man than this, that a man lay down His life for his friends" (John 15:13).

OFFERTORY PRAYER.   Gracious Lord, in our offerings may our willingness to give match the measure of thy blessing.

PRAYER.   Deliver us, O God, out of our darkness into Thy light; and bring us ever to see clearly what Thou hast ever faithfully purposed. Thou hast called us into Thy service; send us not empty away. Fulfill in us all Thou hast intended when Thy hands shaped us, and by Thy grace fit us wholly to Thy mind in Christ Jesus.—Paul Scherer

LECTIONARY MESSAGE

Topic: Interruptions
TEXT: Mark 5:21–43
Other Readings: 2 Sam. 1:1, 17–27; Ps. 130; 2 Cor. 8:7–15

Jesus' life was filled with interruptions. Does he ever plan a day, as we are called upon to do, and then never see the plan realized because of the many interruptions? Yet he never seems to be frustrated by the interruptions. Rather, he turns the interruptions into opportunities to help struggling people and further the kingdom of God.

In the text, Mark uses master strokes to show us what was likely a typical day in the life of Jesus and how he handled the invasions of his time. He is met by a multitude of people, all likely wanting some special treatment from him. One man gets to the Lord first. Maybe he was able to do so because of his position in the community. As president of the synagogue, Jairus would hold a special place in the pecking order. Likely he was a man devoted to his Jewish heritage and religion. Certainly he was seen as a leader to be followed. Now, in a desperate moment he falls at the feet of Jesus and petitions him to cure his gravely ill daughter.

In that moment, this leader of the people laid aside any opposition he might have felt for Jesus, and in a last-ditch effort to save his daughter's life, he put himself at the disposal of the Lord. William Barclay rightly describes this man when he says that he laid aside his prejudices against the itinerant preacher-healer, forgot his pride fostered by his position in the community, ignored what his friends would think, as he cast away his dignity and begged at the feet of Jesus for the very life of his child.[1] Surely what he did

would create problems for him. But this important community man discovered what we all must learn. He found that it is only when we trust Jesus without reservation and in spite of all opposition that we receive the Lord's concern and help. Mark tells us that Jesus heard the plea of Jairus and immediately went with him to minister to the darling of his heart.

The journey to the house of Jairus had not progressed far before there was another interruption. A pitiful woman with a long-standing blood problem, who had spent everything on a search for medical help, brought the journey to a halt. Knowing that she should not be in the crowd because of her disease, and knowing that she should never publicly intrude on a man, she readily broke the rules in order to find relief for her malady. Like many of us, she did not want to be identified as one who needed what Jesus had to give. She desired to remain anonymous, to just blend into the crowd, never answering for her faith or identifying with him who brings healing and change to all circumstances of pain in life. But Jesus found her out.

Again we see the compassion of Jesus as he turns aside from his journey of mercy in behalf of Jairus and takes the time to meet the need of this desperate woman.

Twice in a very short time Jesus was interrupted in whatever schedule he had in mind for his day. Once he was openly accosted by an important man who in other circumstances might have been his antagonist. Then he was invaded by a desperate, nameless woman who had tried everything else and came to him as a last resort, hoping against hope that he would be able to help her. Jairus's bold action of open faith was met with answering love and help, as was the timid, quivering faith of the desperate woman.

These interruptions tell us several things about Jesus. They tell us that Jesus is never so busy or so scheduled that he does not have time for people from every walk of life and with every degree of faith in him. They tell us that whatever Jesus lays his hand on lives. The woman was given a new lease on life. Jairus's daughter was restored to health. Again and again Jesus lays his hand on a situation and healing comes, giving life fresh

---

[1] William Barclay, "The Gospel of Mark," in *The Daily Study Bible* (Philadelphia: The Westminster Press, 1956), pp. 126–28.

and powerful. He lays his hand on ambition and turns Saul into Paul. He lays his hand on a ruptured relationship, and it is healed. He lays his hand on a torn marriage, and it is made whole again with new life and purpose. Indeed, it is because of the interruptions that came to his life that we see how much he cares and how much he can do to make us whole and alive again.

These interruptions in the life of the Lord tell us that interruptions in life are opportunities for service that we must not ignore. They indeed become doors to our spiritual growth and healing.–Henry Fields

SUNDAY: JULY SIXTH

SERVICE OF WORSHIP

Sermon: The Real Meaning of Freedom

TEXT: Luke 15:11–24; also Gal. 3:23–26

We Americans have built a society that has given an unprecedented measure of freedom to each of its citizens. I can do whatever I want as long as I do not interfere with your pursuit of what you desire. And in this land of plenty, there is a veritable supermarket of desire where we are little more than consumers.

Our problem, with regard to freedom, is that we may not even know what true freedom is. The teenager can hardly wait for the freedom of the adult. The adult longs to be a teen again. The poor would love the freedom of the rich, but the rich remember what it's like to be free of worry and to get a full night's sleep. How we look at freedom depends on where we stand, and it makes freedom very hard to define.

I. The New Testament is never confused about the real meaning of freedom, however. The biblical view is that freedom—genuine personal freedom—consists in knowing that we are the children of God and then living joyfully out of that knowledge without having to be guided by any external constraints.

a. Consider the story of the prodigal. The younger of two sons wanted to be totally free. He was tired of being told what to do—when he could come and go . . . and with whom. He wanted to get away where no one could give him orders anymore. He wanted to be free!

You know what happened. The boy went off. He was totally free—or thought he was.

b. Then, everything changed! This young man who had wanted total freedom—wanted it so badly he could taste it, wanted it so badly he was willing to hurt his family and everyone else to get it—decided that it was not freedom he wanted after all. What he really wanted was total subjection.

There is a form of religion that caters to this sort of personality and is built upon this psychology. It is the form of religion that, with its strict code of behavior and its sense of supermorality, thrives on getting hold of people who once were ready to go to the other extreme; they become very obedient, docile slaves in somebody else's moral system.

c. Is that freedom? That certainly is not what Paul said. Paul said that it is foolish to return to slavery once you have been set free in the Son (Gal. 3:25–26). It is the same point Jesus made in this parable.

"No," says the father, "you can't be a child again. You have to be an adult now. It's time to grow up." So he calls for a ring and puts it on his finger. It was the ancient symbol of adulthood and authority. Then he called everyone together and said, "This is my son! He was lost and now he's found. He was dead and now he's alive!" For the boy-now-become-man, it was time to learn to live with a new kind of freedom—the responsible freedom of sonship.

II. Having real freedom does not mean having complete freedom. It means living freely out of whatever situation we happen to be in. It means accepting the limitations of our lives and not feeling hampered by them.

a. Consider the prodigal after his homecoming. Here's what his new freedom was like. He rose early in the morning, before daybreak. After breakfast, he went to the fields to superintend the work of his father's servants. During the heat of the day, the sweat ran down his face, and his clothes stuck to his body. He came in in the afternoons dirty and grimy, scorched and burned by the wind.

b. Yet, he was free. He was no longer the prisoner of his passions or his circumstances. He was home—and glad to be there. When he came in from working all day, he was thankful to have a cool bath. He craved the food at his mother's table. He cherished the conversation after dinner and the stroke of his father's affirmation on his shoulder as he passed. He loved to stroll in the moonlight and think about life.

He remembered his escape to the far country—the fickleness of his friends, the feeling of desperation, the sense of destitution when the money ran out. He was thankful to be home—and glad to be free!

III. Do you see? Real freedom—our freedom in Christ—is not the freedom to do anything we choose to do. It isn't even the freedom to remake the world—and everyone in it—the way we would like them to be.

a. Real freedom is the freedom of forgiveness and restitution, the freedom of acceptance and renewal, the freedom to be who we are in joy and peace and love. Real freedom is the freedom Paul spoke about in Galatians—not to be slaves of the law anymore. That only produces lives of anxiety and jealousy and desperation. It is the freedom to be sons and daughters of God, so that we can experience the fruits of the Spirit—love, joy, peace, patience, kindness, goodness, trustfulness, gentleness, and self-control (Gal. 5:22–23).

b. Freedom is not the freedom to do nothing. It is not the freedom to be anybody or anything we want. Freedom is the ability to be happy with who we are as human beings and to give thanks for our human situations—knowing that God loves us and accepts us and is preparing us for our eternal destinies in Christ Jesus.

Anything else is not freedom but only an illusion of freedom. The way the prodigal son was made to be his father's son and not his slave—this is what we, too, were made for. And when we finally discover that and integrate it into our self-understanding and way of relating to the world, we will experience the joy and excitement the prodigal must have felt when he strolled in the moonlight and realized how good it all was!

God does not want us to be His slaves. He truly wants us to be His sons and daughters, through Jesus Christ our Lord.—Gary C. Redding

Illustrations

IS THIS FREEDOM? I almost laughed. I think you will too. Here was a lovely young mother in my office—a baby in her arms and a slightly older child systematically dismantling my office and her mother's nerves.

This harried mother had only a few minutes to talk. She was due to pick up her third child from the preschool when she left. She apologizes for her hair, which she had not had time to properly fix that morning. She also was embarrassed about her dress. It was clean when she left home but now showed traces of milk and juice and two or three flavors of baby food.

We had already discussed what she came to see me about. She was at the door, readjusting one child on her hip and pacifying the other to keep him from whining. Then she said, "Wow! When I think that five years ago I was dying to get married and move out of my parents' house so that I could be free, it almost blows my mind!"

Freedom is relative, isn't it?

To live in the land of the free is a blessing indeed—surrounded by burglar alarms, medicine cabinets, and our fears of hypertension and heart attack, insanity, insolvency, and unemployment!—Gary C. Redding

STAND FAST. Certainly Roger Sherman, Oliver Wolcott, William Williams, and Samuel Huntington of Connecticut, all signers of the Declaration of Independence for their colony, must have given thought to these published words of the Reverend Judah Champion of Hartford, when he said, "For heaven's sake and our own, let us arouse, my countrymen, and act up to the dignity of our character as free-born Americans. Let us be steady, prudent, firm and united, trusting in the Lord. Now, by the love of God to perishing sinners . . . By all that Christ hath done and suffered to purchase our privileges and eternal salvation . . . By all that is dear and sacred . . . By all your regard to the sacred Trinity, to yourselves, to posterity, and to your country, we beseech and adjure you to stand fast in the liberty wherewith Christ hath made us free. Amen."–Robert F. Williams

SERMON SUGGESTIONS

Topic: The Holy Place and Redemption
TEXT: Lev. 16:2–3
(1) The ark and the mercy seat were together the place of holiness. The only attitude with which we can approach the mystery of Jesus' death is the attitude of awe. (2) The ark of God and the mercy seat were together the place of loneliness. One man, one solitary man, had the right of entrance to them. Jesus Christ, upon his cross of death, meets our loneliness and conquers it. (3) The ark was the place of forgiveness.–Chalmers Coe

Topic: Prayer
TEXT: Eph. 6:18–20
(1) *What we should not expect of prayer:* (a) that we shall receive everything we ask for; (b) that God's guidance will make us infallible; (c) that prayer will change God's mind. (2) *These are true functions of prayer:* (a) to make us God-conscious; (b) to enable us to enter into God's creative activity.

Worship Aids

CALL TO WORSHIP.   "O magnify the Lord with me, and let us exalt his name together" (Ps. 34:3).

INVOCATION.   Tune our hearts, O God, to sing your praise. We love you because you first loved us, and we wish for all the universe to join us in praise of you. Purify our hearts, so that we may worship you today and serve you tomorrow in spirit and in truth.

OFFERTORY SENTENCE.   "God was making all mankind his friends through Christ. God did not keep an account of their sins, and he has given us the message which tells how he makes them his friends" (2 Cor. 5:19 TEV).

OFFERTORY PRAYER.   Lord, make this message effective at home and abroad through our faithful personal testimony and through our faithful financial stewardship.

PRAYER.   O God, Creator of all good, if we are honest we have to confess that we are wealthy. Though we may be poor in the world's goods, as people count wealth, we have, each of us, overwhelming riches: our human heritage, our national treasures, the natural beauty of this world, the gift of friends and of others who love us. Life itself we have received from you, as well as our personal gifts and potentials. Greater than any other gift is the gift of your Son and all the treasures of truth and life that come to us through him. Whenever we are tempted to imagine that any of our blessings have come simply because of what we have done or deserve, deliver us from the evil of ingratitude, and help us to acknowledge with joy as the Source and Goal of all that we are and have.

LECTIONARY MESSAGE

Topic: Two by Two
TEXT: Mark 6:1–13
Other Readings: 2 Sam. 5:1–5, 9–10; Ps. 48; 2 Cor. 12:2–10

The time of their internship was drawing to a close. For many months the Twelve had followed Jesus from place to place and marveled at the mighty healing deeds of mercy he performed. They had heard his call to the multitudes to draw close to the Father. They had listened to words that had never been spoken with such power before. They had also seen those occasions when response to him was hindered by unbelief. But always they had been in his presence when great things were done. Now it was time for them to learn that his work could be extended through them. So he called them and began to send them out two by two (6:7).

I. This was a watershed event, because for the first time Jesus was sending out others to carry his message and do the work of making people whole. Granted, it was a temporary mission, but it was a first. It was a pattern that can still be followed with certainty that it will accomplish more than can be done by one lone individual. It is still a method that produces mighty results when it is followed.

Up to this time the predominant word of Jesus had been "come." He had called the disciples from various labors, inviting them to come and follow him. Now he injects another verb, one that places responsibility on the shoulders of the followers. They are to "go." It is true that there could have been no going unless they had come and learned of him and from him. Such is still the case. We of this age are called to come and see, but the result of seeing is that we might go and tell what we have seen and heard. This sending out of the Twelve was the beginning of the intention of Jesus to arouse the nation. Evidently it had its effect. Verse 14 tells us that Herod heard about what was happening as people were changed through the work of the disciples and thought John the Baptist had come back from the dead.

Nations are still aroused and directed Godward as followers of Jesus go out and do his work in this fashion. In fact, they will never be changed until they are impacted by the declaration in word and deed of the gospel of Christ.

II. "Take nothing for your journey except a staff only; no bread, no bag, no money in your belt. Just wear sandals and do not put on two tunics" (6:8–9). "Travel light," this says. It may also indicate that the journey was not going to be a long one. But another thought comes from commentators. It seems that there was a habit of rabbis and religious leaders to take a bag with them to collect subscriptions for their gods. They would go from village to village and many times come back with overflowing bags of money. It was as if they were saying, "It will cost you to receive my learning and help." Jesus is telling his followers that they are to go and give, not get. That is still the intent of the church. When we become more interested in keeping the masonry and instruments of worship than we are in meeting the needs without price, we have failed to fully follow the Lord. Like those early witnesses, we are to not be encumbered with that which will prevent us from genuinely doing Christ's work in a waiting world.

III. Jesus tells his followers also to be ready for defeat (6:11). He knew that they would go to places where they would not be received. He had been there. Nazareth's rejection was fresh in his mind. But he knew and had experienced the truth that one rejection does not mean defeat. Shaking the dust off your feet is a call to put the defeat behind you and go on. That is still the call of the follower of Jesus. We will not always be successful in our adventuring for him. Like our Lord, we will find that there are those places where no great works can be done because of their unbelief. Such is never to destroy our continuing efforts. Move on. Try again, for there are yet many who await the saving power of Jesus that we have the privilege of sharing when we go out two by two.
—Henry Fields

SUNDAY: JULY THIRTEENTH

SERVICE OF WORSHIP

Sermon: Body Building
TEXT: Luke 2:52

Luke says in the verse that is our text, "And Jesus increased in wisdom and in stature, and in favor with God and man."

Notice the second phrase. Luke says that Jesus increased in stature. This is physical growth. This morning, I want to share with you some thoughts out of God's word about growing up physically.

I. More to Faith Than Just Being Religious
a. As there are people who make a sharp distinction between faith and the mind, even so there are people who separate faith from the body. They imply, "It doesn't matter how I take care of my body. It doesn't matter what kind of shape I am in physically. The only thing essential is that I have faith."

First Corinthians 6:13 says, "The body is not for immorality, but for the Lord; and the Lord is for the body."

In Phil. 1:20, Paul expresses the urgent desire that "Christ shall even now, as always, be exalted in my body."

b. Do you think you can have faith in Christ and do what you want to with your body? Not at all. For the Bible says that if you have faith, then you will recognize that the body is the Lord's, you will realize that the body is the temple of the Holy Spirit, and you will therefore discipline your body and develop your body and nourish your body and build up your body so that it can be used to glorify God!

That's why eating right is important. That's why exercise is important.

There is more to faith than just being religious. Faith, real faith, will lead you to develop your body.

II. More to Health Than Not Being Sick

a. Viktor Frankl is one of the leading psychotherapists of our day. When he was an inmate at Auschwitz during World War II, Frankl observed a strange phenomenon. Survival did not appear to depend on the health of the inmates. Many of the young and healthy and strong would die. On the other hand, many who were old and frail and sick would survive. What, then, was the key? Those who did survive had a strong sense of purpose and hope. Frankl concluded that where there is a driving passion or a great purpose in life, the physical body is more likely to survive. There is more to health than not being sick.

b. Norman Cousins, former owner-editor of the *Saturday Review,* returned from Europe with a nontreatable illness that left him paralyzed and immovable. He was told by his doctor that his chances for recovery were one in five hundred. With no other hope before him, Cousins asked the doctor if he could treat his own illness. The doctor agreed. So Cousins moved out of the hospital into a hotel. Tucked away in his comfortable hotel room, he took time to straighten out some of the primary relationships of his life. And then he developed a program of laughter. He sent out for old Marx Brothers movies and obtained old reruns of "Candid Camera." For two hours a day he watched funny movies and laughed. He said, "The more I laughed, the better I got." After a while all his symptoms disappeared, and he returned to work. It was ten years later when he wrote his best-selling book which proclaimed that there was healing in laughter.

c. Centuries before Frankl made his conclusions and Cousins wrote his book, the writer of Proverbs declared, "A joyful heart is good medicine, but a broken spirit dries up the bones" (Prov. 17:22).

Developing physically into wholeness is important. And the keys in developing physically and remaining healthy are the attitudes with which you approach life and the feelings that you allow to control your thinking.

There is more to health than not being sick.

III. More to Sickness Than Today

a. Dr. Paul Tournier, a celebrated Swiss physician and psychiatrist, noted once, "Most illnesses do not, as is generally thought, come like a bolt out of the blue. The ground is prepared for years, through faulty diet, intemperance, overwork, and moral conflicts, slowly eroding the subject's vitality. Man does not die, he kills himself."

When you body breaks down, when illness comes, when physical exhaustion sets in, it is not because of what you did yesterday or today. It is because of what you have been doing for the last few weeks and the last few months and the last few years.

b. The Bible says, "For whatever a man sows, this he will also reap" (Gal. 6:7).

Because there is a law of consequences written into the framework of our universe, our bad habits will eventually wreak their havoc on our bodies. There is more to sickness than today.

IV. More to Life Than Health

a. I do not want you to think that illness and poor health are automatically signs of lack of faith. The Bible says that sometimes when you try to develop your body physically, and sometimes when you have the right attitudes in life, and sometimes when you do practice good health habits, physical problems still come. When it happens, don't despair. Just remember that there is more to life than health.

The ultimate goal in life is to serve God, whether you are physically strong, or physically weak, whether you are well or sick.

b. God has used those who are strong and physically sound to do his work. But God also uses broken things. It takes broken soil to produce a crop, broken clouds to give rain, broken grain to give bread, broken bread to give strength, and sometimes God uses broken bodies to serve him more effectively. You do need to care for your body. You do need to strive for good health. But when your body is weak and your health poor, the larger challenge is to do what you can with what you have.

c. Developing physically is important, and having positive attitudes and good habits will help you to do it. But even if your body is broken by disease or limited by handicaps, you can still honor God with your body if you are willing to "do what you can." Will you make that commitment today? Will you say to God who made you, "I will commit myself to you today, where I am, with what I have." That commitment can be the beginning of a new walk with God for you.—Brian L. Harbour

Illustrations

APPETITE CONTROL.   Temptation was especially brutal to Mrs. Evelyn Couch of Birmingham, Alabama, in the area of appetite control. Fannie Flagg tells us about Evelyn in her novel, *Fried Green Tomatoes at the Whistle Stop Cafe.* Evelyn—who had a weight problem—was visiting her friend, Mrs. Threadgoode, and eating her Baby Ruth candy bar when she started to cry. Mrs. Threadgoode asked what was wrong, and Evelyn replied, " . . . I just cain't seem to stop eating. I've tried and tried, every day I wake up and think that today I'm gonna stay on my diet, and every day I go off. I hide candy bars all over the house and in the garage. I don't know what's the matter with me."—David Albert Farmer

IMMUNIZATION AGAINST ADVERSITY. Not freedom from temptation but a serene fortitude in the face of disappointment and chagrin should be our goal. If you have evaded all unpleasantness in life, your happiness is placed in unstable equilibrium by the constant dread that some unavoidable disappointment is just around the corner. If you have faced pain and disappointment, you not only value your happiness more highly, but you are prepared for unpre-dictable exigencies. Just as we can immunize ourselves against certain bodily diseases by stimulating our reserves to over-activity by taking graduated doses of toxin into our bodies, so can we immunize ourselves against adversity by meeting and facing unavoidable chagrins of life, as they occur.—W. Beran Wolfe, M.D.

SERMON SUGGESTIONS

Topic: If I Sat Where They Sit
TEXT: Ezek. 3:15
What I (preacher-pastor) would do if I say where they (they lay people) sit: (1) I should sit well up toward the front of the church. (2) I should want to put on the collection plate a weekly offering which in some real sense represented me. (3) I should feel elated and eagerly expectant as the minister stood up to preach—to bring forth treasures new and old from the unfailing resources of the Faith. (4) I should wish to greet any stranger seated near me, when the period of worship came to an end.—Edgar DeWitt Jones

Topic: Why People Go to Church
TEXT: Heb. 10:24–25
(1) To worship God. (2) To find forgiveness. (3) To find fellowship. (4) To find power —spiritual power for this difficult task of living.—Adapted from Leslie D. Weatherhead

Worship Aids

CALL TO WORSHIP.   "Lord, who shall abide in thy tabernacle? Who shall dwell in thy holy hill? He that walketh uprightly, and worketh righteousness, and speaketh the truth in his heart" (Ps. 15:1–2).

INVOCATION.   God of forgiving grace, we come to you that we may forget—forget past failures and past victories. We also come to you that we may remember your past mercies and our past conceit. In this forgetting and remembering may we find a truer sense of what you are and what we are.

OFFERTORY SENTENCE.   "The silver is mine, and the gold is mine, saith the Lord of Hosts" (Hag. 2:8).

OFFERTORY PRAYER.   O God, may we never forget thy ownership of all things and our stewardship of all that we fondly call our own. Bless us and bless our offerings as we remember.

PRAYER.   God of wisdom, we thank you that you have given to us an ever-flowing source of refreshment for our lives. Your word, like water, enters our parched existence, bringing vitality, growth, and fruit. Because we have studied, meditated, and applied the truths of Holy Scripture, we have often had answers to our questions, courage to rebuff our temptations, and power to meet the challenge of victorious living. We do not congratulate ourselves, but thank you for giving this means of help.

We acknowledge that we have not always sought your word. We have many times leaned heavily to our own understanding when your better way was clearly marked. We have suffered sin's betrayals and have lived to regret following short-sighted advice, fleeting pleasure, and destructive cynicism.

Forgive our folly, we pray, and set us on paths attended by your presence. So let us find life's true meaning and the joy of doing your will.

LECTIONARY MESSAGE

Topic: The Pride of Fools and the Death of a Great Man

TEXT: Mark 6:14–29

This Scripture is a drama that reveals what happens when pride usurps principle, causing the innocent to suffer. It is a vivid picture of power used for personal gain with disregard for anyone who gets in the way. It is a tragedy as dark and devious as any play ever written.

Notice in the opening scene (vv. 14–16) that King Herod has learned of the miraculous powers of Jesus and that there is much speculation as to who Jesus is. Some persons said Jesus was Elijah, others called him one of the prophets of old, but Herod had someone else in mind. "John, whom I beheaded, has been raised from the dead," he said, and Herod had many reasons to reach that guilt-ridden decision.

In scene two (vv. 17–20), we learn what occurred between John the Baptist and Herod. Herod had John arrested because John bluntly stated, "It is not lawful for you to have your brother's wife." Herod had cast off his first wife, the daughter of Aretas IV, the Arabian king, to marry Herodias, his brother's wife.

Herod feared John, sensing that he was a holy man. What John said perplexed Herod, though he gladly listened. Herod thought it best to put John in jail for a while: the people were easily stirred up. Herodias had stronger feelings about John. She was the sort of a woman who thought nothing of flouting convention and living above the law, but she did not care to be held up to public ridicule by someone acting like a prophet. Herodias was determined to have John the Baptist permanently silenced, but without Herod's approval it could not be. She would bide her time, then move with swiftness when she could.

As scene three opens (vv. 21–29), preparations are under way for Herod's birthday party. It is to be a stag event for the government and military officials of the kingdom; the leading men of Galilee would be present.

Herodias sees her chance. She suggests her daughter, Salome, dance as entertainment, and with wine flowing, Salome dances suggestively to the approval of all present. In the heat of the moment, Herod makes a rash promise to Salome, "Ask for anything you want, up to half my kingdom and I will give it to you."

In reality, Herod Antipas was not so much king as tetrarch of Galilee and was in no position to give away any of his kingdom. Yet with this foolish vow, Herod unknowingly threw the ball into the court of Herodias. Salome was a dancer, and thinking was not what she did best, so she went to her mother, the ethical pygmy, who believed no violence is too small in the service of revenge, for an answer. Without batting an eyelash, Herodias replied, "Ask for the head of John the Baptist." Salome hurried into the king and delivered the request, asking for the head of the Baptist at once on a platter.

Herod, who had been showing off how powerful he was all evening, was in a tough spot. A king tricked by his own oath is a favorite motif in legend. Herod was too proud to recant. Even though he deeply regretted his foolish vow, the order was given, an executioner was dispatched, and John the Baptist, greatest of all men who ever lived (Matt. 11:11), perhaps never even knowing why he was to be executed, was silenced forever. John's head was delivered to Salome, who once again did not know what to do. Naturally she turned to her mother, delivering the head to Herodias. As the curtain comes down on this drama, the Scripture records:

when the disciples of John heard of this, they took his body and laid it in a tomb.

It takes courage to stand up for principle in the face of opposition. John the Baptist epitomized a sense of oughtness and was brave to declare what his conscience could not disallow: no person, no matter how powerful or weak, is exempt from the moral imperatives of the Ten Commandments.—E. Lee Phillips

SUNDAY: JULY TWENTIETH

SERVICE OF WORSHIP

Sermon: Well-Timed Temptations

TEXT: Luke 4:1–13; also Deut. 26:1–3, 16–19

I am well acquainted with temptation as are, I suspect, most of you. As well as I know temptation, she or he has never spent any energy trying to get me to do good things; oh, what temptation presses us to do may seem—at first—to offer great rewards, but temptation is only interested in having us do what will bring us and others harm. Temptation whispers to us and hovers over us, obviously, at our points of weakness and is merciless in trying to persuade us to do what is not best.

What I've noticed about temptation through the years, and this trait is especially evident in the story Luke tells us about Jesus' sojourn in the wilderness, is that temptation's appearances are calculated; there is nothing random or coincidental about them. We're talking *well-timed temptations!*

In this story from the Third Gospel, temptation is personified. It is the devil himself who speaks the luring words to Jesus. And I want you to notice *when* the devil speaks. Listen carefully to Luke's story.

I. Jesus was "full of the Holy Spirit." Jesus was returning "from the Jordan." What had happened at the Jordan? Jesus had been baptized there! Jesus was "led by the Spirit" into the wilderness. Do you follow Luke's emphasis here?

This was a "spiritual high" for Jesus. He was elated—almost overcome with the reality and the joy of God's presence with him.

He must have felt, then, that all was right with the world.

a. You've been there, haven't you? So full of the reality of God's love for you and God's presence with you that you couldn't think of anything else, had no room to feel anything else? What a wonderful awareness. We all wish such times would come around more often.

b. Here Jesus was, on the spiritual high of his life, feeling led to go to the wilderness, of all places, for some uninterrupted communion with God. The wilderness was not a pleasant place to go; in fact, it was considered a frightening place, and not too many people would go there voluntarily. But Jesus felt he had the resources to be able to survive whatever he might encounter there.

II. Luke also reports: (Jesus) ate nothing during those days, and when they were over, he was famished. In that state of mind and body—not when he was feeling full and strong and ready for anything—the devil shows up.

a. Remember, one of the tempter's devices about which we have to be most careful is that what we are encouraged to do, at first, doesn't sound like anything bad; it sounds like something good for us. Jesus was in a bind. He wasn't just hungry; he was famished, starving, and the devil says, "I don't see any food around here; there's nothing to eat for miles, but I have an idea about how you can get hold of some food right away." How thoughtful of the tempter to be concerned about Jesus' plight. What a nice guy!

b. We have to remember, as we rehear and rethink this very familiar story, that part of what was happening to Jesus during his time in the wilderness was a clarifying of his calling. God was making known to him in those long and lonely and frightening hours, which had begun—paradoxically —when Jesus was so very enthusiastic, the shape of the task he would have to undertake in order to be God's person in what was ahead. So, in the larger picture, the devil is suggesting that Jesus use his powers for his own purposes.

c. In the wilderness, Jesus is coming to grips with the proper use of the power that God is bestowing upon him. He will be a leader among the people of God; he is coming to grips with that fact, but how will he use his authority? The temptation to sell himself and his cause by the inappropriate use of his power and influence were great. Jesus could have used his power in s self-serving manner and, thereby, could have become great in the eyes of the people, who nearly always hunger for a powerful leader. *Or* he could use the power at every turn only as God directed him; this, of course, is what he dedicated himself to do.

III. During this time of acute inner turmoil, the devil showed Jesus in an instant all the kingdoms of the world. And the devil said to him, "To you I will give their glory and all this authority; for it has been given over to me, and I give it to anyone I please. If you, then, will worship me, it will all be yours."

a. The devil is brazen and has no reticence whatsoever about openly seeking Jesus' allegiance. If Jesus follows him, look what control and popularity will come to him. But, if Jesus is faithful to God, what then? Will he ever get out of the wilderness? Will his power get him anywhere at all? Will anybody know his name? Will anybody respect anything he has to say? Not necessarily. Not necessarily.

b. Even so, Jesus' loyalty is singular. He is devoted to God alone, and his rebuttal of his tempter—again—is based in Holy Scripture: "It is written, 'Worship the Lord your God, and serve only him.'" Only God! Not the devil. Not power—real or desired. Not presumed grandiosity.

Notice that once Jesus speaks his mind

based on the teaching of Scripture, the tempter leaves him alone—at least for the time being.

IV. There is another temptation about which Luke wrote. Finally, in Jesus' mind, the devil took him to Jerusalem and placed him on the pinnacle of the temple, saying to him, "If you are the Son or God, throw yourself down from here, for it is written, 'He will command his angels concerning you, to protect you,' and, 'On their hands they will bear you up, so that you will not dash your foot against a stone.'"

a. How absurd! Jesus would never fall for something crazy like this—no pun intended. But he was tempted. Jesus must have preferred to think that he would not face harm when he began to say publicly what he felt God was telling him to say to a society that would, undoubtedly, be hostile to his ideas. But God's people don't put God to the test; they don't tell God what God has to do; they don't agree to take on certain ministries *if* God will promise them that nothing bad could possibly happen when they're doing the will of God.

b. That's not part of the deal. That's not the way God works, and Jesus countered the devil simply by saying, "It is said, 'Do not put the Lord your God to the test.'"

But in this instance, the devil had been quoting Scripture himself. Imagine that! He had been trying to get Jesus with the Bible—fighting fire with fire, you know. Jesus heard the devil, but he didn't fall for it.

Well, on that last, "Bug off," the tempter left Jesus alone . . . for a while at least—until, as Luke recalled it, "an opportune time." The tempter never left Jesus alone for long; at his every moment of concern and anxiety, the tempter was there to press Jesus to turn away from God's path.

V. As they were with Jesus, the devil's temptations of us are always well timed! Make no mistake about it, and don't be caught off guard. If you are God's person, prepare to be tempted because you *will be* tempted to do other than what God wants and asks of you. And the greatest temptations you will ever know will come when you are at your worst, at your weakest moments.

a. Being tempted is no sin. When we know that we are being tempted, that is not an indication of something wrong with us or our faith. The sin is in going the way of the tempter.

b. We must remember God's love for us and our commitment to God—even when we are feeling beaten down and overwhelmed. If, in that state of mind, we can counter the devil's offer with God's word, the tempter will leave us be—until the next opportune moment.—David A. Farmer

Illustrations

GOING WITH THE CROWD. Do we wait to take our cue from others, so that we may go with the crowd, echoing their cries, being captured by the prevailing mood? Once having begun to march with them, it is hard to stop and break the ranks. When they all cry, "Hosanna!" or as they would now say, "Three cheers!" it is not hard for us to say and do the same. But so often the crowd today is not for Christ. They may not shout, "Crucify him!" as they once did. We might then be stirred to protest. Now they are simply politely incredulous, much too busy to be bothered, or frankly quite indifferent, since it is none of their business.—John Trevor Davies

ROCK BOTTOM. Religious nurture implies at least a preliminary knowledge of cardinal doctrines and practices. Contrary to a widespread notion, what one believes in deeply and passionately is of major importance. A growing body of truths, tested and validated by experience even if not explicitly stated, is a rock against which deprivation, poverty, tribulation, and death itself dash in vain.

In the next place . . . a sound philosophy is morally sensitive. No cleavage between accepted moral standards and conduct is permitted to develop. No attempt is made to condone inexcusable behavior. An evil practice is abandoned as soon as its nature is discovered. New insights into the demands of life are gained by him who obeys the dictates of a tender conscience. Only to him who does what he believes to be right is fresh moral light given. Our ideals are clarified and redirected by the exercise of the moral judgment we already possess.—Karl Ruf Stolz

SERMON SUGGESTIONS

Topic: A Plea for Simpler Living
TEXT: Ps. 116:6
(1) An unburdened life. (2) An unpretentious life. (3) An uncrowded life. (4) An unhurried life.—A. Leonard Griffith

Topic: Opening Your Eyes on a New World
TEXT: 9:25
The formerly blind man saw a new world. When our spiritual eyes are opened: (1) We see a special, spiritual world with new appreciation. (2) This new world is characterized by the love of God and of neighbor. (3) Christ is the Light of the new world.

Worship Aids

CALL TO WORSHIP. "How amiable are thy tabernacles, O Lord of hosts! My soul longeth, yea, fainteth for the courts of the Lord: my heart and my flesh crieth out for the living God" (Ps. 84:1–2).

INVOCATION. How good it is to be here, O God, your people together, singing, praying, and listening for your word in Scripture and sermon. We confess that we do not always know how good it is, and our joy ebbs and flows. Build within us now good experiences and memories that will sustain us in times of stress and longing and opportunity in the days to come.

OFFERTORY SENTENCE. "Let us be thankful, then, because we receive a kingdom that cannot be shaken. Let us be grateful and worship God in a way that will please him, with reverence and fear" (Heb. 12:28 TEV).

OFFERTORY PRAYER. Our Father, we are thankful that we can offer the perishing fruits of our labor in the service of your kingdom that will remain forever. Raise these gifts as an acted prayer that your kingdom may come and your will be done on earth as it is in heaven.

PRAYER.   Clear our vision this morning, we pray, Lord. We are so blinded by what is visible around us that we fail to see the things of the spirit that make the large difference in how we live and move and have our being. We need this morning to be able to see beyond the darkness of what is material into that which is luminously spiritual. All about us are barriers that prohibit our view of the wide vistas you desire us to see. Enable us this morning to see beyond the barriers that we may envision what is real and eternal.

- Let us see beyond the barrier of the quick satisfaction of hate to the long joy of forgiveness.
- Let us see beyond the appetite for more to the pleasure of self-control.
- Let us see beyond greed to the luxury of giving.
- Let us see beyond blinding pride to the healthiness of humility.
- Let us see beyond profit to usefulness, past the heat of desire to the light of renunciation, past the glaring light of power to the beauty of service, past the poisonous growth of selfishness to the wonder and power of selflessness.– Henry Fields

LECTIONARY MESSAGE

Topic: Handling Life's Interruptions
TEXT: Mark 6:30–34, 53–56

The apostles, who had been commissioned by Jesus to go out two by two and minister to the people, healing, casting out demons, and preaching repentance, finally returned and reported on their mission to Jesus. So many people were coming and going they barely had time to eat. Jesus wisely suggested they go away for a while and rest in a lonely place. Healing, like preaching, can be energizing, but it can also be exhausting. Jesus knew the mind seldom achieves what energy denies and that physical exhaustion is the great crippler of many a noble cause. We all have a responsibility to maintain our health, so that God may make use of the bodies we are given. Stewardship of health is fundamental to the active life of faith.

So Jesus and the disciples went by boat to a quiet place, but the people saw them and ran along the shore. When they landed, the crowd was there to greet them. Jesus was not irritated by the persistence of the crowds, even though the purpose of the trip was cut short. In fact, Jesus had compassion for them because he saw them as sheep without a shepherd.

Some of the greatest opportunities in ministry will come in awkward moments when the need of another will surmount your need for quiet, and in that hour one must reach outside oneself, using the compassionate love of God from within for the mercy of the moment. Sheep are easily led astray and without a good leader face many perils. Thus Jesus saw himself in a shepherd role, tenderly and empathetically responding to the needs of the people with teachings that would help them find the green pastures of salvation and the still waters of peace.

Later one day, after five thousand had been fed on five loaves and two fish, Jesus and the disciples crossed in a boat to Genesaret, and the scene was virtually the same as before. Jesus was recognized by the crowd around the shore, and this time they brought their sick.

The more Jesus did for others, the more seemed needed to be done. If he fed them, they wanted more food. If he healed them, there were still more to be healed. If listeners caught a glimpse of the holy and sensed the nearness of God, then they wanted to hear more.

"Over here, Jesus, it's my invalid mother." "This way Jesus, my child is lame." "Jesus, Jesus, just let me touch you. I am blind and I cannot find you." And wherever Jesus went the sick were laid in the open marketplace of city or town, and even those who touched the fringe of his tunic were healed.

Imagine, no hospitals, no clinics, inadequate medicine, no mental institutions, and Jesus faces the full array of illnesses in his day: leprosy, deafness, deformities, headaches, tumors, boils, goiters, birth defects, insanity, and retardation and healed them all. Whence the power?

Maybe had we the power in our sinful condition we would misuse it; it might ruin us. Not so with the pure, sinless Son of God, the man of prayer. Jesus' pattern in healing was always to heal the whole person, to examine the motive as well as the complaint and lead the person not only to a healthy body but to a healthy relationship to God. The forgiveness of sins and the healing of the body are inextricably linked.

How approachable are you? These passages tell of a Savior who was accessible, who did not withdraw from the needs of others but rather welcomed them as opportunities for ministry and with the power of God met every need. More like the Master let us ever be!–E. Lee Phillips

SUNDAY: JULY TWENTY-SEVENTH

SERVICE OF WORSHIP

Sermon: The Missing Ingredient
TEXT: Acts 19:1–7

Our churches are filled today with people who are living as if Pentecost had never happened. Historically, they are on this side of Pentecost. Spiritually, they are on the other side, for they are trying to live their Christian lives without the Holy Spirit.

Many Christians in today's churches are living their Christian lives as if they did not even know the Holy Spirit existed. They are grieving the Spirit. They are quenching the Spirit. They are neglecting the Spirit. There is a missing ingredient in their lives.

The seriousness of the problem becomes apparent when you realize what happens when a Christian tries to live without the Holy Spirit. There are two tragic consequences.

I. First of all, discipleship without the Spirit will lead to wandering. When you don't know where you are going, you are going to get lost. Because we cannot see the whole scope of life, because our understanding of life is so limited, most of the time we don't know where we are going. We're lost. We need someone to guide us, someone to give us directions, someone to show us the way. The Holy Spirit is given to the Christian to serve as our guide through life.

a. The Holy Spirit guides us through *God's Word.* Paul wrote to young Timothy, "All Scripture is inspired by God, and profitable for teaching, for reproof, for correction, for training in righteousness; that the man of God may be adequate, equipped for every good work" (2 Tim. 3:16–17). This is the guidebook for the Christian life. As we

read it, study it, and learn it, the Holy Spirit will use it to guide our lives.

b. The Holy Spirit also guides us through our *circumstances.* In our circumstances, if we will look deeply enough, we can discern the finger of God opening doors of opportunity for us. It is through those very circumstances that the Holy Spirit is guiding us.

c. The Holy Spirit guides us through our *sanctified common sense.* At the Jerusalem Council in Acts 15, the leaders of the church come together to deal with a sticky problem, how to relate the Gentile Christian to the Jewish Christians. After much prayer and consideration, Luke says that they made a decision. Acts 15:28–29 says, "For it seemed good to the Holy Spirit and to us to lay upon you no greater burden than these essentials." That is sanctified common sense.

d. The Holy Spirit guides us at times through *closed doors.* Twice in Acts 16, the Holy Spirit closed a door on the apostle Paul. He wanted to go to Asia, but Luke says they were "forbidden by the Holy Spirit" (v. 6). Then, they wanted to go to Bithynia, but Luke says "the Spirit of Jesus did not permit them" (v. 7).

e. The Holy Spirit also guides us through our *companions.* When Paul was converted on the Damascus road he cried out, "Lord, what shall I do, Lord?" And the Lord told him, "Arise and go on into Damascus; and there you will be told of all that has been appointed for you to do" (Acts 22:10). And it was through a man named Ananias that the Spirit gave instructions to the apostle Paul.

Jesus has given the Holy Spirit to every believer to guide us into truth. He guides through God's word, through our circumstances, through our sanctified common sense, through closed doors, and through our companions. But when we grieve the Spirit, and quench the Spirit and neglect the Spirit, there will be a missing ingredient in our lives. And the result will be a wandering around in life with no clear direction for no precise purpose.

Discipleship without the Spirit leads to wandering.

II. But there is a second result. Discipleship without the Spirit will not only lead to wandering. It will lead to weakness. The Holy Spirit was given not just to enlighten us but also to empower us.

The Holy Spirit was given to empower us. Jesus said to those first disciples, "But you will receive power when the Holy Spirit has come upon you" (Acts 1:8). And that power will enable us not only to change our attitudes but also to change our actions. He will not only enlighten our minds. He will also empower our lives. But when we grieve the Holy Spirit and neglect the Holy Spirit, there is a missing ingredient in our lives. The result is weakness.

III. There are two things that every Christian needs to experience an abundant life: an accurate perception of life and an adequate power of life. Both of these are available through the Holy Spirit who indwells your life.

So the question of the hour, "How can I be filled and controlled by the Holy Spirit?"

a. The first step is to *believe*. You must believe that the Holy Spirit exists. Sometimes we have problems believing what we cannot see. I cannot see the Holy Spirit, but I can see His work. I cannot see the Holy Spirit, but I can experience his power and purpose in my life. The Holy Spirit is the permanent, powerful presence of God in this world today. You must believe that.

b. The second step is to *desire*. In the beatitudes Jesus says that whoever hungers and thirsts after righteousness will be filled. To be filled with the Holy Spirit, to come under his control, you must not only believe that He exists. You must be willing to ask God to let the Holy Spirit fill you and control you. You must desire it.

c. The third step is to *repent*. After Peter preached his Pentecost sermon, the people cried out, "What must we do?" Peter answered, "Repent . . . and you shall receive the gift of the Holy Spirit" (Acts 2:38). As a glass filled with dirt cannot be filled with clean water, even so the life filled with unconfessed sin cannot be filled with God's Holy Spirit. You must be willing to confess your sins and get them out of your life before God's Spirit can control you.

d. The fourth step is, by faith, to *appropriate* the Holy Spirit who is available to you. When you believe the Holy Spirit exists, when you desire to be filled, when you confess your sins, you have done what the Bible says you must do. Then, you simply appropriate the Holy Spirit into your life and begin to live under his control.

The question of ultimate importance for every person is, "Are you filled with the Holy Spirit?" If not, there is a missing ingredient in your life.—Brian L. Harbour

Illustrations

WHERE IS THE HOLY SPIRIT?   At a certain Christian school the teacher taught her class to repeat the Apostles' Creed clause by clause, each pupil having his own clause. They would begin class each day with this group recitation of the Apostles' Creed.

One morning the recitation began with the first boy who said, "I believe in God the Father almighty, maker of heaven and earth." The second boy said, "I believe in Jesus Christ, his only Son our Lord." Then there was silence. As the teacher looked up to see what had happened, one of the pupils said, "Teacher, the boy who believes in the Holy Spirit isn't here today."—Brian L. Harbour

FAITH IN THE HOLY SPIRIT.   Holy Spirit is the Inspirer of mankind in wisdom, courage, and love. Sometimes the New Testament uses the name Comforter: *con-fort,* "with strength." The Greek noun translated "Comforter" is *paracletos,* a word hard to translate, meaning perhaps (as we have already suggested) Helper or Apostle. The King James Version once translated the same Greek *paracletos* by "advocate." In the Roman courts an *advocatus* was one who stood by an accused man to defend and strengthen him. Another New Testament name for the Holy Spirit is Pneuma, meaning "breath," almost as that word is used in the hymn: "Breathe on me, Breath of God." Whatever the name, there is promise of wisdom, courage, and love beyond man's native endowment; and the promise has been fulfilled.–George A. Buttrick

SERMON SUGGESTIONS

Topic: New World Symphony
TEXT: Isa. 65:17–25

What are these warring factors over which God promises victory to those who are his? (1) The brevity of life. (2) The perversity of self-defeat. (3) The warring environment: In God's new world, that realm of life into which he calls us, even the environment will be conducive to the fulfillment of his good purposes.–J. Ithel Jones

Topic: Parable of the Sower
TEXT: Matt. 13:1–9

(1) *The causes of failure.* (a) Lack of spiritual perception: some seeds fell by the wayside. (b) Lack of depth in character: some fell on stony ground. (c) Impressions come to nothing when the mind is subjected to dissipating influences, and yields to them: some fell among thorns. (2) *For the permanence of religious impressions:* (a) Sincerity of purpose. An honest and good heart. (b) Meditation. They keep the word which they have heard. (c) Endurance. They bring forth fruit with patience.–Frederick W. Robertson

Worship Aids

CALL TO WORSHIP. "Show me thy ways, O Lord; teach my thy paths. Lead me in thy truth and teach me: for thou art the God of my salvation; on thee do I wait all the day" (Ps. 25:4–5).

INVOCATION. God of grace, give us the gift of listening on deep levels that we may hear the voice of God in quietude and respond in commitment because we love the Lord that much.–E. Lee Phillips

OFFERTORY SENTENCE. "Thou are worthy, O Lord; to receive glory and honor and power: for thou hast created all things" (Rev. 4:11).

OFFERTORY PRAYER. Father, you have given to each of us gifts through which wealth is placed into our hands. Inspire us this morning to give gifts to you through your church as we bring our offerings and dedicate them to the use and betterment of mankind throughout the world.–Henry Fields

PRAYER. O Lord, our God, we pray thee, grant thy blessing especially upon all that are gathered together in this place today. May those who have come from darkness, and sadness, and who are weary and heavy-laden, find indeed that they have come to the right place. O thou that hast made thy yoke easy and thy burden light, grant, we pray thee, to fulfill to them today the promise of strength, that as their day is their strength shall be. Grant, we pray thee, that they may be glad that there is one place where burdens, touched of God, may roll away; where the low-lying clouds are pierced by faith; where men may see beyond their hovel, and beyond their poverty, and beyond their cares and tearful days, the bright and unclouded future.–Henry Ward Beecher

LECTIONARY MESSAGE

Topic: Letting God Use What You Have
TEXT: John 6:1–21

In this passage of Scripture, Jesus and his disciples have passed to the far shore of the Sea of Galilee, and there many pilgrims on the way to Passover in Jerusalem meet them, hoping to observe healings. John records that Jesus did five things:

First, Jesus observed the crowd of five thousand following him and turning to Philip asked if Philip knew where they could buy enough bread to feed the crowd. Jesus knew Philip was slower than the others and wanted to help him imagine how he might solve the situation, though Jesus had a plan in mind. Philip typically replied that eight months' wages would not be enough for each person to have a bite.

Andrew, Simon Peter's brother, found a boy with five small barley loaves and two fish and brought them to Jesus, saying, "How far will they go among so many?"

Jesus did not answer Andrew's question, but using unusual common sense when working with an active crowd, instructed the disciples to have the people sit down on the green grass. Mark tells us (Mark 6:40) the disciples had the people sit in groups of fifty and a hundred.

Then, Jesus took the two loaves and gave thanks and they were distributed to the people. The same pattern of blessing was followed with the two fish. No gift is too small for thanksgiving to God, and by example, Jesus showed the quieted crowd the importance of prayer.

We never know how great a small contribution to God might become. Certainly this lad's mother, going about her daily tasks, probably never thought his lunch would be used to feed thousands. Nor was it likely the little lad had any notion of the possibilities of his gift. But the boy was willing. God is dependent on small, humble, gifts to build his kingdom, for, like a mustard seed, they can by faith become a great, arching tree in the economy of the Creator (Matt. 17:20).

The fourth thing Jesus did was to make certain that no food was wasted. Instructions were given that all which was left over was to be gathered up. Twelve satchels full were gathered, a satchel containing just enough food for the day.

When the people added up all that had transpired they felt that Jesus was the long-awaited Prophet that was to come into the world. Jesus knew they wanted to make him a king by force, so he dismissed the crowd, sent the disciples away, and withdrew into the hills to be alone for a while.

Notice how deftly Jesus takes time for individuals yet also knows how to handle a crowd. Events do not control Jesus; Jesus controls events. It is nowhere recorded that Jesus was ever flustered. No one ever threw anything at Jesus he could not handle.

The scene now shifts. As darkness comes, the disciples go down to the lake and set out on a boat without him, and a squall arises. The lake is five miles across, and when they are well over halfway across the disciples see what appears to be Jesus walking on the water and they are terrified. Jesus makes a significant statement: "It is I; be not afraid." Mark has it: "Be of good cheer. It is I; be not afraid" (Mark 6:50). After Jesus' words, he is gladly taken aboard, and before they know it the boat has reached shore.

In between these lines you will find there was a numinous quality about Jesus in the eyes of his disciples. Jesus was compassionate, authoritative, gracious, approachable, yet there was about him the mystical, the miraculous, the wholly other. John knew, and from the very first line of his Gospel he is trying to tell us, that Jesus is the Word of God incarnate, whose power knows no limit. Could we not say Jesus comes walking across all the rough waters of our lives, bidding us to be unafraid, to be trusting children of faith, looking to God for sustenance and peace? One of the saddest facts of the Christian church is that so many of us have been so reluctant to give all we have for use by the living Christ. Is there something holding you back, a real tempest within that needs to be dedicated to God?–E. Lee Phillips

SUNDAY: AUGUST THIRD

SERVICE OF WORSHIP

Sermon: What the Church Needs Now
TEXT: John 12:1–8

The Bible claims that love is the greatest and most abiding value in all the universe. Our churches do need bigger programs, better buildings, more members, and greater commitment. But what the church most needs now is–love!

The kind of love we need is displayed by Mary, whose story John recorded (12:1–8) as occurring in the village of Bethany just a few days before Jesus came to Jerusalem to be crucified.

The scene as John painted it seems domestic and intimate. Mary sat at the table and loved Jesus for his love, his care, and his fellowship. Then, impelled by an overwhelming sense of thanksgiving and love, she quietly arose, stood before him, and anointed his head and feet with a very expensive perfume.

The whole action revealed an impulsive response of devotion, costly and authentic in its affection. The attitudes reflected by Mary in this story authenticate the depth and extent of her love. Where love is genuine, it nourishes patterns of behavior that indicate its reality.

I. Mary's Love Made Her Generous

a. Verse 3 describes the perfume as "very costly." Verse 5 amplifies this as being "three hundred pence," almost a year's wages for a working man in those days. How costly would it be to give your annual income for such a gift as that! Obviously Mary must have scrimped and saved over a long time to procure so costly an offering. The suggestion (which we shall pursue later) is that she had put it aside for some special purpose but was compelled to present it immediately to him now.

b. Authentic love breeds a generous spirit—a spirit willing to sacrifice, to surrender self-interests. It shows up in extra effort, extra time, and extra giving, without complaint, as an expression of devotion to God. And it also means a generosity in relationships.

c. A generous spirit means forgiveness for our fellow church members when they hurt and injure us. In the kingdom Jesus expects our behavior toward others to match his toward us. The generosity of his grace comes not because we deserve it but because we need it! So must we show forth the reality of our love by like behavior in the church. Those who love the Lord the most are those who are the most generous—generous with forgiveness and friendship and gently sensitive to the needs of others. If you are callous, cold, and critical, always demanding your rights in the church but insensitive of others' rights, I must challenge the reality of your love for Christ.

d. To love means to be willing to sacrifice. It means a spirit of generosity seen as the attitude that swiftly forgives and is quick to encourage the best in others. Those who crush and squash others with hard and bitter spirits proclaim the hypocrisy of their claimed love for the Lord. The harsh, narrow, critical Christian is a contradiction in terms.

II. Mary's Love Made Her Humble

a. In Jesus' day the house servant would bid travelers welcome by washing the dust from their tired feet, covered only by simple sandals. When Mary anointed Jesus she took the humble servant's part, saying, "What others will not do, I shall, because I love him."

That's why the church needs an increase in genuine love today. So many in the church are simply unwilling to serve where the real needs are! We prefer the high spots to the humble corners for our service. Quiet service in the choir requires humility and submissive loyalty when you are not asked to sing the featured parts. Much hard work must be done behind the scenes in every church on committees and in the hundred necessities needed to keep programs flowing smoothly. Such service is seldom in the public eye, and it is never easy to enlist some members in fulfilling it.

b. Judas criticized Mary's actions, seeing a waste in the apparently useless sacrifice of the precious perfume (John 12:4–5).

Jesus saw behind the surface of the deed to its motive and reality. He discerned this to be an act of pure love from the heart. He does not hold us responsible for what we can do. We may not have the gift of preaching or of evangelism. If we are not called to lead, we are not responsible to lead. But we are responsible to do quietly what we can do where he has placed us.

c. Jesus sees the service of the humble. He notes the fidelity of those who serve quietly in the inconspicuous places in his church. He evaluates motive and faithfulness and capacity higher than public prominence when he judges our behavior.

d. Jesus noted that her love led her to sense his special need for acts of devotion right then. He was not to be with them always, and Mary sensed his need for a loving act of affection as he faced the cross. She knew this would have meaning for him then and would thus be much more valuable than if it were kept for burial anointings.

III. Mary's Love Made Her Sensitive

a. All the Gospel writers sandwich this little story, with its beauty and encouragement to Christ, between the tales of chief priests and scribes plotting to kill Jesus and Judas's agreement to betray him. The experience of these days weighed heavily on the Savior's shoulders.

He faced the cross in only a few hours' time. Already the shadow of its suffering stamped an agony in his soul. In just a little while he actually cried out, "Now is my soul troubled . . ." (John 12:27), but Mary noted his hurt while he sat at supper. And she said, "I have saved this for a gift of love to anoint his dead body, but he needs it now! He goes directly to Jerusalem to be our sin-bearer; we must tell him now that we love him." That is what this gift meant for Mary. And for Jesus it meant encouragement, support, love, and inspiration to fulfill the Father's will, a sacrificial and generous, humble and genuine expression of affection that revealed Mary's sensitivity to Jesus' needs.

b. When others act ugly and evil, if your love for Jesus is pure you may also anoint the Savior! You support his purposes and nourish his glory when love makes you generous, humble, and sensitive.

The church needs more love, and so does Christ. Our love both to Christ and his church may be tested by our willingness to spend time in his presence and to match that sacrifice of time with the discipline of loyal service in the lowly place, sensitive to his need to have us love him because he first loved us.–Craig Skinner

Illustrations

CONTEMPLATION. An old farmer spent thirty minutes each day sitting quietly in his parish church on his route to the fields. Knowing him to be illiterate, unused to verbalizing prayer, and somewhat simple in his ways and mind, friends asked what he did there each day.

Slowly the old man replied, "We have a stained-glassed window over the pulpit. It shows Jesus dying on the cross for my sins. I look at that beautiful window and use it to settle my thoughts on the Savior. Than I close my eyes and think of him hanging there, meeting all the cost of my salvation.

"Then I look at him. And he looks at me. And we love each other."–Craig Skinner

CHURCH AND PERSONAL TROUBLES. It was a happy fortune in the early days of my ministry to have a pastorate on the coast of Maine, where my friendships included a group of sea dogs, the old, weather-beaten ship captains who had acquired their wisdom from sailing the seven seas in all weathers and climates. They had the farseeing eye; the grim, tight lips; and the experience of men who had to master the destructive forces of nature. Most of them were men who had sailed the old square-riggers or the four- or five-masted schooners.

As a land lover I had always expected that in a storm you would head to shore as a place of safety; but I found that the philosophy of the old sea captains was drastically opposite. "What," they would say, "head to shore and dash the ship on the rocks and reefs? No, not in a storm–always head to deep water and open sea. There you can ride out the storm."

In the storms of life I often think of this philosophy. Running to the shore is dangerous; head out to the open sea. Make for the deep water–outride the storm. It is no wonder, then, that a great Christian leader once said to me, "When the church is discouraged, it is exactly the time to strike out on a big adventure." In life, when the criticisms come, head out into the deep."–Benjamin P. Browne

SERMON SUGGESTIONS

Topic: Weighed and Found Wanting
TEXT: Dan. 5:1–31, esp. v. 27
(1) Belshazzar's Feast (Then). (2) Belshazzar's Feast reenacted (Today). (a) The excesses. (b) The consequences.

Topic: Conversion of Saint Paul
TEXT: Gal. 1:15–16; Phil. 3:7
Paul might have continued his early course in life but for the fact that somehow he was not satisfied and that he had heard

disquieting talk about Jesus, whom God revealed to him as his Son. The difference that made: (1) It saved Paul from himself. (2) God gave Paul something to do in the world. (3) Paul discovered the unity of all mankind in Christ.–D. M. Baillie

Worship Aids

CALL TO WORSHIP.   "We have not a high priest who is unable to sympathize with our weaknesses, but one who in every respect has been tempted as we are, yet without sin" (Heb. 4:15 RSV).

INVOCATION.   In these still moments of worship we seek to walk for a while in your presence, Father. Quiet our noisy lives, calm our frenzied diversion, gentle our riotous ways, bring calm to our racing thoughts and peace to our troubled souls. Let the music of wonder at your presence flow over us like rivers of refreshing water. Bring the light of your truth to bear upon our darkened understanding, that shadows of wrongness may be chased away.–Henry Fields

OFFERTORY SENTENCE.   "Keep your life free from love of money, and be content with what you have, for he has said, 'I will never fail you nor forsake you.'" (Heb. 13:5 RSV).

OFFERTORY PRAYER.   Lord, we know that if we love you enough no other love can compete with what is right. So fix our hearts on you, O God, that everything we gain and control will be under your lordship.

PRAYER.   Almighty God: you love us, but we have not loved you; you call, but we have not listened. We walk away from neighbors in need, wrapped up in our own concerns. We have gone along with evil, with prejudice, warfare, and greed. God our Father, help us to face up to ourselves, so

that, as you move toward us in mercy, we may repent, turn to you, and receive forgiveness; through Jesus Christ our Lord.– *The Worship Book*

LECTIONARY MESSAGE

Topic: What God Requires of Us

TEXT: John 6:24–35

Here we encounter the intellectual and spiritual power of Jesus Christ as he appeals to the mind and heart in confrontation, dialogue, and explanation. How do you turn the desire of hearers from one thing to another? How do you take what you know people want and turn them toward what they need, without repelling them? How can Jesus Christ present himself as one offering more than Moses and cause others to respond positively to him? The answers to these questions are in these eleven verses that, like the entire Gospel of John, appeal to the mind and the soul, present the lordship of Christ, and leave us breathless in their audacity, profundity, and unshakable truth.

The crowds had been following Jesus and got into boats and went across to Capernaum, where they found him on the other side of the lake. These searchers asked Jesus three questions and made one response.

First, they wanted to know when he got there. Jesus turned the question on them and told them they were looking for him not for spiritual reasons but to be fed. They were more interested in food than faith. Then Jesus made an even more startling statement by telling them "not to work for the food that spoils but to seek the food that endures unto eternal life." "This food the Son of Man will give you," Jesus explained, "for the Father has authorized him to do so."

This brought a second question from the crowd and a second response from Jesus. "What must we do to do the work of God?" they ask, with an emphasis on doing. Jesus replies, "The work of God is to believe the one he has sent," thus turning the emphasis from outward works to inward faith and leading them to ponder his challenge. The crowd soon sensed Jesus was referring to himself, and they wanted credentials. They knew Jesus had mysteriously fed a large crowd from no adequate supplies. So they asked if Jesus had a miraculous sign to give them that they might see and believe? After all, they reminded Jesus, our forefathers ate manna in the desert: "Moses gave them bread from heaven to eat."

Jesus, never missing a beat, replied that "it was not Moses who has given you the bread from heaven but it is my Father who gives you the true bread from heaven. For the bread of God is he who comes down from heaven and gives life to the world." Manna gave nourishment, but it did not give life. God offered to give them the latter, not as material substance but as a living Personality. Jesus is showing them that God is offering that lasting Gift to them in him. And at that the crowd responded, "Sir, give us this bread always."

Jesus questioned the crowd's motives, turned their attention to deeper matters, then challenged them toward faith, belief in the Son of Man. The dialogue went back and forth. The crowd eventually said, "You have done no more than Moses did—why should we turn from him to you?" Jesus' entire response was to move them from temporary bread to eternal sustenance through him, the true bread. The crowd wanted bread; they needed God. They wanted a sign, the sign was before them. Jesus says, "Eat of the bread of this world and sooner or later you will die; believe in the one God has sent and you will have the food that endures forever."

John is always moving one from fact to faith, from the temporary to the eternal, from doubt to belief, for whoever believes in Jesus Christ may have eternal life. John finds the purpose of life wrapped up in allegiance to the Christ.

The struggle in this passage is in Jesus' urging the crowd who comes looking for him to turn from a physical mind-set to spiritual reality. Faith is the key, for the bread of life who has come from heaven to give life to the world is before you. What did Jesus give us? He gave us himself. Nothing else is needed.—E. Lee Phillips

SUNDAY: AUGUST TENTH

SERVICE OF WORSHIP

Sermon: The Power of Religion

TEXT: 1 Cor. 1:18–24; James 1:26–27

When Jesus called Christians to become "doers of the Word," he projected a definition of religion that we need to heed. He distinguished false from true religion and suggested that authenticity is measured in ministry: "to care for orphans and widows in their distress." Who has been embarrassed with religion in recent years? One need only mention the congressional review of the militant theology, weapons arsenal, and sexual abuse of David Koresh; the poison gas production and attack of Asahara Shoko and his billion-dollar kingdom of Om in Japan; or the sexual license and the fraudulent TV kingdom of Jim Bakker. The burning cross of the Ku Klux Klan suggests Christian origins, although nothing could be more foreign to the Spirit of Christ than the promotion of racial hatred. Just the title of a recent article, in *Christian Century,* "Dealing with Criminal Religions," is a commentary on the state of religion today. Not even "Christian" religion always bears a resemblance to the moral qualities that Paul listed as the gifts of the Spirit in Gal. 5:22–23: "love, joy, peace, patience, kindness, generosity, faithfulness, gentleness, and self-control"; but religion does seem to have a strange connection to power. Religion may well be the most powerful mover and shaker of world history, especially when its power is translated into political clout and military revolution. The most violent wars, the most cruel torture, and the deepest hatred are driven by religious zeal from the earliest records of human history to the present moment. Religious zealots at the time of Christ viewed themselves as agents of divine wrath against the enemies of God is Israel. They burned with hatred toward the Roman occupation and committed acts of murder and sabotage. Paul attributed his persecution of the church to zeal for the Law.

Harvey Cox revisited *Religion in the Secular City* twenty years after his best-selling book to find that religion had not gone down for the final count. The revival of fundamentalism in the Moral Majority and the rise of Latin American Liberation Theology are two examples not only of the ability of religion to survive but the power of religion to fuel major political movements in the modern world. Religion came back with a vengeance in the 1970s with a strange contradiction: rejecting the modern world, yet making alliances with the electronic media and current politics to achieve its purposes. The trend is to reject secularization while becoming thoroughly secular in political action, revising the gospel to favor the rich, and easily accepting war as a means to bring in the Kingdom of God.

I. *Religion is a powerful presence in the modern world.* Gibbon, on the decline and fall of the Roman Empire, described the Roman attitude toward the multiple choice of religions: "The various modes of worship . . . were all considered by the people as equally true; by the philosopher as equally false; and by the magistrate as equally useful." When Constantine came to prefer Christianity above other religions, he found a useful tool in managing the population under his charge. The variety of religions had always served a useful function in Roman government. For the first time in history, the Church entered into a marriage of convenience with the State—each able to exploit the influence of the other over the people. The Radical Reformation was right in calling this marriage "the Fall of the Church." Christianity at that moment became just another religion, and we have never quite learned the primary lesson of Christian history that the power of the gospel is sufficient.

The public appetite for controlling God and for simple solutions to highly complex problems and its reluctance to bear personal responsibility make easy prey for corrupt religion. If my generation was too skeptical of religion, too much like the philosophers, this generation is too gullible, giving to cultic movements in political power that which they lack in spiritual depth. Political entrepreneurs of every persuasion seem always ready to use religion to convince the public of a divine endorsement of a political candidacy, movement, or party. After a while the slow, tedious process of depending on the power of the Spirit to convict and to convince is abandoned for the authority of law and the power of the state.

If religious zeal is the problem, religious indifference, apathy, is not the solution. We cannot avoid the radical nature of the call to discipleship, but we can choose the focus of our commitment. The tendency to lean away from commitment for fear of being viewed as religious fanatics is the sin of moderation. If the church is obedient to the call of God, she needs no other strength. The church always has a "bully pulpit" to sway opinion and to move the course of history, but power alone is not enough. We need to measure the morality of power to determine its source and direction.

II. *The power of Christ measures down to the need of the world.* Jesus was never interested in measuring up to the political expectations of Messiah in his time, but he did measure down to the deepest hunger and the most impoverished cases of human deprivation. Jesus was confused with the Old Testament prophets largely because he imitated their preference for the underdogs above the religious elite. Thus, Paul observed to the church at Corinth that the strange power of God comes incognito. It is manifest in a cross. The wisdom of God appears to be foolish, and the power of God appears to be weak, but Paul preached the cross—foolishness to the Greeks and a stumbling block to the Jews. When offered the kingdoms of this world, Jesus passed. When the people came to crown him king, he walked away. The one crucified "King of the Jews" wore only a crown of thorns. His Kingdom was not of this world—not because God rejects the physical world, but because the Kingdom of God is not of the same political order of kingdoms in this world. James measured the truth of religion by its effect on the weakest members of society, widows and orphans, and its refusal to be allied with the temporary structures of this world. True religion measures down to the lowest and weakest residents of the world, not up to the high and mighty.

The power of the gospel is incomparable. It is the power of God for salvation. The power of faith to move mountains can never mean the surrender of will and decision to any human leader of an institution, no matter how charismatic they may appear to be. Faith is the commitment of will and mind to the leadership of God in Christ. Christ never asked that we follow blindly, just faithfully. He never promised the kingdoms of this world, only the Kingdom of our God. —Larry Dipboye

Illustrations

GOVERNMENT AND RELIGION.   We are sometimes told that government has no purpose but an earthly one; that, whilst religion takes care of the soul, government is to watch over outward and bodily interests. This separation of our interest into earthly and spiritual, seems to me unfounded. There is a unity in our whole being. There is one great end for which body and mind were created, and all the relations of life were ordained; one central aim, to which our whole being should tend; and this is the unfolding of our intellectual and moral nature; and no man thoroughly understands government, but he who reverences it as a part of God's stupendous machinery for this sublime design. I do not deny that government is instituted to watch over our present interests. But still it has a spiritual or moral purpose, because present interests are, in an important sense, spiritual; that is, they are instruments and occasions of virtue, calls to duty, sources of obligation, and are only blessing when they contribute to the health of the soul.—William Ellery Channing

THE GROUND OF HOPE.   If we need something to buttress us in the inevitable struggles of life, there is nothing that can help us more than the conviction that each one of us is sought by Him who made the Pleiades and Orion, that each of us is truly known as no finite man can ever know us, and that, in spite of our feebleness and sin, we can become channels of God's universal love. Even the unjust happenings of the present life cannot dismay us, because this life is not all. If God really is, then a future life is required in order that the manifest injustices of the present life may be redressed.

One natural result of this kind of intelligent faith is an almost boisterous joy. The classic expression is found to be, "We know that in everything God works for good with those who love him, who are called according to his purpose." Persons with this vibrant faith will face hardship, misunderstanding, and loss of loved ones, and all will face the death of their own bodies, but the triumphant faith takes these exigencies into consideration.

This faith is so strengthening that it ought to be uniting. The chasm between a merely secular conception of the world and any conception in which the Personal Basis of the moral order is recognized is so great and so crucial that those who believe in the latter are foolish to let their particular differences divide them. Moslems and Christians and Jews and many more need to know that they have the greatest things in common. The question of the particular banner is secondary.—Elton Trueblood

SERMON SUGGESTIONS

Topic: Making Prayer Effective
TEXT: 1 Sam. 12:23

There can be no question of the healing and helping power of right prayer. My recommendation: (a) Be concerned. (b) Trust God. (c) Keep on praying. (d) Follow up your prayer with study and work.—Nels F. S. Ferré

Topic: The New Commandment of Love to One Another
TEXT: John 13:34

(1) The novelty of the law—"That ye love one another." (2) The spirit or measure of it —"As I have loved you."—F. W Robertson

Worship Aids

CALL TO WORSHIP.   "Blessed is every one that feareth the Lord; that walketh in his ways" (Ps. 128:1).

INVOCATION.   Almighty God, our heavenly Father, we meet in reverence before you in worship. Forgive us for not walking in reverence before you at all times. Cleanse our thoughts, forgive our sin, according to your mercy in Christ Jesus, and help us to be more obedient and loving children of yours.

OFFERTORY SENTENCE.   "Whatsoever ye do in word or deed, do all in the name of the Lord Jesus, giving thanks to God and the Father by him" (Col. 3:17).

OFFERTORY PRAYER.   Our Father, put such love in our hearts that what we say and do, whether in church or outside, may truly respect our Savior and cause others to love him, who know of him only through what we say and do.

PRAYER.   O God our Father, whose Son forgave his enemies while he was suffering shame and death: Strengthen those who suffer for the sake of conscience; when they are accused, save them from speaking in hate; when they are rejected, save them from bitterness; when they are imprisoned, save them from despair; and to us your servants, give grace to respect their witness and to discern the truth, that our society may be cleansed and strengthened. This we ask for the sake of Jesus Christ, our merciful and righteous Judge.—*The Book of Common Prayer*

LECTIONARY MESSAGE

Topic: The Everlasting Bread of God
TEXT: John 6:35, 41–51

The Johannine Gospel is a spiritual Gospel, doctrinal rather than ethical, theological not biographical, forever dealing not simply in facts but what is behind the meaning of the facts. Every time John records a miracle he records a discourse following it.

When Jesus is teaching truth he does not mince words, he brings home the relationship of the soul to God in brave assertions calling for decisive response. Jesus never dilutes the truth to pander to popularity.

Finally, Jesus become messianic in interpreting the miracle of feeding the five thousand. In self-affirmation he proclaims the first of several "I am" statements unique to this Gospel of condensed truth. "I am the bread of life," Jesus declares, "and he who comes to me will never be hungry and he who believes in me will never thirst."

Jesus gets foundational. This is bottom line. Bread and water sustain life—without them you cannot go on. When Jesus speaks of life, he is making a spiritual reference. Real life is in a relationship of intimacy and trust with God, and apart from Jesus Christ no one can experience that new relationship with God. The hunger and thirst of the human soul are uniquely satisfied through faith in Christ Jesus.

Jesus threw down the gauntlet, and there were people present who became very literal and missed the point. They doubted and rebelled. In essence they said, "How can Jesus make a claim to have come down from heaven? We know his parents and watched him grow up."

As usual Jesus met them head on and admonished them to stop grumbling. Then he made a telling reference to grace: "No one comes to me unless God who has sent me draws him." Next, Jesus goes a step further to indicate that whoever is drawn to God he will raise up in the last day. In the work of salvation the Father and the Son are totally one, the son receiving and guarding all who come to him because he is completely devoted to God's will. The doing of the Father's will is the purpose of his coming into the world (John 4:34).

"Those who hear God's call and learn the truth from God will come to Jesus." Jesus further asserts, "Anyone who believes in me has everlasting life."

Then again, Jesus resumes his pivotal vow to be the bread of life and contrasts the bread he is with the manna their forefathers ate in the desert: they ate and died. But

Jesus says, "I am the bread that comes down from heaven. If you eat of me you will not die, you will live forever." As if that were not enough, Jesus adds another startling assertion: "This bread of life is my flesh, given for the life of the world."

Jesus' language has plainly turned sacrificial (John 1:29). He is referring to his death and does so in two ways. It is voluntary, ("I will give") and vicarious ("for the life of the world") (Isa. 52:13–53:11, 12; 49:6). Here Jesus is taking the widest possible view for those who might benefit from his death (John 3:16–17).

Faith in the Lord Jesus Christ is sung about, affirmed, and proclaimed from Christian churches throughout this world every Sunday, if not oftener. Jesus' self-affirmations come as hard sayings to many minds, and not all who come to believe are "drawn" by the same presentation. One might come at an evangelistic rally, another might respond through a class for seekers, another after years of intense struggle. Faith can be costly, but the Savior Son of Calvary, who voluntarily laid down his life for *all* who will believe, saves completely, finally, and eternally. No one else does. No one else could.–E. Lee Phillips

SUNDAY: AUGUST SEVENTEENTH

SERVICE OF WORSHIP

Sermon: "It's Just Not Fair"

TEXT: Eccl. 3:16–4:3; also Matt. 7:24–29

I. In this text, the philosopher comes up with yet a different argument for the emptiness of his life. Remember, now, he's already decided that the false and elusive centers of life won't hold. Work, learning, success, fun, history, family, sex, acquisition . . . he's hustled them all and decided it's like trying to catch the wind. And he's decided that God puts us on this treadmill of living that is going nowhere and to no purpose.

Now, he turns to a different disappointment. "Moreover," he says, "I saw under the sun that in the place of justice, wickedness was there, and in the place of righteousness, wickedness was there as well" (3:16).

"Okay, we're stuck with what God has designed–a fixed and recurring scheme of things. But of all the things that keep on repeating themselves, here is the worst– the injustice and wickedness and pain of life."

Now, in verse 17, he decides that maybe God will sort things out and judge between the wicked and the righteous . . . hold people accountable. But his fragile faith won't carry that idea very long, so he slips back to despair. "We're all animals, anyhow," he says in verse 18. "God cuts us slack to show our real identity. We're no better than the animals, and our eternal destiny is just as uncertain." He has no real confidence in a life beyond the grave.

So we live and die like animals. What's the use of talking about meaning in a world like that?

Here's the old philosopher's conclusion (4:1–3): "The world is full of oppression . . . the pride and power of people can be heartless and devastating. Better dead than alive in such a world–in fact, better unborn than to come into such a mess." He says it again in chapter 7: "The day of death is better than the day of birth" (v. 1).

So it's complete disillusionment that we find in this section of Ecclesiastes. In his old age, our philosopher steps back a few paces to look at the human experience, and in his detachment, he's become a pretty cynical observer.

In our worst moments, this can be the sentiment of every philosopher or Solomon or Job or Jane among us–except that our worst moments are probably not times of cool detachment. It's when we're slapped around by life and stinging with its hurt that we're apt to say through gritted teeth, "It's just not fair!"

And because it's not fair, life can feel pretty empty . . . and hopeless.

So, as I read this section of Ecclesiastes, the feeling here is claustrophobic . . . trapped . . . helpless in a world of animal instincts.

But look! Two-legged animals *are* different. We make choices. We do by calculation and decision a lot of what other creatures do by instinct and nature. It's *our* nature to decide.

Our philosopher is right—wickedness and injustice often replace goodness and fairness. Oppression is real; the misuse of power is real—the tears of victims are legitimate. But an awful lot of that is reality because we human animals choose injustice and wickedness and selfishness and sin.

Of course, God gave us the freedom, so, indirectly, it's God's fault, and you can shake your fist at God if you want. But mostly, the choosing is ours. It's as the Jewish writer Elie Wiesel noted after the death camps of World War II, "Where was God at Auschwitz or Treblinka or Buchenwald?" The answer to that question is another question, said Wiesel: "Where was man?"

Where was the man or woman who could do justice, love mercy, be honest, show courage, and act out of love? Those men and woman were *there*—choosing injustice, wickedness, selfishness, and sin.

So God gives you life and freedom. He doesn't ask you whether you'll accept it or not . . . just what you'll do with it.

II. In the light of that, let me remind you of two things that today's Scriptures tell us.

a. First of all, *we live with limits.* Our Ecclesiastes philosopher has some truth for us here. Life does not let us have absolute and unhindered freedom. Winds and tides impose limits, ignorance imposes limits, sin—ours and others'—imposes limits; the interconnectedness of our humanity imposes limits as we make bad judgments with their ripple effects.

All of those limits we must live with.

Also, in the givens of things, you and I have learned some truth. We human types are black, white, red, yellow, brown; we're female and male; we have families who've blessed us and flawed us; we may live in a society that gives us choices and votes, or we may live in totalitarianism, which makes choices for us and without our consent.

So life is not bestowed on us with total freedom. There are times when we have little choice about what is. There are times when we have *no* choice about what is.

What, then, shall we do with this truth, this reality?

Well you can shake your fist against the God who created reality in such a way. Or you can hole up in cynicism and whine about the unfairness of it all. Or you can do what one of the men in Jesus' story does here in Matt. 7—shrug your shoulders, throw up your hands, let it ride, *que sera sera*.

b. Take a look at that story now, because there's a second thing to be known about life and freedom, and it's here in this story; namely, *there is a way to live with limits.*

Matthew and Luke both have this little parable; it ends Jesus' longest teaching section—the Sermon on the Mount and the Sermon of the Plain. What's Jesus offering in his teaching? A way of life in relationship with God. A friendship and partnership with a loving God who will equip you to live meaningfully—in a real world.

All through this section of Matthew, it's reality—sin, selfishness, person-to-person conflict, enemies, family, money, sexuality, worry about the future; that's mostly what the Sermon on the Mount is about. And Jesus believes that in the life of discipleship you can learn to live in the real world with sanity and direction and lasting purpose.

How? In personal relationship with God: in receiving, by faith, God's love and forgiveness; in making Jesus Christ not only your role model but your daily friend and supporter. The Sermon on the Mount is for *disciples*—it's not a set of ethical guidelines addressed "to whom it may concern." So Jesus, here at the end of it, tells this little story to say, "Here's a way of living in this world, in a world with limited choices (sometimes, of no choices), you can make this choice—to build your life on faith and not confusion or despair."

Jesus is a carpenter; he knows about buildings. The story has integrity. One builder takes a hard look at reality. Flash floods are going to hit, high winds will come. He's got to build on a rock-solid foundation. When life leaves him vulnerable and exposed and without choices, he has already *made* the choice that will help him survive.

The other builder may know about storms and flash floods, but he's decided that the way to deal with reality is to just let it ride. In a world of limited choices, he gives up the one main choice he's got—*something solid* to build on.

Now, Jesus doesn't say he's an evil man; he calls him "foolish." He's not wicked, just careless. That's not the way to live with the limits of this world.

Right now—today—you can make the choice. You can stand with our philosopher in Eccl. 4—life "under the sun," period— nothing higher or deeper than this world and secular reality. If that's your choice, then believe him when the philosopher tells you twice in the same text what to expect: "no one to comfort them" (4:1).

There is another choice, and Jesus offers it to you—the foundation of personal faith and of daily discipleship. I remember a story about a rich man who employed a builder to build a house. "Make it the finest house you can build; spare no expense," he said. The builder went to work, and when he was finished, he felt pleased with his work—until the rich man said, "The house is yours . . . but only if you live in it." Then, the cut corners and botches and weaknesses reminded him that he could've built it better.

You're going to live in what you build. Every house will be tested by the storms and will be exposed to the harsh realities of life. You're going to live in your house, built on the foundation you choose. What will it be?

I'll give Nietzsche credit—he said that if you've got a *why* to live for, you can bear with almost any *how*. He had that right.

What's your *why* this morning? Will it hold when limits are real and answers are scarce?

Jesus offers you why for living in the solid foundation of God's love. Why not take it?— William L. Turner

Illustrations

"SOUL MAKING." If, then, the evil in human life finally reveals its nature according as it becomes or fails to become a phase in the fulfillment of God's purpose, we must conclude, so far as the present life is concerned, that there are both good and evil suffering, and that there are redeemed and unredeemed sinners. Any revision of the verdict must depend upon lengthening the perspective out until it reaches a new and better conclusion. If there is any eventual resolution of the interplay between good and evil, any decisive bringing of good out of evil, it must lie beyond this world and beyond the enigma of death. Therefore we cannot hope to state a Christian theology without taking seriously the doctrine of a life beyond the grave. This doctrine is not, of course, based upon any theory of natural immortality, but upon the hope that beyond death God will resurrect or re-create or reconstitute the human personality in both its inner and its outer aspects. The Christian claim is that the ultimate life of man—after what further scenes of "soul-making" we do not know—lies in that Kingdom of God which is depicted in the teaching of Jesus as a state of exultant and blissful happiness, symbolized as a joyous banquet in which all and sundry, having accepted God's gracious invitation, rejoice together. And Christian theodicy must point forward to that final blessedness, and claim that this infinite future good will render worthwhile all the pain and travail and wickedness that has occurred on the way to it.—John Hicks

A CREATIVE VIEW. In the Italian Alps I used to love a certain deep, ever sunless gorge, through which a resounding mountain torrent was continuously fighting its way, without rest, without fruit. Why did I love it so? Doubtless because I realized, amidst that sterile-seeming uproar, that, down far away, this torrent would spread itself out as a sunlit, peaceful, fertilizing river, slowly flowing through the rich plain of Piedmont.—Baron Friedrich von Hügel

SERMON SUGGESTIONS

Topic: The Lord's Continuing Mercy
    TEXT: Ps. 107:1
    (1) When we suffer calamities—opportunity to rebuild. (2)) When we fall into temptation—a promised way of escape. (3) When

we become unfruitful—restoration and growth in grace.

Topic: The Irreparable Past
TEXT: Mark 14:41–42

(1) The irreparable past. (2) The available future: (a) The duty of Christian earnestness —"Rise"; (b) The duty of Christian energy— "Let us be going."—F. W. Robertson

Worship Aids

CALL TO WORSHIP.   "Cause me to hear thy lovingkindness in the morning; for in thee do I trust; cause me to know the way wherein I should walk; for I lift up my soul unto thee" (Ps. 143:8).

INVOCATION.   Eternal Spirit, hope of the souls that seek thee, strength of the souls that find thee, we worship thee, praying for that inner refreshment and renewal, which only thy presence can bring. Through another week the world has towered above us with its huge problems and has assailed us with its turbulence, and we have grown anxious, fearful, perplexed, inadequate. We need some shepherd to lead us in green pastures and beside the still water, restoring our souls. Surprise us today with some unexpected gift of thy grace, some needed insight and guidance, some vision of new possibilities, some fresh resource of strength and courage. Let this visit to thy sanctuary be to some of us the beginning of a new era, as though once more at the burning bush thy voice said to us, "The place whereon thou standest is holy ground."--Harry Emerson Fosdick

OFFERTORY SENTENCE.   "Seek ye first the kingdom of God, and his righteousness; and all these things shall be added unto you" (Matt. 6:33).

OFFERTORY PRAYER.   O God, you know better than we know ourselves what we seek so desperately in this world. Help us to seek what we truly need and in finding it arrange all of life according to priorities that are real and good. Draw us to you, so that we may gain and use all things of earth for your glory, for our spiritual growth, and for the blessing of others.

PRAYER.   O God, we cannot fathom the mystery of thy being, but we rejoice that thou knowest us and the temptations that try us, and the sorrows that beat upon us and cast us down, and the pains of body and of mind that cloud our spirits and make sad our world. Leave us not as those who are fatherless and outcast, but bring us thy dawn, and shed light upon our path. When we are wounded with mental and physical distresses, be at hand to heal and save. When the cares and troubles of life threaten to kill the soul, let thy Spirit sustain us and create for us an inner world of hope and faith and love, where we may take refuge and hear thy voice speaking to us to warn, to comfort, and to guide. Save us, O Lord, from the weaknesses of self-pity. In misery and suffering let us turn to thy pity, which alone can strengthen, cleanse, and uplift. Let not failure or sorrow embitter us, or shut us off from those about us, but may we find a cure for our own griefs by pouring the oil of consolation and the wine of gladness into other lives. Grant us brave hearts and true. Inspire us with firmness to carry out every holy purpose. Forbid that we should waste the time that is left in vain regrets for the past, or vague dreams of the future, but let us be up and doing, knowing that though we may fall, thou wilt not cast us away. May we gather up the fragments of time and opportunity which remain, that nothing be lost. Grant that we may see thee, not only in the thunder and tempest and earthquake, not only in the great moments of spiritual exaltation, but also in the commonplace duties, in the familiar relationships of life. May our home-life be fortified with the spirit of love and mutual helpfulness. Remove from our midst all wrath and clamor and evil-speaking, and bitterness and estrangement, and make us gentle and easily entreated, the children of a forgiving God. May we know, with a spiritual knowledge, that thou art Love, and that dwelling in Love we dwell in thee, through Jesus Christ our Lord.— Samuel McComb

LECTIONARY MESSAGE

Topic: The Way of Wisdom

TEXT: John 6:51–58

Solomon was reputed to have been the wisest of men. He demonstrated this wisdom in the request that God give him wisdom rather than power and wealth. Yet Solomon did not continue to live by wisdom. He failed through his marital excesses and his idolatry.

I. Wisdom recognizes God's gift (v. 51). To most people in first-century Palestine, Jesus was an ordinary human being. He might have appeared wiser than most, he could do amazing things, but he was still just a man. Thus, when he claimed to be the living bread that came down out of heaven, it was difficult for them to take his claim seriously. Human nature cannot accept such a claim. Wisdom from God is needed to recognize God's gift. Such wisdom is available to those who seek it. They are to ask God and he will give it generously and without complaint (James 1:5). The psalmist stated, "The fear of the Lord is the beginning of wisdom" (110:10). Wisdom acknowledges God and God's greatest gift.

II. Wisdom sees beneath the surface (vv. 52–53). Jesus called upon his hearers to eat his flesh and drink his blood. These were people who wanted a repetition of the feeding in the wilderness when God sustained his people for forty years. Now Jesus had miraculously provided food for the crowd. They wanted him to do it again and again. They failed to understand Jesus. They could not see beneath the physical surface to the true life, the spiritual.

We, also, are a visually oriented society. We tend to think that what we see is the true reality. We fail to see that there is something more significant beneath the surface. It requires wisdom to probe these depths. Jesus claimed that man does not live by bread alone (Matt. 4:4), but conventional wisdom claims that he does. It is easy to spend all of our time and energy in earning physical necessities, and we forget the spiritual aspect of life. Jesus called the person who does this a fool (Luke 12:20). Wisdom realizes that the relationship with God has first priority. And it knows that such a relationship comes only through faith in the one who claimed to be the living bread.

III. Wisdom perceives the way to eternal life (vv. 54–58). Jesus came to bring life. "In him was life" (John 1:4). He gives life to those who eat his flesh and drink his blood (v. 54). To eat his flesh and drink his blood is to enter into an intimate relation with him. It is to have absolute trust and commitment.

Eternal life means to live forever and to be raised in the last day, but it is more. It is also a new quality of life that becomes reality the moment one commits one's life to the Lord Jesus Christ. It is physical life now, but it is also life that is lived in conformity to the will and purpose of God. It is life that is pleasing to him, and therefore is the richest of all life that one can live. It is to abide in Jesus and to have Jesus abide in oneself (v. 56). God's desire is that people share in this eternal life. Wisdom enables one to see the way to this life through commitment of oneself to Christ. Wisdom recognizes God's gift, sees beneath the surface, and perceives the way to eternal life.—Clayton K. Harrop

SUNDAY: AUGUST TWENTY-FOURTH

SERVICE OF WORSHIP

Sermon: The Sun in the Doorway

TEXT: John 19:26–27; also Luke 23:46

What most of us fear about death, when we think seriously about it, is the separation it entails. We don't want to be removed from the people we love or the life we know.

Even Jesus acknowledged the reality of death as separation.

The story is set like a small drama at the heart of the passion narrative, which for the early church was the most important part of the gospel story. Jesus was suffering on the cross. Among the faces of the crowd gathered around the crucified men, he saw two he knew—those of his mother and the beloved disciple John.

In the gathering twilight of his pain, he spoke to them.

"Mother," he said, "there is your son."

And, to the beloved disciple, "Son, there is your mother."

It was an act of terminal provision, of tying up loose ends. Death was the end of something. Jesus knew he was going through the doorway.

But there was another aspect of Jesus' death. He was not only terminating something, he was beginning something.

"Father," he said, "into thy hands I commit my spirit."

As though someone waited for him there in the darkness. As though the darkness was not darkness at all.

As though, through the doorway, he could see the sun shining, see its rays falling on the doorsill, see it waiting to envelop him, warmly and invitingly, the moment he stepped from the room.

He wasn't afraid to leave things behind, because he knew there was a paradise on the other side of the door.

"Now, that may be okay for Jesus," you say, "but not for me. I am no saint, and I am certainly not the Son of God. I can't see what is on the other side of that doorway, and going through it scares the dickens out of me!"

Does it?

Have you ever stopped to consider what passing through death will be like—what the actual moment of dying will entail?

Professor Edwin Shneidman of Harvard University, who has written a great deal about death and dying, says it will be nothing. That's right—*nothing*.

If we were conscious of passing through death, says Professor Shneidman, we would not be dead. And, as we have no conscious experience of it, it cannot really be said to have happened at all. Our dying, in other words, is an instantaneous thing, a transformation that occurs so quickly that we don't know anything about it.

To return to our metaphor, it is like passing through a door. One never thinks about the doorway itself. The doorway is only the

passage between two worlds, one inside and the other outside. There is no content, no substance, to the act of going through.

Therefore it is not in itself something to dread.

John Dryden, the eighteenth-century poet and playwright, said it succinctly:

Death in itself is nothing;
But we fear
To be we know not what,
We know not where.

What we really fear about death, in other words, is the unknown beyond it. Suppose we do not like it there. Suppose there is nothing there, that the doorway of death opens onto a blank wall! That would be a bit of a fix, wouldn't it?

"Let Professor Shneidman and John Dryden talk as they like," you say; "as for me, I want to stay on this side of the door."

I am not so sure.

The evidence is mounting that there is something on the other side of the door and that, for most of us, at least, it is something good. And the evidence is not all coming from religious sources—from preachers and devotional writers who speak out of the context of faith. Much of it today is coming from doctors and psychologists who have worked with hundreds of persons in various stages of dying.

You have surely read about their work and the testimonies of many people they have interviewed. What they say is that there is life on the other side of the door—beautiful life, apparently. Many people have died long enough to discover it. They have died clinically—with no pulse or heartbeat—and then been revived. And during the time of their deaths they have had fantastic experiences of living beyond the moment of death.

Most of these persons have spoken of the joy of life after death. Some have heard beautiful music. Many have been reunited with loved ones. Many have had experiences of the presence of Christ or of other religious leaders from the past.

One of the happy effects of the publication of these testimonies is the encouragement it has given other persons to share their own experiences of a similar nature. Before, they were afraid they would be accused of hallucinating, of having wild dreams. Now they can speak without shame of what they have seen and felt and heard.

A former student of mine had a child who drowned. He was floating facedown in the swimming pool when they found him. His flesh was blue and he had no pulse. But someone gave him CPR, and, to everyone's amazement, he returned to life.

"Franklin," the little boy kept mumbling as he regained consciousness.

"Franklin?" gasped his parents.

Franklin was the name of the boy's grandfather, who had died before the boy was born. But no one in the family had ever called him Franklin, and they said there was no possible way the boy could have known his name. Yet the child described his grandfather perfectly, and insisted he had seen him.

A woman in Texas told me about the death of her seventeen-year-old son Chris. Before he died, Chris began talking to his grandfather as if the grandfather were in the room with him, though he had been dead for several years. Moments before he slipped away, Chris began saying the Lord's Prayer in a very loud voice. The sound filled the room with a great power, so that everyone there, the family members and the nurses, was gripped by the experience. Then he was gone.

When my wife's mother died, one of our former schoolteachers came to the funeral home to visit my wife. "I had to come to share something with you," she said. "I had a very serious illness a few years ago, and the doctors thought I was gone. I revived after a few minutes and got all right. But during those minutes I was with my grandmother, who had been dead for years. It was so peaceful and beautiful there that I didn't want to come back."

The woman's face was radiant as she told the story. The memory still inspired her. "Don't worry about your mother," she said. "She is in a world more wonderful than you can imagine!"

Perhaps this is what Jesus was trying to say to the disciples in the Upper Room.

"There are many rooms in my father's house," he said. "I am going ahead to prepare a place for you. Don't be afraid to come through the door."

Do you remember how the martyred Stephen died, in the book of Acts? The stones were raining down upon him, crushing his body and opening great bloody lesions on his flesh. He raised his eyes to heaven and said, "Lord Jesus, receive my spirit"—just the way Jesus died on the cross, saying, "Father, into thy hands I commit my spirit."

There is a world of love and healing on the other side of the doorway—a world of incredible beauty and peace and joy. We do not need to be afraid of it.

Sometimes I think this is why Jesus made all those postresurrection appearances to the disciples—to the men on the road to Emmaus, and the followers in the Upper Room, and Thomas, and the ones who were fishing that morning in Galilee. He wanted them to know that death is not the monstrous finality we so often interpret it as being—that things are not always what they seem to our earthbound imaginations—that life is in God's hands and we can trust him for the future.

When we know that—when we live by that belief—we approach death with a new attitude. We are even able to go the way G. K. Chesterton described the early Christians as going—as though they smelled the grave afar off like a field of flowers.

Or the way Leslie Weatherhead, the famous London pastor, saw a man in his parish go. At the end, said Weatherhead, the man must have thought his pastor's hand on his was trying to restrain him from dying, for he cried, "Don't hold me back. I can see through the gates. It's marvelous."

Or the way a young man I knew died. John's body was eaten up with cancer. He had suffered for months. In the final days, his wife had stayed constantly by his side, and so had his mother. They had all talked together about their faith in God and how important that was. A few moments before John died, his mother kissed him on the lips and went out of the room to leave him alone with his wife. As she was passing through the door, she said, she felt John's spirit soar past her in a mighty rush, and heard him say, "Hurray!" A few seconds later, her daughter-in-law came out and said, "John's gone. He smiled and died peacefully."

Can there be any doubt that John saw the sun in the doorway? Or the face beyond the door?

By the grace of God, it's what we all have to look forward to.—John Killinger

Illustrations

ADVERSARIES, YET VICTORY. Bunyan's description of the Christian journey through life is one of the most realistic ever produced. There are giants to be fought at nearly every turn in the road, and the Pilgrim trembles to see at the very gate of heaven a byway to the pit. But there are experiences of victory, and a vision of the gates of glory at the end.—Daniel Day Williams

THE SOUL TAKES A FORM. Samuel Cox of England, a well-known biblical scholar and student of biology, visited his indoor marine aquarium. On the surface of the water he saw a tiny creature, half fish and half worm, not an inch long, writhing, seemingly in mortal agony. With convulsive efforts it bent head to tail on one side and then the other, twisting and turning with extraordinary effort for a creature so small. Thinking that the insect was near death, Cox was about to throw it out of the aquarium so as not to pollute the water when suddenly right under his eyes its skin split from end to end and there sprang out a delicate fly with slender black legs and pale lavender wings. Balancing itself on the floating discarded skin, as on an island, it preened its gossamer wings and flew out an open window.

What a dramatic spectacle of nature's creative and metamorphic powers! It is also a striking illustration of two separate and distinct environments, each requiring a different type of body. The watery environment of the worm would have brought instant death to the beautiful and delicate fly. And who would have believed that the humble worm would one day take to itself gossamer wings and soar into the air to feed upon the flowers?

So man has a physical body superbly equipped for a physical existence; but within him, says Paul, is the potentiality of a spiritual body fitted for a spiritual existence. All around us in nature varied forms appear to meet the demands of life. In the words of the biologist Cox, "The quality of life determines the form it assumes, the form changing as the life changes and rising as the life rises."—John Sutherland Bonnell

SERMON SUGGESTIONS

Topic: Appointments with God
TEXT: Amos 4:12
(1) The Lord will meet us at the Cross. (2) The Lord will meet us at the Church. (3) The Lord will meet us at the Treasury. (4) The Lord will . . . meet us at the Judgment. Note: The first three are voluntary, but we have no choice in the fourth.—J. E. Ledbetter

Topic: Holy Alliances
TEXT: Mark 10:9
Like so many of the Master's sayings, its application goes far beyond the original intention. Some of these God-made alliances which Christ here dares us to break: (1) Religion and character. (2) Faith and reason. (3) The human soul and Jesus.—James S. Stewart

Worship Aids

CALL TO WORSHIP. "Lift up your heads; for your redemption draweth nigh" (Luke 21:28).

INVOCATION. Lord of life, some of us come to worship today uncertain of ourselves, of directions to take, decisions to make, priorities to embrace. Help us to catch a vision of your purpose for us in this place and set about fulfilling it to your honor and glory.

OFFERTORY SENTENCE. "Provide for yourselves purses that don't wear out, and save your riches in heaven, where they will never decrease, because no thief can get to them, and no moth can destroy them. For your heart will always be where your riches are" (Luke 12:33–34 TEV).

OFFERTORY PRAYER. Look into our hearts, O God, and tell us what we love. If we love you little, help us to love you more. If we care too little about the people around us, help us to be more concerned. If we are too much wedded to the things of this world, free us from our idolatry and set our hearts on the enduring riches of your kingdom.

PRAYER. Lord Jesus, you understand the sufferings of the weak and the oppressed. Although you are strong, you allowed yourself to be taken prisoner. You were the victim of bullying and illtreatment, punishing blows and insulting words. You suffered an agonizing death for us and for our sins. Be near to those who suffer innocently as political prisoners and give peace and comfort to them by your presence.

O God, the father of the forsaken, the help of the weak, the supplier of the needy, you teach us that love toward the race of man is the bond of perfectness and the imitation of your blessed self.

Open and touch our hearts that we may see and do, both for this world and that which is to come, the things that belong to our peace. Strengthen us in the work which we have undertaken; give us wisdom, perseverance, faith and zeal, and in your own time and according to your pleasure prosper the issue; for the love of your Son, Christ Jesus.–Lord Shaftesbury (1801–85).

LECTIONARY MESSAGE

Topic: The Words of Eternal Life
TEXT: John 6:56–69

The believer seeks to live in close fellowship with God. This union does not come automatically. It requires effort on the part of the individual and obedience to the ways of God.

I. A vital attachment to Jesus (vv. 56–59). For many, association with God is connected with a certain place or a certain time. When the Temple was built in the days of Solomon, it was seen as the place where the people would meet God. They were assured that he dwelt in the Temple. They could go there with the confidence that he would listen to and answer their prayers. For the Temple was above all else a house of prayer. Not only could the Israelite be assured that God would listen to prayer from one of the covenant people, but even the "foreigner" could come and pray with the assurance that God would hear and answer. Isaiah called the Temple a house of prayer for all nations (Isa. 56:7). The psalmist desired to dwell in the house of God (Ps. 84). It was for him the place where he might live in the presence of God.

For people today, meeting God may be associated with a church facility. It may be related to the regular time of worship. For others, however, the meeting with God is not necessarily associated with one time or one place. It comes through a vital attachment to Jesus. They recognize him as the giver of eternal life, and they delight to "eat his flesh and drink his blood." Prayer is vital, but the place of contact with God is the person of Jesus Christ himself.

II. Life through the Spirit (vv. 60–65). So long as Jesus is seen as any other mortal, he is not the means of fellowship with God. Indeed, under those circumstances he may be an offense. Only as one sees him seated at the right hand of the Father does this vital attachment to him bring the reality of close fellowship with God. Jesus knew that his ascension to the Father might be a scandal to some, but for others it was the assurance that what he had said was true. God is Spirit. And worship of God must be in spirit and truth. Times and places may be important, but it is the inward relationship with the Father that gives vitality to worship. Jesus said that it was the spirit which gives life (v. 63). Physical life may exist without this vital connection with Christ, but eternal life cannot.

III. Confession (vv. 67–69). During his ministry, many followers found it difficult to remain with Jesus. He was not what they desired him to be. He did not fit the established mold. His words were difficult to understand and his requirements were costly. He was opposed by the leaders of the community as well as the political leaders. In such circumstances, people were called to evaluate their loyalty to him. Some answered by turning away.

People today may be attracted to Christ for a variety of reasons. Often it is because of what they think they may profit from him. And this attraction continues for a time but only until they begin to realize he is not what they thought him to be. True, he promises many wonderful things, but his demands are great. And so people turn back from following him as people did of old.

But had Jesus' ministry failed completely? What about the Twelve, who had become his close companions? Would they also go away? No. Instead, they responded with a confession of who he is. Peter answered Jesus' question with the words, "Lord, to whom can we go? You have the words of eternal life. We have come to believe and know that you are the Holy One of God." This is the confession God desires. There is no one to whom one may turn other than Jesus. He is the way to God, and those who come to God come through him. He speaks the words that convey eternal life. He gives new life now, and he promises continued life in the future. He is also the Holy One of God. He is separate from the created order just as the Father himself. There is no sin or fault in him. He is the one upon whom we can depend to bring us into the close relationship with God that is the greatest desire of the godly person.—Clayton K. Harrop

SUNDAY: AUGUST THIRTY-FIRST

SERVICE OF WORSHIP

Sermon: Work in Christian Perspective
TEXT: Col. 3:23

Work has become almost exclusively an economic concern. This is unfortunate. We in the church have allowed the definition and values given to work to be drawn from the wrong sources.

In reality, work is a theological concept, not an economic one. The idea of human labor was born in the creative mind of God. Thus, in order to understand the meaning of work, our attention must be focused on the truth of Holy Scripture.

I. The Nature and Significance of Work

a. Though the command to work is written into the creation accounts of the Old Testament, the best insights into the nature and significance of work are to be found in the New Testament. Paul wrote to the Colossians, "Whatever you do, work at it with all your heart, as though you were working for the Lord and not for men" (3:23 TEV). This may well be the most precise understanding of work ever offered from a Christian perspective.

In the New Testament, the only distinction between types of work is that between work done for other purposes. Notice what distinctions this understanding destroys. Gone is a comparison of different types of work on the basis of physical versus mental labor, manual skills versus supervisory abilities. Gone also is an evaluation of various types of work based upon amounts of remuneration. All that matters is how or whether the work is offered to God.

The New Testament view of work makes no distinction between sacred and secular tasks. In fact, the New Testament apparently has no concept of secular employment. When work is done for the Lord, any work, it becomes sacred.

b. The church in its corporate life should model as well as teach a view of work. The key doctrine is the priesthood of every believer. Each individual in the church is important, and each position of service within the church is important. No type of work can be called more significant than another if both are done for the Lord. Thus, the church operates with a recognition that all of us are about a holy business of seeking to do what we believe God has called us to do and with an openness that allows for every member to function as a priest.

II. The Purpose of Work

a. As you would expect, one's understanding of the nature of work will directly affect one's grasp of the purpose of work. Our desire is to see both the origin and the goals of work in Christian perspective. Paul wrote to the Ephesians, "The man who used to rob must stop robbing and start working, in order to earn an honest living for himself and to be able to help the poor" (4:29 TEV). We are to work in order to sustain life for ourselves and for our families and in order to be of help to others.

b. The New Testament offers no condemnation of income. But the New Testament is harsh in its judgment on the accumulation of goods for the sake of accumulating goods. The labor of our hands is not to build monuments to ourselves but to do ministry for others. The purpose of work is income—but income over which the Christian acts as a steward to see the sustenance of family and self and to see to the help of those in need. Quite frankly, my fear is that though intellectually we know the Bible is right, experientially we live more in response to the economic determinism of Karl Marx's *Das Kapital* than to the moral teachings of the New Testament.

c. Again let the church model what it teaches. Let us be a community of believers dispersed to assume all kinds of employment but united in an agreement of our major business.

Through the work we do and with the products of the work we do, we can be about the central tasks of meeting human needs in Christ's name and bringing all of life into subservience under Christ's lordship.

III. Life does not consist of work alone.

a. As Christianity speaks to the nature and purpose of work, so does it address itself to the restrictions that must be placed on work.

In our society life's meaning has been too exclusively identified with employment. That is why vacation periods are often either not used or used to do some different kind of work. That is also why retirement is frequently viewed as failure.

Work is certainly an important dimension of life, but life does not, must not, consist of work alone. Some things are worth far more than a particular job. Morality and personal integrity are more valuable than work. Family solidarity and healthy intrafamily relationships are worth far more than any one job. A good relationship with the church is of greater significance than a particular position of employment. These are some of the components of life that are worth quitting work to enjoy. Of course there does not have to be a conflict between work and any one of these. But when there is conflict, let us not make a mistake about which is more important.

b. Work is important, but it is not so important as to demand the entirety of life. The truth is that when our total allegiance and energies are devoted to any temporal concern, this is sin. God alone is absolutely worth living for or dying for.

The institutional church has responsibilities in relation to its members just as the members have responsibilities in relation to the institution. No one person or group must be expected to do everything. The church is a community that functions best when each member of the community works within it according to his or her God-given abilities. Work here is important, but even here work must have restrictions.

c. To be able to view one's work from the perspective of faith and at the same time to be able to look up from one's work and see reminders of faith is the way life should be. I hope those who labor in our city will be able to understand their work not so much from within the narrow perspective of a particular job but from the broader perspective offered by that community in which the Scriptures are read, faith is nurtured, worship is offered, and ministry is performed. I believe it is from that perspective that work may be best understood. "Whatever you do, work at it with all your heart, as though you were working for the Lord and not for men."–C. Walton Gaddy

Illustrations

FAITH AND WORK.   I have read that Philip II of Spain had a window built into the office where he worked so he could see his private chapel next door. Anytime that he was working at his desk, considering the affairs of the nation, he could look at the cross on the altar in his place of worship. Worship and work, religion and labor, were not neatly segmented but beautifully blended within the life of this Spanish ruler. His labor for the state was informed by his love for the Christ. Here is a model worth pondering; a posture toward work and faith worth emulating.–C. Welton Gaddy

WORK—A DOG'S LIFE.   "Yours must be a dog's life!" someone said to a traffic officer at a busy intersection. "It would be if I were a dog," the policeman answered. "But I'm not a dog; I'm a saver of lives. Already I've saved three today, right here at this corner. How many have you saved?"–Roy L. Smith

SERMON SUGGESTIONS

Topic: Found Among Sinners
TEXT: Isa. 53, esp. v. 12
(1) The mother of our Lord was an ordinary human being, though God blessed her in special and remarkable ways. (2) At his baptism Jesus identified himself with the sinners he came to save. (3) In his ministry, our Lord was called a friend of sinners. (4) In his death, Jesus was numbered with the transgressors-for us.–Author unknown

Topic: Toward Spiritual Renewal
TEXT: 1 Cor. 3:11, 10
(1) The foundation for spiritual renewal is

laid once for all in Jesus Christ, but each person must continually take care how he builds on it. (2) Spiritual renewal must also come through the Christian family. (3) Spiritual renewal involves letting Christ be Lord. He must become the effective head of the church.–Nels F. S. Ferré

Worship Aids

CALL TO WORSHIP.   "Be of good courage, and he shall strengthen your heart, all ye that hope in the Lord" (Ps. 31:24).

INVOCATION.   Creator God, alert our senses to your world. Let sight and sound, taste and touch remind us that you have made us and have given us the good earth as our home. May all that is within us and all that surrounds us glorify your name.

OFFERTORY SENTENCE.   "Let your light so shine before men, that they may see your good works, and glorify your Father which is in heaven" (Matt. 5:16).

OFFERTORY PRAYER.   Shine on, O God, through the offerings we bring; shine on and get glory to yourself; shine on and bring the world to your feet in obedience and praise.

PRAYER.   Eternal God, who givest us the day for work and the night for rest, grant us health of body, clarity of mind, and joy of soul, that we may do whatsoever our hands must do with our whole strength. Deliver us from the bitterness that poisons, the frustration that maddens, the futility that deadens. We would work to make our dreams real, and dream to make our work worthwhile. At the end of the day content our hearts, that in thy gift of rest we may be prepared for the labors of thy kingdom here on earth, through Jesus Christ by whose work we have been redeemed.–Samuel H. Miller

LECTIONARY MESSAGE

Topic: Pure and Undefiled Religion
    TEXT: Mark 7:1–8, 14–15, 21–23

We are creatures of habit. Or to put it another way, much of what we do in life daily is based on tradition. We go to bed at a certain time and we arise at a set time. We watch the same programs weekly on television. We follow a set routine in much of life's activity. And if someone were to ask us why, we would simply say it is because we have always done it that way or because our parents did it that way. It is tradition, habit.

The same thing can enter into religious practice. We go to church at a set time each Sunday. The worship service follows a set pattern. Again, it is based on tradition, not anything specified in God's Word. We tend to be critical of other people when we see them practicing their religious traditions without realizing that we do the same thing. There is nothing inherently wrong with tradition. But tradition must always come under the judgment of God's Word. And before we criticize the traditions of others, we must evaluate our own.

I. Human tradition or divine commandment (vv. 1–8). Jesus' disciples were criticized because they did not follow the traditional practices of the day. The washing of hands before eating was specified for the priests in the Old Testament (Exod. 30:19). The Pharisees had sought to make their nation into a kingdom of priests and to impose this ritual upon all the people. Thus, when they observed that Jesus' disciples did not follow these traditions, they were disturbed and questioned Jesus about why his disciples were being irreligious. His response was that these were human traditions and not God's commandments. The danger with human traditions is that they tend to replace what God has said. This was true in Jesus' day, and it can be true in our day. Isaiah had recognized this and sought to make the people aware that their worship was outward with no inner content (Isa. 29:13). It is

easy for us to focus our attention on outward tradition and miss the importance of the inner content. Tradition always threatens the commandment of God.

II. What defiles (vv. 14–15, 21–23). The human tendency is to center attention on the outward. It can be seen and, when necessary, blame can be placed on it. Thus, when we fail we seek to excuse ourselves and place the fault elsewhere. We blame our heritage or our environment. Or as a last resort, we often say, "The devil made me do it." The truth, of course, is that what was done comes from within and not from some outside influence. To be sure, the outside influence may encourage our behavior, but it is not the final cause of it. What poses a temptation to one person may be of no significance to another.

What enters the body from outside cannot cause religious defilement. It may cause disease, but it cannot affect one's relation with God. The people of Jesus' day had very strict regulations about what might be eaten. Jesus taught that these rules were meaningless insofar as one's relationship with God was concerned. External things cannot defile. Only those things that come from within can bring defilement. This is why Jesus placed so much emphasis upon the inner person, as did the prophets of the Old Testament. Evil acts and practices come from within and show what the person is really like. And it is these very things that affect the relation of the individual with God.

Tradition may be good or bad. When one relies upon it rather than upon God, it is harmful. When we allow that which is outside to control our lives, then we are in danger of bringing forth the types of conduct that defile us before God. James understood that religion had two dimensions: the outer and the inner. True religion was to help people in their needs, but it was also to keep oneself unstained by the world (1:27). We neglect either aspect to our own detriment.–Clayton K. Harrop

SUNDAY: SEPTEMBER SEVENTH

SERVICE OF WORSHIP

Sermon: Finding Solid Ground
TEXT: Ezek. 28:1–9, 25–29; also Heb. 13:1–8

Churches that want to grow will make it easy to come to church.

That's why I was struck with Psalm 15. It starts out, "O Lord, who shall sojourn in the tent? Who shall dwell on the holy hill?" It is referring to the Temple in Jerusalem, and about how hard it is to get into it. The Temple was not open to everybody. You had to meet certain requirements in order to worship in the Temple.

I. Most people who know these things say that this psalm is an "entrance psalm." It was used as a liturgical preceding entry into the Temple. The rest of the psalm is an elaboration of what it means to do right, and to walk blamelessly: Do not slander, do not speak evil of someone, or reproach a neighbor. It says the person who does right is the person who builds up community, doesn't tear it down. There are words that hurt, and words that heal. Those who do the right speak the words of healing.

a. But they are not silent. They speak out against the wrong, they praise those people who do the right. And finally, they "do not put money out at interest, and do not take a bribe against the innocent." It refers to charitable loans, money that you give to the poor because they need it, or to help somebody through a tough time. In other words, we are not to profit from somebody else's misery.

b. This definition of doing right is found throughout the Bible. It is, in fact, a foundational ethic of the Bible. You come across it everywhere. You heard it in the other lessons read for you this morning. What caught my attention is that apparently you don't get into the Temple until you do these things.

II. But what about the law? What about morality? If we emphasize grace, does that mean we just tolerate everything? Do we just accept people the way they are and not expect anything better from them? Make no demands upon them? Have no expectations about their behavior? There is always this tension, especially in a church that emphasized grace. What about morality?

a. Grace is given to you to empower you to turn around and to do something with your life. So conversion is just the beginning. Conversion is the start of a journey. You ought to be going someplace with your life. You ought to be getting better. You ought to become more loving.

b. That's what characterized Wesley's preaching, this emphasis that Grace is given to you so you can do something with your life. Grace is stronger than anything else in your life. It's stronger that bad habits, bad upbringing, bad environment, bad parents, bad luck. In the hymn "O for a Thousand Tongues to Sing," written by his brother, Charles, it says,

> He breaks the power of canceled sin,
> he sets the prisoner free; . . .

You can begin a new life. That's what grace is for. Grace is the power that sets you free–to do good, and to become better.

III. The Old Testament lesson is a wonderful affirmation of this testimony about God's will to set us free. The Jews are in Babylon in exile. They are in bondage. But Ezekiel sees that the real bondage is not that they are held by the Babylonians but that they're held by fatalism, the idea that I can't do anything about my situation. I am the product of forces greater than I am; therefore all I can do is hunker down here in Babylon and wait it out. We will always be exiles. We will always be in this bondage. Things are never going to change. My life is always going to be the same.

a. The fatalism was condensed into a saying that went like this: "The fathers have eaten sour grapes and their children's teeth are set on edge." That has a lot of truth to it, incidentally. Psychology has taught us that, and we ought to take it seriously. There are moral consequences to our actions that reverberate throughout the community and the generations. Any adult who says, "What I do is my own business," is being morally irresponsible. The point of the proverb, "The fathers have eaten sour grapes and their children's teeth are set on edge," is that life is a community, and what I do affects you, and what you do affects me.

b. But the problem with those people in Babylon was that they were saying if my present suffering is the result of someone else's sins, then I just have to sit it out. There's nothing I can do about it. In their language, "God is not finished with the punishment." That is the idea Ezekiel attacks. So our text begins, "What do you mean . . . 'The fathers have eaten sour grapes, and the children's teeth are set on edge'? As I live, says the Lord God, this proverb shall no more be used by you in Israel." No more excuses that something up there, some power greater than myself, is preventing me from the life that God has created for me. This proverb, this excuse, shall no more be used by you.

c. The stunning revelation of the psalm is that what you do affects your relationship with God. It reveals that God's availability is linked to our morality. We always assumed that God would be there when we needed him, if we needed him. Don't call us, we'll call you. But it doesn't work that way, according to these Scriptures. They say our morality, the way we live, has something to do with God's availability. That's why they ask the question at the door of the Temple, "O Lord, who shall sojourn in the tent? Who shall dwell on thy holy hill? He who walks blamelessly, and does what is right . . ."

IV. I thought about what that means to us. I had to admit that this is strange to me, and I assume to you, too. We know about God's love and grace, God's forgiveness. I came to the conclusion that what we know about God is not only what we have experienced in our life, but what others have experienced in their lives. In fact, the Bible is a record of how others have experienced God in their lives. The authors of the passages we have wrestled with this morning know about God's grace. They have experienced God's grace. But they have discovered something else about God, something that you and I may be resisting.

a. We may be resisting it because we are modern men and women, shaped by the modern world's fascination with human freedom and autonomy. So we believe that morality is a personal thing, a matter of individual conscience. Morality, in the words of our day, is a matter of life-style. So we may resist it because we are so thoroughly modern. Or we may resist it because we don't want to hear it. We come to be church to be comforted, not to be challenged.

b. So if your world is shaky, or if God is not real to you, or if you suspect that God has abandoned you, then consider this. God's availability is linked with your morality. So maybe you don't need more grace. Maybe you have sufficient grace, and what you need now is to use the grace that God has given you—to do good, and to be better. —Mark Trotter

Illustrations

CREATIVE REVERSAL. In a purely physical world, selfishness is the only practicality and self-preservation the essential purpose. A Dillinger in a materialistic order is thoroughly practical, provided he can get away with it. But if life means something more than to fill one's body and to satisfy the passions of the flesh, self-preservation becomes turned about and, through the preserving of the finer attributes of life, through service to the welfare of the race, the individual finds his own fulfillment.—David Seabury

HEALTH IS "MANY SPLENDORED." Mental health—some of us believe—includes all the healths: physical, social cultural, and moral (spiritual). To live, to love, to care, to enjoy, to build on the foundations of our predecessors, to revere the constant miracles of creation and endurance, of "the starry skies above and the moral law within" —these are acts and attitudes which express our mental health.

Yet, how is it, as Socrates wondered, that "men know what is good, but do what is bad"?—Karl Menninger, M.D.

SERMON SUGGESTIONS

Topic: Which Way Shall I Take?
TEXT: Isa. 42
(1) Why we are sometimes paralyzed by indecision: (a) We may have tried and failed before; (b) We may want to be absolutely sure that we are making the best possible

choice; (c) We may simply hate the responsibility of making up our mind. (2) However, something can be said in favor of one who deliberates: (a) Some people do choose too quickly. (b) Some decisions are made too quickly from lack of experience. (c) Some people make some decisions too quickly because they are too naive, too gullible. (3) Then, if this means that God's way must be the best way, what can we do? (a) Be sure that you are really committed to follow God's will. (b) Know your Bible. (c) Seek the personal leadership of God in your life. (d) Value the counsel of your fellow Christians, that is, those who are more than worldly-wise. (e) Be willing to act on faith.

Topic: When Fatalism Is Fatal

TEXT: John 3:7

(1) It is the nature of nature to change. (2) It is not only the nature of nature to change but it is the nature of human nature as well. (3) Not only does nature change, not only does so-called human nature change, but it is the nature of God to expect change.— Gaston Foote

Worship Aids

CALL TO WORSHIP.   "Hear my cry, O God; attend unto my prayer. From the end of the earth will I cry unto thee, when my heart is overwhelmed: lead me to the rock that is higher than I" (Ps. 61:1–2).

INVOCATION.   Our Father, save us from our disappointments, as we realize that every disappointment is an appointment with you. Today, as we meet for worship, many things have gone wrong for many of us, but what we do now is right for all of us. So renew our spirits; make straight our paths; and give us joy in your will.

OFFERTORY SENTENCE.   "Ye ought to support the weak, and to remember the words of the Lord Jesus, how he said, It is more blessed to give than to receive" (Acts 20:35).

OFFERTORY PRAYER.   Our Father, we want to give, we need to give, and we are determined to give. Help us to know our true ability, and grant to us the grace to let this knowledge guide our giving.

PRAYER.   Long have we heard that Jesus is the way, the truth, and the life, Father. Grant us the grace that enables us to follow him, to learn from him, and to live in him as we venture into the days before us.

Give us the vision to walk in his ways. Open our minds to truth that we may not fall into falsehood. Fill our hearts with love that we may overcome hate and its attendant ravages. In him may we live lives of righteousness, peace, and love.

Help us, Father, to translate Christ's Spirit into deeds of compassion and service. May we never be merely hearers of his word and not doers of it also. Generate in us a compassion for the needs of our fellow pilgrims which will go forth to care for their need. Give us a concern for the burdened which will strengthen us to help them carry their heavy loads. Give us a caring for the lonely which will populate their loneliness with friendly presence. Give us a heart for the lost which will go out into all climates to lead them gently into the fold of your grace and forgiveness.

Father, in a world which is a mixture of good and evil, light and darkness, pray keep our faith and hopes burning bright, that we may be light-bearers in the darkness and the bringer of good news with all its promise and hope to people everywhere.—Henry Fields

LECTIONARY MESSAGE

Topic: Concern for Others

TEXT: Mark 7:24–37

It seems to be a fact of life that we divide humankind into camps. In the ancient world it was Jew and Greek, Greek and barbarian, slave and free, rich and poor. Today it is "us and them," whoever "us" may be and whoever "them" may be. Our divisions may be on the basis of religion, race, social or economic status. We tend to be attracted to those who are like us and put aside those who differ from us. It is difficult to remember that God is not a respecter of persons (Acts 10:34). He bestows his blessings upon all people (Matt. 5:45). This understanding has spurred the interest in missions, in evangelism, and in many of the social programs that are commonplace today.

I. Help for a Gentile (vv. 24–30). Jesus did not share the common feelings of his day with regard to other people. We are told that his countrymen showed an aversion to Gentiles and Samaritans and strong support for fellow Jews. In addition, riches were looked upon as an evidence of being pleasing to God. Illness and misfortune were indications of grievous sin. Yet, even in the Old Testament, it was taught that the poor were a special concern to God (Prov. 22:22–23).

Mark tells us how Jesus had withdrawn to mainly Gentile territory and a Gentile woman approached him seeking help for her sick daughter. But the disciples wanted Jesus to send her away (Matt. 15:23). It was all right for Jesus to heal Jews, but they did not want him to be bothered by other people. It is easy for us to share their attitude. Our resources are limited. We have only so much time and energy. Therefore, it seems wise to use our time and resources for the benefit of those like ourselves.

This Gentile woman could not be called a child of God in the same sense as a Jew. From the Jewish viewpoint, she should not share in the blessings that God provided. She seems to have realized the difference as well and did not demand to be recognized in the same way as a Jew. She simply wanted a small portion of the benefits that God could provide. She sensed that God was able to care for all. His provisions were not limited. After her expression of confidence in God, Jesus healed her daughter.

Our God has an infinite storehouse of blessings, more than are necessary for one group of people. He intends for all to benefit from his mercy. But he has chosen to rely upon us to be the hands and feet that share his blessings with others. We dare not look on the outward appearance of people to think about how they differ from us. We need, as did Jesus, to look on the inward part and see how all are like us, in need of God's grace and mercy. Only then can we adequately share God's love with others.

II. Help for the helpless (vv. 31–37). Many people have not been blessed with physical health. They lose their sight, their hearing, their ability to move around. Our modern world has become increasingly aware of and sensitive to the disabilities that affect people. We are concerned to see that they have equal opportunity for education, for employment, for enjoying life to the fullest.

Such concern has not always been expressed. Often those who were disabled were put outside as being useless and a burden. They were looked upon as being cursed by God because of their affliction. Jesus expressed a deep concern for such people, and much of his ministry was in healing those who were afflicted. He sought to alleviate human pain whenever and wherever he found it. Part of his mission was to assist people in every circumstance of life.

Jesus' example should give direction to our lives. We may find it difficult to help others. We are often overwhelmed by the need we see about us. We watch television and see the miseries of people around the world. And there seems to be little that we can do to deal with this human suffering. It is true that, as with Jesus, we cannot assist every suffering person. But God has given us resources that enable us to assist some. And he expects us to share with those in need. James claimed that faith is not real unless it seeks to help others (James 2:1–10). Jesus stated that when we seek to meet human need, we are actually ministering to him (Matt. 25:40). We are to be at work helping those who cannot help themselves. This is the practical outworking of faith in our lives.—Clayton K. Harrop

SUNDAY: SEPTEMBER FOURTEENTH

SERVICE OF WORSHIP

**Sermon: The Key to a Good Life:
The Real Story of the Ten Commandments**

TEXT: Exod. 19:16–20:20

The Ten Commandments. For many of us, the very words denote harshness and repression. Are the commandments really negative? Did God give them to the ancient Hebrews as an affliction, as a burden to bear?

I. This isn't the impression we get when we read the story of the commandments in the book of Exodus. There, in the midst of a high drama, with the people of Israel standing around the foot of Mt. Sinai in the thunderstorm and Moses going up into the clouds to meet with their God named Yahweh, the commandments are bestowed as a blessing. They are given to constitute a bond between Yahweh and his people.

a. There are rules in the moral universe that are fully as real and important to know as the rules of the physical universe. The created order is not entirely chaotic and unpredictable. And the better we know and observe those rules, the more they will work for us to produce favorable consequences. I cannot leap off a housetop without running counter to the law of gravity and risking serious injury. And by the same token I cannot disregard God, kill another human being, or commit adultery without going against the moral nature of things and hurting myself.

b. Viewed in this light, we can understand why the ancient Hebrews were so proud of the commandments, why they inscribed them on bits of parchment and sewed them into the sleeves of their garments or wore them in bands around their heads; and we can appreciate the enthusiasm of the psalmist:

Blessed is the man
who walks not in the counsel of
the wicked,
nor stands in the way of sinners,
nor sits in the seat of scoffers;
but his delight is in the law of the
LORD,
and on his law he meditates day
and night.
He is like a tree
planted by streams of water
that yields its fruit in its season,
and its leaf does not wither.
In all that he does, he prospers.
(Psalm 1:1–3 RSV)

II. "But what about Christ?" someone asks. "Didn't he do away with the law? Aren't we under grace today, and not under the law?"

a. It is true that law and grace are opposites in our vocabularies. We remember that Jesus frequently opposed the scribes and Pharisees, who were the sworn defenders of the law in his day. We are the heirs of the teaching of the apostle Paul, especially in Romans and Galatians, that the law can become an instrument of sin, binding burdens impossible to bear, and that only the grace of God is able to save us for eternity. And we still get goose bumps at the war cry of the Reformation, "Salvation by grace alone!"

b. But we need to go back and restudy the Gospels to see that Jesus never rejected the law. Our only glimpse of him as a young man is that picture of him as a youthful scholar of the law, arguing with the learned doctors in the Temple. And it was the thoroughness with which he knew and loved the law that enabled him to argue so effectively with the scribes and Pharisees. His confrontation with them was not over the law's existence but over its interpretation.

Jesus saw better than anyone the mistake of turning the law into an instrument for paralysis and condemnation. But he never suggested abandoning the law.

III. It is important, therefore, to study the commandments, and to learn to live by them today. The coming of the Spirit of God has not canceled them. Instead, it has put a new heart in us and enabled us to fulfill them. If the law was ever our enemy—and the scribes and Pharisees had made it one—it is now once again our friend. Now we can understand it and perceive its blessedness. Now we can behold what a gift it is. Now we can echo the conviction of the psalmist, "I will never forget thy precepts; for by them thou hast given me life" (Ps. 119:93).–John Killinger

Illustrations

RULES.   There is something about most of us, of course, that doesn't like rules. We are instinctively rebellious, like the little tomboy sitting on the front porch sulking when her daddy came from work. "What's wrong with Puddin'?" he asked his wife. "Oh," said his wife, "she just found out today that there's a law of gravity, and she's mad about it."–John Killinger

EVERY PROBLEM HAS A SOLUTION. The last Commandment, "Thou shalt not covet," really sums up the other nine because it teaches that the outer must correspond to the inner. If you wish abundance or any good thing, you must have it in your consciousness first, because the outer will always correspond to the inner. Although Moses gave this Commandment some eleven or twelve hundred years before Jesus Christ, it also sums up the Sermon on the Mount because Jesus came and took it and amplified it. The whole teaching of Jesus is that the outer is but the result of the inner. As you believe, so do you express.

If you want peace, harmony, love, abundance, and health in your life, then you must begin by changing the inner, and the way to do that is to believe that God is working through you. Quietly turn to him, and claim that he is guiding, strengthening you, opening your way. Quietly believe it. That is the secret of life, and that secret will open any door, bridge any gap, remove any obstacle, retrieve any mistake, shut out any sin, and clear up any grief, because it is claiming and realizing his Presence, and in his Presence is fullness of joy.—Emmet Fox

SERMON SUGGESTIONS

Topic: When the Lord Stands Up to Plead
TEXT: Isa. 3:13–15, also Pss. 6, 13, 35, 80:4; 89:46; 90:13; 94:3; Rev. 6:9–11; Hab. 1:2

(1) There come times when God breaks the silence, for God is committed to his people for their good. (2) If we will not learn God's lessons in the quiet of the sanctuary or in the ordinariness of daily living, then we must learn them in the upheavals of suffering, for God reacts against all that harms his people and responds in mercy toward manifold human need. (3) That teaches us: (a) that our real security is in God; (b) that evil will be punished; (c) that right will triumph.

Topic: Forget to Remember
TEXT: Various verses
(1) Forget the past (Phil. 3:13). (2) Forget the cost (Phil. 3:8).–Jack Finegan

Worship Aids

CALL TO WORSHIP.   "Sing praise to God, sing praises: sing praise unto our King, sing praises. For God is the King of all the earth" (Ps. 47:6–7a).

INVOCATION.   O God, as we attempt to magnify your name in our worship, may we also determine to magnify your name in the ways we go about achieving the laudable goals that life and opportunity place before us. To that end, grant us the will and the power to bring the manner of our living into harmony with our professed ideals.

OFFERTORY SENTENCE.   "And he said unto them, Take heed, and beware of covetousness; for a man's life consisteth not in the abundance of the things which he possesseth" (Luke 12:15).

OFFERTORY PRAYER.   Gracious Lord, spare us the mistake of seeking the reward for tithes and offerings in mere material gains. Grant us the joy of giving because it is right, because your kingdom grows through our gifts, and because the good news goes forth on the wings of our faithful stewardship.

PRAYER.   O God, you made us in your own image and redeemed us through Jesus your Son: Look with compassion on the whole human family; take away the arrogance and hatred which infect our hearts; break down the walls that separate us; unite us in bonds of love; and work through our struggle and confusion to accomplish your purposes on earth; that, in your good time, all nations and races may serve you in harmony around your heavenly throne; through Jesus Christ our Lord.—*The Book of Common Prayer*

LECTIONARY MESSAGE

Topic: Following Jesus

TEXT: Mark 8:27–38

A small child is filled with questions. In fact, parents and others may become irritated by the continual questions that come from the lips of an inquisitive child. This, however, is how the child learns. While many of the questions may be trivial and seem foolish, they are of great significance for the development of the child.

I. Who is Jesus? (vv. 27–30). Adults also ask questions. The scientist in the laboratory, the doctor in the office, the technician in the shop all seek answers to questions that are of desperate concern to one or many individuals. But the most important question ever asked is the one Jesus asked his disciples, "But who do you say that I am?"

The disciples had followed Jesus for many months. Now they had withdrawn from the crowds, and they were put to the test. Jesus first asked what other people were saying about him. The disciples knew very well what people were saying. And people had a good impression of Jesus. He was of great importance, comparable with the prophets of God of previous generations.

But what about the disciples? Did their understanding of Jesus go any deeper? Peter answered, probably for the entire group, "You are the Christ." For them, light had broken through the darkness. They had come to realize that Jesus was more than the crowds thought. He was more than a prophet. He was the Messiah, long promised by God and eagerly awaited by the people. It is equally important for people today to answer the question, "Who is Jesus for me?" It is not enough to say he was an important person. We must echo the words of Peter and understand that Jesus is the Christ of God sent to bring eternal life.

II. Understanding Jesus' mission (vv. 31–33). The confession of Peter was a great step forward, but he lacked understanding. Jesus stated that he had come, not to lead a revolt against Rome and set up an earthly kingdom, but to die. It was a great shock to those men to hear Jesus talk about his coming suffering and rejection, his being killed. They believed that the Messiah would live forever (John 12:34).

Jesus knew the mission for which he had come into the world. He had not come to be served but to serve, to give his life as a ransom for human sin (Mark 10:45). He could fulfill his work only by sacrificing his life. And he refused to allow anything to turn him aside from that goal. Not even the best intentions of his closest friends could alter his commitment. When Peter insisted that Jesus was mistaken, Jesus had to call this leader of the apostles "Satan." Peter could see only from the human point of view, not God's.

We are like Peter many times. We want God to be what we imagine him to be. We want him to do what we think is right. Jesus could see from God's perspective and, therefore, he was willing to go to the cross. We recognize, with our hindsight, that this was truly the best. It has brought for us abundant life.

III. Understanding our mission (vv. 34–38). Peter did not understand his own mission either. Thus, Jesus had to show him what God expected of him, and what God expects of his followers in every generation. To follow Jesus meant to deny self and take up a cross. Self was no longer to be the master of one's life. The cross was the instrument of execution. Jesus claimed his followers must die to self and become his followers. Following was a continuous, lifetime process.

Jesus understood how easy it is for us to get our priorities wrong. We seek to do those things that will benefit our physical life. We want to prolong it, to make it as painless as possible and as enjoyable as possible. Jesus stated that those who make this physical life the center of all interest and endeavor have lost the meaning of true living.

Only as this life is submerged into the life and activity of God can one learn the true meaning of living. One may "gain the whole world," but it is of no profit.

Jesus insisted that one's life is measured by the response that is made to him (v. 38). When we turn from him and refuse to follow him, he promises that he will be ashamed of us. Our mission is to follow him faithfully now so that he will acknowledge us when he comes in the glory of his Father. In this way we will show ourselves to be his true followers.—Clayton K. Harrop

SUNDAY: SEPTEMBER TWENTY-FIRST

SERVICE OF WORSHIP

Sermon: When God Disturbs Our Religion
TEXT: John 3:10

Religion, we are told, has become a hot topic in election campaigns. Every political candidate wants to be perceived as being on the side of religion. That is the side of the Good Guys: to query anything that smacks of religion puts one in the category of the Bad Guys. It is assumed that this is the message of the Bible.

In fact, what we find in the Bible is that time and again religion is attacked as the enemy of the living God. In the Old Testament it is not only the religions of Israel's neighbors that are denounced, but also the religious practices of the Israelites themselves. Listen to the voice of God speaking through the prophet Isaiah.

Then read the Gospels. Have you ever noticed that the fiercest words of Jesus seem to be reserved for leaders of religion? What disturbed his contemporaries, and still should disturb us, is his insistence that, at the heart of true religion is a daily communion with the God of infinite love and a reflection of that love in our dealing with others.

I. So we are wrong if we think that by placing ourselves in the ranks of his disciples we are therefore automatically among the Good Guys, exempt from the judgment that falls on the Immoral Majority of those the King James Version calls "publicans and sinners."

a. Because religion is, at its best, the most glorious and satisfying dimension of human life, when it is corrupted it becomes one of the most vicious. Fanatical religion, which is raising its ugly head across the world today, has been responsible for some of the bloodiest wars in history. It is fanatical religion—Christian, Jewish, Muslim, or any other—that has surfaced today and is a clear and present danger.

b. According to the Bible, then, whatever else God judges, he certainly judges the quality of our religion. This is where his presence, and the words of Jesus, should disturb us most. As preachers have discovered, no one ever objects to a sermon denouncing hypocrisy—for a hypocrite is always someone else, not me.

II. So let me introduce you to the real subject of this sermon, the man who was at the receiving end of a sharp and sudden barb of Jesus.

a. Churchgoers are familiar with the third chapter of John's Gospel. But we may not have thought much about Nicodemus, who slipped in one evening for a talk about religion. He began the conversation most courteously: "Rabbi, we know that you are a teacher sent by God; no one could perform these signs of yours unless God were with him." Immediately, according to this account, Jesus confronted him with the necessity for some kind of upheaval in his religious life. "Unless a man has been born over again he cannot see the kingdom of God." Nicodemus is baffled, and Jesus presses home his disturbing attack. Eventually Nicodemus stammers, "How can these things be?" And Jesus answers in almost scathing tones: "Art thou a master of Israel, and knowest not these things?" In a modern version it sounds even more abrupt: "What?" said Jesus. "Is this famous teacher of Israel ignorant of these things?"

b. Why, then, was Jesus so rough with him? What was wrong with Nicodemus's religion? It was not hypocritical. It was not fanatical. In many ways it was like ours, we may think. Yes; and like ours in that it was a little too satisfactory, a little too drab and conventional, and much too resistant to challenge and change. It's not just false and demonic religion that God disturbs. It's good religion that we settle down with. It's the religion we have fitted into our way of life—helpful, comforting, guiding, but not really dynamic or developing.

Do you never have that feeling of something missing, of a new experience of God's grace that is hovering out there waiting to be discovered? There are moments in worship, for instance, when many of us seem to glimpse a new, and perhaps simpler, Christian life, a presence of the Spirit that would mean being truly born again—"new every morning." We long to break through the images that have satisfied us too long, to find new light streaming in on the theology with which we have settled down. We glimpse what it might mean, in Paul's words, to grow into "the measure of the stature of the fullness of Christ."

III. As often happens, I was drawn to this text because I heard it speaking to me. God was disturbing my religion. "Art thou a preacher of the gospel, trained in theology, a student of Scripture—and knowest not these things?" And if I say, "What things, Lord?" he seems to speak to me of the power of the Spirit to keep breaking up dead patterns of devotion, stale theology, convenient compromises, wrong-headed prejudices, and to offer me a constant rebirth. Surely, he says, you should know that this is what matters—more than all the machinery of religion in which you are involved.

a. "Art thou a good Presbyterian and knowest not these things?" Isn't that what he is saying to those in our mainline churches who are not hypocrites, and not fanatics, but loyal supporters of the historic denominations? What we ought to know is that the heart of true religion is not the organization, or the ritual, or loyalty to the best traditions, or support for the good causes, necessary as all these things are, but a lively contact with the Spirit of God, who blows through our world like the wind, sometimes soft as a zephyr, sometimes strong as a hurricane, bringing to each one of us the daily possibility of new life in Christ.

b. Among those, ministers and laypeople,

who have led this congregation for one hundred fifty years, have been men and women who heard this challenge, who were faithful to the gospel transmitted across the years since Pentecost but were also awake to the call of the living Spirit to be constantly born again, revising their ideas, recognizing new opportunities, presenting to all within and around the Christ who satisfies the soul. Our constant rebirth in him is no remote mystic experience. This church has not been led by mystic dreamers, but by those who listened to the apostle James's words about faith: "If it does not lead to action, it is in itself a lifeless thing."

IV. I believe Jesus loved Nicodemus. I believe he respected his position as a "Master in Israel" and was not just being sarcastic. I believe he loves you and respects the religion that you sincerely hold. But I also believe that for all of us there is something more to come if only we let him disturb the religion with which we have settled down. We must be ready each year, each month, each day to be born again in the love and service of Christ. That is the overarching religious issue for us all.—David H. C. Read

Illustrations

FAITH AND DOUBT.   Faith will always be doubted. Doubts are the odds that faith must meet. Otherwise faith would be a dead certainty, not faith. Someone has quipped that doubts are like the measles: health is served if they "come out." Well, they are a more serious issue than measles, much worse than a child's disease; but they are safer when they are acknowledged, and they are dangerous when they are hidden in the pretense which says, "I am not troubled by doubts."—George A. Buttrick

NEWBORN!   Maybe Nicodemus had six honorary doctorates and half a column in *Who's Who,* Jesus said, but if he couldn't see something as plain as the nose on his face, he'd better go back to kindergarten.

"I'm telling you like it is," Jesus said. "I'm telling you there are people on Medicare walking around with the love-light in their eyes. I'm telling you there are ex-cons teaching Sunday School. I'm telling you there are undertakers scared silly we'll put them out of business."

Jesus said, "I'm telling you God's got such a thing for this loused-up planet that he's sent me down so if you don't believe your own eyes, then maybe you'll believe mine, maybe you'll believe me, maybe you won't come sneaking around scared half to death in the dark anymore but will come to, come to life."

What impressed Nicodemus even more than the speech was the quickening of his own breathing and the pounding of his own heart. He hadn't felt like that since his first pair of long pants, his first kiss, since the time his first child was born or the time they'd told him he didn't have lung cancer but just a touch of the flu.

Later on, when Jesus was dead, he went along with Joseph of Arimathea to pay his last respects at the tomb in broad daylight. It was a crazy thing to do, what with the witch-hunt that was going on, but he decided it was more than worth it.

When he heard the next day that some of the disciples had seen Jesus alive again, he wept like a newborn baby.–Frederick Buechner

SERMON SUGGESTIONS

Topic: Needed: An Adequate God
TEXT: Exod. 20:3 and Ps. 135

(1) The idols we serve: pleasure, fame, power. (2) The tragic betrayals by the "gods" we foolishly worship. (3) The abundant life the true and living God wants us to enjoy.

Topic: But—Is God Personal?
TEXT: Isa. 40:25; Heb. 1:1–2

(1) Alternatives to a God who is personal: (a) A god who is impersonal. (b) A God who is subpersonal. (c) A God who is suprapersonal. (2) The only God with whom I can have daily relationship is *personal*. He must be One whose will meets mine, demanding the highest from me, and supporting me at the point of my inevitable weakness. He must be One who, as my Father, encourages

me and chastens me, and who, as my Friend, stands by me. And this kind of God is revealed in Jesus Christ.–Elam Davis

Worship Aids

CALL TO WORSHIP.   "Be thou exalted, Lord, in thine own strength: so will we sing and praise thy power" (Ps. 21:13).

INVOCATION.   Lord, you are the Alpha and the Omega, the first and the last, our Creator, our Redeemer, our eternal Ruler. All that we are and have and hope for is in you, and we praise you. Give us hearts that are joyful and willing to serve you as we go singing of your power and your love.

OFFERTORY SENTENCE.   "As ye have therefore received Christ Jesus the Lord, so walk ye in him: rooted and built up in him, and established in the faith, as ye have been taught, abounding therein with thanksgiving" (Col. 2:6–7).

OFFERTORY PRAYER.   Father, our faith and love overflow into tithes and offerings that we now bring to you. We thank you for every blessing that enables us to present these tokens of our stewardship.

PRAYER.   We have heard, Father, that you love the little children of the world. This morning we are grateful that we have the opportunity to think with the children and learn from the children as we gather in worship. Remind us that we who have walked a long distance from childhood have been called by Jesus to become as little children, to possess their faith in God and their trust in his care and leadership. Some of us have forgotten that call. We have tried to manage life in our own wisdom, knowledge, and strength, and it isn't working. Call us to you anew this morning that we all might appear before you as little children anxious to hear your words of guidance and love.

Thank you for the ones who dedicate themselves to serving the children of the church and the community. Grant them wisdom, courage, and patience to face each challenge brought by the children to their door and the ability to manage them in such a way that the children will be able to function well in the world. Enable those of us who are older to be sensitive to child fears, child failures, and child expectations. May we not disappoint the little ones but rather surprise them with the joy of new discovery, new positive experiences, and new challenges. Show us how to make Jesus real to them. Let our words about him ring true. Let our lives be lived in constant contact with his ways. Let our love for them be the very love of Christ which wins and supports and helps to grow in God-likeness.

Now as we commit this hour to you we do so knowing that it will be followed by other hours filled with dismay, doubt, and misunderstanding. But let each of us gain sufficient strength and determination here this morning that we may commit ourselves to making even the most difficult time periods of trust and faith and undying hope. Meet us, Father, fill us with your spirit, and send us forth into the world to do your will among the children of every age as we serve you.—Henry Fields

LECTIONARY MESSAGE

Topic: The Way to Greatness
TEXT: Mark 9:30–37
Other Readings: Prov. 31:10–31; Ps. 1; James 3:3–4:3, 7–8a

The word *great* implies that someone has done an extraordinary feat, has done something few if any others have done. When we think of the word *great* our minds focus on famous people, star athletes, politicians, those who have wealth, people who make headlines. Jesus had a different definition of greatness. Jesus taught that the way to greatness was through serving others, not in being served. Modern persons whom Jesus would consider great are people who receive little public acclaim: discovers of vaccines that cure diseases, humanitarians, advocates for the impoverished. Our text

today lets us look into a private session Jesus had with his disciples. His missional intent was not to leave a series of propositions or wise teachings. He wanted to leave behind a band of persons on whom these propositions were written, people whose lives lived out these ideals and goals. This is the second time in Mark that Jesus taught them about his suffering and that he would arise in three days. Though they did not understand, they were afraid to ask him to explain what he meant. They knew a great deal, but they were afraid to know any more. The human mind has a great facility for rejecting that which it does not wish to see.

I. Facing the End (9:30–31)
This is the second announcement of Jesus' approaching passion (8:31). The disciples found it hard to accept that Jesus would not be a political messiah, that he would not alter the political scene. Mark says that this was a very private session between Jesus and the disciples. They were beginning their journey toward Jerusalem and to the Cross that awaited him there.

It may surprise us that the disciples were afraid to ask him what he meant. If they had asked what he meant, it might have messed up the neat package they had wrapped for Jesus. The disciples would have had to change their way of thinking about Jesus. They knew he was the Messiah, but their ideas were no different from those of the people. If they had really known what he was saying, it would have messed up their way of thinking. They might not have been nearly as comfortable following him. We, too, do not accept the Cross of Jesus as the supreme revelation of God.

II. True Greatness (9:33–35)
As they traveled toward Capernaum, the disciples proved they did not understand the true meaning of Jesus' messiahship. Though Mark does not describe the discussion among the disciples as they traveled, Jesus asked them what they were arguing about. Who likes their secret thoughts or discussions to be made public? What may seem significant and highly important in private conversation often seems foolish when revealed in public. The disciples had been arguing among themselves about who would be greatest.

Though they refused to answer him, Jesus revealed that they were arguing over who would be the greatest. The disciples must have felt very foolish to have this deeply personal aspect of their lives brought into the open. His simple teaching is that the person who wants to be first must be the last of all, and the servant of everyone. The way to greatness is always through servanthood, ministering to others, not through prominent positions. When people act in selfless ways, it is so rare that it is remembered. While this is a simple truth, it is yet quite profound. If Christians could practice this simple virtue, it would solve every economic problem, every political problem; it would eliminate the divisions and disputes among people in the world, including those in the church. The disciples' true ambition must ever be to be a servant, without receiving recognition for their actions. The reward comes in knowing that one is doing the will of God.

III. Helping the Helpless (9:36–37)

Jesus continues dealing with worthy and unworthy ambition as he places a small child in the midst of the disciples. If we want someone to advance our career or our position in life, a child is not the one to help do it. Children cannot give these things but must have things done for them. We should cultivate the friendship of persons who cannot do things for us, but for whom *we* can do things. To receive a child is to receive Jesus himself. The final test for a society and for a Christian is what we do for children.

The way to greatness is in serving those who cannot do things in return for us. Do we have worthy ambitions? Are we striving for acclaim or for ministry or service to those who cannot further us in any way?–Jerry M. Stubblefield

SUNDAY: SEPTEMBER TWENTY-EIGHTH

SERVICE OF WORSHIP

Sermon: Pass the Salt

TEXT: Matt. 5:13–18

Some years ago, I was making calls on people who had been visiting our church and had shown an interest in becoming members of the church. One woman I called on will never be forgotten. She was the youngest septuagenarian you could imagine. She confided that it had been a long time since she had really studied it. Indeed, she had been away from the church for many years, but now she wanted to commit her life to Jesus Christ anew.

At the end of the conversation, she confessed she had some reservations about church people and church activities, but she knew that as a Christian, one needed to be a part of the church. Without thinking it through, I welcomed her into the church by saying, "You are one salty lady." Then as an afterthought, I mentioned that to me being salty was high praise. Well, the explanation was obviously not adequate, because she called several friends and relatives and told them about the irreverent reverend who had called her salty. She later told me that they all assured her that she was not salty but very sweet.

That is an encounter that stands out in my mind because it was the odd beginning of a close friendship but also because it sheds light on one of the most important questions we will ever ask: "What does it mean to be a Christian?" It could also be phrased, "What does it mean to be a member of the Church of Jesus Christ?" If it means more than another expression of our civic involvement, there must be a unique image of what it means to be a Christian. Indeed, the New Testament uses several images that take us further than we want to go. Perhaps none is more strange and wonderful than when Jesus charges his followers to be the "salt of the earth." *What is needed–if God's saving mission, begun by Jesus, is to continue–is nothing less than salty people* who have not lost their zest.

I. It is a strange image but, if we have ears to hear, I think it still may speak volumes to us. First, it speaks to the question I hear every week: "Am I valuable?" Some of us never seem to go past that question. Salt was of immense value. It was payment for Roman soldiers (that is where the word *salary* comes from) and seen as a symbol of the divine. On Jesus' lips, the word connotes the Worthy One who loves us and values us despite our feelings. Our value is given to us. "Red and yellow, black and white, they are precious in his sight," is a truth we sing as children and search for as adults. What a difference it would make if we could receive the salt of self-worth and pass it on.

II. This image of salt speaks to another question: Are there any values that continue over the centuries and across continents to endure and prevail? It is common for us to decry the decline in moral standards but feel at the same time powerless to live by and pass on these same values. It is here at the conclusion of the Sermon on the Mount that Jesus tells us that we will do the impossible through the power of the Kingdom of God in us. We are to be the salt that preserves and passes on the values that go beyond basic instincts. These values are both glorifying to the Creator and liberating for the creature.

This all sounds very high-minded and somewhat ethereal. Are Christians of any value in and for the world? John 17 records what might be accurately called the Lord's Prayer. The one we give that name is more a model of prayer for his disciples. John 17 recorded Jesus' agonizing, yet triumphant, prayer that we would be *one,* and serve God in the world. God has provided what it takes, in Christ, for us to be a saving influence, to be salty people. We are precious (as all are) in his sight, preserving the Kingdom values, penetrating the world.

There was a popular song that spoke of being the "living legacy of the leader of the band." The leader of the band of twelve has promised that his Spirit will be in us. That Spirit is the salt of the precious, invaluable life of God in us. Jesus does not say you will become the salt; rather, you are the salt! You are valuable. Some of us cannot hear that too often. We doubt it constantly. God created you in his image; Christ died for you. Can you, can any human be lacking worth? Can there be a higher calling than to pass it on?

Yet it seems a truth we never freely learn. A fifteen-year-old boy volunteered to teach a Sunday school class for four-year-olds. When asked what he had scheduled for the first lesson, he replied, "Well, the lesson plan says, 'Show them that each person is an individual with different potentialities and abilities; there is value in our difference . . . ' If that doesn't work, we'll make clay bunnies." Well, its easier to make clay bunnies than to recognize the values God had given each person. When Jesus said, "You are the salt," it was both singular and plural. The whole church is called to be the salt, but no individual "can sit it out." Every pinch of salt is important. One child said salt is what makes food taste bad when you don't put it in. In the same way, believe it or not, the work of Christ suffers when you say God can't use you because of some shortcoming, or you're of no value because of your age. "You are," said Jesus, "the salt of the earth."

III. Jesus did not need to explain to a group of fishermen the greatest property of salt in the ancient world. In kegs they layered the fish with salt to preserve it.

a. As the salt of the earth we are called to *preserve* the values that really count. This does not mean that we are museum keepers protecting every human tradition. That has been the church's problem. We have often kept traditions and lost people—majored in minors. There is a story that Presbyterian ministers used to wear hats in the pulpit following the great example of John Calvin. No one remembers how the tradition started until it was discovered that Calvin preached in an old cathedral where pigeons used to roost in the rafters. His hat was a necessary defense. A tradition was born that didn't need to be preserved when the pigeons were gone.

What we are called to preserve through God's spirit is people. In the early centuries of the church, those who were baptized had a pinch of salt placed on their tongues. Perhaps it was a reminder of the body of Christ's call to preserve the savor of commitment in the convert. It was also a reminder to the church to *be* the church. We are also called to preserve the value of the Kingdom here on earth. That means taking costly stands on our belief that life is a gift and all people are valuable. That means fighting forces that would dehumanize any . . . including the handicapped, the aged, the widow, the orphan.

b. Of course that's the key: if the salt is of value . . . if the salt is of value, if it is to preserve, it must *penetrate.* The quality of life described in the Beatitude will make no difference at all unless it penetrates the people, institutions, and structures of the world. God at work in our lives means a salt that bites and stings as well as heals. God brings judgment as well as grace. How can we know the comfort of God's forgiveness if we deny the strength of God's judgment on our sin? A novelist reminds us that it does not say you are the honey of the world, you are the salt of the earth! Being the salt of the earth, being the church of Jesus Christ, means taking a stand against what we believe is evil or dehumanizing. The worst is not rejection for a stand we have taken; the worst, Jesus says, is being insipid, flat, bland . . . salt that has lost its zing.

What are the greatest dangers facing our church? That we won't make the budget, that our programs won't be successful? No, the greatest dangers are that we will curve in upon ourselves, that we will huddle together, becoming a comfortable "Christian ghetto" or, on the other hand, that we will be in the world, but not to penetrate, not to witness of Christ's love in word and deed, but to mingle. If we are to be the church, bearers of salt, we must penetrate the world.

In the final analysis, the salt is the good news of Jesus Christ that penetrates our lives and begins the lifelong process of making us "new creations." That very process is stunted when we try to hold on to that message that turns the world upside down. We can not contain that salt in the precincts of the church; we cannot tame it, make it smooth and sweet. If we are to return its penetrating power in our own lives, we must be prepared to pass it on.–Gary D. Stratman

Illustrations

A RADIANT FAITH.   Oliver Wendell Holmes once said, "I might have entered the ministry if certain clergymen I knew had

not looked and acted so much like undertakers." Robert Louis Stevenson once entered in his diary, as if he was recording an extraordinary phenomenon, "I have been to Church to-day, and am not depressed."

Men need to discover the lost radiance of the Christian faith. In a worried world, the Christian should be the only man who remains serene. In a depressed world, the Christian should be the only man who remains full of the joy of life. There should be a sheer sparkle about the Christian life; and too often the Christian dresses like a mourner at a funeral, and talks like a specter at a feast. Wherever he is, if he is to be the salt of the earth, the Christian must be the diffuser of joy.–William Barclay

THE CHURCH, THE GOSPEL, AND SOCIETY.   Do not worry about church statistics. It is a matter where the Church can afford to be indifferent to its own aggrandizement if it can but get access and influence with its gospel. The Church's numbers can only be increased by thinking about numbers and much more than we do about the gospel.–P. T. Forsyth

SERMON SUGGESTIONS

Topic: A Yoke for the Young
TEXT: Lam. 3:27
(1) *The significance of yoke-bearing:* (a) The yoke signified restraint. (b) The yoke means constraint as well as restraint. (c) The yoke suggests fellowship. (d) The yoke means service. (2) *The satisfaction of yoke-bearing:* (a) It will save you from many regrets. (b) There are joys in the yoke of Christ that cannot be found in the service of sin. (c) It is good that one bear the yoke in the days of youth, because then we learn more rapidly and impressions are more lasting. (d) There is enrichment in store.–W. W. Weeks

Topic: Living with Style
TEXT: 1 Cor. 16:23
(1) It involves living thankfully. (2) It involves living usefully. (3) It involves living courteously. (4) It involves living magnanimously.–John N. Gladstone

Worship Aids

CALL TO WORSHIP.   "Arise, O God, judge the earth; for to thee belong all the nations!" (Ps. 82:8 RSV).

INVOCATION.   Our hope is in you, O God, for the putting right of all things wrong. Open our eyes to see through faith that you are at work even when present circumstances seem to deny it.

OFFERTORY SENTENCE.   "But ye, brethren, be not weary in well doing" (2 Thess. 3:13).

OFFERTORY PRAYER.   We confess, our Father, that there are times when our words, our deeds, and our gifts seem futile, and we are tempted to give up in discouragement. Make us strong and faithful in our stewardship, we pray, with the assurance that you will cause our efforts in due time or in eternity to succeed.

PRAYER.   O Creator God: it is fitting that we offer up our heartfelt thanks for this wonderful fall day which shares with us its beauty and offers the promise of harvest and plenty:

For the earth which is our home; for fruit and vegetable; clear, flowing streams; and creatures of the field which share their food with us;

For the family of humankind to which we belong; for the families in which we were born and live each day; for love and affection, tenderness and caring; for the shelter a home provides against the storms of life;

For the family of God, the church universal, comprising all those who put their faith in you and who have given themselves to righteousness, justice, goodness, and love, and who have committed themselves to making a positive difference in the world;

For the family of God which gathers in this place, our own congregation where both joys and sorrows are shared, the truth is sought, souls are nourished, and weary travelers are encouraged and refreshed;

For Jesus of Nazareth, called the Christ, who, more than any other who has ever lived, has revealed your true nature of love, mercy, and grace; Jesus who has taught us the ways of God, who made the ultimate sacrifice, and who holds the promise of everlasting life.

For all these wondrous blessings, we offer up a heartfelt prayer of thanksgiving and a song of praise, O God.

And now, we intercede for those who have been made weary by life: the sick, troubled, grieving, distressed. Be with each one of your children as they need you.—Randy Hammer

LECTIONARY MESSAGE

Topic: Being a Faithful Disciple
TEXT: Mark 9:38–50
Other Readings: Esther 7:1–6, 9–10; 9:20–22; Psalm 124; James 5:3–20

Being a faithful disciple requires not only being faithful to Christ but being tolerant of those who differ from us but who are trying to do the work of Christ. It also means that the Christian will avoid all temptations to sin, even if it means going through life with only one hand, one foot, or one eye.

A faithful disciple of Jesus functions in the world much as salt does. We are to flavor the world in which we live. Christian principles are taught but also practiced by Christians. As faithful disciples we are to live at peace with one another. We should live in harmony with one another.

I. The Inclusiveness of Discipleship (9:38–40)

John felt that those who were not a part of their company should not be trying to cast out demons.

Intolerance can come from some good sources, from loyalty, from confidence in the truth proclaimed, the desire to keep the truth uncorrupted. Our narrow idea of truth may come from our loyalty to the means than the ends, to organization than to the gospel it was organized to serve, to the institution than to God, to the parochial and regional than to the universal. Jesus uses this incident to teach about the inclusiveness of discipleship. This is a problem modern Christians face as we criticize, fail to have fellowship with other Christians who might worship different than we do or do things in ways we do not do them. There are some great lessons we can learn from this event. We need to be more tolerant of others.

People have a right to their own thoughts. This is a right that we as Christians should respect. There are multiple ways to God, not just the way we found Him. We must remember that truth is always bigger than any one person's grasp of it. As a person has a right to their own thoughts, they also have the right to do their own speaking. Before judging a belief or a doctrine, it must finally be evaluated by the kind of people it produces.

Being tolerant means that a Christian cannot entirely condemn another's belief that makes that person a good person. While we may condemn a person's beliefs, we must never hate the person. Jesus teaches that those who do His work belong to Him.

II. Rewards and Punishments of Being Faithful Disciples (9:41–42)

Mark shows the enormous significance of being faithful in discipleship by the illustration of the cup of water. Any kindness shown, any help given to the people of Christ will not lose its reward. Our motive in helping is that the person in need belongs to Jesus Christ.

To help is to win the eternal reward. To cause a weaker brother or sister to stumble is to win the eternal punishment. For one to sin is bad, but to teach another to sin is infinitely worse. To have a great millstone placed around one's neck was a Roman form of capital punishment. It would mean certain death.

III. The Necessity for Faithful Discipleship (9:43–48)

Being a faithful disciple is one goal that is worthy of any sacrifice. It is a goal for which everything must be sacrificed. The ultimate sacrifice is to enter the kingdom of God. What is the Kingdom of God? The Kingdom of God is a society upon earth in which God's will is as perfectly done in earth as it is in heaven. To enter the Kingdom of God is worth any sacrifice, any discipline, any self-denial to do the will of God. Jesus has warned against offenses to others. Just as intense are offenses to oneself.

Often it is the good that is the enemy of the best. Ambition and the lure of fame call for surgery if one is to seek first the Kingdom of God. It may be necessary to excise some habit, abandon some pleasure, give up some friendship, cut out some thing that has become very valuable to us. This rooting out must occur if we are to know real life, real happiness, and real peace.

IV. Faithful Disciples are Salty (9:49–50).

There are three ideas found here. Each is a pithy saying. Being salted by fire refers to Jewish law that every sacrifice must be salted with salt before offering it to God. This made the sacrifice acceptable to God.

Salt is good. It serves to lend flavor to things and was the earliest of preservatives. Christians who have lost their Christian flavor cannot do their function as a preserving force in the world.

Unless Christians have the salt of Christian gospel, we will not be at peace, either in the church or in the world at large. Only if we have salt in ourselves can we live in real fellowship with others.—Jerry M. Stubblefield

SUNDAY: OCTOBER FIFTH

SERVICE OF WORSHIP

Sermon: Jesus' Prayer for Christian Unity
TEXT: John 17:20–26

One of the most powerful movements sweeping across the Christian world is the quest for Church unity. Many Christians have seen the fragmentation of the Church as a scandal and a factor that harms its witness to the world. The fighting within the Church between Christians about correct doctrines and Church practices is an affront to our Lord. As we gather at the Communion Table we join other Christians around the world who worship on this day with a prayer for Christian unity.

Let's look for a moment at a part of our Lord's high priestly prayer for his Church and how this prayer might guide us in our quest for unity. Jesus' prayer began with a personal plea that he might glorify his Father in the ultimate sacrifice on the cross (17:1–5) which lay before him. Next he prayed for his disciples, that they might be consecrated to God's truth in order to serve Christ as he sends them into the world (17:9–19). Jesus then offers his prayer for all future believers, which includes you and me and other Christians around the world. All believers who read these verses (vv. 20–26) overhear the Lord's prayer for them.

I. Even as Jesus faced the most difficult experience in his earthly life, his prayer reveals a quiet trust in his Father's presence and guidance. With the certainty of the cross before him, rejection by the crowds around him, and desertion by the disciples who were closest to him, Jesus maintained his confidence in what God would do in the future.

a. But Jesus' prayer not only reflects his certainty about his Father but his confidence in the disciples. Even knowing his disciples' fears, ambitions, struggles, and weaknesses, Jesus did not lose trust in them. He had chosen them after long hours of prayer, and he was convinced that God would use them as instruments to spread the good news throughout the world.

b. Jesus prayed for the unity of the future Church. He prayed that the future growth of the Church would not inhibit its unity. What then is the debate about whether or not the Church should be united? The last will and testament of our Lord was a prayer for the unity of the Church. All the debate about whether or not the Church should be united is superfluous, if we really want to follow the intention of our Lord. The unity of the Church was our Lord's basic desire.

c. Notice also that the text reveals that Jesus prayed for a unique kind of unity for his Church. He prayed that the future disciples in the Church would be united as he and the Father were united. "May they all be one, as you Father, are in me, and I in You" (v. 20). Jesus' unity with his Father was based on a unique personal communion of the Son with the Father. The Church's unity is a reflection of the unity within the Triune God.

II. The basis of the Church's unity, as it is modeled after our Lord's unity with his Father, is rooted in the nature of God and Jesus' obedient love. The Father was "in" Jesus, and Jesus was "in" the Father. As the Father has "sent" the Son, so Jesus "sends" his disciples into the world (v. 21).

a. If Christians loved one another as Jesus loved his Father and the Father loved the Son, this same expression of love would be evident in the life and work of the Church. The motivating power of God's love that guided the ministry of Jesus would be then the dominating expression of the Church's mission. The disunity of the Church continues to be a compelling argument to the world that the Church has lost sight of its redemptive mission to share God's love as it claims to have experienced it in Christ.

b. Our model for the unity in the Church comes from our Lord. Jesus Christ extends God's grace to all persons. Jesus called all persons to experience the Father's love. Instead of exhibiting Christ-like love, we often draw circles and exclude persons from the Church. We often want to include only those who think as we do or act as we do. Only those who fit in certain theological boxes or believe along our rigid patterns can be included in the fold. Jesus encountered this attitude in the Pharisees, who built their religion on exclusiveness. Their religion erected walls and fences to keep people out. But this was not the kind of religion Jesus proclaimed. Rather than excluding persons, Jesus reached out to include them. Rather than pushing people down, Jesus reached out to lift them up. Rather that crushing people with heavy burdens, Jesus sought to liberate them. He does not want to build walls that separate but doors that open to include others.

III. The reason that Jesus prays for the unity of the Church is so the world might know the true nature of God as one. Note the three stages through which God manifests his glory.

a. First, Jesus received glory from his Father. What was this glory? This glory was revealed through Jesus' Incarnate life, words, and ministry. This glory may have a reflection of Jesus' obedient love of his Father. Glory may have been a reference to Jesus' death on the cross. When Jesus spoke about his death, he usually spoke of being "glorified" (John 11:4; 12:23).

b. Second, Jesus transmits this glory to his disciples (vv. 22–23). As Jesus had reflected the light from his Father, the disciples were to be lights to show others the way to the Father. Sometimes the disciples would suffer as the Lord had suffered. The ministry of the Church is not to call attention to itself but to lead people to God.

The Church's task is not to erect fences so that we can keep out those who don't think or act as we do. Instead, our role is to glorify God and lead other persons to find God.

c. Third, ultimately Christ's glory will not be realized in this world but in the eternal glory that he has gone to prepare for his disciples. During times of tribulation, the disciples can take hope in the love and promise of God (see Rom. 8:18–25; 2 Tim. 2:11–12). God's glory will not be fully manifested in this world, but it will be known as we depart this life to dwell eternally with God.

IV. In a few moments we will commune at the Lord's Table. Jesus extends his invitation to all of his followers to come and commune at his Table. We come to the Table at his invitation, and in acknowledging Jesus as our Lord and Savior, we affirm that all other Christians who come to this, the Lord's Table, are our sisters and brothers in Christ. Those whom our Lord has included, let no one exclude.–William Powell Tuck

Illustrations

THE BASIS OF UNITY.   Love in the New Testament is not a sentimental and affectionate emotion as we so commonly interpret it. There are three words in Greek for love, three words that we have to translate by our one word *love. Eros*–"erotic" comes from it– that is one. In vulgar use it meant sexual lust; in Platonic philosophy it meant the yearning of the soul for the realm of the gods. The New Testament never employs that word; both in vulgar and in philosophic usage it had connotations that would not do. *Philia*–that is another Greek word. It meant intimate, personal affectionateness and friendship. The New Testament does use that, twenty-five times, when intimate affectionateness is meant. But the great Christian

word for love is something else: *agape.* Over two hundred and fifty times the New Testament uses it, and agape means nothing sentimental or primarily emotional at all; it means understanding, redeeming, creative goodwill.–Harry Emerson Fosdick

MAKING A DIFFERENCE.   In a CBS special several years ago, Bill Moyers told about a man in New York City who decided he would try to do something to help the hungry. As he went to work each day in New York City, he distributed a hundred sandwiches to the street people. The street people soon learned about his kindness, and they lined the sidewalks waiting for him to hand them a sandwich. After a TV segment which showed the man handing out sandwiches to the people, Moyers observed, "New York City's population now runs in excess of eleven million people. A hundred sandwiches will hardly scratch the surface of the need. But while Sam may never move his world very far, at least the direction he is moving it is forward."–William Powell Tuck

SERMON SUGGESTIONS

Topic: Good News for You
   TEXT: 1 Kings 19:4; Eph. 2:8–10
   (1) *The fallacies of legalism:* (a) That human beings can be perfect; (b) That coercion can change the human heart; (c) That we can save ourselves. (2) *The saving truth of the gospel:* (a) The promise and comforts of the gospel are for such a person as you. (b) A place of useful service is for such a person as you. (c) This is an amazing truth, but it shows the grandeur of the grace of God.

Topic: Christ's Love
   TEXT: Rev. 1:5
   (1) It is timeless. (2) This timeless love was demonstrated and proven in the great act of time. (3) Our praise is the fitting answer to this great love.–Alexander Maclaren

Worship Aids

CALL TO WORSHIP.   "Let my mouth be filled with thy praise and with thy honor all the day" (Ps. 71:8).

INVOCATION. Father, we are thankful for this world in which we live, for its beauty, its vastness, its supportive wealth, and its many challenges. As we view all the demands of life on this earth, we are made aware of our littleness. Yet, through Christ we know the greatness of your love which gives worth and meaning to our small lives. This morning, as we worship, may we find sufficient faith to see you more clearly, sufficient confidence to know that we can worship you only—love strong enough to serve you always and enough wisdom to acknowledge you as lord in all of our life situations.—Henry Fields

OFFERTORY SENTENCE. "And he said unto them, Take heed, and beware of covetousness: for a man's life consisteth not in the abundance of the things which he possesseth" (Luke 12:15).

OFFERTORY PRAYER. Help us, Father, to declare your faithfulness by our own faithfulness in our giving. Whether our gifts are great or small, may they be used for your glory as they are blessed by you for the ongoing of your kingdom among people of the world.—Henry Fields

PRAYER. O God the Father of our Lord Jesus Christ, our only Savior, the Prince of Peace: Give us grace seriously to lay to heart the great dangers we are in by our unhappy divisions; take away all hatred and prejudice, and whatever else may hinder us from godly union and concord; that, as there is but one Body and one Spirit, one hope of our calling, one Lord, one Faith, one Baptism, and God and Father of us all, so we may be all of one heart and of one soul, united in one holy bond of truth and peace, of faith and charity, and may with one mind and one mouth glorify you; through Jesus Christ our Lord.—*The Book of Common Prayer*

Topic: Till Death Do Us Part
TEXT: Mark 10:2–16

Other Readings: Job 1:1; 2:1–10; Ps. 26; Heb. 1:1–4; 2:5–12

The issue of divorce was one of vital interest in Jesus' day as it is today. The Phar-isees try to trap or trick Jesus. They wanted Him to contradict the teachings of the Jewish law as it regards divorce. Divorce was a common practice among the Jews of Jesus' day. There was much discussion about divorce among the rabbis and in society. In contrast to the issue of divorce is the Jewish ideal of marriage. Jesus responds to the question of the Pharisees by doing three things: He speaks of the purposes of God and the moral and spiritual realities of the marriage relationship; He places profound emphasis on the permanence and sanctity of marriage; and He provides a significant picture of Himself as the champion of women. Mark follows this section concerning divorce with an emphasis upon children. Jesus is shown not only as a champion of women but also of children, neither of whom had any basic rights in Jewish society. They were considered the property of the man, who could do with them as he chose.

I. The Question of Divorce (10:2–5)

The issue is raised in reverse order. Before discussing the question of divorce, one should consider the divine intention of marriage. What was God's intent for marriage? Moses' granting a certificate of divorce may have been an attempt to control divorce, to reduce it to a law, and to make it more difficult.

The Pharisees were trying to trick Jesus, to get Him to take a position opposite that of the Jewish law. A man could divorce a woman for almost any or no reason. Jewish law said that a woman could *ask* her husband for a divorce but only under unusual circumstances. Deut. 24:1 gives the Jewish law for divorce. This passage says that a man could get a divorce from his wife for only one reason, adultery and adultery alone. This was the position held by the rabbinic school of Shammai. The school of Hillel held that divorce could be granted for lesser reasons: if the wife spoiled a dish of food, if she spun in the streets, if she talked to a strange man, if her husband heard her speak disrespectfully of his family, or if her voice could be heard in the next house. Thus divorce was for the most trivial reasons, or for no reason at all.

Women were hesitant to marry because of the insecurity of marriage. By speaking on such a heated question, Jesus was striking a blow for women. In Jewish law a woman was considered a thing, with no legal rights whatever. Having no legal rights or standing, she was at the complete disposal of the male head of the family. Jesus' emphasis here is that the loose sexual morality of His day must be mended.

II. God's Purposes for Marriage (10:6–9)

In the mind of God, marriage was a permanent relationship that made two people one. Actually, the marital union made the couple unique. The marital bond was not to be dissolved by human laws and regulations. Marriage, in God's sight, is meant to have an absolute permanency and unity that no Mosaic regulation with a temporary situation could alter. Moses allowed a man to write a divorce certificate and put his wife away. But this was done because of the hardness of their hearts.

God's purposes in marriage were for a spiritual and physical union in marriage. Marriage is not a matter of temporary convenience or pleasure but of God's holy purpose. Too many enter marriage as if it were a money-back-if-not-satisfied purchase or for a thirty-day trial period. Christian marriages require a deep commitment by both husband and wife. Jesus repeatedly empha-sized that institutions were made for people and not people for institutions.

III. Jesus Blesses the Little Children (10:13–16)

Jewish mothers often brought their children on their first birthday to be blessed by a distinguished rabbi. No one knows why the disciples did not want the little children to be brought to Jesus. Jesus was the kind of person who cared for children and for whom children cared. You can tell much about the character of a person by how little children respond to them. He may have smiled easily, laughed in a warm way.

It may seem strange that Jesus said that the kingdom of God is like little children. A child has characteristics that fit one for the Kingdom of God. Children are dependent and receptive. They must depend on adults for all they receive. They respond to love and kindness.

Children are humble, not having learned to think in terms of place, pride, or prestige. That comes later in their development. A child is obedient; their natural instinct is to obey. Children trust others. They accept authority and they have confidence in other people. A child has a short memory, has not yet learned to bear grudges and nourish bitterness.–Jerry M. Stubblefield

SUNDAY: OCTOBER TWELFTH

SERVICE OF WORSHIP

Sermon: What Can We Expect from God in a Crisis?

TEXT: Dan. 3:17–18, 26–27

The story is simple. Three young Hebrews, men entrusted with certain government posts, refused to bow down and worship the golden image of a heathen god, even though the king ordered it. The king threatened to cast them into a burning fiery furnace. No matter! They trusted God to deliver them and so informed the king. However, they made it plain that if God did not choose to deliver them, they would still not bow to the king's order. They were thrown into the furnace of fire, and while they were in it a fourth figure appeared—a divine figure. Then they came out intact, without even the smell of the flames upon them. As a result, King Nebuchadnezzar became a worshiper of their God.

What is God saying to us through this story? "I will be with you, my faithful people, when the fires of trouble get hotter and hotter for you." We can assume, therefore, that God will be with his faithful people in all their crises, whether they be great or small.

I. In our various life situations, God will compel us, as he did the young Hebrews, to confront the issues of decision. Choices have to be made. We go along with no painful confrontations for a long, long time, but eventually we come up against matters that we cannot take for granted.

Sometimes the issue will be clear. It was so for the young men in our story. They were ordered to repudiate one of their most hollowed religious traditions, the conviction expressed in the ancient Shema: "Hear, O Israel: The Lord our God is one Lord." To bow in worship before the golden image would have signified their denial of the one Lord: Yahweh, creator of the heavens and the earth, the God of Israel. They have been cooperative at levels where their religious heritage and faith were not put in jeopardy, but they would not, they could not, cooperate where they would have to deny their God.

Your life may not be threatened, but your job or your popularity may be at stake when someone with power over you demands that you violate what represents obedience to God in your life. The matter is clear-cut, and you may have to answer in the spirit of Martin Luther, "Here I stand . . . I can do no other . . . God help me! Amen."

But there are other times when the issue will be confused, when we are not confronted with a clear choice. We don't know, and perhaps cannot know at the time, what is the right course to follow. It is not a matter of our being double-minded persons, who are rightly regarded by James as unstable in all their ways. We are simply not infallible, and we do not at the time have the wisdom to make a decision that leaves no room for doubt. We take seriously the best advice we can get, and we try to leave our passing feelings as much as possible out of our decision. We know full well that we may be wrong, dreadfully wrong, but the time for decision has come; we would wait if we could, but we cannot.

II. However, we can trust God to help us make a good decision when matters of life and death, as well as matters of lesser importance, face us.

God gives courage to face the consequences of a right decision. Of course, we do not always know all of the consequences —good or bad—of a right decision. "If I had only known!" we sometimes lament in painful retrospect. But the three young Hebrews knew precisely what was in store for

them. They knew what the king did not know—that the true and living God had a stake in their faithfulness to him, that their God held the power of life and death, not only over them, but also over Nebuchadnezzar, and that God could mightily use their example to strengthen others.

But what happens when we have to make a decision in some gray area, when right and wrong do not stand out in such stark contrast as black and white? This is where many of us have to live every day. Some of us do not enjoy the luxury of a simplistic ethic.

In these days, none of us can hope to live with a comfortable conscience. Life is too complex, and we are too involved in everything about us to have a comfortable conscience. But we can have a comforted conscience, knowing that the grace of God will cover our imperfections. We have to learn that absolute faithfulness is not, in the final analysis, what moves God to help us. We can trust God to give us courage to make some kind of responsible decision.

III. Where can we find the necessary bravery to carry through when we must decide? It is simply in the assurance that God will be with us whatever may come.

Though the main question is not deliverance, he often does deliver us. "Deliver us from evil" is a legitimate prayer. James asserted, "The prayer of faith shall save the sick." The four Gospels are full of stories of God's deliverance of individuals from physical ills. All of us have known of persons who credited their recovery from sickness or their escape from danger to God's intervention. Shadrach, Meshack, and Abednego believed that God could deliver them from the wrath of King Nebuchadnezzar, and God used them to show that he was superior to all earthly powers. Perhaps their faith was shaken a bit when they were bound hand and foot and brought to the furnace of fire and yet no sign of God's deliverance appeared. God can and does often literally answer our prayers. With God all things are possible.

But we must not think that God has to deliver us literally from all evil, all suggestion of harm. We can hardly insist that the writer of the book of Daniel would have us believe that. The second book of Maccabees, describing events that occurred during the very time the book of Daniel was written, tells the story of seven brothers who died in flames one after the other for their faith in God and their loyalty to him. Their mother said to the seventh of them, as he made ready to die, "Accept death, so that in God's mercy I may get you back again with your brothers." So he died, as did the others, believing that "the King of the universe will raise us up to an everlasting renewal of life, because we have died for his laws."

The main point is this: the presence of God with us regardless. The young Hebrews could not be sure that God would spare them from the flames of the king's wrath; they could only be sure that God would be with them in the midst of the flames or anywhere else. The proud, gloating king, looking into the fiery furnace, saw not three figures, but four, and the fourth looked like a divine figure—"a god," Nebuchadnezzar called him.

God does not have to spare us from suffering, pain, rejection, and persecution—if only he be with us in it! God may deny us some things, even life, that he may give us himself and all that the gift of himself includes.—James W. Cox

Illustrations

COMMITMENT. In the second century after Christ, Polycarp, a venerable Christian, faced such a choice when he was commanded by an authority to renounce Jesus Christ. He replied, "Eighty-six years have I served him, and he has never done me wrong. How can I now deny my King who has saved me?"—James W. Cox

NEVERTHELESS. The love of God and the love of self are curiously intermingled in life. The worship of God and the worship of self confronts us in a multitude of different compounds. There is a taint of sin in our highest endeavors. How shall we judge the great statesman who gives a nation its victorious courage by articulating its only partly conscious and implicit resources of forti-

tude; and who mixes the most obvious forms of personal and collective pride and arrogance with this heroic fortitude? If he had been a more timid man, a more cautious soul, he would not have sinned so greatly, but neither would he have wrought so nobly.—Reinhold Niebuhr

SERMON SUGGESTIONS

Topic: Let's Go!
TEXT: Exod. 14:15; Matt. 28:18–20; Luke 24:19
(1) If we do not go forward, we will likely go backward. (2) We must go forward. (a) In our trust of Christ who calls us to faith in God's saving power; (b) In the challenges of Christian living. (3) We must hesitate only in order to prepare adequately for the tasks before us.

Topic: Members of One Body
TEXT: Rom. 12:3–8
(1) One is not above the other. (2) Each is a part of the other. (3) Each has a job he can do acceptably.—Chalmer E. Faw

Worship Aids

CALL TO WORSHIP. "In God is my salvation and my glory: the rock of my strength, and my refuge, is my God" (Ps. 62:7).

INVOCATION. Almighty God, with whom we have ever to do, open our hearts to your truth and our eyes to the needs the Holy Spirit would have us see. Then give us the courage to act with justice and love, a people who sought the face of God in worship and then began to serve as Jesus did.—E. Lee Phillips

OFFERTORY SENTENCE. "Behold I am coming soon, bringing my recompense, to repay every one for what he has done. I am the Alpha and the Omega, the first and the last, the beginning and the end" (Rev. 22:12–13 RSV).

OFFERTORY PRAYER.   Knowing that we shall all give account of ourselves for our deeds, grant that we may be careful about how we live and how much we keep and spend and give.

PRAYER.   Bless us, our Father, in all our work and in all the relations of life. Sanctify the life of the home. May its memories abide with us to strengthen us in the hour of temptation, to comfort us in the hour of sorrow. May children love and honor their parents, and may parents be tender and considerate with their children, knowing how delicate is the child soul, and how easily harshness casts it down. Pour out a spirit of kindness and goodness in the home, that all the members of it may be bound each to each in bands of mutual love and service that may not be broken. Bless us in the larger world where we toil and suffer. We thank you for work and the opportunity to work. Grant that our labor may be congenial to us; that we may do it with ease and a sense of mastery. Let us not be enslaved to our tasks, but may we feel ourselves greater than they, and ready for still nobler efforts. Save us from sullen discontent, from fruitless war with the circumstances of our lot. Make our hearts obedient, that by the untoward things of experience we may win a larger and freer life. Give us the spiritual vision and a desire to pass beyond ourselves, to think of the needs of others, to make the world a little better than we found it. Put within us Christ's yearning for the redemption of the world. Kindle within us his passion for the souls of men. Uphold us with the faith that you have called us into fellowship with him, and your coworkers in the achievement of your purpose of good.– Samuel McComb, adapted

LECTIONARY MESSAGE

Topic: Cheap or Costly Grace?
   TEXT: Mark 10:17–31
   Other Readings: Job 23:1–9, 16–17; Ps. 22:1–15; Heb. 4:12–16
   Some accuse the modern church of emphasizing cheap grace, not costly grace.

There are those who say that much preaching and calls for discipleship do not emphasize the Cross and what it costs God for us to have redemption. The modern church is concerned that they might offend someone, so they often place few demands or requirements upon those who would become members. Thus church membership and being a part of God's kingdom do not have the deep meaning they should have. Jesus was always cautious in inviting people into discipleship that they might not understand what was required of them. He placed high demands upon those who would be his disciples. Not everyone who heard his message responded in a favorable way. Even his own disciples did not fully understand or grasp the kind of Messiah he was to be. People seek religion for a variety of reasons. Some are facing a personal crisis, some are pressured by people who love and care about them, others are attracted by other believers, and some like the minister and the members of that church.

   I. A Man Comes to Jesus Seeking Eternal Life (10:17–22)
   Mark tells us little about this man. Matthew and Luke add other facts: he was young, rich, and a ruler. This man was dissatisfied with his life; he wanted something he did not have, something he could not find through his present way of living. His discontent was with a whole way of life. His way of life had not brought any real sense of satisfaction to him, or deep meaning to his life.
   He came running and tried to flatter Jesus by calling him "Good Teacher." Without catching his breath, he asked Jesus what he must do to inherit eternal life. He came to Jesus in a very emotional state. Possibly he felt that Jesus could quickly tell him how he might know the assurance of eternal life.
   Jesus reminds him that only God is good. He sought eternal life on the wrong terms: what he could do to have eternal life, not what God could do. The man had kept all the commandments that deal with his relationship to other people.
   In reciting these commandments to him, Jesus asks him if he had defrauded anyone; defraud is not one of the Ten Commandments. Often the rich had gained their

wealth by fraud, taking advantage of others. This man was respectability *par excellence.* One can be respectful and not do anything. Each commandment Jesus asks him about are negatives. The essence of Christianity is doing things, positive things, with one's life and influence. He was respectable in that he never took anything from anyone. It is Christian to give everything to someone.

Jesus' basic question to the man was, "How much do you want real Christianity?" The man's wealth was the prize he valued most. When confronted by Jesus, the man was not willing to give up his wealth so he could inherit eternal life, which was a gift from God.

When Jesus looked at the man, it was a gaze filled with love. This kind of love seeks deliberately to help, to meet another's needs. It was not the look of anger but the appeal of love. His look of love also sought to pull the man out of his comfortable, respectable, settled life into the adventure of being a real Christian. It was also a look of grief, for he saw the man choose to fail to be what he could be.

II. The Danger of Riches (10:23–27)

Here Jesus goes against popular Jewish morality that believed that prosperity was a sign of God's favor and was also the sign of a good person. Wealth was proof of excellence of character and favor with God. When Jesus spoke these words, he used humor to drive his point across. The camel was the largest animal seen in the land, the eye of a needle was the smallest opening of which the people commonly spoke. When you think about it, it is a ridiculous idea.

The axiom in this passage is that the person who trusts in himself and his possessions can never be saved. When a person substitutes riches for being, riches can imprison a person in a world of illusions. It is easy to develop a false sense of security. Those who trust in the saving power and redeeming love of God enter freely into salvation.

III. Christ Is No Person's Debtor (10:28–31)

Jesus gives a warning against all pride. Ultimate judgment belongs to God who alone knows the motives of a person's heart. He gives a warning that the judgments of heaven may upset the reputations of earth.

The rewards of discipleship are both in this time and in the age to come.–Jerry M. Stubblefield

SUNDAY: OCTOBER NINETEENTH

SERVICE OF WORSHIP

Sermon: Keep On Being Converted

TEXT: Phil. 2:5–13

What has God been doing with your life lately? Are you sensitive to what he has been doing with you, and for you, and through you? Or are you even reluctant to think or talk that way?

Paul frequently did this kind of reflecting. One of those occasions was when he shared his testimony in behalf of his defense before King Agrippa. He recounted how God dealt with him while he journeyed toward Damascus. In moving words, he declared, "I was not disobedient to the heavenly vision!"

Now if you follow the account of this remarkable man, you will recognize that he was not perfect. Sometimes his life and his attitudes fell short of the Christian ideal, and his teachings did not contain on every occasion the fullness of the gospel. Perfection he never claimed, but obedience to the vision he strove for. Perhaps you remember his words: "I do not consider that I have reached perfection, but I am pressing on to see if I can capture it, the ideal for which I was captured by Christ Jesus" (Phil. 3:12 Williams).

In the Scripture read today, Paul earnestly admonished the Christians at Phillipi: "Work out your own salvation, with fear and trembling; for God is at work in you, but to will and to work for his good pleasure" (Phil. 2:12b–13).

I. When we read these words from Paul, we must be careful to avoid two possible misunderstandings. To be told to "work out our salvation" may cause us to think of salvation as obtained through human effort rather than by Divine gift. The other misunderstanding to avoid is the distortion of the nature of salvation itself.

a. As you heard in the reading of the Scripture, Paul's exhortation to work out your own salvation was preceded by that marvelous description of what God has done in Christ. It bears reading again; indeed, it is a passage the Christian would do well to place in memory so as never to forget its message (Phil. 2:5–11).

Paul urges persons already recognized as Christians to have an inward disposition that will direct them in their manner of life. He points them to the mind of Christ Jesus and describes what Christ did. In his description he gives a brief but high view of the incarnation and the atonement.

Christ first existed in the form and nature of God. Then he "emptied himself"; that is, he gave up his divine rank and took on the form of a man.

Not only did Christ empty himself, refusing to seize for his own the glory that belonged to God, and become man, he took on the form of a servant, humbled himself and subjected himself to death on a cross. Paul does not explain it. He merely affirms it. "Christ died for us!"

And then did you hear Paul's last affirmation? Paul's conclusion comes after this "therefore." Because of what Christ has done, God acts and we should act.

God has highly exalted him and bestowed on him the name which is above every name, that at the name of Jesus every knee should bow, in heaven and on earth and under the earth, and every tongue confess that Jesus Christ is Lord, to the glory of God the Father (Phil 2:9–11).

It is not confession that makes Jesus Christ Lord. God has made him Lord. When you understand this truth, you will not be apt to make the mistake of thinking of salvation as being attained through human effort.

b. But then if salvation is the gift of God in Christ, why does Paul talk about working out your own salvation? Here he obviously speaks of salvation not in the sense of repenting of sin and receiving Christ as Lord, for indeed the ones to whom he writes already have done that. He wants them to experience the fullness of salvation by following out the Christian life in such fashion that God's will and pleasure may be fully realized in them. Repentance, confession, and receiving Christ as Lord is not the end of the matter. It is the beginning. Work out the fullness of salvation. What does God still want to do with you, for you, and through you? Are you prepared to let his will and his pleasure direct your life?

When Paul spoke of working with "fear and trembling," he did not intend to create any doubt about salvation or a fear that it might be lost. To fear God may mean to reverence him, to be in awe of him, to be open to being taught and led by him. Let our fear not be the kind that would cause us to want to hide from God, like Adam in the garden, or to somehow escape his presence and his judgments. To be afraid of God is not what we desire. To be fearful of displeasing him may help us be alert to our weaknesses and more faithful to our commitments.

II. Did Paul always live according to the counsel he gave? How do you account for the times of his frustration and failures? You and I probably more nearly identify with Paul when we read his words written to the Christians at Rome. He confessed: "I do not understand my own actions. For I do not what I want, but I do the very thing that I hate . . . I do not do the good I want, but the evil I do not want is what I do" (Rom. 7:15).

a. Have we not been there with Paul? We do some stupid action, and immediately we ask ourself: "Why did I do that?"

For Paul, to confess that he could will what was right and yet not be able to attain it was to confess that sin is never far away. It is not adequate to explain our foolish and evil actions by saying "the devil made me do it!" We are responsible, and God holds us accountable. No wonder, then, that with fear and trembling, we need to strive all the more seriously to attain the ideal to which God calls us.

b. And how shall we strive? How shall we run with perseverance the race that is set before us? The race began when we confessed that Jesus Christ is Lord. That race will not end until we join him in glory. Between hear and there, we, like Paul, must press on. Sometimes the road will be rough and steep and we shall grow weary. Sometimes we shall be confronted with things about ourselves we have not known, and fresh repentance and change will be required. We will need to keep on being converted along the way.

III. Generally we use the term *conversion* to refer to the experience we call "the new birth." It is perfectly right that we should. But all of us know that we are not born full grown. Christian character is not automatic. There is a sense in which conversion means "changed," "a turning around," "a revolution." We may need to be converted in this sense many times on our Christian pilgrimage.

a. At least, that was true for one whose faith and commitment led him to become recognized as the most prominent of the disciples. I speak of Peter. He left the fishing boat to follow, and he proclaimed boldly his loyalty. At the Last Supper Jesus said, "You will all fall away this night." Peter declared, "Though they all fall away, I will never fall away." But before the dawn of a new day, Peter denied him three times. On a housetop in Caesarea, Peter slept one day. God spoke to him in a vision. The heavens opened and animals appeared as if on a great sheet let down from heaven. A voice said, "Rise, Peter; kill and eat." But Peter's response was negative, "I do not eat what is unclean." But the voice said, "What God has cleansed, you must not call common." When Peter awakened, he knew that God had dealt with him and that he now must become an apostle to the Gentiles. A radical conversion had occurred.

b. The Peter in the Gospels is not the Peter we see in Acts. The new Peter is penitent, converted, Spirit-filled. He gives evidence that he has continued to let God work in his life to will and to do his pleasure.

Peter demonstrated truths that Paul taught, even before Paul taught them. Peter, like Paul, pressed on. He did not give up in the struggle toward the ideal. It was as if he was in a tug-of-war, going forward three steps and back two, but always pressing forward. Peter grew. He began to exhibit the evidence of the Holy Spirit in his life.

IV. We can learn from the teachings of Paul and the experiences of Peter and Paul. We need to be "born again" only once. But

shall need to be converted, changed, renewed many times. We accept Paul's urging –"Keep bringing your life into submission to God's spirit. Keep on letting his will and his pleasure be done in your life."

What has God done for you, with you, through you lately? What does he want to do–even this week?–G. Willis Bennett

Illustrations

GRACE IN THE DUNGEON.   There are many who say, "I am caught in a web of circumstances that bind me hand and foot. How can I have abundant living under those circumstances?" In answer I refer you to a passage which tells of those who "find grace in the dungeon" (Jer. 31:2 Moffatt). If you find grace at all, you must find it in the dungeon. You are caught–you are not able to get out of the dungeon; then the only thing to do is get the dungeon out of you– to find grace in that very dungeon. –E. Stanley Jones

A SELF-CONFESSED FOOL.   A dear old man told me how he dealt with himself, and I have never forgotten it. He was so gentle and wise, he must have felt my thought about him. Here is his story:

"Up until a few years ago," he said, in a rare mood of intimacy, "I was a most irritable man. When anything went wrong, I fussed and fumed and flew off the handle. My influence, such as it was, religious or otherwise, was worse than undone. I suffered in health, in business; I was miserable and made others miserable.

"One day I pulled myself up and said, 'Look here, you are just a plain fool.' In the Bible, as you know, it is a sin to call our brother a fool. 'You are a fool,' I said to myself, and I observed it. 'If your religion, or failing that, your common sense, does not cure your fussy temper, what has it done for you? What is it worth?'

"In short, I gave myself a dose of fool-medicine, and it worked. I made up my mind that I would bring all my strength of will, and all the grace of God I could get, to bear upon my temper. While I do not want to boast, it has been a long time since I found myself fretting and worrying. I cannot tell you the difference it makes in my own life and in the happiness of others."—Joseph Fort Newton

SERMON SUGGESTIONS

Topic: Remember the Lord Your God
TEXT: Deut. 8:1–10, 18
(1) His redemptive chastisement. (2) His gracious providence. (3) His inescapable commandments. (4) His loving purpose.

Topic: What's in a Nickname?
TEXT: Various
(1) The Thunderer, Mark 3:17. (2) The Rock, John 1:42. (3) The Encourager, Acts 4:26.—John N. Gladstone

Worship Aids

CALL TO WORSHIP.   "I will sing of the mercies of the Lord for ever: with my mouth I will make known thy faithfulness to all generations" (Ps. 89:1).

INVOCATION.   Eternal Father, you gave to us of earth your special Son, that we might know you, love you, and be delivered from our sins. Fill our hearts today with the joy of those who remember and trust; and we will lift our voices in glad praise to you this day and forever.

OFFERTORY SENTENCE.   "For God so loved the world, that he gave his only begotten Son, that whosoever believeth in him should not perish, but have everlasting life" (John 3:16).

OFFERTORY PRAYER.   Lord, when we think of all the needs about us of body and soul at home and abroad, and the provision of faith through our Lord Jesus Christ, not a mite would we withhold.—E. Lee Phillips

PRAYER.   We come to Thee, O God, with words of thanksgiving on our lips. We thank thee for thy gifts. They are as varied as our needs, as manifold as our desires. Our hearts cry for love, and thou hast given us the love of parent and of friend, that have been as thy benediction on our lives. Our minds crave light and knowledge, and thy Spirit has kindled a lamp within us. We long for the vision of beauty, and thou hast revealed thyself gloriously in the open page of Nature. May we take these gifts, not for their own sake only, but as steps with which to mount upward to thee, who art the perfect of love and truth and beauty. Bathe us in thy re-creating life, that we may cast off all meanness, all despair, all sin and shame, and enter into the secret of thy eternal gladness. Help us to turn our earthly blessing to ends divine.—Samuel McComb

LECTIONARY MESSAGE

Topic: The Way to Great Discipleship
TEXT: Mark 10:35–45
Other Readings: Job 38:1–7; 34–41; Ps. 104:1–9, 24, 35c; Heb. 5:1–10

This scenario is similar to that of Mark 9:30–37, only here it is not a discussion among the disciples but is the direct request of James and John. There is inbred in all of us the desire for fame and fortune. Most would not be so bold or brazen as to verbalize it as James and John did. We either are more modest or do not want to presume to be so bold as to ask for such prominent positions. The disciples were ordinary men, not a group of saints. This story shows their humanity. We do not know what prompted them to ask for these prominent places. A certain amount of ambition is good; it keeps us striving for worthwhile goals. Ambition keeps us working at our tasks, helps us successfully face the moral temptations that come to all of us at times. We do not want to disappoint either ourselves or those who look up to us.

Jesus uses this occasion to teach them about the true nature of greatness, of servanthood.

I. The Request of Ambition (10:35–40)
Jesus' first response to them is that they do not know what they are asking. They were seeking something in the spiritual world that can come only by spiritual processes within themselves. What they were asking for could only be given through

particular, specific acts and experiences. They would have to earn these prominent positions through the kinds of lives they lived.

In Matt. 20:20–23 the mother of James and John, Salome, makes the request for them to occupy the two chief places when Jesus comes into His glory. She and they misunderstood the nature of the kingdom Jesus would establish. They felt He would establish a political kingdom. James and John, along with Peter, were in the inner circle of disciples often spending special time with Jesus. By this request, they are locking out Peter. The Scripture does not tell us anything about the reaction of Peter to this selfish request they made. This action showed how selfish they were in making such a request.

They had ambition for first place in an earthly kingdom. This event shows that even those in the inner circle with Jesus failed to understand what Jesus was teaching them about His future kingdom. Their idea was that the Messiah would have earthly power and glory. Though misguided, James and John still believed in Jesus. They show an amazing confidence and loyalty to Him. Even in their confusion they show that their hearts were in the right place. Never for a moment did they doubt Jesus' ultimate triumph.

Jesus showed them His standard for greatness. If you want to be great, be the servant of all. "Can you drink from the cup I am drinking or be baptized with the baptism I am baptized with?" They affirmed that they were able. History proves that they were able and did undergo severe suffering and even death for Christ. He was reminding them that the way to greatness was through suffering. The Christian's cup and baptism involve denying to self and taking up one's cross. It means we are to follow Jesus without reservation. A part of the Christian's saving force in the world is a Christ-like sensitivity to human needs that sometimes brings real pain into life. It mean putting ourselves into conflict with evil and dangerous powers. The standard for greatness in the Kingdom is the standard of the Cross.

James and John were asking Jesus to grant them things that belonged only to God. For Jesus the will of God was always supreme.

II. The Way of Service and Salvation (10:41–45)

The actions of James and John aroused deep resentment and anger among the other disciples, the way we would respond under such circumstances. In worldly kingdoms the standard of greatness was power. In Jesus' kingdom the standard was service. Greatness consists not in reducing others to your service, but in reducing yourself to their service. What the world needs is people whose ideals are service. What would happen if our lives were measured only by the amount of real service we have rendered to people? Would we be considered great?

The phrase "to give His life a ransom for many" has been variously interpreted. The supreme example of Jesus' own service was the giving of His life, and in this way He served as a ransom for many. For Jesus His death was not an accident, not a tragedy, but an offering from which people would receive great blessing. Jesus is saying that it cost His life to bring people back from their sin into the love of God. The cost of our salvation is the Cross of Christ. Something happened on the Cross that opened for us the way to God.—Jerry M. Stubblefield

SUNDAY: OCTOBER TWENTY-SIXTH

SERVICE OF WORSHIP

Sermon: Why Pray?

TEXT: Luke 2:25–35; also Matt. 7:7 RSV

"The curse of so much religion," George Meredith is quoted to have said, "is that men cling to God with their weakness rather than with their strength."

Do you believe that?

As I look into my own life, I have to admit, "Yes, it is true—too true. I have often clung to God in weak resignation." I have said, "Why concern myself with this or that? God knows what he is doing." Or I have said, "I'll be satisfied with what I am and what I do. Why be rash and try to play God?"

Many things I read in the Bible disturb me. I read the words of Jesus, "Ask, and it will be given you; seek, and you will find; knock, and it will be opened to you." These words disturb me when I discover that I am to ask and keep on asking; seek and keep on seeking; knock and keep on knocking. Keep on praying? Some of us have hardly prayed about some things for the first time!

The need to pray—prayer defined by the literal meaning of the English word *pray*—is a basic and continuing need of everyone. More than that, God himself needs our prayers to help him do some things that would not be done without those prayers.

But here is our temptation. We can have our devotional fervor turned on or off by the latest theologian or philosopher we have read. The need to pray, however, is persistent. We may put to sleep that need with a massive dose of hyper-Calvinism, or we may bind and gag it with a brash Stoicism, but the need stays with us.

I. We should not be surprised if an imp sits on our shoulder and whispers, "You can't change God's mind. So why pray?"

That assertion is frighteningly close to the truth. Some of the words of the Bible almost say that. "For ever, O Lord, thy word is firmly fixed in the heavens," says the psalmist (119:89 RSV). But he doesn't quite say, "You can't change God's mind." He does tell us that Jehovah differs from the gods of the heathen, for the Lord is predictable. He is faithful and reliable.

Or, consider what Paul has to say: "For those whom he foreknew he also predestined to be conformed to the image of his Son. . . . And those whom he predestined he also called; and those whom he called he also justified" (Rom. 8:29–30 RSV). This tells us that God's mind is made up about one thing in particular—the redemption of humankind. His eternal purpose is a purpose of love and grace. When Jesus came, he underscored that fact. Who would want it different? We are resigned to that. No, more than being merely resigned to it, we can welcome it, embrace it, affirm it with our whole being.

On the other hand, there is that aspect of the will of God that is not welcomed, not embraced, not affirmed. When God visits us with suffering, sorrow, and death, we indeed "wince" and "cry aloud." Will meets will. Our mind struggles with the mind of God. There is a modern reenactment of the ancient drama of Jacob wrestling with the angel, the Ninevites repenting so that God will repent, or Jesus saying in anguish, "Father, if it be possible, let this cup pass from me" (Matt. 26:39).

The audacity of it is breathtaking. Do I, a mortal, dare to put on my shoes and stand up to God? The deed is done when I don't like what is happening to me or to someone else and register my complaint with God, or even when I am bold enough to confront God with the restless yearnings of my heart. Am I being blasphemous or insolent to pray in that manner?

If so, then Epictetus, the Stoic, sounded better than many Christians when he prayed, "Give me what Thou desirest for me. For I know that what Thou choosest for me is far better than what I could choose." Brother Lawrence, who practiced the presence of God, would practically agree with Epictetus, for he said that he regarded the hours spent in the kitchen as valuable as those spent in prayer.

Some philosophers and some saints would make a prayer a matter of submission only. Why fight, they seem to say, for the last chapter of this story is already written, and we know how it will come out.

P. T. Forsyth saw it differently. He said, "We need not begin with 'Thy will be done' if we but end with it."

Does God really want us to confess our impatience, to ask him questions, and to beat a path of protest to his throne of grace? It should not surprise us if he does. We are not better than our Lord. What more vivid example have we of wrestling in prayer than the picture of a solitary figure, the Son of God, praying through the night hours?

The Bible and our Lord in particular plainly teach that prayer is petition, asking, though it may have other meanings too. It seems clear also that some things simply would not happen apart from our prayers. The theologian Emil Brunner declared, "God awaits our prayer, and because He longs to extend His Kingdom not only over men but through men and with men, God accomplishes some things only when they are asked for; God earnestly awaits our prayer. We dare believe that our prayers make possible for us some action of God not otherwise possible."

Can we say that God is any the less concerned with the asking than with the receiving? Is he less concerned with the seeking than with the finding? Is he less concerned with the knocking than with the open door? No, "He is the hunger, as well as the food." It is as much Christian to pray boldly as it is to yield graciously.

II. Now, quite naturally we are interested in what happens as the result of our prayers. We are practical enough for that! What does happen?

If you pray, something will happen to you. The one who prays finds a hand to guide him when the way is dark. He discovers he can go on in spite of failure, sickness, and even sin. He hears God say, "Thy sins be forgiven thee" (Matt. 9:5) and "I will never leave thee, nor forsake thee" (Heb. 13:5). We need that! Without seeking and finding the help of God one might wander a lifetime in the dark, or fold up in defeat every time a strong, opposing wind should blow, or despair of ever being at peace with God.

These are perhaps our most urgent needs, these crises of the spirit, but they are not our only needs that God meets through prayer. Some of you may know that as a recent and dramatic experience.

Jesus said, "You did not choose me, but I chose you and appointed you that you should go and bear fruit and that your fruit should abide; so that whatever you ask the Father in my name, he may give it to you" (John 15:16 RSV). What might appear to be a selfish prayer may be nothing of the kind. It may really be God's indirect way of doing a significant work for his kingdom.

Prayer does cause remarkable things to happen in the life of one who prays. It can also lead to happy consequences in the lives of those one prays for. Pray for someone, and you will come to love him, care what happens to him, and, if possible, do something concrete to help him. But that is not the limit of such prayer. God uses our prayers to help those for whom we pray, even though they do not know we have prayed for then, even though we may have no contact with them except through prayer.

One of my seminary professors spoke in a class of the effect of intercessory prayer. He said that God had given him a special ministry of praying for some people whom others had given up praying for and that he had seen some of them become converted. There are many people whose lives are different because someone prayed for them, the doctrine of free will notwithstanding.

What shall we say of the prayers of those whose concern moves beyond the needs of the individuals they know? Some are distressed by the sins of mankind, by our universal fallen state, by the pain and anxiety that a world subjected to futility inflects on its inhabitants. Are these who mourn in this way truly blessed, as Jesus said they were? Do their lifelong prayers make sense? Will their faith that rebels at last move the mountains of sin, suffering, and death?

Let us turn back the scroll of the centuries. A man of Israel bows to the ground in an agony of prayer. This man had not meekly acquiesced in the humiliation of his people before the world. He had not accepted the perdition of the heathen as a final judgment of God. He found no meaning and redemption in trying to be a well-adjusted personality in the kind of world he lived in. His prayer for a Messiah who would change what is mean and spiritually distasteful became the passion of his life.

And God gave the man a hope in his striving. God revealed to him that in his lifetime he would see the Christ. Years pass. Jesus is born. Inspired by the Spirit, this man Simeon came to the Temple. where the infant Jesus was being presented to the Lord. He took the child in his frail arms, which now felt new strength. Tears of joy filled the sad, ascetic eyes as he blessed God and said, "Lord, now lettest thou thy servant depart in peace,/according to thy word;/for mine eyes have seen thy salvation/which thou hast prepared in the presence of all peoples,/a light for revelation to the Gentiles,/ and for glory to thy people Israel" (Luke 2:29–32 RSV).

This man's prayers poured into the stream of God's purpose, as did the prayers of many others, and surely helped to bring to pass what God had willed. The Redeemer came. At last, he came! What a glorious fulfillment! But there is more.

The last prayer has not been prayed, and the last battle has not been fought. The martyrs pray, "How long, O Lord." Many other devout hearts pray, "Thy kingdom come, thy will be done in earth as it is in heaven." Some pray in the words of the Seer, "Come, Lord Jesus." And with the whole creation "groaning in travail," "nature, also, mourns for a lost good."

I have often wondered how one could be properly concerned about God's will for the present life and at the same time pray for the hastening of the Lord's return. I knew a pastor who periodically preached and prayed publicly for the second coming of Christ. His concern about it always seemed to coincide with a new crisis in his personal difficulties. He seemed to value the Parousia as a kind of *deus ex machina* to extract him from the messes he repeatedly got himself into.

Who will be the persons who "have loved and longed for his appearance"? I think it will be those who are so concerned about the ultimate triumph of God's purpose that they throw themselves, their strength, and their prayers into the burning challenges of the hour, with the intrepid expectation that what is but half-finished today will be completely fulfilled in God's great tomorrow.

Why pray? The magnitude of the need of my own life, the incompleteness of the lives of those I love and know, and the burden of

the world's sin and suffering leave me with no alternative but to pray—if I care and God cares. God wants my prayers, asks for them, inspires them, and, amazing though it may seem, will, through those prayers, find his hand strengthened to accomplish his purpose of grace.

Simeon of old fulfilled his stewardship of prayer. Our stewardship is yet unfulfilled. So we and others must pray "until he has put all his enemies under his feet" (1 Cor. 15:15 RSV).—James W. Cox

Illustrations

GOD'S WILLINGNESS.   Prayer is not informing God of something he does not already know or pleading with him to change his mind. Prayer is the opening of the soul to God so that he can speak to us. "Prayer is not overcoming God's reluctance; it is laying hold of God's willingness."

It is essential to any real understanding of prayer that we get this sequence straight. God speaks, and summons us to respond.— Georgia Harkness

PROVISIONS.   Dr. H. H. Rowley told a moving story of God's provision through prayer.

In response to an appeal for more liberal support of foreign missions, an elderly lady who lived in an almshouse placed in Dr. Rowley's hand an envelope with an extra gift of seven shillings, six pence for foreign missions. Dr. Rowley, her pastor, knew that she could not afford such an amount from her meager allowance, since she had already given generously to missions. He begged her to take it back, arguing that as the Lord was pleased with Abraham's willingness to sacrifice Isaac, but did not require it after all, so the Lord would be pleased with her willingness without her gift. With quiet dignity she refused, saying that she was not giving the money to her pastor.

A few days later a wealthy lady sent Dr. Rowley a check for five pounds of service he had done for her. She requested that the money be used for his work as he pleased. He went to see the lady in the almshouse. As he was leaving, he asked if she would do him the service of allowing him to leave with her a small gift, telling her of its source.

Immediately she burst into tears and told him that at the moment when he had knocked at her door she was on her knees, praying that God would somehow send her something to meet her need. She had no food and would receive no more money for three days.—James W. Cox

SERMON SUGGESTIONS

Topic: Redemption Is Real
TEXT: Ps. 114
(1) God's people experience it (vv. 1–2). (2) Nature expresses it (vv. 3–6). (3) Let all the earth recognize it (vv. 7–8).—Chalmer E. Faw

Topic: How Believe in a Good God in a World Like This?
TEXT: John 16:33
The higher our concept of God, the more perplexity we face. Why, then, do we believe in a good God? (1) To some of us it is impossible to explain the goodness in the world on the basis of no God. (2) As we have grown older, we have come to take mystery for granted. (3) What we call evil, plain, tragedy, plays a positive role in life. (4) Some of us believe in a good God because we long since have given up early childish, naive ideas of God that we once held. (5) The contribution of Christian faith to the problem of evil has lain not so much in supplying a theory to explain it as in furnishing a power to surmount it. Jesus himself never said I have explained the world, but he did say, I have overcome it.—Harry Emerson Fosdick

Worship Aids

CALL TO WORSHIP.   "A day in thy courts is better than a thousand" (Ps. 84:10).

INVOCATION.   Grant, O God, that we may see each day of our lives in the light of this day. May sabbath glory transform every common task and sanctify all our

thoughts and purposes. To this end, may your face shine upon us as we worship you today, so that we may acceptably serve you tomorrow.

OFFERTORY SENTENCE.   "Christ . . . hath given himself for us an offering and a sacrifice to God for a sweet smelling savor" (Eph. 5:2).

OFFERTORY PRAYER.   Our Father, you have given your dearest and best for us, yet he yielded himself up willingly to do your will and for the joy that was set before him endured the cross. May your example and his show us what love can do when it is real.

PRAYER.   Almighty God, Father of all mercies, we your unworthy servants give you humble thanks for all your goodness and loving-kindness to us and to all whom you have made. We bless you for our creation, preservation, and all the blessing of this life; but above all for your immeasurable love in the redemption of the world by our Lord Jesus Christ; for the means of grace, and for the hope of glory. And, we pray, give us such an awareness of your mercies, that with truly thankful hearts we may show forth your praise, not only with our lips, but in our lives, by giving up our selves to your service, and by walking before you in holiness and righteousness all our days; through Jesus Christ our Lord, to whom, with you and the Holy Spirit, be honor and glory throughout all ages.—*The Book of Common Prayer*

LECTIONARY MESSAGE

Topic: How to Seize the Day
TEXT: Mark 10:46–52
Other Readings: Job 42:1–6, 10–17; Ps. 34:1–8 (19–22); Heb. 7:23–28
Do you ever feel life is passing you by? Bartimaeus knew that feeling. The whole world seemed to pass him by as he sat beside the road blind and begging. But unobserved within Bartimaeus something was

happening. He was getting prepared to seize the first opportunity to change his life for the better. He prepared to seize the day, and that day came. Mark 10:46–52 records the events of that day, and they become for us a pattern for personal growth.

Three observations need to be made before we examine the pattern of Bartimaeus's personal growth. First, growth happens in spurts. No doubt Bartimaeus had spent a number of days beside the road with nothing happening. Then the growth came all in one day. Growth is dynamic and not constant. Second, genuine growth occurs at God's initiative. It was Christ's nearness that precipitated the events that gave Bartimaeus new life. God gives the growth. Third, genuine growth can be sabotaged by us and others. As soon as Bartimaeus began to cry out, "Jesus, Son of David, have mercy on me," others shouted for him to be silent. With these observations in mind, let's watch to see how we might imitate Bartimaeus as he seized his day of salvation.

I. *Develop a holy dissatisfaction.* Bartimaeus was not the only beggar between Jericho and Jerusalem that day. But as far as we know he was the only beggar to be healed. "Luck," you say? The great Dodger shortstop Maury Wills used to say that luck happened when opportunity met preparation. The Puritans spoke of developing a holy dissatisfaction for anything in your life that wasn't fully God's will. Bartimaeus no doubt was not satisfied with the roadside. He wanted his sight back. Even as he did the most responsible task he was able to do, he silently, unashamedly prayed for healing. He did not despair that the problem was insurmountable or that he should just accept his weakness. We too need to cultivate holy shames and dissatisfactions for any aspect of our lives that hinders us from what we know to be God's best for us. However, it is not enough to keep that desire silent.

II. *Declare your desire.* "When he heard that it was Jesus of Nazareth passing by, he began to shout, 'Son of David, Jesus, have mercy on me.'" Bartimaeus overcame any sense of self-consciousness and shouted his heart's desire. Shameless confession to God brings new life. We must confess to others our need and desire for change. Note that

Bartimaeus's desire was nearly sabotaged. "Many rebuked him and told him to be quiet." Some people will not take your declaration seriously. When that happens, we must do what Bartimaeus did.

III. *Outshout your discouragers.* Far from withdrawing into silence, Bartimaus "shouted all the more, 'son of David, have mercy on me.'" We must expect resistance from within and from without. We will have to outshout discouragement. To cease would be sin. Prayerlessness is sinfulness. Prayerfulness is blamelessness. Persistence in prayer is not about overcoming God's reluctance, but rather it clarifies for us what really is important to God and what is the surest way to His glory and our good. Something amazing happens when we outshout the discouragers.

IV. *Discover your encouragers.* Jesus stopped the Jerusalem-bound pilgrimage and said, "Call him." In the midst of his discouragers, Bartimaeus found his encourager, Jesus. How often Jesus stands up for people when no one else will. Note also that once it became clear that Jesus was an encourager of Bartimaeus, at least some of the discouragers converted! Their "Shut up!" became "Cheer up! Get up, he's calling for you." We must find and join to folks who will support our growth. Encouragement in the name of Jesus is the mission of the church. Our witness to the roadside people is "Get up, cheer up, he's calling for you." How shall we respond to the urging call of our encouragers?

V. *Move forward to accept the call to change.* Growth will require more than insight, it will require action. "Throwing his cloak aside, he jumped to his feet and came to Jesus." By discarding his cloak, Bartimaeus was leaving behind his former existence as a beggar. That cloak would have provided his bed at night and his begging position each day. Inaction or clinging to previous comfort zones would have prevented Bartimaeus from seizing the opportunity presented by the call of Jesus. The old things passed away so that new things could be grasped. No one can move forward without simultaneously leaving something or someone behind. That move will demand honesty.

VI. *Be honest with the Lord.* "What do you want me to do for you?" Bartimaeus knew what he really wanted, and he answered Jesus with a few honest words, "Rabbi, I want to see again." Real reverence keeps honesty central. Prayer that fails to be "gut level" honest simply fails. There are no answers to dishonest prayer. This is the second time Jesus asks this question in this chapter. He first asked it of James and John in verse 36. Both times it was asked Jesus received the answer he wanted, the honest answer. The Spirit of Christ always asks this question, "What do you want me to do for you?" We must answer him honestly if we want the new growth only he can initiate. The growth will require our obedience.

VII. *Act in obedience to his words.* "Go, your faith has healed you." There is creative power in God's words. The words of Jesus to Bartimaeus created new sight. The word *go* means to take up the new life that your faith has provided you. The absence of the experience of God can deafen us to the call of God and the power of his word to direct us to new life. Faith heals as we act in obedience to Christ's words. Obedient faith experiences the creative power of those words.

Christ's command created a new life for Bartimaeus and can create genuine growth in us. There is an inherent opportunity for genuine growth whenever we put ourselves within the hearing of the speaking of the gospel. Notice what Bartimaeus did in response to his restored eyesight.

VIII. *Be grateful by being faithful.* Following, fellowshipping, and witnessing are ways to be grateful for what growth God has given. Bartimaeus chose to express his gratitude by joining Jesus and the disciples on their journey to Jerusalem. He became a living document that there is new life in following Christ. Jesus had no fresher or more grateful witness as they entered the gate called Beautiful that evening.

IX. *Conclusion.* The story of Bartimaeus is good news for two reasons. First, it contains good advice for seizing opportunities for genuine growth. Second, it contains the good news that God always finds a way to demonstrate his mercy and power in the lives of those wanting and willing to cry out for new life. God will not forsake us or leave us.—Roderick K. Durst

SUNDAY: NOVEMBER SECOND

SERVICE OF WORSHIP

Sermon: Sharing Dominion with God
TEXT: Gen. 1:26–31a; Rom. 8:19–22

In the very first chapter of the Bible, we are told that God, after creating the world and all its bounty, entrusted to humankind dominion over all creation. "Have dominion over . . . every living thing that moves upon the earth," God said (Gen. 1:28). God is still the owner of creation, mind you, yet he lends it all to us for our benefit and enjoyment. We share dominion with God to whom creation rightly belongs. But what exactly does that mean?

I. To share dominion with God is to act on God's behalf. The psalmist says that in creating us in his own image, God made us a little lower than himself and crowned us with glory and honor (8:5). Being created in the image of God means in part that the

Creator has given us dominion over the works of his hands.

We are the stewards, or caretakers of the earth. A steward is one who acts in place of another. Jesus told a parable about a wealthy landowner who went on a far journey and entrusted his estate to tenants. When the owner finally returned, he found that some of the tenants had been faithful in protecting what belonged to him. Others had been unfaithful. The ones who had been faithful were rewarded. The ones who had been unfaithful were punished.

Such is the way with us. God created the world and then entrusted it to tenants. Some of us have been faithful in caring for what belongs to God. Most of the world have been careless and unfaithful.

Consider the example of a church camp or retreat center. Every camp or retreat center must have a capable, dependable caretaker. The caretaker does not own the camp. He cannot do with the camp—the buildings, lake, swimming pool, trees, etc.—as he pleases. He cannot sell the camp. He had better not desecrate it. The caretaker will be held accountable for the manner in which he manages that which belongs to another. For he acts on behalf of God and God's church. So it is with us. Our temporary dominion means we act on behalf of God. We may be held accountable.

II. To share dominion with God is to use only what we need. Human dominion is limited. We should not squander or be careless in the way we use creation. In the beginning God said, "I have given you every plant yielding seed in its fruit; you shall have them for food" (Gen. 1:29).

Without getting on a soapbox, I would point out to you that this particular text calls for a vegetarian diet. As the writer of Genesis saw it, there was to be no killing of man or animal. Human dominion was meant to be peaceful, free of violence. God's world was meant to be a heaven on earth. The requirement of a vegetarian diet and the command against killing animals for food was altered after the flood.

There are many people today who will not eat meat for religious and ethical reasons. They do not believe in the meat factories where the cattle are housed and then slaughtered. Believing that all life is sacred, they cannot think of eating one of God's living creatures.

Others eat a vegetarian diet for health reasons. We know that those whose diets consist only of fruits, vegetables, nuts, and grains are much healthier. They feel better to boot.

I admire anyone who can maintain a strict vegetarian diet. There are times when I wish I could. But the point I set out to make here is that sharing dominion with God means using only what we need. It means being frugal in our use of food and other earth resources, being careful not to dump so many leftovers down the garbage disposal. If we can get by sometimes without eating meat, then let's do it. Let's not waste water, or electricity, or gasoline, or heating oil. Let's not cut down a tree unless we have to.

The Native Americans have a lot to teach the rest of us about the proper use of the earth and its resources. The Native American writer Marilou Awiakta writes, "We have never really understood that we are one small part of a very large family that includes the plant world, the animal world and our living relations . . . everything is in physical and spiritual connection—God, nature, humanity. All are one, a circle. . . . Respectful care brings abundance. Lack of care brings nothing. If you take, you must give back—return the gift." As Christian stewards, we are called to use only what we need and not squander the precious bounty of the earth.

III. To share dominion with God is to respect and protect what rightfully belongs to God. Marilou Awiakta continues in her book, "Way back in the beginning of time, the Creator puts the Law in Mother Earth and all she gives us. If you take from her, you have to give back respect and thankfulness. If you don't do that, why then she quits giving."

Chief Seattle (1854), another Native American of the last century, who has profoundly influenced our concept of ecology, said, "You must teach your children that the ground beneath their feet is the ashes of our grandfathers . . . the earth is our mother. Whatever befalls the earth, befalls the sons of earth. . . . This we know. The earth does not belong to man; man belongs to the earth. . . . All things are connected like the blood which unites one family. . . . Man did not weave the web of life; he is merely a strand in it. Whatever he does to the web, he does to himself." Did you know that every person in America produces an average of twenty-five pounds of trash per week? Only 10 percent of this garbage is recycled. Every hour Americans throw away 2.5 million plastic bottles. Every three months, we throw away enough aluminum cans to rebuild our entire commercial air fleet. And every Sunday, 500,000 trees are made into newspapers that aren't recycled.

The apostle Paul, in Romans, states that all of creation groans and suffers pain because of the sinfulness and carelessness of humankind. "We know that the whole creation has been groaning in labor pains until now," he says (8:22). In Paul's view, all of creation longs to be redeemed and set free from the powers of sin, evil, and death. When humankind is fully redeemed, so shall creation be redeemed and set free.

What is the point here? The point is, as Christian stewards we need to act responsibility and respect, preserve, conserve, and recycle the good earth the Creator has given us.

Two boys got into a fight one day many years ago. One was rich, had nice clothes, lived in a beautiful house, and ate the best food. The other boy was poor, his clothes were ragged, and he had very little to eat. Not surprising, the rich boy won the fight easily. The poor boy complained, "If I had good food to eat like you, I could have won." This experience was the turning point in the rich boy's life. He would decide to give his life to helping the poor. He became one of the world's most famous men. His name was Albert Schweitzer.

It was the humanitarian-missionary-doctor-writer Albert Schweitzer who, perhaps more than any other of this century, instilled a reverence for life and reminded us that all life is sacred. The earth and all forms of life around us are a sacred trust from God.

In sharing his dominion with us, God allows us to act on his behalf, he expects us to use only what we need, and he calls us to respect, preserve, and protect this planet that serves as our home, and that will serve as the home for our children, grandchildren, and great-grandchildren. Will you be a faithful steward as you share dominion with God?—Randy Hammer

Illustrations

ENVIRONMENT.   *USA Today* reported that scientists predict a limited number of plants and creatures will be living on Earth in two to three hundred years. They include flies, weeds, starlings, grackles, rats, raccoons, and cockroaches.

Notice what is missing? Humans. Careless ravaging of our planet will make it uninhabitable for all but the hardiest creatures.

Two to three hundred years seems a long way off to us today. We will not be around to fall victim to the final devastation that makes Earth uninhabitable, but our descendants will.

Earth is a marvel of the universe. Ours is perhaps the only planet of its kind. It may be the only planet among billions that supports intelligent life.

The ultimate waste of humankind would be the careless destruction of intelligent life on Earth. When God created our world and called it good, He likely did not intend for us to destroy it.

If we—the so-called intelligent life on Earth—do not take the stewardship of our environment seriously, our planet will commit suicide.—Dale L. Rowley

ECOLOGY.   In his book *Spiritual Ecology,* published in 1990, Jim Nollman quotes the wisdom of the American Indian. According to the Great Law of the Haudenosaunee, the six-nation Iroquois confederacy, the leaders of the tribe respected their obligation to those who would live 150 to 200 years in the future. Their law reads: "In our every deliberation we must consider the impact of our decisions on the next seven generations." This is in sharp contrast to the materialistic, greedy, selfish, wasteful outlook of our times.—Robert B. Watkins

SERMON SUGGESTIONS

Topic: The Everlasting Arms
    TEXT: Deut. 33:27
    (1) Our refuge in God. (2) Development through God (33:3a). (3) Our fellowship with God (33:3b).—W. W. Weeks

Topic: All Saints and All Sorts
    TEXT: 3 John, v. 11
    (1) *Gaius.* He speaks to us about the hospitality in the Church. (2) *Diotrophes.* He speaks about the abuse of power in the church. (3) *Demetrius.* He speaks to us about the testimony of goodness in the Church.—John N. Gladstone

Worship Aids

CALL TO WORSHIP.   "You know what hour it is, how it is full time now for you to wake up from sleep. For salvation is nearer to us now than when we first believed" (Rom. 13:11 RSV).

INVOCATION.   Almighty God, our heavenly Father, we come to thee in the midst of the crises of our times and of our personal lives, asking thee to give us a clear view of thy purpose for our lives, the strength to live up to that vision, and the wisdom to live as those who have already won the victory through thee.

OFFERTORY SENTENCE.   "Although the fig tree shall not blossom, neither shall fruit be in the vines; the labor of the olive shall fail, and the fields shall yield no meat; the flock shall be cut off from the fold, and there shall be no herd in the stalls: Yet I will rejoice in the Lord, I will joy in the God of my salvation" (Heb. 3:17–18).

OFFERTORY PRAYER.   Heavenly Father, help us to keep our stewardship and gratitude intact in the bad times as well as in the good. May we always find reason to rejoice, knowing that you are a faithful Father. May we rejoice in the little that we can bring as well as in the abundance.

PRAYER.   All thy works praise thee, O Lord, and thy saints give thanks unto thee. On mountain and field and flower and sky thou hast set thy glory. The hearts of men and women and little children thou hast filled with happiness. "The whole round world is bound with golden chains about thy feet." O give us spirits attuned to the harmonies of thy universe, that this day we may join in the swelling chorus of praise that ever magnifies thy name. Lift us up into thy joy, before which sorrow hides her face and pain and fear fly away.

We bless thee for thy self-revelation in Jesus Christ, our blessed Lord and Master. We have stood in his presence and have heard him say, "He that hath seen me hath seen the Father." In him thou hast come among us, cleansing our soiled hearts, healing the wounds of body and of mind, giving rest to the troubled conscience, and opening the blind eyes to the beauty and brightness of the world. As we listen to his voice, grief becomes a scorn of ills and the weaknesses of life become our glory. As we look into his face we seek nothing but that we may love him with all our hearts and serve him with all our might. O Christ, thou Son of God, let the Spirit which bore thee to the Cross abide in us! Touch us with the power of thy surrendered life, that we, no longer the servants of the world, may become the children of God!–Samuel McComb, adapted

LECTIONARY MESSAGE

Topic: Finding Our Mission

TEXT: Mark 12:28–34

Other Readings: Ruth 1:1–18; Ps. 146; Heb. 9:11–14

Jesus generated and encouraged questions. People felt confident that he would receive their questions respectfully and would answer them wisely.

People ask questions of teachers for four different reasons:

1. Because they want to know the answer. Ignorance pursues instruction.
2. Because they want to show what they know. Arrogance pursues a platform.
3. Because they want to humiliate the teacher. Anger seeks satisfaction.
4. Because they want others to learn the right answers from a teacher they respect. Wisdom seeks to reproduce itself.

Jesus was often asked the first three kinds of questions, but finally in Mark 12:28 he is asked the fourth kind. Of all the commandments, which is the most important? Jesus answered by prioritizing two commands. He said that the commands to love God and to love people are the very hinges on which hang all the commands (Matt. 22:40; Deut. 6:5; Lev. 19:18). This composite summary command has two implications. First, love for God must never be separated from love for people. Second, genuine care for people issues from a devotion to the One God. First John says, "We love because he first loved us. If anyone says, 'I love God,' yet hates his brother, he is a liar. For anyone who does not love his brother, whom he has seen, cannot love God, whom he has not seen" (1 John 4:19–20).

One of the best-selling job hunter's handbooks of the nineties has had for several years a section of pink pages at the back. These pages are entitled, "How to Find Your Mission in Life." The essence of the author's contention is that you cannot find the right job until you know what your mission in life is. Step One in finding your mission is to worship God and love your neighbor. We must be committed to mirroring God's love to those around us. We live to make this planet a kinder place no matter if the other guy cuts us off in traffic or doesn't bring our clippers back. With these fundamental commitments, finding our mission becomes a process of blending our greatest joy with our greatest concern.

The command to love God comes from the book of Deuteronomy. Deuteronomy means "the second law." It was the second coming of the God's instructions to the congregation of Israel. It was the spiritual preparation provided through Moses immediately prior to entering the promised land. Upon its reception and understanding, the Israelites were, as Jesus says in verse 34, "not far from the kingdom of God." When we align our total selves with this command, we find ourselves edging into what our life has always seemed to promise. Herein lies deep fulfillment in fellowship with the God and Father of Jesus Christ.

The second commandment is found in Lev. 19:18. The purpose of Leviticus was to guide the nation of Israel in how to enjoy continuous fellowship with holy God. Fellowship with holy God means living in compassionate community with our neighbor. Our standard of response is no longer tied to our neighbor's behavior. We do not return "tit for tat." No matter how we are treated, we will still love. Keeping this command demands that we give good for evil. There is no room for revenge or hatred if we believe that God is able to keep the books fairly (Rom. 12:19; 1 John 3:13–15). Through the resurrected Christ we experience the forgiveness that sets us free to forgive others.

Maturity is no longer measured by how long we can hold a grudge. Maturity now is measured by our ability to restore offenders to relationship. Fellowship with holy God means making and remaking lasting relationships. We become unwilling for anything to separate us from the loving fellowship we have in God's presence (Rom. 8:35). We become willing to take the initiative in every instance to go to our neighbor to repair injured relationships (Matt. 18:15). We simply have no toleration for tears in the fellowship. Our anticipation is that we will experience Christ's presence in such reconciliation meetings (Matt. 18:20).

Conclusion: Jesus spent his life as the definitive demonstration of what life looks like when it is lived in constant obedience to the greatest commandment. His life therein became the most attractive life ever lived. Our capacity to have that attractive life comes from abiding in Christ (John 15:7–8). His death defined the depth of the love God has for us and we can have for others. His resurrection made this life, his life, new life available to us by faith.—Roderick K. Durst

SUNDAY: NOVEMBER NINTH

SERVICE OF WORSHIP

Sermon: How Shall We Live?
TEXT: 2 Thess. 3:6–13

The Old Testament says in the Song of Solomon, second chapter, verse 15, that there are little foxes that spoil the vine. The ancient Israelites recognized that image. In the spring, there were young foxes who could get into the vineyard and start nibbling at the buds. Before long there was no fruit in "due season." Likewise there are times when our lives as Christians seem to be nipped in the bud. We do not flourish spiritually. Paul knew that the Thessalonians had come into an experience of new life, but were now beginning to have trouble with "little foxes" destroying the bloom of what God wanted to produce in their lives.

I. Paul goes so far as to name one of these foxes. He calls that little fox "Busybody." We may complain that the scripture is not clear enough, but maybe the problem is the words are too clear.

a. Paul warns that this little fox, "Busybody," is destroying not just the vine of one Christian. We think we should save our concern for the truly big sins, for the things that can hurt people and destroy families. But somehow the person who leaks information about what's going on in other people's lives and even carry rumors about, does great damage. Paul is saying in effect, "Let us root out the 'Busybody' in ourselves and let us be aware of what the 'Busybody' can do in the community of faith." The Busybody is a little fox that can do great damage.

b. Here is the second fact about this fox. He's not only little, he's very subtle. We always begin by saying, "I probably shouldn't say this, but . . ."; "I don't want to judge, but . . ."; "I'm not completely sure of my facts, but . . ."; "I'm not completely convinced that God wants me to say this, but . . ." That tiny word *but* does the subtle work of opening the way for the little fox that does unbelievable damage.

c. It began to bring destruction to the life of the church in Thessalonica, and it can destroy us as well. What then does Paul say to the question of how we should live? His response to those who were busy about other peoples' affairs and beginning to spread rumors could be paraphrased in these words: "Be busy about the work that God has given you." "Busy" is not always bad. We have work to do in our lives. It is unique to us, and no one can do it for us. When we are about the work, we tend to have less time to comment on all those in the neighborhood, the classroom, or the church. Paul is telling us to be busy about those things that we have been given to do.

II. Another danger that was in Thessalonica is also present in us. We, too, easily move from being actors to being directors. I know that there are many movie actors who

now go into directing, but I'm not commenting on that at all. We are given the grace to act out our own life. Deep trouble comes when we take over the job of directing the lives of others, spend less time acting out what God has given us to do. Don't put down that which God has given you to do.

a. Jesus said, "I must be about my Father's business." When we begin to follow this same Jesus, we learn that God has given us a part in His saving and healing work. In Eph. 2:10, it says we are saved so that we might do good works in this world. Today we hear a lot about "being saved," and the natural reaction is, "Saved for what?" It's a good question. A partial answer is that we are saved so that we may be a part of the good work that God has for us here and now. Our vocation is a high and holy calling; we have the possibility of making a difference in this world.

b. The scripture also reminds us that we will be held accountable for every word that we speak that tears down, detracts, and destroys. As we come to an understanding of the work that God has given to build up, not to tear down, our values change. What others would call "menial labor" can be blessed and be part of God's plan. We are able to move forward not engaged in idle talk about others but getting on with the work of God's Kingdom.—Gary D. Stratman

Illustrations

NOT A JOB, BUT A CALLING.   A group from our church went to a retreat in Michigan. The speaker was the president of Princeton Seminary, who lifted up for us one of the great themes of the Christian faith that gets so easily lost in the shuffle. The Latin word *vocatio* was used to remind us that we all have a "calling." It's more than our job. Our jobs are only, at best, a part of our vocation. You have a place to serve. You have gifts that have been given to you. Vocation is not just for a few. Every Christian has been called.

In the book *Working*, by Studs Turkel, there are interviews with many, many people about their work. One women interviewed said, "What we really need more than anything else is not a job but a calling."

In Jesus Christ, we have been called. What we're to be about is not minor or insignificant, but a part of God's work on this earth. Do we dare slight it?—Gary D. Stratman

WHAT MAKES UP LIFE.   Life is not made up of great sacrifices and duties, but of little things; in which smiles and kindness and small obligations, given habitually, are what win and preserve the heart and secure comfort.—Sir Humphrey Davy

SERMON SUGGESTIONS

Topic: The Faithfulness of God
    TEXT: 2 Tim. 2:13; Gen. 18:25
    (1) Seen in the dependability of nature, the trustworthiness of creation's working system. (2) Seen in the higher level of moral certainty and ethical stability. (3) Seen in the more intimate area of experience—in the Divine-human relationship.—J. Wallace Hamilton

Topic: The Loneliness of Christ
    TEXT: John 16:31–32
    (1) *The loneliness of Christ:* (a) Caused by the Divine elevation of his character; (b) Felt by Christ in trial. (2) *The spirit or temper of that solitude:* (a) Its grandeur; (b) Its self-reliance; (c) Its humility. "God is near you. Throw yourself fearlessly upon him."—Frederick W. Robertson

Worship Aids

CALL TO WORSHIP.   "Make thy face to shine upon thy servant: save me for thy mercies' sake" (Ps. 31:16).

INVOCATION.   In the sanctity of these moments, in the holiness of this place, visit us, Father, with the power of your Spirit and love. Call us to repentance that we may turn from our sins. Keep our minds from indifferent wandering that we may live focused lives. In this hour, fix our affection on you that we may go back to the world to serve in your name.—Henry Fields

OFFERTORY   SENTENCE.   "For unto whomsoever much is given, of him shall be much required: and to whom men have committed much, of him they will ask the more" (Luke 12:48).

OFFERTORY PRAYER.   Giver of every good and perfect gift, provider of our every need, we thank you that we have the opportunity to share with others the bounty of your blessing to us. May our gifts and tithes bring hope, truth, healing, and help to people here and around the world.—Henry Fields

PRAYER.   Our Father, we worship and love thee; and it is one point of our worship that thou art holy. Time was when we loved thee for thy mercy; we knew no more; but now thou hast changed our hearts and made us in love with goodness, purity, justice, true holiness; and we understand now why "the cherubim and seraphim continually do cry, Holy, Holy, Lord God of hosts."
    We adore thee because thou art holy, and we love thee for thine infinite perfection. For now we sigh and cry after holiness ourselves. Sanctify us wholly, spirit, soul, and body. Lord, we mourn over the sins of our past life and our present shortcomings. We bless thee thou hast forgiven us; we are reconciled to thee by the death of thy Son. There are many who know that they have been washed, and that he that beareth away sin has borne their sin away. These are they who now cry to thee to be delivered from the power of sin, to be delivered from the power of temptation without, but especially from indwelling sin within.
    Lord purify us in head, heart, and hand; and if it be needful that we should be put into the fire to be refined as silver is refined, we would even welcome the fire if we may be rid of the dross. Lord save us from constitutional sin, from sins of temperament, from sins of our surroundings. Save us from ourselves in every shape, and grant us especially to have the light of love strong within us.
    May we love God; may we love thee, O Saviour; may we love the people of God as being members of one body in connection with thee. May we love the guilty world

with that love which desires its salvation and conversion; and may we love not in word only, but in deed and in truth. May we help the helpless, comfort the mourner, sympathize with the widow and fatherless, and may we be always ready to put up with wrong, to be long suffering, to be very patient, full of forgiveness, counting it a small thing that we should forgive our fellow-men since we have been forgiven of God. Lord tune our hearts to love, and then give us an inward peace, a restfulness about everything.—Charles Haddon Spurgeon

LECTIONARY MESSAGE

Topic: Because God Is the Audience
TEXT: Mark 12:38–44
Other Readings: Ruth 3:1–5; 4:13–17; Ps. 127; Heb. 9:24–28

Jesus made two things whenever he taught in Jerusalem: disciples and enemies. He ended his public teaching ministry on the temple courts in Jerusalem, again making disciples and enemies. He gave an earnest warning to the crowd against the "religion for show" that was too common among "the teachers of the law." When God becomes our audience instead of people, everything changes in our approach to religion. This warning and the widow's story that follows give key insights into practicing a religion that truly pleases God.

I. *Avoid any abuse of position if you want a rewarding religion.* In five indictments Jesus clearly defined the faith of the scribes as only "for a show." He asserted that these jurists and judges of religious law liked to wear their flowing robes of office inside and outside the courts. More people could be impressed that way. These interpreters of the Mosaic laws had developed an addiction for preferential greeting in the supermarkets, preferential seating in the synagogues, and prolonged prayer, if it was in public. Imagine a pastor wearing his baptismal robes to get quicker service at the bank, the surgeon wearing her smock and mask to get the better seats at the theater, or robed choir members expecting to be invited to the front of the line at the Department of Motor Vehicles. Now imagine how many and how deeply people are turned off

religion and even God whenever religion is practiced in that manner. No wonder Jesus insisted, "Such men will be punished severely" (Mark 12:40b). No wonder the crowd delighted to hear Jesus' teaching! No wonder Jesus was crucified within the week!

II. *Avoid religious showmanship if your aim is to please God.* Jesus said that God was not interested in watching what the Pharisees had to show. God isn't the only one who quickly turns away from a religion for show. A religion for show is just that—"for show." It doesn't do any good for anybody. It's like the cardboard television sets or microwave ovens sometimes displayed in model homes by decorators. They don't do anything. They are just for show. Religion, however, is supposed to do something. Religion is supposed to do good. The prophets always warned that worship wears God out when it habitually neglects righteous living and compassionate service. The acid test of religion is whether or not it cooperates with God in ministering to the friendless, homeless, and loveless. The religion of these scribes not only wore God out, it made him angry—angry enough to punish severely.

III. *Don't let the letter of the law smother its intention.* In the fifth of six indictments, Jesus accused the interpreters of the law of "devouring widow's houses." At first this indictment seems out of place with the other accusations of pious showmanship. However, the Hebrew laws gave little or no inheritance rights to widows. Hebrew women had no legal standing to inherit their husband's estate at his death. If the couple had no children to inherit or if she had no living relatives, her house could be devoured in the system of religious law. To defend such an inheritance, a widow might need to expend much in legal fees. A widow's rights might be deftly denied in court by a shrewd jurist who knew the necessary scriptural proof text or rabbinical precedent. Her needs could be consumed by others in the name of God as *corban,* which was a contemporary irrevocable trust that guaranteed income to the scribe while "justifying" neglect of family (Mark 7:11). Widows could be convinced to will inheritances to their scribes. And it was all legal! However, when immorality is legal, the law should be changed, not the moral. It is now illegal in

California for attorneys to be included in their client's wills since such professionals have undue influence and conflict of interest in such outcomes. Ministers should have been included in that law. One pastor made it a matter of conscience never to allow himself to be included in the will of any parishioner, no matter how insistent.

No wonder Jesus challenged the Pharisees and scribes, "Go and learn what this means, I desire mercy and not sacrifice" (Matt. 9:13; Hos. 6:6). If we are going to make God choose between proper order of worship and genuine care for the hurting, he'll take the latter every time. Legality can never replace morality. If we must choose, choose to cooperate with God and prioritize mercy. Make sure religion looks after those who have no rights.

IV. *Make sure the poor profit from your religion.* Good showmanship always has its earthly rewards. Even Jesus said so. If what the Pharisees wanted was applause from their peers, then they certainly received their reward. But they would receive nothing from God. Whenever we turn religiousness to our personal benefit we are becoming committed to the kind of pious showmanship that makes God walk out. Is it any wonder that Jesus sentenced the scribal producers of such a moral gong show to eternal condemnation? The Pharisees were devouring the defenseless whom God was seeking to feed (Deut. 10:18).

V. *Practice what you preach whenever you find opportunity.* Jesus found an immediate opportunity to practice what he had just taught. He pointed out a poor widow worshiping in the Temple (Mark 12:41–42). Could this widow have been one of those widows whose household had been devoured by the teachers of the law? She may have thought, "They may be able to take away my house, but I will always have the Lord's house." She determined that nothing would come between her and worship. She wanted to participate fully in worshiping

God. Giving is a part of worship, so she gave what little she had. She worshiped God with a sacrifice of praise. Jesus used her act of giving to define the measure of one's giving in terms of what's left to the giver. No doubt her act and condition brought to memory the stories that Mary and Joseph had told about the widow Anna who had welcomed the infant Jesus' presentation at the Temple years before (Luke 2:36–38). Perhaps Judas was sent rushing into the crowd after her to refill her purse from the Master's mercy purse (John 12:6). I think that Jesus became her Kinsman Redeemer that day. Perhaps Judas complained about spending so much on the widow just as he also complained about the woman who spent so much on Jesus.

Jesus so impressed the disciples with the divine concern for widows and orphans that the early church's first social ministry had to do with meeting the physical needs of the widows in the congregation. James was inspired to define true religion as religion that looks after the widows and orphans (James 1:27). Religion is on track when it has a component of helping the poor. It acts in covenant with the least. The true religion of the second- and third-century Christians caused them to wade out into rivers at night to rescue abandoned babies, mostly girls, who had been cast away as unwanted by parents. Such religion garnered the reluctant respect of even the most hardened Christian-haters in Rome. These are the good works that cause men and women to thank God (Matt. 5:18).

VI. *Conclusion.* Good worship yields good works. Good works draw men and women to worship in gratitude. The good works and words of Jesus drew even Pharisees, like Nicodemus, to new life and worship. Worship and life become whole when we make the God and Father of Jesus Christ our audience. This salvation equips us for the good works that please God.–Roderick K. Durst

SUNDAY: NOVEMBER SIXTEENTH

SERVICE OF WORSHIP

Sermon: He Judgeth Me

TEXT: 1 Cor. 4:1–5 ASV

From the United States Supreme Court's far-reaching decisions to proverbial back-fence gossip, all of us are involved daily in the matter of judging. We both judge and are judged.

By far the greater amount of judging that daily goes on is informal and unofficial. This may be conscious or unconscious, sometimes malicious in intention and sometimes not intending, yet doing, immeasurable damage.

Paul found himself the victim of the judgments of Corinthian Christians and wrote a classic paragraph on the subject in its broader scope. In 1 Cor. 4:1–5, Paul writes about the three basic courts of judgment before which each one of us finds himself: the general public, his own conscience, and the Lord God. The outline to the paragraph can hardly escape the reader; the courts themselves cannot be escaped by any one of us. We appear before each whether we choose to do so or not, whether we know it or not. They are basic, inescapable, and all-important realities in each life.

I. The Judgments of Others

It is an easy observation that the judgments of others are often wrong. Jesus, the only sinless person this world has ever known, was condemned and crucified as a traitor and blasphemer. He was not wrong; his judges were.

a. There are two basic reasons why the public is so often wrong in its judgments. It often is wrong because it does not know better. No court is in position to render a verdict until it has the necessary facts in hand. We never have all the truth about the other person. We simply do not know enough to be infallible judges.

b. A second and more serious limitation on us is moral. We are not good enough to hold the fates of other people in our hands. Often we judge amiss because we are lacking in integrity. Prejudice and bias cause us to be too hard on those whom we dislike and too easy on those whom we like.

c. There are two extremes that Paul avoided and that we may well avoid. Under the criticisms of the Corinthians, Paul avoided the extreme of indifference and that of bondage. By neither word nor action did he say that their judgments meant nothing to him.

The court of others is right often enough that it cannot safely be ignored. Even when this court of others is wrong, it is important to give it a reasonable respect. The Christian is in the world for the good he can do; the good he can do is bound up with the influence he has on others; his influence is affected by what others think and say of him. It is important, then, the Indian-like one keep an ear to the ground to know what others say of him.

The other extreme is that of slavery. One may so fear the criticisms of others that one is controlled by them. One may be so paralyzed by the criticism of others that one is afraid to speak or act on convictions. One's convictions are silenced by fear of being convicted! Hypocrisy in religion roots in the longing to please others.

Paul refused to ignore or be enslaved to the judgments of others. He respected them, but he refused to bow before them. Their judgments he termed a "human day," for that is the actual Greek for what is translated "human judgment." Apparently Paul was contrasting the "human day" or man's judgments, with "the day of the Lord" or God's judgments.

II. Conscience or the Court of Self

Paul recognized a second court, as inescapable as the first. He recognized, too, the fallibility of this source of judgment. He said, "Yea, I judge not myself. For I know nothing against myself; yet am I not hereby justified" (1 Cor. 4:3–4 ASV). Paul presumably intended a hypothesis, "though I know nothing against myself," as the Greek of his sentence would allow. Even though his conscience should not convict him, yet he would not be acquitted.

a. Conscience is subject to the same two limitations that characterize the court of others. It may be uninformed, and it may be dishonest. Even in its function as judge, conscience is often wrong. Often we think right what is actually wrong. Sometimes we are unfair to ourselves, condemning ourselves unjustly. Conscience must be instructed and enlightened. As may be true of the court of others, conscience may have a moral lack. We tend to be too easy on ourselves and too hard on others. What we condemn in others we tend to explain in ourselves.

b. To forget that conscience is fallible may be disastrous. We hear it said, "It doesn't matter what one believes, just so he is sincere." Only in religion, where it hurts most, does one think so loosely. Sincerity is indispensable, but it is not enough. In mathematics, architecture, and medicine one would never say that it does not matter what one believes. Certainly one would not say this when his bank account is being totaled, when his house is being built, or when he is undergoing surgery. A teacher would be "fired" for saying that two plus three equal seven—no matter how sincere he may have been.

c. A cherished freedom of worship is popularly expressed as the freedom to worship according to the dictates of one's own conscience. Certainly we do not want to be forced to worship according to the dictates of any religious or political group, but the above statement leaves much to be said. To begin with, conscience does not dictate; it judges a past act. Could conscience dictate, it would not be a safe dictator. The freedom we should cherish is the freedom to worship as God dictates, as he speaks to us through convictions that are instructed and enlightened. Only to the extent that we are submissive to God in enlightened faith will conscience function as a trustworthy judge.

III. The Supreme Court, the Lord Our God

Paul rested his case before God himself as the true and final judge. He would respect the judgments of others and of his own conscience, but he would bow before the authority of God alone: "He that judgeth me is the Lord." This judgment is always right, and it is final.

a. God is not subject to the limitations of knowledge and character that limit the other two courts. God knows us as we are, and only he knows us as we are. It is a para-

dox, yet true, that each of us is both better and worse than others think. But God knows us as we are. At the same time, each is better than others know. There is contrition over sin, yearning to give oneself to that which is pure, true, and worthy. The best of this is known to God alone. God alone sees us at our worst and at our best. He alone knows us fully enough to judge us finally.

b. Not only does he so know us, but his judgments are right. When God condemns us, it is because there is no alternative. His conditions are never arbitrary; they are determined by our needs. When God justifies the sinner, he does a creative work. When God justifies the sinner, he "rightwises" him; that is, he redirects him. In justification God gives the sinner not only new standing but new life. The justified sinner is one who has accepted God's rejection of him and then God's acceptance of him. God justifies the sinner; he does not justify the sin. So, in condemning and in justifying, God is just and right.

c. God's judgment is final. There is no appeal beyond this Supreme Court. What matters if one should have the praise of men and an easy conscience, if at the last he must hear the Lord's judgment: "Depart from ye that work iniquity?" What matters if one should fare poorly in the court of others and feel himself unworthy of Christ's presence, if at the last he hears him say, "Well done, thou good and faithful servant; enter thou into the joy of thy Lord?"

IV. Conclusion

With Paul's strong reminder that our judgment rests inescapably and finally with the Lord, we may certainly combine the picture given us in Heb. 4:12–16 of him with whom we have to do, that is, him with whom is our account. He is there pictured as one who knows us completely, who is a high priest who understands us with sympathetic love, and who invited us to a throne of grace.

Because he knows us fully as we are, we cannot hope on our record to stand his judgment. Were there not forgiving grace, there would be no hope. But there is that hope. We are invited to his throne of grace, where we may find mercy and grace to help in time of need. Before him we must stand; there is no option. We have but one hope, his forgiving grace. Our only hope is a sufficient one. It is all we have; it is all we need. May we thank God that he that judges us is the Lord!—Frank Stagg

Illustrations

THE LORD'S POWER TO SEE. The Lord with whom our account rests is a "judge of the intents and purposes of the heart." There is no creature which is not naked and open to his eyes. He has a power to see what no eye of man can see. X-ray may "see" through flesh or steel; radar may "see" through fog and darkness; the telescope may "see" stars billions of miles away; and the microscope may "see" tiny particles otherwise unknown to man. But only God can see the intents and purposes of the heart.—Frank Stagg

DAY OF JUDGMENT EVERY DAY. Why, for us every day is a day of judgment—every day is a Dies Irae, and writes its irrevocable verdict in the flame of its West. Think you that judgment waits till the doors of the graves are opened? It waits at the doors of your houses—it waits at the corners of your streets; we are in the midst of judgment.—John Ruskin

SERMON SUGGESTIONS

Topic: The Way of Holiness
TEXT: Isa. 35:8
(1) A high way. (2) A strait and narrow way. (3) A plain and obvious way. (4) A safe way.—J. N. Norton

Topic: On Graduating in Gratitude
TEXT: Various
(1) The false gratitude of invidious comparison, Luke 18:11. (2) The selective gratitude of natural happiness, Luke 17:15–16. (3) The mature gratitude of victorious faith, Luke 22:17.—John N. Gladstone

Worship Aids

CALL TO WORSHIP. "The joy of the Lord is your strength" (Neh. 8:10).

INVOCATION. Lord, God move in our hearts as never before. Help us to understand our purpose in this world, our security as believers, our responsibilities as disciples, our possibilities as obedient followers of the Lord Jesus Christ.—E. Lee Phillips

OFFERTORY SENTENCE. "It is in God's power to provide you richly with every good gift; thus you will have ample means in yourselves to meet each and every situation, with enough and to spare for every good cause" (2 Cor. 9:8 NEB).

OFFERTORY PRAYER. Our Father, we know that we can give only what we have. You have always endowed us with some gift for providence or grace that we can offer on the altar of the church's stewardship. Receive, we pray, what we bring to you in love and gratitude.

PRAYER. Here we are again, Father, a congregation of souls seeking the experience of being filled with your presence and power which enables us to meet life with courage and faith. Some come here this morning filled with joy and happiness because they have experienced life at its best and have known some of its deepest joys. Enable them to cherish the moment, that it may be a strength to them in other times of their lives.

Some gather in this sanctuary today mellowed by events which have caused them to face large issues of good and evil, perhaps for the first time in their lives. Strengthen them in faith for the first time in their lives. Strengthen them in faith that they may ever choose high good after the fashion of Christ and shun base evil, lest it fray and even destroy the delicate fabric of life's best for them. Some have journeyed here today under the burden of loss and sorrow. Forces beyond human control have invaded life and taken away life's loves and life's stability. In the sacredness of this hour let those sorrowing hear again the promise declaring that "weeping endures for the night, but joy comes in the morning." Bless them with assurance that they are not alone. Fill their despair with your strengthening presence and turn their blinding tears into prisms through which they see the glory of your new dawn of hope and life beyond despair.

Some have come seeking the road that leads to forgiveness and salvation, Father. Let some word be spoken which will open the gate leading to the need and desire of their hearts. May old debasing habits be broken here today and removed so that they will no longer enslave your child. May tempting sins be overcome in Christ's power and may lostness be swallowed up in the coming home of those who have strayed from the fold and become lost in the darkness of life. Make this a glorious day as we worship here in Jesus' name.—Henry Fields

LECTIONARY MESSAGE

Topic: Three Hoping Skills
TEXT: Mark 13:1–8
Other Readings: 1 Sam. 1:4–20; Ps. 16; Heb. 10:11–14 (15–18), 19–25

Power does corrupt and absolute power corrupts absolutely. I would assert that hopelessness corrupts and absolute hopelessness corrupts absolutely. Hope is at the core of all coping skills. Without hope we cannot cope with life. Coping skills are essential for daily survival. Hoping skills are cloned and honed as we learn the eschatology of Jesus. Eschatology is that branch of biblical truth that deals with God's plan and lordship of the future. Eschatology tells us to hope in the Resurrected One who will return. Three hoping skills are found in the first eight verses of Mark chapter 13, sometimes called the Little Apocalypse. Jesus' intent is that by applying these hoping skills as Christian eschatologists, we can practice an open-eyed hope that enables the strong coping skills necessary for faithful living and ministry.

I. *Be alert to enchantment with human achievement.* In verse 1, the disciples sought Jesus' affirmation of the magnificence of the temple buildings. "Look, Teacher! What massive stones! What magnificent buildings!" Jesus was probably as impressed as anyone by Herod the Great's sermons in stone. The temple area restoration, begun in 20 B.C., was intended to restore the glory of Solomon's Temple. The Jewish historian-philosopher Josephus described some of the massive stones as being as large as 45 cubits by 5 cubits by 8 cubits. The 162 columns in the temple courts were nearly 50 feet high and took three men with outstretched arms to span their circumference (about 27 feet). Such massive construction suggests centuries, if not eternity. Architects for major financial institutions know their building materials must be massive enough to promote confidence and a sense of reliability in the hearts and wallets of their customers.

Architecture can enchant, but buildings do fall. Herod's temple would be burned by the Romans in A.D. 70. Jesus foresaw this event and the danger of placing ultimate comfort in anything temporal. With canny insight Jesus disturbed his disciples' illusion of temple permanence. "Do you see all these great buildings?" "Yes," they nodded. "Not one stone here will be left on another; every one will be thrown down." In fact, when the Roman soldiers stumbled with their golden booty in A.D. 70, the golden coins and talents of the temple treasury spilled down between the cracks of the floor's massive stones. The soldiers tore down every stone to recover all the gold.

Every time human achievement enchants Christianity to peaceful slumber, some great evil shatters our sleep. The British apologist Alan Richardson asserted that Christian apologetics suffered a decline in the eighteenth and early nineteenth centuries due to Christianity's being overimpressed with technological and scientific achievements. Classical Protestant liberalism bought into the spell of unlimited human progress and the ability of humanity to build the kingdom of God by solving every earthly ill. Then came World War I, the war to end all wars. Then came World War II. Now in the mid-1990s, every continent seems touched by war. Christian hoping skills stay alert by enjoying human achievement but knowing that we must look beyond human ends to the One who stands at the end. A Christian worldview is informed by the great eschatological truths. Christ will return. Nations and individuals will give an account. Satan and death will be cast into the lake of fire. Those whose names are found in the book of life will be transformed with creation into a new community. Such a worldview rejoices in the hope of God's faithfulness. Like faith, hope comes by hearing the Scriptures.

II. *Be alert to deception by keeping your eyes*

open to Scripture. Many Christians intentionally avoid reading the Book of Revelation. Its apocalyptic, symbolic language and numerology confuses and frightens them. They know people who are absolutely absorbed with projecting the date of Christ's return or identifying the Antichrist. Some were friends with Harold Camping, the founder and radio scholar of Family Radio, who projected September 1994 as the month of Christ's return. We all know people who are "eschatomaniacs," so occupied with the end-time prophecies that they are unable to get along with present things and people. But is "eschatophobia" the solution? Fear of prophetic passages limits our hoping skills. The point of Christian eschatology is that, even through times of active persecution, Christians might hear the call for "patient endurance and faithfulness" (Rev. 13:10). Jesus warns us to keep our eyes open, including open to all the insights the Bible contains. The alternatives are deception or apathy. "Many will come in my name, claiming, 'I am he,' and will deceive many" (Mark 13:6). The history of the Jonestown Massacre reveals that deadly deception began when the members and leaders of the People's Church in San Francisco closed their eyes to the contradictions between the words of Jesus and their beloved Reverend Jones. Keep your own eyes open. Read the Word, all the words. Keeping your eyes open to the Scriptures is an incredible coping skill and an antidote to deception.

III. *Be alert but not alarmed.* Forewarned is forearmed, so Jesus warned his disciples that the experience of war, earthquake, and famine would precede the end. But this preceding would be like a false labor before real birth. Stay watchful, but do not rush to the hospital at the first pain. What sorrows the Lord must have foreseen at the many saints who would become so alarmed at the imminence of the end-times as to sell their homes and quit their jobs. Paul exhorted the Thessalonians that the best way to cure these second-coming alarmists is to insist that eschatomania is not an entitlement to free food. "If a man will not work, he shall not eat" (2 Thess. 3:10). Hunger is an effective way to induce reality.

Church history is replete with individuals and communities who committed strange acts and even horrible atrocities in the name of Christ's return. As the third millennium approaches us, many will again succumb to such thinking as a way of coping with their fear of the future. Instead of trusting that the God who brought can keep us, they will insist on being supplied with a detailed eschatological calendar. Instead of being ever ready for Christ's return, these foolish virgins will have no reserves if their calendar is delayed. Theirs will be a future of dismay, despair, and disillusionment. Caring ministry will be required. Scripture will need to be lovingly applied to their wounded minds and hearts. We should imitate the inner core of the disciples. Peter, James, John, and Andrew made it a point to sit at the feet of Jesus and learn (Mark 13:2). Ask questions and search for his answers. None who keep calling on his name in this way will be put to shame.

IV. *Conclusion.* The world has a right to expect Christians to out-hope their troubles. Christians expect trouble, but we expect Christ more! Nothing shall separate us from the love of God in Christ Jesus. None need be without this hope. None who calls upon the name of the Lord shall remain hopeless.

–Roderick K. Durst

SUNDAY: NOVEMBER TWENTY-THIRD

SERVICE OF WORSHIP

Sermon: Thanks Be to God

TEXT: Ps. 103; also 2 Cor. 9:1–15

If we were asked this morning to make a list of everything we are thankful for this Thanksgiving, we would probably all be very mindful of our spiritual heritage and the importance of God in our lives. But if some roving reporter stopped us at the shopping mall tomorrow and asked, "What are you particularly thankful for this Thanksgiving?" there is a good chance we would name our health, or our children, or our land of plenty, or a good job, or any of a dozen other things, and never think to mention God or Jesus. Isn't that right?

I. When the word *Thanksgiving* is mentioned, we tend to think of it in terms of a cornucopia of blessings—"amber fields of grain" and "purple mountains' majesties," a table loaded with turkey and sweet potatoes and mincemeat pies, a healthy, happy family gathered together in the dining room, a home filled with the warmth of an open fire and cheerful, lifting voices, a good bank account to support everything, and enough position or status in the world to satisfy our personal needs. "Count your many blessings," runs an old hymn, "name them one by one; count your many blessing, see what God has done."

a. But what about the person who has come upon hard times and doesn't appear to have much to be thankful for? Is that person left out? Suppose it is someone facing an operation for cancer. Is this a time to be thankful? Suppose it is someone who will be eating Thanksgiving dinner alone because the dearest person in his or her life died six weeks ago. Will this person feel thankful? Or maybe it's someone who has recently lost a job, and the coming of the holiday season is hardly a cause for rejoicing. What is the basis for this person's thanksgiving?

b. The Bible reminds us that there are two levels of thanksgiving open to us. One is the level of thanksgiving for the provisions of life—for food and shelter and interpersonal relationships and all that. The other is the deeper level of thanksgiving for our rela-

tionship to God. The first is important, the Bible says, but it is not nearly so important as the second, for our relationship to God is the most important gift in life. "Bless the Lord, O my soul," intoned the psalmist, his "steadfast love" is "from everlasting to everlasting." The Hebrew word *hesed,* here translated "steadfast love," is the word most frequently used to express God's lovingkindness to the Hebrew people through the ages. God gives us everything we need, said the apostle Paul, so that we in turn are able to supply the needs of others; but at the base of everything he gives us is the gift of his Son, who, though he was rich, became poor to bring us into richness (2 Cor. 8:9). Wherever we make our lists, therefore, in church or in the shopping mall, the first gift we ought to remember in our thanksgiving is God's steadfast love and the Son he sent into the world to die for our sins.

II. The real spirit of thanksgiving, Paul said to the people of Corinth, is enlarged not by receiving more from God but by giving away to others out of what God has given us.

a. When we realize what God has done for us, in other words, it triggers such an explosion of joy and gratitude in our minds that we want to share everything we have with other people. The Corinthians were taking up an offering to help the poorer saints in other locations. Paul had been bragging about their generosity everywhere he went. He knew they would come through, as they had before, for the relief of fellow Christians in other parts of the empire. And what they were doing, he said, would overflow in "many thanksgivings to God"—not just their own, but the thanksgivings of many other people.

b. True thanksgiving, then, is more than a holiday when we count our many blessings. It is a time when we remember our relationship to God who is the source of all blessings, and in our remembrance become so excited that we reach out to create more blessing and excitement in the world around us.

III. A proper thanksgiving brings us back to a sense of God and the holy. It reminds us of what is important in life. It emphasizes turning the world into God's kingdom. It gives thanks for Jesus before everything else in our list of blessings.

a. There are two ways of looking at life. We can look at life as a merry-go-round or we can look at it as a journey. Many people look at it as a merry-go-round, with pretty colors and fantasy-like boats and swans and seashells to ride in, and lots of brass rings to be grasped for prizes. But the life lived as a merry-go-round doesn't really go anywhere. It only moves around and around in the same path. The Christian view of life has always regarded it as a journey, the way John Bunyan did in his great book *Pilgrim's Progress,* with mountains to climb and rivers to cross and sloughs of despair to make our way through. And at the end of the journey stands the Creator of everything, waiting to receive us in love and rejoicing.

b. If we are thankful only for the abundant gifts in our lives—for food and shelter and clothing and automobiles and TV sets and puppy dogs and beautiful houses—we are looking at life as a merry-go-round. We are happy as long as the merry-go-round is turning and the music is playing and there are brass rings to grasp. It is when we are thankful above all for the gift of the Lord Jesus that we see life as a journey reaching out before us and know that our relationship to God is the most important thing in life. Then thanksgiving takes on a new dimension, a deeper dimension, and we realize it can occur in the face of death, or when we are poor and jobless and there is no food on the table.

c. It isn't any wonder that the Apostle, surveying the marvel of such a faith, exulted in his letter to the Corinthians, "Thanks be to God for his inexpressible gift!" All the other things—mere things—are good, and we cannot but be grateful for them. But Christ, the faith, eternal life, the journey—these are beyond price, and they are the real objects of our thanksgiving.—John Killinger

Illustrations

THE BREATH OF LIFE.   Heaven knows terrible things happen to people in this world. The good die young, and the wicked prosper, and in any one town, anywhere, there is grief enough to freeze the blood. But from deep within whatever the hidden spring is that life wells up from, there wells up into our lives, even at their darkest and maybe especially then, a power to heal, to breathe new life into us.—Frederick Buechner

AFLAME WITH FAITH.   Here is the imperative call that I hear again and again: Come to the Cross; come to the Table of the Lord; come to the point of decision; come to penitence, that the realm of my thoughts may be purified and strengthened, so that from them may spring the waters of the good life. Nothing could do more for us as would-be Christians than a response to this imperative call. Nothing would be more likely to better our condition than to guard and discipline those thoughts that come to us; rejecting out of hand those that are unworthy, transmuting those that are the raw material of good into acts of good, and above all this, educating ourselves to think honestly, to think purely, and to think with charity.—Donald Soper

SERMON SUGGESTIONS

Topic: Behold, Thy King Cometh unto Thee

TEXT: Isa. 61:1–7

(1) As royal preacher of redemption. (2) As royal creator of a new world.—Johann Michael Reu

Topic: Christ's Kingdom Demands a Fearless Confession

TEXT: Matt. 10:24–33

(1) For Christ's sake, to whom we belong. (2) For the Gospel's sake, which we must proclaim. (3) For the world's sake, which we must overcome. (4) For the Father's sake, who shall protect us. (5) For our own sake, whom Christ is to confess.—R. C. H. Lenski

Worship Aids

CALL TO WORSHIP.   "The Lord is king! Earth, be glad! Rejoice, you islands of the seas! Clouds and darkness surround him; he rules with righteousness and justice!" (Ps. 97:1–2 TEV).

INVOCATION.   Almighty God, who in time didst send thy Son, who lived the perfect life and died the obedient death and was raised in miraculous Resurrection; we pause this day to recall his marvelous ascension. Show us again that Jesus Christ still lives, that just as he left us, so shall we one day see him and, grasping his nail-scarred hand, be joined forever in an eternity of joy. —E. Lee Phillips

OFFERTORY SENTENCE.   "The earth is the Lord's, and the fullness thereof; the world, and they that dwell therein" (Ps. 24:1).

OFFERTORY PRAYER.   O Lord, your holy word and our own good sense tell us that all that we are and all that we call our own belong to you. Help us to find ways of living and sharing with others that will reflect this truth. May your blessing be upon *this* way to that end.

PRAYER.   You have given us eyes, O Lord, and we see so little; ears, and we hear so little; hearts, and we love so little. The world around us is a treasure-trove of gifts: dancing leaves and smell of smoke; geese on the wing and children playing; fields of grain and kitchen larder; cars and boats and buildings and houses; fast-food chains and TVs and shopping centers; friends and families and a nation of plenty. Why are we so often unhappy and discontented? What is missing in our lives amidst all this abundance? Is it you, O Lord? Have we reveled in gifts and missed the giver? Have we accepted the evidences of your love and forgotten the love itself? Forgive us, O Lord, and turn us again to wholeness and perception. Let the mind that was in Christ Jesus be in us as well, to walk humbly in the world and to see everything with the eyes of

children, who rejoice in dandelions and colored leaves, who skip rope and ponder the clouds, who dwell in the day they have without trying to save it up for tomorrow. And let us live with true thanksgiving in our hearts, remembering your love and your presence, which would turn even the desert into a paradise, and which are freely ours in him who said, "You have eyes, can't you see? And ears, can't you hear?"—John Killinger

LECTIONARY MESSAGE

Topic: Mixing Politics and Religion
TEXT: John 18:28–37
Other Readings for Christ the King: 2 Sam. 1:4–20; Ps. 132:1–12 (13–18); Rev. 1:4b–8

Birth is the natural way to become a citizen of a country. Rebirth is the supernatural way to become a citizen of heaven. The apostle Paul laid claim to citizenship with Rome and heaven (Acts 22:28; Phil. 3:20). Dual citizenship means that we must find the right mix of politics and religion. Jesus did mix religion and politics. Rather than rejecting earthly governing authorities, Jesus affirmed and interacted with them. We who follow Christ as King simply cannot abdicate involvement with earthly politics. When Paul encouraged the Philippian believers to conduct themselves in the world worthy of the gospel of Jesus Christ, he used the Greek word for conduct that forms the root of our word *politics.* The essence of our life in the world, then, is to mix politics and religion in a way so worthy of the gospel that people are drawn toward heavenly citizenship.

There are three approaches that Christians have used to mix politics and religion. All three are modeled in John's record of Jesus' first arraignment before Pilate (John 18:28–37).

I. The church-state perspective of the Jewish leaders saw the Roman government as the enforcers of religious law. The government should obey the dictates of religion. The elders of the Sanhedrin ordered the Temple police to arrest Jesus for a series of ecclesiastical trials. On the basis of these midnight trials, the leaders brought Jesus to Pilate for execution. As the chief Roman authority in Jerusalem, he alone had authority to execute criminals. When Pilate asked for the charges, the accusers replied, "If he were not a criminal we would not have handed him over to you" (v. 30). Such courtroom statements are not uncommon in nations that practice a church state form of government. When two Christians were on trial for vandalizing an exterior mosque wall, a capital crime in the largely Islamic state of Pakistan, the prosecutor simply said that the accusers' testimony could not be doubted since the accusers were fine Muslims. The Christians were exonerated after the media voiced outcries from all over the world and because the accused were discovered to be illiterate and therefore unable to commit the crime with which they were charged. Our continent's early settlers were pilgrims seeking a land outside the tyranny of the English church state. History indicates that no church state, be it Christian, Islamic, or Buddhist, has been able to avoid the tyranny that violates consciences with Inquisitions. The church-state approach aims at theocracy, but it always falls terribly short due to sin and selfishness. The New Testament urges us to await the true theocracy which God will construct as heaven and earth are made new in the *eschaton*.

(Please note that only John's Gospel uses the expression "the Jews." The synoptic Gospels use the more precise phrase "council of the Sanhedrin and elders." A literal translation of John's account would mislead the reader into thinking that more than the Jerusalem Jewish officials are meant by John's expression. His choice of words no doubt represents a time when the early church was enduring great pressure from official Judaism but should not be understood as an anti-Semitic reference since John and, for that matter, Jesus, were Jews.)

II. If the church-state approach to mixing faith and government falls short, so does the state-church approach of Pilate. The state-church form of government deifies government and often perceives the constituting documents of that state as divinely inspired. As fine as our Constitution is, we must remember that it has been amended more than twenty times. Pilate saw religion at best as an agent to strengthen the rule of Rome and at worst as something to be tolerated. All persons within the Roman spheres of authority were required to offer annually a pinch of ritual incense with the words, "Caesar is Lord." Enforcement of this policy upon the Jews in Palestine had proved so bloody and counterproductive that Jews had been exempted from this participation in Roman civil religion.

Pilate's orders were to carry out a policy of noninterference and toleration of Jewish affairs unless Roman control was threatened. For this reason, Pilate's first response to the Jewish elders was to refer Jesus back to their own jurisdiction. However, when they indicated that they were calling for an execution, Pilate was forced to deliberate the case, because capital trials were matters solely for Roman justice.

In the initial interrogation of Jesus, Pilate determined that Jesus had no intention of challenging Roman authority. "My kingdom is not of this world. If it were, my servants would fight to prevent my arrest" (John 18:36). Remember that at the arrest the night before, Jesus had cut short Peter's attempt to fight for his king. Jesus revealed to the disciples that he could have called twelve legions of angels and that one day, with a trumpet's shout, he would call those angels (Matt. 26:52–53). "But *now* my kingdom is not of this place" (v. 36). From this response, Pilate made two conclusions. Jesus was a king but of no capital threat to the government Pilate administrated. Though he tried every legal means to get the crowds to accept less than crucifixion, Pilate knew he ultimately authorized the execution of an innocent human being. No amount of hand washing is ever able to cleanse when we disobey our consciences under peer pressure and practice the so-called "tender mercies of injustice." The state-church model always fails because, when push comes to shove, God and conscience are made to take a backseat to the interests of the state and the politician's career.

III. Peter said that mixing faith and government would be so difficult that believers would feel like resident aliens in their own countries (1 Pet. 2:11). In Christ's approach to mixing politics and religion, two steps must be followed. We learn these steps from Jesus' words to Pilate. Jesus declared that he was born to be king. So we must first affirm his kingship in our lives and then we must always side with the truth. The truth may not be easy to determine, but once we know it we must side with it. The truest patriotism that Christians can offer any earthly government is to be reliably truthful. When Jesus said, "Everyone on the side of truth listens to me," wasn't he inviting Pilate to change his politics and become a disciple? (John 18:37). If Christians are committed to Christ, Jesus said they must also be committed to the truth in any issue. No matter what side we start out on, once we know the truth we must move to that side. Such movement is the authentic profile of courage that verifies that Christ is our king.

How then can we discern truth? Pilate ended the arraignment with the question that should be on our minds, "What is truth?" Our ability to discern truth is directly related to the statement of Jesus that "if you hold to my teaching you are really my disciples. Then you will know the truth, and the truth will set you free" (John 8:31-32). "Everyone on the side of truth listens to me" (John 18:37). Scripture quickens our consciences to discern and profile truth. As we study the facts and evaluate concepts and data, Jesus will show us how to stand. No nation can ask for better citizenship than to have people who can be absolutely relied upon to stand up for the truth in any issue.

IV. Conclusion: The moment I abdicate my responsibility to listen to Jesus by siding with the truth, I am imitating Pilate and not the Apostles. If I try to wash my hands of mixing politics and religion in this way, then I am really washing my hands of Christ's leadership. There is an incredible freedom in making up our minds ahead of time that in every issue encountered, we will acknowledge Christ's lordship by siding with the truth. To be such is to be the light and salt of the earth.—Roderick K. Durst (N.B.: All quotes are NIV or personal translations)

SUNDAY: NOVEMBER THIRTIETH

SERVICE OF WORSHIP

Sermon: Bless the Lord

TEXT: Ps. 103:1-7, 19-22

It may seem strange in this Advent Season to select a text from Israel's Psalter in order to prepare us for Christmas—for God's gift of Christ to us.

My choice may seem all the more strange when we notice the highly individualistic and private content of Ps. 103.

"Bless the Lord, O my soul and all that is within me—bless his holy name!"

How can this psalm of personal piety prepare us for the universal and cosmic event of Christmas, and in what way is it able to address the pressing ecological and political issues of our time?

Does not this text tempt us away from all these issues in order to welcome us to the safety of a privatistic shelter, that is, to invite us to a docetic withdrawal from the real world into a pietistic haven?

Moreover, why choose a Torah-psalm—a psalm of praise and thanksgiving, a doxology, whose sole focus is the urging to the soul to bless the God of goodness and salvation?

Is not there much more reason to select a psalm of lament, to reflect on the cruel ways in which God often deals with us, and to reflect with Albert Camus on the silent indifference of God toward many of us, when we experience so frequently a seemingly absurd world, gripped by "the slings and arrows of outrageous fortune"?

I have neither an easy nor a solid answer to these questions.

I don't even know how I traveled in my own life the road from complaint and doubt to thanksgiving and gratitude.

However, one thing I do know: my journey from complaint to blessing and gratitude is not simply the result of the resignation of old age; rather it is the fruit of a fundamental change in my perspective on reality, that is, a new conviction of what really counts in life. For example: Ps. 103 helped me to discover why I always prefer to listen to the fugues and cantatas of J. S. Bach in my office, even while heavily preoccupied with the scientific study of the Bible.

Indeed, this psalm made me aware that our concentration on anthropology, sociology, and rhetoric and on the so-legitimate concerns of blacks and women remains empty unless we remember from day to day that our personal life and action are anchored in the majestic reality of God—in the God whom the psalmist urges us to bless because he has blessed us and continues to bless us.

Moreover, Ps. 103—along with the Psalter as a whole—teaches me that all my speech about God is empty unless it is simultaneously speech with God.

In other words, the Psalter teaches us that theology without doxology disintegrates into "religious voyeurism" and into ideological theological bickering, which suffocates the praise of God by his people.

And so Ps. 103 is for me a profound commentary on Bach's music: for perhaps no theologian has grasped the priority of the majesty and tender mercy of God better than Bach, the musician.

Within this context we must realize that our blessing of God is not a world-avoiding privatistic exercise. Rather it poses to us the question of what constitutes our identity in the world: Where is our life anchored? Whence does it derive its selfhood and stance in the world? And what does it dare to hope for?

The urging of the psalmist to bless the Lord is motivated by an appeal to our memory: "Bless the Lord, O my soul and forget not all his benefits" (v. 2). Our blessing of the Lord, then, is a daily remembrance of the ground of this blessing, that is, in the words of the psalmist: "He made known his ways to Moses, his acts to the people of Israel" (v. 7).

Indeed, our blessing of God in our life of prayer is able to transform "the habit of our being," that id, to change our customary habit of plaintive routine into a life of gratitude.

For we must be aware that the fruit of blessing the Lord constitutes our true blessedness, our true happiness, which cannot remain hidden. For, when I bless the Lord, my experience of blessedness shifts my perspective on reality: it enables me to relativize things that the world around me deems to be of ultimate importance; moreover, it makes me remember that the glory of the Lord of my life—and not my own glory—constitutes my true selfhood. And finally, in blessing the Lord with all my soul, my own blessedness may possibly make me a blessing for others—for all those around me who feel betrayed and abandoned by the God of blessing; those for whom the God of blessing has become a God of curse.

However, while we bless the Lord we should not forget that this blessing cannot be a blessing of private fulfillment, for the psalmist reminds us in his final line that God's blessing of us contains as well a hope. Thus he calls on all creation to bless the Lord: "Bless the Lord, all his works, in all places of his dominion" (v. 22).

And so my blessing of the Lord can only then be authentic when it realizes its provisional nature. Our thanksgiving, then, must necessarily include the urgent petition that God's sovereign majesty and steadfast love—which the psalmist so frequently emphasizes—will lift the burden of suffering of the oppressed of the earth, and that God will complete the fullness of his blessing by embracing his groaning creation in his loving arms.

It seems to me, then, that Ps. 103 evokes in us what Bach understood so well and what the *Westminster Shorter Catechism* expresses so well when it defines the chief end of a person's life in these terms: "A person's chief end is to glorify God and enjoy him forever."

Thus Ps. 103 points us in this time of Advent to the God of Israel, who at Christmastime promises not only to reaffirm his steadfast love to us, but also to bring new hope of blessing to his confused and suffering world.

And so may we, driven by this hope, join the psalmist in praise:

"Bless the Lord—O my soul and all that is within me—bless his holy name." —J. Christiaan Beker

Illustrations

PSALM 103 EXTOLLED.   This psalm is one of the finest blossoms on the tree of biblical faith. Its roots reach deep down to where the most powerful springs of biblical piety flow, and by the noble and serene tones in which it praises the grace of God, it has enriched both poetry and life in the course of the centuries. The man who speaks in this psalm is able to talk from personal experience that has led him through adversity and suffering caused by sin till he was able to enjoy the full sunlight of the grace of his God.—Artur Weiser

WHY WE FORGET.   It is generally true that all that is required to make men unmindful of what they owe to God for any blessing, is that they should receive that blessing often and regularly.—Richard Whately

SERMON SUGGESTIONS

Topic: God's Instruction to the Soul
    TEXT: Isa. 1:18
    (1) He touches through conscience. (2) The soul is instructed by the providence of God. (3) God instructs by the revelation of Jesus Christ: (a) In his example; (b) In his forgiveness; (c) In the new life he promises and implants and supports by God's spirit.—W. J. Knox-Little

Topic: Salvation, Our Advent Song
    TEXT: Luke 1:68–79
    (1) Grounded in the mercy of God. (2) Revealed in the coming of Christ. (3) Imparted by the remission of sin. (4) Reflected in our service and praise.—R. C. H. Lenski

Worship Aids

CALL TO WORSHIP.   "O send out thy light and thy truth: let them lead me" (Ps. 43:3).

INVOCATION.   As we meet to worship thee, O God, we look to thee to dispel the darkness that lurks in our hearts, the folly by which we so often let ourselves be guided. Chart our paths for us and shine upon our ways with true wisdom.

OFFERTORY SENTENCE.   "Blessed are they that do his commandments, that they may have right to the tree of life" (Rev. 22:14).

OFFERTORY PRAYER.   We have promised much, Father. We have built our budgets to minister in your name, we have undertaken projects which enhance worship. We have committed to missions that need large support. Convict us of the need to keep our promise, support our church, provide for worship projects, and do your mission around the world as we give tithes and offerings week by week. Take what we give this morning and do your mission around the world as we give tithes and offerings week by week. Take what we give this morning and bless it with your spirit that it may be used for your glory.—Henry Fields

PRAYER.   Father, we give thanks for life's blessings, those blessings that fill our lives every day, those blessings that keep us on life's way, those blessings that lift the soul and stir the heart, those blessings that you have given from your open hand and heart.
    Our pondering reminds us that the blessings you give are those ingredients in life that we seldom think about, life's common things, without which there would be no life. The sun, the stars, the wind, the rain, the sea, the sky, the fields and forest—all of these we use and too often seldom really see

with children and the aged, fathers and mothers, shelter and warmth, love and protection, goodness and kindness, work and play, faith and worship. Then there is the security and peace we enjoy, liberty and freedom, companions and friends with whom we company. And we cannot forget schools where we learn and churches where we are molded into the higher self you have made us to be. We cannot forget the sacrifice and service of many who make our lives pleasant and healthful. Nor must we leave out the faith we possess as well as that which others have in us and in God, along with a devotion which is inspiring and uplifting to us in our weaker moments.

We are thankful for these blessings that lift the level of our lives when we meditate upon them, when we reach out open hands to receive them in gratitude, and when we reach out open hands to give to others all that we have become because of the blessing visited upon us by your gracious and providing Spirit.

Accept our thanksgiving for all the blessings we have listed among us, and generate in us a desire to be a blessing to you and others as we commit life to Your care and keeping.—Henry Fields

LECTIONARY MESSAGE

Topic: The Promise of God
  TEXT: Luke 21:25–36
  Other Readings: Jer. 33:14–16; Ps. 25:1–10; 1 Thess. 3:4–13

What a strange text for the first Sunday of Advent! And what an appropriate and fitting text for the first Sunday of Advent! With these words, we are reminded that Bethlehem, as focal to the Christ Event as it is, is only one chapter in God's story of salvation. The Event, as it is, is only one chapter in God's story of salvation. The celebration of Advent properly reaches back into the promises of the prophets. But at the same time, Advent points forward to the ultimate fulfillment of God's plan. Advent is for us a holy time—a time to remember the first coming of God's son—and it is also a time to voice our deepest conviction

that the ultimate return of God's Son is yet to come.

That ultimate return, in many ways, will mirror the initial arrival of Christ in Bethlehem. God's present and future promise holds for us the certainty of crisis, the assurance of hope, and the weight of responsibility.

I. *Crisis is certain* (vv. 25–27). Every part of the Christ Event is marked by crisis. At the birth of Christ the question was asked, "Is this truly the fulfillment of God's promise?" Then those who heard him speak and saw him minister were forced to ask, "Can I believe? Will I believe that this man is who he claims to be?" At the Resurrection, the questions continued: "Could this be true?" And even today, the questions rise from deep within: "Is he really coming back?" The questions call us to personal crisis. Will we believe? Can we believe?

But there is more. The Gospel writer reminds us that there is cosmic crisis as well. All creation groans under the weight of sin and all creation awaits the fulfillment of God's plan. As that time approaches, the entire cosmos reflects the crisis inherent in encounter with the Creator. Christ was born in Bethlehem in a time of crisis. His life and ministry confront us with crisis. And his ultimate coming will be marked by that same kind of crisis.

II. *Hope is sure* (vv. 28–33). The natural response to crisis, whether personal or cosmic, is fear and dread. But surprisingly, the Gospel writer calls us to hope. In anticipation of Christ's coming, we are invited to stand up and lift up our heads, because we know that our redemption is near. With confidence and hope, the people of God understand that cosmic crisis points to the arrival of God's kingdom.

Let it never be said that the Christian faith lacks realism. Every tenet of the faith reminds us that suffering is real and costly and devastating. Every word of our Lord challenges us with the pain and disappointment of living in this kind of world. But every word of somber realism is clothed in a word of hope. Certainly, the crisis is real. Yet God will win in the end. Without question, pain and sorrow will grip the lives even of God's people. Yet God's hope is sure. The coming kingdom of God is the reality that compels God's people of promise to see hope in the midst of crisis.

III. *Response is required* (vv. 34–36). The theological realities of crisis and hope find their conclusion in the ethical demands of readiness and preparation. Because this is a time of crisis, it matters how we live. Because of the certainty of our hope, it matters how we live. The proper response to both crisis and hope is watchfulness, personal discipline, and breathless anticipation. True belief, in every case, ushers forth into obedience and faithfulness.

The events of Bethlehem teach the same truths. Christ forces us to choose; every word and every action of his life draws us into personal crisis. Even in crisis, he both grants his hope and calls us to hope. And finally, he refuses to allow us to keep his call at arm's length. Rather, his words cut us to the heart and demand the response of true faith and obedience. As with Bethlehem, so also with the ultimate coming of God's Son. As important as Bethlehem is, there is yet another chapter of the story to be written.—Barry A. Stricker

SUNDAY: DECEMBER SEVENTH

SERVICE OF WORSHIP

Sermon: Hope That Meets Us Again—And Again

TEXT: Phil. 1:3–11

Halford Luccock tells of a New England dinner party some years ago. A man who spent his summers in Maine fascinated the other guests with the story of a little town called Flagstaff. The state planned a dam and Flagstaff was to be flooded by the large lake formed by the dam. As a consequence, all improvements and repairs to the town stopped. Why paint a house if the deluge threatened it within six months? Why repair anything if it faced destruction? So, day by day, week by week, the town become increasingly bedraggled, dilapidated, woebegone. And then the man made a telling observation: "Where there is no faith in the future, there is no power in the present."

"Where there is no faith in the future, there is no power in the present." The little passage we read a moment ago from Paul's letter to the church at Philippi comes from prison. It bespeaks power in the present because of faith in the future. It is written by a man innocent of any violent crime—a man who in another of his letters writes of the tortured life he lived in behalf of the Gospel, but whose experience with shipwreck, beatings, starvation, and betrayal seem seldom to get him down. Indeed, in the face of the worst life can dish out, Paul seems frequently to be at the edge of rejoicing!

Why? How, in face of all the discouragement rampant in his churches, all the virulent resistance to his message—how, as he struggled with what must have been some serious wound or physical disability—how could Paul continue to plow through dangerous and painful circumstances with such radiance and courage?

It is because Paul had faith in God's future that he possessed such power in the present. When Paul anticipates what he calls "the day of Christ," as he does with those Philippines, he speaks out of the confidence of an Advent, a breaking in, an all-embracing restorative and compassionate presence alive and at work in his life amid every circumstance, regardless of how we might judge it from a human point of view. For the New Testament hope begins with trust that through even the most troubling, painful, and apparently loveless of circumstances, there—yes, even there sharing the pain, eager to grant us the strength to endure—there presides One who lovingly grasps, sustains, and bears us through. Indeed, there presides one who will not finally let the frequently chaotic and tragic circumstances of our lives have the last word.

Where does that hope come from? Well, for us, as for Paul, it comes from the foot of the Cross. The hope we claim, the hope we pray for, the hope we confess, the hope we live for during Advent is rooted and grounded in the hope affirmed on Good Friday and Easter. No Passion? No Advent! No Easter? No Christmas! It is because of the trust we commit to One who conquers with forbearance and love even the violent crucifixion of the likes of Jesus that we dare hope even amid the things that are killing us.

Now, here is the beauty part. That Easter —that Advent hope grounding the gospel—is not something in the far-off, never-never land of fantasy and fairy tale. It is not some dream world off in the distance, not a foggy utopia, some pie in the sky by and by. It is hope meeting us in real life right now. For Christians down the ages, for you and for me, it is a hope born of an indefatigable love that breaks in upon us again—and again.

Do you see what this means? It means, first of all, no human relationship, no matter how badly damaged, distorted, stretched, warped, crushed—no human relationship is finally beyond repair. Oh, I know that sounds gibberish and fantasy. I know in many lives here there is a brokenness among family, or friends, that seems irreparable. I know there is grief, guilt, despair, over the fissures and chasms dividing some of us from those we love and have lost, or who love and have lost us. And I do not exclude myself. But the hope meeting us time and again is one bearing that most gracious and releasing of mysteries, forgiveness. It is true, is it not? Here is how one commentator describes it:

"When somebody you've wronged forgives you, you're spared the dull, self-diminishing throb of a guilty conscience. When you forgive somebody who has wronged you, you're spared the dismal corrosion of bitterness and wounded pride. For both parties, forgiveness means the freedom again to be at peace inside their own skins and to be glad in each other's presence." That is a hope we wait for, yes—but even more, a hope that meets us again and again.

And the Advent hope, meeting us again and again, is hope grounding what the purpose of this church calls "striving for righteousness, justice and peace." The world as

God would have it—a world finally reconciled and at peace—such a world, friends, comes finally as a gift from God. And part of the gift is the courage, the serenity, the good humor to stand and strive for the loving dominion of God right now.

Nelson Mandela has an autobiography on the bookstands. He has to be one of the heroes of our time. Yet while Mandela suffered in prison for decades under the apartheid regime, Bishop Desmond Tutu faced that evil regime with a faith in the future generating power in the present:

"I want the government to know now and always that I do not fear them," Tutu proclaimed. "The resurrection of our Lord and Saviour Jesus Christ declares for all to know that life will triumph over darkness, that goodness will triumph over injustice, and that freedom will triumph over tyranny. I believe fervently what Paul meant when he said, 'If God be for us, who can be against us?'" That hope meets and undergirds us in our striving for God's future again—and again.

And be assured Christ's Hope meets us time and again in our trials and in our rejoicing. Surely in our trials, as John Carmody affirms in his little reflection entitled "Cancer and Faith." Contemplating the God beckoning him amid his terminal illness, Carmody confesses, "If I am, if I really exist and am not a dream, then I rest in God." And like Paul rejoicing ebulliently in prison, Carmody affirms his confidence in Hope grasping him from someplace other than how he happens to feel today, or what the oncologist reports to him this afternoon or tomorrow. It is a hope and a presence independent of and from beyond the threat of his illness and the crisis of his life—yet a presence enfolding and bearing him through it all.

And, of course, in our rejoicing as at a wedding, we know the Eternal One stands with us because of the solemnity of the occasion, the richness of the possibilities, the joy of two people promising to serve each other representing the gospel itself.

So, friends, on this second Sunday of Advent, this high moment anticipating Hope, I invite you to this Holy Table. For here in these symbols of bread and wine we witness a Hope shining through—incredibly—a body broken and blood spilled: Hope emerging triumphant. Indeed, at this table we share a Hope from Love's future providing power for the present—again and again. Come. For all is ready.—James W. Crawford

Illustrations

HOPES AND CHAINS.   Real hopes always have chains attached to them. Hopes are wings, we are told. We have all seen great hopes act as wings to life, giving lift and buoyancy to hard days and long years. All true. Yet a cherished hope binds one as by a chain to obligations implicit in the hope itself.

It was in that deep sense that Paul had hope of Israel. Because that hope in the God of Israel, revealed in Jesus Christ, sang within him, he willingly wore chains. The iron chains on his body were only the symbols of a deeper and stronger chain. He was the slave of Jesus Christ. "The love of God constrainth me," he wrote. Because of his hope for men, for Israel, for the world, he bound his life under great obligations, as the servant of all.—Halford Luccock

FINDING GOD.   Act up to your light, though in the midst of difficulties, and you will be carried on, you do not know how far. Abraham obeyed the call and journeyed, not knowing whither he went; so we, if we follow the voice of God, shall be brought on step by step into a new world, of which before we had no idea.—John Cardinal Newman (1801–90)

SERMON SUGGESTIONS

Topic: They That Wait upon the Lord
TEXT: Isa. 40:28–31

(1) An unexchangable God as the antidote to all despondency and the foundation of all hope. (2) The unwearied God giving strength to wearied people. (3) Wearied people lifted to the level of the unwearied God and to his likeness.—Alexander Maclaren

Topic: The Kingdom of God Is Within You
TEXT: Luke 17:20–30

(1) It does not come with observation—it is spiritual. (2) In it you must suffer many things—it is marked by tribulation. (3) It cannot be understood by those who care only to eat, drink, and marry—it is not fleshly. (4) Yet in the end it shall shine like lightning from one end of heaven to the other—its hidden glory shall be revealed at last.—R. C. H. Lenski

Worship Aids

CALL TO WORSHIP.   "The Lord is nigh unto them that are of a broken heart; and saveth such as be of a contrite heart" (Ps. 34:18).

INVOCATION.   Father, make us aware of our brothers and sisters who worship with us. As we bring to you our own needs and problems, help us to bear one another's burdens and in this way fulfill our Lord's law of love.

OFFERTORY SENTENCE.   "Blessed be the Lord, who daily loadeth us with benefits, even the God of our salvation" (Ps. 68:19).

OFFERTORY PRAYER.   Our Father, we do not know how wonderfully we have been blessed: So, many of thy blessings are beyond our knowledge or ability to appreciate. Open the eyes of our understanding and help us to recognize the marvelous gifts of thy grace and to walk in the assurance of the presence with us of thine unseen angels.

PRAYER.   Blessed art thou, O Lord our God, the God of our fathers, who turnest the shadow of death in the morning; who hast lightened our eyes that we sleep not in death. O Lord, blot out as a night-mist our iniquities. Scatter our sins as a morning cloud. Grant that we may become children of the light, and of the day. Vouchsafe to keep us this day without sin. Uphold us when we are falling, and lift us up when we are down. Preserve this day from any evil of ours, and us from the evils of the day. Let this day add some knowledge, or good deed, to yesterday. Oh, let us hear thy loving-kindness in the morning, for in Thee is our trust. Teach us to do the thing that pleaseth thee, for thou art our God. Let thy loving Spirit lead us forth into the land of righteousness.—adapted from Lancelot Andrewes (1555–1626)

LECTIONARY MESSAGE

Topic: Preparing for the Promise

TEXT: Luke 3:1–6

Other Readings: Mal. 3:1–4; Luke 1:68–74; Phil. 1:3–11

That God's promise comes to pass is sheer grace. But God's desire to involve human beings in the fulfillment of his promise may be an even greater gift of grace. God invites his people to join him in joyful preparation. The King is coming! The kingdom is near! God's people share in the celebration. But more than that, God's people share in the preparation. That is their mission, at the same time both privilege and duty. It is their God-given role to usher in the moment of God's salvation and hope.

God affords the same opportunity to his people today. As was true during the first Advent of Christ, the people of God today share in the joyous task of preparing the way for the kingdom to break into hearts and lives. What an act of grace for God to allow us to share in his work of eternal salvation! We see that same grace in the gospel even as the miracle of Bethlehem approaches.

I. *The moment is right* (vv. 1–2A). Why the mention of names of obscure and famous? The Gospel writer takes great pains to remind us that the fulfillment of God's

promise is tied to history. The promises of God are fulfilled in history. The names of real people and real places remind us that the Word will become flesh in human space and time. Even more than that, that time is the *right* time. This moment is the moment that has been chosen by God. The promise is about to be fulfilled and the moment is theologically ripe. God has determined the timing, and this moment is his moment.

Jesus' later ministry continues this theme of the right time. Jesus reveals his identity at the time he determines. And Jesus lays down his life at the time he determines. But now, as the plan of God unfolds, this moment—in the fifteenth year of Tiberius Caesar—is the moment that God has chosen. For that reason alone, this time is the right time.

II. *The messenger is willing* (vv. 2b–3). In that holy moment, the word of the Lord came to John. From the beginning, God has graciously proclaimed his word through the agency of human messengers. And in keeping with the rich tradition of prophets and proclaimers, John is prepared, set apart for his task, a willing vessel in the hands of his God. The last of the old, John proclaims God's demand for repentance in anticipation of the coming kingdom. His proclamation is grounded in the past, anchored to the present, and focused on the future.

III. *The message is fulfilled* (vv. 4–6). John draws his message from Isa. 40:3–5. In keeping with ancient tradition, the message demands that preparation be made for the arrival of the King. Rough places are to be made smooth, and crooked paths are to be straightened. Indeed, life itself is to be put in order because the King is coming.

The task of preparing for the coming kingdom falls not only to God's messenger, but also to those who would be God's people. The clear presentation of the message compels others to become messengers themselves. The message in every age continues to echo the same truth: God's promise will come to pass and God's people are compelled to share in the glorious time of preparation.—Barry A. Stricker

SUNDAY: DECEMBER FOURTEENTH

SERVICE OF WORSHIP

Sermon: Being Ready for Christmas
TEXT: Matt. 1:18–25

Let me ask you a question: Are you ready for Christmas? Usually when we talk about getting ready for Christmas, we talk about deeds we have to do. However, I'm not talking about deeds, I'm talking about attitude. When I want us to be ready for Christmas, I want us to have that kind of openness this Christmas to the coming and doing of God in our lives.

Enter Joseph, an often neglected member of the Christmas story but one who played a most vital part. Here was a man who lived with an openness to God. If he hadn't been open and committed to God, then Joseph would have been a very insignificant part of our Christmas story, and the whole story would have been changed.

But because of Joseph's approach to the Christmas event, he was ready for Christmas. How do we know he was ready for Christmas? What is it that we have to do and be in order to have the right attitude toward Christmas?

I. To be ready for Christmas we need to trust God, confident that he knows what he's doing.

a. Joseph was a man of faith, but he was not a man whose faith was always easy. There were those moments when it was difficult for him.

I'm sure Joseph had a lot of questions he wanted to ask about the situation. But in spite of that, the story tells us that Joseph took Mary for his wife and did what God told him to do. He was someone who didn't understand all that was going on, but he did understand one thing: God could be trusted. In the midst of all of it, he would at least trust him to know what he was doing. Because he did, Christmas happened.

b. Now we are people of faith, but at times it gets difficult to keep. As we look at all that's going on in the world, and as we look at what happens in our own personal lives, it gets hard to hold on to God.

There are those who laugh at any thought that God might be in this world, much less in control of it. How can you talk of love in the face of so much hate? How can you talk of good in the face of so much bad? How can you talk of peace in the face of so much war? How can you praise God in the light of so much suffering?

Does God know what he is doing? We might wonder about that. Despair and hopelessness can creep into our spirits. Then Christmas comes! Christmas reminds us that God can be trusted, for in those days there was darkness over the face of the earth, too. There was heartbreak and misery and suffering and pain. It seemed as if God was far away, but he wasn't. Instead, God was right there in the middle of them, and into that darkness, the flicker of a little light spread into a tremendous flame. God was there.

c. What can a baby born in some out-of-the-way stable do? Nothing but grow up and change the world, that's all, because God was in it. In our darkness, Christmas causes us to remember that God is still with us and that he is still at work in this world. We can trust him. He has not forsaken us. We can live this Christmas with a sense of openness because we can see it—if we have the eyes to see it—love and joy and peace and life because God is here! He is here with you now! We can trust him!

II. To be ready for Christmas, we need to be carers for others.

a. Joseph's part in the Christmas story was to care for Mary, to minister to her every need, and that Joseph did. Because Joseph cared, Christmas happened.

b. Christmas is the time when it seems that we do reach out to care for others in special ways. We have many good causes at Christmas: the Joy Fund that seeks to provide toys for needy children; food baskets for the hungry; presents for prisoners behind bars; gifts for lonely people in nursing homes; and much more. All this is good.

Of course, caring for others and for their needs ought to be a yearlong way of life. Christmas tells us about a God who cared so much for us that he was willing to come down, even at the risk of his life, to minister to us. Christmas calls us to the same kind of doing, the same kind of caring. The needs are all around us. The hungry are here, thousands each day, dying for lack of food.

c. The most alive people I know are those who have gotten themselves off their hands and are ministering and caring for others. To be ready for Christmas is to be ready to care, to minister, to reach out to touch the life of someone else for God's sake. Are we ready for that?

III. To be ready for Christmas, we need to be givers to God of all that we are.

a. I wonder if anybody told Joseph how dangerous it would be to serve as the earthly father of Christ? Right after the birth of Baby Jesus, he had to take Mary and the baby and run for his life into the land of Egypt because of Herod. The king was insecure and jealous and sought to do away with this baby he felt would be a threat to his throne.

He began searching for him, killing babies two years of age and under. Joseph had to run for his life. It was dangerous. Would Joseph be willing to risk his life? Would Joseph be willing to do all that God asked? Joseph was. Whatever God needed him to do, he was willing to do.

b. Has anybody ever told us that there is a cost involved in being a Christian? There is! There will be those in this world who will not like those of us who are Christians. There are values in this world that stand against everything we value as Christians. We might lose some popularity if we stand up for what we believe is right and best and just. It will cost us time as we immerse ourselves in the ministries of Christ. It will cost money as we support the ministries of Christ with our finances. It might cost us our lives, as we stand up to fight against prejudice, the rise of racist organizations, injustice, and wrong.

Are we willing to give God everything he needs from us in order to see that his will be done? Christmas is not as meaningful to many because they cannot say to God, "Whatever you want, I'll give; wherever you lead, I'll go; whatever you ask, I'll do." To be ready for Christmas, we can offer to God no less than everything he wants.

c. There are a lot of activities that you and I have to do to be ready for Christmas.

But while there are a lot of things I have to do, I hope that I'm ready for Christmas. I hope that in my attitude I am living on tiptoe, looking in every place and in every experience for the coming of God in a new and special way, for God is with us.

As we trust him and care for others, as we come to the place where we are willing to give ourselves to him, he can come in new and special ways.–Hugh Litchfield

Illustrations

SURPRISE ENDING.   One of my favorite Christmas stories was told by Dina Donahue in *Guideposts* magazine. It was about a nine-year-old boy named Wally Purling. Wally was big for his age and was also a little slow mentally. But although big, he wasn't a bully. Everybody liked him. He was nice to all the little kids; in fact, he took up for them all the time.

They were doing a Christmas program in his school, and Wally wanted to be in it. He wanted to be a shepherd, but the teacher had another part in mind for him. She wanted him to be the innkeeper because he was so big. Wally took the part home and studied it and practiced it hard.

The night came for the play, and everything was going smoothly. It came to the time when Mary and Joseph knocked on the door of the inn and Wally opened the door and said, "What do you want?" Joseph said, "We need a place to stay for the night." "You've got to find it somewhere else; the inn is full." "Are you sure?" Joseph asked. "We've come a long way, and it's cold." "No. There's no place here, go someplace else." "But my wife is going to have a baby, isn't there some corner we can hide in?"

At this point in the play there was silence, one of those embarrassing silences that made you believe that somebody had forgotten his line. Wally stood there, not saying anything. The prompter whispered, "No, begone!" So Wally said, "No, begone!" Joseph put his arm around Mary and turned to walk away from the inn.

It was at this point that this Christmas play took an unusual twist. Wally was big, but he had a heart just as big, and he couldn't stand seeing Mary and Joseph walk away. He suddenly said, "Wait a minute, Joseph. Bring Mary on back. You can have my room. I'll sleep in the cold."

There were those who said that the Christmas story was ruined, but I think not. In that little event was caught the whole essence of it: a boy willing to sleep out in the cold so that Mary and Joseph could have what they needed for the coming of the Christ child. Maybe we would enjoy Christmas a whole lot more if we were willing to sleep out in the cold for Christ, if we had to.—Hugh Litchfield

EMMANUEL.   "For we preach Christ crucified," the Apostle Paul wrote to the church at Corinth, "a stumbling block to Jews and folly to Gentiles." He could as well have written "We preach Christ born" or "We preach Christmas" because the birth presents no fewer problems than the death does both to religious people—"the Jews"—and to everybody else—"the Gentiles." Christmas is not just Mr. Pickwick dancing a reel with the old lady at Dingley Dell or Scrooge waking up the next morning a changed man. It is not just the spirit of giving abroad in the land with a white beard and reindeer. It is not just the most famous birthday of them all and not just the annual reaffirmation of Peace on Earth that it is often reduced to so that people of many faiths or no faith can exchange Christmas cards without a qualm. On the contrary, if you do not hear in the message of Christmas something that must strike some as blasphemy and others as sheer fantasy, the chances are you have not heard the message for what it is. Emmanuel is the message in a nutshell, which is Hebrew for "God with us." Who is this God? How is he with us? That's where the problem lies.—Frederick Buechner

SERMON SUGGESTIONS

Topic: Securely Guarded
TEXT: Various
(1) A proclamation, Deut. 32:10. (2) A prayer, Ps. 17:8. (3) A promise, Zech. 2:8.—W. W. Weeks

Topic: The Sufficiency of Jesus Christ
TEXT: Luke 7:10
(1) Is the gospel of Christ sufficient for the needs of the human soul, or shall we look for something else? (2) Are the teachings of Christ sufficient for the world's problems, or must we look elsewhere? (3) Is the power of Christ sufficient for the program of the church, or shall we look for something else? —J. Clyde Turner

Worship Aids

CALL TO WORSHIP.   "O send out thy light and thy truth: let them lead me; let them bring me unto thy holy hill, and to thy tabernacles. Then will I go unto the altar of God, unto God my exceeding joy" (Ps. 43:3–4a).

INVOCATION.   Gracious Lord, you have been our willing teacher, and we have been your laggard learners. Inspire us today with an openness of heart to understand, and an openness of will to do.

OFFERTORY SENTENCE.   "Blessed be the Lord, who daily loadeth us with benefits, even the God of our salvation" (Ps. 68:19).

OFFERTORY PRAYER.   O God, we confess that we are rich in many ways—some of us in money; some of us in education; some of us in friends; some of us in spiritual gifts. Help us to use responsibly what has been impoverished by greedily hugging to ourselves what could be a blessing to others and a glory to your name.

PRAYER.   O God, thou art Life, Wisdom, Truth, Bounty, and Blessedness, the Eternal, the only true Good. Our God and our Lord, thou art our hope and our heart's joy. We confess, with thanksgiving, that thou hast made us in thine image, that we may direct all our thought to thee and love thee. Lord, make us to know thee aright, that we may more and more love and enjoy and possess thee. And because, in the life here below, we cannot fully attain this blessedness, let it at least grow in us day by day, until it all be fulfilled at last in the lift to come. Here be the knowledge of thee increased, and there let it be perfected. Here let our love to thee grow, and there let it ripen; that our joy, being here great in hope, may there in fruition be made perfect.—Adapted from Saint Anselm

LECTIONARY MESSAGE

Topic: Proclaiming the Promise
TEXT: Luke 3:7–18

Other Readings: Zeph. 3:14–20; Isa. 12:2–6; Phil. 4:4–7

What is it about the Good News that makes it so good? John's proclamation of God's message would cause us to wonder. Certainly, the Good News is unexpected, grace-filled, and life-giving. The Good News is God's invitation to life full and free. The Good News is the story of what God has done in our behalf. And for those reasons, that news is truly good. But the Good News is also overflowing with words of judgment, challenge, and confrontation. The ministry of John reminds us of the danger of hearing only half the story. His proclamation is full and complete. Because that's true, his proclamation reminds us that the Good News is sometimes also the hard news.

In every case, God's challenge is met by his own grace. Still, we need to hear well the entire proclamation of Advent.

I. *Hard words* (vv. 8–14). "Hear the Good News, you snakes!" Few of us would dare to begin our proclamation with such words. And even fewer of us would dare begin our Advent proclamation with such words! And yet, those words are as much a part of God's promise as any others. The lesson here is that we demonstrate our true embrace of the message through ethical living and gracious giving. Anything less is a sham.

John is quite clear. It is not enough to have the right name. It is not enough to claim the best ancestry. It is not enough to rely on education or occupation or social standing. The message of repentance here bears fruit. Proper preparation for God's promise means that human lives will be different. Those with money, those with power, and those with position are all called to submit to the revolution about to begin.

These hard words call for radical change. These hard words are costly. These hard words remind us yet again that the promise of Advent cannot be enjoyed from a distance. These hard words get inside us and turn our lives right-side-up. These are good words because they remind us of our true standing before God. These words are good because they remind us of what God both expects and demands of His people. We can hear these hard words because they are true words.

II. *Good news* (vv. 15–18). Why would the people wonder if this messenger named John might be the Christ? Perhaps their expectation comes from the fact that John speaks the truth. In his message, there is no artificial theological sweetener. There is only truth. And that in itself suggests to the people that this might in fact be the one of promise. Hearing the truth is rare in every day. But John understands well both his identity and his role. He is the preparer and the proclaimer. The Christ is indeed coming, but his name is not John. And the truth that this Christ will speak is even more searing than the message of John. Certainly, the Christ is coming to save and heal, but he is also coming to judge and to cleanse.

Again we ask, What is so good about this Good News? John's words are Good News because they proclaim the fact that God has kept his promise. The full plan of God is coming to pass and that full plan included both judgment and grace.—Barry A. Stricker

SUNDAY: DECEMBER TWENTY-FIRST

SERVICE OF WORSHIP

Sermon: A Christmas Meditation
TEXT: Luke 2:29

The celebration of Christmas in our churches draws almost all of its material from the story of the birth of Jesus as it is told by Luke in his Gospel. It is to Luke that we owe most of the details—the annunciation to Mary, the journey of Mary and Joseph to Bethlehem, the birth in a stable, the shepherds out in the field watching their sheep, the appearance of the angels to the shepherds and their announcement to them of the birth of the child, and the hasty visit of the shepherds to Bethlehem to see the babe in the manger and to spread the report of what they had seen.

There is only one feature that often figures in our celebration that is not in Luke's account—the story of the wise men who followed the star and came to visit the newborn king, bringing their gifts of gold, frankincense, and myrrh. This story is told only in the Gospel of Matthew. In the older and more elaborate church calendar, it was separated from Christmas and celebrated on a day of its own called the Epiphany, meaning the first appearing of the newborn king to the Gentiles. This was celebrated on the twelfth day after Christmas and it was a major holy day, as we can gather from the fact that Shakespeare took the name *Twelfth Night* for the title of one of his plays. Apart from that, as I have said, everything else in the story as we recall it in our celebration comes from Luke.

On the other hand, however, there is one episode in Luke's account that we have neglected and that may set our view of Christmas in a different light. The celebration of Christmas in the church nowadays has turned it very largely into a children's festival. Now that may seem right enough. After all, the principal thing in Christmas is the birth of a child, and what could be more appropriate than to bring children into the celebration? They surely enjoy it, and their presence perhaps brings something of the meaning of the occasion home to us older ones.

But there are no children in Luke's story.

By contrast, the first articulate human celebration, according to Luke, came from two old people, two very old people who were nearing the end of their lives. These were Simeon, who by his own account was waiting for his departure, and Anna, whom Luke calls a prophetess and who, as he tell us, was eighty-four years old.

This episode, which occurred on the visit of Mary and Joseph to the Temple for the ceremony of purification prescribed in Lev. 12:2–8 and the presentation of the firstborn prescribed in Exod. 13:2, 12, could be read as the Lukan equivalent of the Epiphany, which is traditionally associated with Matthew's account of the visit of the Magi. It could perhaps also be read as the conclusion of the nativity, which is completed when the newborn child is recognized for who he is. Simeon and Anna are not only an integral part of the story—though they are omitted in our Christmas theatricals—they are also Luke's last word, the word he wants to leave us with. What is he saying to us with it? I suggest there are three things.

First, to put it in a very general way, Simeon and Anna were waiting and, as Luke suggests, they were representatives of a large community of people who were waiting. They were fitting representatives because through the long years they had surely learned to wait. It is said that patience is a virtue, but it is not a virtue we acquire at birth. To the contrary, the early years of our lives are characterized by impatience. We don't want to wait; we demand instant satisfaction of our wants. And in a culture that is youth-oriented, this attitude tends to be disseminated through the population at large. I will cite two examples.

First, at a time when the old were seen as the repositories of wisdom and as those who set the mores of society, as was the case in my now far-distant youth, we were taught that if we wanted something we should save our money until we had enough to buy it. Today the order is reversed; the current rule is "Buy now, pay later." The other example is, of course, to be found in the realm of sex. In the olden days we were taught, more by example than by precept, that the sexual impulse should not be gratified at its first stirring, despite its urgency, but held in restraint until it could be exercised within the permanent and personal relationship of marriage. But today it is, "Why wait for marriage?"

The prevailing mood of impatience makes it all the more difficult for us to endure the waiting that, paradoxically, is forced upon us more and more by the conditions of modern life. We hear much of the accelerated pace of life. But have you noticed how much of our time we have to spend in waiting? Almost everywhere we go we have to wait, often in line, as at the post office, the bank, the motor vehicle office, even the police station where we go to pay our parking ticket. The most visible symbol of the accelerated life is, of course, the automobile. The automobile enables us to go places far more quickly than the old horse and buggy. But I read recently that in New York City an automobile travels at an average speed of eight miles per hour, which is much slower than a horse-drawn carriage and only twice the speed at which an able-bodied person can walk. It is not surprising that the people of New York City have not become renowned as paragons of patience.

But Simeon and Anna were not only waiting for the long stretch of their years to come to an end. They were waiting for the fulfillment of a promise. This is the second point that stands out in the story. It was clearly important for Luke, for he mentions it in connection with each one of them. They had a promise to their waiting, and it is in the context of this promise that they greeted the infant Jesus. It is noteworthy that Luke does not define the promise as the coming of the Messiah. He puts it in somewhat broader terms: Simeon, he tells us, was waiting for the consolation of Israel, and the people to whom Anna spoke were, he says, waiting for the redemption of Jerusalem. At the end of his Gospel, Luke describes in a similar way Joseph of Arimathea as one who was waiting for the kingdom of God (Luke 23:51).

What Luke is telling us with these expressions is that if we are to understand the birth of Jesus we must look at it not merely in the unusual manner of its occurrence and the extraordinary events that accompanied it, as Luke himself has related them, but in the context of the whole purpose of God with his people and, beyond them, to all people. This is the theme of the song that Luke puts into the mouth of Simeon. Strange as it may seem, Simeon says nothing about the child he holds in his arms; his joy is that

> . . . mine eyes have seen thy salvation
> which thou has prepared in the presence
>   of all peoples,
> a light for revelation to the Gentiles,
> and for glory to thy people Israel.
>   (Luke 2:30–31 RSV)

Perhaps the strangest thing in the story of Simeon is that the first sentiment he expresses after holding the newborn babe in his arms is willingness to take leave of this life: "Lord, now lettest thou thy servant depart in peace" (Luke 2:29). By this he showed that, having been sustained by the promise through all the years of waiting, he was assured that the prospect of his participation in the fulfillment would not be obliterated by his death. He knew that the meaning of Christmas is the promise of the new that reaches beyond the barrier of death.

The birth of a child is always, of course, an event of promise. No one can look at a newborn babe without feeling that. We would all repudiate the man (if he ever existed) who is said to have been visiting a young couple who had just received their first baby and, when asked if he would like to see the baby, replied, "No thanks; I have seen one before." It has been said that the birth of a child is the nearest thing in our experience to the creation of the world in the beginning. And the child whose birth we celebrate at Christmas is, as Paul says, the firstborn of the new creation; he is the one appointed and equipped to bring creation to the destiny for which it was created. That is what these two old people recognized. Christmas is not an occasion for remembrance of the past, however picturesque it may have been. It is the seal of the promise of God that God will fulfill his purpose in creation and bring it to a glorious consummation, in which we hope to participate. The celebration of Christmas is an occasion for the renewal of this hope.—George S. Hendry

Illustrations

CHANGE AND PAIN.   At every stage in the growth of this planet, from whirling flame to modern society, change and pain have gone hand in hand. If at any point in cosmic history God had respected the integrity of old structures and balances, man would not even exist today. The whole enterprise would have stopped short, the memorial to a Creator whose nerve had failed.

Somewhere ages hence when man, or whatever man in the providence of God has become, stands on the frontiers of greatness which you and I cannot even begin to imagine, he may look back across the ages at what we call undeserved suffering, at famine, tempest, earthquake, and myriad natural disasters, and see in the afflictions not the punishing fist of the Judge, but the restless fingers of the Creator.—William Muehl

THE PERFECT FAITH.   To stand in the darkness and yet know that God is light; to want to know the truth about a thousand mysteries, the answers, anywhere, and yet to know beyond a peradventure that God is not hiding from us anything which it is possible and useful for us to know; to stand in the darkness and yet know that God is light—that is a great and noble faith, a faith to which no man can come who does not know God.—Phillips Brooks

SERMON SUGGESTIONS

Topic: The Decisive Babies of the World
TEXT: Isa. 9:6–7

(1) When we center our attention on the decisive babies of the world, a mood of expectancy and hope arises. (2) This message speaks not only to our need of hope in days of discouragement, but to our sense of personal helplessness in the face of the world's catastrophe. (3) We have spoken of Jesus as though he were one of the decisive babies of the world, but to us, as Christians, he is *the* decisive baby of the world.—Harry Emerson Fosdick

Topic: Modern Substitutes for Christ
TEXT: John 6:68

Let us wipe the thought of Jesus from our mind and face a few of our practical problems without him and let us see how we fare. (1) Consider, for instance, temptation. (2) Let us turn to the sense of guilt that oppresses us all at times. (3) Let us consider our need in the hour of bereavement.—W. E. Sangster

Worship Aids

CALL TO WORSHIP.   "This is the day which the Lord hath made; we will rejoice and be glad in it" (Ps. 118:24).

INVOCATION.   Deepen our joy, Father, as we come to this sacred day of remembering the time when Christ was born. Let the hour recall for us the wonder of the moment, the permanence of the gift you gave, and the love that was shared from eternity to us.—Henry Fields

OFFERTORY SENTENCE.   "For ye know the grace of our Lord Jesus Christ, that, though he was rich, yet for your sakes he became poor, that ye through his poverty might be rich" (2 Cor. 8:9).

OFFERTORY PRAYER.   On this special day may what we give reflect what we believe to be the meaning of the Christmas event. Give meaning to our gifts today just as you did to those given long ago by wise men.—Henry Fields

PRAYER.   Like humble shepherds we come before you this morning, Father. We have heard the good news of the message bearers and in these sacred moments we want to really see what has come to pass, that has been made known to us. For some of us the message has been sounded for so long that it has become dulled with the hearing. Let us hear it now as if for the first time. Let its truth sink deep into our souls and call us to a new understanding of love and service and faith and giving. Send us all from this meeting together in your presence to tell abroad the things that we have seen and heard which the Lord has made known unto us.

Like wise men we come this morning. May our greatest wisdom be that we understand how little we really know. We can bring our descriptive gifts, our designated presents, and understand that these are of great value to the Lord. But may we bring also a seeking mind, not just to see some strange event, but to behold a new beginning, a new era when Christ in truth and fact reigns in our lives and hearts and through us makes a difference in the world around us. Make us wise enough to return to him time and again, knowing that in our own wisdom we cannot begin to manage life as you intend it to be lived. From far and near we come, Lord. Bless us as we pray, we in this holy hour in this holy place.

Like lost pilgrims we come this morning, seeking the one who can direct us on our pilgrimage of faith. Deliver us from getting bogged down in the minor issues of belief. Open our hearts and minds and lives that we might scale the high mountains of truth and view the vistas of wonder which you long to reveal to us. Be the light for the way, the hand that guides, the spirit that forgives and the one who saves us to the uttermost, we pray.–Henry Fields

LECTIONARY MESSAGE

Topic: The Pronouncement of the Promise
TEXT: Luke 1:39–45 (46–55)

Other Readings: Mic. 5:2–5a; Luke 1:47–55; Heb. 10:5–10

It would be difficult to comprehend fully the reason behind the confidence and assurance of Mary and Elizabeth. In the unfolding drama of Advent, God has given them central roles to play. Surely, they are filled with unsettledness and fear and wonder. But their initial fear and doubt have given way to confidence, trust, and a desire to be faithful. Together, these two women share the experience of holy encounter with God.

In one sense, Mary and Elizabeth are unlikely characters for God's drama. But in another sense, they are no more unlikely than the other characters who appear in other scenes. For us, they serve as yet another reminder of his plan. And the experience of Mary and Elizabeth is the very same experience of God's people today. His promise today continues to include the presence of his Spirit and his own blessing for those who truly believe that God will do what he has promised.

I. *Blessed are those who cooperate with God* (vv. 39–42). Seeing Mary approaching, Elizabeth is filled with God's spirit. And out of that experience she loudly pronounces God's blessing upon Mary and upon the Christ child she will bear. Mary has willingly cooperated with God. Mary has given herself completely to God. Because of her willing spirit, God's plan will come to completion through her. God's power is absolute, yet He has determined to call for human cooperation as his plan is made known. For that reason, Mary's willingness to obey is central to the Advent story. And for that reason, Mary is blessed. God's people today are blessed as well when they cooperate with God.

II. *Blessed are those who see God at work* (vv. 43–44). Elizabeth too is blessed. Possessing the spiritual sensitivity to see God's hand, Elizabeth is aware that God is at work around her. She understands correctly that she herself is favored because God's chosen one stands in her presence. God has graciously allowed Elizabeth the opportunity to see and understand that he is at work. The response, for both Elizabeth and the baby in her womb, can only be joy. God's people today are blessed as well when they are able to see God at work. And the response to that can only be joy.

III. *Blessed are those who believe that God will fulfill his promises* (v. 45). The focus of Mary's response to God can be found in her obedience. Beyond that, however, Mary's faith is demonstrated in her willingness to believe that God is able to do just what he has promised. We would do well this Advent to remember just how impossible God's word to Mary had been. From her point of view, God's promise was absurd and unlikely and ridiculous. And yet, she chose to believe. What a testimony of strength and courage! God's people today are blessed as well when they choose to believe that God will fulfill his promises. God will fulfill even his promises that seem absurd and unlikely and ridiculous.

IV. *Blessed are those who understand the true nature of God's kingdom* (vv. 46–55). E. Stanley Jones referred to Mary's song as the most revolutionary document in the world. Indeed, it is clear that Mary has grasped the true nature of the coming kingdom. The song proclaims the downfall of the proud and the exaltation of the lowly. Mary's song is about the mighty being cast down and the humble being lifted up. The song is about the hungry being filled and the rich being sent away empty. The essence of Mary's song is that God desires and intends to usher in a time of heavenly revolution. Though that is not often how we think about Bethlehem, that is exactly what happened on the first Christmas.

Amazingly, Mary is able to recognize the true nature of the kingdom. Steeped in rich biblical imagery, Mary's song pronounces the purposes and blessing of God. God's people today are blessed as well when they understand the true nature of God's kingdom.–Barry A. Stricker

SUNDAY: DECEMBER TWENTY-EIGHTH

SERVICE OF WORSHIP

Sermon: Living in God's Eternal Purpose

TEXT: Eph. 3:1–12

In this passage we have the most sublime communication ever given to a human, revealed by one who calls himself "the very least of all the saints" (3:8). In order to appreciate the truth here revealed, we need to know what it is God's "eternal purpose" to do for his creation. Paul uses many synonyms for the revelation: cause, mystery, promise, intent, and eternal purpose. When a person comes to the Bible meaning to find spiritual truth and enlightenment, he must give himself to it in a personal way, not attempt to open a deep mystery of God with a purely objective, scientific, or documentary study, for, as Paul states in verse 5, it is now revealed "by the Spirit."

I. We need to be aware of the problem that the revelation is meant to solve.

a. We must begin by recognizing why the acceptance of the Gentiles in Jesus Christ is a clue to the unity that God provides for all persons everywhere. The unity of all things is now revealed throughout Christ Jesus, that those who were far off are now made nigh by the gospel. There has been a deep, thoroughgoing split between God and his created beings because of the work of his prime opponent, Satan, who has fomented and perpetuated the rift between good and evil, even to the extent of fostering warring and evil spirits within each human being, but especially between those who have learned to love God and his people and those who deny him in their hearts and seek to harm their fellow humans.

b. There are multiple names for the disunity, the opposition of those who help and those who hurt one another. The rift is evidenced in sin, murder, war, robbery, envy or jealousy, anger, cheating, lying, slavery, incest, and adultery. These and their variations strongly force people apart and prevent the joint operations necessary for beneficial society. These are the work of Satan, who was described with all his host in Milton's *Paradise Lost,* and who was seen in all his crafty deceptiveness in C. S. Lewis's *Screwtape Letters.*

c. The difficulty of bringing about the kind of unity humanity needs is seen by every parent, every teacher, and every pastor. It is the reason for military forces, governments, courts, and systems of "justice." Healing the basic disunity of human beings is sadly needed. When a man requested to be excused from jury duty, the judge reproved him by saying, "What if every citizen were like you, sir?" The man responded, "If every citizen were like me, Your Honor, there would be no need of courts."

d. Yes, the separation that matters is not only that between Jew and Gentile, which Paul specifically addresses, but the one between human and human; it is not only racial, gender-based, or age-related. The pervasiveness of harm caused by this radical split should become our unrelenting compulsion, as we seek to conquer it by him of whom Paul writes. It should force us to overcome the "mystery of evil" with the mystery revealed to Paul, who, though he considered himself the least, was made a minister of the promise in Christ through the gospel, the energy of God.

II. By the same energy, we must minister by lives of hope, grace, fellowship, and service—to fulfill the glory in Jesus Christ.

a. God healed—and can continue to heal—the great separation between all "Jews" and all "Gentiles," who are "strangers to the covenant of redemption." That healing is the key to his power to work in today's hearts and minds, today's families, today's communities, today's nations, today's world.

b. In this letter we see the solution to the mean and destructive separatism of nation from nation and of class from class. We see the pattern for all true community when each "esteems the other better than himself," we see the true Christian universality, when all seek not power of life over others, not profit at the expense of others, but joyous work for the benefit of all. All rests on the acceptance of the truth that "God is in Christ, reconciling the world to himself." Surely in the hierarchy of truths, this one tops everything and correlates all of it.

c. Life becomes a school of dedication, each moment exposing a spark of God's love as the learning is shared. There is a cosmic glow about Jesus Christ. It is the living, cosmic Jesus Christ who is the center of a great drama of unity, in which everything in Heaven and on Earth is to become one in Him. The Christian must be thoroughly Christian: Christian doctrine, Christian experience, and Christian ethics are inseparable.—John R. Rodman

Illustrations

FAITH AND STEADFASTNESS.   I was brought up with the doctrines of Calvinism, and a cardinal belief of Calvinism found expression in the resounding phrase "the final perseverance of the saints." By that was meant that a real believer can never finally fall from grace. The Arminians may believe that a man can be "saved today and lost tomorrow," but to Calvinists that is salvation by luck, not by grace! It is a comforting doctrine, and I still believe it. Knowing my own wayward heart, and the frailties of men in general, I know well that we can falter and fail and fall. We can turn our backs on God in stubborn disobedience, but he will never, never turn his back on us or cast us out of his strong everlasting arms.

It is a comforting doctrine, but not a sentimental doctrine. We are not released from making every effort to be steadfast, persevering, patiently enduring Christians. We must learn to remain strong and steady under the fierce winds of change, doubt, temptation, bitter disappointment. A faith that lacks steadfastness is useless to ourselves, the Church, and the purposes of God. One of John Wesley's secrets of success, it is claimed, was his "kingly neglect of trifles." He adamantly refused to allow any "trifles." such as frustrations, setbacks, sufferings, to deflect him from the main business of his life, his Master's business. "I love one that perseveres in dry duty," he once said. So too, does God! Saint Benedict of Nursia created his monastic family on the basis of *stabilitas,* "steadfastness," and the vow of his monks was to that and nothing more. It should be every Christian's vow. The grace of God will never fail us, and we should make every effort not to fail the grace of God.—John N. Gladstone

A FITTING ANSWER.   A man in the South, a Negro handyman, was asked by his white employer, a bank president, "John, why are the colored people spending all of their money going to court to get equal rights? All of the money and power and government in the South are on our side. How do you hope to get the things you want if we fight you?" The Negro thought a moment and answered, "S'pose God say so?"—Gardner Taylor

SERMON SUGGESTIONS

Topic: The New Road from Bethlehem
TEXT: Matt. 2:12

The wise men had been warned and they accepted the heavenly guidance. But you may think of it as being more than an indication of an altered itinerary, more than a topographical detail. After we have truly seen Jesus, something takes place in the soul which alters everything. (1) Here was a new experience. (2) The new experience entails a new responsibility and a new service of humanity.—Philip W. Lilley

Topic: The Power to See It Through

TEXT: Philem. 24; Col. 4:14; 2 Tim. 4:10

Here is the story of a man who made an excellent beginning and a wretched ending: Demas, my fellow worker; Demas; Demas forsook me. Obviously the qualities which make a good start possible are not identical with the qualities which see life through to the end. (1) Staying power is always associated with a certain central integrity of conscience. (2) Staying power is always associated with the experience of being captured by a cause, laid hold on by something greater than oneself to which one gives one's loyalty. (3) Staying power is commonly associated with profound resources of interior strength replenished by great faith.—Harry Emerson Fosdick

Worship Aids

CALL TO WORSHIP.   "The Spirit and the bride say, Come. And let him that heareth say, Come. And let him that is athirst come. And whosoever will, let him take the water of life freely" (Rev. 22:17).

INVOCATION.   Almighty God, thou who didst raise Jesus Christ from the dead, touch the dead and dying elements of our lives and usher us into the abundant life that thou hast promised to those who love thee. Remove from our hearts any destructive fear of the future, whether of the life that now is or of the life that is to come. Let our openness to thy Spirit and our worship of thee give thee access to our hearts, our homes, our work, and our play.

OFFERTORY SENTENCE.   "A man's life consisteth not in the abundance of the things which he possesseth" (Luke 12:15).

OFFERTORY PRAYER.   O God, we know that we cannot live by bread alone, but there are those who will not live because they have no bread; and there are those who are already dead in trespasses and sins because they have not received the bread of life. We bring you our offerings, that some may have bread and that some may have your quickening word. Bless us all as we give, and bless those whose hunger is satisfied and whose spiritual need is met because we care.

PRAYER.   God, we pray for thy Church, which is set today amid the perplexities of a changing order, and face-to-face with a great new task. We remember with love the nurture she gave to our spiritual life in its infancy, the tasks she set for our growing strength, the influence of the devoted hearts she gathers, the steadfast power for good she has exerted. When we compare her with all other human institutions, we rejoice, for there is none like her. But when we judge her by the mind of her Master, we bow in pity and contrition. Oh, baptize her afresh in the life-giving spirit of Jesus! Grant her a new birth, though it be with the travail of repentance and humiliation. Bestow upon her a more imperious responsiveness to duty, a swifter compassion with suffering, and an utter loyalty to the will of God. Put upon her lips the ancient gospel of her Lord. Help her to proclaim boldly the coming of the Kingdom of God and the doom of all that binds us. Multiply the God-conquered souls who open their hearts gladly to the light that makes us free, for all creation shall be in travail till these sons of God attain their glory.

We pray thee for those who amid all the knowledge of our day are still without knowledge; for those who hear not the sighs of the children that toil, nor the sobs of such as are wounded because others have made haste to be rich; for those who have never felt the hot tears of the mothers of the poor that struggle vainly against poverty and vice. Arouse them, we beseech thee, from their selfish comfort and grant them the grace of social repentance. Smite us all with the conviction that for us ignorance is sin, and that we are indeed our brother's keeper if our own hand has helped to lay him low. Though increase of knowledge bring increase of sorrow, may we turn without flinching to the light and offer ourselves as instruments of thy spirit in bringing order and beauty out of disorder and darkness.—Walter Rauschenbusch

LECTIONARY MESSAGE

Topic: The Promise Fulfilled
TEXT: Luke 2:41–52
Other Readings: 1 Sam. 2:18–20, 26; Ps. 148; Col. 3:12–17

The events of Bethlehem separated from the later life and ministry of Jesus would be nothing more than a pleasant story. But within the context of Jesus' life and ministry, the events of Bethlehem take on eternal significance. What happened at Bethlehem matters specifically because Jesus lived out his calling. What happened at Bethlehem matters specifically because Jesus fulfilled the promise of God. We can see God's promise fulfilled as Jesus teaches, performs mighty works, walks resolutely to the cross, and then is raised from the dead. But we can also see growing evidence of fulfillment as Jesus journeys to the Temple as a twelve-year-old boy.

I. *Jesus honors the past* (vv. 41–42). With his family, Jesus chooses to celebrate custom and honor heritage. Later he would remind his followers that he had come to fulfill the Law. But even here, as a twelve-year-old boy, Jesus keeps the tradition of God's people. We are reminded by these verses that this story known as the Christ Event is no new plan, but that it fits perfectly with God's desire from the beginning. By honoring the past, Jesus is already fulfilling and verifying the promise of God.

II. *Jesus embraces God's call in his life* (vv. 43–47). Even as a child, Jesus possesses depth of insight and understanding. Already he is aware of the purpose behind his presence. Significantly, Mary and Joseph find Jesus in the Temple both answering questions and asking questions. And those who hear him are amazed. By beginning to embrace what God has in mind for him, Jesus is fulfilling and guaranteeing the promise of God.

III. *Jesus abides with the Father* (vv. 48–49). The inner passion of this young life is to be about the business of the Father. Evidently, Jesus senses an inner desire to be about the things of God. And his extended presence in the Temple demonstrates both his desire and his willingness to give Himself to those matters. What his parents interpret as youthful misjudgment is actually a profound picture of proper priorities. Throughout his life, Jesus abides with his Father and thereby he fulfills the promise of God.

IV. *Jesus fulfills his purpose* (vv. 50–52). The entire purpose for Jesus' ministry revolves around his relationship with God and his relationship with human beings. Understanding that purpose, Jesus continues to mature and grow. Growing in wisdom and stature, and growing in favor with God and with others, Jesus demonstrates his resolve in becoming the person God has called him to be. As he would make clear later in his ministry, this calling is a calling that he will willingly accept. And even here as a young boy, Jesus is consciously and intentionally seizing the purpose that is uniquely his.

The promise of God will one day come to full completion. We can believe that because of what we know about Christmas. We can have confidence in that reality because of what we see in the life and ministry of Jesus. God has promised a Savior. God has invited his people to join in the preparation for the promise. God's people have been faithful in proclaiming the promise. The pronouncements of blessing have been sounded. And now the ultimate fulfillment of the promise is certain. The King has come! The kingdom of God is near!—Barry A. Stricker

SECTION III.
Messages for Communion Services

Topic: The Bread of the Angels
TEXT: Ps. 78:9–31

This psalm, like Psalms 105–107, is a "reminder" psalm, dealing with the history of Israel and the failure of the people to be faithful to God. The heading of the psalm calls it a "Maskil"–a Hebrew word meaning "instruction." The early verses of the psalm suggest that it was written to enhance the transmission of the faith from generation to generation. "I will utter dark sayings from of old," says the writer,

> things that we have heard and known,
> that our fathers have told us.
> We will not hide them from their
> children,
> but the glorious deeds of the Lord, and
> his might,
> and the wonders which he has wrought.
> (vv. 2–4)

What the writer proceeds to recall is God's rescue of Israel from the Egyptians and his care for them in the wilderness. But the Israelites were restless. They rebelled against God because they wanted food. "Can God spread a table in the wilderness?" they demanded. "God made water gush from a rock. Can he also give bread, or provide meat for his people?"

God did give bread and meat, says the writer. He opened the doors of heaven and rained down manna. No one is quite certain what manna was, though it is suspected that it was a whitish substance that forms on the tamarisk bushes of the desert of Sinai and other Middle Eastern deserts and is capable of sustaining human life for several days at a time. It may well have saved the Israelites from starvation at various intervals of their wilderness wanderings. "The grain of heaven," the psalmist calls it, and "the bread of the angels." And God gave them quails to eat–apparently an abundance of quails, as thick as the sand of the seas. God did spread a table in the wilderness. And still the people sinned and rebelled, wanting more. Finally, says the psalmist, God's anger could not be restrained, and he slew the strongest men of Israel–probably through wars and skirmishes with other tribes in Canaan. The Israelites forgot what God had done for them, and as a consequence they suffered constant defeat and humiliation.

Now what does this have to do with us? Why should what happened to a tribe of nomads in an ancient desert have any meaning in a day of computers and rocketry? It doesn't–unless the psalmist was right, that the story needs to be passed down from generation to generation, so that we don't make the same mistakes.

We know something of wilderness don't we? Maybe not literal deserts, but deserts of the spirit, certainly. Life isn't always what we bargained for, is it? How many times have I seen a man or a woman, unhappy in some luckless marriage, weeping with head in hands and crying, "This isn't what I expected at all!" Or how many times have I heard parents agonizing over some wayward, rebellious child, "We never thought that having children would come to this!"

How many of you, when a job was lost, when bills were due, when depression set in, when expectations were dashed, said, "Oh, I don't think I can make it, life is too hard!" Life is often more than we bargained for, isn't it?

To the ancient Israelites, the desert was an evil place. Not only was it a place without plants and food, a place of scorching heat by day and icy wind by night. It was a place inhabited by demons, by evil beings that sought the lives of those who trespassed there. It was *anti*-life. And don't our lives seem that way sometimes? They get into wilderness places that actually seem to be anti-life. Our souls are screaming inside us, our ears are bursting, and to die would be a relief.

And then the psalmist's question becomes real to us: "Can God spread a table in the wilderness"? Can God enter these desert places with our souls and care for them there? What can he do that would possibly make a difference when we feel this way?

Only the heart of faith can answer such a question. Do you know what I mean by "the heart of faith"? I mean the heart that has learned to trust God despite all outward circumstances. This is what the psalmist was concerned about; he wanted his children and their children after them to understand that God is faithful even when we are feeling neglected and hurt and cast away. The heart of faith is the heart that remembers the goodness of God even when life seems to be all pain and frustration. It is the heart so fixed on prayer and love that it rejoices in small things while bearing large burdens.

There was a woman who had had many troubles. I forget what they all were. She had gone through a divorce, I think, and had lost her job. She was feeling desperately unhappy. As a child, she had always gone to her father with her problems, so she called up her father in Florida and asked if she could come to visit. He said, of course. "She drove down to Florida and poured out her troubles to him. Afterward, they went walking by the ocean, and strolled out to the end of a pier as they watched the sun setting over the water. Holding her father's arm, she gazed at the colors in the sky and said, "If all the good moments in life were put together, they would last perhaps twenty min-

utes, wouldn't they? "Yup," said her father, patting her had. "Precious, aren't they?"

You see the difference? That's the heart of faith. The small moments are precious. The manna in the wilderness. The quail when there is no meat. The little gifts of God that remind us he is there—or *here*.

"The grain of heaven," the psalmist called the manna. "The bread of the angels."

And here we are at the Lord's Table again. We don't have the bread of the angels. We have the bread of the Son himself. "Your fathers are the manna in the wilderness," said Jesus, "and they died. This is the bread which comes down from heaven, that a man may eat of it and not die. I am the living bread . . . if anyone eats of this bread, he will live forever; and the bread which I shall give for the life of the world is my flesh" (John 67:49–51).

I said that the psalm is a reminder psalm. The Table too is a reminder. "As often as you do this, do it in remembrance of me." God *can* spread a table in the wilderness, can't he? He can speak to us in the darkest passages of our lives, because his only Son passed through the darkness too. Have you thought it was all over for you? Is your life a mess? Do you blunder on from day to day, hurting those you love and despairing of finding the way out? This bread and cup are for you. They are reminders of the Lord's presence, even in the wilderness of life. And they will give you strength, like manna in the wilderness, for going on.—John Killinger

Topic: It Isn't Easy to Be Still
TEXT: Ps. 46:20
The English poet, W. H. Davies, has a poem entitled "Leisure." Two lines of it are:

What is this life if full of care,
We have no time to stand and stare?

How apt these words are in describing the world of our time! The Psalmist wrote: "Be still and know that I am God."

Are we ever ready to be still? Can any of us create conditions under which God can get through to us?

I. *We must learn to be still and look upon the beauty of this world.* All around us lies the grandeur of the world of nature. A mountain climber in the Swiss Alps had stopped to rest halfway up, and being a cynic he scratched on a rock the words: "There is no God" (from Ps. 14:1). When he reached the top, he was struck with awe and wonder as he looked out upon the snowcapped minarets and the endless peaks and crags. On his way down, however, he stopped by the same rock and revised what he had written: "The fool says in his heart there is no God" (the whole of verse 1).

II. *We must be still and look at and consider the lives of those around us.* How often people meet us or pass in front of us and we do not even see them. Be still, and realize they are not just some other human beings! Through the heart and soul of every person who is kind, honest, and helpful, God is working. We must never forget that we are all God has to work his will through.

Now this suggests a further need: be still at times and ask ourselves not only, what do we see in others, but equally important, what do others see in us? It was said of Henry Drummond, the great Scottish scientist and Christian of the nineteenth century, that "wherever he was, whether in the cluttered laboratory or the dingy classroom or the crowded railway station, he always appeared like golden embroidery on homespun gray."

III. *Another suggestion: We must be still in order to sort our our priorities.* What is the real source of your daily strength and mine? The Psalmist said: "Be still and know that I am God." What he really meant was: "Give in and admit that I am God." Stop running your own show in your own way and by your own limited wisdom and power.

Remember Jesus' parable about the Pharisee and Publican who came simultaneously into the Temple to pray. Jesus is here telling us that our lifestyle is framed by what we set up as our highest priority in the presence of the living God. Some people, however, set up as their chief priority social respectability or denominational exclusiveness (only we know how to worship God right). I think of a town in which I once lived where a lady pointed to the stately Gothic church on the town square and said with a sense of superficial pride: "That is the church to be seen in on Sunday morning in this town." As the great Scottish divine Samuel Rutherford remarked, "Your heart is not the compass God steers by." Or as the Chinese Christian Madame Chiang Kai-shek asserted: "There is a limit to one's physical assets; there is no limit to one's spiritual resources."

IV. *To be still is like that old sign at the railroad crossing: stop, look, and listen.* And in the matter of being still, the thing we tend to overlook is listening. There is much God wants to say to us, but we don't listen; we come with an armful of demands: Give us this and give us that. The greatest heroes of the Judeo-Christian faith were those who said in the deep stillness of life: "Speak, Lord, for your servant hears."

What disturbs many of us in these times is the absence in so much of our public worship of an urgent wish to be still. No one is engaged in readying themselves for the declaration of a word from God. There, before us, is the Bible, symbolizing the Word of God as the "only infallible rule of faith and practice." There is the pulpit where the Word of God is proclaimed and interpreted. And there is the Holy Table where that same Word is demonstrated in action in the Sacrament. Before such holy things, who should be otherwise than STILL? Everyone of us knows the 23rd Psalm, where the focus of the writer's song is upon God and his shepherd:

The Lord is my shepherd,
I shall not want;
He makes me lie down in
green pastures.
He leads me beside still waters.

The next verse comes as a sort of corollary to our tarrying beside still waters—"He restores my soul." Only in the quiet of God's presence, as we listen, are our lives given new resolve to be and to do what he wants us to become for his sake and our own sake and for the sake of our world.— Donald Macleod

Topic: Strutting His Stuff
TEXT: Job 2:1–10
Gardner Taylor, retired Pastor of the Concord Baptist Church in New York City, was asked what image he has of God and Dr. Taylor said, "First I see Personality, and I find it very hard not to see personality apart from gender, so I continue to use the male pronoun, but I do not believe God's

personality includes the female gender as well and is, in fact, more than gender. God is personality and that personality is marked by compassion and intelligence. God is a personality with mercy and wisdom."

Dr. Taylor got that image of God from the long discussion about the personality of God in the Bible. Much of that debate about who God is comes in this book of Job. Look at the way the whole book begins. It begins with giving us a slice of one possibility for God's personality in the opening discussion. God is hanging out with his crowd at the mall. They are talking and joking about how things are going. And then one of the fraternity comes in late. Hey there Satan, what's happening? Satan says, "Not much." God says, "Where have you been?" Satan says, "Just cruising around. Here and there. Just kind of checking things out." They have had this conversation before and God has allowed Satan to take away all of Job's material blessings and now this God gloats, "Didn't I tell you what a winner my servant Job is? Did you see the way he adores me, still worships me? There ain't nothing he wouldn't do for me. He loves me. Wow, isn't that a kick." God strutting around bragging about his servant Job. So Satan says, "He still only does it cause it pays. He only hangs out with you cause you take care of him. So you let me waste a few cows and a couple of his children died, he still hasn't really suffered." You know what they say, "As long as you've got your health, you have everything." He still has everything that is important to him. You saw those reports of the people on the ferry that capsized, how it was every life for itself. He still has his life. If you really want to see how devoted Job is to you, put a little hurt on his body and see how he does. Now that would really be adoration if he worships you then.

The story of Job begins with a definition of God as personality, but it is a personality that is exactly like yours and mine in that it can be tempted not only to do that which is less than good, the God in this story of Job is a God who can be tempted by the best to destroy that which is good. Satan tempts God in this story and God yields to the temptation to sacrifice the good for the possibility of the better. In the story of Job, even God is tempted by the better, by Satan say-

ing that Job's worship now is nice but it would mean even more if you could get Job to worship you in the midst of physical pain. Even Job's wife says, "Just give up, Job, and curse God and die."

So while Job and his friends are discussing the whole theological issue of God's justice—whether or not the bad things that happen to us are God's retributive justice and the good things that happen to us in this life are God's rewards for good behavior, which Job never is willing to accept—surrounding that story is the possible discussion of a God who can be tempted to sacrifice the good for the possibility of the better.

And we are still very much caught up in the necessity of this debate over the nature and personality of God. The more international and cosmopolitan we become, the more politically correct we become, the more tempted we are to say something like, "It doesn't really matter who God is or what we call him, we all worship the same God and are going to the same place." And yet, it is out of what we believe about God and the personality of God that we shape how we are to live and how we are to die. A college recruiter from Harvard told a group of high school seniors, "Harvard has terminated its ties with the religious community which founded it. It is now seeking to preserve three links with the past: the pursuit of excellence, the values of openness, and the contribution of service." But how does one establish excellence if it is not in comparison with some God-given standard? How can one achieve excellence by the way of openness? It is only by commitment that one obtains the means to accomplish greatness. How does one determine what is service to others until one has an understanding of the purpose and destiny of human life? Isn't there that story about the Boy Scout on the corner helping widows across the street. Someone asks how it is going. He says, fine, he has helped four widows cross the street. The other says, that is very good. The Boy Scout says, yes, and three of them did not want to go. How can you be of service until you know what is really needed. It is out of what we understand God to value that we discover what we are to value. It is out of what we believe God will keep and preserve for us that we seek to accumulate treasures. It is out of what we understand the personality and nature of God to be that we can live in fear and guilt or joy and hope. So indeed it matters to us where we get our picture and our understanding of the personality, the compassion and wisdom of God.

That is what makes this table and this meal so central for us as Christian people. It is where we see the personality, the compassion, the power, the love and the wisdom of God. That is why we continue to cling to this scandal of the Cross that in this one person, Jesus, God has shown us Himself. For in the love and grace of Jesus Christ, we have seen the Father and know that God is not out to condemn the world but to save the world and that his love and mercy are gifts to all who will simply stop trying to "justify themselves," as Dr. Larson put it, and begin to live on the good news that God has already prepared a way into his kingdom for us and a life in his service for each of us who are ready to enjoy it.

Here at this table in the life of Jesus Christ we see that all of our goodness can never stand before and never add a thing to the holiness of God, and all of our evil in this world is nothing but a live coal in the middle of the ocean of God's mercy. Here we see ourselves not in comparison with each other, but before the power and wonder of God's love, and hear that invitation, "Come unto me, and join me at the banquet feast of the people of God. Come then to the joyful feast of the people of God."–Rick Brand

Topic: Rebounding from Rejection
TEXT: Isa. 53:1–3

Rejection hurts. Sometimes we try to pretend it does not matter, but it does. When we say, "I could care less," we often really mean, "I wish I did not care so much!" No matter how we try to explain it away or depreciate the source, being rejected by others causes us excruciating pain.

For many, rejection starts early in life. It might begin with the gnawing suspicion that parents favor one child over the other. Some who do not lose the battle of sibling rivalry, simply never experience the esteem-building approval of their parents. Nothing they do is ever good enough for their parents.

Others feel rejection when they do not excel in sports. There is intense anxiety when children line up for the choosing of teams for a ballgame. Adults often forget how painful it is to be the last one chosen or not to be chosen at all.

Or, who can forget the longing to be popular–perhaps the most powerful drive of the adolescent experience? Do you remember what it felt like not to be tapped for membership in the honor society . . . not to be awarded the part in the school play . . . not to be asked to sing the solo part? Do you remember your first infatuation and the pain of discovering that your heartthrob did not even know you existed?

Yet rejection is hardly kid's stuff. Some of us can still remember the anguish of opening letters of rejection from the college or university of our first or second choice. Many who never made it to college–or who made it but did not finish–often carry a self-imposed stigma.

Adults know rejection. The only difference is that the stakes are higher in adulthood. Acceptance is essential to our success on the job. Being bypassed for a long-anticipated promotion or losing a position only adds to the fear of future failure. Even the very successful worry about staying on top.

Marriage certainly offers no guarantee of acceptance and affirmation. The truth is, some of the most painful experiences of rejection can happen between husbands and wives. Constant criticism, withheld affections, lack of encouragement, and total shutdown of communication cause many a spouse to feel put off or put down.

One middle-aged woman who just received her divorce papers said to me: "I feel totally rejected. I feel like an orange with all the juice squeezed out. The best years of my life are gone, and all that's left is a broken heart and shattered dreams."

Rejection is one of the most painful–and universal–experiences of life. It makes us afraid. Memories of rejection in the past make us leery, cautious, and restrained. We flinch with fear of what people can do or say to hurt us. The last thing we want–the last thing we will allow–is to get close to anyone again. Why should we put ourselves in a vulnerable position and risk being devastated again?

Deprived of deep, meaningful relationships, this fear of rejection also robs us of courage. We become solicitous and compliant. Like a chameleon, we begin to blend into the background of other people's values and attitudes.

Often we are willing to do almost anything to keep approval and acceptance coming our way. We hedge our convictions, adjust our values, and keep our opinions to ourselves in order not to do or say anything that will cause others to reject us. The result of that intense psychological maneuvering is that we depend upon other people far too much. The drive to be liked ends in panic over the possibility of being rejected.

Isaiah's prophesy foresaw the rejection of the Messiah. He wrote:

He was despised and rejected by
men, a man of sorrows, and
familiar with suffering. Like
one from whom men would turn
their faces he was despised,
and we esteemed him not.

(53:3)

In the life of Jesus, this prophecy came true. He was misunderstood by his family, rejected by the leaders of Israel, and denied and betrayed by his disciples.

How did he cope? How did he avoid playing his life to the crowds in order to win their acceptance and approval? How did he withstand the disappointment of his own family's displeasure? How did he keep it all together even when his closest friends turned on him? What was the secret of his ability to withstand the pain of rejection?

Without appearing overly simplistic, the Gospels make it clear that, for Jesus, pleasing God was the first priority of his life. That was all that was ultimately important to him.

It helped see him through all the difficulties with his family. For instance, following his first REAL confrontation with his mother and Joseph, Jesus courageously declared the intent of his life: ". . . I must be about my Father's business," he said (Luke 2:49).

On another occasions, when his family became concerned about his welfare, and came to take him home, Jesus responded:

Who are my mother and my broth-

ers? . . . Then he looked at those seated in a circle around him and said, "Here are my mother and my brothers! Whoever does God's will is my brother and my sister and mother" (Mark 3:33–35).

In other words, Jesus found his support and affirmation in those who view things from the perspective of God. Others were simply unable to comprehend the significance of a life concerned only with pleasing God. It is still true that oversensitivity to other people's attitudes is often due to our desire to please the wrong people.

When Peter would have stood in his way to prevent his going to Jerusalem to face the full fury of those determined to destroy him, Jesus replied: "Get behind me, Satan! . . . You do not have in mind the things of God, but he things of men" (Mark 8:33).

In his benevolent attempts to persuade Jesus to avoid the certain rejection of Israel's leaders, Peter had played into Satan's hands. In his response, Jesus reminded his friend that we will never be free to the potential hurts of rejection until pleasing God becomes our first priority.

Even when he suffered the ultimate rejection of men, Jesus remained true to God. The prophet Isaiah describes the pain that resulted in verses 7 and 9.

Luke, however, reminds us of how secure our Lord was in the Father's love for him. When rejection had run its course and his enemies had done everything they could do to him, in the end Jesus committed himself to His Father's keeping. His final words were: "Father, into your hands I commit my spirit" (Luke 23:46).

Our goal as Christians is not to win a popularity contest but to serve the Master. Obedience to him often will run counter to the values of our friends and work associates. We will sometimes get into trouble because of what we believe. Our stand on certain issues may bring criticism and hostility. Our priorities will make us targets for ridicule.

I am convinced that the reason so few of us share our faith is that we fear rejection. Think of the times you have not talked about what Christ means to you because you feared being labelled a pious prude. Recall those times when you remained silent while a person's character was assassinated with gossip or ideas were expressed that were contrary to your convictions. It happens almost every day.

That reluctance to do battle for truth reminds us that we are playing our lives to the wrong audience—concerned with pleasing the wrong person. In fact, when we decide to please the right person—Jesus Christ—for the right reason, in the right way, rejection may be a sign that we are making an impact.

Living to please God may seem like a momentous step. It will mean breaking lifelong patterns and letting go of false securities. At its basic level, the fear of rejection is rooted in our profound need to be loved and the false notion that other people ought to love us as much as we need to be loved. Yet only God can meet that aching need.

The elements we share in the Lord's Supper—the bread and the cup—remind us how severed is the pain of rejection. The broken body—the spilled blood—underscore the incredibly high price of rejection.

Few things make us more aware of our need for the Lord than rejection. The only final cure for the frowning face of rejection is his smiling face of love and acceptance. These elements also remind us of how secure we are in God's love for us.

The prophet also sounded that note of Divine acceptance. Earlier, he had written:

Come now, let us reason together, says the Lord; though your sins are like scarlet, they shall be as white as snow; though they be red like crimson, they shall become like wool (Isa. 1:18).—Gary C. Redding

ILLUSTRATIONS FOR COMMUNION

A SPECIAL LOVE. What is it that distinguishes God's covenant love from the noblest forms of human love? It is so splendidly spontaneous. Love is not forced from God by some power outside, not seduced from God by our lovable personalities. Quite the opposite. God's love goes out to men and women who are sinners, who are utterly unworthy of love divine, cannot demand that love, become God's beloved simply because he wants it so, can love God only because he loves them. This kind of love we Christians find "new," discover in its most radical form, when God gives us his only Son—to reveal that love and to live it in very death.—Walter Burghardt, S.J.

AS JESUS LIFTS US UP TO GOD. We often speak of Jesus as dying for us; we sometimes speak of him rising for us; we rarely think of his ascending for us. But that was a thought in the minds of his early followers. They could not think of their Jesus as doing anything for Himself only. Wherever he was and whatever he was, he was for them. And after his ascension they thought of him as for them toward God. You remember how Paul states it as the climax of what Jesus does for Christians. "It is Christ Jesus that died, yea rather, that was raised from the dead, who is at the right hand of God, who also maketh intercession for us."—Henry Sloane Coffin

RESTING IN GOD. As attachments lighten and idols fall, we will enjoy increasing freedom. But at the same time our hearts will feel an even greater, purer, deeper ache. This particular pain is one that never leaves us.

Authentic spiritual wholeness, by its very nature, is open-ended. It is always in the process of becoming, always incomplete. Thus we ourselves must also be always incomplete. If it were otherwise, we could never exercise our God-given right to participate in ongoing creation. The course of our lives is precisely as Saint Augustine indicated: our hearts will never rest, nor are they meant to rest, until they rest in God. This precious restlessness is mediated by and manifested through our physical being, through the combined minute strugglings of the cells of our brains and bodies as they seek harmony and balance in their endless adjustment to circumstances.

Our fundamental dis-ease, then, is at once a precise neurological phenomenon and a most precious gift from God. It is not a sign of something wrong, but of something more profoundly right than we could ever dream of. It is no problem to be solved, no pathology to be treated, no disease to be cured. It is our true treasure, the most precious thing we have. It is God's song of love in our soul. —Gerald G. May, M.D.

REMEMBER! I recall Rabbi Abraham Joshua Heschel's startling affirmation: Much of what the Bible demands can be summed up in a single word–*remember!* Ancient Israel was a community of faith vitalized by memory, a people that knew God by reflecting not on the mysteries of nature but on its own history. To actualize was to retain within time and space the memory and the mystery of God's saving presence. And Elie Wiesel, that remarkable Jewish storyteller who feels guilty because he survived the Holocaust, has reminded us that, for Jews, to forget is a crime against justice and memory: if you forget, you become the executioner's accomplice.–Walter J. Burghardt, S.J.

SECTION IV.
Messages for Funeral Services

SERMON SUGGESTIONS

Topic: A Christmas Message of Peace
TEXT: Luke 2:1–14, 21–32

The death of a loved one is never easy, but to experience the death of a husband and father at Christmas is especially difficult. While the rest of the world is celebrating the birth of the Christ-child, those of us here will always connect this season with the death of John. At this moment, we are having a difficult time connecting with the joy, the glitter, the excitement of the season. The warmth and hope of Christmas seems like a distant echo to us. So why read Luke's account of the birth of Jesus? Why bring Christmas to a funeral?

Because, if the message of Christmas cannot speak to us at this moment, if it cannot address this deep hole in our spirits, it cannot speak to us at the better times of life.

If I were asked to name one word that summarizes the message of Christmas, it would be *peace*. When the angels appeared to the shepherds, they blessed them with the peace born of God's favor. Many of the carols we sing at this season of the year speak directly of or paint the picture of peace—"Silent Night," "Away in the Manger," "O Little Town of Bethlehem," and so on. God came to bring peace on this earth. It is peace that a broken and hurting world needs desperately. It is a sense of peace that those of us gathered in this place want, for our world has been disrupted by death. We would like for the tumultuous voices of pain and grief to be silenced. We long for that sense of stability and order that death has

taken from us. Today we felt like crying with the prophet, "My soul is bereft of peace; I have forgotten what happiness is" (Lam. 3:17 NRSV).

One of my favorite Christmas carols is "It Came upon the Midnight Clear." One of the verses reads like this:

> All ye, beneath life's crushing load,
>   whose forms are bending low,
> who toil along the climbing way with
>   painful steps and slow,
> Look now! for glad and golden hours
>   come swiftly on the wing:
> O rest beside the weary road, and hear
>   the angels sing.
> Will you rest with me beside the weary
>   road of grief for a moment and hear
>   afresh the angels' song of peace?

In Scripture, the word for peace comes from the Hebrew word *shalom*. That word means far more than the absence of conflict, though it surely means that. In its fullest sense, shalom, or peace, describes a sense of wholeness, or completeness, or well-being. It is of that peace the angels sang. It is that peace that surrounds us today.

When I visited John in the hospital shortly before he died, Betty related to me her lifelong concern for his salvation. She also shared with me that the day before he slipped into his coma, he asked God to forgive him and to come into his life. He accepted God's offer of peace. The broken relationship between God and John was reconciled. She related to me how after that experience, John seemed so much more at peace with himself and what was happening to him. We can celebrate that John found that peace God offers to each of us.

We can also celebrate that John is now at peace. His lifelong struggle with illness is now over. Because of his new relationship with God, we are confident that John is secure in the arms of God. For him all sickness, strife, pain, and death are no more. As John heard a voice from heaven say, "Blessed are the dead who from now on die in the Lord . . . they will rest from their labors" (Rev. 14:13 NRSV).

We can celebrate God's promise of peace in the midst of our pain and grief. In John's Gospel, after the crucifixion of Jesus, the disciples lock themselves in a room to be alone with their fears and grief. Suddenly Jesus appears in their midst and says, "Peace be with you." From that moment everything changed for them. Jesus' presence transformed their sense of hopelessness and despair to one of hope and excitement. His presence gave them new direction and purpose for living.

When the angel appeared to Mary telling her that she was chosen to give birth to the Messiah, the angel told Mary the name of her son was to be Immanuel, "God with us." Over and over in Scripture, salvation is described as the presence of God among his people. Israel was delivered from Egypt because God intervened in person in their behalf. Moses was able to lead the people through the wilderness, because God was in their midst as a pillar of fire or cloud. Joshua was able to win battles because God was with him. When God is present, all is well.

The message of the Christmas story is that God is present. Jesus is in our midst. Even in the middle of chaotic circumstances, we can live with hope, joy, and purpose, because God has not abandoned us. The same God in whose presence John now stands is with us. He will lead us through the darkest valley and give us rest and strength. The psalmist writes,

There are many who say, "O that we might see some good!
Let the light of your face shine on us, O Lord!"
You have put gladness in my heart more than when their grain and wine abound.

I will both lie down and sleep in peace;
for you alone O Lord, make me lie down in safety.

(Ps. 4:6–8 NRSV)

The angels' blessing of peace does not have to sound as a distant echo for us this Christmas. If we listen closely with our hearts, we will experience the presence of God with us. In his presence we will find strength, hope, joy, and life.

May the peace of Christ rule in your hearts this Christmas.–Jim Holladay

Topic: God in the Times of Life
TEXT: Eccl. 3:1–15

"For everything there is a season, and a time for every matter under heaven. . . . He has made everything suitable for its time; moreover he has put a sense of past and future into their minds. . . . I know that whatever God does endures forever. . . . That which is, already has been; that which is to be, already is; and God seeks out what has gone by."

The writer of Ecclesiastes describes well the human condition. Every time I hear the words of this passage, I am reminded of the amazing ambiguity of life. Life and death, war and peace, love and hate, gain and loss, joy and mourning all occur side by side at all times and in every place. Even as we gather to mourn the loss of our sister Gladys, in another place another family gathers to celebrate the birth of a new son or daughter. As we concern ourselves about how we will adjust to life without our loved one, another family wonders how they will adjust to the presence of a new family member.

Life is seldom one-dimensional. Even at this moment, those of us in this room experience a complex range of emotions. We are sad, because we will miss the strength, the dedication, the joy that Gladys brought to our lives. We are relieved that she did not suffer in death. We are angry because her death seemed so unnecessary. We have both given to one another and received words of comfort.

Yet our primary experience today is grief and mourning. These are powerful feelings and experiences. Grief can overwhelm our thoughts and our dreams. Grief barges in on our lives when we need to focus on other matters. Grief can sap our strength and cause us to wonder if life is really worth all this struggle and misery. Grief can obscure our vision of God's presence.

Over the next weeks and months, as you struggle through the process of grieving–a process that can lead to a deeper affirmation of life, living may become more complex and confusing. You may experience sadness in the middle of celebrations. You may find yourself laughing when you think you should be crying. You may wonder when life is going to get back to normal.

Here it is time to be reminded of the words of the writer of Ecclesiastes. All of these experiences are a part of life. Normal living means moving back and forth between dancing and mourning, death and birth, love and hate, war and peace, crying and laughter. What is normal? It is living each day with the realization that it holds potential for good and bad, success and failure, tragedy and triumph.

Now you may be asking, "Where is the comfort in that? Are we not supposed to be here to receive words of support and encouragement? How am I supposed to look forward to the future?"

And you are not alone in asking those questions. The writer of Ecclesiastes wondered about the meaning of life as observed in the human experience. Indeed, he concluded at one point that "all is vanity," and that "the dead . . . are more fortunate than the living."

Yet he did not fall into despair nor allow his grief to overtake him. Though he could not find meaning in the consistent inconsistency of human existence, he did affirm that life has meaning. In the midst of the ups and downs of life, the writer discovered a source of hope, a place to stand, a consistent center.

Hear again his words:

"God has made everything suitable for its time; moreover he has put a sense of past and future into their minds, yet they cannot find out what God has done from the beginning to the end. . . . That which is, already has been; that which is to be, already is; and God seeks out what has gone by."

No matter what came his way in life, the writer discovered one thing was constant. No matter how undependable others may be, one thing could be counted on. No matter how unpredictable today may be, one thing was predictable. The writer discovered that God's presence and God's concern was a given, whether he was laughing or crying, living or dying, dancing or mourning. What gave him hope, what gave him a reason to live, was finding his strength and his reason for living, not in the circumstances of life, or in other persons, but in the wisdom, strength, and presence of God. It was his understanding that his life was in God's hands that gave him the courage and strength to face whatever the day may bring.

In his letter to the church in Rome, the apostle Paul wrote, "We do not live to ourselves, and we do not die to ourselves. If we live, we live to the Lord, and if we die, we die to the Lord; so then whether we live or whether we die, we are the Lord's. For to this end Christ died and lived again, so that he might be Lord both of the dead and the living" (Rom. 14:79 NRSV).

Like the writer of Ecclesiastes, Paul reminds us that our lives are in God's hands. Gladys knew that all the days of her earthly life. She knows that completely today. As we struggle through this loss and the grief that comes with it, let us hear Paul and the writer of Ecclesiastes remind us to trust our lives to the Lord. When circumstances sap our strength and threaten to turn hope into despair, let us turn our lives toward the Lord who holds the past, present, and future in his hands. Let us trust our way to the Lord who knows us better than we know ourselves. Let us remember, when we feel most alone, that God will not abandon us. He will seek us out, because we are his. When we feel most alone and pained by our separation from Gladys, let us remember that Christ is "Lord of both the dead and the living," and in him we are never finally separated from one another.

In the days and weeks to come, do not run from pain or joy. Do not try to avoid the valleys or the mountaintops. In whatever time you are experiencing, trust your life into the eternally present hands of God. He is present and loves you through all the times of life.–Jim Holladay

Topic: Remembrance of the Dead
TEXT: Matt. 25:31, 34–40

Many among us have taken part in services in memory of victims of violence who were killed because of their religious beliefs and of their preaching in word and action the biblical message of redemptive love. At times we may have marked the occasion with programs red in color, signifying the blood of martyrs; other times we have preferred the green of hope. We have never been able to present a scroll that could list all those who throughout history have given their lives that we might be liberated.

When we honor those forebears, we do so having made the passage from initial devastation to peaceful remembrance. We can even rejoice that these men and women were so struck by the gospel message that they cared enough for others to sacrifice their own well-being in serving them.

For many here at this assembly the death of someone we love may be too recent for us to consider these moments of contemplation a celebration. We can at least be grateful for the Church's encouragement to us tonight to pause and recall memorable times with those who are now safely in the hands of God.

Well-meaning friends often urge us to seek distractions, to move on with our lives. The Gospel suggests actions that are memorials of loving care, signs of our faith that in reaching out to others we are following in the steps of the first Christians. I doubt that any one of us could have been more tempted than Mary to ask, "Why?" as she kept the death watch of her son with John and other disciples. Yet, after a quiet, somewhat hidden life she accepted the commission, "Woman, behold your son," and widened her motherhood beyond that of Jesus to the Church being born. Certainly, her remembrances were both bitter and sweet, like gall and honey; on that Friday the peace and well-being associated with the mystery of resurrection were yet to come.

Yet, even before that assurance of Sunday morn, Mary and John turned outward to each other in faithful obedience to the testament of Jesus. That care, that compassion of two sorrowing persons for each other, was soon extended to the frightened gathering in the Cenacle, then to puzzled followers as the Easter message spread, on to the cheering thousands at Pentecost. Mary and John, united at the moment of the violent death of Jesus, continue to inspire us with their role in the founding era of a community pledged to justice through peace, to a sect whose members in their love and care for one another were always open to welcoming others.

In any naming of the dead we all know the list of the faithful is incomplete; any roll call is limited. Tonight as we name loved ones, let us think of them as representative of those no longer in need of any conversion of life. May we ask for the grace we need so we too will hear one day, "Truly, I tell you, just as you did it to one of the least of these who are members of my family, you did it to me."—Grace Donovan, S.U.S.C.

Topic: The Strength of Love: A Funeral Meditation for Faye (Chris) Moyer

TEXT: The Song of Songs 8:6–7

Regardless of what others might think or say, we pastors are a fortunate lot! Why? Because we can extend our hands in open sensitivity, and people will place the key to their hearts and lives in our palms. What a blessing we have! You open your homes to us. You open your lives to us. You gift us with your joys, and share with us your sorrows. Who else can claim such an honor and such a blessed privilege? As a pastor I have received blessings untold, from countless names and faces. They have been there, the people of God, offering the graceful opportunity to share their laughter and their tears. Time and again, I've been invited to remove my shoes and step upon the sacred soils of human triumph and tragedy. I've been there to see the beaming smiles of new parents, and have seen the tears shed by the sick, the dying, the bereaved.

We pastors are fortunate indeed! And it is all because of people like you. Opening your wounds; pouring out your anxieties; grafting our lives to your own. Let the world scoff and scorn! But let it also see that there is a Christian community. Alive! In love! Sharing and bearing the cross of human compassion and concern!

And once again, by the grace of God, I was invited into the sacred soils of the love shared by Jim and Chris. Don't ever take that privilege for granted! To be welcomed in this way is nothing short of a blessing. Whenever we are invited into the private sanctuary of another's personal pain or joy or sorrow, we should enter reverently. Enter quietly and listen as they tell you of the ups and downs, the highs and lows, the give and take of what life has been. We must enter with our hands extended and hearts open, ready to receive the gifts such persons will give. So, I'll tell you of the gifts I received from Jim and Chris.

This was no mere fairy-tale romance! No prince on a white steed or damsel in distress. What they shared with me, the gift I received, was the power of honest, courageous, and steadfast love. Jim and Chris shared a "love as strong as death." This love is genuine. Honest enough to admit to shortcomings and inadequacies. Courageous enough to face the trials and tribulations of life. Steadfast! Enduring years of illness, shattered dreams, unfulfilled desires! They have gifted us with a living testimonial to the power of such love!

Dare I even say it?! Jim and Chris enjoyed a love that "burned like a blazing fire, like a mighty flame!" That flame continued to burn throughout the dark night of uncertainty. The fires of their love touched your lives. When you were cold, it gave warmth. When you were in your own personal darkness, it gave light. And if you ever doubted that love could abide, the glowing fire of their love removed such doubt!

The "mighty waters" of their personal pain never smothered that flame of love! The rivers of anxiety, of sickness, and of struggle could not "wash it away"! Chris sustained Jim with her loyalty and love. Jim nurtured Chris through his presence and expressed concerns. And as I watched this couple in those last hours, I couldn't help but thank God for their lives, their loyalty, and their love. As I watched Ann, Jeff, Steve, and Mary Alice, I couldn't help but feel that somehow, through some act of God's grace, this family had been consecrated by the love of these two people. But there was another gift that I received.

I entered Chris's room to give. But as I left her side, I felt that I had been gifted. Gifted with her warmth and acceptance. Gifted with her smile and gentle manner. Gifted with her support and encouragement. Even more, I had been gifted with her love! Are you aware that the name *Faye* means "Faithful"? In the heart and life of this precious woman, you and I were gifted with a faithful friend. What more praise could a person receive than to say that in

every act, in every thought, in every gesture of concern, this woman lived up to her name—"Faithful!" The name *James* means "May God protect"! In their marriage, within their family, with their friends, this couple embodied the union of their names: "May God protect the Faithful!" Through Chris's love, our faith has been strengthened; through Jim's compassion and care, we have indeed been "protected"!

Jim, the love you shared with your wife is "as strong as death"! No! It is stronger yet! For the love you have shared is nothing less than the love of God poured into your hearts and lives. And look at the love of God, radiant in the life, and death, and resurrection of Christ!

Death is a mystery we cannot fully comprehend! Death has separated you from your beloved wife. And I know it's painful. I know that you will miss her dearly, and even long for her presence. But I also know that Christ has tasted death, and by the grace of God, now lives and reigns supreme. I believe that Christ will be with you, to share your sorrow and to ease your pain. I know that God's love broke the chains of death's grip. I believe that because Christ lives, Faye shall live also. I believe that one Day the love of God which is stronger than death, will call us from death to life. And, I believe that on that Day we will be reunited with those who have gone before us in death.

In this world of skepticism and doubt, I believe in the promises of God. God will not leave us alone in the hour of sorrow and loneliness. Our Lord never abandoned Chris, and He will never forsake you! On this day, while your hearts are heavy with grief, this is God's Word of promise to you: "Be strong and of good courage; be not frightened, neither be dismayed; for the LORD your God is with you wherever you go!"

Jim and Chris have taught us how to love. Now, we return that love to Jim, Ann, Jeff, Steve, and their family. Let's surround them with steadfast love and loyal devotion in the days, weeks, and months ahead. Give them a shoulder to lean on and a sensitive heart to listen. Offer them your friendship and your care. Such love will truly honor the memory of Chris, and fill the lives of her loved ones with an even greater courage and hope.

Such love reveals the grace of God, restoring the broken heart. In a world growing colder each day, such love burns like a blazing fire and like a mighty flame! And with such love, we show the world that our Christian hope is greater than the grave. Our Christian love is stronger than death!

Remember Chris. Not as a person of fear, but as a woman of deep faith. Remember her. Not as a failure, but as a fighter. Remember her. Not as a loner, but as a lover. Remember Chris. *Never* a coward, *always* courageous. And always hold within your heart the memory of how, time and again, she invited you to enter and enjoy the sacred soil of her life and love!–Albert J. D. Walsh

ILLUSTRATIONS
FOR FUNERAL SERVICES

WRESTLING WITH GOD. Nikos Kanzantzakis tells of an earnest young man who visited a saintly old monk on a remote island. He asked him, "Do you still wrestle with the devil, Father?" The monk answered, "Not any longer, my child. I have grown old, and he has grown old with me. He no longer has the strength. Now I wrestle with God." "With God!" exclaimed the young man in astonishment. "Do you hope to win?" "Oh, no, my son," came the reply, "I hope to lose."–John N. Gladstone

GOD REVEALED. Only in one place can we find an assurance that God is love, and loves us eternally, and that is in Christ. He is the Revealer of God to men, and Guide of men of God. "God is Christ-like, and in Him is no un-Christ-likeness at all," was Michael Ramsey's way of putting it. "God," said Paul, "proves His love for us in that, while we were yet sinners, Christ died for us." In Jesus Christ, incarnate, crucified, and risen from the dead, the love of God is communicated to our wondering hearts, and we are forever sure that nothing can ever separate us from it.–John N. Gladstone

TO EXPERIENCE IS TO KNOW. I remember once near Interlaken waiting for days to see the Jungfrau, which was hidden in mists. People told me it was there, and I should have been a fool to doubt their word, for those who told me lived there and they knew. Then one day the mists were gone, and the whole great mountain stood revealed. Next day the mists were back, but now I had seen, and knew myself that it was true. Men and women, let us trust the saints, the people who have a right to speak about the fellowship of Christ, because they have lived in that country all their lives. Yes, and let us trust our own moments of vision: what matter if there are days when the mists come down and the face of God is hidden? We have seen, and we know forever that this is real, so real that by it we can live and die.–James S. Stewart

NOT ENVY, BUT HUMILITY IN HEAVEN. We know that we shall not all be equal in glory; the equality . . . lies in this, that each soul is fulfilled to its full extent with the delights of God's house. And we know that there can be no murmuring or envying in that manifestation of the sons of God. We shall, I imagine, have no time to say, "Who could have thought of seeing you there?" We shall be too engrossed in the reflection, "Who would have thought of seeing me here?"–Ronald A. Knox

SECTION V.
Lenten and Easter Preaching

SERMON SUGGESTIONS

Topic: The Triumphal Entry

TEXT: Matt. 21:1–11

There was a time in my childhood when, with wild expectation, I awaited one particular weekend. There was a time when I just couldn't wait for Memorial Day. In my hometown the celebration began on Friday evening, with a fabulous carnival, and ended Sunday evening, as the skies above our little town exploded with the light of a thousand bright burning stars. There were reds, and blues, and golds. But for me the real joy came Saturday afternoon, as one hundred screaming fire trucks and marching bands made their way down the south side of Chestnut Street.

It was enough fun to make you give up a frog hunt, or even a ball game with those bullies from the next block! There was a time in my childhood when I'd count the colorful floats and join my pal—Davey—as we marched side by side with real soldiers, carrying rifles that smelled of oil.

And most of all, there was a time when I held my breath as Old Mack came by in his shiny white car—propped up in the back seat like a cigar store Indian. But proud! Old Mack's eyes held the wisdom of a thousand years—I swear. And there was a time in my childhood when I honored Old Mack with my right hand over my heart.

Old Mack! The people sitting on their lawn chairs, and on the curbs, would rise to their feet as Mack's shiny car went rolling by. They'd put their hands together and make a sound like thunder claps on a still summer's night. Old Mack would keep those eyes, heavy with wisdom, fixed straight ahead. I wasn't sure what he saw—but I was certain he'd get there! Women wiped tears from their eyes, and old men stood at attention, raising hands like boards to their tired brows, as Mack went rolling by.

There was a time in my childhood when I —well—I'm somewhat ashamed to say it. Well, I sort of worshiped Old Mack. He was my hero! A valiant warrior who courageously survived the "war to end all wars." Some people even said he was like a savior, who had put his own life on the line to snatch his fellow soldiers from the jaws of hell itself.

And there was a time when I felt proud of our town for treating Old Mack with honor and respect. There was a time when I was certain Old Mack was loved beyond question. And I was just as certain that people would go to their deaths to preserve him, and all that he stood for. There was a time in my childhood when I knew that I, too, would die for Old Mack.

But time has this way of testing our characters and commitments. I also believe time has a way of making us eat our faithless words. And there was a time in my childhood when I faced that day. Yet, not alone. I faced it with a town—a community —people I thought cared—like me—a caring community.

Was it Douglas MacArthur who once said, "Old soldiers never die, they just fade away"? Well, I suppose he was wrong. Because one evening, somewhere back behind the sports page, my father read aloud: "Old

Mack dies at the age of 97. Community drive started to raise funds for Chestnut Street monument." And from the kitchen my mother simply sighed, "Poor soul!" I sat glued to my seat, waiting for my parents to talk about giving something to the cause. But Dad merely chuckled at the comic strips, and my mother mindlessly whistled along to the tune of Tennessee Ernie Ford!

Even though in the privacy of my own home, I felt shame. Surely my own parents would never turn their backs on the one who had given his very life for the freedoms they told me to cherish! How could they so quickly forget this man whose life had been devoted to others?

Then one day the test of my commitment came. A knock at the front door. All alone I opened to find a woman, wearing a wide-brimmed hat, holding a blue can. And staring at me from the heart of that can were those wise old eyes of Mack, the fallen hero! Tipping the can she said, "I'm collecting for the monument, son. Are your parents home?" In a flash I said, "No!" But before I could shut the door, she said, "Then, can you give something?"

I could almost feel my face go flush. Suddenly I recognized that hat! It was Mrs. Waters. Third house on the lefthand side of Bakker Street. So, she *knew* that I had a paper route. And that meant that she also *knew* I had money! All I could see was that baseball glove I'd been scrimping for—for what seemed like years! I'm telling you, it was tough. There I was, caught in the clinches of commitment. What would it be? Old Mack? Or the glove?

They say that ignorance is the lesser part of valor. So I was determined to be *really* ignorant, and go for the glove. "No," I said, rather sheepishly; "I don't—I mean, I can't—I mean—no!" And once I felt safe behind closed doors, I went slinking off to my room —to count my money, and to dream of that glove.

Weeks later I overheard this conversation between my parents and some of their friends. It seemed that the committee couldn't raise enough money to put up a matchbox, much less a monument, to honor the memory of Old Mack. But believe me, that wasn't the worst of it!

The funds would also have covered the cost of a nice burial plot for Old Mack in the local War Heroes Cemetery. And without those funds, the old warrior—that valiant savior whose eyes had beheld a million flags waving and whose ears had once heard a thousand voices cheering—that caring comrade came to his rest among the vagabonds, drunks, and the general low-lifes of our small town. Old Mack slept in some unmarked grave, in the community cemetery, disparagingly called "The Town Dump"!

Well, there was a time in my childhood when I felt the joy of a parade. There was a time when I found security in a caring community. And there was a time when I believed that people in my town were deeply committed to one another, and to this courageous old warrior.

Do you understand? There was a time when I was certain Old Mack would never be forgotten—and that people would sacrifice life and limb to save the cause for which he had risked his own life. But that's only because there was a time in my childhood when I confused the pleasure people feel at the parade with the passion of genuine commitment!

You know, someone once said that "time is our most astute teacher." And they must be right. Because with time I learned much about Old Mack; and even more about life. I discovered that Old Mack had lived alone for years: no family, no friends. Once a year a local VFW would come calling on Old Mack, in the guise of friendship and in the costume of community care.

But, no one really cared. We just loved *what* Old Mack made us feel; and *how* Old Mack made us feel. And each year, after the lawn chairs were folded and packed away, and the fire trucks were settled and silent in their houses—Old Mack sat alone in his dark, dreary room. You see, I learned much about Old Mack. But I learned even more about caring and commitment and community.

I learned that real community can only be found where people are truly committed to one another. And I learned that genuine compassion and care can only be forged on the anvil of commitment. More than that, I discovered something about personal character.

It now seems to me that people can claim to honor and respect many things without nurturing a sense of genuine commitment. Most of us will joyously clap hands for our war heroes. And while we cheer the victors, we all too often ignore the victims. I'm referring to those lost and lonely souls in our Veteran's Hospitals. *And* it seems that many of us will just as quickly praise the Lord with our lips while our hands avoid contact with the lost, the lonely, and the loveless in other sectors of life.

And so, there was a time when I thought being a committed Christian meant nothing more than regular church attendance and daily digestion of a good dose of Scripture. There was a time when I believed that commitment to Christ meant nothing more than witnessing to the world of his wonder. And there was a time when I felt that following Christ merely meant being faithful to the church's cause.

Well, frankly, they are all important—to one degree or another. But what I'm learning—day by day—is that being a Christian means nothing less than placing our character in the shadow of Christ's cross—*every day.* And I'm also learning that the depth of our Christian character is measured not so much by our pious behavior as it is by our commitment to answer Christ's call—placing our shoulder beneath the cross of Christ-like compassions.

Do you remember the story? It ended like this: "Then the crowd that went ahead and the others that came behind raised the shout: 'Hosanna to the Son of David! Blessings on him who comes in the name of the Lord! Hosanna in the highest!'" And that was just fine. Like all those clapping hands and joyous hollers for Old Mack. That was just fine.

But I suppose the pressing question is, Were any of those parade-pleasers really committing to Christ and his cross? Or maybe that's no longer the issue. Perhaps the real questions is, Are you and I committing to Christ, and his community, and his compassion—and his cross?!

We are all aware that Lent is a time for reflection and repentance and renewal. But it can also be a time of deepening our commitment to Christ's cross, at the same time allowing his Spirit to deepen our Christian character. And it can be a time for strengthening the bonds of Christian community, while broadening the base of Christ-like compassions.

That means, of course, that we can all become more fully involved in ministries of concrete care—to the sick, and the sorrowing, and the sinful. Perhaps then we will also discover—quite by surprise—that we can arrive at Easter morning with a more Christlike character as the gift of our gracious God.

Because if my experience is accurate, then it must also be true. The depth of our Christian character will be measured, not by our performance at the parade, but by our willingness to lean hard and place our shoulder beneath the weight of Christ-like compassions.—Albert J. D. Walsh

Topic: Blessed Are the Strugglers
    TEXT: Luke 6:17–26; Jer. 17:7–8
    If you are struggling today—and many of us are—*you are* in the right place! Church is the place for people who struggle.

Have you ever noticed the special place in Jesus' heart for people who struggle? This trait of our Lord's is very obvious throughout the Gospels, though, for some reason, it is often virtually overlooked.

In the pain and confusion of our lives, it's difficult for us to conceive of a God who cares about us and our struggles.

But the God who is revealed in Jesus Christ—in the life and ministry of Jesus from Nazareth—is not only concerned about the trials of people like us, but also is preoccupied with what hurts us and diminishes the quality of our lives. Indeed, there is a special place in the heart of Jesus, yea in the heart of God, for strugglers like us.

Among Jesus' most treasured teachings are what we call "The Beatitudes," those sayings that begin, in most of our English translations, "Blessed are . . ."

Beatitudes is a Latin word that means "the blesseds" and refers to the way these sayings begin; the Beatitudes are blessings. The New Testament scholar Ray Summers sees the Greek word in question, *makarlol,* as a word of acclamation and says that it should be translated "congratulations!" However you translate it, the word seeks to bestow some kind of divine blessing upon those to whom it is addressed.

I remind you of the importance and the

power of the spoken word—especially to bless or to curse—in the ancient Jewish mind-set. These blessings from our Lord, which we call the Beatitudes, are alive with divine power sufficient to cause them to become reality, and his first hearers knew that better than we do.

Most scholars seem to believe that the Beatitudes point to the end of time as the arena for their fulfillment. There is, in much of biblical—especially New Testament —teaching, the idea that matters can never be made entirely right in this world as we know it; therefore, accounts are not fully settled until a new heaven and a new earth have been created.

Finally, those persons who are faithful to God—regardless of how hopeless their plights and their projects may seem in this world—will receive, by God's own hand, what they most need, what they most desire.

Each of Jesus' blessings in our text is spoken in reference to those who struggle with a very specific life crisis. Did you notice? "Blessed are you who are poor. . . . Blessed are you who are hungry. . . . Blessed are you who weep. . . . Blessed are you when people hate you. . . . exclude you. . . . revile you. . . . defame you. . . ." *Blessed are the strugglers!*

You don't hear anything in Jesus' teaching like "Blessed are those who succeed in all they undertake." Or, "Blessed are those who have it all together, all the time." Or, "Blessed are you who are perfect, who defy every expression of weakness, whose relationships are always successful, who never have financial difficulties, who always display a stiff upper lip."

Why did we ever let ourselves buy into an undying admiration of a kind of struggle-free, trouble-free person (who absolutely must be fictitious, by the way)?

We know better, but we have an image of up-and-coming people, prominent people, people we want in leadership positions as those who do not struggle. We rarely see ourselves as in that group of to-be-admired folk, but we always want to be.

The truth is that Jesus had little to do with the up-and-coming folk of his day—those who seemed and wanted to appear struggle-free—not because he disliked them, but because they wanted nothing to do with *him.*

Jesus has nothing against the rich and famous, as if their influence and their financial situations place them out of the reach of his love. Jesus' complaint against them as a group—and certainly there were expectations to this—was that they trusted in their possessions and their positions more than in God and, at bottom, loved what they had more than the God who had given them life.

Those to whom Jesus most easily related, and it remains so today, were the people who had needs, tremendous needs: people who had failed in some sense; people who were confused. You name it. They were imperfect people; they were strugglers. The thing was, they knew it; they admitted they were strugglers. And they didn't feel above talking to someone who was interested in helping them.

The prophet Jeremiah said it very well: Blessed are those who trust in the LORD, whose trust is the LORD. They shall be like a tree planted by water, sending out its roots by the stream. It shall not fear when heat comes, and its leaves shall stay green; in the year of drought it is not anxious, and does not cease to bear fruit (Jer. 17:7–8 NRSV).—David Albert Farmer

Topic: "Who Says You Can't Have It All?"

TEXT: Eccl. 4:4–16; 1 John 2:15–17

I. Some things you can't do—there are limits—reality is reality.

So the question is, Can you put your mind to it and figure out how to be happy with life? Our Scripture section for this morning starts and ends with that now familiar refrain: "It's all empty and a chasing after the wind."

I think he's a pretty cynical old guy. Somebody once suggested that the reason Mark Twain often wrote so bitterly was that he felt so deeply. That's Ecclesiastes.

He starts by saying that whatever you've earned . . . or learned . . . or accomplished in your life thus far, it won't be enough. His parable comes at the end of our text. A poor young man comes out of prison to replace an aging king, and he wins the favor of the masses. But he'll pass off the scene, too, and not everybody will have good memories of him. Public favor is a fickle and fading thing, so today's successes and glories are temporary. The point of all this seems to be: don't be overimpressed with your own achievements—after a while, most others won't be too impressed with them—and don't make success the crown point of your life.

You can have it all . . . and still come up empty. This is not a word Americans want to hear! We are intoxicated with success, but a lot of us never really learn what that is. It's probably because we don't know the meaning of another word—and that word is *enough*.

It's an old story, says our Ecclesiastes philosopher. Back in chapter 1, he writes, "Our eyes cannot see enough to be satisfied; our ears cannot hear enough to be satisfied." Over in chapter 6, he writes, "All human toil is for the mouth, yet the appetite is not satisfied." And here in chapter 4, he says, "I say that all toil and all skill in work come from one person's envy of another. This also is vanity and a chasing after wind" (v. 4).

So our philosopher uses a couple of proverbs to talk about alternatives.

- Fools fold their hands and consume their own flesh (v. 5).
- Do nothing, then you're at the mercy of circumstance.
- Better is a handful with quiet than two handfuls with toil, and a chasing after wind (v. 6).
- Get the necessities of life, then chill out. You don't need two handfuls when one will do.

A third option: It's to answer the question in verse 8. That question is, "For whom am I toiling?" "What am I doing all this for?"

The answer to that question is *not* success, because that turns out to be a real disappointment. The world is full of people who *thought* success would be "having it all" but discovered that they had everything to live with and nothing to live for—it was a hollow victory.

But the bottom-line question remains, "Why am I doing what I'm doing with my life and work?"

So, what is spiritual reality about where you are? And will that help you understand what it's all for—this stuff and strength of your life?

II. I think so. Let me tell you two things about strength and spiritual reality, about the gospel and whatever "all" you have this morning.

a. First of all, *your strengths are blessings.* Blessings—that's a spiritual word, right! It assumes there's a connection between all the stuff and strengths of life—and God.

Carlyle Marney said that people in the West, in America, "exploded out of the Garden of Eden with a hammer" in our hands. We "hammered, twisted, melted, congealed, braided, shaped, organized, traded, harnessed, mastered the stuff of this present world." But over our shoulders we kept having to decide, "What about God? What about the spiritual part of life? Because, though we thought we could abandon the spiritual, we found that the spiritual would not abandon us."

Our New Testament reading this morning makes the spiritual and material connection. In 1 John 2:16 it says, here's what's in the world: the desire of the flesh—the "sensuous"; the desire of the eyes—the "materialistic"; the pride of riches—the "egotistical." All of that is real, but *temporary,* says John. It's already passing away. So don't let your first love, your core loyalty be to the "things" of this world. That belongs to God.

b. One other thing about strengths and spiritual reality: *your strengths are opportunities* (vv. 9–12).

We are not alone in this world; what to do with our strengths? Share them, says our philosopher. We don't live forever in this world, what to do with our stuff? *Share it* is the answer.

It's not a world of ones alone, but of twos and threes and thousands! It makes no sense to use our strengths for selfish ends alone. Did you hear the end of our New Testament text?

The world and its desire are passing away, but those who do the will of God live forever (v. 17).

Don't waste the strength and stuff of your life—they are blessings from God—share them with others. You may change some lives; you may lead some people to Christ, you may shape some minds, you may meet some needs and solve some problems.

That is spiritual reality about our strength

and our stuff. We've been blessed—don't hoard it, pass the blessing on!—William L. Turner

Topic: On The Way to Calvary— A Bureaucrat

TEXT: Matt. 27:1–2, 11–26

Here's Pilate's story on the road to Calvary. What's in it to match up with our hearts and minds as we bare them to the fresh winds of the Spirit during these days before Easter?

From the perspective as a Christian, two conclusions grow out of Pilate's story–I wouldn't set them in concrete, but they're grown out of my personal brooding over this familiar story.

I. First, Pilate *made some wrong equations.* For instance, he made *legality* and *morality* the *same.* Rome could do that and, like Mary Poppins, never have to explain!

Laws must be enforced. That's necessary in any civilized society. But to assume that something's inherently right just because it's legal is naive. The British made this equation in India, and Gandhi said, "You're wrong. Legality and morality aren't always the same thing." In my Alabama boyhood, there was a whole Southern legal system that was morally wrong . . . but perfectly legal. In places like the USSR, China, South Africa, we've seen whole national systems that were quite legal . . . and morally bankrupt.

Pilate acted legally, but his decision was morally wrong. Pilate equated legality and morality, and that can be a wrong equation. We American Christians must go on resisting the temptation to bless any political status quo of the right, left, or center that may be the antithesis of our own spiritual and moral values.

Pilate also equated neutrality with justice. "I wash my hands; it's up to you; whatever happens is not my fault." Then his soldiers went right out to plait the thorns, drive the nails, and plant the cross! "I'm neutral," said Pilate, and George Orwell might have called it "doublespeak"—saying one thing and getting the opposite result.

We need a fresh vision of the Bible's God. He is not neutral. He takes sides—with slaves in Egypt, with the poor in the land, with the weak and the disinherited. In Jesus of Nazareth, the Bible's God sides with the hungry, the thirsty, the naked, the homeless, the sick, and the prisoner (cf. Matt. 25:31f.).

Clearheaded Christians ought to know better than to make Pilate's equation–neutrality equals justice. That helped to crucify Jesus . . . and it still does great damage.

Washing our hands in the name of being neutral and trying to push away responsibility is *not* the same thing as a Christian commitment to dealing with the world's reality.

Jesus didn't make these equations, and he went to the cross–but the cross of suffering for what is right goes on saving and re-shaping the world. Pilate did make the equations, and he walked away from responsibility.

So the issue becomes, "Are we with Christ . . . or with Pilate?"

II. The other conclusion about Pilate's story–he *asked some right questions.* "Are you the king of the Jews?" That's the first question asked by Pilate in all four Gospels. Jesus could have said, "No, not in the political sense that you're talking about, but yes, in the deepest level of human need for the love and forgiveness of God." In John's account of Jesus' trial, Jesus said something to Pilate about truth, and Pilate responded by asking, "What is truth?" (John 18:37–38). I've always thought that was his bureaucratic cynicism oozing out. He's a jaded man, with no hold on anything lasting. "What is truth, Jesus of Nazareth? Who knows about that anymore? Who knows about ultimate reality?

So, where is that truth that can give meaning and direction to our human existence?

And our morning's text here in Matthew records the other right one: "What then shall I do with Jesus who is called Christ?" (v. 22).

For me, they always go together: "What is truth?" and "What shall I do with Jesus?" The second is a direct response to the first.

For someone here this morning, these are *beginning* questions. You've come here without Jesus Christ as center and Savior of your life. Until now you have centered your life in surface realities–things, power, expectations, ambition–and now you're learning that those are sorry substitutes for Truth. Great! This is the moment God's been waiting for with your life. He'll fill that emptiness with himself, if you'll let him. The Truth you've been looking for is available through Jesus Christ; don't stay trapped with Pilate in your cynicism and despair!

For the rest of us this morning, these are ongoing questions. "What is truth about my world, and what are my Christian intentions in it?"

- Where there is sin in all its ugliness, what shall we do *with* Jesus?
- Where there is pain and injustice, what shall we do *with* Jesus?
- Where people live in alienation and hopelessness, what shall we do *with* Jesus?

On the way to Calvary, there was a man named Pilate. You can walk with him. On the way to Calvary, there was a man named Jesus. You can walk with him. In a world of sin and injustice and suffering and need, those really *are* your choices.—William L. Turner

Topic: How Do You Answer the Crucial Question?

TEXT: Mark 8:28–35

I. In the first place, I believe the Cross deals most adequately with our incessant question about the love of God and human suffering. If God is God, if God is love, if God is all-powerful, why this deeply troubled world of ours? Why this suffering? Why these terrible human conflicts? Why the incessant pain of betrayal? Every major religion in the world begins with this passionate human cry: Why, God, this human misery, so much caused by ourselves?

The Christian faith, I believe, asks the same question this way: not so much "why?" but especially, "where?" "Where was this supposedly all-loving and powerful God when the likes of Jesus was tortured and crucified? Where was God when Jesus died?

This is what I believe: And I shall begin at the Cross. Where was God when Jesus died?

You see, our God is in it with us. Our God is sunk in human life, amid all of our brokenness, tragedy, bizarre incidents, and good intentions gone sour. We have all heard it said, "I love Jesus, but I cannot stand God." We have heard the plaintive cry, "I wish God knew what it was like to be me." This Cross affirms no distant, invulnerable, standoffish Deity, no aloof, impervious God, deaf to our desolate pleas here. Just as we confess God present on Calvary, so we confess God mixed up in pain with our own worldly and personal crises of relationship and conflict.

II. In addition to this God of Jesus standing with us amid the tragedy, suffering, and anxiety of our human condition, we see at the Cross the most incredible, humbling, and unimaginable of personal transactions: the release, the freedom, the liberation that true love always brings to troubled and injurious human situations, the fresh beginning inaugurated by this mystery we call "forgiveness."

How can I describe it? How does the Cross bring about forgiveness? What is going on here?

And here we move from the area of human suffering to the region of human sin. And what is this thing called sin? Well, one little girl says, "Sin means knowing that what you are about to do, think, want, or say is really bad, but doing, thinking, wanting, or saying it anyway." Sin is the damnable propensity to put ourselves near the center of virtually everything. It is this tilt toward making ourselves, or our gender, or our family, or tribe, or nation, or religion the measure of all things. It is the opposite of sharing and serving and caring and giving ourselves away.

To use the expression of that time-honored confession from the Anglican *Book of Common Prayer,* "We have done those things we ought not to have done and we have not done those things we ought to have done, and there is no health in us."

How can we get off the treadmill? How can we break this constant subverting of our highest aspirations and hopes? How can we find release from the consequences of our human irresponsibility and the guilt that goes with it?

I believe we are released, liberated, freed for service and living of radiant creative lives by the loving act of forgiveness. I believe that when we truly love one another we will go to any length to restore ruptured relationships. A wounded love can respond in many ways. It can grow cold. It can go another way. It can withhold itself. It can wreak vengeance. And yes, it can at great risk and terrible peril hazard humiliation or rejection and offer forgiveness. And that is what the love of God has done at the Cross of Christ. That unconditional love bearing with us through our sin and our suffering cleans our slates, enables us to begin again, refuses to balance scales. It does not seek justice by weighing and debating the things we have messed up. It dissolves all that junk in a healing, re-creating love offering a new beginning, a fresh start in a restored relationship.

That grace you know, I know, we know enables us to treat one another compassionately, with humor and understanding. As John writes, we love because God first loved us.

III. Last, God's hope. Let me tell you a story that essentially binds together everything we have said this morning. It is a story from the life of the Scots preacher H. H. Farmer. Dr. Farmer writes:

Many years ago I was preaching on the love of God; there was in the congregation an old Polish Jew who had been converted to the Christian faith. He came to me afterward and said, "You have no right to speak about the love of God, until you have seen, as I have seen, the blood of your dearest friends running in the gutters on a gray winter morning." I asked him later how it was that, having seen such a massacre, he had come to believe in the love of God. The answer he gave, in effect, was that the Christian gospel first began to lay hold of him because it bade him see God—the love of God—just where he was, just where he could not but always be in his thoughts and memories—in those bloodstained streets on that gray morning. It bade him see the love of God —not anywhere else, but in the midst of just that sort of thing, in the blood and agony of Calvary. He did at least know, he said, that this was a message that grappled with the facts; and then he went on to say something the sense of which I

shall always remember, though the words I have forgotten. He said, "As I looked at that man upon the Cross, as I heard him pray, 'Father, forgive them, for they know not what they do,' as I heard him cry in his anguish, 'My God, my God, why hast thou forsaken me?' I knew that I was at a point of final crisis and decision in my life; I knew that I must make up my mind once and for all, and either take my stand beside him and share in his undefeated faith in God . . . or else fall finally into a bottomless pit of bitterness, hatred and unutterable despair."

It is this empty Cross, made so by God's power, a power that does not stop the worst from happening—but rather takes the worst we can do to one another in our sin, through our suffering, yea even death itself, and transforms it into the very act redeeming, saving, restoring us—making hope where there is no hope; opening doors we thought slammed; whispering yes where we heard a shouted no. Here, at the Cross, we witness a hope that will not be destroyed, a hope bearing us through and promising a future when everything else denies a future. Now that's power!—James W. Crawford

Topic: The Clothes of Christ
Text: Luke 2:7; Rev. 1:13
Ferdinand Hodler, the great Swiss artist, refused to paint the Matterhorn. It was, he said, too great for his canvas. This subject, the clothes of Christ, is too great for any canvas. The text is all of the New Testament; a text too long to be read in its entirety. But it is possible to highlight some significant verses that point the way. One might begin with the first reference to the clothes of Christ and compare it with the last reference to the clothes of Christ.

I. The first is found in Luke, chapter 2, "And she gave birth to her firstborn son, and wrapped him in swaddling clothes, and laid him in a manger, because there was no room for them in the inn" (Luke 2:7).

The last is found in Rev. 19, beginning at verse 11, "Then I saw heaven open, and behold, a white horse. He who sat upon it was called faithful and true, and in righteousness he judges and makes war. His eyes are like a flame of fire, and on his head are many diadems. He has a name inscribed which no one knows but himself. He is clad in a robe dipped in blood, and the name by which he is called is 'The Word of God.'"

See the contrast between his first clothes and his last clothes. When I was young and read that about swaddling clothes, I thought they were something special, something very different and unique. That's not the case. That was the perfectly ordinary garment of the Jewish baby. When a baby was born in that day, they rubbed him with oil. They sprinkled salt upon him because of old tradition. They wrapped strips of cloth like bandages very tightly, binding his legs and arms to the body. They thought that would give strength to the infant. Those were the swaddling clothes. They were perfectly ordinary. It is to the credit of the wise men that they were not fooled by that but still fell down to worship him, an ordinary-looking baby in ordinary clothes.

This last picture of the clothes of Christ is quite extraordinary. Here is a vesture dipped in blood, monogrammed with the phrase "The Word of God." Put them side by side, and they teach us two things about Christ. He was so much like us and then he was so much unlike us. Those seemingly contradictory ideas are absolutely essential to understanding Jesus. They are the key. If you don't know those two things, you will never understand him. He was so much like us! He was so much unlike us!

In many fields of knowledge there is a key. Nobody understood early Egyptian history because nobody could read hieroglyphics. Then they found the Rosetta Stone. That stone has the same paragraph written on it three times, in three different languages. Two of those languages were well known. One was Egyptian hieroglyphics. The Rosetta Stone was the key that unlocked our knowledge of ancient Egypt.

The theory of relativity developed by Einstein was the key that opened up modern physics and science. So here is the key to understanding Christ. He was so much like us. He had a body like our bodies. He didn't have a body like the Roman god Janus, with two faces, one looking forward and one

backward. He didn't have a body like your second-grade teacher who had eyes in the back of her head. He had a body like ours: two eyes, two ears, two arms, two legs. Cut him, and he would bleed. Deny him rest, and he would grow tired. Deny him water, and he would be thirsty. Deny him food, and he would be hungry. Wound him, and he would die. He was so like us. But he was so unlike us. He was tempted as we are tempted, but he never sinned as we sin. He prayed as we pray, but he never *had* to pray the way we *have* to pray. He grew hungry as we grow hungry, but he never made food the essential thing in his life. He worked as we work, but he never made work the central thing in his life. He loved, but he never let it degenerate into lust. Here was one so much unlike us. It's marked by the vesture dipped in blood.

Some say it is the blood of vengeance: the blood of his enemies. He *is* God's avenger, the executor of the wrath of God upon men. We may interpret it that way. But others say it is his own blood, his precious blood, his atoning blood, that would make this the costliest garment ever worn.

One of the most expensive fabrics in the world is vicuna. It's make from the hair of the throat of certain goats. If you had a dress made out of that, it would cost you thousands and thousands of dollars. Not long ago they were selling gold lace in London at $151.20 a yard. They are rags compared with this vesture dipped in blood, His precious blood.

So we learn in his ordinary first clothes and his extraordinary last clothes, how much like us he was and how much unlike us he was.

II. Then let us compare his work clothes and his clothes of wonder. He wore a carpenter's apron. He came to fill the next to the lowest place in the social structure of his day. He did not come as a great spiritual leader might have been expected to come. He did not come as one of the priesthood of that day. He did not come as one of the scribes of that day. He did not come as a great political leader, as a king or a governor. He did not come as a great military leader, as a general or a commander. He did not come as a great business leader, a banker or merchant. He did not come even as a schoolteacher, or a physician, or one of the professions! He came as a carpenter. The only thing lower than a carpenter was a tanner. Perhaps he would have come as a tanner, except then he would have been barred from the Temple where many of his deeds were done. So, he came as a carpenter.

He wore not only the apron of a carpenter. In the upper room, he put on the towel of a servant and washed the disciples' feet. That was the lowest job. The servant who was given the least place in the house was the servant who waited at the door to wash the guest's feet. That's the place he took.

It made headlines in the newspapers and was recorded in the history books that John F. Kennedy said, "Ask not what your country can do for you, but what you can do for your country." The sentiment was expressed far better by Jesus, who said, "I came not to be served, but to serve." "My father works," he said, "and I work."

After the Resurrection Jesus met his disciples by the sea. He fixed their breakfast. The risen, glorified Christ did not think it beneath his dignity to do that. He built a fire. He cleaned the fish. (What a dirty job that is!) He cooked their breakfast. He did not think it beneath him to do that.

And in his work he showed us the splendor of work, the dignity of work and the sin of indolence and laziness. The Thracians of ancient Greece thought work was a sin and a shame, so they lived by war. Our Lord thought differently.

There's a book entitled *Dress for Success.* Executives at IBM really believe in that. They require their people to dress in a certain way.

Jesus in his carpenter's apron, Jesus girded with towel, hardly seems dressed for success. But then once, once, we see him in robes that befit him. On the mount of Transfiguration he was changed. His garments shone as the light. Those robes of light fit him as perfectly as the carpenter's apron had. They fit him because we associate light with life. Without light there would be no life on this planet. We associate light with beauty. All of our colors are drawn from a little narrow space on the spectrum of light. We associate light with protection and safety. Now through the laser, we associate light with healing. How appropriate that Christ, who is our life, and who gives a new

definition to beauty, and who is our protection and who is our healer, should be robed in a garment of light. They say that clothes make a man. Of course, it's not true. Clothes do tell you something about the man. If you see a teenage boy who has always been careless about his appearance suddenly begin spending an hour at the mirror combing his hair, you know something about him. You know he's found a girl.

You see someone who is a very meticulous about his appearance, and you know that here is someone who is concerned about detail. You see a person who is careless about his appearance, and you know this is someone whose mind is on larger things and has not thought for details.

III. We learn a lot about Christ from the clothes that he wears; from his ordinary clothes to his extraordinary clothes, from his work clothes and his clothes of wonder. We learn the most from his dying clothes and his deathless clothes.

There was that purple robe they put on him, to mock him. Where did they get that? That was the uniform of an officer in the Roman army! When they put it on him, it was at the same time paradoxical and proper. It was paradoxical because he was the Prince of Peace. They meant to mock him. They put on the Prince of Peace the uniform of war. Yet war and peace are always opposite sides of the same coin. He is the Prince of Peace. He is also the Captain of our salvation. He is the Lord of Hosts. His church marches like an army with banners. There *was* a certain appropriateness to what they did when they put the scarlet robe on him.

Then at the cross, they took his seamless robe and gambled for it. That touches us. It was his only possession, and they took it. He didn't own a home. He didn't have any money. He didn't have any land. All that he owned was that one seamless robe, and they took it. Not only was it his only possession; it was a very special possession. It was a seamless robe. That tells us that is was made with special care, by his mother perhaps, or by some friend and supporter who believed in what he was doing. When they took it, they marked indelibly the difference between him and themselves.

He was one who was always giving, and

they were those who were always taking. He had little concern for possessions, and they had concern for little else. He lived by destiny, and they lived by chance. You and I have to choose which will be the pattern for our lives. Will we be givers or takers? Will we be people who have little concern for that which is material or people who have concern for little else? Will we be people who live with a sense of spiritual destiny, or will we be people who live by chance? Having taken his robe, they then crucified the unclothed Christ.

The artists have been people of great sensitivity. They have always draped the body of Christ on the cross. The fact of the matter is, they stripped him and nailed him there! They did it to humiliate him. They did it to bring him shame, but they failed. He had an inner dignity they could not touch! Sometimes when I have been going somewhere to speak, I have put on my jacket and said, "I've got to put on my dignity." But Christ did not put on his dignity, and they could not take it off. Christ had an inner dignity that they could not take away from him. They stripped him of his possessions! They stripped him of his robe! But they could not strip him of his dignity!

God saw the unclothed Christ, and he put on him robes so splendid that they're beyond description. Rev. 1:13: "dresses in a robe reaching down to his feet, and with a golden sash around his chest." God clothed him—clothed him with power and might and beauty and glory and honor!

Now see the most wonderful thing of all. It's in the chapter with which be began. "There followed him, riding upon white horses, men and women dressed in fine linen, white and clean." Where did they get those robes? You know. He put his robe on them: his robe of righteousness—his robe of purity, his robe of sinlessness. He put his robe on them! He puts his robe on us!—over the rags of our self-righteousness—over the filth of our sin! He put his robe on us!

> I got a robe!
> You got a robe!
> All God's children got a robe!
> When I get to Heaven
> Gonna put on my robe!
> Gonna walk all over God's Heaven!
>   —Robert C. Shannon

Topic: Christ Arose, So What?

TEXT: 1 Cor. 15

Many people misunderstand Easter. The holiday for them is colored eggs, bunnies, new clothes, a break from school, and possible church attendance for the first time that year. But isn't Easter more than that? Isn't Easter about Jesus, who died, rose from the dead, and is alive today? Yes, but so what? What difference does it make to me that Christ is alive?

The meaning of Easter is a theological matter. The fact of Easter is a historical matter. The benefits of Easter are a personal matter.

I want to address the benefits. What difference does the resurrection make in your life?

I. *It gives significance to your personal life.* Have you ever felt you are only a number, a cog in the corporate machinery? Have you ever felt you did not matter?

But the resurrection of Jesus Christ shatters those negative thoughts with a powerful benefit: *You matter to God.* That is the good news of Jesus Christ.

"Now, brothers, I want to remind you of the gospel I preached to you, which you received and on which you have taken your stand. For what I received I passed on to you as of first importance: that Christ died for our sins according to the Scriptures, that he was buried, that he was raised on the third day according to the Scriptures" (1 Cor. 15:1, 3–4 NIV).[1]

The point is that Jesus died and rose again for you. In other words, if you had been the only person on Earth, Jesus would have died and risen again for you. Why? Because you matter so much to Him.

II. *It gives meaning to your present life.* Thomas Aquinas wrote, "There is within every soul a thirst for happiness and meaning." Everyone wants his or her life to count and to make a difference in the world.

Many people unfortunately have never found purpose for their lives. They search,

---

[1] From the Holy Bible, New International Version, copyright © 1973, 1978, 1984 by International Bible Society. Subsequent references are marked NIV.

hunt, and strive for answers but always came up short.

Good Friday was the worst day in history for disciples. All their hopes and dreams were destroyed. They turned, with heads down, and walked back to their old stations in life. Their once full, meaningful lives now were empty. But that was Friday. The disciples learned that the resurrection followed the crucifixion. And that changed their lives.

They saw firsthand the resurrected Christ. "And that he appeared to Peter, and then to the Twelve. After that, he appeared to more than five hundred of the brothers at the same time, most of whom are still living, though some have fallen asleep. Then he appeared to James, then to all the apostles, and last of all he appeared to me also" (1 Cor. 15:5–8 NIV).

The resurrection gave new meaning to these men's lives. Life was put in a new perspective. They were given a new direction. These men were changed forever. They went forth with a new zeal. Life once again became worth living.

III. *It gives hope to your future life.* Many people have no hope beyond death. That is a horrible way to live—and a horrible way to die.

Fortunately, it is not the only way.

While the Bible is the most reliable textbook on life after death, the greatest proof is Jesus Christ's resurrection. Our link to life after death is Jesus' own resurrection. If Jesus has been raised from the dead, resurrection indeed is possible.

Jesus said, "I am the resurrection and the life. He who believes in me will live, even though he dies; and whoever lives and believes in me will never die. Do you believe this?" (John 11:25–26 NIV).

Paul elaborated on Jesus' words: "But the fact is that Christ did actually rise from the dead, and has become the first of millions who will come back to life again some day" (1 Cor. 15:20 TLB).[2]

Peter said, "Now we live in the hope of eternal life because Christ rose again from the dead" (1 Pet. 1:3 TLB).

Death is a doorway to life for believers. We will face death. We cannot escape that fact. But we can see beyond death because of the resurrection of Christ. We can be like the man whose tombstone bore the words "Gone away with a Friend." It will be that way for us because of the resurrection.

IV. *It gives victory to a defeated life.* Note Paul's words: "How we thank God for all of this! It is he who makes us victorious through Jesus Christ our Lord! So, my dear brothers, since future victory is sure, be strong and steady, always abounding in the Lord's work, for you know that nothing you do for the Lord is ever wasted as it would be if there were no resurrection" (1 Cor. 15:57–58 TLB).

The cross appeared to defeat Jesus. Had Satan won the battle? Did evil conquer righteousness? Had wrong demolished right? Had hate smothered love?

People only see the cross at times. However, the cross isn't the last part of God's plan.

The fog of life's experiences sometimes causes us to see only *our* crosses. We are bombarded with defeat. We feel crushed and destroyed. We think the walls are caving in on us. We want so desperately to win.

We can win through Jesus Christ.

Do you want to win? Do you want victory in your life, whether it be conquering a bad habit or rebounding from a loss? You can know you have that victory because of Jesus' resurrection.

The resurrection of Jesus Christ does make a difference in your life. It provides the greatest benefit of all time to humankind.—William Richard Ezell

ILLUSTRATIONS

MEANING OF EASTER.   A Sunday school teacher asked her class the Sunday before Easter about the meaning of the holiday.

"Easter is when all the family gets together, and they have a big turkey and sing about the pilgrims and all that," replied one student.

"No, that's not it," said the teacher.

"I know what Easter is," a second student responded. "Easter is when you get this pine

---

[2] Verses marked TLB are taken from The Living Bible. Copyright © Tyndale House Publishers, Wheaton, Illinois, 1971. Used by permission. Subsequent references are marked TLB.

tree and cover it with decorations and exchange gifts and sing lots of songs."

"That's not it," the teacher repeated.

Then the third student responded: "Easter is when Jesus was killed, put in a tomb, and left for three days."

"He knows! He knows!" the teacher said ecstatically to herself.

But then the boy went on: "Then everybody gathers at the tomb and waits to see if Jesus comes out, and if he sees His shadow he has to go back in for seven weeks."—William Richard Ezell

THE REAL CROSS.   We live so far from the cross that it is hard for us to see it for what it was. Certainly it was nothing like the burnished crosses that we put in our chancels. How much more appropriate it would be if we had a rough-hewn, blood-stained, wooden cross above that table, and if we must have a picture, to have men of our own day about it, farmhands and fisher-folk, steel puddlers and sharecroppers, clerks and taxi-drivers, and preachers and priests, and businessmen and engineers and soldiers. For we all had a hand in it. The cross unhappily seems so far off and so unreal when really what it is and what it does is so contemporary. The people about it were people like us.—Clayton E. Williams

EVIL MOST DANGEROUS.   A friend who saw Buchenwald from the inside tells how the walks that led up to the gas chambers were themselves attractively decorated, outside. There is no evil so dangerous as the evil which justifies as good.—Clayton E. Williams

DYING TO SIN, LIVING TO GOD.   To the death that is sin we have been dying since our baptism. And the dying is never ended. For dying to sin is not something negative; dying to sin is turning to Christ and turning to Christ is a constant conversion. If sin is rejection, dying to sin is openness: openness to God's presence poured out on us through every flower that opens its chaliced petals to us, every breeze that caresses our skin, every man or woman whose eyes meet ours, the awesome presence of the Holy One himself tabernacled within us. In dying to sin, we live to God.—Walter J. Burghardt, S.J.

SECTION VI.
Messages for Advent and Christmas

SERMON SUGGESTIONS

Topic: What Are You Expecting for Christmas?

TEXT: Isa. 40:1–5; John 12:20–36

I love this season of the year—from the moment it starts to the moment it ends! I love everything about it! The candles, the carols, the cards, the presents to be bought, the stockings to be hung all evoke tones of excitement and anticipation . . . and I'm truly sad when it's all over!

I know there are plenty of Scrooges among us who every year denounce the commercialization and the crassness of so much of modern Christmas celebration. And I agree, to some extent, that we frequently overdo it. Sometimes, some of the music is too loud and incessant. Often, the decorations are too big, too brassy, too tawdry, too much. It's a season that brings with it much tension and stress. And we're saturated with it all, long before Christmas Eve.

I am reminded of the story C. S. Lewis wrote more than thirty years ago, "Exmas and Christmas." It takes place on the island of Niatirb, which is Britain spelled backwards. Every winter the Niatirbians celebrated a festival they called Exmas.

They packed the marketplaces in all sorts of weather in order to get ready for the celebration. They looked for cards and gifts for their relative and friends.

As the days counted down, the preparation began to take its toll. Many of the people grew pale and weary. They looked as though they were under tremendous strain.

Some even missed the big day altogether because they were so exhausted, or they had gotten sick from overeating and drinking.

But there was another holiday held on the same day as Exmas. The Niatirbians called it "Christmas." It was a holy day, but it was difficult to keep it holy because Exmas was so distracting.

The point of Lewis's story is that there are really two different holidays celebrated on December 25. One is celebrated by almost everyone in the United States—that is Exmas. The other is celebrated by the followers of Jesus—it is called Christmas.

And because both holidays fall on the same date, people often confuse them. For instance, one of the classic holiday stories is *How the Grinch Stole Christmas.* In the story, a nasty creature called the Grinch steals all the presents, decorations, and food in the little town of Whoville. By doing this, he thought that he could prevent Christmas from coming.

But of course, he found that Christmas comes even without presents and food. Just like many other people, the Grinch was confused. He did not steal Christmas. He stole Exmas.

If you steal all the presents, there is no Exmas. But Christmas still comes. Take away reindeer and stockings, and there is no Exmas. But Christmas still comes. Exmas is made of greeting cards, trees, reindeer, cookies, and parties. Take these all away, and you have eliminated Exmas. But you still have not touched Christmas.

Christmas is not presents and fruitcake. Christmas celebrates the coming of God's

Son into the world. When we celebrate Christmas we remember that God came to earth so that the world could see Him, hear Him, and know Him. Christmas reminds us that God still invites us to meet Him and know Him. And that's an altogether different matter than Exmas.

Now don't misunderstand me. I am not saying that Exmas is bad and only Christmas is good. Is spite of C. S. Lewis's rather jaded description of it, and even though it may have gotten out of hand in contemporary culture, Exmas is still a nice holiday. Families get together, kids still burst with excitement, houses and stores are beautifully decorated. The music is uplifting and inspiring. People even talk about love and peace.

Exmas is great, even if it is a lot of work. But it can also be very distracting. The danger is that it is very easy to get so busy preparing for Exmas that there is no time left to prepare for Christmas. In fact, the two holidays are so different, preparing for one is radically different than preparing for the other.

That is what Advent is all about, and that is why we are observing Advent. Exmas can become so all-consuming that we never think about Christmas until it's past. Advent, however, represents a conscientious and disciplined effort by Christians to keep the focus upon the primary event of history –the coming of our Savior into the world.

At Christmas, it's easy for us to become like the people who once greeted President Franklin Roosevelt at a gala ball. He was tired of shaking hands and smiling his big smile and saying all of the usual inanities at such an occasion. So, he decided to do something outrageous.

Convinced that no one was listening anyway, the President greeted each person by saying, "I murdered my grandmother this morning." Everyone responded with a smile and a nod and said things like "Wonderful!" "Lovely!" "Keep up the good work, Mr. President."

One diplomat, however, did listen and actually heard what the President had said. He leaned over and whispered in Roosevelt's ear, "I'm sure she had it coming to her!"

If, from time to time, we do not deliberately force ourselves to see what God is doing, and to listen to what God is saying, then we will likely never really know the God who has gone to such lengths to make Himself known. To prepare for Exmas is to get ready for a party. But to get ready for Christmas is to get ready to meet a Person.

Jesus entered the world at Bethlehem nearly twenty centuries ago. And because He lives today, we can still meet Him–if we are prepared. And preparation is the key that allows us to hear and open our hearts so that Christ can come in and have fellowship with us. So, getting ready for and counting the days until Christmas really means getting ready and counting the days to meet our Savior and Lord. And that is our primary vocation during Advent.–Gary C. Redding

Topic: The Dream We Covet
TEXT: Luke 2:13–14

Sometime during this Christmas this question will be asked, possibly by you. It may be as you sit by the fire with the ones you love. It may be as you celebrate a joyful moment. It may be as you sit and contemplate all that Christmas means to you. Then the question comes: Why can't it be like this always? Why can't Christmas last all year long? For there is something about the Christmas spirit that strikes a responsive chord in us and causes us to think about the fact that the world could be better than it is.

Christmas is a time for dreamers to dream about a world that is not but can be. At one time, most of us were dreamers. When we were young we were going to change the world, remember? We were going to dash out into it and right all the existing wrongs. Out we went with good intentions, but we bumped into a harsh reality. The world is not easy to change, and often people don't want to change. Because of that, we began to see our dreams fade into the background. They were impossible dreams anyway, weren't they? So we got down to the business of trying to survive in this world.

But Christmas keeps coming back. Christmas keeps coming to try to stir up the forgotten ashes and embers of those dreams.

Christmas causes us, if just for a moment, to wonder, Why can't we have a world where peace and love and joy are the way it is? Still, all the time we dream, inside our minds lies the thought that it's impossible.

The angels were wrong, weren't they? For they came bursting onto the scene crying out, "Glory to God in the highest, and on earth peace, good will toward men" (v. 14 KJV). We say, "What a dream!" Oh, that it could be! How we would love a world like that! This is the dream we covet: peace on earth, goodwill toward men. But can it ever be? Was Christmas wrong? Was the song of the angels a pipe dream, or can it really be?

I. *It's a dream about peace on earth.* When Christ was born, there was peace on earth in the sense that no wars were being fought within the Roman Empire, which included most of the known world; Rome was in charge. We see that because Mary and Joseph went to Bethlehem to register for taxes. There wasn't anything they could do about it.

There was no war outwardly, but inwardly, within the hearts of people, there burned violence, mistrust, and hatred of their Roman conquerors. Though no war was being fought, the seeds of it were certainly there. Into the midst of that unhealthy, tense atmosphere, the angels sang of peace on earth, and others said it couldn't be. But they sang it because, since Christ was born in Bethlehem, there could be peace on earth.

If there is one thing this world needs, it's peace. We certainly don't have it. There is trouble all over the world. Place your finger almost anywhere on a world map, and you will find trouble there. Our world lives on the brink of war. Even today, we talk almost matter-of-factly about a limited nuclear war. The prophets of old warned against crying out, "'Peace, peace,' when there is no peace" (Jer. 6:14). We don't have to worry about that today. Nobody is crying peace. We know that it is not here.

Yet we want it. In any survey taken that asks people what they want most, the number one answer is usually peace. We dream of it, we sing about it at Christmas, but do we think it's possible? Are we doing anything to see that the dream comes true?

We who sing for peace at Christmas, do we give anything to see it come to pass? Have we given up on peace? Do we still believe it's possible? Sometimes, to cry out for peace in our world seems to be like a lone voice crying in the wilderness. To cry out for peace will not meet with responsive ears. To call for us to take the risks for peace will not always be met with affirmative nods. To be those who try to be peacemakers is not always popular. But the alternative to peace is insanity. We need to dream of peace.

II. *They dreamed of goodwill toward men with whom God is well pleased.* There wasn't much goodwill in those days. Many, like the Romans, didn't believe in God. Many, like some Jewish people, didn't take him seriously. As a result, there was ill will among the people. They mistrusted one another, were suspicious of one another, hated one another. Then the angels sang "good will toward men," and the Jews said, "You've got to be kidding. Goodwill toward the Samaritans? Goodwill toward the Romans? Goodwill toward the Greeks? Not on your life!" But the angels sang on: "Good will toward men" because Christ is born!

We need goodwill among people today. Wouldn't it be nice if we could have a brotherhood of humanity in which we treated one another with dignity and respect, regardless of color of skin or origin of birth or place on an economic ladder? Wouldn't it be nice if we could get along with one another? We don't seem to be able to treat one another well.

An editorial told about a number of handgun deaths in 1980 across the world. In every country around the world there were less than one hundred handgun deaths—except the United States. In the United States, there were over ten thousand. We are violent. We do not get along. We treat one another harshly.

As for marriage, there is now a 51 percent divorce rate. Some young people coming to be married want the words "till death do us part" taken out of their marriage ceremony. They want instead "till love dies," as if they know that when they get married it will probably not last.

At Christmas, for just a moment, we begin to feel closer to one another. We treat the poor a little bit better, trying to take care of their needs. We are even friendlier toward our neighbors, and a lot of times we even get along better in our homes. Maybe we can get along.

III. *It's a dream of total commitment to God.* Here's is the key to the angel's song: Glory to God in the highest. That meant that all worship and honor went to him; that meant that everybody needed to love him. Everybody needed to worship him. Everybody needed to serve him. If that happened—glory was given to God in the highest—then peace on earth, goodwill toward men could happen.

That's the secret! The secret is not that you and I on our own will go into this world and by some miraculous, superhuman effort bring peace on earth and goodwill toward all people. The secret is that this God who has come in Christ will bring peace if we will let him use us. But can it be? We dream of it. If only everybody would love God, what a nice world that would be! But in order for that to happen *we* have got to give glory to God, and that means you and I have got to take God seriously. You and I have got to believe his way of life. You and I have got to put him first in our lives.

The danger of Christmas is that we will go on worshiping the baby Jesus. Babies are pretty. But Jesus grew up and looked at us from a cross and said, "Follow me. Take up your cross daily. Leave it all behind and follow me" (author's translation). Are we willing to worship that Christ? For until we are, the dream is impossible.

Can Christmas last always? Maybe it can. Maybe it can last for us if we try to live day by day by giving glory to God and seeking his dream.—Hugh Litchfield

Topic: Hitch Your Destiny to This Star

TEXT: Jer. 33:12–16

If you had to pick one day in the whole year on which to locate and celebrate the birth of Jesus, the Church did well to pick December twenty-fifth, very near to the winter solstice—the day of the longest night. It is the time of year when our anxieties are deepest and our need for Christ's hope seems greatest.

So, really, winter and its approaching hazards are the perfect backdrop for the Christmas story. Because it shows that what is at stake in faith is survival. *Survival.*

I used to think of faith as making life better. But for me today, faith is what makes life possible! I came to understand why a star high above earth, looking, as it were, right down at Bethlehem, has become the most inspiring image from the entire Christmas story. Christ's star inspires security in our hearts no matter what the insecurities outside may be.

In Matthew's Gospel story, the star was the signal that brought the world's attention to an obscure village near the Mediterranean Sea, in a country that was a plaything to the Roman Empire, and before that of the Babylonian Empire, and before that of the Assyrian Empire, and before that of the Egyptian Empire. It shone down on a people truly battered by history, trampled by armies careening from one exploit to another. For this country, survival counted for everything.

For us survival has come to mean "doing what you have to do." Survival has come to mean "dog eat dog." Survival has come to mean "looking out for number one" and being in a real hurry to do it or lose your ground to competitors.

But for Israel, survival meant trying to see itself in a divine perspective. Unlike those of other nations that conquered it, Israel's king did not claim to be divine. Rather, the people held the king, starting with King David, accountable to God—for something Israel called righteousness. And when things went wrong, someone—some prophet—always called for a self-searching to find the ways in which their behavior had drifted away from something Israel called righteousness. They took time for this—they took time to do this.

This star shone down on Bethlehem—on "The City of David," as it was regarded—in a country as occupied with God as it was preoccupied with its enemies, a nation that kept faith with a God who promised to lift them back up, and who indeed kept faith with them. Their God was the companion of survival, not an inconvenience to it. It is like cause and effect. Righteousness was the key to survival, not an impediment. Righteousness is a burden to us, but not to Israel.

Israel may have had many burdens, but righteousness was not one of them, because

God gave them room to err and to learn and to find their way. No fault was ever held against them permanently by God, but their self-searching made them know that God's love was from everlasting to everlasting—what we call forgiveness.

This was a survival faith—a faith forged in the fight for survival—driven by the twin engines of God's high expectations of righteousness, on the one hand, and God's eternal forgiveness, on the other hand. Only with this survival faith could Israel survive the suffering caused both by its own sins and by outside forces. You can certainly see why mere survival, under such desperate circumstances, felt so much like triumph.

Jesus himself, as he stood on the threshold of Jerusalem and his own bloody demise, pictured the very same destiny for Israel and all communities of faith when he warned the people that at first "nation will make war upon nation—there will be great earthquakes, and famines, and plagues in many places—in the sky terrors and great portents." Then finally, "When you see Jerusalem encircled by armies, then you may be sure destruction is near." All these figured as inevitabilities requiring what he had from the prophets and in turn gave us—a survival faith.

So this star over Christ's cradle is not meant as any mere decoration over a baby's crib. It shone down on David's city, King David's city, David who was accountable to God—so it is just as much David's star, it is Israel's star, it is Isaiah's star and Jeremiah's, and Jerusalem's star. It could be Boston's star, your star. It is the star of hope because it promises survival—not mere self-improvement and job success. It promises self-searching integrity and giant-killing might—not the hurried and anxious striving for self-satisfaction that is our destiny today.

Christ's star connects three important things—righteousness, forgiveness, and our survival. Salvation comes to this—truth and honesty and fairness before God are still expected even when all else is going up in flames. God wants a commitment to righteousness from us even under widespread conditions of unrighteousness. The behavior of others is no excuse for our misbehavior.

The presence of violence in the streets and armies at the borders does not exempt us. Because that righteousness is the leaven that transforms the whole loaf, the whole world—righteousness is the miracle-working germ that cures all.—Richard N. Chrisman

Topic: A Name to Remember
Text: Matt. 1:21

"Thou shalt call his name Jesus." By the time a baby is born, parents very often have chosen a name—or perhaps I should say two names, if they are wise. Occasionally, a name may almost seem imposed on them. Something makes them certain right away that this is what it must be. So it was with Jesus. The name had come to Joseph in a dream. The Bible takes dreams seriously—as does modern psychiatry. And when you dreamed of an angel, you would be sure to pay attention. So these words would be burned into Joseph's heart and mind: "Thou shalt call his name Jesus."

You might expect the messenger of God to give an extraordinary name for an extraordinary child. When the prophet Isaiah had a son, he reported that the Lord had said to him: "Call his name Maher shal-al-hash-baz." That's the kind of name that raises questions and must be quite a burden to carry through life—even back when they didn't have all these forms to fill out. (And think of the problems the hymn-writers would have had if Joseph had been given that name for Jesus!) Jesus was, in fact, a very common name among the Jewish people, although not exactly as we have it now. Jesus is the Latin spelling of the Greek Yesous, which was, in turn, a modification of the Hebrew Joshua. Since you didn't come here on Christmas morning for a lecture in etymology, let me just say that the name given to this little boy was Joshua, and when he went to school there would surely be other Joshuas around. After all, wasn't one of the great heroes of the Hebrews called Joshua, and isn't there a Bible book with his name?

I think God wanted him to have a very common name. For he was to be truly one of us, sharing in all joys and sorrows that we know, subject to the same dangers, feeling the heat and the cold, being hungry and thirsty, laughing and weeping. So the baby got the familiar name Joshua just as the baby of Elizabeth, Mary's cousin, who was born about six months before, got the name John, which today is even commoner than Joshua.

It isn't the name you are given that determines the person you are going to be. Even people who are saddled with absurd or meaningless names can live them down—and even make them lovely for those who know them. Recently I heard about a baptism in Scotland where a little child received the name Pindonah; for that was what the father said when asked, "What is the Christian name of this child?" Afterward he complained bitterly to the minister, "You told me you might not remember the name, so I wrote it out and pinned it on her. And that's what I said when you asked me: 'It's pinned on her.'" What's in a name? I trust that little Pindonah will grow to be a lovely Christian woman.

Yet there was something in the name given to Mary's child—and our text tells us what it was. The name Joshua means in Hebrew "The Lord will save," so, from the moment of his birth the Son of Mary was called "Savior," or "Deliverer." Thus we read: "Thou shalt call his name Jesus: for he shall save his people from their sins." And from that day till now the name Jesus has been lifted high above all other names on earth. It is the Savior's birth we celebrate today.

I notice that at this season journalists are searching for some signs of light to report among the gloomy news that reflects what's happening in the modern world. And, of course, there are some. As Flora Lewis pointed out in Friday's *Times,* there are many terrible things that haven't happened. But I would suggest that the brightest sign of all is the persistence of the name Jesus across the centuries and around the globe, and the saving power that it proclaims. The name given to a little Jewish boy in a stable in Bethlehem nearly two thousand years ago has become a name to remember. It is probable that more men, women, and children know that name today than ever before. However it is pronounced—Jesus, Hesus, Yesous, Jesu—it is an instant bond between those who love him. And in what we call the "secular world," the name of Jesus cannot be forgotten. Even when it is used as an expletive (and I confess that, although tolerant of cuss words as a way of blowing off steam, I will not use, and hate to hear, this beloved name abused), unwitting tribute is being paid to the unforgettable Christ.

A good part of our attempt to live the Christian life could be described as remembering the name of Jesus. In a time of joy, like Christmas Day, we remember him, and the joy has a deeper meaning. In a time of gloom and depression of spirit, we remember him, and he shares the burden and leads us through. In a time of strong temptation, we remember him, and, like Saint Paul, hear a voice that says, "You have not so learned Christ." In a time of guilt, we remember him and may hear the voice that said, "Neither do I condemn thee; go and sin no more."

> How sweet the name of Jesus sounds
> In a believer's ear!
> It soothes his sorrow, heals his wounds,
> And drives away his fear.

Around the world, there has been a revival of a prayer used by a Russian monk. It's called the "Jesus Prayer" and is simply the repetition of the words "Lord Jesus Christ, Son of God, have mercy on me, a sinner." It's a good way to begin or end a day, or to seek strength at any moment wherever we happen to be.

"She shall bring forth a son, and thou shalt call his name Jesus; for he shall save his people from their sins." What better day to remember the name of Jesus than his birthday? For our carols and readings don't simply take us back to the manger: they lift our hearts and minds toward the day when "at the name of Jesus every knee shall bow . . . and every tongue confess that Jesus Christ is Lord, to the glory of God the Father."–David H. C. Read

Topic: Christmas Eve Greeting

TEXT: John 1:1–5

As we have heard the Gospels describing the birth of Jesus read tonight, we have heard an emphasis on much of the action indeed taking place at night. The magi followed a star blazing brilliantly at night. Who knows but what Herod in his plans to wipe out the male children under the age of two did not keep counsel by night. And of course, we find the child himself born during the night.

Nighttime and darkness seem always to be a piece of the Christmas mood and tone. I suppose we might even say from time to time ourselves that we celebrate Christmas in a dark time. And to say and believe that is nothing more than to conform what the Gospels themselves imply about the first Christmas: Jesus was born at night in a dark time.

Nonetheless, just a few moments ago we sang a wonderful carol including words describing Bethlehem that night: "Yet in thy dark streets shineth/the everlasting light."

And if Phillips Brooks has it right in that carol, if we consider ourselves living in dark times, another truth breaks through our pessimism and discouragement: the shining of an everlasting light.

We cannot get through Christmas without celebrating that "everlasting light." Nearly eighty years after the death of Jesus, a little community of Jesus-movement people reflected on the meaning of the life begun in Bethlehem in terms of Light shining in the darkness. That little group knew the fury and contempt of the religious authorities as well as the harsh mistrust and oppression of the civil authorities. They were rejects. For them the world seemed a dark place. They lived, to use their own metaphors, amid a threatening and turbulent midnight.

And yet, the spokesperson for the troubled little community, though living as if saturated by darkness—the spokesperson, John, speaks of Christ in terms of "Light." Remember? "In the beginning was the Word . . . and the Word was life and the life was the light of all. And light shines in the darkness and the darkness did not overcome it." Through his Gospel, John speaks of this Bethlehem gift as light—unquenchable, invincible, imperishable light.

Is it that conviction that brings us here tonight? Is it this eternal metaphor of "Light in darkness" drawing us out in the dark and in this threatening weather to testify again in dark times with our brother John? I wonder. I tell the officers of the church year after year of serving a New York congregation during the course of the so-called Christmas bombings of North Vietnam during the War in 1972. That Christmas Eve was not so different from this one—wet, soggy, miserable—and still the people poured into our confined sanctuary, squeezed into the pews, lined the walls, sat on the floor in the center aisle—agnostics, atheists, men and women who would not set foot in a church on a bet, Jews, Muslims, Buddhists. Why? Why that night? The music? To be sure. To hear the story? Perhaps. To sing the carols, maybe. To hear the preacher? Hardly. They came, this universal mob, because they knew we were going to light candles during that service, and by heaven they needed a light to hang onto in a dark world. Nothing sectarian about that. You did not have to buy any religious doctrine to light a candle, to hold it, and finally trust in the great Christmas affirmation that a capital *L* Light shines and the darkness has never put it out.

And so it is tonight. Wherever you are from. Whoever you are, wherever you go to church or synagogue, or whether you never do, welcome to this gathering of men and women testifying, in the first place, to what has been called the greatest story ever told. It is a gorgeous story told in narrative form. But there is another reality standing behind that story, another set of facts and symbols and truth: Light amid darkness; Light shining, as this great Cross testifies—Light shining through everything that would try to crush and extinguish it, not even terror or failure, not rejection or death. Indeed, it is this Cross that tells us the truth about the babe in the manger. And that is why tonight we all can testify to light gleaming amid the darkness—real darkness—whether it be of poverty, homelessness, or depression; whether cancer, loneliness, and family dissolution; light beaming amid the darkness of unemployment, near bankruptcy, and betrayal; yes, to light shining beyond the midnight of alcohol and drug dependency, AIDS, and war.

It is Christmas Eve, friends. The Love, the Peace, the Compassion, the Grace—this Word of God has come among us—this Word is life to all of us, this Word is Light to all of us—Light that shines in darkness and the darkness has never put it out.—James W. Crawford

Topic: Taking the First Step

TEXT: Luke 2:39–52

Charles Kettering, corporation analyst and executive, once said to a group of students, "We need to pay more attention to the future. Most of us will spend the rest of our lives in it."

The last of anything brings recollection and evaluation, retrospection and inventory. And on the flip side is anticipation—a new year. And there is excitement or dread in that. Our imagery is of a clean slate—perhaps a giant eraser that rubs out all the old year's mistakes and frustrations—a chance to start over.

Of course, there's no such eraser. There's always a lot of spillover—good and bad—from yesteryear. But the turning of a calendar corner *is* important.

There was a day when our Lord Jesus looked his future squarely in the eye.

When they had finished everything required by the law of the Lord, they "returned to Galilee, to their own town of Nazareth. The child grew and became strong, filled with wisdom; and the favor of God was upon him" (vv. 39–40).

At that point, it sounds as though Luke is ready to jump ahead to the exploits of John the Baptizer. In fact, it's good sequence and makes complete sense if you just move past verses 41 to 52 and take up with John in chapter 3. Instead, we get a bonus. It's too short and too sparse to satisfy our curiosity after two thousand years, but this little story is the only thing that breaks the silence between our Lord's birth and his baptism, a silence of thirty years. The childhood of Jesus, some have said, is like a walled garden from which we've been given this single flower.

Now, Luke is the only gentile author in the New Testament. Theophilus, to whom he writes his Gospel and his book of Acts, is likely Greek or Roman. Yet, especially in Luke's account, Jesus of Nazareth is a true child of Israel. He was circumcised at eight days, and he was dedicated to God at six weeks. His story takes place either just before or at the actual time when he became bar mitzvahed—son of the law. Then, at age thirty, his public life begins. At each stage of his development, Jesus is in lockstep with Judaism.

But there's something else as well. This little experience is like the foreword in a book: it gets us ready for what's coming later. It is Jesus, looking at his future—where

he'll spend the rest of his life—and taking the first, conscious step toward that.

Luke doesn't say it's Jesus' first or only visit to Jerusalem for Passover, but this one is memorable. It's a week's celebration, so it's not unusual that Jesus and his parents should get separated. Women traveled first, then men came along later. The children would be with friends or other relatives in the larger crowd, and it might be that when they camped at night, the whereabouts of the children would be noted.

So Jesus' parents missed the boy at day's end, and it took them three days to locate him. He's staying with family or friends in Jerusalem at night, or he's in a different camp, but the impression is that during daylight he's in the Temple, listening and asking, the typical rabbinic method of education.

This trip to Jerusalem—*this* Passover—there's a singlemindedness in Jesus that brings him into tension with his family. They say, "We've missed you—been worried about you." He says, "You should've known where to look. I've been in my Father's house" (or "about my Father's business"; the exact language is uncertain). But in the Gospel accounts, these are the first words to come from his lips. They are words of intention about his future.

I. As we move quickly now into the new year, there may be two or three things to be learned here: *conviction,* for example, personal conviction. To this point in his story, Luke has the words about Jesus' specialness on others' lips—Mary, Joseph, Elizabeth, Zechariah, Simeon, Anna, some shepherds and angels. Now Jesus claims this specialness for himself. Here are the stirrings of his own identity.

Relationship with God begins in such a moment for us all. There comes a day when the testimony of all around you—no matter how true—becomes secondary to the hunger and the choosing of your own heart. And it isn't easy to come to this conviction.

It's important to feel special! It's important to know that the love of God is the giving and valuing force in this world that makes each of us someone special. Faith is born in this conviction of specialness, of grace, of God's calling me to companionship.

The conviction that is stirring in Jesus

here is nothing less than his very identity. Who am I? How shall I relate to God? And what is the Father's business as it bears upon my life?

Remember this about the future—there are vices and virtues in us all that are neither yet. They're possibilities—*until* we decide to obey them. And when you decide to obey . . . to start living out of conviction, don't be surprised if others don't understand. Jesus' conviction here sets up tension with his parents, and that would continue throughout his days.

But I ask you, as you step into the future, by what convictions are you living your life? I pray that grace and specialness and commitment to the Father's business are at the top of your list.

II. There's something else here: *trust.* "My Father's business," "my Father's house" —there was no way for him to *fully* understand that at this moment in his life. So how do you live your way into a future? How do you start *toward* before you know what that fullness will look like?

By trust . . . that the God who called you to faith and conviction, called you to journey and that on that pilgrimage you will not be deserted. How could Jesus have known that the Father's business would mean the temptation and the struggle of the cross? He couldn't. So he lived in the unknown by trust. The same voice that said, "I must be in my Father's house," also said at the end of life, "Into thy hands I commit my spirit." Those two statements can only be bound together by the rope of trust. When life tests your convictions about specialness and grace and purpose, you can survive by trust in the almightiness of God's love and care.

III. There's one other thing here: *awareness.* He says it in Jerusalem: "my Father's business." But he *learns* it in Nazareth.

What does God use to shape our lives? Most often, Nazareth and the routines of everyday life there. To be aware of that is to know that each day has possibility, and every circumstance may be God's teachable moment as he molds our lives. Obviously, though he traveled to and from the holy city of Jerusalem, Jesus spent most of his life in and around Nazareth.

Where is God at work? In the plain deeds of a carpenter's shop, in the routine relationships of a small town, and in a family where he learned his images and stories. What he preached abroad, he started to learn in Nazareth.

So, as you take a step into your tomorrows, keep the awareness strong that spiritual maturity doesn't grow in the soil of the unusual or the spectacular. It grows in the commonplace, the everyday. When you look at how Jesus turned out, there must've been some not-so-usual people in Nazareth —mother, father, rabbi, friends. And God used what was at hand to shape his life . . . I believe God still operates that way.—William L. Turner

ILLUSTRATIONS

AN ETERNAL FOUNDATION. In the Christian world, and largely in the non-Christian world as well, we orient our reckoning of time around this Christmas world as well; we orient our reckoning of time around this Christmas event. We count our days and years *post Jesum Christum natum*—from the birth of Christ. For many, this is a banal custom. Yet for us who believe, it is an essential indicator: the story of our life is no longer to be separated from the story of the child in Bethlehem. We no longer merely count our days; we live our days "after the birth of Christ." After the birth of Christ—that changed the outlook and orientation of our lives. We may—we are supposed to—begin our calendar days with this beginning. In our earthly real flesh, we are no longer wordless, and therefore not worthless; we are no longer God-forsaken people eaten away by worries. Our temporal like has its eternal foundation—Jan M. Lochman

WHOSE BIRTHDAY? A family celebrated Christmas each year by singing "Happy Birthday" to Jesus, baking a cake for him, and setting an extra chair at the table to remind them of his presence.—Bill Cashman

DIVINE CONDESCENSION. When we speak of God coming down to earth, we mean (among much else) that He had something to communicate which was of the utmost importance. If that communication was to take place, He had to come down to our level, to see through our eyes, to stand alongside us, to share with us in our deepest experiences. Only so could He teach us what was in the Mind of God. Only so could He be to us what God for ever is.—Frederick Donald Coggan

THE POINT OF CHRISTMAS.   In the cartoon strip "For Better or for Worse" the younger sister, Lizzie, rejoices as she tells her big brother, "Look! I got nine dollars an' eleven cents to spend on Christmas!" Lizzie's brother, Michael, replies, "You can't buy something for everyone with nine dollars an' eleven cents, Lizzie!" But with supreme confidence Lizzie exclaims, "I'm gonna try!" Walking away, Michael answers sarcastically, "Well, they're sure gonna be cheap presents." But Lizzie reminds us of the point of Christmas with her answer to Michael: "Nothing is cheap, Michael, if it costs all the money you have!"

So we are reminded that nothing is cheap about Christmas in God's eyes, either. After all, He gave us everything He has—Himself! —Ed Mitchell

MANGER AND CROSS.   Yesterday a beautiful poinsettia plant was delivered to our home. No gift could be more meaningful to a Californian. It was sent by a young and highly gifted Methodist preacher. Three years ago I had appointed him to a splendid church. He was very happy. Then came news that his little son was seriously ill. It was cancer, and there was no hope. Death would come swiftly. The little boy is still alive, perhaps to suffer a few weeks more. The minister and his lovely wife have carried on. He preaches to increasing congregations. He ministers to his people in the thousand ways that characterize a good minister of Jesus Christ. Every night he sits for hours holding his son in his arms. The pain seems less when the father holds him close. The father sleeps on a mattress on the floor beside his boy so that he can take his son in his arms again whenever the boy cries out. He does not talk about his sorrow. He prays. He serves. He sends poinsettias at Christmas. That is what happens when a man bows before a Manger and kneels before a Cross.—G. Bromley Oxman

GO AGAIN TO BETHLEHEM!   Sin cannot ultimately defeat Him. The idea of some automatic human progress (which warmed the heart of our Victorian fathers) may be impossible for us, but this world is still *God's* world.

Be sure of it by going again to Bethlehem. In all the growing madness of things, in the frustration and bitterness of the hour—come and pause by the manger and hear the truth of your most holy faith. This Baby is Almighty God. He will grow and struggle with this world, and, as He leaves it at the last, having lived the perfect life for our example, this He will say to all who care to listen: "Be of good cheer; I have overcome the world."—W. E. Sangster

SECTION VII.
Evangelism and World Missions

SERMON SUGGESTIONS

Topic: Forgiveness and Its Limits

TEXT: Matt. 18:10–22

Limits: Library books back within three weeks; taxes paid by a certain date; mortgage payments to the bank within ten days of the due date, or add 5 percent to the bill. Everything in life has limits, does it not?

Everything, that is, except the capacity of God to forgive. People sin and sin and sin, but God forgives. Listen to the parable again: One of your sheep goes wandering off somewhere. Wouldn't you leave the ninety-nine on the hills and go after the lost one? No, you wouldn't; that does not make any business sense at all. You've got to protect your investment; ninety-nine sheep in the hand is worth more than one in the bush! But God doesn't think that way. God is perfectly happy to wander the hills, eon after eon, searching for the little lost sheep. And when He finds one, He rejoices.

This is so sweet it is almost sloppy. Does God require the sheep to say, "I'm sorry"? Does God spank the little rascal so it won't do it again? Does he tie a rope around it? Apparently not. God simply takes it back and rejoices that the sheep is home once again. Next day, He's out after another "poor, wandering one."

So Jesus tells us another story, a little different this time. Suppose your brother or sister in the church does something to you. Here's what you do: Go to him or her first privately, and tell the wrong. If he listens to you, then you have gained your brother back. If he doesn't listen to you, then take a couple of others with you, and try again. If it still doesn't work, then tell the story to the church, and let them try to reconcile you. If the person won't listen to the church, then "let him be to you as a Gentile and a tax collector."

Now, we're talking limits. Three strikes and you're out, just like in baseball. I try to work it out; I and a couple of others try; then the whole church tries; and then I'm not obligated to forgive anymore. That's more than fair. After all, if the person were really serious about his faith, he'd listen to reason after all that.

But, wait a minute. Listen to the end of this second story closely. Verses 18–19 say that if we bind sins on someone—if we say, "You have done something wrong, and you haven't repented of it, so we're not forgiving your sins"—if we bind sins, then God does so, too. And if the church, or even two of three of us gathered here pray the same way, then God agrees with us. If we agreed not to forgive, then God agrees. That sounds a little strange, doesn't it. Verse 14 said that God doesn't want anyone to perish; verse 18 seems to say that if we want to bind sins on someone and send them to Hell, God will agree. And verse 20 is even more strange: "Where two or three are gathered in my name, there am I in the midst of them." See, the reason they were gathered in verse 17 was to treat some unrepenting sinner like a Gentile and a tax collector. Can you really imagine Jesus throwing someone out of the church? Can you see Jesus refusing to forgive?

He must be playing around with the

words here. Look back at verse 17 again: "If he refuses to listen even to the church, let him be to you as a Gentile and a tax collector." Let's ask ourselves how Jesus treated Gentiles and tax collectors. Well, as it happens, Matthew's Gospel is full of them. When Jesus was born, who came to see the baby in Matthew? The three wise men, who were Persian astrologers–Gentiles. When Jesus started his ministry in Galilee, Matthew pointed out that the region was called "Galilee of the Gentiles" because so many non-Jewish people lived there. One of Jesus' first healings was of the slave of a Roman centurion. So Gentiles were OK. What about tax collectors, those renegade Jews who robbed their own people for the Romans? Well, one of Jesus' own disciples was a tax collector–a man named Matthew. The Pharisees got onto Jesus, saying that he was the friend of tax collectors and other law-breakers. So if Jesus said, "Treat him like a Gentile and a tax collector," what did he mean? Love him–forgive him–put your arms around him.

It probably took a few minutes, but Peter figured that one out. You can see the wheels turning, the smoke coming out, and then he says, "Now, wait a minute, Lord. You told us this nice little story about the sheep, and then this story about three strikes and treat them like a tax collector. Will you tell us straight out, how many times am I required to forgive my brother? Suppose he does the same thing to me seven times in a row? Is that enough forgiving?" And Jesus' famous answer, "Not 7 times, but 70 times 7." In other words, there are no limits on your forgiving, either.

There are some questions we ask whose answers we really don't want to hear. Does the wife of the adulterous husband really have to forgive him every time? Are we really supposed to forgive murderers? If it were up to us, would we forgive Saddam Hussein or Adolf Hitler? Every fiber in our body, every ounce of our humanity says "No. If you forgive these people, then there is no justice. If you don't make them pay, then right and wrong don't matter, and we all might as well shoot each other as not. If I forgive the thieves who stole my son's bicycle, then what's to stop them from stealing my van or my house?" When we ask Jesus,

"How often should I forgive," we want to hear, "Three strikes and they're out, and you're off the hook," and for centuries the church has pretended that Jesus could really say that.

But we know the answer before we ask the question. We just don't want to hear it. God's forgiveness is unlimited. He will search for the lost sheep every day for all eternity. Jesus' forgiveness is unlimited, and he died to prove it. If we are Jesus' disciples, if we truly wish to live as he lived, then we will tell ourselves to do what few people in history have done–open our ears and listen to what he says. Our forgiveness is also supposed to be unlimited. God gives us the strength to listen, to hear, and to obey.–Richard B. Vinson

Topic: The Tragedy of Backsliding
TEXT: John 6:66–71

A revival just isn't a revival without a sermon on "backsliding"! In a not-too-distant past, one of the stock emphases of revival times focused upon this sin. It was a term popularized by John Bunyan in *The Pilgrim's Progress.*

Bunyan would feel right at home among most contemporary churches. Among most Baptists, Methodists, and Presbyterians, more than one-third of our members are unaccounted for!

The text illustrates the meaning of backsliding. The crowds had been eagerly following Jesus. But then, he begins to say some "hard" things. That is, he begins to say some things with which the crowd does not agree–perhaps, does not understand, or both. As a result, they leave Jesus behind to find a smaller, less demanding Savior.

Then follows a pathetic scene in which Jesus turns to the Twelve and asks if they, too, are planning to desert him. The very question suggests that backsliding is a real possibility in the life of every Christian. Not a single one of us is above the temptation of letting our love for Christ grow cold. Nor are entire churches free from this possibility.

The Bible does not hide the reality of this sin of backsliding. In the parable of the sower and the seed, this sin is illustrated in the seed that falls on rocky soil and quickly springs up, only to fall away.

And these are they likewise that are sown on stony ground, who, "when they have heard the word, immediately receive it with gladness; and have no root in themselves, and so endure for a time: afterward, when affliction or persecution arise for the world's sake, immediately they are offended" (Mark 4:16–17).

In the same parable, we are also warned of the choking effects of worldly cares and the deceitfulness of riches: "And these are they which are sown among thorns; such as hear the word, and the cares of this world, and the deceitfulness of riches, and the lusts of other things entering in, choke the word, and it becomes unfruitful" (Mark 4:18–19).

The melancholy scene of Peter denying Jesus should be proof aplenty of the nearness of this sin. Paul writes to the Galations who have fallen away in the persuasion of false teachers: "You ran well; what has hindered you now?" (5:7).

But, backsliding is not just a fictional or biblical problem. The modern church is riddled with backsliders. Look at any church directory that is more than a year or two old. Not only will you notice what the years have done to each of us, but another sadder fact will strike you.

There will be pictures of those who, at the time the directory was published, were active. But, where have they been lately? What happened to them? What is the impact of backsliding upon a Christian?

I. What happens to the backslider?

a. First, when you cease to be fervent for the Lord, when you grow lax and lazy in the work of the church, when you ease off in your personal prayer life and devotions, when you grow careless in your support of the work of your church with your tithe, it is a natural and inevitable consequence that you also forfeit the joy of your salvation.

It would be helpful to remember David's anguished plea to the Lord after his sin with Bathsheba. He had grown cold toward the Lord, and then cried in utter despair, "Restore to me the joy of my salvation" (Ps. 51:12). The contemporary church is full of members who are full of the things of the world but starving to spiritual death for a real relationship with God.

The exact reason why does not matter. What does matter is that the terrible spiritual cost is too much to pay, whatever the reason.

b. Another effect of backsliding on the Christian is the loss of meaningful fellowship in the faith. The story is old, but it illustrates this point.

A revival evangelist visited a man who had not been in church for years. They both sat before the open fire for a while, just staring into the flames. Finally, the minister took the tongs and, reaching over, grasped a flaming coal and rolled it away from the other logs.

They both continued to sit in silence while the coal, apart from the others, slowed turned from red-hot to a faint glow and then a cold, black cinder. It was his first words in several long moments when the man turned to the minister with tears in his eyes and said, "I'll be in church Sunday, Preacher."

People drop out of church for various reasons. I heard of one man who stopped going to church because a girl joined Sunday morning and then participated in the Lord's Supper that night before being baptized. The man–a deacon–stomped out of the church that night and–when I heard about him–had not been back for over a decade.

What a tragedy! A man became a backslider for over a decade over such a small matter! How effectively the devil does his work in the lives of God's people.

c. A third effect of backsliding is its negative impact upon the church of Jesus Christ. It means there is one less Christian to do the work of the Lord in the local community. It means the other members who are sincerely trying to carry out the mission and fellowship of the church must carry your load. It means the rest of the church will have to spend time putting out the brushfires backsliders often start with a critical tongue toward the pastor, the deacons, other church members, or the church in general. And all because one Christian is not right with God!

Casey Stengel was still managing baseball when most men of his age were sitting back in their easy chairs admiring their trophies. The unique spirit he brought to the game has been permanent in its impact.

One day he was hitting some balls to a rookie in right field who missed every fly ball. Then Casey hit some on the ground, and he missed those too. Casey called him in from the field and advised him, "I want to show you how it is done. You hit some balls to me."

The rookie lofted a few fly balls to Stengel, who also missed them. Stengel jogged in and chided the rookie, "You messed up right field so bad nobody can play it!" Then the manager walked off the field.

The contemporary church and witness may owe its weakened, compromised state more to those who have dropped out than to those who have stayed with it. After all, those who carry the burden of the Christian faith today often are forced to carry more than their share. Be careful how you criticize the church if you are not actively participating in her life!

But even worse than hurting yourself or hurting your church, backsliding will hurt your Lord. Think again about the picture illustrated in the text. Imagine the Lord saying with sadness in his voice, "Will you also go away?" Even though we know that no one else has the words of eternal life, too many of us do turn away for such small and petty reasons.

II. a. Admittedly, some backslide because of incomplete conversions. In some cases, there was no genuine confrontation with the Savior. This was so in the text. Jesus tells the crowd, "You seek me, not because you saw the miracles, but because you ate of the loaves and were filled" (6:26).

In our day, the satisfaction of immediate need too often results in conversion that is not real. Perhaps that explains what the writer of 1 John meant when he wrote, "They went out from us, but they were not of us; for if they had been of us, they would no doubt have continued with us" (2:19).

b. Another factor in backsliding is often some looming sin. The writer of Hebrews refers to this: "Therefore, since we are surrounded by so great a cloud of witnesses, let us lay aside every weight and the sin which so easily besets us" (12:1a).

Obviously, there are many in whose hearts God has done a work of grace. Yet they have apparently turned their backs upon Jesus and his church. In many of those situations, the problem is "the easily besetting sin"—that sin which the Christian has not confessed and forsaken, that sin which

the Christian continued to secretly cherish and feed—and even practice—after conversion, that sin that he or she simply could not abandon!

And after conversion, it continued to grow like a dreadful cancer. Finally, it has become so big—it has become so poisonous, so infectious—that it has literally threatened the spiritual welfare of the believer!

If that is your case, listen! Your sin does not have to do that to you! Jesus came to do battle with sin. He defeated the power of sin in the world and in your life! Your sin is not bigger than God's ability to forgive it and to remove it from your heart!

c. Another cause for backsliding is simply the living of these days. Living becomes difficult, stressful, challenging, hard, even painful. Life takes its toll on our spiritual commitment. Christians lose their joy, their enthusiasm, their interest!

There are some times and events in every person's life that need to be marked with a red flag—areas of high potential for spiritual backsliding.

Young people—red flag high school and college years. That's when you're gaining your independence. You are out from under your parents' watchful eye. You have wheels. You can go and come as you please. The temptation is strong to drop out of the church and let your spiritual life suffer.

Red flag the early years of marriage. Love is often blind concerning the spiritual nature of marriage. Are both you and your marriage partner Christians? Are you both of the same denomination? If you are on your way to the altar, have you carefully discussed this vital area of life? Have you prayerfully decided in which church you will plant your life and your family's?

Red flag the achievement years—the years when you begin your own business or when you begin to climb the corporate ladder of success. All of a sudden you will seem too busy—or too tired—for regular worship and church participation. Your tithe will seem too big for your church. After all, you think, they don't wisely use what you already give!

We often put a blue or pink bow on the mailbox or door when a baby is born. But a red flag should also be raised over this event! Children do not keep parents from church, but parents often use children as an excuse for backsliding. Don't let the devil lull you with this one: "We'll get active in church when the children get older. We know they need to be in Sunday school." They surely do . . . and so do their parents!

The biggest red flag should be hoisted over the home in which more and more excuses are given for decreasing participation in church and a dwindling spiritual life. Start listening to yourself, and if your excuses are just that—excuses—if the ox always seems to be in the ditch, then either fill in the ditch or kill the ox! Excuses will soon cripple a spiritual life!—Gary C. Redding

Topic: Imprisoned by Illusions of the Past
TEXT: Exod. 16:1–3

After being enslaved for four hundred years, Israel was freed from the bondage of Egypt. It had taken ten plagues to break the powers of Pharaoh, but finally millions were following Moses toward the land promised to Abraham. After departing, the prodigy of Jacob were to face great challenges. The barrier was no longer the chariots of Pharaoh but the unbelief within their hearts.

God's purpose for his children was a prompt entry into the land flowing with milk and honey. The Lord wished for Israel to leave and never return to the bondage of Egypt, physically or spiritually. Though Israel exited as a free people, the covenant congregation retained spiritual tendencies to return to the land of slavery.

Contemporary Christians, liberated from spiritual bondage by the cross of Jesus Christ, resemble Israel by being less than free from the pitfalls of worldliness and evil. The disciples of Jesus, like Israel, are called to leave and never return to the boundaries that are imposed by our disobedience. Like Israel, believers are called to come out of Egypt and stay out.

I. *Illusions of the past are powerful when provisions fall.* Nostalgia causes a longing for days and things of the past. Nostalgia makes some desire old automobiles, outdated gas company signs, and antique bathtubs. Nostalgia makes others hang old implements on the living room wall.

Nostalgia includes a significant element of illusion. When desiring relics of the past we forget the hardships that accompanied the good old days. For instance, when we long for that 1957 Chevrolet Bel-Air coupe, we forget that the classic Chevy lacked air conditioning, automatic transmission, power steering, and AM-FM stereo radio. If our wish for the old car were to come true, we would soon discover that we miss the smooth ride and other comforts developed since the 1950s.

The Israelites had a nostalgia of sorts when they thought back to the abundant food of Egypt (v. 3). These illusions were triggered by the food shortage in the Desert of Sin. Even though just a month before, the Israelites had experienced the miraculous interventions of God, they were now under a test of their faith. In the days preceding this incident, they had consumed all the bread they had carried out of Egypt. The plagues were fine, crossing the Red Sea on dry ground was great, but now they were hungry, and there was nothing to eat. With parched lips and empty stomachs, they began to think back about how things used to be. They remembered the good old days sitting around banquet tables in Egypt. They had never been hungry in Egypt, it seemed.

In their musing, the slave's gruel of Pharaoh seemed like a choice leg of lamb. The coarse, moldy bread of bondage was recalled as baked goods of the finest quality. In the illusion prompted by Satan, they could smell the loaves just pulled out of the oven. Of course the illusion was missing a few realistic details. In Egypt they had suffered the slaughter of their children. They had borne the heat of the day in back-breaking labor to build the storage cities and monuments to Pharaoh's lofty pride. When the supplies of food ran out and stomachs began to growl, the look back to Egypt was transformed from the horror of fact to the deception of illusion.

When hardships come, the illusion of past comforts presents itself as an alternative, and a return to past life-styles is prompted. The recovering alcoholic under stress of marital problems may think that he can relax by taking one drink. Just one. Instead of remembering the sickness, financial problems, and worse marital problems related to the bondage of alcoholism, an illusion of ease and comfort is recalled. When confronted with difficult teenage children, some parents may begin to question their commitment to the church and Jesus Christ and think that past days were full of tranquil times. There is the temptation to chuck the present spiritual discipline of prayer and seeking the Lord's will and attempt to go back to old ways of faithless living.

II. *Living between miraculous interludes.* The grumbling of the Israelites caused a rift in their relationship with the Lord and established a pattern of behavior in their lives that would be difficult to break. At the next trial, instead of being stronger, they would be weaker and more susceptible to disobedience to their loving heavenly Father.

The succeeding chapters reveal that after the powerful plagues and parting of the Red Sea the Lord had miraculous plans to feed his people. Soon the manna from heaven was to fall for bread, and quail would be sent to provide choice meat to appease aggravated hunger. Thereafter God was to bring his chosen people to the southern border of Canaan and show them into the land of promise.

Although their hunger was great, God was even greater. The Lord had not abandoned his people, he was soon to act to meet their every need. The trials of hunger were intended to build the faith of the covenant people as they saw their every need provided for in their trust of the Lord. Instead the people clung to illusions of past comforts, and these thoughts and actions left an indelible destructive print upon their spiritual lives.

In today's struggles believers face the same challenge of faith. In the midst of trials believers are not to despair of faith but to believe in the One who is greater than the world. We are not to conclude that we are in the valley of death but in an interlude between God's miraculous provisions. The miracles may not be as noticeable as the parting of the Red Sea, but they will be decisive acts of God on our behalf all the same.– Ken Cox

Topic: The Church—Ministry, Mission, Evangelism

TEXT: Matt. 28:16–20; Luke 4:16–20

We are not here to entertain ourselves; that is not why we come to church. Neither are we here simply or primarily to perpetuate our institution–though that is a powerful temptation in this day and time. Rather, when we Christians come together, we must strengthen ourselves; we must do what is necessary so that we are inspired and invigorated as a result of being here. But making this a good and effective and useful place to be is a means to an end and never an end in itself.

Our ultimate goal as a community of faith is to become focused and energized while we are *here,* while we are gathered together, so that we can be effective in getting the message of church out there, beyond these walls. If you come to church for worship and you are heartened, let us say, but not enough happened while you learned and worshiped and prayed, the essential is lacking.

The very word for "church" in the New Testament is *ekklesia,* which, literally, means "called out ones" and from which we derive our English word *ecclesiastical,* used, of course, to refer to church-related matters. The Church is Christian people *called out* of the world–yes, that is a part of who we are. We are called *out of* the world because we are not to be conformed to this world. But the called-out ones are sent back into the world for ministry and service in Jesus' name. The cycle is not complete until the called-out ones have gone back to places of hopelessness and struggle and despair carrying the message of our Lord, Jesus Christ, and filled with his presence and purpose.

I know of no better summary of the ministry of the church, *our* mandate for ministry, then Jesus' own testimony as to what he was about in terms of ministry. This is what we said at the outset of his ministry, and we know that he lived by this throughout his brief career. As Luke reports it, Jesus said, "The Spirit of the Lord is upon me, because he has anointed me to bring good news to the poor. He has sent me to proclaim release to the captives and recovery of sight to the blind, to let the oppressed go free" (Luke 4:18 NRSV).

If you have ever wondered what it is you're supposed to be doing as a Christian, wonder no more.

This directive for ministry is nothing easy, but it is very clear. This is what the

Church must be doing; if we are the people of Christ, this is what we must be doing: bringing good news to the poor, proclaiming release to the captives, and recovery of sight to the blind, freeing those who are oppressed. The Church is constantly *preoccupied,* not with itself, but with those who struggle and hurt in every way, especially with those whom society has cast aside as, essentially, insignificant or unimportant. About whom are we talking? The homeless, the hungry, the jobless, the chronically depressed, persons dying with AIDS, alcoholics, drug addicts, bigots, those who believe that they must keep their true identities concealed—especially from the religious community—the hated and the dispossessed in other countries and cultures, the affluent who in spite of their material resources and influence see no value in life. We are called to reach out to those who have no hope, those who can find no good reason to live, the unattractive and the seemingly unredeemable. These were the people with whom Jesus was consumed. These were the people for whom Jesus, the head of the Church, lived and died!

We go out to minister to these people, first, to try and soothe their pain, give them shelter and food to eat, befriend them, sit with them, wait with them. We meet them, and we take them where they are. We, first, *live out* the message of God's love for them, and—then—maybe we'll have the opportunity to speak the message of God's love to them. *Maybe* we'll have that privilege; there is no guarantee that we will, but perhaps we will earn the right.

Remember Jesus' words: "Go therefore and make disciples of all nations, baptizing them in the name of the Father and of the Son and of the Holy Spirit, and teaching them to obey everything that I have commanded you. And remember, I am with you always, to the end of the age (Matt. 28:19–20 NRSV).

We call this passage of Scripture "The Great Commission." It is the Church's mandate, but the Church has often forgotten that—according to the example of our Lord—we earn the right to point people to faith by, first, making an effort to address their needs. To try to make disciples without getting to know and care about people is artificial, superficial, and cold. The caring comes before the telling and the baptizing and the teaching.

When we do get to tell people our message, what will we say? What is the message of the faith, the essential message of Christianity? In fact, there is much to say if we get to the business of teaching people "everything" that Jesus commanded, but there is a foundational message upon which, I believe, everything else is built. This theme is the treasure of the Christian Church, and it has come to us because of God's revelation of Godself and God's message through Jesus Christ: God loves us, every single one of us, and there is nothing you can do to change that basic fact of reality; further, this God who loves us wants us to celebrate life to the fullest and so offers us a way for that to happen.

Now, in a world that is so blatantly impersonal and tragedy-tainted, a world that so often leaves us feeling lonely and questioning our value as human beings, what better message could there be? What word do people need more than this word? There is no fact that any of us need to know more than this fact. And not only does this message transform our lives, but also, as the Church, we get to pass on to others this same good news. This message is ours to know, to experience, and to tell.

When we are performing ministry and proclaiming the message, we are doing evangelism. Honest evangelism is nothing contrived or assaultive; it is, rather, the natural outgrowth of caring and sharing our faith in God through Jesus Christ. And the only formula there is is that we know people and reach out to them before we speak.

We are the Church. We are the people who carry in the very fabric of our being the love of God. Let us, then, be about our business.—David Albert Farmer

ILLUSTRATIONS

THE POWER OF A PROMISE.   Maggie and George are the central characters in Thornton Wilder's 1940s play *The Skin of Our Teeth.* There is a terrible struggle going on between them.

George is a fine man. He's made his way

up from almost nothing. He's been an excellent father, a pillar of the church. He has all the best interests of the community at heart.

And Maggie is as fine a woman as you could ever hope to meet. She lives for her children. She is the acting president of the Excelsior Mother's Club. She does needlecraft so well that people want her to go into business.

They have been married for a long time. For most of that time, there has been a war going on. Some strange things have happened to George during the years. For one thing, he has fallen in love with another woman. As we meet him, he is about to leave Maggie, once and for all, and finally find happiness.

George says: "Maggie, I'm moving out . . . of everything. For good. I'm going to marry Miss Fairweather. I shall provide generously for you and the children. In a few years, you'll be able to see that it's all for the best. That's all I have to say. . . . You're a fine woman, Maggie, but . . . but a man has his own life to lead in the world."

Maggie responds: "Well, after living with you for five thousand years I guess I have a right to a word or two, haven't I?"

George answers: "I want to spare your feelings in every way I can, Maggie."

But Maggie answers calmly, almost dreamily: "I didn't marry you because you were perfect. I didn't even marry you because I loved you. I married you because you gave me a promise. . . . That promise made up for all your faults. And the promise I gave you made up for mine. Two imperfect people got married and it was the promise that made the marriage."

"But, Maggie," says George, "I was only nineteen."

"Still," Maggie says, ". . . when our children were growing up, it wasn't a house that protected them; and it wasn't our love that protected them—it was that promise."—Gary C. Redding

CLEAN THROUGH THE WORLD.   While she was a millionairess living in a swanky New York apartment, Gert Behanna was miserable. So miserable, in fact, that she tried to take her own life more than once. "I

failed at everything I tried to do," she told a seminary audience. "Even when I tried to commit suicide, I failed."

But she heard the Word of God, responded to it, and was gloriously saved. Describing her conversion experience, she talked about kneeling by her bed and asking Christ to do something with the shambles of her life. "When I stood up again," she said, her face beaming with joy, "I felt like I had just taken a spiritual shower bath!"—Lucien E. Coleman, Jr.

LIGHT FOR OTHERS.   The mighty Mississippi River lay dark and forbidding across my path. Someplace in the darkness was a ferry that represented my only hope of getting across.

Stepping from my car into darkness that felt as if it was trying to swallow me, I walked to a long utility pole with a feebly burning lantern set at its base. Its soft glow scarcely penetrated the darkness.

Attached to its handle was a slender rope. The rope disappeared upward into the darkness, only to reappear and stop at hand level.

I took the rope, pulled gently, and slowly the lantern began to rise, taking its soft glow into the midnight blue sky.

Before long, I heard the sound of the ferry. They had seen the signal light and were on the way to take me across the river.

Many times I have needed help through hard or impossible situations. During those times, God has faithfully provided someone or something to light the way, so help and deliverance could come.—Ernie Perkins

SIN'S PAYOFF.   Sin always starts with the best but ends with the worst. In spite of inflation and devaluation, sin still pays the same wages—death. A man still reaps just what he sows. We may not see it now, but we will see it sooner than we expect—the worst is yet to come. And the day will come when we will hate ourselves for thinking we could sin and get away with it. With sin, the worst is yet to come; but for the Christian, the best is yet to come. God always saves the best for the last.—Warren W. Wiersbe

BORN AGAIN. Here are some of the new birthmarks: "He that is born of God loveth the brethren." Is that mark on you? Here is another: He that is born of God abideth in Him." That is another mark. Is that on you? Here is another: "He that is born of God overcometh the world." Is that mark on you? Here is another: "He that is born of God keepeth himself in the love of God." Is that mark on you? Here is another: "He that is born of God hath the witness in himself."–Gipsy Smith

SECTION VIII.
Preaching from Ephesians

BY RICHARD B. VINSON

The letter to the Ephesians presents a set of puzzles to the biblical interpreter. On the one hand, it is full of long, rolling phrases and wonderful twenty-five-dollar theological words you can really chew on. On the other hand, for believers who prefer parables and aphorisms, it is a thick book easy to pass over. On the one hand, Ephesians gives us some marvelous texts: saved by grace through faith; Christ created in himself one new humanity in the place of two; one Lord, one faith, one baptism, and so on. On the other hand, Ephesians gives us some troublesome texts: wives be subject to your husbands; slaves obey your earthly masters with fear and trembling.

Three books, more than others, shaped these sermons. Andrew T. Lincoln's commentary in the Word Biblical Commentary series (1900) and Markus Barth's two-volume commentary in the Anchor Bible series (1974) make a good pair, especially since the two authors disagree on many points. They both have extensive discussions of the text and full bibliographies. Walter Wink's trilogy on the Powers contributed a very powerful hermeneutical tool for dealing with the "in the heavenlies" parts of Ephesians. My debts to these three scholars will be clear when you read the sermons.

Topic: We Are Somebody
TEXT: Eph. 1:1–14
We are here today to celebrate something about ourselves, something hard to imagine and easy to forget. According to Ephesians, our celebration of this fact is one of our most important jobs as a church. So let's do

it well; borrowing from Jesse Jackson, repeat after me, please: We are (We are) Some-*body* (Somebody). You sound tentative —say it like you really mean it: We are Somebody!

I. Who Are We?
We have an identity problem, not so much an individual identity problem as a corporate one. I know who I am: I can tell you my profession, my address, my social security number. It's our corporate identity that is unclear. I know who I am, but I'm not sure who we are, or what "we" I really belong to.

We are Christians. But nothing about that term is a meaningful identifying marker. Gallup polls show that most of the country agrees with many of the premises that are supposed to define us, but our own attendance records show that most of these believers are absent. Denominational markers are perhaps worse. I am a Baptist, but so is Jesse Helms. I suppose there are some advertising groups who have me pegged as a member of a particular purchasing cohort; that may help them send me junk mail, but it doesn't help me. I've moved so many times in my life that neither my place of birth nor my present community defines me. The only members of my family in my community are the ones who live in my house, so family is not a helpful marker either; I'm not a member of a clan who know themselves as a certain type of person. Companies complain that there is no loyalty within organizations anymore. Surely I'm overdoing this, but one gets a mental picture of a nation of isolated persons riding to work with the headphones on, working in front of a terminal with the radio on, and then eating fast food on their couch with the TV on.

We have a corporate identity crisis—this is not really news. It is not news that most of us would like to belong to a meaningful group that would help to define us. Small groups flourish as people seek the support and coherence of a place where "everybody knows your name." The church in the New Testament is sometimes presented as such a place, but our reading in Ephesians goes one better. We are all members of one Person; not just group members, but the body of Christ.

II. God's Chosen

Ephesians goes at this from different angles in this long opening prayer. God blessed us, chose us, set our destiny—not as individuals, but collectively, as members of Christ. Being God's children, our being "holy and blameless before God," or being flooded with the blessings of God's love—God gives us all those things together. We experience them only together.

This is hard to imagine, since it is different from most things that happen to us. A department store may send you a flyer because you, like thousands of other folks, have a certain kind of credit card or live in a certain place; but you still pull the thing out of your own mailbox, and it doesn't make you feel like part of a group. God blesses us, chooses us, aims us toward God's goals as part of a group, really as part of a single person, Christ. There's an old gospel song, "I'm on my way to Canaan's land; if the preacher don't go, that won't hinder me; I'm on my way, praise the Lord, I'm on my way." It's not true: my salvation and yours are bound together. If you don't find God, my joy will not be full. From the beginning, by God's choice, I belong to us, and we belong to Christ. We are Somebody!

III. Bound for Christ

Ephesians presents this as something that God did but also as something that is in process. We are aimed at Christ, who is God's plan, God's model for success. We are bound up in Christ by God's choice, but we are also aimed at Christ. Unity in Christ is a fact in God's choice but a goal in our lives. This is where our celebration is so impor-

tant. Nearly everything about our lives tries to separate us from God and from each other. We are encouraged to think of ourselves as consumers, filling our shopping carts. We are encouraged to think of ourselves as spectators to be entertained, being filled with what the world thinks is interesting or amusing. Unless we say it again and again, we will not believe it; and unless we say it; the world will never hear it. We were created to live united with God, united with one another, bound together by the character of Christ.

IV. Bound with the Spirit

Some have had that dream, of a society where we'd all be fitted together like the parts of a Body, with Christ as our head. But how do we know that such a dream is realistic? By this: God has given us the Spirit, both as a mark of God's authenticity on us and as a down payment, a first step toward becoming Christ. Think about those moments when in worship we have seemed to you like a big family, united in our concern for someone, or united in a song of praise sung from a hundred hearts, or united in a moment of godly grief, when we all sat stunned by the public naming of a sin we'd all shared. God sends us the Spirit to teach us that we're not fooling ourselves or the world. We are Somebody, even if we forget. We are Somebody, even if we have a long way to go before we really look like Jesus. We are Somebody—say it with me—we are Somebody! By the grace of God, by the gradual enfolding into Christ, by the presence of the Spirit—we are Somebody!

Topic: The Ways Things Are
TEXT: Eph. 1:15–22
Our reading today tells us The Way Things Are. I hear your thoughts: What can it know of my situation? What could a first-century writer know of cyberspace, multinational corporations, media campaigns? What could this book tell me about my children, my spouse, my relationships, my job? It's full of demons and angels and miracles and blinding lights, which may have been the world once upon a time, but which don't seem to help me. We read the papers or listen to talk shows to learn about The Way Things Are, and believe me, it's not too good.

THE MINISTERS MANUAL FOR 1997

I. The Powers

That's what we think—all Bible talk is preacher talk, removed by two millennia and several revolutions from the real world —and the first glance at our reading will seem to confirm our suspicions. "I want you to know," says the author, "God raised Christ from the dead and seated him at his right hand in the heavenly places, far above all rule and authority and power and dominion." Those last four things are names of spiritual critters, Powers with a capital *P,* malevolent beings that control The Way Things Are. We don't hear this very well. Maybe we think we're supposed to believe in the Devil and demons and all, but don't know what good it does us. Or maybe we've given all that up with the bogeyman; it's stuff good for a thrill in a horror movie, but nothing real.

But it is. This is the truth, my age-of-technology brothers and sisters: there are spiritual forces bigger than we are that control The Way Things Are. When human beings get together and form big institutions, and the institutions get a name and money and power, they begin to have a force and a life of their own. Example: a young woman goes into TV journalism, let's say, full of idealism—going to bring the unvarnished truth to the viewers, going to stick to real issues and not play what sells. Why is it that the best way to control her idealism is to give her a raise and a stock option in the network? Why will being an insider inevitably bring her around to the values of the institution?

I've picked on a media institution, and I don't mean to say that they are worse than the rest of us. It will almost certainly happen in any institution; make a person a part of the structure, and he or she will be made more and more in its image. Walter Wink says that big institutions have spirituality; think of it as the whole being more than the sum of its parts. People can be replaced, but the institution goes on.

II. Christ Rules

Oh, you say, I believe that. The System— of course. You can't fight the system. Bureaucracies, corporations, governments— they're bigger than all of us, and no one can win. Not according to Ephesians. The Powers control the world, according to Ephesians, but not Christ. They thought they had

him on the cross, but God showed what real power was when God raised Jesus from the dead and seated him in heaven. Ephesians uses the image of a seated ruler, with a footstool carved to represent the different parts of the empire—as if a ruler rested his or her foot on the globe, symbolizing world domination. Christ's foot rests not just on the world but on all the Powers.

III. Christ Rules for Us

So what, you say? What does mythology have to do with us? Christ is in charge—does that really change my life? Does that release me from the power of the government, the bank, the stock market? Yes, it does. Christ rules for us, says the text. In Christ, we too have been released from slavery to the power. Christ is our Lord and no one else in fact.

They say television controls our opinions, monopolizes our time, ruins our ability to concentrate, shapes our values. But it is powerless over us if we turn it off. They say that the values of the institutions for whom we work control us, forcing us to pursue profit more than good, forcing us to value productivity more than persons. But they are powerless over us if we are willing to walk away rather than act contrary to Christ. Even the mighty sword of government, the rule of Caesar, can be overcome. Brother Martin told us that if a people refused to be treated as second-class citizens, then those laws would be exposed for the lies they were. It took suffering and hard work, but things changed.

This Scripture text is not a recipe, but a photograph; not a plan, but an analysis. This is the truth: There are forces, Powers, that control The Way Things Are for the world. But God raised Jesus and placed him above the Powers, to rule the Powers for us who are included in the Body of Christ. That fact, that truth, liberates us from the lies of the Powers—you are all in my power— sets us free to live under Christ. How we live free—that's another text and another sermon. But for today, it matters that we are free. It's a message to all the prisoners in the Gulag: your captors have a new master; the doors are open, and you can go.

Topic: Resurrecting Zombies

TEXT: Eph. 2:11–22

I write this sermon just a few weeks after

someone bombed the federal building in Oklahoma City, knowing that by the time you read it, there will be other tragedies that will be fresher on your mind. They always leave us with a bad mix of emotions—anger, confusion, depression, despair—the more so the closer we are to the events. Christians find it hard to be very much like Christ in response to such horror. Most agreed with the call for instant execution of any and all connected with the bombing.

I. We're All Zombies

But there is a serious call in this passage to something greater than revenge, something greater even than justice. It begins with an evaluation of what we are, the second in this letter. We humans, it says, are zombies. Zombies, as any fan of B-movies knows, are corpses animated by the spell of some wicked person who uses a fetish or an evil crystal or something of the sort. They are especially dangerous because they are dead. There's always a scene in the movie where the good guys try to kill them, chopping off arms, and so forth, but it does no good. How can you stop a dead person?

That's what we humans are, says the author, zombies. We are corpses, dead in sin, and animated by the spirit of the Powers of this age. It's a cruel parody of God's creation, in which people were made out of the good earth and brought to life by God's breath. We are made from dead flesh, wallowing in the passions of the flesh, and brought to life by the noxious breath that animates The Way Things Are. Is this not true? Do we not live and breathe profits and acquisitions? Do we not live by the spirit of this age, which tells us to gain, to control, to hoard? Ninety-nine percent of our lives, subtracting the few minutes in church when we are actually paying attention during the prayers, can we claim to be controlled by anything other than the values of our world?

It is only degree that separates us from the mad bombers of this world. We, too, have done acts of cruelty; we have hated; we have been angry enough to consider killing someone or wish them dead, even if we never acted on it. All of us, all humans, controlled by the Spirit of the Age, have the moral sensitivity of zombies. Only degree separates us, I say, and the grace of God, for God has rewritten the normal Hollywood ending to the zombie movie.

II. We're All Transformed Zombies

Usually, after the good guys fail to stop the zombies by attacking them, they discover the secret fetish or magic crystal, and once they destroy it, the corpses crumble back into the earth. If we followed out the analogy, God would destroy the wicked powers, burning them with holy fire, which is what we want to happen to mad bombers. But God has other plans. God resurrects zombies. God puts them through the true death and true resurrection of Jesus Christ, transforming them. God redeems zombies, making them truly alive, giving them, in fact, the eternal life of Christ. Instead of spreading death and destruction, God fits them for good works, giving them a purpose and a dignity. God, who placed people in a good world so long ago, who gave us a good purpose, has redeemed our corruption through Christ.

The bombers can be redeemed, you see; that is the message of the gospel. How do we know? Because God has redeemed us, who were just as much zombies as they, even if we never set off a bomb. God made us into something new, filled us with a clean spirit, and set us to a good purpose, even if we don't live like it very often. "We are what he has made us—it is the gift of God—by grace you have been saved." The transformation, thank God, depends on God's power, and so it can happen to anyone.

Can we pray for the redemption of the bombers? More to the point, unless we had relatives or friends in that tragedy, can we pray for the redemption of our enemies? Anyone can look for revenge; most Americans are taught to value justice. But only the grace of God, only the heart of Christ, only the resurrection of the Spirit, can redeem us to the point where we can pray for the redemption of those who do us harm. Hard, but not unthinkable—it is one of the "good works" to which God has created us.

Topic: One for Two
TEXT: Eph. 2:11–22
I. Racism Lives

Racism is a sad human universal. All the world has always divided humanity into us and them. Circumcised and uncircumcised, Greeks and barbarians, blacks and whites; the divisions change over time and culture, but we humans seem always to have an "us" and a "them." We treat them, the others, with suspicion. We create customs or pass laws that keep them at a distance and at some disadvantage from us. And just when we think that things might be improving, something happens to show that racism still infects our society.

My hometown had the Whites Only and Colored Only signs removed during my childhood, but the attitudes were much more permanent. The director of a home health service says that many of those who call to request a nurse or a sitter still refuse to accept a person of another race. Schools may be desegregated, but students still tend to hang together in single-race groups. And despite all the government interventions, despite all the rhetoric over forty years, despite all the marches and protests, all things political and economic, from jobs to housing to loans, are easier to come by in this country if you are not a member of a minority. And despite the fact of continuing discrimination, there is a growing feeling that "we have done enough for them."

II. It Can Be Cured

We need a new vision, a new reason to keep fighting this disease. We need a reason to believe that our efforts could actually help, that our energies are not wasted on a incurable human failure. Enter Ephesians, with this mural of humanity being cured from racism. At the beginning, there's the "us and them," the aliens and the citizens, the strangers and the members of the covenant, the circumcised and the uncircumcised. At the end, there's only one group, all citizens, all members of one family, and united so tightly in their worship of God that they could be compared to a temple. No more strangers, no more aliens, no more "other." It's a vision to set us thinking: Must humans be racists? Is this a curable disease?

Yes, he says, God in Christ makes "one new humanity in the place of two," which sounds utterly simplistic. The world was not then and is not now neatly divisible into two groups who dislike each other. Instead, racism is a snarl of divisions over skin color, language, class lines, education, and beliefs. In this day, "circumcised" would have included Jews who hated and fought other Jews, to say nothing of the divisions within

the "uncircumcised" category. How can this letter give us a solution if it does not even fairly state the problem?

III. Person by Person

Actually, Eph. 2:15 says "one new *anthropos* in the place of two." "Humanity" translates *anthropos* accurately, but it obscures the fact that the noun is singular—"one new person in the place of two" is better. "One new person in the place of two" is what happens when two people, of different races or classes, become Christian friends. The attitudes of both shift; they learn to depend upon each other, and because they do, it is no longer as easy to hate the whole class to which their friend belongs. And if the two are both aiming to become more and more like Christ, the means and motivation to be patient, to forgive, to sacrifice for the other will be present. What a vision: one new person in the place of two, person by person, being changed by Christ's love operating their friendship.

IV. Redeeming the System

I can hear some of my teenager friends mocking me. "Yeah, why can't we just all get along?" It's more complicated than that, too, I know. We may be friendly, person to person, and still allow more systemic racism to exist. But Ephesians say that Christ put an end, in God's eternal plan, to all the laws dividing us. That doesn't mean we don't have to work to end racism, but it should give us hope that the effort is worthwhile. It's the vision that gives us hope: seeing a mural in our minds of persons laying aside their hatred two by two, and of whole societies striking down the legal and physical barriers to equality—seeing this will help us to keep going.

Note, please, that both personal and systemic racism are demolished by Christ in the mural. It seems to me that the disease can't be cured without attacking both simultaneously. Church groups should, for example, take on person-to-person projects that put believers of one race in close contact with believers of another race. But they must also struggle against the systems that help to create and perpetuate racism. To do one without the other is futile. Ephesians itself speaks of slaves and masters treating each other with Christian love and respect without ever challenging the institution of slavery, and that left the door open for the whole sad spectacle of slavery and segregation in the South.

V. Unity and Diversity

One more thing about this mural. Because it is a Christian picture, it paints the final scene as the union of all persons in Christ. The dividing wall of which he speaks in verse 14 and "the law with its commandments and ordinances" in verse 15 was the Torah, the Law of Moses. In other words, to be included in the glorious union of the final scene, Jews will need to quit living by the Torah, will need to give up those things that define them as Jews. That, of course, was absolutely unthinkable and impossible for many Jews, even for many Jews who came to believe in Jesus. Why did becoming a Christian mean that they needed to stop living as Jews? It brings up a sticky question: to cure racism, is it necessary to erase all our differences of culture?

I don't think so. On the friendship level, it doesn't work that way. Christian friends can learn to appreciate and to understand each other, and both change some in the process, but neither changes into the other—they each become something new. They become, in fact, Christ, as Christ is filtered and refracted by all the things that make each person who she or he is.

And on the system level, the elimination of racism doesn't have to result in the loss of differences. I think of the Church of the Holy Sepulchre in Jerusalem, used by Christians of several different types. I was there one Pentecost Sunday to hear the liturgy being sung simultaneously in four different languages in four different spots in the church. Maybe a more ideal vision of unity would be one congregation singing in one language, and maybe that's what God's ultimate future holds for us. But in the meantime, it was awesome and inspiring to be in that place, near to the rock where Christ died, and hear God's praises voiced together, yet with such diversity. However fractious and bumpy the compromise governing the Church might be, on that morning it held, and that great building became, for me, a holy temple, filled with God's praise.

Can you see the vision, too? Can you see a place where, in Christ, there is no "other,"

no "alien," no "stranger"? Racism is not the final truth about humanity. God has already determined that our final end will be in unity, not division, and in love, not hatred. Let the vision move you and unite you with all God's people, person by person. Let the vision move all of us to eliminate all the dividing walls and laws that continue to separate us. Let us not grow weary until we are one place, one holy temple, all singing God's praise, each in our own voices.

Topic: How We Can Be One

Text: Eph. 4:1–6

I have a book on my shelf, Frank Mead's *Handbook of Denominations,* which is a guide to about two hundred of the religious groups in the United States, giving a little history and a brief description of the beliefs and practices of each one. But two hundred is nowhere near all of the different types; if you just think of all the independent, one-of-a-kind churches, it boggles the mind. Reading from the yellow pages: God's Blessing Center, Holy Tabernacle of Jesus Christ, Life Line Gospel, Movement of Jesus, One Accord Holiness, Christian Faith and Victory, Christian Fellowship, Christian Heritage, Christians United, and so on.

What a potpourri! In the face of that fact, and in the face of the fact that even within denominations, there are sometimes factions within factions, what are we to make of all this "one body, one hope, one baptism" stuff? When Ephesians was written, there weren't so many different types of Christians, but there were enough options already for the author to know that "one church" was a lot harder than it sounds. How is our church one with all those other churches? And for that matter, how is our church one, because you all know as well as I do that we have lots of different points of view on lots of different topics?

I. Prayer for Unity

It's a prayer, it seems to me, and an exhortation. A prayer, because Ephesians here is really calling on the power of God to make something true, and an exhortation, because to make it true will also take some work on our part. Be one, Ephesians is saying, be one by letting God make you one.

Begin with the prayer part, the eternal truth part, down in verses 4–6. All those "one" things are statements of faith about the way God has made us a church. Body-Spirit-hope go together. We are a Body, the Body of Christ. God took us, individual lumps of clay, and molded us into a Body, bringing us alive by breathing into us the Spirit, the breath of God. Remember back in the second chapter of Ephesians, where we're told that we were zombies, living dead, controlled by the evil Powers? Well, God undid that, making us alive, giving us living flesh instead of dead, filling us with a holy spirit.

We all feel united in worship, when the Spirit lifts us to God and binds us together. We feel it as we use the gifts God has given us, ministering in God's name. We feel it when someone comes to faith and is united with God's saving grace. And those moments, remember, those are a down payment, a mere taste of what life eternal will be like. That is our hope, which the Spirit guarantees for us. All of us in this room, and all of us worshiping around the globe, all of us are bound together by the same Spirit and given to same promise to hope for. We are alike that way.

Lord-faith-baptism also go together and are another way to think about how God makes us into a church. We come to confess Jesus as our Lord, and we are baptized on that confession. That is how all of us begin our Christian pilgrimage. Now, thinking about all those groups again, we know that baptism is done differently among them, and that in fact one of the reasons for so many different kinds of church is a different definition of baptism. But do we not all see it as the beginning of our walk with Christ? Even in this room there are differences in when and how we were baptized: some in a river, some in a baptistery, some in other denominations, some as children, some as adults. Do the differences make us less a church?

And if we need another, Ephesians gives us one more way to think about how we are alike. We are all God's creations: not just us Christians, but all the people of all the world. God made us all, and God's plan, remember, is to unite us all in Christ. Our mission as a church is to live out that unity so that the rest of the world can see that it is possible. Now, unity can include diversity;

the mere number of churches or the variety of styles of worship could simply reflect taste. Unity can include diversity, but it cannot include animosity. If Baptists won't call Catholics sisters, or if one type of Baptist won't call another type brothers, then we're not living up to the way God made us.

II. Challenge to Unity

So Ephesians gives us some hints for improvement—the exhortation part. God has called us to be one, has made us a Body through the Spirit, has baptized us into faith in our Lord. But if we have strayed from that, here are some methods for coming back.

Humility and gentleness will help. These words describe a poor person in the Old Testament, people who depend on God because they have nowhere else to turn. They put their lives and future in God's hands and believe that God will take care of them. But in the time of Ephesians, these words meant to be like a slave, weak and helpless. Nobody wanted to be "humble and gentle." Instead, they wanted to be aggressive and forceful. So do we, I think, and that's why we can't get along with one another. To be one, we must be readier to listen and to learn, and less insistent on having things done as we think God wants them done.

Patience and "bearing with one another" will help as well. Think of a couple, married for a long time, where each has quit trying to change the other and has simply adjusted. She bears with his faults and he with hers. Living under the same roof forces you to do this if you are to remain together. That happens in a church, too, as brothers and sisters in the faith learn through experience about their strengths and weaknesses. But to learn patience with one another, you must spend enough time together to need patience. The same goes for relationships between churches. Who needs patience if all we ever do is an occasional Thanksgiving service? We need to set ourselves challenges that we can only do together and then spend enough time with one another that we take off our company manners—then we'll learn patience!

The biggest help, then, will be to make unity a priority. "Make every effort," says Ephesians. We mostly make little effort, doing only what comes easily. We should do the hard thing; we should take up a project so big that we could only complete it with the help of other churches. And then we should pray for the Spirit to give us unity, to keep bonds of peace, while it is going on.

Topic: The Gifted Church
TEXT: Eph. 4:7–16
I. You are Gifted

You are a gifted church, do you know that? Do you know how blessed you are, how providentially fortunate you are to be sitting in this place, surrounded by this group of people? Now, we all know about Lake Wobegon, where all the women are strong, all the men are good-looking, and all the children are above average. But this is not false praise. This is simple fact—we are a gifted church. Look at verse 7: "But unto every one of us is given grace according to the measure of the gift of Christ." Who is gifted? Every one of us—not just some of us—each and every one of us. Who gave us the gifts? God did—that's what's behind the "is given." And what did God give us? God gave us grace—that word itself means "a gift"—God gave us a gift, but not just any gift. God gave out presents in the way Jesus gave gifts. When asked for wine, Jesus didn't just give a bottle, he gave over a hundred gallons. When asked for food, Jesus didn't give a half a sandwich, he gave enough bread and fish that five thousand families could have enough and more left over. When asked for love and compassion, Jesus gave everything he had. You are a gifted church: in fact, you've got more gifts sitting in this room than you can count, because that's always the way that God gives—abundantly, lavishly, outrageously.

And God gives what you really need, too. God's gifts to this church are exactly suited to what we face. That's why Ephesians quotes that strange little verse from Psalm 68 in verse 8. If Christ ascended—if he went up—and then gave gifts to everyone, what does that mean but that he had first been down? If he went up, he must have been down first. And where was Christ when he was down? He was down among folks like us, down among the sinners, down among the needy people. He lived here. He knows people. He faced what we face: hunger, sickness, death, high taxes.

II. The Gifts You Have

At this point in the text, we've heard that God gives great gifts to each of us, gives them to us in bushel baskets, and gives gifts that we can really use. Then we read the list in verse 11, and we think we've been tricked: "And he gave some, apostles, and some, prophets, and some, evangelists, and some, pastors and teachers." I'm no any of those things, I can hear you thinking; I'm not a pastor or a missionary or an evangelist or a prophet.

I'm not an apostle, you say, but you are. What were the apostles, anyway, but people who bore witness to their encounter with Christ? Apostles were men and women who knew Jesus personally. Apostles were men and women who could say, "Jesus is alive—I know he is." Any of you certain that Jesus is alive? Do any of you have a testimony about how, maybe in a dark time in your life, the love of Christ became very real to you? Any of you have a story about how, perhaps during a worship service, you were cut to the heart because you knew there was something Christ was calling you to do? That's what an apostle is, and that's what some of you are; I know, because I've heard you tell of it. And those experiences you have had are gifts from God, not just for you, but for all the rest of us in this room. We will need you apostles to tell us about the living Christ, to give us hope in our dark times, until the day when we all stand united before Christ, perfect in our knowledge of the living Son of God.

I'm not a prophet, you say, but you are. Prophets are men and women to whom God gives a message to tell to others. Prophets say, "I think we ought to get involved in a mission trip to Costa Rica, because that would be God's will for us." Prophets sometimes say, "I think we ought to go out on a limb on this—it's the right thing to do," and sometimes say, "I really think we ought to stay away from this." Some of you are prophets, because I have heard you and seen you as you prodded and nudged some of the rest of us to get on with something. You prophets were able, through God's gift, to look ahead and see us meeting the goal; you knew that with God's help we could do it.

And we need you desperately. A church

need lots of prophets, all trying as hard as they can to listen for God's will for the church. Lots of prophets, not just one or two. Somewhere the idea has gotten loose that a church has one prophet who gets the word from God and passes it down to the people, but that's wrong. A church needs lots of prophets, because none of us is able to hear God perfectly. If we listen to one prophet only, we'll hear only as much as one person can hear from God. No, we need lots of prophets, so that, as verse 14 says, we will no longer be children, blown this way and that by one man's opinions. We need lots of prophets who will speak the truth in love to one another, so that we can be the strongest and healthiest body of Christ we can be.

Some of you are evangelists. Evangelists to us means Billy Graham Crusades or somebody's TV show, but that's not what it meant in Ephesians. An evangelist is someone who shares the gospel with another. Have any of you ever told my children about Jesus? I know you have, and that's the gift of evangelism. What God gives us, I think, is first, the gospel to share and, second, the opportunity from time to time to share it and, third, the courage in that moment to speak up. And we need you evangelists. Think about it: there's a chain of testimony that goes all the way back to the Apostles, one person telling another, all the way down to you. If we ever stop sharing the gospel, then we are robbing not just the people who might listen to us, but all the generations that come after us. We need lots of evangelists, until that day when the whole world will grow up into Christ, who was its beginning.

And the last gift: pastors and teachers, two parts that really go together to make one gift. The word *pastor* means "shepherd," and simply means someone who cares for another with the love of Christ. A teacher passes along what he or she has learned about God and Christ. We can think of plenty of examples: deacons, Sunday school teachers, VBS workers, and so forth. They all tell about God and try to give God's love to others. But the same thing happens on an informal basis, too. Does anyone ever ask you what you think about some religious topic, and you tell them, to the best of your

knowledge, what you've learned? Do you ever notice anybody hurting, and to the best of your ability, try to comfort them? That's a Christian calling, brothers and sisters. That's a moment where, if we will be open to it, the Spirit of God will give us what we need to give to them.

We are a gifted church. God has given great, wonderful gifts to each of us, gifts that we really need, gifts in incredible amounts. God has given them to each of us. I don't think I'm exaggerating to say that probably, if you keep your eyes and ears open, you will regularly see the chance to be each of these things to someone. Don't say, "I can't do it," because God says you can. Don't say, "I'm not gifted," because God says you are. Don't say, "I won't do it," because God knows we need you, and God has put you here with us to hold us up. Say, "Yes, I will use my gifts, I will do what God enables me to do."

Topic: Cleaning Out the Closet
TEXT: Eph. 4:17–32

This is the way it used to be, two thousand years ago, when people were converted to Christianity. They would be taught about their new faith for a while, and then they'd be baptized. They would go to a river, if they could, or a pond or lake if a river wasn't handy. The person to be baptized would take off his old clothes and enter the water naked. After he'd been baptized, then he'd come out of the water and put on new clothes; often they'd give him a white robe to put on as a symbol of his new life in Christ.

This is why Ephesians can remind readers about their conversion in this sort of language: "You were taught to strip off your former way of life, your old self, and to clothe yourself with the new self, created according to the likeness of God." Once upon a time, Christians had done this, literally. Now, our baptisms didn't happen that way, but I think we can still see the point. Becoming a Christian means putting off the old way of life and putting on a new way, and we can think about what that means by thinking about changing our clothes.

I want to carry that metaphor a little further, and think about cleaning out the closet. Periodically that's something we all have to do. That needs to happen in our faith as well. We may have stripped off the old way of life a long time ago, and we may have been living as Christians for years. But from time to time, you find that somehow you have collected some spiritual coats and shirts and shoes that you really don't need. These are ugly old things that are inappropriate for God's people. But somehow we have them now. We need to clean out the closet, get rid of them once again.

I. Old Overcoat

Ephesians starts with falsehood–lying. "Putting away falsehood, let all of us speak the truth to our neighbors." Now, I doubt seriously that any of us makes a practice of lying to others. Sometimes children go through a stage when they have trouble telling the truth, but they usually get corrected out of it. I've known some adults, even some Christians, who had trouble with the truth. But most people, Christians or not, learn that the world goes along better if we stick to the truth.

The interesting thing is that Ephesians uses the word *lie* to describe the whole way of life that people have when they are not Christians. All the world outside of Christ runs on one great lie, and it goes something like this: Life is supposed to be fun and entertaining for me; anything that makes it easier or more fun is good, and anything that makes it harder or more boring or less fun is bad. And that lie is so much a part of this world–every commercial, and the average American sees literally billions of them over a lifetime, every commercial is a thirty-second reinforcement of the great lie. Life is supposed to be fun and easy for me. That's like an old overcoat that we keep trying to throw out of our closet, but every time we look, there it is again. We just have to keep trying to clean it out.

II. Pesky T-Shirts

Anger too, which I think of as a little T-shirt, needs constant attention. It's normal, sometimes even OK, to get angry. If you and I read reports about a fire at a chicken plant, we get angry if we learn that exits that could have saved lives had been blocked or locked. That's needless, senseless, irresponsible behavior. Anger against actions like that is a motivation to get things changed for the better.

But most of the time my anger is over somebody getting in the way of my plans. I wanted to go forty-five down this road, and the joker who pulled out in front of me is only going thirty, and it makes me mad. Now, there's nothing "righteous" about that. The text says, "Don't let the sun go down on it." Get rid of it that day. It's like a little T-shirt you put on. The joker in the car makes me mad–one T-shirt. The student who's talking in class makes me mad–another T-shirt. I'm still mad over something my wife said to me three weeks ago–another T-shirt. Pretty soon I'm so wound up in this emotion that I can't do the work of God. Don't let them stack up on you like that. Get rid of it that day. Let the day of your anger also be the day of your reconciliation.

III. Work Pants

Then it mentions theft: "Thieves must give up stealing." Again, I'll bet that you gave up stealing a long time ago. We all usually learn to respect personal property pretty young. But, again, Ephesians means more, because the opposite of stealing is working so that you'll have something to share with the needy. I think the word for this broader kind of stealing is *materialism*. The world wants to give us a pair of work pants with big pockets. On a tag on the back pocket of these pants, there's a motto: "Work hard, so that after you pay the bills, you can buy yourself something nice." That's the most natural thing in the world, but Christian work pants have a different motto: "Work hard, so that after you pay the bills, you can help somebody else." God expects us to help the less fortunate. But it takes constant reminding of ourselves so that we don't put on the wrong pants out of the closet over and over.

IV. Dangerous Boots

Last of all, the text mentions evil talk. It means hurtful words, poisoned words that can tear a person down. I'll bet none of us are deliberately cruel in our speech. I'd be willing to wager that there is not a person in this room who would deliberately try to cut someone with words.

But we can do it without meaning to. My son used to have a pair of boots that he loved to wear. The only problem with them was that the heel and soles were very hard rubber. If he was sitting in your lap and kicked his feet, those boots would bruise. If he was playing with other kids, he could hurt them without meaning to. We've got to watch the way we talk and the way we act, to make certain that we don't bruise people without meaning to do it. It might not even be in the words, but in the tone we use. Ephesians says to let our words "give grace" and to act kindly toward one another, "tenderhearted." We need to throw out any words or tones or actions that could hurt without meaning to hurt and, as Christians, try to talk and act to build others up.

It's a lifetime project, cleaning out our spiritual closet. Every time I turn around, I find myself with some unwanted, inappropriate stuff to discard. Confess it to God—get rid of it—and put on the right stuff.

Topic: "This Is a Great Mystery"
TEXT: Eph. 5:21–33

Recently I heard a young woman, married almost two years, give a sermon on this text. She began by saying that she thought that the women's liberation movement had taken from women about as much as it had given, and that one ought to take this text literally. There can be only one leader in a marriage, she said, and that should be the husband. Submission may seem hard for women, she said, but think of the task Ephesians assigns to the husbands; they must love their wives as much as Christ loves the church, must nourish and care for them and be tender to them. "I feel sorry for you men," she said, "because that is an awesome responsibility."

Pick up many recent commentaries on Ephesians, or something written on feminist or womanist interpretation, and you get a quite different approach. Ephesians, without argument, uses God to validate a husbands-in-charge-of-wives type of universe, and this is a step away from the liberation of Gal. 3:28 and a step closer to the values of the world in which the church lived. How could the author of Eph. 2:11–22, with its clear vision of the leveling, unifying force of the gospel, have ignored its implications for the home? (I've saved the slavery text for another time, but the same point can be made.) For many interpreters, the question becomes how much of Ephesians one can salvage.

One sort of salvage effort focuses on verse 21: "Be subject to one another out of reverence for Christ." Some argue that whatever the author says to one spouse can be applied to the other. There are problems with this: verse 21 is connected to verse 20 and is neither a separate sentence (as in the NRSV) nor an introduction to the section on husbands and wives (as some commentaries treat it). And the bigger problem: if the author meant for mutual submission to be the rule, why bring up wifely submission separately and confuse the issue?

Recognizing that there are problems with any line of interpretation, I make the following presumptions. First, there is much in Ephesians for which we should be grateful, and it is worth a struggle. Second, because it is not possible to obey the original intent of every biblical command—consider the rules on animal sacrifice as an obvious example—we must learn how to deal with those that present great difficulties.

In my view, as a husband of almost twenty years, marriage is a great mystery. I am surprised at irregular intervals at how much I misunderstand my wife. There have been no set patterns that have always worked between the two of us or between us and our three sons. We've had to try out ways of relating to each other, of handling problems, of parenting, and then modify, discard, supplement, and evaluate. That last sentence makes it sound so cool and professional, but I confess that it has not been so. As in most other families I know, the decisions to modify, discard, supplement, and evaluate are often stressful and agonizing. And we've had it easy, compared with many; we've not suffered through the loss of a child or lengthy unemployment or catastrophic illness.

Through it all, sometimes my wife has led me and sometimes I have led her, and sometimes our children have a better idea than either of us. With all due respect to the author of Ephesians, he and I both have blind spots, and my wife has helped me to see, if not correct, some of them. I also believe that my wife, whose commitment to Christ and to Christ's values is obvious to all who know her, can hear God's directions better on some issues that I can. Mutual submission, to me, makes more sense than constant wifely submission.

Furthermore, I am as yet incapable of

loving my wife as Christ loved the church. I would like to do that, and through practice and correction, I hope to love her better in the future than I do now. But in the meantime, why should I insist on her literal obedience to verse 24 when I cannot literally obey verse 25? But you may say that while both verses are goals, they are still directional indicators; she should be growing more submissive, I more Lord-like. That's exactly the point, it seems to me. If I were to become more like Christ to my wife, what would that mean but becoming more and more like a servant and less and less like a master?

And finally, as a firm believer in the idea that each Christian is gifted by Christ to serve each other (Eph. 4:7–16), I believe that my wife and I are called to be Christ to each other. Is she free from the charge to love me as Christ loved the church? I hope not, for we are called to be "one flesh" in verse 31, and the only hope I have for us ever to reach that point is through the work of Christ in each of us. Therefore, it seems to me that our calling is to serve each other, to love each other, and to lead each other under the direction of the Spirit.

This is not as simple as "my word is final," but it is more true to the way that it seems to me Christ has worked in my life. It is not as simple as either obeying this passage literally or discarding it completely. But, again, my Christian life has rarely been lived at either end of that spectrum. Most times I follow what I think I know of God's will, full of anxiety that I have misunderstood, certain that I could easily repeat errors of judgment I've made in the past. Following Christ is a great mystery, in marriage as in all other things. Maybe that's why it keeps me wanting to turn the page, to read the next chapter, to follow the trail of the Spirit as my wife and I are led toward Christ together.

Topic: Parenting and Beyond
    Text: Eph. 6:1–4
Some of us here are parents, or have been, or are grandparents as well as parents; some of us here have never been parents; but all of us need to understand that we have a stake in raising the children of this church. I would argue, in fact, that we all have a stake in all children everywhere, but the point is easier to see if we think of the future of this Christian fellowship. How will it have a future, if not the children? And how will they be our future, if we do not teach them the values that bind us to this fellowship? So let us, each of us, this morning think of ourselves as parents and teachers of the young, and listen to what we must do in that role.

I. Discipline
First point: parents must create discipline in their children. Speaking to the children, Paul says that they should obey their parents, and quotes the fifth commandment to back that up: "Honor your father and your mother." That's the children's half of the equation. But we know that respect must be earned and nurtured. Parents have to help their children to obey and honor them, and this happens through discipline.

Discipline does not always mean punishment. It means steady, firm control, and it is a lot of hard work. In teaching, for example, you want the kids to study regularly. You want to teach them to put some time into the subject daily, rather than to cram just before a test. So you assign daily work or tests, and the students gripe about how much work that is. But the work is really for the teacher, who has to grade all that stuff all the time.

The same is true, is it not, with parents. It takes a lot of energy to check up on your kids, to make certain they are doing the tasks you assign them. It's much easier to just let them go and let them get away with things. But then they would not learn the discipline of daily life, of getting tasks done day by day. So take heart, parents; when you think, "Why do I bother trying to get them to do what I ask?" there is a higher purpose. You are teaching them to respect order and discipline, including the order and discipline of God.

And what about those here today whose children are grown? Well, most of you are still involved, in one way or another, as care-giver to your grandchildren or to the children in this church. Parents, certainly, bear the primary responsibility to raise their children in the faith. But each of us, because we are a family of God, have some responsibility, too, to do all we can to make certain that the next generation is raised up in the Lord. Even if the children we deal with are not our own, we still should model the steady, encouraging sort of discipline that helps children learn to be responsible.

II. Patience

Second point: Ephesians recommends patience to us. "Do not provoke your children to anger," it says, and if it were to have put that command into positive form, it would be telling us to be patient.

Patience is not passive but active. Patience is a little boy in line waiting for ice cream with his older brother. The smaller is chanting, "I want vanilla! I want vanilla!" But when they reach the front, the shop is out of vanilla. So the older boy buys two strawberries, and says, "Look, Peter, pink vanilla!" Patience is active, looking for ways to head off conflicts before they start. Patience is also encouraging, like a former boss of mine who put up with a great many dumb mistakes when he could have done things faster himself; but he was patient and kept telling me that I could do it, and pretty soon I could.

Mostly, though, patience is a matter of perspective. Children live in the now almost exclusively. A half-hour is an eternity to them, and next week might as well be in another lifetime. The longer we live, though, the more we realize that things have been bad in the past and have gotten better; things have been good in the past and have gotten worse; that the only thing that stays the same is change. Patience is a lesson that can be learned only by living long enough, and it is a great gift to give to your children. And those of you who have lived long enough to have grown children can teach us newer parents and our children a lot about patience.

III. Teaching

Third point: the text says that we must be teachers, bringing our children up in the discipline and instruction of the Lord. How many of us would say that our parents pointed us toward our own faith? How many of us can also name other important Sunday school teachers or church members who were always symbols in our minds of what Christians ought to be? I can remember only a few lessons from my own Sunday school experience, but I remember lots of teachers. I put my pennies in a bank shaped like a globe and learned that they would

help people in China learn about Jesus. I can't even remember learning "Jesus loves me" or "Jesus loves the little children," it happened so long ago, but my faith in a God who loves me deeply and who loves all persons equally no matter what their race grew from those experiences.

We are all of us teachers of the next generation, whether we mean to be or not. By our interest, our encouragement, our patience, our discipline, we teach our children to love and to trust God. Or by our indifference to those things, we will teach our children that loving and trusting God is not so important. Psychologists tells us that children sense how important faith is to adults even before they can put the contents of faith into words. It is a task for parents, first, but then also for the whole family of God. Let us dedicate ourselves to it.

Topic: No Partiality

Text: Eph. 6:5–9

This is one of those texts that ought to stop us cold, but which we often jump over easily, or ignore, or "morph" into our world. It isn't about employers and employees, though; it is about slaves and masters, and the idea of a Christian writing to other Christians who owned slaves and saying, "Treat them well," instead of, "Let them go," ought to stop us cold.

I. Slavery Then and Now

It is true, as the commentaries point out, that slavery in the first century was not one-size-fits-all. Slaves who worked in the mines lived short, terrible lives. Other slaves, known to us from popular literature of the time, lived very well. If fortunate enough to be the business manager for a wealthy man, a slave might own other slaves, might make enough money to buy his freedom, might even inherit freedom and citizenship upon the death of his master. It is also true that, because there was no middle class in ancient times, there was little difference, economically, between a free person on the bottom of the society and a slave.

So slavery was not the worst thing in the world. Some poor people, in fact, sold themselves or their children into the ownership of the wealthy, knowing it was their only chance to live. Would I do the same, if I thought it would keep my children from starving? Very likely so. The moral to be drawn from this is that we do not know the specific situations of the slaves and masters this author had in mind and should not heap blame upon his head.

But—but—texts such as this one, and the parallel text in Colossians, and above all 1 Tim. 6:1–2, were "texts of terror" in the history of the church, and that should stop us cold. Maybe when the author of Ephesians wrote, this was the best he could do for his readers. Maybe telling the masters, "Free your slaves," was simply out of the question. But slavery continued long after it was unnecessary, with thousands kidnapped from their homelands, shipped like cattle to the New World, sold like dry goods. And the slavers and the slave owners justified themselves with these texts. My own denomination was begun in order to allow slave owners to become Christian missionaries. At church services slaves were exhorted with these texts to be submissive, obedient, willing workers, to know their place in God's order, and to set aside all dreams of freedom.

II. Blind Spots

First lesson: we all have blind spots. The author of Ephesians, who said to the masters that there is no partiality with God, did not or could not take the next step and say there should be no partiality among Christians, no "slave and free." Paul, writing to the slave owner Philemon, told him that he must accept his slave Onesimus "as a slave no longer, but as more than a slave, a beloved brother." This author could not, and my Baptist ancestors could not, and I know in my heart that they were not worse people than I, nor am I less captive to my culture than they were to theirs. Where are my blind spots? Which oppressed group do I ignore with a clear conscience?

III. Redemption, Not Courtesy

Second lesson: a true Christian response to oppression goes beyond "be nice to them." Ephesians demands that masters stop threatening slaves but allows the system of slavery to stand: The Way Things Are. But a more completely Christian response will say that any system that promotes oppression must be redeemed, changed, resurrected. Any system that makes zombies out of people, turning them

into slaves and owners, must be overwhelmed by God's power and redeemed. So we must always be on the alert for groups that are powerless or repressed to whom we are told that we ought to do a good turn now and then. Our ultimate task, under Christ, is not to make their lives easier under the system but to redeem the system through the Spirit's power.

IV. We'll Be Overcome

Final lesson: We all have blind spots; we're all tempted just to act nice to the oppressed and stop there. But the power of the gospel is the power that raised Jesus from the dead; the author of Ephesians knew that. And so through the movement of the Spirit, freedom will come. God can and will break through our prejudices. God will break past our culture, even when we use the Bible to reinforce it. God's movement is toward freedom, toward the unity of all persons under God through Christ. God will redeem us, blind believers that we are, because with God there is no partiality.

Topic: Honest Underwear and Spirit Swords

TEXT: Eph. 6:10–17

I. Spirit Problems Need Spirit Tools

Make a list, if you please, either on the back of the order of service, or in your head. Pick five problems you're having right now —any five at all. They could be serious or not, work, house repairs, relationships, children—whatever. Take a minute and do that now.

Got them? Question: How may of the five would you consider spiritual problems? I have a friend, for example, who has a new boss who does not listen to anyone who was there before, wants to change every procedure, and is hiring new folks right and left. Her problem is whether the time she's invested in her job is worth staying and putting up with Know-it-all, or whether she'd be better off jumping ship. That's an economic problem, right? A problem of balancing time, income, benefits, and so on? But all those are really spiritual problems. How hard will it be to see her programs changed? How much of herself is invested in the job? Does she have the energy to make a move, or the energy to stay?

Our problems worry us, sap our spirit,

turn our spirits to dust and stone. That's not news. This section says, though, that we fight not just against our own self-image and fading resources but against evil spiritual forces. Whether we want to use the name Satan or whether we want to think of The System or The Way Things Are, we all know the feeling of being a cog in a machine. Try to work with some giant corporation; try to fight racism; try to get the government to protect some helpless person, and then tell me what you feel. Is there not a feeling that The System doesn't care whether you live or die and would just as soon crush you as look at you?

So my friend not only has to deal with her own energy but also the feeling that she's worthless, that there are a million other better-trained, younger, smarter people out there who will snap up any job she'd be interested in. She has to listen to the sinister whisper from the Powers that the only way to win in this life is to play the game by Their rules—that's The Way Things Are. Cheat, lie, steal, run over others, flaunt yourself, sell yourself, exaggerate, promise them the moon, finders keepers. We wrestle, not just against the weaknesses of flesh and bone, but against the cosmic powers of this present darkness.

God be praised, we are not helpless in the struggle. God has given some tools for the struggle. Ephesians uses a military metaphor: spiritual armor. Put it on, so that you'll be able to withstand the charge of the cosmic powers.

II. Honest Underwear, and So On

The armor comes in pairs, beginning with underwear—yes, underwear. The belt was a leather apron worn by soldiers under their armor as sort of a foundation garment—leather underwear, that's even better. What's the foundation, the very beginning of the struggle? Truth. Honesty. You have to begin by shaking off the lies of the Powers. We are told so many by our world: we're consumers, our aim in life is pleasure and leisure, other people exist to meet our needs. Or we're worthless scum unless we are a financial success, or unless we look like the pictures in magazines. Begin with an honest look at who you really are: a sinner, weak and wounded, saved by the grace of God.

The belt is paired with the breastplate, the big piece of armor buckled on the front to protect your torso. Its name is righteousness—right standing with God. See how it fits? Once we know who we truly are, then we know that in Christ, through God's grace, we have been accepted. We are right with God, and that is powerful armor indeed. Let that protect you when the Powers begin to whisper in your ear and try to entice you to their side. You belong to God. You wear God's breastplate. Let no one tell you otherwise.

The shield and the helmet are the next pair. The shield was a big rectangle that the soldiers held in front of themselves and the next man in line, overlapping the edges. It reminds us that we have a resource in our Christian brothers and sisters, and a ministry to them. They can help us in our struggle, and we must help them. The shield's name is faith, and it will be their faith in God and in you that will carry you through your hardest spiritual battles. It is matched by the helmet named salvation. Salvation is God's gift alone. It is what our faith is in. We put our faith in God's ability to win over evil, and salvation is God's promise to bring that about.

So far these are all protective devices. The underwear was to hang everything on, and the breastplate, shield, and helmet were to turn aside the blows of the enemy. Our offensive weapons are our shoes and sword. The first one will absorb the punishment, but the only purpose in doing so is to let the shoes carry us close enough to use the sword. They are also matched. The shoes are our willingness to share the gospel, and the sword is the gospel itself. In this wicked world, we must be willing to keep living right, to keep talking right, and to keep spreading the word of Christ's love. And when we do, God promised to make it effective. It is the Spirit's sword, not ours. Our words don't save people, God's Spirit does. But we must be ready to share.

III. Facing the Battle

Will these bits of armor help you with your list of problems? I believe they will. Will they make your problems go away? No; it isn't called a battle for nothing, and many of our struggles last a lifetime. Will these bits of armor mean that you will always win? It depends on what you mean. Jesus had to go to the cross; Paul had to endure stonings and imprisonments. My friend may lose her job. But those aren't defeats, even if they are terrible, painful events. In God's eyes, the only real defeat is to sell out to the other side. And that may happen; maybe some of you feel as if you have done that. Under pressure from the Powers, you have joined up with them, adopted some of their methods, lived under their rules. You have breathed in their noxious breath, the evil wind that makes people into zombies—consumers, sex objects, workaholics, users.

What are you wearing today? Do you wear the colors of the enemy? Have you put on the lies that the Powers try to sell you? Take them off, and dress yourself in God's armor. Put on your armor, pick up your sword, and take up your post once more. We need you, and you need us. Close ranks with us, and help us to share the gospel, the Spirit's sword, the only sword that brings life instead of death. Help us as we face the Powers to redeem them, for that is our task.

SECTION IX.
Resources for Preaching on Prayer

BY ROGER LOVETTE

When President Ulysses S. Grant left the presidency he was financially a broken man. He had trusted the wrong people and they had stolen all his investments. His family had nothing. So he wrote his memoirs and paid back all of the debts he'd incurred and was able to leave his family well secured after his death. But during those hard days of writing and trying to keep going financially, Grant developed cancer of the tongue, which would finally take his life. One of the great stories of courage is the battle that General Grant fought with cancer. One day a friend of his, General Howard, came to visit the ailing Grant. Howard hoped to cheer up his very sick friend. So the general began to talk to Grant about the great battles they had fought in together. This conversation did no good. Grant just sat there depressed. Finally Grant put up his hand, shook his head, and said, "Howard, tell me something about prayer."

The people who wander in on Sunday mornings need many things. But one subject will always strike a note in their lives. They need to hear something about prayer. Why? Many do not know how to pray. Some need the same kind of teaching Jesus taught his own disciples. Some of us yearn for spiritual power that seems to elude us. Some of us need to brush aside the everydayness in which we almost drown and focus clearly on what really matters. Others need proper definitions of prayer to clear up misunderstandings and faulty definitions. Prayer can help with many of the concerns of our lives.

The preacher who stands on Sunday and gives his or her people some solid understandings about prayer will enable them to grow and mature in their spiritual lives.

Topic: Prayer As Basic
TEXT: Ps. 19:14
Sometimes we make the spiritual life too complicated. The common people heard Jesus gladly because he brushed away the clutter and dealt with the basics of their lives. One of the mistakes that we make in church is assuming too much about the practicalities of prayer. Most folk, like Jesus' disciples, say, "Lord, teach us to pray."

Once during the Civil War, after a terrible rainstorm, the chaplain went from group to group. All the soldiers were trying to pull their cannons out of the muck. The chaplain put his hand on the shoulder of one soldier and said, "Brother, are you saved?" Covered in mud, straining to get his artillery unstuck, the soldier roared back, "Don't ask me riddles! I'm stuck in the mud." Jesus never provided riddles; neither did his forebears in the Old Testament. They did provide some basic handles for encountering God.

Ps. 19:14 provides us with the basics of prayer. "Let the words of my mouth and the meditation of my heart be acceptable in thy sight, O Lord, my rock and my redeemer."

I. These words are a prayer for help. We find in him two strong words: *Rock* and *Redeemer*. President Abraham Lincoln understood this during the terrible days of the Civil War when he said, "Again and again, I am driven to my knees. There is no other place to go."

We all pray for help. We live in a world of great uncertainty. We, too, have needs. We pray because we mess up our lives and we are all like sheep who have gone astray and turned everyone to our own ways. We pray because alone we know that things just do not work out.

Archimedes once said that if he could find a place to stand he could move the world. We have that place—God is Rock and Redeemer. The old hymn is right: He is our firm foundation. Prayer provides help. He is Rock and Redeemer.

II. These words are a prayer for healing. We pray that the words that come from our mouths and the meditations that spring from our hearts will find an acceptance in God. We pray for healing. As Agnes Sanford used to say, we pray for the healing of our memories. We also pray for the healing of our thoughts and fantasies and dreams and even our nightmares.

These words mean there comes to all of us that very great grace that touches our words, thoughts, and even the subconscious forces of our lives with healing and acceptance.

And so as we pray we bring whatever thoughts and meditations that are uniquely ours to this throne of grace. God provides us the healing we need. Our words, deeds, and thoughts find an acceptance in God Almighty.

III. These words also provide a prayer of hope. This prayer was offered at the place of sacrifice. Offering is not simply some check we write or some coins we place in the offering plate. Our real offering becomes our words and deeds. Our great hope is that what we bring, flawed though our lives may be, will find an acceptance in God's eyes.

This acceptance means that we do the right in our words and even in our meditative thoughts. One translation says, "May they be a delight in your presence. May what we do and say bring the Lord God a great joy."

The hope is that in who I am and in what I do there can come to be a rightness, an authenticity, that squares with the One who calls us. Out of the Second World War there comes the story of a Japanese kamikaze pilot who ploughed his plane into a Navy ship near the shore and then crashed. The sailors and the chaplain dragged sixty of their own men onto the little island nearby and buried each one. As they turned back to their boat, someone called out, "I see one more." Tired, nauseated, exhausted, the men trudged over to find the body of the Japanese soldier who had caused this terrible tragedy. There was great silence on that little island. Would they leave the enemy soldier or bury him? The chaplain spoke: "Men, we must do the right thing this afternoon. Some of you will say he was a suicide and that his order was to fly into one of our ships and to kill all of our boys. And this is true. He was a human being. Together, with him, we are all members of the same human family. I find no hatred in my heart for him. If you search your own hearts you may find the same thing. I want us to bury him just as we buried all our brothers here today. I want us to bury him and to remember that on a God-forsaken island in the Pacific one day we faced the challenge of basic human kindness and passed the test at least once in our lives. We will not give him a Christian burial. That would profane both his own faith and ours. But we will kneel, and pray to God in hope that this act will somehow unite us beyond the conflict and madness of what we have done out here. When we have finished burying him, let us mark the spot with a headstone. We do not know his name. But we will simply inscribe his grave: Japanese Pilot and the date. It is my hope that this act of reverence might just be the right thing to do in the light of eternity."

The chaplain captured the essence of the prayer some old psalmist had written years before. Even after all these years these words are a guide for us all. "Let the words of my mouth and the meditation of my heart be acceptable in Thy sight, O Lord, my strength and my redeemer."

Topic: Prayer As Balance
TEXT: Matt. 6:2

When we think of prayer we usually think of bowing one's head and bending a knee. To pray is to talk to God, and this is true. But prayer is a varied activity. One man likened prayer to a three-legged stool. He said that if the stool does not have three legs it is out of balance and there is no support. He also observed that if one leg is longer than another we have no way to be supported. A tilted stool is of little help.

Prayer that is balanced has three legs. All three legs are equal and all are of the utmost importance. The three legs are the closet, the house, and the sanctuary.

I. *The closet.* Jesus cautioned us to enter the closet and pray privately. He warned us about public displays that make prayer other than communication with God. We recall his story of the two who went into the Temple to pray: one wanted all to hear. Jesus commended the other man who, alone and out of hearing distance, whispered, "God, be merciful to me a sinner."

Jesus was forever leaving the crowds and his disciples to pray alone. Jesus knew that it would be easy to get lost if he did not find some quiet time for solitude and prayer.

We all need some prayer time when we listen to the silence. To go into the closet is to shut the world out and to face God alone. There is a motto at Lake Wales in Florida that says: I come here to find myself—it is so easy to get lost in the world. The closet, away from the noise of the world, is important when we talk to God.

II. *The house.* But there is another leg to prayer. The Bible also says, "When two or three are gathered in my name—I am there." Jesus called twelve disciples into a circle of intimacy. If closet prayer provides solitude and quiet—praying with a small group begins to meet our needs for intimacy. Community develops as we bow our heads together.

Early Christian worship took place in the homes of the believers. There were no church buildings until the end of the third century. Little closets of home fellowships were all they had. They broke bread with glad and generous hearts. In that small-group setting they would learn to trust and to love. They would weep with those who wept and rejoice with those who rejoiced. They were known and they came to know one another.

Church school classes, small groups, retreat settings provide this function. Many have called the small-group experience their private church. Such circles of love

and acceptance provide places where we can be loved and affirmed and accepted and even judged. We learn trust and love in the small-group setting.

III. *The sanctuary.* The third leg of the stool of prayer is the sanctuary. Jesus went to the synagogue weekly, as was his custom. He called the Temple a house of prayer and drove out the money-changers when they perverted its use for wrong purposes.

Just as we need the closet and the small circle—we also need the larger group. Christ taught the multitudes. He often healed the sick in large settings. Amid thousands he proclaimed, "I am the bread of life."

Why do we need the sanctuary? To be reminded of the diversity of the people of God. "In Christ there is no east or west, in him no south or north." We need that holy perspective that reminds us that seven thousand have not bowed their knees to Baal. There is strength in traveling the road with others.

We also need the tradition that comes to us through the corporate worship of the church. The great traditions of hymns, prayers, and doctrine are handed down in the sanctuary of corporate worship.

So we return to the church for weddings and funerals as well as Sunday services. We are surrounded by the saints of the ages. We have stained glass and music and the richness of the years that give us an anchor for the shifting sands of our lives.

In the Temple Isaiah heard a voice that changed his life. "Who will go?" There, surrounded by the treasures of his faith, he responded, "Here am I—send me." We need the sanctuary as part of our prayer life.

No one leg can ever do the job of praying. The closet is important but never enough. Prayer is never a permanent retreat from the world. Neither is prayer an evasion or an escape. We pray, as did Jesus on the Mount of Transfiguration, to receive energy for the tasks ahead. Vision and task are always united. Prayer cannot make us hermits —it turns us outward toward the world. From closet we must venture forward to the public square.

The house also has limitation. The small group, like the closet, has its limits. The small group can become closed and elitist. Prayer groups can degenerate into gossip sessions. Groups can provide healing and growth for persons or provide destruction through manipulation and oppression. Groups have life cycles—they do not last forever. Small groups alone cannot meet all of our prayer needs.

But just as closet and house have their limitations—so does the sanctuary. The large-group setting cannot always serve as a place of solitude. We cannot expect the large gathering of the church to take the place of the closet or the house church. One hour a week on Sunday cannot meet all our prayer needs.

Like the stool, prayer stands on three legs. Make your prayer life a balanced experience. We all need the closet, the small group, and the corporate worship of the church. Such balance makes strong Christians able to face whatever the world throws our way.

Topic: Prayer As Discovery
TEXT: Luke 11:1–13

Jesus called twelve disciples. Ordinary people with ordinary problems. Can't you see them doing as we would do, off in some corner, whispering, "What do you think he meant by . . . ?" Or one would say, "Did you notice how he touched that leper or how he spoke to that woman in the middle of the day as if she were a real person who counted?" One might say, "Did you notice this morning how he doesn't seem to get uptight the way we do? Lord knows, he has reasons." They said to one another, "What is it that keeps him going? What do you think happens out there in the hills when he is alone? I wonder what his secret is." And out of all those questions they came with a request. Maybe, the disciples reasoned, it came because he prayed. And so they came together to discover the secret of his power. "Lord, teach us to pray . . ."

And so the Lord began, patiently, once again to teach them about the source of his power. He taught them to pray—and in their praying they would discover many things that would infuse their lives with the power he had found. We can make the same discoveries they did as we begin to pray.

I. We discover that we are heard. Jesus remembered his Old Testament. "I have heard the murmurings of my people . . ."

Exodus had said. God hears. He listens to the murmurings. When people hurt, God listens. Or again: "If my people who are called by my name will pray and seek my face, I will hear . . ." God hears. And out of that rich background of his heritage he told them, "When you pray, go into your room and shut the door and pray to your Father who is in secret; and your Father who sees in secret will reward you. He hears and he cares."

But it isn't only words. There are many occasions when we can't put our longings or hurts into words. We do not know what to say. Paul tells us, "Likewise the Spirit helps us in our weakness; for we do not know how to pray as we ought, but the Spirit himself prays for us with sighs too deep for words."

One of the things that gave Jesus his power was that he knew he was heard by his Father. When we pray we begin to discover that we, too, are heard.

II. As we pray we discover that we are loved and accepted. To be loved is to be taken seriously. Jesus was free because love set him free. From his baptism on, he remembered the voice that whispered, "You are my beloved." In the light of that promise he moved out into a larger world.

More than once Jesus called his disciples beloved. It was as hard for them to accept as it is for us. Do you recall Aldonza in *The Man of La Mancha*? Don Quixote kept calling this poor woman with a very shady past by a new name: Dulcinea. Old, ugly Aldonza had lived a terrible life. But Don Quixote kept calling her this strange new name, Dulcinea. She asked him why he said such ridiculous things like giving a fancy name to someone who only worked in the kitchen. He told her he believed in her—that she had great worth. Slowly, Aldonza begins to believe the wonderful things the don says about her. "Could I be," she wondered, "Dulcinea?" At the end of the play, the don is old and lies dying and confused. He doesn't remember anyone's name. She begs him to call her Dulcinea. He asks, "Is it so important?" Through tears she says, "It means everything, my whole life. You spoke to me and everything was different. You called me by another name—Dulcinea. And when you spoke the name, an angel seemed to whisper, Dulcinea, Dulcinea . . ."

It changed her life to discover that she was loved and accepted. When we come to that quiet place, near to the heart of God, we come to reckon with this incredible truth: we really are beloved.

III. Prayer also helps us realize that we can be changed. Prayer does many things, but one thing is certain: prayer changes the pray-er.

In Mark 11 Jesus said to his disciples that if we say to the mountain, "Be cast into the sea—believe it and it will be so." So, in summary he said, "as you pray believe in what you ask for and it will be so." This passage is not about mountain-moving.

Prayer is about the mountains in our lives that stand so stubborn and hard in the middle of our journeys. All those things that hinder us and make us take the side roads that seem so difficult. Sometimes there are habits. Sometimes there are people we need to forgive. As we pray we are changed—the mountains in our lives really do move. Prayer changes the pray-er.

IV. Prayer leads to another discovery—that we can be stretched. Real prayer is more than an exercise in selfishness. Real prayer stretches the pray-er. Prayer sent David Livingstone to Africa. Prayer sent Lottie Moon to China even after a Baptist Mission Board said they could not appoint a woman. It happened because, years before, the Lord Jesus, out in the hills, discovered some stretching of his own. Under that strength, he was able to move back into life —to touch lepers, the rich, children, women, and the poor. Because he was stretched, he helped them stretch the possibilities of their lives, too.

V. As we pray we discover that we are enabled. Remember the lesson from the Garden of Gethsemane. Jesus faced the cross and death as he prayed. After he finished, he shook the sleeping disciples and said, "Rise, and let us be going." He was able to face the worst the world could offer because he found a power through prayer.

Charles Bracelen Flood has written a great book about what happened to Robert E. Lee after the Civil War. Lee lived five years after the Civil War ended. He became president of the nearly defunct Washington College. He would use his new position to create a model educational institution that would exemplify for a deeply wounded na-

tion the healing power of compassion, generosity, and reconciliation. He was enabled after the greatest defeat of his life.

Jesus taught his disciples that wonderful things would happen to them as they prayed. They would make many discoveries. They would come to know that they were heard, loved, and accepted, that they could be changed. They would be stretched in ways they had never dreamed. And, in the hard places of their days they would be enabled.

Topic: Prayer As Love

TEXT: Luke 11:5–13

All of us have felt strength and power because someone prayed for us. We call this kind of praying intercessory prayer. Someone has called intercessory prayer "prayer with names on it." Dr. Fosdick's definition may be the best of all. He called our prayers for other people "love on its knees."

To love, then, is to pray. To bring someone's name before the throne of grace is to love them. Our parable in Luke 11 gives us some clues as to how we make our prayers a matter of love.

I. Prayer as love means persistence (vv. 5–8). A man and his family were fast asleep. Way after midnight someone knocked on the door. "Who is it?" the sleepy man asked. "Your neighbor. I have company and nothing to feed them." The man tried to get him to go away. It was too late. The neighbor would wake up his children and animals. But the neighbor who knocked kept knocking until finally the man got up and gave him what he needed. Jesus said the man gave his friend who knocked on his door what he needed because of the man's importunity. Strange word. Importunity means to be persistent, to be urgent or demanding. He beat on the door and did not stop until he got what he needed.

This does not mean that we pester God until he finally throws up his hands and gives us whatever we ask. Persistency means that God knows we mean business. This is the test of our sincerity. Our motives are clarified, and we come to know what really matters.

II. Prayer as love means petition (vv. 9–10). Our petitions are to be specific. We name real names and talk about real hurts. None of us are half as interested in Occupant Only mail as we are in some handwritten letter with our name on the envelope.

Jesus teaches us here that if we ask and seek and beat on the door for something special, our prayers will be heard. The man in the story wanted two loaves. His friends were hungry. He needed bread for the table. We are to be specific when we pray. Call out real names and real needs, and you will be heard.

III. Prayer as love means promise (vv. 11–13). What we have here is a clear picture of God. He is a good parent. He will not give us scorpions or serpents—harmful things.

So God will always be consistent with his nature. He will never give us harmful things. A little boy prayed after school one day, "Make Springfield the capital of Massachusetts." God did not change his geography. He never acts contrary to his will.

Neither will God destroy our sense of responsibility. He is a good parent. He will never do for us what we can do for ourselves. One day Bishop Fulton Sheen was asked to pray about a certain matter. He refused, saying, "There are some things you have to do for yourself." We all have to pray our own prayers, pay our own taxes, and make our own love. God will never do for us what we can do for ourselves.

Neither will God allow us to set limits on what he can do. Like the father in the story, he will respond in love and in care. He will keep his promise. We can count on him.

Most or all of us have experienced this prayer called love. Indeed, intercessory prayer really is "love on its knees." Someone prayed for us and we found the strength to go on. Someone cared and lifted us up or we would not be here today.

Begin your journey with prayer as love. It will always be marked with a persistency that knocks on the door as long as it takes. This prayer will always be marked with petition—asking, seeking, and knocking. This prayer is always marked with a great promise. How much more will your heavenly Father give to those who ask!

Topic: Prayer As Preparation
Text: Matt. 26:41

Dr. David Poling asks an intriguing question about prayer. "Why do athletic teams," he wondered, "always pray just before the game but never in practice?" Such praying isn't limited to athletics. Before all the events in our lives we pray: "God help!" We get in a jam and we cry to God for deliverance.

The big question is, How do we learn to pray in practice as well as just before the game? Would it not be better to pray before we face the crises of our lives?

Jesus is our model. The greatest struggle of his life was the cross. He prepared himself and his followers in the Upper Room when he broke the bread and said goodbye. He prepared himself as he made his way to Gethsemane, where he prayed as his disciples slept. After that prayer time he turned to face his arrest and death. He said to his sleeping disciples, "So, could you not watch with me one hour? Watch and pray that you may not enter into temptation; the spirit indeed is willing, but the flesh is weak" (Matt. 26:40b–41).

What we learn from studying Jesus' prayer life is that he was able to pray right before the game because he always prayed in practice. On the edge of his death he simply did what he had always done—lift up his longings to the Father. Prayer, then, for Jesus was preparation for the future.

Matthew understood this when he wrote his Gospel. Jesus prayed at the beginning of his ministry. Prayer would form a vital part of the Sermon on the Mount. When John was arrested and later beheaded, Jesus prayed. When his own troubles began, he prayed on the Mount of Transfiguration, in an Upper Room, in the Garden, and even from the Cross. He was able to face it all because prayer was a golden thread that was stitched into his life from the beginning.

Jesus' words on the eve of his death provide us with help that prayer might become preparation for us too. "Watch and pray that you may not enter into temptation . . ."

I. The first word is *watch*. The original language has a sense of urgency we do not find in English. "Keep awake," he admonishes. This word *watch* is sprinkled throughout the New Testament. It was a serious charge for a soldier to be caught sleeping on duty. Halford Luccock used to say the worst *ism* was not communism, fascism, or secularism but somnambulism—drowsy, drugged, senses dulled.

The word *watch* also meant vigilance. We are encouraged to be alert, ready, with our eyes wide open. Prayer as preparation enables us to watch with vigilance long before the hard times come. Jesus said, "Watch!"

II. The second word that Jesus used was *pray*. Watch and pray. Jesus was able to face his last great difficulties because he had prayed all along. One of the rules of faith is that if we have prayed in practice, it is altogether appropriate to pray before the big events of our lives.

To pray is to rely on God. Someone asked a little boy if he said his prayers every night. He shook his head: "Not every night. Some nights I don't need nothing." Across our on-again, off-again prayer habits, Jesus challenges us to pray without ceasing.

Madeleine L'Engle writes in one of her books that there was one summer when four generations in her family spent the same summer under one roof. They went all the way from a tiny infant to an eighty-nine-year-old great-grandmother. She said twelve people in the same household got claustrophobic and tense many times. She discovered a spot ten minutes from the house that was far enough away she could hear no voices and sounds from where they lived. That quiet place had a small brook and a green meadow, and no one was in sight. She would slip away, dangle her feet in the brook, look at the foliage, listen to the birds sing, lift herself up to God in silence. "Slowly," she wrote, "the impatience and frustrations would fade away." She would walk back up the road to the house in peace.

We all need some circle of quiet where prayer puts everything back in perspective. We refocus the lens and peace returns. We, too, are able to walk back up the lane to our responsibilities once more.

III. The third word that Jesus used here was *temptation.* "Watch and pray lest you enter into temptation . . ." Jesus knew there were temptations in practice as well as in the big game. He faced the enemy death because, day after day, he had faced the little temptations of his life.

This word *tempt* means "trial or test." There in the Garden he was engaged in the greatest struggle of them all. Thy will . . . my will . . . My way . . . Your way.

We are tested again and again as Christians. Falling away is the central problem for the people of faith in any age. But Paul wrote to weak, erring, frail Corinth, "No temptation has overtaken you that is not common to man. God is faithful, and he will not let you be tempted beyond your strength" (1 Cor. 10:13).

Like us, the disciples learned the hard way about stumbles and falls. But when they put the words of Jesus together they kept the words of our text. They saw prayer as preparation for all of life and not just the big battles. They were to watch, every day, with eyes wide open. They were to pray during practice and not just before the big events of life. And when temptation came—usually when they least expected it—they would stand firm. They would discover the strangest of truths. Despite the leaky roof and faulty wiring and erratic plumbing, the house of their lives was built on a rock. They watched and they prayed—and even when temptation came—they stood firm. To pray is to be prepared for whatever life brings. The old gospel song is right: "Watching and waiting, looking above, . . . / Filled with his goodness, lost in his love."

Topic: Prayer As Thanksgiving
TEXT: Ps. 124

We can never properly understand prayer if we leave out thanksgiving. Doxologies and praise to God flow through the Old and New Testaments. Thanksgiving, our faith tells us, cannot be consigned to one holiday in the year. Thanksgiving is the golden thread than runs through most of the prayer life in the Bible.

The psalms abound in thanksgiving. Psalm 124 calls us back to prayer as doxology. The origin of this psalm is unclear. We do know that some great crisis in the life of the nation precipitated these words. The crisis was so grave that the writer compared it to a flood that was about to drown them all.

And in the middle of all their difficulties, a note of thanksgiving and victory is sounded. Listen to the doxology that shines out of the middle of a national crisis.

I. We must not underestimate the enemy (vv. 1–5). Israel's enemies were a cruel and angry mob (vv. 2–3), a raging torrent of engulfing waters (vv. 4–5), and a fowler's trap in which birds were caught (v. 7).

God's people were in grave danger of annihilation. Their praises were sung against a dark background of danger. How different from much of today's gospel. We preach that as long as we are Christians, difficulty will not happen to us. Often we underestimate our enemies.

One of our greatest enemies is the self. Pogo once said, "We have met the enemy and he is us." Karl Menninger said it in *Man Against Himself.* There is within the heart of all of us the great tendency to wreck and destroy ourselves and those we love. This self-destruction is forever with us.

Paul recognized this when he said within all our hearts there is this great rift: "What I want to do, I do not do—what I do not wish to do—that I do." The enemy within would destroy us if let loose. We cannot underestimate that destructive power.

But there is also the enemy without. Alvin Toffler has said that change is occurring at such a fast pace that we are left scared, depressed, and confused. The enemy without immobilizes many of us.

Every major institution in our time is under attack. Church, school, government, business, and family. Nothing seems to be right or wrong—everything seems to be a thousand shades of gray.

Many in our time feel besieged and overwhelmed as did the people in Israel. *Exile* is a word that we can understand. "Fightings within and fears without"—words that we can sing with great passion. Against this backdrop of trouble, the psalmist gives us a hopeful word.

II. We cannot underestimate the power of God (vv. 6–8). We can sing the doxology because we do not face the present or the future alone.

Listen to the psalm: He will help us escape. He will help us through whatever we face. He will bring the release that we need.

It does not matter that we are weak. God has always done his best work with the vulnerable. In our weakness we discover this other grace—the power of God.

In the middle of the traumas of our lives we can sing a doxology. We sing because God will sustain us as he sustained the people of God long ago.

We have recently celebrated the fiftieth anniversary of the end of World War II. One of the heroes of that war was a man named Eddie Rickenbacker. He and his companions were shot down and were adrift at sea. A young man in that little life raft was named Johnny Bartek. He had saved a little New Testament, and with that little book as their center, the shipwrecked men began to pray. They felt their prayers were answered. A seagull came and they killed it, and that nourishment kept them going until help arrived.

Dr. John Sutherland Bonnell, longtime Presbyterian minister, heard that story and asked Johnny Bartek, "Johnny, what did the New Testament do for you?" Bartek said, "Well, it kept us steady. We did not lose our heads and crack up. It kept us sane." Then the pastor said, "But what if the seagull had not come in answer to your prayers?" Bartek replied, "Then we would have died like men and not like cowards."

Prayer always leads us back to doxology. Like the psalmist, we cannot underestimate the power of evil within or without. But that is not the last word. Neither can we ignore the power of God that is ever present with all his children.

On good days and bad we can say with the saints of the ages: "Thanks be to God!"

Topic: Prayer As Reality

TEXT: Ps. 136

Many view prayer as a turning away from the world. They say that prayer is pie in the sky by and by. They charge that prayer is a diversionary ritual that does not face real life. Consequently, many people have given up on prayer as irrelevant.

The biblical record views prayer as rooted in reality. Out of the depths the people of God offered their petitions, and again and again they testify that they were heard.

Psalm 136 is such a testimony. The exile had ended. Finally they trudged back home. For years they had prayed to return home, and finally their prayers were answered. When they returned home, everything around them needed attention. It was a time of transition and rebuilding. In such a hard time, Psalm 136 came into being. In time, it became one of their most popular psalms. They used these words at Passover and at New Year celebrations. The words are an antiphonal poem in which, back and forth, priest and people speak to one another. This psalm is not all that original. They claimed it as one of their favorites because it summarized the longings of their hearts and the difficulties of their lives.

If ever there was a prayer that dealt with reality, Psalm 136 does just that. It became a buoy thrown out to people who felt they were drowning.

Twenty-six times the same phrase is sounded: "For his steadfast loves endures forever." On twenty-six occasions he met them at the junctures of their lives with an incredible promise: "His steadfast love endures forever."

This term, *steadfast love,* came from the Hebrew root *chesed.* For the Hebrews there were two meanings to this word *chesed.* On at least three occasions in the Old Testament this word meant "shame or reproach or defilement." It could be translated, "The Lord is ashamed of us. . . . The Lord judges us by his reproach. . . . The Lord does not like us as we are." The other meaning of the word *chesed* was "steadfastness." God could be counted on in times of need.

Churches divide themselves under one of these two definitions. Either God judges and condemns and turns away from us, or God is a God of steadfastness. He holds us up and cares for us despite who we are and what we do. Here we struggle with the very nature of God. Is this God enemy or friend, judge or friend?

Twenty-six times the psalmist hammers out his understanding of the nature of God. He chose the second definition—God was friend. God really is loving-kindness, mercy, and grace.

I. We discover his steadfast love in the created order (vv. 4–9). The Hebrews knew that what God had created was good. Adam and Eve looked out on a vast landscape of wonder and delight. They knew, as Joseph Sittler has said, the world was to be regarded as a place of grace.

One of the great biblical words is *behold.* "Look! See!" They were to open their eyes. In times of slavery, rebellion, wilderness wanderings, promised land—even exile—they discovered a steadfast love.

II. We also discover his steadfast love in our own history (vv. 10–15). They saw God as one who delivered them when they were in need. Listen to their litany: "Who struck Egypt through the firstborn. . . . And brought Israel out from among them. . . . Who led them with a strong hand and an outstretched arm . . . who divided the Red Sea . . . and made Israel pass through the midst of it . . . and overthrew Pharaoh and his army in the Red Sea.

They discovered in their own stories that the God of the universe had stooped down and touched them with his goodness. They did not deliver themselves. There are no self-made people. God leads his children.

As we think back on our own pilgrimages, Egypts, Pharaohs, Red Seas, impossibilities, and difficulties, and wilderness roads—we have made it through. Those exiles knew they never would have made it back home without the stubborn, steadfast love of God. This is our story, too.

III. We discover his steadfast love in the exits and entrances of our lives (vv. 16–22). He led them through the wilderness—they had never been there before; he stuck down great kings—whose names they could hardly pronounce; he gave the new land to them as a heritage—it was a place they had never been before.

These new entrances, like rebuilding a land or walking through the door of old age or taking a new job or facing the uncertainty of the future, are scary. Our whole age seems to be built on fear. We fear for our children, for our retirement, for our health, for our government, for our safety—for where the world is going. And flowing through the madness of our time is this great promise: "For his steadfast love endures forever."

IV. We also discover that God's steadfast love is very personal (vv. 23–25). The psalmist reminded them: "He remembers us. . . . He rescues us. . . . He gives food to all flesh." These are all personal words. We are remembered. Our needs are met. He feeds us as he fed our forebears in the wilderness.

Truman Capote was a brilliant writer whose personal life was haunted with many difficulties. He said that on the nights when he was depressed he would have a conversation with his imaginary Siamese twin. "First, now let's say a prayer. The one we used to say when we were growing up and our dog Queenie used to sleep with us. We would get under the quilts and pull them up over our heads because the house was so cold. And then we would pray:

Now I lay me down to sleep,
I pray the Lord my soul to keep.
If I should die before I wake,
I pray the Lord my soul to take. Amen."

Then Truman would say good night to himself. Then he would say, "I love you." His imaginary twin would respond, "I love you, too." Then he would say, "You better, because when you get right down to it, we've got each other. Alone. To the grave. It's all we've got." That's the tragedy, isn't it? He said the Siamese twin would always reply, "You forget, Truman. We've got God, too."

Prayer at its best is reality. It meets us in the junctures of our lives and we are reminded God is there. We've got God, too. His steadfast love endures forever.

SECTION X.
Children's Sermons and Stories

January 5: Stay on the Right Road

Object: Model of a street sign (that can be switched)

Once a minister went to visit the home of a church member. He located the address, knocked on the door, but was very surprised and embarrassed when a complete stranger answered the door. He apologized for being at the wrong house and retraced his steps to find the problem. He discovered that someone had switched the street sign like this *(flip sign from "right street" to "wrong street")* and had directed him down the wrong road.

Jesus taught that living was like taking a trip to a place we have never been. Jesus warned that some people would confidently give us wrong directions on our life's journey. Jesus promised to show us how to make the trip correctly. Listen to Matt. 7:13–14.

Jesus warned that the wrong paths of life would be crowded. Most of us don't like to be alone, so we are tempted to make decisions that will put us on pathways that are occupied by the popular crowd. Another word for crowd is *mob*, and mobs can be dangerous. Mobs of people are like stampeding elephants. They will rush down the wrong road and be unable to change direction even though the path will lead the whole crowd over a cliff. If someone wants to change their life once they are part of a mob, they will find it next to impossible. Most people are swept along the wrong path with the crowd that used to make them feel comfortable.

Jesus said that the right pathway for our lives began with a narrow entrance. This is the gate of accepting Jesus as Savior and Lord. Jesus said only a few people were on the right road, but he was with them for the whole journey. So we may feel we are in the minority for standing for things that are good and right, but we should never feel alone, for the Lord has promised to be with us.

A challenge for any traveler is to follow directions to a place that they have never been before. Along the way, the traveler may wonder why the trip is taking so long or question whether they have missed a turn. Jesus promised that if we got started on the right road and listened to him carefully always, he would guide us down the road of great joy.—Ken Cox

January 12: The Artist

Objects: A painting and a photograph

Today I would like you to show you two pictures. *(Show a painting and a photograph.)* This is called a painting, and this is called a photograph. What is the difference? . . . The photograph is a picture of something that a person saw when looking through the lens of a camera. And at the right moment, the photographer snapped the picture. The painting is a picture of something that an artist saw, either in front of him or in his mind. Then, over a period of time, the artist transferred what he saw to a canvas. So, which is the harder thing to do: take a picture or paint a picture? . . .

To paint a picture, you need to remember several things. First, you cannot make a picture by covering the canvas with one color.

And the second thing to remember is that when you use several colors, there must be a sharp variation between them so that the forms in the picture can be clearly seen.

Sometimes we need to do the same thing in life. For example, the people around us may be doing things that hurt others. We might say that they are painting a picture of an unfriendly person—we might even say they are being brats.

Now, you can do two things. You can add your color and variation to that picture by doing the same thing; or you can change the picture by using different colors—colors of love and kindness and saying nice things about people. The choice is yours. Just like a photographer or a painter, you decide what you want to put into your daily picture that other people will see in you. And the nice thing about it is that every day we have a new canvas to use. If we did not like the picture we painted yesterday, today we can start over and make a better picture of how we think life should be seen.—Kenneth Mortonson

January 19: Jesus Prayed All Night

Object: A picture of an owl or a ceramic model, etc.

This is a picture of an owl. Owls are "nocturnal" creatures; that is, they come out at night. People are called "night owls" if they like staying up late at night. I have stayed up all night just a few times in my whole life. Some of you may have stayed up all night at a slumber party or while laughing and giggling at a summer camp.

Jesus stayed up and prayed all night. Listen to Luke 6:12. This verse indicates the importance that Jesus placed upon praying. Prayer is something that should be very important to us.

From time to time churches hold special times of prayer, and members take turns praying all night. Prayer meetings are held to identify people that are in special need of prayer. During prayer meetings, we may pray for people that are in the hospital or for those who have had an accident and need a special blessing from the Lord.

It is not necessary for us to pray all night, but we should set aside a special time each day to pray. Having a special time of prayer each day keeps us from forgetting to pray. We pray at mealtimes to thank the Lord for our food, but we also need time when we can talk to the Lord about other needs without being in a hurry. God is always with us, and we can talk to him like our best friend. We should always be honest with the Lord. If we have done something wrong, we can ask for forgiveness and the Lord will always grant it. Jesus prayed when there were special decisions that he had to make. Jesus also prayed for his daily bread and told all of us to do the same thing. Whenever we pray, whether it is over a meal or during the afternoon, God hears us. To talk to a friend across town we can use our telephones. To talk to God in heaven we use the special privilege of prayer.—Ken Cox

January 26: The Spiral Notebook

Object: A spiral notebook

I am sure that most of you have seen a notebook like this. *(Show them a spiral notebook.)* It is different from what we call a two- or three-ring notebook. The difference is that the pages of the spiral notebook cannot be removed from it without tearing them or destroying the wire that holds the pages together. Now notice that the spiral that unites the pages is really just one continuous wire, curved to make a spiral, and that each turn of the wire runs through one of the holes in the paper.

This little notebook reminds me of life. Each page is like a day in our life. What we do today is recorded in time, and once the day is past, we cannot change what is on the page. But life is not a single day. Each day is important to our total life. Each day teaches us new things about ourselves and about how to live. We need to take the good we learned and let it guide us as we live the next day, the next page. You see, because we are Christians, we have a spiral that will hold life together. It is our faith in God through Jesus Christ. He is the one who tells us the right things to do. He is the one who shows us how to correct our past mistakes. He is the one who tells us those mistakes are forgiven and that we can flip the page of yesterday and start anew today. He is the one who said, "Lo, I am with you to the end of time" (cf. Matt. 28:20).—Kenneth Mortonson

February 2: David's Insides Are Better Than His Outside

TEXT: 1 Sam. 16:1–13

Hello, boys and girls. Today I'm going to tell you a story about a young boy named David. David was the youngest son in a family full of boys. All of his big brothers were very brave. They were also very big and strong. They were smart and very good-looking, too. Because David was the youngest, he usually got stuck with the jobs that no one else would do, like watching the sheep.

One day, it was time for God to choose a new king. He sent a man named Samuel to find the new king in Bethlehem where David and his family lived. Samuel told David's dad that God wanted one of his sons to be king. Jesse, David's dad, was very excited. The only problem was, they didn't know which one to choose. So Samuel had Jesse bring all of his sons to Samuel. All seven of David's brothers visited Samuel, but Samuel said they were not the ones to be king. God told Samuel, "Don't look at what the guys look like on the outside. Look at what they are like on the inside. That is what I'm worried about."

Because Samuel did not choose any of the older sons, Jesse sent for young David. As soon as David arrived, God told Samuel, "David is the one." After several years, David became king. He was not perfect. As a matter of fact, he made a lot of mistakes. There were times when he disobeyed God and other times when he did exactly what God told him to do.

It is important for us to remember that God does not look at what we look like on the outside. He does not care if we are big or small, what color hair we have, or how many freckles. God loves us and wants us to love God and each other. This is what makes us pretty on the inside. This week, try to love one another and God in a special way so you will be pretty on the inside.–Lou Ellen Rich

February 9: The Staple

Object: A stapler

Does anyone know what this is called? (Show a stapler.) Do you know what is it used

for? . . . In order for a stapler to fasten two papers together, you need this little gadget, and within it, you need a row of staples. (Show.) In the stapler the staples have a U-shape. When you staple the papers, one of those little U-shaped wires is pushed down and then, after it has pierced the papers, it hits a little slanting dent in the bottom that pushes the ends of the wire together to form a staple that will hold the papers together. This is a very useful little gadget.

If you were a staple, which would you rather be: a staple in the stapler attached to all the other staples, or a staple that has been pushed out and bent and is holding some papers together? . . . Why? . . . Let me tell you what I would think if I were a staple. Staples are made to hold papers together. While it might be nice to just sit in the stapler with all the other staples, that is not fulfilling the purpose for which I was created. I may not like the idea of being pushed down through the papers and then bent into a new shape, but if that is what it takes to make me into what I am supposed to be, then that's all right. I will only be useful when I am pushed and bent.

Now, we are not staples. But each one of us does have a purpose in life, and part of our job, in growing up, is to discover what we are supposed to be. There may be some hard times, and we may have to do a lot of changing, but in the end we will only be happy when we can be useful as God wants us to be.–Kenneth Mortonson

February 16: What Color?

TEXT: Rom. 10:8b–13

Object: A Ping-Pong ball with half painted one color and the other half left white

"For there is no distinction between Jew and Greek; the same Lord is Lord of all" (v. 12).

(Hold the ball so that one group of children sees the colored side and the other sees the white side. The groups might have to be seated opposite each other.)

Good morning. What is the color of this ball? (The children on one side will say, "Black," or whatever color you have painted it, and the others, of course, will say, "White.")

Why do some of you tell me it is a color

and the others tell me it's white? How can that be? Can you both be right? Of course you can. How? You might both be right if I have painted half the ball one color and left the other half white. And that is exactly what I have done.

We are quite tempted to divide people according to what makes us different. Some of us are female and some are male. Some have light skin and others darker skin. Some have red hair and others black hair. We are all different in one way or another.

Sometimes we let our differences make us feel better than others. Our reading today tells us that everybody who believes in Jesus is loved the same by God. There is nothing that makes one person better than another in God's eyes.

The ball may be white, or it may be another color. The fact is, it is still a Ping-Pong ball. We may be female; we may be male. We may be A-students or we may be D-students. We may be good at throwing and catching a ball, or we may be poor at doing that. No matter what—God loves us each the same.

This is a lesson that many adults never learn. Jesus taught his followers to respect all people regardless of their differences. That is a hard lesson for some of us to learn, but it is an important one. Thank you for helping me tell about this important lesson again.—Children's Sermon Service Plus!

February 23: Daniel Was Committed to God

TEXT: Dan. 1:8

Object: A can or box of food with a nutrition label

This can of food has a label that identifies the nutrition facts of its contents. You may have noticed people reading cans and boxes in the store or at home. Some people refuse to eat certain food, not because of its taste, but because of its contents. For instance, one of my favorite foods, peanut butter, is high in calories and fat. I can't eat peanut butter as often as I would like because I will get too chubby.

A young man named Daniel lived long ago, and his life is described in the Bible. In fact, a book of the Bible is named after him.

One thing that Daniel is noted for is refusing to eat certain foods. Daniel refused to eat some food that was given to him, not because of its taste, or even because it would make him gain too much weight. Daniel refused to eat because he wanted to be obedient to the Lord. Listen to Dan. 1:8.

Daniel refused to eat the royal food because he had been taught that it was a sin to eat certain foods. In Daniel's day, God had commanded that some foods were not to be eaten, and to do so would have broken God's commandments. So, when Daniel would not eat the food that was placed before him, he was demonstrating his commitment to be obedient to God. Daniel knew that God loved him and had a special plan for his life. Daniel did not want to do something wrong and spoil God's plan for his future or displease the Lord.

In our day, the Lord has not placed restrictions on special foods. We may eat the foods of our choice. However, we demonstrate our commitment to the Lord by being obedient in other areas. We demonstrate our commitment to God's commandments and plan for our lives by refusing to cheat, steal, or lie. Instead we are truthful and seek to do good things for the Lord's glory.

Daniel was used in a very special way by God. Even though he was a young man, the Lord began to change many of the problems of Daniel's people through him. When we are obedient to the Lord, God can use us in special ways to help with the problems of our day. God wants to bless the people of our land, and he can use committed people to help in a mighty way.—Ken Cox

March 2: Ruth Helped Naomi

TEXT: Ruth 1:16

Object: Two coffee cups

These are coffee cups. Adults like the taste of coffee, but that is not the only reason they drink coffee. Coffee time is an opportunity to visit and listen. Sometimes while having a cup of coffee, persons can solve their problems. Not all problems can be solved over coffee, but it is helpful to be together.

One of the most beautiful stories in the Bible is the Old Testament book of Ruth.

Ruth and her mother-in-law lived in the land of Moab and were having very difficult times. Their husbands had died, and they were all alone in the world. Ruth's mother-in-law was going to make the difficult journey back to her home, Judah, and told the younger Ruth that she should stay in Moab, where life would be easier. Ruth had nothing to gain by going with her mother-in-law, but she was unselfish and refused to leave her mother-in-law all alone in her time of need. Listen to Ruth 1:16.

By not leaving her mother-in-law, Ruth made a decision that was pleasing to God. Ruth understood that their problems couldn't be solved easily, but by staying together through the hard times, they would have better lives. As the story turns out, Ruth and her mother-in-law worked together, and the Lord richly blessed their lives and descendants.

You can help someone just like Ruth did. We may not be able to solve all of a friend's problems, nor should we even try. One of the worst things that we can do is give advice to someone who is going through hard times. The good and kind thing that we can do for a person with problems is to listen to them and be with them. This is especially true for persons as they get older, like grandparents. One of the finest things we can do for our grandparents, or a neighbor who is older, is to take time to visit them.

Remember the lesson of the coffee cups. People like coffee times, not only because of the taste of the liquid, but because those moments together provide an opportunity to draw strength from one another.–Ken Cox

March 9: Broadcasting

In one of his parables, Jesus told about a farmer who went out to plant his seed. As he did so, said Jesus, some of the seed fell on good ground, and some among the weeds, and some among the rocks. Today, when the farmers plant their seeds, they know exactly where the seed will go. Because of the machinery they use, the seeds are all in a straight row. But back in the time of Jesus, they did not have such machines. Instead they carried their seeds in a bag, took a handful as they walked along, and cast the seed out in a circular motion. This was called broadcasting.

It is interesting to remember that today, when people produce radio and television programs that they send out, we say they are "broadcasting." They just send it out without being able to control where it will go. It goes everywhere.

But this does not mean that there is no control over where the words or pictures go. The control is at the receiving end. We turn the dial to the station or channel we want. And if we do not like what we see or hear, we can turn it off.

The same thing applies to what people "broadcast" when they are near us. If someone is calling you names, you can walk away or turn it off by ignoring them. If someone is saying nasty things about someone you know and like, you don't have to listen. Walk away. And if you don't do that, then refuse to listen to what is being said. Just because someone says something about another person that does not mean it is true. Remember, you can control what you let into your mind.–Kenneth Mortonson

March 16: Two Hands

This morning I want you to look at something that is very important to you. It is something that is always with you and you use it every day. Can anyone guess what I am thinking about? . . . You have two of these things, and they have fingers. What is it? . . . Of course, your hands. I wonder why God gave us two hands? We have only one head and one nose and one tongue. But we have two eyes, and therefore we can see better. Close one eye and notice that you cannot see as much as with two eyes. We have two ears because we need to hear what is happening all around us. Life would be different if we could only hear sounds on one side. This is also true of our hands. We can do so much more because we have two hands. For example, we can write more easily because one hand can hold the paper as we write with the other hand. It is easier to carry a long board with two hands. It is easier to learn how to ride a bicycle when you can hold the handlebars in two hands. It is easier to use a fishing pole or a golf club or a baseball bat when you have two hands. Life is just so much easier and we can do so many things when we have two hands.

But with our hands, we also have a responsibility to use our hands carefully. For example, we use our hands to eat, but it is our mind that tells our hands what to bring to our mouth. We can form our hand into a fist and hurt someone, or we can extend our open hand in friendship. Some people are so taken with what they have created with their own hands that they worship it (Cf. Mic. 5:13). Others have learned to fold their hands to help them pray to God and to worship him. So be careful how you use your wonderful hands.–Kenneth Mortonson

March 23: Run the Race

TEXT: Heb. 12:1–13

"Let us run with perseverance the race that is set before us" (v. 1).

Object: Running shoes

Good morning! This morning I brought some running shoes to show how we are to live our Christian lives. How many of you like to run? *(Let them answer.)* Running is fun and running is exciting! I love to run.

Some people run in long races. When we run a long way, we can get quite tired at times and we might want to give up. But we keep going. The word here is *perseverance*. It means to keep going, to keep on doing things and not give up–even if it hurts. It's a wonderful, big word.

One nice thing about being a member of a congregation like this is that there are many people who help us "run the race," or keep going with our lives. They are interested in us, and they cheer us on. It's like running in a long race, and they are on the sidelines encouraging us.

Dear Jesus: Thank you for the people in our lives who cheer us on in what we do. Amen–Children's Sermon Service Plus!

March 30: The Last Enemy

TEXT: 1 Cor. 15:19–26

The last enemy to be destroyed is death (v. 26).

Object: Picture of a tombstone or grave–even a picture of Jesus' empty grave

The apostle Paul says that the last enemy to be destroyed is death. Can you tell me what death is? *(Let them answer.)* Death is when the life goes out of something that is living. I had a pet that died. The life was gone, and only the body was left behind. I was very, very sad. Death is a cruel enemy.

I knew I would never play with that pet again. Never again would he come when I called him. Never again would he let me pet him. Never again would I see him run and jump and play and do all the funny things he did when he was alive.

On this day Jesus defeated death. He died so that we might not die. In other words Jesus died so that we can live eternally. People still die. It makes us very, very sad. But the promise of Easter is that death is not forever. There is the resurrection of the dead to look forward to. Someday I will leave this body behind and join Jesus. You will too. That's wonderful news.

Meanwhile we still have death. It is still an enemy. But it is an enemy that has lost its sting and its power because of Jesus and Easter. Easter is the biggest celebration of the year because the most important thing in the world has been done: Death has been defeated. This is a wonderful thing to know about–especially when we lose someone very important to us.–Children's Sermon Service Plus!

April 6: Watch Your Words

TEXT: Ps. 19:4

Object: An enlarged comic strip with empty "word balloons"

It's impossible to know what is happening in this comic strip that I have photocopied out of the newspaper. I have taken some Liquid Paper and deleted the words in the "balloons" that reveal what the characters are saying. In a cartoon strip the artist draws the pictures and determines what the cartoon's message will be by inserting the words. The words are the finishing touch that completes the meaning of the cartoon. Without the words, no matter how funny the drawings, we can only guess at what the comic strip says. By putting different words in these balloons, we can completely change the meaning of this comic strip.

The words that we speak are just like the words in a comic strip. What we are thinking in our minds soon finds its way into words that come out of our mouths, and what we say determines the course of our lives and shapes others too. When God created the heavens and the earth, he spoke them into existence. God's words are very powerful and are creative and destructive.

Our words are like that too. What we say can do a lot of good or a lot of harm.

Our words can make or break a person's feelings about themselves. For instance if you see a new person your age in your neighborhood, what you say can help or hurt them. If you say, "I don't know you, you look funny, and your shoes are goofy," then that newcomer to our city can feel pretty bad. On the other hand, if you say, "My name is Ken, I can be your new pal, and I will introduce you to my friends and you can play with us," those friendly and kind words can make a stranger feel welcome and happy. And that's not all. When we make someone else feel bad, our hearts grow sad with anger or harshness. But when we build up others with positive and kind words, we feel good inside.

God has commanded that we think wholesome thoughts and be very careful with what we say. Remember, thoughts turn quickly into words, and our words are very powerful in determining the quality of our lives and others. Listen to Ps. 19:14. Let this verse be our prayer always.—Ken Cox

April 13: Music Notes

Every Sunday, when we gather together, we sing some songs. This morning I want you to look at a song sheet. *(Open a hymnal or some other music book.)* What do you see? . . . *(Words, lines, and musical notes.)* Now, just concentrate on what we call the musical notes. If you look closely, you will see that each note is in a special place on the lines. And some notes are different. Some notes have a line, like a flag, at the top. Sometimes that little flag connects two notes together. Some notes are solid black, and others have a white center.

There are two reasons for these differences. The position of the note on the lines indicates what sound should be given to the note, and the shape of the note indicates how long the note should be played or sung. We sometimes call this latter condition the value of the note. So position and value determine how we put all the notes together, and that gives us the music for our song. And if you have an orchestra playing, or a choir singing, where different people play or sing different notes at the same time, you

have something very special when it is done right. All this comes from a sheet of music with its many notes. Now, the person who produced the original sheet of music is called the composer. That person decided what sound was to be produced, and the people playing or singing have to follow the notes to produce the tune.

Life is like a sheet of music. God has in mind a certain kind of life that he wants us to live. In the Bible, he tells us what we are to do and as we play those notes, so to speak, we produce the life that the composer, God, wants from us. But he wants different things from each person. We all have our own special value and position in life, and when people do what God wants them to do, we make beautiful music together.—Kenneth Mortonson

April 20: Pray for Something Specific

TEXT: Jer. 33:3

Object: A shopping list

This is a shopping list. Most folks make out a list like this when they go to the grocery store. The list helps them remember everything that they need at home.

A different shopping list has to be made out for each trip to the store, because what we need at home has changed. One day we may be out of peanut butter, the next day we might have used up all the jelly. So, we check the pantry and refrigerator and make out the list for what we should buy.

What we pray for should reflect what we need the same way our shopping list does. When we pray we ask our heavenly Father in Jesus' name for what we are lacking in life. We should never fail to ask the Lord for what we need. We should pray for our food and housing to be supplied. We should pray for protection and strength. The Lord loves us and has promised to supply our needs. We should pray a prayer of thanksgiving when our needs are met. His word instructs us to ask for great things. Listen to Jer. 33:3. Whether the need is great or small, we have the privilege of asking God for it.

What we pray for should change from day to day like our shopping lists. If we are saying the same prayer over and over again without thinking, we are not praying as we ought to. This kind of praying is called "useless repetition" and indicates that we are not seriously asking the Lord for what we need.

One way that the Lord intends for our faith to grow is through the answers that he grants to our specific prayers. If we pray without thinking, and fail to look for answers, we will not notice how God is working in our lives. However, if we pray for something we need in particular and expectantly look for God's filling of that need, the Lord will reward our diligent seeking with an answer that will strengthen our faith.

When we go to the store, we list exactly what we need. When we go to the Lord in prayer, we should ask him specifically for what we lack.—Ken Cox

April 27: The Button and the Buttonhole

This morning I want you to look carefully at this shirt. How many buttons does it have? . . . *(Be sure to count the ones on the sleeve also.)* And how many buttonholes are there? . . . There are the same number of each because a button cannot do what it is supposed to do without a buttonhole. And to know that this little cut in the material is a buttonhole, you need to know how the button is used. The two go together and each one gives meaning to the other.

Have you ever wondered why God created boys and girls, men and women so that they could help each other? Men and women are different in many ways. For example, if a man does not shave, he will grow a beard. A woman does not grow a beard. This may come from the fact that long ago, the man went out into the cold to hunt for food. The beard helped to keep his face warm. The woman remained at home, caring for the children of the family.

Now, the point I want you to remember is that we are like the button and the buttonhole. In order to make life complete, boys and girls, men and women need each other and we are to help each other become what God wants us to be. Since we need each other, we had better be kind and gentle to one another. We need to understand each other and not expect everyone to be exactly the same. Remember the buttons. They came in all sizes and shapes and color. Remember the buttonholes. They also came in different sizes and are made of all kinds of

different material and colors. But no matter what the color or size of each, together they do a wonderful job of doing what they were created to do.—Kenneth Mortonson

May 4: Mustard Seed Faith

TEXT: Luke 17:5–10

"If you had faith the size of a mustard seed . . ." (v. 5).

Object: A small seed (perhaps even a true mustard seed from the Holy Land)

I am amazed at how a small seed like this can grow into a huge plant. Every tree you see and every large plant began as a small seed. God uses the forces of nature, the sun, rain, and the soil, to nurture the seed into becoming a plant—sometimes a very large plant.

What is the largest plant you have ever seen? *(Let them answer.)* Do you know how small the seed was for that plant? It was probably very small indeed—perhaps as small as this seed.

Jesus said that faith is very much like a small seed. It doesn't take much faith to do wonderful and powerful things. A person with a little faith can do very much.

Unlike this seed, however, one cannot see faith. I can see the seed; I can't see faith. I can touch the seed; I can't touch faith. And yet faith is very powerful!

Faith is what you are learning in Sunday school, at home, and in church. Faith means trusting Jesus and believing in Jesus. What you are learning about faith is some of the most important learning you can have in life! I'm glad you have faithful teachers to tell you about our important Christian faith!

Dear Lord: Help our faith grow as you help all things grow. Amen.—Children's Sermon Service Plus!

May 11: Mothers Are Very Powerful

TEXT: Isa. 66:13

Object: A little cradle

A popular movie tape is the action adventure film. In this kind of picture the leading character, a hero, has extraordinary power and goes about doing colossal things. In one such movie I saw Arnold Schwarzenegger swimming underwater while on the surface of the water he grabbed a rocket launcher and fired it over and over again like a cap pistol. Now that's power, action, and adventure!

But I don't believe Arnold Schwarzenegger is the most powerful person around. One of the most famous sayings about powerful people is regarding mothers. Yes, mothers. *(Begin rocking cradle.)* It goes, "The hand that rocks the cradle is the hand that rules the world." So, no matter how strong the heroes may be in action adventure films, we know that our mothers that we are honoring today are more powerful still.

Mothers are powerful because of their influence. Mothers shape us and mold us the way an artist carves a statue. Abraham Lincoln, the sixteenth president of our country, said, "All that I am or hope to be, I owe to my angel mother."

Mothers are powerful, not because they can shoot a rocket launcher like a pistol, but because of their kindness. Listen to Isa. 66:13. The Lord wanted to convey the message that he was going to be kind to his people, so he used the example of a caring mother. We must remember that we can make positive marks on people's lives not because we can beat them up but because we can shape them through kindness and caring.

There is one other saying about mothers that has come down through the years. It is an old proverb stating, "God could not be everywhere, and therefore he made mothers."

Let's recognize the real power in our lives as we remember and honor our mothers.–Ken Cox

May 18: Forever!

TEXT: Heb. 13:1–8, 15–16

"Jesus Christ is the same yesterday and today and forever" (v. 8).

Object: A diamond ring (or an object that looks like a diamond)

Good morning! Today I brought a diamond with me because they say, "A diamond is forever!" In other words, a diamond lasts a long time. Do you believe that? *(Let them answer.)*

Many things do not last long. It seems like everything changes. People grow to be bigger and bigger, so they need new clothes and bigger shoes. People move to different homes. Telephone numbers sometimes change. Buildings fall down and others get built. It sometimes seems like *everything* is changing! Only diamonds last a long time.

Diamonds do last a long time, but, like everything else, they will also change. You and I know someone who does not change. Jesus *never* changes. People come and go and things change all the time, but Jesus always stays the same. Jesus is the same as he was 2,000 years ago, and Jesus is the same today as he will be 2,000 years from now.

I'm glad to know Jesus, who is so strong that he doesn't change.

Dearest Lord Jesus: You knew me when I was very little and you loved me then. You love me now as well. We thank you for your love. Amen.–Children's Sermon Service Plus!

May 25: Stained Glass Windows

Why do we have windows in our homes? . . . They help us to see outside. They let light in and they can be opened to let in fresh air. But not all windows are the same. In many churches, you will see a special kind of window. Why is it called that? . . . Because the glass has been stained with different colors so that the light will still shine through but when you look at it you cannot see outside. What you see is the design on the window.

There are two interesting things about a stained glass window. The first is what I just mentioned: you cannot see through the glass, but the light can come through. The second thing is that the light coming through the glass enables us to see a special design. That means that if you went outside right now and there were no lights on in the church, you would not be able to see the beauty or the design of the window. So this is what I want you to remember. In order to see the windows in our church, light must be shining through them.

This reminds us of something that is very important as we try to be Christians. Because we live with Jesus, a special light or spirit is present with us. When that light shines forth from us and people look at us, they will see more than you or me as a person. They will see the image of Jesus in our life. Jesus said, "Let your light so shine before [people], that they may see your good works and give glory to your Father who is in heaven" (Matt. 5:16). When Jesus makes a difference in our life, we must let other people see that difference by the way we live in God's world.–Kenneth Mortonson

June 1: The Baseball Cap

Object: A baseball cap

Who can tell me what this is? . . . *(Show the children a baseball cap.)*

That's right. This is a cap; or, to be more accurate, a baseball cap.

This baseball cap is designed to be used in a special way. How many of you know the correct way of wearing a cap like this? . . . *(Give to someone to put on.)*

The correct way to wear this cap is with the visor in the front. Do you know why? . . . Because the purpose of the visor is to shade the player's eyes and to help him see better when he is outside in the sun.

You see, a cap is used when you are outside. Therefore, many people think it is not polite to wear a cap inside. It is like sitting in a house with your hat and coat on. That action says to the people you are with, "I am anxious to get out of here and be outside. I am not even going to bother taking off what I wear outside."

It is important to think about what our actions say to other people. What we wear and how we wear our clothing communicates to the people around us. If a person came into the worship service wearing his pajamas, it would be like telling the preacher, "I plan to sleep through your sermon today."

So, the lesson from the cap is simply this: Remember what things are for and use them correctly. And remember that how you use whatever you have tells other people how you feel about them.–Kenneth Mortonson

June 8: We Should Share Our Faith

TEXT: Philem. 6

Object: A bag of peppermints, candy, etc.

We are taught to share what we have. If a friend comes to visit our house, we are to share our toys with them. We are being selfish if we keep things just for ourselves. When we share our toys with a friend we have twice the fun because we have someone to play with. I want to share something

with you this morning. *(Pass out peppermints so that all the children get one piece of candy.)* Before you eat this peppermint get permission from your parents. It's okay this once to have the peppermint in church if your parents approve.

Sharing is giving to others the good things that we have. The Bible encourages us to share our faith. We share our faith by telling others about our belief in Jesus as our Savior and Lord. Listen to Philemon 6.

Foreign missionaries are persons who share their faith in another nation. Many of these missionaries to other countries have to learn to speak another language and live where customs are strange. Home missionaries work in the United States in places like inner-city neighborhoods of large metropolitan areas like New York or Houston. These home missionaries may feed the hungry and provide shelter for the homeless. Whatever the country, customs, or needs that are dealt with, the goal of the missionaries is to share the gospel of Jesus Christ.

We have an obligation to share our faith. All Christians do. We must not be selfish with our faith. If we share our belief in Jesus, we become happier because we will have more Christian friends. We must see ourselves as missionaries in our neighborhoods. So, don't forget when you are sharing your toys, time, or even a piece of peppermint candy, to remember to share your faith in Jesus too.–Ken Cox

June 15: Lost Ones Found!

TEXT: Luke 15:1–10

Object: A new coin (If you can, arrange to get a roll of new coins and pass them out at the end of the children's sermon.)

"I have found the coin that I had lost" (v. 9).

Jesus once told a story about a woman who had a coin such as this. She needed the coin because she was very poor. Something happened, however, and she lost the valuable coin.

Have you ever lost something that was important and you just couldn't find it anywhere? *(Let them answer.)* That's how this woman felt. She felt so bad about her lost coin. That coin was so important to her.

Everywhere this woman looked she could not find the coin. She looked under the bed.

She looked under the rug. She looked in the kitchen and in the bedroom. She looked in every pocket of every dress. She swept out her house, hoping she could find the shiny coin—but there was no coin! She felt very bad about that. She even started crying. But —just then—she saw something shiny. It was the lost coin! It was the coin! She was as happy as a person could be!

She was so happy she called her neighbors and friends and anyone who would come to rejoice with her. Her lost coin was now found. She was very happy!

Jesus told this story because he was really telling about people. God feels about people the way this woman felt about her coin. God is so very happy when any boy or girl starts believing in God.

Every person—each one of us—is very, very important to God.

Dearest Lord: Thank you for looking for and finding us. Amen.—Children's Sermon Service Plus!

June 22: David Wasn't Perfect

TEXT: Ps. 51:1–2, 10

Object: Humpty Dumpty picture, broken egg, etc.

There is a nursery rhyme about an egg that goes like this:

Humpty Dumpty sat on a wall,
Humpty Dumpty had a great fall,
All the king's horses and
all the king's men
Couldn't put Humpty Dumpty
together again.

These verses teach us that when some things are broken, it is impossible to put them back the way they were before.

David is one of the greatest heroes in the Bible. When he was young he was chosen by God to be king, and he gained a mighty reputation because he triumphed over Goliath on the battlefield. These great things about David would give the impression that he was perfect. David wasn't perfect. One of the stories about David in the Old Testament was of how he was forgiven by the Lord after breaking the commandments of God.

After becoming famous, David hatched an evil scheme. David had a woman's husband murdered during a battle and took the lady to be his wife. To make matters worse, David tried to hide his crime. However, God knows everything that happens on the earth, and the Lord was fully aware of the wrong that David had done. God sent a prophet named Nathan to inform David about the seriousness of his crime. After hearing Nathan explain how God was upset with him, David confessed that he was wrong. After confessing and paying for his sin, David was restored to fellowship with the Lord.

One of the psalms records the words of David as he told God how sorry he was for committing and covering up this sin. Listen to Ps 51:1–2, 10.

We can learn a lot from David's mistake. We should not do the things that we know are wrong. When we do, someone is always hurt, and we upset the Lord who loves us. If we do make a mistake we should immediately confess our wrongdoing and not try to hide it from the Lord. The longer we hide our errors, the worse they become. Finally, we should trust the Lord to put our lives back together again. Humpty Dumpty couldn't be repaired, but by the grace of God, we can be restored to productive lives because God loves us and will forgive us when we ask him to.—Ken Cox

June 29: The Ballpoint Pen

Object: A ballpoint pen

How many of you know how to write? . . . What do you use when you write? . . . Some people use a pencil. It is easier to correct what you have written with a pencil. All you need is a good eraser. But I think most grownups write with a pen. And today most people use what we call a ballpoint pen. Have you ever seen the inside of a ballpoint pen? . . . Let me show you what it is like. Here is a tube that contains ink, and at the end of that tube there is a metal tip with a little metal ball at the end. It is hard to see, but it is there. That little ball puts the ink on the paper as it rolls along. That is why it is called a ballpoint pen.

So you see, this tube inside the pen must be there with ink in the tube and a little tiny ball that rolls in order for someone to write with it. Both parts are essential. If the ball is stuck for some reason, you cannot write. If the ink is all used up or dried up, the pen will not work.

Sometimes, people are like the empty tube. They have nothing to share with other people. But a Christian is someone whose life is full of good things that they are willing to share.

Sometimes people are like the stuck ball, they are stubborn and will not move. They think they are right, no matter what other people say. Now a Christian is steadfast, but that is not the same as being stubborn. A ballpoint pen that continues to work is steadfast, for it is always ready to write when called upon to do so. The stubborn person is rigid. The Christian person is someone who is always willing to discover new truths about life with God and in God's world. Like the little ball, they keep turning and looking and discovering how wonderful life is, and as they do so, they leave their mark on the world around them.–Kenneth Mortonson

July 6: What Made Goliath Weak?

TEXT: 1 Sam. 17:26

The Bible tells about the exciting life of a young man named David. David became the hero of his country, Israel, because he conquered a giant named Goliath.

The giant Goliath was very strong. He stood over nine feet tall and wore armor that weighed over a hundred pounds. Goliath's spear was huge, and he was an expert in fighting with it. The Scriptures state that Goliath had been trained as a warrior since he was a child. Goliath was so frightening that the entire army of Israel trembled in fear because of his threats. With a loud intimidating voice, Goliath dared the whole nation to send just one person out to fight him. Goliath made the army of Israel ashamed because no one was brave enough to answer the challenge.

David happened to come to the battlefield one day on an errand to bring food to his brothers in the army. David heard Goliath's loud challenges and knew immediately that Goliath could be defeated. David grasped that Goliath was a weakling, even though he appeared strong, because he was guilty of taking the Lord's name in vain. David had heard Goliath say disrespectful things about God. David had been taught from childhood to respect God and to never speak his name without being reverent. As soon as David heard Goliath's foul talk, he knew that Goliath couldn't win, because his sin would make him weak. Listen to 1 Sam. 17:26.

All that David took into battle was his shepherd's staff, a slingshot, and five stones that he carried in his pouch. Primarily, David was armed with his belief and trust in God. Sure enough, Goliath lost the fight even though he was covered in armor and held his huge menacing spear. David won because of his faith in God.

We should not think that people are strong and beyond correction just because they can frighten us with their strength. If we are threatened by a bully like Goliath we should hold on to the right actions we have been taught, knowing that God will be with us to help us be winners in life.–Ken Cox

July 13: Dust Masks

Object: A dust mask

Have you ever seen a person wearing a mask like this? *(Put on a dust mask.)* Where was the person when you saw him or her? . . . Do you know what this mask is called? . . . It is a dust mask. Now, sometimes, in very cold weather, someone may put on a mask like this when they go outside to help warm the air they are breathing; but the main use of this mask is to catch dust. When people are cutting the grass, or sawing wood, or sanding a floor, they will use this mask to catch the dust or pollen and keep it from entering their lungs. Did you know that everyone has a kind of dust mask that is with us all the time? Where is it? . . . That's right. There are little hairs in your nose; and these help to filter the air we breathe. They, like a dust mask, catch the dust that is in the air and keep it out of our lungs. You know there is a lot of dust in the air. We see it on our furniture in any room that has not been dusted for a long time.

God has so made us that we have ways to keep nasty things out of our body. He has done this because we cannot inspect every bit of air that we breathe every day. But there are other things in life that can do nasty things to us if they get inside us. Here, we have to use what we call willpower. That means that we have to filter out things that might hurt us. For example, your parents may tell you that you are not to watch certain programs on TV. They are trying to teach you that some things are not good for you to watch. Seeing a lot of violence in a program may cause you to think that it is OK to hit or hurt someone. That is the wrong thing to have in your mind, so you have to use the filter of willpower and turn to another program. It is a good thing that God has given us ways to keep us safe.–Kenneth Mortonson

July 20: Philip, A Famous Witness
TEXT: Acts 8:34–35
Object: A light bulb

This is a light bulb. We take these for granted now, but the invention of the light bulb was an exciting advancement years ago. The inventor of the light bulb, Thomas Alva Edison, became famous because of his innovations. Schools have been named after Thomas Edison, and his name stands for hard work and persistence.

A famous man in the Bible was named Philip. Philip is well known because of his faithfulness in telling others about Jesus. Philip told people about Jesus wherever he went. On one occasion, Philip was walking down a road near Jerusalem when he met a man from Ethiopia driving a chariot. The chariot driver was reading a scroll of the Bible but didn't understand the Bible. Philip got up in the chariot and informed the man that the Bible was speaking of Jesus. Because of Philip's witness, the man from Ethiopia believed in Jesus and was baptized in some water beside the road.

We can become famous in telling others about Jesus. People that we meet every day are like the man in the chariot and do not understand about Jesus. They need someone they know and trust to explain that Jesus loves them. These people can find that we are helpful, not pushy, in sharing what we believe. We can gain a reputation for carrying the good news of Jesus in a kind, compassionate way.

Witnessing or telling others about Jesus is something that all of us can do. We don't have to be a genius or an inventor of new products to be famous. We can become famous by telling our friends about Jesus just like Philip.–Ken Cox

July 27: The Bible Is an Heirloom
TEXT: 1 Cor. 11:2
Object: An heirloom

This necklace has been handed down through four generations within our family. It was first worn by our children's great-grandmother. When something is valued and passed down like this, it is called an "heirloom." Heirlooms may be jewelry, books, furniture, or anything precious that is given from generation to generation.

The Bible is just like an heirloom. The only reason that we have the Bible today is that it has been valued and handed down from generation to generation.

During some sad days in Old Testament history, the books of the Bible were almost lost. A king by the name of Josiah discovered the books of the law and began to teach them and live by them again (2 Kings 22:10 ff.). The Bible must be cherished by each generation or it will be lost.

The apostle Paul understood the importance of not only passing down the Bible but obeying the scriptures. Listen to 1 Cor. 11:2.

So, we have the Bible because it has been regarded as precious and handed down to us. Now, we need to treat the words of the Bible as precious. We treat the Bible as a precious possession by taking time to read the Bible. We also strive to obey the teachings it contains. It is only through knowing and obeying the scriptures that we are able to pass the Bible along to someone else.–Ken Cox

August 3: Colored Pencils
Object: Colored pencils

Is there anyone here who likes to draw? . . . How many like to draw with colored pencils? . . . I have several colored pencils that I'd like you to look at this morning. Here is a red one and a blue one and a green one. I can tell what color the pencil will put on my drawing just by looking at it. In a sense, the colored pencil is true to itself. It has to be in order for it to be useful to me. That is, when I want a red color in my picture, I will take a red pencil to produce that color. If I did not know what color would come from each pencil, then I would have a terrible time trying to color a picture.

I think that God wants us to be like the colored pencil. He wants us to be true to who we are. Jesus said, "For no good tree bears bad fruit, nor again does a bad tree bear good fruit; for each tree is known by its own fruit" (Luke 6:43, 44). Or as we have been seeing this morning, each colored pencil is known by its own color.

Let me show you what that might mean in the way we live each day. The Bible tells us that we are to love one another. If that is important to you then you will do all you can to show your love for others. For example, when someone does something nice for you, what is the right thing to do? . . . Say thank you. Suppose you want to be a friend to someone, and you have a candy bar in your lunch box that could be broken in half. What might you do for your friend? . . . Right. Showing love for others means sharing what we have with them. That is one way you can add the color of Christianity to your life. And it applies to so many things. For example, when a family loves their church, they will share what they have with the church.—Kenneth Mortonson

August 10: The Lord Knows What Tomorrow Holds

TEXT: Jer. 1:12

Object: Binoculars, telescope, etc.

These are binoculars, and their function is to make things that are far away look close. Binoculars are very good to have in a football game when you're way back in the cheap seats.

The technology available today to see things that are far away is amazing. With telescopes, distant planets in our solar system can be seen. Using satellite technology some scientists recently saw some comets crashing into Jupiter, which is millions of miles away from earth.

As capable as we are to see things far away, there is no device that can see into tomorrow. There is no human invention available to forecast the future. Those magazines at the supermarket that make predictions about the future are just making up wild stories. None of those tales is true.

Years before he came into the world, God announced the birth of Jesus. The birth of Jesus came about just as God foretold through his prophets. The Lord reported in advance the birth of Jesus in Bethlehem and that he would be in the family line of King David. Whatever the Lord announces in his word is certain to come true because God keeps his promises. Listen to Jer. 1:12.

The Bible contains another pronouncement about Jesus. God has revealed that Jesus is coming back. Jesus' return to earth is called the "second coming." We know that Jesus will return one day because God has promised it. None of the prophecies of the Bible has failed, and the foretelling of Jesus' return will come about just like the Bible says.

We don't know what the future holds, but we know who holds the future. Furthermore, in the Bible we are told how to live by faith until all of God's promises are fulfilled.—Ken Cox

August 17: The Buckle

Object: A buckle

Who can tell me what this is called? *(Show them a buckle.)* And what is it used for? . . . Right. The purpose of a buckle is to hold two straps together or to form a clasp for a belt. Usually a buckle is made of a metal frame and a movable metal tongue. In order for the buckle to work, there must be holes in the end of the belt. Since there are several holes in the belt, it can be adjusted to make the belt fit a variety of sizes. Once the belt is in place, it will stay that way as long as the owner of the belt needs it. I am very thankful for my belt. *(Tell of a time when you used a belt.)* I have a pair of pants that are a little too big for me and they would keep sliding down if it were not for my belt. That belt solves my problem. And my belt is always ready to help me, whenever I need it.

We need to be like a belt to God. We never know when he might need us to do something special for him. Every one of us has a special talent and we may have to wait a long time before God gives us an opportunity to do something special. But we better be ready at all times to do whatever we can. When we see someone who needs help, God wants us to help them, if we can. And when we help them, we are helping Jesus.

He said, in effect, "Whenever you do something special to someone in need, it is like you are doing it to me" (f. Matt. 25:40). When we show love for someone else, especially because we are Christians, then we are showing our love of Jesus who loves everyone.–Kenneth Mortonson

August 24: Jesus Healed Sick People
TEXT: Mark 1:34a
Object: A thermometer

This is a thermometer. A thermometer lets us know when someone is sick. When a temperature is above normal there is an infection or other problem that must be treated. Sick persons want to get well, because when we are sick we feel bad.

When Jesus ministered on earth he healed people of their sicknesses. Listen to Mark 1:34a.

God gave Jesus the ability to heal people so he could be seen as very important. When people knew Jesus could heal them, they looked to him for the answer to life's problems. After Jesus healed someone, he would preach and teach about how to live for God.

When Jesus healed someone from a disease, he eliminated a major problem in their lives. However, regardless of how sick we might be, we have an even greater problem than our illness. That problem is our sin. We commit sins when we do wrong things or turn to our ways instead of God's ways. Unforgiven sin is our biggest problem.

Jesus healed people to show that he had the ability to forgive them of their sins. Jesus still heals today when we pray to him, but he doesn't heal in every single case. However, Jesus forgives sin each and every time a person asks for forgiveness, and thus takes care of life's biggest problem. The Bible teaches that all who believe in Jesus have eternal life. Let's be sure we put our trust in God by believing in Jesus.–Ken Cox

August 31: Don't Forget to Love Yourself
TEXT: Matt. 22:39

Good morning, girls and boys. How many people in here love someone or something? We all have someone in our lives that we love. It may be a parent, a brother or sister, maybe a friend or a teacher. We all have someone we love.

Sometimes it is very easy to love other people. Maybe they do nice things for us. Some people make us laugh and we like being with them. We give them presents on their birthdays and at Christmastime. We call them on the phone or go over to their houses to play. We do nice things for them because we love them. We love them.

In the Bible Jesus tells us that the most important thing we can do is Love God with all of our heart. That is a very important thing to do and sometimes it is a very easy thing to do. God gives us a lot of things. We get to enjoy all of nature that God created. God gives us friends and family to love. God can be easy to love.

After Jesus tells us to love God, he tells us to love our neighbors. Sometimes that is easy and sometimes that is difficult. Sometimes we love our neighbors. They are kind and fun, and they are easy for us to love. Other times, we might have to really work hard to love our neighbor. Sometimes we want to be mean to them because we do not like them or maybe they do not like us. Sometimes it is very difficult to love our neighbors, but it is important that we try our hardest to love them.

Jesus tells us that we should love our neighbors like we love ourselves. Sometimes we forget that we should love ourselves. God made us and cares about us very much. Each one of us has special talents. Some of us are very funny. Some of us sing very well. Others of us are very smart. Some of us are very nice. We all have something very special that makes us unique. There is no one else in the world exactly like you are. We need to love ourselves because God loves us too.

Remember this week that you are very special. God loves you very much. God also loves our neighbors because they are special too.–Lou Ellen Rich

September 7: Squirrels Get Ready
TEXT: Matt. 24:44
Object: A picture of a squirrel or ceramic model, etc.

This is a picture of a squirrel. Squirrels live in trees and they're really fast. Squirrels dart across roads and run up the side of trees faster than anything I have ever seen. In addition to being fast, a common characteristic of squirrels is getting ready for things to come.

Squirrels prepare for the harsh cold of winter by storing up food in their tree homes. They will put in enough pecans or nuts during summer to get them through the scarce food supply of winter. If they didn't take these steps of preparation, they would starve during the winter months.

We must learn a lesson from squirrels. Squirrels get ready for something even though they don't have calendars or weather reports. There is something inside them that makes them get ready.

The Lord has told us to get ready for his coming. Listen to Matt. 24:44. So, we must be ready when the Lord comes back. We do this by telling others about Jesus whenever we can and by being obedient to the Lord's commandments. Let's always be ready for the Lord's return.–Ken Cox

September 14: Listen to Your Elders
TEXT: Prov. 23:22

Object: An old book

By looking at the faded cover of this book and the darkened edges of its pages, it's easy to see that it is very old. I have discovered that even though it's old, it is full of very useful information. I use this book often, and I am very careful with it so I can use it for many years to come.

Our society values things that are brand-new. Some have called our country a "throwaway" society because if something gets old, we just discard it. For that reason, some might look at the cover of this book and just toss it into the trash. But in doing so, they would lose a treasury of knowledge. We also treat senior citizens that way. We don't throw them away, we just don't pay as much attention to them as we should, preferring instead to heed a younger person who seems to be more in style. Our heavenly Father advises us to respect people that are advanced in years. Listen to Prov. 23:22.

As our fathers and mothers advance in years they should be listened to very closely. Senior adults have been through many life experiences and have learned what is good and bad. If we don't listen to them, we are doomed to learn everything "the hard way." This unfortunate way of discovering the truth is called the school of "hard knocks,"

because learning without listening can be very painful.

Senior adults will not force their ideas upon us, but if we ask for their help, they will give us the benefit of their wisdom. God is like that. Jesus describes himself as standing at the door of our hearts patiently, politely knocking. He wants us to open the door of our minds and hearts and pay attention to his direction. God also says that he speaks in a "still, small voice." If we are willing to pay attention, God will present his wisdom through various channels.

If you are lucky, old books like this, which are a treasure, can be rescued from the trash heap. And if we are willing to ask and seek advice from our elders, we will learn and be blessed by God.–Ken Cox

September 21: The Carving
This morning I want you to look at something we see every Sunday. *(Show them a carved surface on the communion table. If you do not have any carvings in your church, bring an example with you.)* This is called a carving, and it is made by taking a piece of wood and carefully removing some of the wood so that what is left represents something. *(Show them the carving again.)* What does this represent? . . . In order to make a carving, you need a sharp tool to remove the wood, and you need to be very careful and you need a lot of patience, for it takes time to complete a carving like this. You also need to know how to carve. One slip can ruin it. You also need to have a pattern to follow. That is, you need to have some idea of what you want to create.

One of the reasons we come to church to learn about God and Jesus and the Bible is because what we learn here shows us a special pattern for life. It shows us how God wants us to live. That means that we are willing to think about what is good and right for life and to seek after it. We know it will take time to become what we want to be as a Christian, but we are willing to work at it and as we go through life, we learn from one another things that help us improve upon the way we live. It is like making a carving. We learn to remove from life the things that should not be there and to bring out the things that should be seen. For example, we are to love one another. That means we must remove hatred and irritating things. It means we must try to bring out kindness. Each person here has a special life with which to create something beautiful. It is hard work, but it is well worth the effort.–Kenneth Mortonson

September 28: Barnabas

TEXT: Acts 4:36

(Prior preparation: you will need to discover what your name means, perhaps have a bookmark from a bookstore with the definition on it.)

Good morning, boys and girls. I have a question for you today. How many of you have a name? Raise your hand if you have a name. Look! We *all* have names. Some of us were named after someone special that our parents loved very much. Sometimes our parents name us after themselves. My dad's name is Jim Ray Rich and so is my big brother's name. Sometimes our parents name us because they think the name sounds cool, like Dakota or Scarlett. They like the way the name sounds. Sometimes we are named after people in the Bible like Mary, Sarah, Joshua, or Jacob. Whatever our names are, they are special because they are our names.

Sometimes our names mean something special. Do you know what my name is? My name is *(here, fill in your own name and its meaning)* Lou Ellen. Do you know what my name means? It means "battle maiden of light." A lot of people think that describes me very well. I like to argue a lot. There are people in the Bible who have very special names. Their names are special because their names describe them. There is a man in the New Testament named Barnabas. We don't hear that name much today, but it was a very special name for a very special person. Barnabas was one of the first missionaries to leave home and tell people about Jesus. He was a very special person, but he was not always called Barnabas. His real name was Joseph. You see, as people got to know him they noticed how very nice and kind he was. He was always encouraging people and helping people. Soon, people began to call him Barnabas, which means "son of encouragement." He was so nice that people began to call him Mr. Nice Guy!! They would see him coming and call

him "the encourager." What a nice man Barnabas must have been!

Sometimes we get called names that are not so nice. Maybe we get called names like "cheater" or "bully" or "liar." We do not like it when people call us these names because it reminds us of the bad things we do. Wouldn't it be great if we were so nice that people called us "helper," "friendly," or "kind"? Jesus would like for us to be known for the good things we do. He would like us to treat each other well, make other people feel special just as Barnabas did.

This week, try to make someone else feel special. Help your family feel good. Be a helper at school. Let people know that Jesus cares about them.–Lou Ellen Rich

October 5: The Wheel

How many of you can ride a tricycle or a bicycle? Do you know why we call them tricycles or bicycles? . . . *Tri* means "three," and *bi* means "two." The word *cycle* comes from a word that means "circle." And the circle is the wheel.

The wheel is a very important invention. Without it we would have no automobiles, as we know them; no washing machines, no elevators–the list goes on and on. The world is a better place because of the invention of the wheel. But, did you know that there was a time when people did not have wheels? A long time ago someone discovered that if you could make a round object that would turn on an axle, then you would have a wheel. Now, the material for a wheel was always present in the world. In fact, the material for everything we have is right here in our world.

This reminds us of something very important. Everything that you need for life is right here in the world that God has created. We don't have to wait for God to place something new in his world. But we do need to take what we have here and use it wisely. In Gen. 1:26, the Bible tells us that God made us in his own image and then let us have dominion over everything. Dominion means making decisions about what to do with what we have. It means using what we have in good and creative ways; in ways that show who we are. It means using our world to let God be seen in us.

Let me share with you something that you can do to show that you are in control of your world. When you have something that you are no longer going to use, don't just throw it away anywhere. That messes up our world. Instead, put the item in the garbage can; or if it is still usable, give it to someone else. When we take care of what God has given us, our world will be a better place.–Kenneth Mortonson

October 12: God Doesn't Rust

TEXT: Luke 12:32–40

Object: A girl's picture, a bank book, a car key

"Wherever your treasure is, there your heart and thoughts will also be" (v. 34).

Good morning, boys and girls. How many of you have ever thought about finding a treasure in your heart? It seems like a funny place to find it, but a lot of people think that their treasure is in their heart. How many of you know what treasure is? *(Let them answer.)* That's right, it could be gold or silver or precious stones like diamonds. But the kind of treasure I am talking about may be riches and may not be riches. For instance, some people consider the most important thing they have to be their bank book. *(Show the bank book.)* When you ask them what is the most important thing in the world to them they will tell you that it is the money they have in the bank. Other people might tell you it's the brand-new car in the driveway. *(Hold up key to car.)* Still others think that the most important thing in the world is their girlfriend. *(Hold up the picture.)* She is by far the most important, and that man would rather be with her than anyone else. She is his treasure, and sometimes he is her treasure. The Bible teaches us that whatever is the most important thing to us is our treasure, and we will think about our treasure more than anything else.

Jesus teaches us that the kinds of things I have mentioned should not be the most important things in the world to us. Our feelings for God should come first. God is our treasure and when we put God first, we will think right about other things. You can lose all of your money. It might be stolen or spent foolishly. You might wreck your car, or it may grow old and rusty. Your girlfriend

may find someone she likes better, or she may move away.

Everything in this world can be stolen, broken, or rusted away. People's feelings change. But God doesn't change or rust, and he can't be stolen or broken. That is why Jesus asks us to put God first and all other things second. Fill your heart with God, and your heart will be filled with joy and never with disappointment. Perhaps you can think about what you call your treasure, and then you can see if God is first in your heart. I know that God wants to be first with you. How many of you will let God be first? Raise your hands. That's wonderful. –Wesley T. Runk

October 19: Praise God

TEXT: Ps. 150

Good morning, boys and girls. How many of you like to make noise? I bet a lot of you like to make noise. When I was a girl, I liked to pretend I was playing the drums. I would get my mother's pots and pans and put them on the couch. Then I'd get two wooden spoons and pretend they were my drumsticks. I'd bang away on those pots and pans until my mother couldn't take it anymore and I'd have to stop. I also liked to dance to the music my father played on the stereo. He'd play classical music, but he like marches and polkas. I'd dance around the living room and spin around until I'd fall down. I'd get dizzy, but then I'd get up and start all over again.

When I went to church, I'd go to Sunday school and play the autoharp when we'd sing. I liked to strum the strings while we sang our songs. I also went to choir at church. We'd get to play the tambourine, the claves, sandpaper blocks, triangles, and xylophones. I loved to make music while we sang. Sometimes we'd sing very fast songs, and sometimes we'd sing slow songs. We'd sing songs about Jesus and people in the Bible. We'd sing songs about God and how God loves us. We'd say thank you to God by singing about the good things God gives us.

In the Bible there is a book called Psalms. It is a book full of poems and songs. Psalm 150 says we should praise God with all kinds of instruments and we should dance and have a good time praising him. God wants to know we appreciate all that God does. God likes it when we sing and play instruments at church. We give God a special offering when we sing and praise him and have fun at the same time.

Remember, girls and boys, when you sing about God in Sunday school and in choir and in church, it is a very special gift that God appreciates very much.–Lou Ellen Rich

October 26: First Fruits

TEXT: 2 Thess. 2:1–5, 13–17

Object: Nice fresh fruit (and perhaps some that is less than fresh)

"God chose you as the first fruits for salvation" (v. 13).

Good morning! I have here something I picked up from the grocery store. It's fresh fruit. I love fresh fruit! When I look at the apples and oranges that I can pick out, I never get the bad ones. I always try to get the best fruit I can. That's the fruit I pick for myself. It's my choice.

You are God's first choice! Just as I would pick the best for myself, so God picks you and me! If you stop and think about it, that is a great honor! We have been chosen by God!

When I was younger and friends would choose up sides to play ball, sometimes I was the last person chosen. It made me feel bad. Sometimes you might be among the last chosen for something as well. But that's okay. You are among the *first* that God chooses!

Keep that in mind if you ever feel bad for not being chosen for something.

Dear Jesus: Thank you for choosing us to serve you. We are glad you have found us important. Amen.–Children's Sermon Service Plus!

November 2: Create Something Good

Good morning, girls and boys. Can anyone tell me who created the world? Did God create the world? Yes, God certainly did. God made all the things in the world now and all the things that are gone like the dinosaurs. God gets the credit for making this world and everything in it, including us! Do you know what's really wonderful? We can create things too. For example, would everyone please make a funny face? Those

were some wonderful funny faces. How many of you like to color? I love to color. I like to draw. Do you like to draw? Do you know that when we do those things, we are being creative? When we make things out of play dough, when we play with our toys and use our imagination, we are being creative.

God gave us minds so we could create things. Sometimes the things we create make people very happy. We can make funny faces and make people laugh. Other times we can draw a pretty picture and someone likes it so much he or she puts it on the refrigerator for everyone to see. We can have fun with imaginary people and places we think about when we play. It is very important that we be creative and use the wonderful minds God gave us. But we must remember, girls and boys, that God wants our creativity to help people. We should try to create good things, not bad.

This week try to remember that we should use our minds to help people, be nice to people, create something good. If you see someone having a bad day, create something good by saying something nice. If you see your parents need help around the house, create something good by picking up your toys or helping out the best way you can. If your teacher is having a bad day, you can draw a card and tell your teacher how much you care for him or her.

Try to use the mind God gave you and create something good this week.–Lou Ellen Rich

November 9: What Is a Tithe?

TEXT: Mal. 3:10

Objects: A dollar, a dime, and an offering envelope

Tithing is a word that we hear very often at church. "Tithing" is giving money to the church that we feel belongs to God. A "tithe" is one-tenth of our income. For each dollar we receive we are to give one dime back to the Lord. *(Demonstrate by showing the dollar and placing the dime into the offering envelope.)* We tithe out of obedience to the Lord's word to us. Listen to Mal. 3:10a.

Our tithes represent what we believe about God and his blessings. When we give one-tenth faithfully back to the Lord and his work, we are saying that we believe that God is the owner of everything, and we are just managers of what he has entrusted to us in his kingdom. A tenth of what we receive isn't very much, but it is enough for us to demonstrate our faith in God.

God has promised to bless us when we are faithful in giving our tithes. Listen to Mal. 3:10b. Now, tithing doesn't make us millionaires, and we shouldn't give to receive something in return. In fact, when we tithe, we have less. But the Lord makes us content with what remains, and that feeling of satisfaction is what some folks are missing when they have so much but still feel like they need more and more to be happy.

The key to tithing is to begin now. So, when you get your allowances that may seem small, give your tithes. Get your parents to help you to determine the amounts. Then when you grow older and have larger incomes, giving a tithe will be an act of obedience that is well established. You will personally experience the Lord's blessing when you tithe, and it is great to have that joy all through your life.–Ken Cox

November 16: Let's Crown Jesus

TEXT: Rev. 4:11

Object: A crown

This is a replica of a crown. Crowns are worn by kings and queens and symbolize their power, position, and strength. In the United States we don't have a king or queen. The head of our government is elected by voters and is called a president.

A president doesn't have absolute power like a king. A king sits on a special chair called a throne, and while on the throne the king makes decisions with unquestioned authority. That means, if the king says to one of his people, "Run that way," off he'll go. If he says, "Do this," it will be done without any hesitation.

The Bible describes Jesus as a king with a very special kingdom. God appointed his son Jesus as king over all God's children. All who believe in Jesus as savior have Jesus as their king. Listen to Rev. 4:11.

Jesus is to be placed upon a special throne in our hearts. That means Jesus reigns or rules in our lives. When Jesus is our king we are obedient to everything Jesus tells us to do. Our instructions come from the Bible. Mother or Dad can tell us about Jesus, but we must ask Jesus individually into our lives to be our Savior. Only we can put him on the throne of our hearts.

We shouldn't be afraid of having Jesus upon the throne of our lives. When Jesus is reigning there, the Bible promises us joy and peace. Thus when Jesus is our king, we are happy and fulfilled.

I hope that Jesus is on the throne of your heart. Remember, you are the only one who can put him there.–Ken Cox

November 23: Thanks to God

TEXT: Luke 17:11–19

Object: A thank-you card (If your church has a postcard of the church, consider giving each child a postcard and asking each to write a thank-you note to someone within the church.)

"Were not ten made clean? But the other nine, where are they?" (v. 17).

When someone does something nice for me, I like to sit down and write a note to that person on one of these. These are "thank you" cards. I send them to thank the person who did the nice thing for me. It tells them that I am thankful for what they did and for who they are.

One day Jesus healed ten people who had a very bad sickness. It was a sickness that caused their skin to become very ugly. People with this skin disease had to leave the town in which they lived because no one else wanted to catch this disease.

Ten people became well because of Jesus, but only one person came back to say "thank you." Jesus wondered where the other nine were. "Were they not thankful?" he wondered.

Jesus does many things for us today. Jesus has given us this church. Jesus has given us one another. Jesus has given us our parents and homes and all that we have. So we say "thank you" the best way we know how. Can you tell me how we might say "thank you" to Jesus for all that Jesus does for us? *(Let them answer. If they can't think of anything, suggest saying thanks in prayer and doing good for others.)*

Dear God: *Thank you!* Amen.–Children's Sermon Service Plus!

November 30: Wake Up!

TEXT: Rom. 13:11–14

Object: A pillow

"Besides this, you know what time it is, how it is now the moment for you to wake from sleep" (v. 11).

Most of us sleep with a pillow under our heads. When we are through with sleeping, we no longer need the pillow. The pillow is great for sleeping, but a time comes when we must be awake. We cannot sleep all the time. That would not be much fun.

Today everyone is awake—right? I don't see anyone else with pillows here. That's good. When we are awake, we can play ball, read, watch television, or listen to music. I like being awake more than being asleep. Do you? *(Let them answer.)*

This time of the year is a time when I really like being awake. Why do you think I like being awake at this time of the year? *(Let them answer.)* It is a time of excitement and looking forward to Christmas that's coming at the end of this Advent season.

Today is the first Sunday of Advent. Advent is that time of the year when we get ready to meet Jesus our Lord. The apostle Paul said it's like waking up from a deep sleep. We want to be alert and ready for Jesus. Jesus comes at Christmas and Jesus comes at the end of the age. I want to be wide awake. I think I'll just put this pillow aside.

Dearest Lord Jesus: Help us be awake so that we can enjoy knowing you as you come to us. Amen.—Children's Sermon Service Plus!

December 7: The Most Precious Gift

TEXT: John 3:16

Object: A lady's wristwatch

This is a lady's wristwatch. Watches are available and inexpensive these days, but fifty years ago during World War II, they were hard to find. During the war years certain food items and valuables had to be rationed. That meant that each family had to take turns buying things that were in short supply.

In the war years, when she was a little girl, Ann Noe remembers getting a very special watch for Christmas.[1]

She tells the story of waking up on Christmas morning and being disappointed when she didn't get the watch that she had asked for. Her mother told her to look in her stocking, and Ann found a small package

[1] *Decision Magazine,* Dec. 1994, p. 25.

way down in the toe of the stocking. When she unwrapped the little gift, she discovered a beautiful watch. Her mom told her that it was to be worn only on special occasions. And for a long time, that's just what Ann did.

Years later Ann learned that the watch had been her mother's. Ann figured out that her mother couldn't find a new watch because of the war shortages, so she purchased a new gold band, put it on her own watch, and wrapped it up for Ann. Ann didn't recognize the watch with the new band on that Christmas morning years before. As Ann grew older the watch became even more precious to her because of the spirit in which it had been given.

At Christmas we are reminded of the unselfish gift of God to the whole world. Listen to this verse. God loved us so much that he gave of himself.

If you really want to enjoy Christmas, try giving instead of getting. The joy of Christmas is in giving, and this might just be your best Christmas ever.—Ken Cox

December 14: Popular John

TEXT: Matt. 3:1–12

Object: A campaign poster or bumper sticker of a popular politician

"Then the people of Jerusalem and all Judea were going out to him [John the Baptist], and all the region along the Jordan" (v. 5).

I brought with me today a poster of a candidate who ran for office. Can any of you tell me who this person is? *(Let them answer.)* Can you tell me what office he ran for? *(Let them answer.)*

People who run for office want you to know who they are. They print thousands of posters and bumper stickers. What else do they do? *(Let them answer.)* They advertise on radio and television. They try to meet as many people as possible. They want to do everything they can to make sure that people know who they are so that people will vote for them and so they get a job in government service. In other words, they want to be popular.

John the Baptist was a very popular man. Did he run for public office? *(Let them answer.)* No, he did not. Why do you think he was so popular? *(Let them answer.)*

John the Baptist was popular because he gave the people something in what he said. He gave them *good news.* He said things that people needed to hear. He said important things. Some of the things John said may not sound like good news as we read about John, but it was to most people. It was *good news* from God and the people knew that John the Baptist spoke as a prophet of God.

That king of *good news* is needed today as well. We in the church try to do everything we can to speak and live the *good news* we have from God. Our children's sermons, our worship service, our sermons, our hymns–all are good news to people who need to hear the good news about God. Thank you for helping me share the good news one more time!

Dear God: Thank you for the good news we have about Jesus. Amen.–Children's Sermon Service Plus!

December 21: Blessed Hope

TEXT: Titus 2:11–14

Object: A doll

"We wait for the blessed hope . . . of the glory of our great God and Savior, Jesus Christ" (v. 13).

How may of you like to play with dolls? *(Let them answer.)* That's great! Many girls and boys enjoy dolls. It's fun caring for a doll as you would a real person. Sometimes dolls can be just like real persons. What are the names of some of your favorite dolls? *(Let them answer.)*

Real babies are just as much fun for adults. When a baby is born, everyone is excited! A baby is someone we can care for and love. But a baby also means *hope.* Would one of you tell me what "hope" means? *(Let them answer.)* When we have hope, we think things will get better. With a baby there is often a lot of hope because a baby might grow up and make the world better. Perhaps the baby will find a cure for a serious illness, or she might build wonderful new buildings. Perhaps the baby will show us how to have less crime, or he might become a powerful man of God. Babies bring us hope.

One baby especially brought hope. I think everyone today knows who that baby is. *(Let them answer.)* Jesus brought the world the best hope ever. He made the world a much, much better place. When he was born, he brought hope. That is why Christmas is such an important, hopeful time.

Dear God: Thank you for the hope that baby Jesus brought us and for the wonderful holiday we have. Amen.–Children's Sermon Service Plus!

December 28: Family!

TEXT: Heb. 2:10–18

Object: Family album

"Jesus is not ashamed to call them brothers and sisters" (v. 11).

I brought this family album with me this morning to show you some pictures of some relatives of mine. These people are all related to me. That makes them special to me and me special to them. It is nice to have relatives.

Some of you have special relatives–brothers or sisters. How many of you have brothers or sisters? *(Let them answer.)* Today I want to tell you about a special brother each of you has.

We know that Jesus is our Savior. Jesus is our King. We know that Jesus is Lord. Jesus is all this. Jesus is the most important person any of us will know. The writer of what we read says that Jesus is "not ashamed" to call us brothers and sisters! Imagine that–Jesus–our brother! What a wonderful way to end the old year and begin the new. We have a heavenly family member–our brother Jesus.

Christmas is a time many families get together. Many will get together tonight to celebrate the New Year. As our families get together we especially want to remember our brother Jesus. How can we remind ourselves about Jesus? *(Let them answer.)* We can say prayers at mealtimes and at night. What about a prayer when we first get up?

I'm so glad we are all related to Jesus!

Dear brother Jesus: Thank you for loving us enough to call us your sisters and brothers. Amen.–Children's Sermon Service Plus!

SECTION XI.
A Little Treasury of Sermon Illustrations

THE DIFFERENCE. A professor of English once delivered a brilliant lecture, "The Literary Excellence of the Twenty-third Psalm," to the Literary Society of the church where he had been brought up as a boy. The old Scots minister, who had been his pastor and teacher in his youth, was the chairman. At the close of the lecture the distinguished speaker asked the old minister to read the psalm. He did so, as he had so often through the years to the members of that congregation, in their sorrows and troubles. A hush followed the heartfelt recital by the white-headed old man. Then the lecturer rose and quietly said, "I may know the psalm—but he knows the Shepherd."—John Trevor Davies

ACHIEVEMENT. Certainly it is a lovely thing when someone has faithfully performed something in his life, be it great or small. Why should he not be permitted to rejoice at this? I too know such a person, who has been fairly diligent, has written books, fat tomes some of them, has taught many students, has quite often got into the papers, eventually into the Spiegal. Goodness! But after all, why not? Only one thing is quite certain: he too has his time and not more than his time. One day others will come who will do the same things better. And some day he will have been completely forgotten—even if he should have built the pyramids or the St. Gotthard Tunnel or invented atomic fission. And one thing is even more certain: whether the achievement of a man's life is great or small, significant or insignificant—he will one day stand before his eternal judge, and everything that he has done and performed will be no more than a molehill, and then he will have nothing better to do than hope for something he has not earned: not for a crown, but quite simply for gracious judgment which he has not deserved. That is the only thing that will count then, achievement or not.—Karl Barth

TO HONOR CHRIST. Anatole France once described how a professional performer was found one day juggling a handful of balls before the cathedral altar. There was not the least irreverence about his deed. This was the one thing he could do well, and he wanted to do his best, in the spirit of high dedication to God. The love of Christ constrained him. His act was a dramatic symbol of his devotion.—G. Ray Jordan

PLANS AND ENTHUSIASM. Martha Berry started her notable institution when she was young. The years went by, and she came to have a thirty-thousand-acre campus and one hundred splendid buildings. Near the end of her long and remarkable life she said, "I believe in having big plans. I furnish the enthusiasm and depend on my friends to carry my plans through. No one of my dreams has failed yet. People respond when you challenge them with a concrete appeal to help young folks. They say I have too much enthusiasm for a woman of my age. Well, I hope I never lose it!" She did keep it till her death. Whoever we are, whatever our particular task in the church, we can cultivate that spirit.–G. Ray Jordan

JESUS' CROSS.   In one of the Irish plays of William Butler Yeats there is a vivid scene which perfectly expresses the objection which the human heart so often and so naturally makes against the religion of the Cross. The scene is in a country cottage in Ireland. The family are sitting together in the firelight of the kitchen, and on the wall there hangs a black wooden crucifix. There is a knock at the door, and when it is opened, in comes a little fairy girl, dressed in green, singing a merry song, the very personification of natural pagan happiness and the spirit of the green woods. Suddenly her eyes fall upon the crucifix, and she stops her singing and hides her face, and cries out, "Take down that ugly black thing."

There is the revolt of the religion of nature against the religion of the Cross. How well it expresses the question that we have all sometimes wanted to ask: Why should Christianity take that gaunt and tragic emblem and set it up at the heart of its message and in the center of its world? Why must Christianity make so much of the death of Jesus, of His Cross?–D. M. Baillie

THE INNER REALM.   It was told of Tauler that once in the city of Strassburg he met a beggar who wished him good day. "Every day is a good day to me," was his reply. "If the sun shines, I am glad; if the clouds rain, I bless God."

"Who are you?"
"I am a king."
"And where is your kingdom?"
"In my heart," replied Tauler.
–Elmer G. Homrighausen

DISCOURAGEMENT.   Did you know that Norman Vincent Peale was so disgusted with the manuscript *The Power of Positive Thinking* that he threw it in the wastebasket? It was saved by his cleaning lady and be-

came an important international best-seller. –Robert Ornstein/David Sobe

TESTIMONY.   Shortly after Holland was overrun by the Nazis in World War II, a group of Dutch Christians were put in jail by the Gestapo. Months later, when one of them was to be released, he offered to take a message to the families of the others. What should they say? One of them finally produced a letter, which in rough translation went as follows:

"Please try to understand that what has happened to us has actually worked out for the advancement of the gospel, since the prison guards and all the rest here are coming to know Christ. In fact, we hear that many of you on the outside have gained courage because of our imprisonment and are speaking the truth more boldly than ever before.

"We hope that we shall not need to be ashamed because of our witness but that we may be bold enough so that Christ's influence will be spread by us, whether we live or whether we die."

Now those sentences should have a familiar ring. For what the writer of the letter had done was to take portions of a letter which Paul had written while he was in prison, 1,900 years before (Phil. 1:12–20), and make them his own. The Dutch Christians, in sending this letter, were testifying that the experience of Paul was their experience, the message of Paul was their message, the God of Paul was their God.–Robert McAfee Brown

THE FORMS OF PRAYER.   *Jesus honored all the dominant forms of prayer.* As for *adoration,* he bowed head and heart before the luminous Mystery: "heaven" is God's throne, and earth his "footstool." As for *confession,* he did not confess his own sin (an item not to be side-stepped), but the sins of his people, in deeper meaning than the words of Moses. "But now, if thou wilt forgive their sin–and if not, blot me, . . . out of thy book." As for *thanksgiving,* and again and again that note is struck ("Father, I thank thee"), for his whole life was praise. As for *supplication,* he daily pleaded for guidance and strength. As for *meditation,* he listened in prayer more than he spoke. As for *intercession,* a form of prayer which raises huge questions for modern man, which we shall not dodge, we here note that he prayed for children, for tempted men, for the family of the dead Lazarus, for his disciples, and for the whole world; so reiterated are these prayers that he is now known as our Intercessor.–George A. Buttrick

A CHRISTIAN EMPHASIS.   Christmas means crowds, children, carols, candy, kindness, for most of us in the Western hemisphere. For Christians, it should mean Christ. Preachers may help rescue Christmas from the secularization that has all but smothered it beneath the tinsel which sentimentalists and salesmen heap upon it, but we would not forgo the sentiment which "gentles" our spirits. Keeping Christmas in the heart, as children do, prepares us for Him who came "a little baby thing" to confound the wisdom that is not wise. While pedantic theological dissertations on the incarnation are out of place in this season, our messages must transmit the central truth that the festival celebrates: God "has visited and redeemed his people" (Luke 1:68), and therefore we rejoice.–David A. MacLennan

SERVING GOD.   General Booth, founder of the Salvation Army, went blind in his latter years; and the doctor didn't know how to tell him about it. He had been lying there on the bed for weeks, and finally the doctor told his son, Bramwell, that he'd have to tell his father. Bramwell went into the old general's room and said, "Dad, the doctor tells me that you'll never see again."

With the tensing of the muscles in his jaw the old general said, "Bramwell, do you mean I'll never look into your face again?"

"Not this side of heaven, Father," Bramwell replied.

Then across the counterpane came the gnarled old hand of the general to take hold of his son's hand. He said, "Son, I've done the best I could to serve my God and my people with my eyes. Now I'll do my best to serve my God and my people without my eyes."–Paul Quillan

CONFESSION OF SIN.   There was a devout lady who in her weekly confession always confessed the same sin of the flesh. Her confessor began to recognize her voice and recall the past confessions. Finally he said to her, "I don't believe I can really give you absolution; you show no firm purpose of amendment, confessing as you do the same sin every week." "Oh, Father," she replied, "That happened a long time ago." "Why, then," he countered, "do you keep confessing it every week?" "Oh," she said, "I just like to talk about it."–James A. Pike

THE MEANING OF "GOD."   In all my experiences I have met no one individual who did not believe in a "power greater than myself." I have had them say, "I do not believe in *God*–I believe in 'Nature,' or 'Universal Law,' or 'Creative Intelligence.'" And that is all right, too. There have been sects which called the Supreme Being "Oom" and "Mobile Cosmic Ether," and while the latter may be a bit unwieldy for emergency use, there is absolutely none who can say they are wrong. There is no reason at all to shy away from an honest evaluation of what God means to you today. Carl Jung has said, "Whether you call the principle of existence 'God,' 'Matter,' 'Energy,' or anything else you like, you have created nothing; you have simply changed a symbol." And this is true. As a matter of fact, we found the student who believes in a Beneficent Power called "Universal law" was often much closer to a God of Love than one who believed in an "avenging Heavenly Father."–William R. Parker and Elaine St. Johns

DEFIANCE.   Defiance, the open and bold resistance to opposition, takes two forms: One form seeks to destroy authority. H. Rap Brown demonstrated that philosophy in the 1960s and the Symbionese Liberation Army in the 1970s. Their only claim was to an inner anger.

The other form of defiance is seen in men like John Wesley Powell, who in 1869 led an expedition through the water-wrought sculpture that is the Grand Canyon. He braved the unknown with defiance. Or consider Rufus Woods, publisher of Washington's *Wenatchee Daily World*, who spent twenty-three years trying to push through the construction of Grand Coulee Dam. It was called "Rufus's pipe dream." But he saw it as a means to turn a desert wasteland into a blossoming and productive paradise. He defied the impossible—and won.

So did others: the men who soared to the moon; a Jonas Salk; a George Washington Carver; and the apostle Paul, who turned the world upside down.—Richard Andersen

GOD'S BEAUTIFUL SOULS.   Of all the colors known to the ancients, crimson was the most beautiful and the most enduring. When they made a crimson robe, it was triple-dyed. First, they dyed the wool, and when it was spun into threads it was dyed in the yarn; and when it was taken from the loom it was dyed in the web. God's most beautiful souls are triple-dyed in disappointment, and pain, and sorrow.—W. W. Weeks

TURNING THE TABLES.   Menelik II was the emperor of Ethiopia from 1889 until 1913. News of a successful new means of dispatching criminals reached him. The news was about a device known as an electric chair. The emperor eagerly ordered one for his country. Unfortunately, no one bothered to warn him than it would never work, because Ethiopia at that time had no electricity. Menelik was determined that his new purchase should not go to waste. He converted the electric chair into a throne.

There was another occasion when an instrument of death became a throne. On a Palestinian hillside about twenty centuries ago, a cross became a throne for one named Jesus of Nazareth. To this day that ancient instrument of torture and death is converted into a powerful symbol of life, hope, and resurrection. Millions of people around the world see the cross as God's way of indicating his refusal to let death and destruction have the final word.—Don M. Aycock

CHRISTIAN MARRIAGE.   Faith in the God of the Bible sets one under a new requirement—the requirement to live according to the Scriptures, rather than according to the will and ways of the world. "If you love me, you will keep my commandments," Jesus says (John 14:15). And faith in the God of Jesus Christ brings with it that powerful and transforming Spirit who enables one so to live (John 14:16–17; Gal. 2:20).

Applied to marriage and home, then, this means that Christian marriages and home life are uniquely different from those in the society around them. George Will once wrote a column in *Newsweek* in which he recalled a statement of Charles Peguy's that "the true revolutionaries in our society are the parents of Christian families." How true that is! Christian families are now so different from the usual families in our society that they are revolutionary.—Elizabeth Achtemeier

ETHICS WITHOUT RELIGION.   Ethics, while originally it grew out of religious motivation and belief, is not the same thing as religion. Renan, it was, who said we are lingering with a code of ethics that has lost its fervor. As he put it, ethical people who have lost their religion are living on the perfume of an empty wave.

People who say we should return to the Sermon on the Mount don't usually see that something a good deal deeper is needed—namely, a live inner sentiment, a vital set of personal values to provide motivation.—Gordon W. Allport

LIFE-CHANGING WORDS.   Dr. Courts Redford recalls that as a boy he was weak, shy, and unduly self-critical. Then one day a loved one said, "Courts, you are God's boy, He is not going to permit anything to happen to you that you cannot handle." These words were like spiritual vitamins, and as Dr. Redford later said, "They changed my life." He kept faith with God and God with him, and a rich Christian ministry has followed.—Theodore F. Adams

BEYOND THE OLD FRONTIERS.   The characteristic feature of the Renaissance period—a feature which I hope has not been lost—was the constant leaping of fixed barriers. Columbus, Copernicus, Erasmus, Luther, Galileo, each in his own field, changed a terminus into a thoroughfare for a new advance of the race. There is a vivid narrative in John's Gospel which says, "Then came Jesus, the doors being shut, and stood in the midst, and said, 'Peace.'" He has always been coming through shut doors. He has always been turning what seemed to be a terminus into a new thoroughfare. Clement of Alexandria well said that Christ has turned all sunsets into sunrises.—Rufus M. Jones

SAVED BY GRACE.   "You have been saved by grace." In any capacity you have to love. In anything that makes you of holy use to others. In whatever is true about you, whatever is noble, whatever is just and pure, whatever lovable and gracious, excellent and admirable. You have been saved by grace. Not by your education, which in these matters can be a wash. Not by your connections. Not by your nationality, except as you have died to country and risen to Christ. Not by your gifts of language and sociability and humor—though one could debate humor, true humor being one of the flowers of grace! "Saved by grace" may sound like a formula, and in our clumsy pulpit hands has often been one. But it is not. If anything, it is more nearly poetry, the haiku of Paul.

We are saved by grace as darkness is saved by sunrise. We are saved by grace as weariness is saved by rest and a warm shower and a lovingly prepared meal. As depression may be saved by spring's longer days, though the wise among us recount that among the most depressed are those who expected spring to make a difference, and it didn't. We are saved by grace as in some measure we are saved from loneliness by friends and good books and all beloved company. As trees are saved from winter's barrenness by leaves and the return of birds upon their boughs. We are saved by grace as mothers and fathers are saved from their children, and children from their parents, by the return of summer days, when children, and they, can get outside and run and play; as parents we are saved from teenagers and teenagers from parents by age twenty, give or take a year or two. As grandparents are saved by Good-bye; thanks for coming; have a safe trip; call us when you get home. We love you. We are saved by grace as winter is saved by crocuses and daffodils. As the dying are saved by a comforting hand, a familiar face. We are saved by grace as someone wronged may be saved by their day in court. As people whose lives are spinning out of control are saved by direction and purpose. Remember the true story of the little girl who asked her parents, "Do I have to do what I want?" We are saved by grace. As the aged and infirm and ill may be saved from sleeplessness and worry by 911—just by its being there. We are saved by grace as we are all saved by music, whether the music is notes on a page or a composition of flowers in the kitchen window, or a loving score of photographs—parents, children, grandchildren, even great-grandchildren—singing across a living room wall. "Saved by grace." Grace is no lazy student's WHEW! that she passed the exam she knew she deserved to fail. Rather, "saved by grace" is a good student's joy that she is alive to take the exam at all, to feel the fresh, brisk air of morning on the way to the exam, and to look forward to coffee and a doughnut in the student union, over a leisurely paper, after the exam is finished. We are saved by grace. Pauline poetry, Pauline haiku.—Peter Fribley

CHRISTIAN TILL IT HURTS.   When Isaac Watts wrote that famous hymn "When I survey the wondrous Cross" he gave it a far better second line than we ever sing in our churches. He wrote:

When I survey the wondrous Cross
Where the young Prince of Glory died.

It is the Young Prince of Glory who calls us to follow him, who rides forth conquering and to conquer and offer us a place in his victorious army. There is nothing soft or sentimental about his demands. He wants all or nothing. Which is it to be?—Joost DeBlank

MOTIVATION IN TENSION.   I served a congregation where, because of our geographical situation, when we opened our doors, there was a constant stream of prospective members and potential new life. Yet we had a constant struggle to develop warmth, friendliness, and unity. Little interest was shown in starting new groups, visitation, and outreach. Later, I served a congregation where it was my unpleasant task to tell members that, given the present rate of decline, we would be dead in a couple of decades because of our geographical location. The realization of that fact could have depressed and defeated the people. Fortunately it had the opposite effect. They mobilized the ministry. Visitation teams, greeters, an overhaul of the church building, and the monthly creation of new classes to meet various age and interest needs all flowed from the stark recognition that, in the words of many laypersons, "If we don't do something and don't do it quickly, this church will be dead in a decade."—William H. Willimon

PATHFINDERS.   No doctrine is a perfect instrument until it has ceased to be an intellectual problem. This is what Paul meant when he exclaimed, "Yea, though we have known Christ after the flesh, yet now hence forth know we him no more." This is not a denial of the doctrine of the incarnation, but rather the removal of it from the realm of speculation, and the placing of it in the foundation of experience. The man who first scooped the heart out of a log and used it as a canoe to carry him across a stream began the mighty fleet of ocean liners. The rushlight and tallow candle were the ancestors of our modern electric lights. The *Twentieth Century Limited* can trace its genealogy back to the tally-ho coach and the oxcart. We have not deserted the faith of our fathers because we have discovered that what they supposed was the terminal is only a way station on the road of human progress, that what they believed was the topmost peak in the range is only one of the foothills. Humanity is still climbing upward, and our children's children will have visions of which we have not yet dreamed.—W. W. Weeks

THE COURAGE TO RISK COMMUNITY. I know that I will always be a staunch Baptist. My Baptist heritage is settled in my bones. My grandfathers and great-grandfathers were persecuted in Europe for being Baptists, and I will not soon reject my heritage as a Baptist. I am a Baptist by conviction, but my heritage as a brother in Christ far surpasses my heritage as a Baptist. In Christ Jesus we need to learn how to risk community with one another. . . . In so doing we learn something very important about God. . . . Think for a moment about our usual patterns of taking sides on issues. Then reflect on the story of a former professor, Dr. Otto Piper of Princeton. During the Second World War he was forced by Hitler to leave Germany in one day, and he ended up with one son in the German forces and one son in the American forces. As he spoke of that situation, he used to say, "I learned something about war," and about "God as a parent who has children on both sides of almost every issue." "I loved my sons," said Dr. Piper, "and it was hard to lose them to the hellish struggles of humanity."—Gerald L. Borchert

RELIABLE STANDARDS.   When John Quincy Adams was president of the United States, he did a dramatic thing. He called both houses of Congress together for a special meeting. He walked up on the rostrum carrying two bushel measures. Holding one in each hand, he said to the audience, "The bushel measure in my right hand came from South Carolina; the one in my left hand comes from the city of New York. One of these bushel measures contains sixty-eight cubic inches more than the other one." He stood silent for a few moments to let the implication sink in; then he slowly placed them side by side on the floor. In the same deliberate way, he walked over to a little table and picked up two one-pound weights, the kind that were used on a set of balance scales to weigh produce. With measured words he said, "This weight in my right hand came from Massachusetts; this other one came from Maine. One of them weighs nearly an ounce more than the other." Again he waited a few moments for everyone to grasp the problem. Then with a resonant voice he said, "Gentlemen, we need a standard measure and a standard weight for the United States of America."

Thus came into existence what is now known in Washington as the "House of

Wonders." Officially, it is the Bureau of Weights and Measures.–C. Roy Angell

LIGHT IN THE WORLD.   We shall be "light" as we are "in the Lord." It is by union with Jesus Christ that we partake of His illumination. A sunbeam has no more power to shine if it be severed from the sun than a man has to give light in this dark world if He be parted from Jesus Christ. Cut the current and the electric light dies, slacken the engine and the electric arc becomes dim, quicken it and it burns bright. So the condition of being light is my keeping unbroken my communication with Jesus Christ; and every variation in the extent to which I receive into my heart the influx of His power and of His love is correctly measured and represented by the greater or the lesser brilliancy of the light with which I reflect His beauty. "Ye were some time in darkness, but now are ye light in the Lord." Keep near to Him, and a firm hold of His hand, and then you will be light.– Alexander Maclaren

OPPRESSION BY DEFAULT.   The church has often criticized the twentieth century for dehumanizing man. Industry, it says, has put man on the assembly line and turned him into a number. Government has lost him in a welter of bureaus and agencies. Apollo flights soar toward the moon, and man, left behind, shrinks into microscopic insignificance.

But religion can lose sight of people as quickly as an insensitive culture can. That is what the parable of the Good Samaritan was all about. We have praised the hero of that story and conveniently forgotten the villains, two pious frauds who left their battered brother in the ditch while they went on about their religious duties.–James Armstrong

THE FACE OF JESUS.   We can have a solid Christology and exegesis, but these can never take the place of the contemplation of the gospel. The gospel transmits to us what most deeply impressed the apostles and the first disciples; it was brought together in the tradition of the first communities to recall what was most significant for the faith and spirit of the Christians. "What we have heard with our ears and seen with our eyes, what we have looked upon and touched with our hands concerning the word of life, we proclaim also to you."

For this reason the gospel is irreplaceable. We find in it Christology as wisdom and the image of Christ as the inspiring message of all discipleship. We find there a person whom we can imitate out of love. This contemplative love, of itself, leads us constantly to the imitation of Jesus, which is the best guarantee of discipleship.–Segundo Galilea

THE INNER LIFE.   The inner life is of infinitely more importance than the outer life. Many now, as in the days of Jesus' life on earth, are careful to keep the outward life respectable and presentable while the inner life of the soul is full of hate, and anger, and envy, and greed–a veritable parallel to those whom Christ declared were whited sepulchers, full of dead men's bones and all uncleanness. A gentleman was one day walking down the street when he passed a store where a man was washing the large plate-glass show window. There was one soiled spot which defied all efforts to remove it. After rubbing hard at it, using much soap and water, and failing to affect it, he found out the trouble. "It's on the inside," he called out to someone in the store. –Louis Albert Banks

THE TIME TO LAY DOWN RULES.   On days when the spiritual flame burns brightly within us, so that there is nothing we so much desire as communion with God, we have perhaps no need of a rule. But it is just then that we should lay down our rules. This is the time for surveying, for taking our bearings and shaping our course; so that, when desire begins to fail and the spiritual flame burns low, the discipline to which we have committed ourselves will still keep us in the right way and in the middle of the road.–John Baillie

THE LAST WORD.   A street in downtown Oxford has a small black cross imbedded in the pavement. A sign nearby tells what it means. In 1555 two British reformers were burned at the stake on the spot where the cross now sits. These reformers,

Hugh Latimer and Nicholas Ridley, tried to renew the church of their day and met death for their efforts. Tradition says that as the fires were lit Latimer cried out, "Be of good comfort, Master Ridley, and play the man. We shall this day light such a candle by God's grace in England as I trust shall never be put out." Latimer was right. His death inspired other people to take up his work and see it through.–Don M. Aycock

GOD AND OUR WORLD.   Long ago Jesus said, "Go ye into all the world." An English churchman, commenting on that phrase, said, "We have made that mean Africa and Fiji and Calcutta, but it means more relevantly the world of computers and biochemistry and politics." God is the God of our world, the world of the here and now, or he is no God at all. He is a worldly God, and we are called to a worldly faithfulness and discipline. God came alive for us as we acknowledge his sovereignty over all things and find him not in faulty definitions and institutions but in the events of every day. In our response to these events we are tried and tested. God is our judge, and history is his judgment upon us.–James M. Armstrong

MISLABELED.   John Roach Straton was a pastor in New York City during the first half of this century. He carried on a feud with the American Museum of Natural History in New York. In the Museum's Hall of the Age of Man was displayed the remains and restorations of fossil men. Straton charged the museum with "mis-spending the taxpayers' money, and poisoning the minds of school children by false and bestial theories of evolution." He demanded that the Bible and representations of Moses be used to replace those "musty old bones." When lightning damaged one of the stone ornaments on the roof of the museum, Straton boomed that this was a divine warning. But when lightning stuck his own church soon afterward, he somehow failed to draw a similar conclusion. I wonder why. –Don M. Aycock

DIAMOND DUST.   "I was passing a jewelry store in one of the big cities the other day," said George Strombeck in a *Christian*

Digest article several years ago, "and saw in the window a diamond cutter. He had a pile of ugly, shapeless stones on the table by his machine. There were no sparkling blue lights, no scintillating gleams. They looked to be just ordinary stones that you would not have picked up from the pavement. In front of him was a small machine made of two disks about the size of a dinner plate. As I watched, he removed the top one and I saw six beautiful diamonds held by small, sunken clamps. The diamond cutter took out each stone, examined it carefully with his magnifying glass, then clamped it back in place. Then he picked up the box of diamond dust, the hardest cutter in the world, and sprinkled the stones liberally with it. When he had replaced the top disk, he turned on the power and it began to rotate. As I watched, I realized that he was using this diamond dust to shape and polish those dirty, ugly stones and make them scintillate and glow so they would be fit for a girl's engagement ring. As I stood there looking, suddenly my eyes ceased to focus and a great truth came over my conscious mind. It rang like a bell. God, too, uses diamond dust to polish and shape human lives. Some of the hardships, disappointments, and frustrations that have come to us are God's diamond dust.–C. Roy Angell

WHO BELONGS?   The Christian church, or let us say more clearly, the community of Jesus Christ, is there and only there where men recognize Jesus the son of the carpenter from Nazareth as their Lord and Redeemer. Everyone who recognizes that belongs to the church of Jesus Christ, and no one who does not recognize and know that belongs to the church. He may like to go to Christian worship serves, he may even have been baptized, instructed, and confirmed, he may even honor Jesus as a particularly holy man, as the most holy and best man that ever lived; but if he has not recognized that Jesus is the Redeemer, his Redeemer, then he does not yet belong to the community of Jesus Christ. He still stands in the entry and waits for the moment when his eyes also shall open and he can say, "Now I also know it: he is my Lord, before whom I unconditionally bow; he is my Savior, whom I unconditionally trust; he is the

One in whom God sends his love and eternal life to me. In this moment he has become a member of the Christian community.–Emil Brunner

CONDITIONING.   A student of psychology–who I fear was only about half trained in the subject–once was arguing with Arch-bishop Temple. The student gave what he thought was the final thrust: "You only believe what you believe because of your early training."

The Archbishop replied, "You only believe that I believe what I believe because of my early training, because of your early training."–Gordon W. Allport

ACKNOWLEDGMENTS

Acknowledgment and gratitude are hereby expressed for kind permission to reprint material from the periodicals and books listed below.

SUNDAY SCHOOL BOARD OF THE SOUTHERN BAPTIST CONVENTION: Each of the following is used by permission.
Excerpt from Dale L. Rowley in *Proclaim,* July–September 1993, pp. 26–27 © 1993, The Sunday School Board of the Southern Baptist Convention; an excerpt from Robert B. Watkins in *Proclaim,* January–March 1995, p. 29 © 1994, The Sunday School Board of the Southern Baptist Convention; excerpt from William Richard Ezell in *Proclaim,* April–June 1993, pp. 18–19 © 1993, The Sunday School Board of the Southern Baptist Convention; an excerpt from Bill Cashman in *Proclaim,* October–December 1992, p. 27 © 1992, The Sunday School Board of the Southern Baptist Convention; an excerpt from Ed Mitchell in *Proclaim,* October–December 1992, p. 29 © 1992, The Sunday School Board of the Southern Baptist Convention; an excerpt from Lucien E. Coleman, Jr., in *Open Windows,* July–September 1993 (September 28) © 1993, The Sunday School Board of the Southern Baptist Convention; an excerpt from Ernie Perkins in *Open Windows,* April–June 1994 (May 1) © 1994, The Sunday School Board of the Southern Baptist Convention.

BROADMAN PRESS: Each of the following is used by permission.
Excerpts from J. Alfred Smith, Jr., *The Overflowing Heart,* pp. 54–57 © 1987, Broadman Press; excerpts from Robert G. Wilkerson in James C. Barry, ed., *Award Winning Sermons,* Vol. 4, pp. 32–37 © 1980, Broadman Press; excerpts from J. Altus Newell in James C. Barry, ed., *Award Winning Sermons,* Vol. 2, pp. 65–70 © 1978, Broadman Press; excerpts from C. Welton Gaddy in James C. Barry, ed., *Award Winning Sermons,* Vol. 3, pp 11–17 © 1979, Broadman Press; Frank Stagg in H. C. Brown, ed., *More Southern Baptist Preaching,* pp. 106–112 © 1964, Broadman Press; excerpts from Hugh Litchfield, *Preaching the Christmas Story,* pp. 23–29 and pp. 106–112 © 1984, Broadman Press.

INDEX OF CONTRIBUTORS

INDEX OF CONTRIBUTORS

SERMON TITLE INDEX

(Children's stories and sermons are identified as cs; sermon suggestions as ss)

SCRIPTURAL INDEX

INDEX OF PRAYERS

INDEX OF MATERIALS USEFUL AS CHILDREN'S STORIES AND SERMONS NOT INCLUDED IN SECTION X

INDEX OF MATERIALS USEFUL FOR SMALL GROUPS

TOPICAL INDEX